D0073303

From Brian and Michelle Palmer, Christmas 2011

The Making of Princeton University

The Making of Princeton University

FROM WOODROW WILSON TO THE PRESENT

by James Axtell

PRINCETON UNIVERSITY PRESS
PRINCETON AND OXFORD

Published by Princeton University Press, 41 William Street,
Princeton, New Jersey 08540
In the United Kingdom: Princeton University Press, 3 Market Place,
Woodstock, Oxfordshire OX20 1SY

Library of Congress Cataloging-in-Publication Data

Axtell, James.
The making of Princeton University : from Woodrow Wilson
to the present / James Axtell.
p. cm.
Includes bibliographical references and index.
ISBN-13: 978-0-691-12686-9 (hardcover : alk. paper)
ISBN-10: 0-691-12686-0 (hardcover : alk. paper)
1. Princeton University—History—20th century.
2. Wilson, Woodrow, 1856–1924. I. Title.
LD4610.A96 2006
378.749′67—dc22
2005034088

British Library Cataloging-in-Publication Data is available

This book has been composed in Adobe Caslon

Printed on acid-free paper. ∞

pup.princeton.edu

Printed in the United States of America

1 3 5 7 9 10 8 6 4 2

I am covetous for Princeton
of all the glory that there is,
and the chief glory of a university
is always intellectual glory.

—Woodrow Wilson

For

SUSAN

as always

Contents

List of Illustrations

Figures 1, 3, 5, 7–9, 12, 14, 15, 18–30, and 32–34 are reproduced courtesy of the University Archives, Department of Rare Books and Special Collections, Princeton University Library; figures 2, 6, 10, 11, 13, 16, 17, and 35 are courtesy of the Office of Communications, Princeton University; figure 4 is courtesy of the Department of Rare Books and Special Collections, Princeton University Library; and figure 31 is courtesy of the Princeton University Art Museum.

Preface

It is a puzzle that universities, charged
with helping to preserve the past,
know so little of their own.

—W. B. Carnochan

—∿—

GREAT UNIVERSITIES are made, not born. Invariably, their infancies and youth are pinched, puzzling, and unpropitious, and their adolescence, even when finally promising, is often bumptious and conflicted. Only in maturity, with realistic ambitions, strong guidance, and good fortune, do good universities achieve the true excellence to which they all publicly aspire. In 1996 Princeton University turned 250 years old, time enough to determine whether it had realized its aspiration to become one of the best universities in the country. By most measures, quantitative and qualitative, it had reached a level of achievement that most rivals could only envy.

Despite the occasion of its bicenquinquagenary, Princeton decided not to commission a history to explain how and why it had made the transition from a good but limited liberal arts college at the turn of the twentieth century to perhaps the best "liberal university" (as Dean J. Douglas Brown dubbed it) at the beginning of the new millennium.[1] A faculty advisory committee concluded that a historian of the modern university would be unduly handicapped by a fifty-year archival restriction on the use of certain official records and would risk the loss of scholarly objectivity by treating a subject so close to the present. The committee also assumed, understandably given the traditional authorship of college histories, that Princeton's

[1] J. Douglas Brown, *The Liberal University: An Institutional Analysis* (New York, 1969); Brown, "The American Liberal University," *PAW*, May 6, 1955, 8–9.

historian would be someone intimately associated with the university, as an alumnus, faculty member, or administrator.

The university sponsored instead a handsome coffee-table book on Princeton's full span, for which veteran foreign correspondent Don Oberdorfer '52 wrote the relatively brief text and photographer J. T. Miller '70 chose the illustrations.[2] Although it has its good uses, *Princeton University: The First 250 Years* does not give a satisfactory historical description or explanation of the modern university.[3] Perhaps most unfortunate, it did not continue the fuller story that Edwards Professor of History Thomas Jefferson Wertenbaker in 1946 had told of Princeton's first 150 years, from its founding as the College of New Jersey in 1746 to its self-designation as Princeton University in 1896.[4]

As Princeton's official bicentennial historian, Wertenbaker had been appointed to chronicle the university's first *two* hundred years. But for reasons that made good sense at the time, the last four chapters he wrote taking the story to 1946 were omitted, presumably to spare the feelings of key subjects still living. When I rediscovered those missing chapters in Wertenbaker's personal papers in Firestone Library, it was also apparent that the story line was left ragged and unfinished because the outcome of World War II was still in doubt (he had to stop writing a year earlier to allow time for the editing and printing of the book) and the university was still on an unusual wartime footing, run largely as a military training camp rather than a traditional liberal arts university.[5] Although the chapters on Woodrow Wilson's presidency were quite thorough and well written, the

[2] In the text that follows, a two-digit number preceded by an apostrophe ('63) indicates the *undergraduate* class (1963) in which the person graduated (or was supposed to after four years). A number preceded by an asterisk (*72) indicates the person's *graduate* school class (1972), when he or she was most likely awarded the Ph.D. This numbering system is not unique to Princeton, but it is seldom explained to the readers of college alumni magazine or histories.

[3] Princeton, 1996.

[4] Thomas Jefferson Wertenbaker, *Princeton, 1746–1896* (Princeton, 1946).

[5] Papers of Thomas Jefferson Wertenbaker, CO 359, box 26, folders 5–6 (175 pp. of revised typescripts), DRBSC, PUL. Other versions of the chapters are in box 20, folder 2, and box 26, folders 5–6.

remaining chapters suffered obviously from thin research and a looming deadline. So the published book ended half a century early, leaving all but sexagenarian or older Princetonians without an explanation of *their* university and what it had become.

This situation appeared to me a personal opportunity. After spending most of my academic career as a student and teacher of colonial American history, particularly the ethnohistory of Indian-European relations, I was ready after the too-busy Columbus Quincentenary in 1992 to return, at least temporarily, to my first love, the history of education. Why I chose twentieth-century Princeton as my subject has puzzled many friends, acquaintances, and even family. Not only did the twentieth century seem to them a long way from my usual haunts and a university very different from Indians, they almost all wondered why a true-blue graduate of Yale (and lighter blue Cambridge) would choose to write about a rival Ivy League university with which I had had no official connections.

To answer their first concern, I reminded them that I regularly teach the whole span of American higher education, as I had once taught all of native American history, and that I was no newcomer to the twentieth century because I had lived through nearly 60 percent of it. Their second concern was somewhat harder to allay because it is so pervasive and persistent. It is a form of what I call the "generic fallacy": "it takes one to know one." In the 1960s and 1970s such an assumption often greeted "outsiders" who attempted to write or teach the history of hitherto-neglected racial and ethnic groups, genders, and sexual orientations. White, male, and "straight" scholars were asked why they presumed to study the emerging histories of black slaves, women, and homosexuals, as if sound historical training, imagination, empathy, disinterestedness, and immersion in the primary record could never overcome the fortuitous "disadvantages" of birth.

By 1996 such blinkered, proprietary thinking had largely disappeared, except, ironically, in one small corner of academe. Only in the genre of college and university histories do we still largely assume that "to know a college you have to have attended it" in some capacity. Since most institutional histories have been and still are written by "insiders" of one kind or another, the assumption is less foolish than outdated because several excellent histories in the last two decades have been written by "outsiders," just as many of the best histories of African and native America and of women have been written by white and male scholars respectively.

I was also unimpressed by such questions and assumptions because I expected my experience as a student (1959–1963) and professor (1966–1972) at Yale to confer two advantages as I wrote the history of Princeton. One was cognitive assonance: I understood what it was like to study and play sports at an all-male and to teach at a newly coeducational elite research university like Princeton. The other was critical distance: since Yale was not Princeton, I would bring a healthy measure of Yale "objectivity" to the project. Only readers, particularly those with a Princeton pedigree, can judge whether my Bulldoggedness has been an advantage or only a predictable impediment.

The question still remains why I chose to write about modern Princeton. The answer begins in the spring of 1958 in my small upstate New York high school, when my junior-year English class was asked to write a research paper on a topic of our choosing. For reasons that I can only guess at this remove, I chose Woodrow Wilson as president of Princeton. I had no personal interest in Princeton—I dreamt of playing basketball for Yale—and even less knowledge of Wilson. But I was fascinated by the notion of a U.S. President who had apprenticed as an Ivy League politics professor and president.

I was especially struck by a photograph in one of my sources—an article by John A. Garraty in *American Heritage*—of Wilson in academic retreat.[6] It shows him striding across campus, in cap and gown, grim-lipped, eyes and head down, to preside over his last commencement in 1910. Yet from my modest research I knew that the first half of his eight-year tenure had been highly successful in remaking the small denominational college into a promising academic powerhouse. He had been defeated by internal enemies—a few "scheming" faculty, trustees, and alumni—only when he tried to move Princeton to a

[6] John A. Garraty, "The Training of Woodrow Wilson," *American Heritage* 7:5 (Aug. 1956): 24–27, 94.

Figure 1. Woodrow Wilson walking to his last commencement as president of Princeton in 1910, bowed but not broken.

residential college, or "quad," system and to locate the new graduate school at the heart of the undergraduate campus.

That image of Wilson apparently sank deeply into my subconscious, for when I saw it again more than thirty years later, I realized instantly that it was a topic I wanted to explore at some length. I didn't need much prompting because I found the photo while relishing five bound volumes of the *Princeton Alumni Weekly* from the mid-1980s that I bought in a Firestone Library sale en route to a Maine vacation. Reading those 105 substantial issues (the magazine then appeared twenty-one times a year) from President William G. Bowen's heyday during the next two weeks prompted me to wonder what, if any, connection there was between my adolescent "hero" Wilson and the enviable and attractive liberal university Bowen was leading to national and international prominence. This book, in large part, is my lengthy answer to that short question.

Despite the framing of my initial question around two presidents, this book is a major departure from most college histories. Although I begin the book and most chapters with Wilson's plans and dreams for his alma mater, I pay relatively little attention to presidents and other administrators. Nor do I organize the narrative around presidential regimes. Instead, I sought to write a book that I—and I imagined most students, alumni, and faculty—would like to read rather than display, shelve, or sell. I also wanted to focus this history of an educational institution on *education*, not on the corporate or corporeal institution per se. One of the unfortunate features of most college histories is their lack of focus on what is most important. The result too often is content clutter, much of it administrative. This is understandable because the vast majority of college and university records are generated by administrators and their bureaucratic offices, and historians gravitate to the most numerous and accessible records they can find. But the histories they write thus tend to give too much coverage to presidential plans, fund-raising campaigns, intramural conflicts, and building construction and not nearly enough to the primary reason for the institution's existence.

In order to concentrate on the *educational* process at the heart of Princeton, I have organized the book topically, but pursued each topic chronologically in order to understand its development and role in the larger educational frame of the university. In an essay written with Princeton firmly in mind, I have argued that the seven essential (though by no means only) features of a great university today are faculty, students, libraries and labs, graduate programs, an art museum, a university press, and resources of sustained distinction.[7] Here each feature, except the last, receives its own chapter. Extraordinary financial resources obviously make the rest possible and probably deserve their own chapter. But the task of making all those dollars make sense and good reading was beyond me (the wayward son of a CPA), so I've spread much of the economic news throughout the chapters where it's relevant to educational developments. Likewise, the often-decisive role of presidents, deans, and trustees is not treated separately but only in the context of the essential academic functions of the university. Alumni, too, are largely absent, except when they affect the university's educational functions, positively or negatively. Although they are one of the university's two main products (scholarship being the other), it is nearly impossible to separate the contribution of their relatively few years at Princeton from the cumulative effects of their previous and subsequent experiences, inheritances, and education.

I've managed to adhere to my original table of contents with but one exception. I had planned to give each of the six elements equal treatment in a single chapter, though I anticipated that in covering more than a century of university history some chapters would run longer than others. As I tackled the topic of student life, however, it quickly became obvious that one chapter would not serve. At Princeton, unlike at many other research universities, the undergraduates were and still are the largest and most important student constituency. Although the graduate population (which has its own chapter) has grown to two thousand, Princeton's more than 4,800 (soon to exceed 5,200) undergraduates continue to dominate the physical scene and command the attention of the faculty and administration.

So it should not have been surprising—but was—that the undergraduates would eventually claim four long chapters of their own: on admissions, the curriculum, the extracurriculum, and the changing landscape of student culture—their dress, slang, religion, politics, and traditions. Given the main audience for college histories—current and former students—I'm hopeful that this extended treatment

[7] James Axtell, *The Pleasures of Academe: A Celebration & Defense of Higher Education* (Lincoln, 1998), chap. 5, "What Makes a University Great?"

of student history and culture will not disappoint readers and that it will chart a somewhat new direction for the genre as a whole.

College histories face another challenge because of their essential nature. As largely internal studies of single institutions, they often assume the form and adopt the tone of "house histories" written to celebrate some anniversary or milestone, which lends an unmistakably chauvinistic air to their story lines.[8] What such histories lack is appropriate context—social, cultural, or intellectual, regional or national. I have tried to locate Princeton in its larger and appropriate contexts as often as possible. Fortunately, since Wilson's day, the university itself has been extremely conscious of its competition and place in what became the eight-member Ivy League, the elite Association of American Universities (of which it was one of fourteen founding members), and, most important, the somewhat presumptuous "Big Three" (Harvard, Yale, and Princeton). Many of its own documents and records use its competitors as benchmarks, of which I have tried to take full advantage. When the university itself failed to draw comparisons, I often sought the data to make my own. Ever since Wilson set the university on a clear course to selective excellence, Princeton and most of its leaders have had an intrinsic interest in sustained quality, a desire to be among the best—if not *the* best—in the areas in which it chose to compete. By those multiple and elevated measures, it is nearly impossible to frame Princeton's story as a house history; I trust I haven't.

Another way I sought to avoid parochialism was to apply my working philosophy from ethnohistory. Approaching Princeton as I would the cultural strangeness of the seventeenth-century Iroquois or eighteenth-century Moravians, I have tried to assume nothing, to ask elemental questions, and to be thorough, balanced, and fair

[8] Richard Angelo, "A House is Not a Home," *History of Education Quarterly* 24 (Winter 1984): 609–18; John R. Thelin, "Southern Exposure: House Histories with Room for a View," *Review of Higher Education* 10:4 (Summer 1987): 357–68; Lester F. Goodchild and Irene Pancner Huk, "The American College History: A Survey of Its Historiographic Schools and Analytic Approaches from the Mid-Nineteenth Century to the Present," in *Higher Education: Handbook of Theory and Research*, vol. 6, ed. John C. Smart (New York, 1990), 201–90, esp. 218–38.

in my search for answers. This has often meant bracketing (temporarily) my Yale- (and William & Mary-) based experience and assumptions until I could learn the available facts about the distinctive Tiger tribe.

Thanks to one of the oldest, largest, and most efficient archives in American academe, Princeton facts are so voluminous that I was forced to make careful selections of the major record-groups and sources I would use to tell my educational story. I quickly discovered that the fifty-year restriction on certain records was virtually no impediment. Most of those records were top-heavily administrative, which I seldom needed because I was less interested in the details of policy-making than in its academic results, and small exceptions to the rule could be had with special permission. If I did need key pieces of information and permission could not be obtained, I could usually find them through other accessible sources. If presidential records fell under the restrictions, for example, I could write to or interview four living presidents; the same was true for faculty whose academic files were closed until death.

In general, however, I eschewed formal interviews, save for occasional e-mail queries on specific topics and three sets of questionnaires I sent to current and former staff members at Princeton University Press, to the alumni of the Graduate School, and to faculty in the Department of Art and Archaeology. I also relied on the full and the edited interviews with alumni conducted by the Alumni Council for the 250th anniversary, and the many rich interviews with Princeton faculty and administrators conducted by William McCleery.[9] Needless to say, I have consulted frequently with countless faculty, administrators, and staff, sometimes seeking materials in their keeping, more often suggestions where I might find paper

[9] The Alumni Council interviews resulted in *Going Back: An Oral History of Princeton* (Princeton, 1996). Cynthia Penney '83 of the Princetoniana Committee kindly provided me and the Princeton University Archives copies of the original transcripts. William McCleery published a number of lengthy interviews in *University: A Princeton Quarterly* and in *PAW*, as well as twenty-five shorter ones in *Conversations on the Character of Princeton* (Princeton, 1986, 1990).

answers to my pertinacious (and I hope not impertinent) questions. By not privileging living sources to which I happened to gain access, I sought to give roughly equal weight and attention to each decade of Princeton's "Wilsonian" century, mostly by using published or archivally accessible materials. If I have occasionally deprived myself of valuable information by my cautious resort to oral testimony, I hope I have also avoided being unduly influenced by misleading rumor, unreliable gossip, and fading memories.

The one published source I found indispensable is the *Princeton Alumni Weekly*. Not only did this editorial independent appear far more frequently than any other alumni magazine in the country (and still does), it has consistently lived up to its masthead goal: "to review without partiality the achievements and problems of the administration, the faculty, and the student body of Princeton University."[10] Although it does not forgo compliments and the occasional "puff piece," it is usually critical and frequently biting, especially in alumni letters to the editor and commissioned feature articles. Moreover, although it is officially independent of the university, it regularly publishes official news from and about the administration and faculty, which is sometimes difficult or impossible to obtain elsewhere. Unfortunately, Princeton's historians have made only random use of the magazine because of its extreme longevity and volume. Until I made an extensive topical index of it from 1939 to 2004, I, too, was unable to take full advantage of its factual and opinionated richness.[11]

I would be remiss if I did not acknowledge the sheer pleasure I have had in researching and writing Princeton's history. Frequent road trips to Princeton to visit archives and libraries, the perfect excuse to buy the first twenty-two volumes of the *Papers of Woodrow Wilson* and countless other books, the opportunity to make my vocation a scholarly avocation, making new friends and acquaintances among faculty, administrators, alumni, and students, even learning

[10] From its founding in 1900 to World War II, *PAW* appeared weekly during the academic year—thirty-six issues. By 1977 it had dropped to twenty-seven issues; in 1988 the now-*bi*weekly was published "only" seventeen times. It currently appears sixteen times. *Best of PAW*, vii.

[11] Computer-disk copies of the index are available in the Archives and in the offices of *PAW*.

to appreciate orange and black as a color combination—all of these have constituted some of my most indelible pleasures over the past dozen years. Although my main task has come to a close, I have cleverly chosen a subtitular end point—the ever-moving present—that will allow me to stay with the project a pleasant while longer.

J. A.
Williamsburg, Virginia

Acknowledgments

The actual writing of a book, as many authors are eager to tell us, is a lonely job, a silent struggle between one's creativity and a stack of blank, white sheets. But before and after the writing, bookmaking is, happily, sociable and collaborative. Certainly in researching and producing this history of a university not my own I have been welcomed and aided, stimulated and corrected, by a large tribe of tolerant Tigers as well as older friends of other stripes. It is a true pleasure to acknowledge and to thank them for their generous contributions.

Frequent research trips to Princeton were made possible by a Friends of the Princeton University Library summer fellowship in 2000 and by the William R. Kenan, Jr. Charitable Trust, which endowed the academic chair I occupy, and the College of William & Mary, whose research leaves and academic freedoms I have long enjoyed. The unmonastic comfort and hospitality of the Princeton Theological Seminary's Center for Continuing Education greatly eased my absences from home.

My first—and often last—stop was the University Archives in Mudd Library. There Ben Primer, then University Archivist (and now Associate University Librarian), Dan Linke, his successor, John Weeren, Nancy Shader, Chris Kitto, Rosemary Switzer, Tad Bennicoff, Gene Pope, and others guided and facilitated my forays into their boundless resources and records. Without their unfailing helpfulness and professional efficiency, I might still be taking notes and ordering xeroxes.

In Firestone Library itself, I was given every assistance by University Librarian Karin Trainer and her staff, Curator of Rare Books Steve Ferguson, Curator of Manuscripts Don Skemer, Reference Librarian Margaret (Peggy) Rich, and Charles Greene, who gave me a backstairs tour of the whole library. Paul Needham showed me the treasures of the Schiede Library and other courtesies. Gretchen Oberfranc, editor of the *Princeton University Library Chronicle*, applied her keen eye and red pencil to three of my articles, which contribute substantially to chapters 7 and 8.

As I tackled each chapter, I came to rely on the help of numerous experts and enablers throughout the university. Registrar Joseph Greenberg opened his well-kept files and statistics to an outsider without noticeable qualms. Dean of the Faculty Joseph Taylor and Associate Dean Toni Turano provided generous amounts of information (and Toni, my former graduate student, good company). Dean of the College Nancy Weiss Malkiel supplied not only documents and publications but a critical reading of the five chapters on the faculty and the students. Dean of Undergraduate Students Kathleen Deignan swiftly and fully answered queries. From One Nassau Hall, President Shirley Tilghman made a timely enquiry on the book's behalf, and her assistant Marcia Snowden lent me several germane reports.

The offices of the Graduate School were equally forthcoming. Dean John Wilson and former Deans Ted Ziolkowski and Alvin Kernan were founts of information and support and, with their wives, hospitable beyond the call. Mary Margaret Halsey commissioned my first Princeton publication, an updating of the 1978 history of the Graduate School by Willard Thorp and others. Associate deans David Redman and Joy Montero and assistant Sandy Sussman speedily answered numerous queries.

In the Art Museum, I benefited from the expertise, trained eyes, and generosity of several: Director Susan Taylor, Registrar Maureen McCormick (whose guided tour was invaluable), Curator of Prints and Drawings Laura Giles, Research Curator of Later Western Art and museum historian Betsy Jean Rosasco, and Managing Editor of Publications Jill Guthrie. Janice Powell, Librarian of Marquand Art Library, gave me wonderful access to her files and memories. John Wilmerding was my "inside man" in the Department of Art and Archaeology and allowed himself to be interviewed during a Maine vacation. Peter Silver (History) and Michael Cook (Near Eastern

Studies) kindly allowed me to relate their pedagogical experiences in the museum.

In writing and revising the chapter on the Princeton University Press, I had the indispensable assistance of Director Walter Lippincott, former director Herbert Bailey, and former controller Bill Becker. Several current and former staffers—too many to mention—kindly answered a questionnaire about the Press and supplied names, dates, and opinions freely. Sales Director Eric Rohmann provided data on a long list of titles, past and present. Frank Mahood and Neil Litt talked with me about book design and production, and Chuck Creesy clarified the computer-technology side of the business and much else. Peter Dougherty, social sciences editor extraordinaire and the new director, has been frank and supportive over many years. Brigitta van Rheinberg, the history editor and mine, has had unwavering faith in this book from the start and has backed it every step of the way, for which I am most grateful.

It has been an education and a pleasure to see the Press in operation on the production side as well. I'm grateful to Debbie Tegarden for guiding a large manuscript through all phases of production; to Eileen Reilly for special attention to its composition; to Frank Mahood for his artistry and skill in design and for humoring an author keen to kibitz; to Jonathan Munk of Bee, Nebraska, for care and precision in copyediting; and to Maria denBoer of Grandville, Michigan, for an index that allows me to locate things that even I had forgotten were there.

Other folks who lent timely assistance were Nancy MacMillan, publisher of the *Princeton Alumni Weekly*, who allowed me to buy bound volumes back to 1939 and lent me a dozen others; John Jameson in the Office of Communications, who supplied several illustrations; Stan Katz in the Woodrow Wilson School of Public and International Affairs, whose forceful articles on Princeton, philanthropy, and higher education stimulated my own thinking; medieval historian William C. Jordan, who clarified the functions and workings of the Princeton University Press Editorial Board; and Edward Tenner, former science editor at the Press, whose article on the Honor System made important corrections to the conventional wisdom. Pat

McConahay and Peter Oppenheimer at Witherspoon Books (alas, no longer in business) kept me well supplied with Princetoniana and shoptalk. John Thelin, my former colleague in higher education, gave some central chapters thorough and imaginative readings. Back home, the staff of William & Mary's interlibrary loan office, headed by Cynthia Mack, did yeoman service in securing fugitive writings on my strange, new obsession.

For the generous gift or loan of books, articles, manuscripts, and other materials, I am grateful to David Hoeveler, Jerome Karabel, Taylor Reveley, Howard MacAyeal, Ralph Woodward, Willis Rivinus, Elizabeth Greenberg, Jessica Lautin, Anne Ruderman, William G. Bowen, Bruce Leslie, William K. Selden, Gretchen Oberfranc, Chuck Creesy, William McCleery, John Mulder, Jill Guthrie, Peter Dougherty, Neil Litt, Alvin Kernan, Ted Ziolkowski, Alan E. Mayers, Russell Marks, Louis Weeks, Angie Lunking, Davison Douglas, Suzanne Hagedorn, W. Robert Connor, the Office of Communications, and many other university offices and staff.

Perhaps my biggest debt is owed to a long-suffering circle of friends and authorities who agreed to read the whole manuscript. Those who read it chapter by chapter, with incredibly good humor, insight, and tactful frankness, were Bruce Leslie, gentleman and scholar of higher education and Princetoniana; John M. Cooper, Jr., Wilson expert, prose stylist, and astute alumnus; Tony Grafton, master historian and keen student of higher education and Princeton; Patricia Marks, former editor of the *Princeton University Library Chronicle* and recent Princeton Ph.D. in History; and Bill Bowen, former president of Princeton and longtime president of the Andrew F. Mellon Foundation. In one fell swoop, former University Secretary Tom Wright and Bob Durkee, his successor, scrutinized the manuscript. All of these eagle-eyed experts saved me from countless sins of omission and commission and burnished many a hapless sentence.

The last person I must thank knew precious little about Princeton when we started, but she has since learned far more than any sensible Wellesley woman could ever want to know. My wife, Susan, has done this with her inimitable good grace, a game spirit, considerable amusement, and (be it said) no little *be*musement. Not only did she lend her keen ear and unsparing eye to the text, she indulged me my intellectual passions and frequent pilgrimages to New Jersey. As the longtime companion of an "Old Blue" Bulldog, she has come to accept his faint but unmistakable orange and black stripes. For all of which this book is dedicated to her and her myriad dedications, of which I count myself blessed to be one.

Abbreviations

Baker Papers	Papers of Ray Stannard Baker, MS 18,601, Library of Congress (microfilm)
Best of PAW	*The Best of PAW: 100 Years of the Princeton Alumni Weekly*, ed. J. I. Merritt (Princeton, 2000)
CHE	*Chronicle of Higher Education*; online at http://chronicle.com
DP	*Daily Princetonian*; online at http://dailyprincetonian.com
DRBSP	Department of Rare Books and Special Collections, Harvey S. Firestone Memorial Library, Princeton University
Marks, *Luminaries*	Patricia H. Marks, ed., *Luminaries: Princeton Faculty Remembered* (Princeton: Association of Princeton Graduate Alumni, 1996)
PAW	*Princeton Alumni Weekly*; online at http://princeton.edu/~paw
PU	Princeton University
PUA	Princeton University Archives, Seeley G. Mudd Memorial Library
PUL	Princeton University Library
PULC	*Princeton University Library Chronicle*
PUP	Princeton University Press
PWB	*Princeton Weekly Bulletin*; online at http://www.princeton.edu/pr/pwb
PWW	*The Papers of Woodrow Wilson*, ed. Arthur S. Link et al., 69 vols. (Princeton, 1966–1994)

Thorp, *PGS*	Willard Thorp, Minor Myers, Jr., Jeremiah Stanton Finch, and James Axtell, *The Princeton Graduate School: A History*, ed. Patricia H. Marks, 2d rev. ed. (Princeton: Association of Princeton Graduate Alumni, 2000)
WW	Woodrow Wilson
WWC	Woodrow Wilson Collection, Princeton University Archives

The Making of Princeton University

CHAPTER ONE

The Dream Realized

In the productions of genius, nothing can be styled excellent till it has been compared with other works of the same kind.

—SAMUEL JOHNSON

WHEN Woodrow Wilson resigned the Princeton presidency in 1910, he was discouraged and emotionally bruised. His failure to determine the location and character of the nascent graduate school and his inability to win support for building residential colleges, or "quads," for all of the college's classes, which he hoped would "democratize" if not eliminate the socially restrictive upperclass eating clubs, had wounded him deeply. A recent cerebrovascular incident that had hardened the lines of his headstrong personality did nothing to prevent or repair the damage. Four years later in the White House, he still had nightmares about the troubles that drove him from the institution he had attended as an undergraduate, loved as a professor, and nurtured as president.[1]

His disappointment was all the keener for having envisioned a brilliant future for Princeton and having enjoyed a string of early successes in realizing that vision. At its sesquicentennial celebration in 1896, the College of New Jersey had officially renamed itself a university. But Wilson, the designated faculty speaker, had been

[1] Edwin A. Weinstein, *Woodrow Wilson: A Medical and Psychological Biography* (Princeton, 1981), chaps. 10, 12; John M. Mulder, *Woodrow Wilson: The Years of Preparation* (Princeton, 1978), chap. 8. On December 12, 1913, Colonel Edward House noted in his diary that Wilson had not slept well the previous night. "He had nightmares . . . he thought he was seeing some of his Princeton enemies. Those terrible days have sunk deep into his soul and he will carry their marks to his grave" (*PWW*, 29:33–34).

scarcely any readier to recognize the larger responsibilities or opportunities of university status than had his faculty colleagues or the stand-pat president, Francis Landey Patton.[2] Yet within a year Wilson had sketched plans for a thorough reform. Six years later, as soon as he became president, he set about resolutely—as he did most things—to make Princeton the best university in the country. In a few short years he reorganized the administration, added trusted deans, and launched major fundraising and public relations campaigns among the alumni. He accelerated the rebuilding of the campus in "Collegiate Gothic" to signal the university's medieval, and particularly English, heritage. He organized the faculty into departments and divisions, recruited a number of senior "stars," hired fifty new "preceptors" to lead small-group discussions and encourage independent reading among the students, and expected all faculty to be scholars as well as teachers. He raised admission and academic standards, revamped the curriculum to balance breadth and depth and to allow only "assisted election" of upperclass courses, and sought in general to subordinate the extracurricular "sideshows" that were smothering "the spirit of learning."[3]

The university Wilson helped fashion during his eight-year tenure strove to be not only *excellent*—that clichéd goal of all colleges and universities—but *distinctive*. No other American university was quite like it, as educator-journalist Edwin Slosson found when he visited and described fourteen *Great American Universities* in 1909–1910. "Here is a university," wrote the Chicago Ph.D., "that knows what

[2] Woodrow Wilson, "Princeton in the Nation's Service" (Oct. 21, 1896), *PWW,* 10:11–31; Theodore J. Ziolkowski, "Princeton in *Whose* Service?" *PAW,* Jan. 23, 1991, 11.

[3] Stockton Axson, *"Brother Woodrow": A Memoir of Woodrow Wilson*, ed. Arthur S. Link (Princeton, 1993), 115; Richard J. Frankie, "Woodrow Wilson: Blueprint for Radical Change," *Journal of Education* [Boston University] 153:2 (Dec. 1970):16–25; Robert J. Taggart, "Woodrow Wilson and Curriculum Reform," *New Jersey History* 93:3–4 (Autumn–Winter 1975):99–114; Thomas Jefferson Wertenbaker, "Woodrow Wilson and His Program at Princeton," in Raymond F. Pisney, ed., *Woodrow Wilson in Retrospect* (Verona, Va., 1978), 74–81; John Milton Cooper, Jr., *The Warrior and the Priest: Woodrow Wilson and Theodore Roosevelt* (Cambridge, Mass., 1983), chap. 7. For Wilson's famous metaphor of "sideshows," see *PWW,* 19:57, 227, 344–45; on "the spirit of learning," see *PWW,* 14:299, 317; 16:50; 18:56–57, 464, 501; 19:283, 297.

it wants and is trying to get it," rather than drifting or slavishly imitating its larger rivals. Yet its originality consisted not in wild, untried novelties but "chiefly in going ahead and doing what others have always said ought to be done." The advent of preceptors, the rationalization of the curriculum, the plan for the "social coordination" of the students in Gothic quads, and the raising of academic standards were all meant to shift "the center of gravity of student life" and to transform Princeton from "one of the easiest places to get into" to "one of the hardest . . . to remain in."[4]

Although Wilson enjoyed considerable success in his first four years, he could not make Princeton into a first-class university as fast or in all the ways he might have liked. Slosson recognized this near the end of Wilson's tenure when he admitted that Princeton was "not among the fourteen foremost universities of the United States if we take as the criterion age, size, wealth, cosmopolitanism, publications, graduate students, professional courses, or public services." Not only was it the second smallest of the fourteen, with the second smallest income (only Wilson's graduate alma mater Johns Hopkins was smaller), it had only forty-eight graduate students (mostly in engineering); no women or blacks; few Jews or foreign students; a largely regional clientele; a cramped, undersized art museum; a five-year-old university press that had yet to publish any books; a small library; and a lot of strenuous athletes. For all of Wilson's efforts, Princeton was "still a college in spirit." But, Slosson predicted, "if it is not a university now, it is going to become one in the fullest sense of the word."[5]

A long century after Wilson assumed the presidency and set off on his path of reform seems a good time to ask, not if Princeton has become a real university—we know that it has—but how he might, from his perch in Presbyterian heaven, regard it through the pince-nez of his own time, goals, and even disappointments. Would Wil-

[4] Edwin E. Slosson, *Great American Universities* (New York, 1910), 75, 76, 77; interview with Arthur S. Link, in William McCleery, *Conversations on the Character of Princeton* (Princeton, 1986, 1990), 77; Axson, *"Brother Woodrow,"* 123; George McLean Harper, "A Happy Family," in William Starr Myers, ed., *Woodrow Wilson: Some Princeton Memories* (Princeton, 1946), 3.

[5] Slosson, *Great American Universities*, 98, 101, 104–5.

son, its intellectual architect, recognize the mature university as a faithful realization of his original design or as a random, even alien, product of American academic evolution?

We don't have to guess at the answer because Wilson's thoughts and values have been thoroughly documented in three extraordinary collections. The first and most indispensable is Arthur Link's sixty-nine-volume *Papers of Woodrow Wilson*, published appropriately by the Princeton University Press between 1966 and 1994. The second and third troves are transcribed interviews with and written reminiscences from most of those who knew Wilson, collected by two of his biographers. Ray Stannard Baker used his interviews and memoirs from the 1920s to write the eight-volume *Woodrow Wilson: Life and Letters*, the second volume of which is devoted to the Princeton years, 1890–1910.[6] In the late 1930s and early 1940s, Henry Wilkinson Bragdon interviewed many of the same people and others for his *Woodrow Wilson: The Academic Years*.[7] Together these sources greatly reduce the need to speculate about Wilson's likely response to his alma mater a century later.

Several of the Princeton colleagues who knew Wilson best suggest that he would have had little difficulty recognizing his handiwork in the new university and would have been comfortable with most—though by no means all—of its features. Henry Fine, dean of the faculty and Wilson's major supporter, told Baker in 1925 that "Wilson *made* Princeton. . . . When he started, Princeton was an unprogressive college—of ancient and honorable tradition, but unprogressive. When he went out it was one of the strongest universities in the country. . . . It has progressed ever since along lines laid down by Mr. Wilson." Seventeen years later, Professor of English Thomas Marc Parrott '88 still maintained that "all the developments since, except the Graduate College, have been based upon foundations

[6] Garden City, N.Y., 1927–1939.

[7] Cambridge, Mass., 1967. Bragdon's useful book must be used with caution because of its numerous factual errors. See the critical review by Arthur Link in the *New England Quarterly* 41:1 (Mar. 1968):118–21, which is reprinted in *PAW*, May 7, 1968, 11, 15.

Wilson laid."[8] With due allowance for the impress of social and academic evolution and a quartet of strong new presidents, can the same be said today, and if so, would Wilson acknowledge or take pride in the continuities?

Perhaps the first thing Wilson would notice about the new university is its size and its newer architecture. Spreading over more than six hundred acres in an exurban setting no longer surrounded by working farms and fields, the campus (a word coined at eighteenth-century Princeton) has almost grown to incorporate the Graduate College, initially—to Wilson's chagrin—isolated above the Springdale golf course and far removed from Nassau Hall, the original college building and now the administrative headquarters.[9] But Wilson was not put off by size alone as long as the university remained on a human scale, fostering "close and personal contact" between faculty and students, and sought the highest quality in all it did. In 1903 he had warned an alumni group in Philadelphia that "the danger to Princeton is the danger of a big, numerically big, university." But by 1910 he boasted to their Maryland counterparts that "almost unobserved, a little Princeton has given place to a big Princeton," in size as well as influence.[10] In just eight years, he had built eight new buildings and, under the guidance of supervising architect Ralph Adams Cram, had not hesitated to raze or move others to bring harmony to the campus and to open sightlines through it.

With some prominent exceptions, the buildings on the new campus probably would please him as well. Since Cram's master plan ensured that Wilson's favorite Collegiate Gothic continued to be used in campus buildings until the late 1940s, the former president could turn his discerning eye on the additions in newer styles. Wil-

[8] Interview with Henry B. Fine, June 18, 1925, Baker Papers, container 105, reel 74; Bragdon interview with Thomas Marc Parrott, Sept. 15, 1942, WWC, box 63, folder 25.

[9] Henry Lyttleton Savage, *Nassau Hall, 1756–1956* (Princeton, 1956); Alexander Leitch, *A Princeton Companion* (Princeton, 1978), 328–33; William K. Selden, *Nassau Hall, Princeton University's National Historic Landmark* (Princeton, 1995); Sean Wilentz, "Nassau Hall, Princeton, New Jersey," in William E. Leuchtenburg, ed., *American Places: Encounters with History: A Celebration of Sheldon Meyer* (New York, 2000), 311–23.

[10] *PWW*, 14:410 (Apr. 15, 1903); 20: 233 (Mar. 11, 1910).

son was no tyro— he knew what he liked. According to Cram and other experts, he had "instinctively a fine sense of proportion and a keen appreciation for good architecture." While he had no technical knowledge, "his appreciation of its quality and importance was unusual in its degree." And he always insisted that "every building," even science labs, "should be beautiful."[11]

So Wilson probably would appreciate the witty, colorful, and curve-blending functionalism of postmodern Princeton, particularly Robert Venturi's Thomas molecular lab (1986) and Wu Hall (1983) and the Computer Science building (1989), which make relaxed bows to the university's architectural traditions. Far fewer would be his favorites among the self-consciously "original" modernist additions between 1950 and 1980. No more than most Princetonians and critics would he relish the relentless linearity, monotonous regularity, and boxy minimalism of the Engineering Quad (1962), the School of Architecture (1963), and Spelman Halls (1973). More to his liking might be Minoru Yamasaki's gleaming and graceful Robertson Hall (1965)—not least because it is home to the school that bears his name—and the imposing, honey-brown, ten-story tower of Fine Hall, named for his indispensable dean. Frank Gehry's flamboyant new science library (2007) would no doubt amaze and appall him at the same time, while Demetri Porphyrios's subtle Gothic rendering of Whitman College (2007) would win instant approval.[12]

More disturbing to Wilson would be not the size of the student body but its composition. Compared to its major rivals, Princeton today is still the smallest institution; although the size of the student body has increased, a corresponding growth of the faculty, coupled with the continuity of the precepts and the addition of the senior

[11] Trustee Henry B. Thompson to Baker, Feb. 27, 1927, Baker Papers, container 116, reel 83; Cram to Baker, Oct. 7, 1926, Baker Papers, container 103, reel 73; Bragdon interview with Cram, May 8, 1940, WWC, box 62, folder 23, p. 2.

[12] Catesby Leigh, "Must the Minimum Be the Maximum? A Critical Look at Campus Architecture, and a Modest Proposal for a Return to Traditional Styles," *PAW*, May 19, 1999, 18–27; Ben Kessler, "Shaping the Campus," *PAW*, May 16, 2001, 24–31; Leigh, "Classic Redefined," *PAW*, Oct. 9, 2002, 12–17; Fred Bernstein, "One Campus, Different Faces," *PAW*, Dec. 18, 2002; 10–14; Raymond P. Rhinehart, *The Campus Guide: Princeton University* (New York, 1999), 64–65, 68–72, 91–94, 101–3, 109–11, 117–19, 122–24.

FIGURE 2. Gordon Wu Hall was built in 1983 as the social area and dining hall for Butler College (1980). Its eclectic and graceful postmodern lines were designed by Robert Venturi '47. The building was underwritten by Hong Kong entrepreneur Gordon Wu '58. It is the only building on campus identified by Chinese characters.

thesis, ensures that "close and personal contact" remain "the greatest good" in a Princeton education.[13] But the conspicuous presence of women, blacks, and international students would, from the perspective of 1910, earn his alarmed disapproval.

As a socially conservative Southerner who had presided over an institution long regarded as the most southern of the northern schools (or vice versa), Wilson would find the presence of several hundred black students particularly disconcerting because he had sedulously discouraged their application in his day. In 1904 he put off one inquiry by noting that "while there is nothing in the law of the University to prevent a negro's entering, the whole temper and tradition of the place are such that no negro has ever applied for

[13] *PWW*, 14:410 (Apr. 15, 1903).

admission." His phrasing was deliberate because the previous year a popular novel had drawn attention to the issue by speaking of the title character's ancestor as one "who was responsible for that clause in Princeton's charter which, unless altered, would forever prevent negroes from graduating from that famous university, and which has made it such a favourite for Southern gentlemen." One of Wilson's classmates who had read the book had to be assured that "the Charter contains no reference to negroes."[14]

Hiding behind the social "temper and tradition of the place" allowed Wilson and Princeton to discriminate against all sorts of potential candidates. In introducing the son of a close Jewish friend, another classmate was confident that "old Doctor Tommy Wilson" would never allow any boy to be "discriminated against because of his race, color, belief or otherwise."[15] Apparently he didn't know the president very well. Although Wilson would eventually appoint the first Jew and the first Catholic to the faculty, he did nothing to halt the unsubtle blackballing of Jewish students from the eating clubs and continued actively to discourage black applicants. In 1909 G. McArthur Sullivan, a student at Virginia Theological Seminary and College, a black Baptist institution in Lynchburg, wrote Wilson, "I want so much to come to your School at Princeton. I am a poor Southern colored man from South Carolina, but I believe I can make my way if I am permitted to come." Wilson's draft reply for his secretary read: "Regret to say that it is altogether inadvisable for a colored man to enter Princeton . . . strongly recommend his securing education in a Southern institution perhaps completing it with a

[14] *PWW*, 14:380 (Feb. 27, 1903); 15:462 (Sept. 2, 1904).

[15] *PWW*, 15:471 (Sept. 16, 1904). For Princeton's long history of discrimination against Jews and blacks, see Slosson, *Great American Universities*, 104–5; Marcia Graham Synnott, *The Half-Opened Door: Discrimination and Admissions at Harvard, Yale, and Princeton, 1900–1970* (Westport, Conn., 1980); Synnott, "Anti-Semitism and American Universities: Did Quotas Follow the Jews?" in David A. Gerber, ed., *Anti-Semitism in American History* (Urbana and Chicago, 1986), 233–71; Jerome Karabel, *The Chosen: The Hidden History of Admission and Exclusion at Harvard, Yale, and Princeton* (Boston, 2005). For scathing indictments of the "snobbish" social scene by two Jewish alumni, see Leon M. Levy to Wilson, c. June 25, 1907, *PWW*, 17:222–24, and Harold Zeiss to Wilson, June 27, 1907, *PWW*, 17:233–34.

course at the Princeton Theol. Sem., which is under entirely separate control from the University." Perhaps more sensitive to the man's feelings than his boss, the secretary avoided any reference to the applicant's color and helpfully advised, "If you wish to attend a Northern institution I would suggest that you correspond with the authorities of Harvard, Dartmouth, or Brown; the last named being, as you undoubtedly know, a Baptist Institution." But he also neglected to mention the local possibility, knowing—as Wilson also knew—that a few blacks had taken graduate courses at Princeton since President McCosh's time while enrolled at the Princeton seminary.[16]

Wilson would be hardly more accepting of Princeton's nonwhite students from abroad. Compared to the literal handful of foreign students from outside Britain and Canada in his own day, the twelve hundred students from around the globe, particularly India and China, would stagger him, for they were barely on his social radar. His handling of an offer to send a number of Chinese students to Princeton on government funds resulting from the Boxer Rebellion indemnity show him once again playing the social "temper" card. To one of his trustees he gave two reasons for declining the offer. One was that "most of the Chinese students come in search of engineering and professional courses, which," he said, "we cannot give them" (although the John C. Green School of Science offered degrees in both civil and electrical engineering). The second excuse Wilson obviously thought the more compelling. "I fear," he said, " . . . that our present social organization at Princeton would be sure to result in making any Chinese students . . . feel like outsiders, . . . set apart for some reason of race or caste which would render them most uncomfortable. There is no door that I can see," he admitted, "by which they could really enter our university life at all, and to

[16] *PWW*, 15:462n2; 19:529 (Nov. 20, 1909), 550 (c. Dec. 3, 1909), 557–58 (Dec. 6, 1909). See also Bill Paul, "Woodrow Wilson and Affirmative Action," *PAW*, Nov. 27, 1996, 47–48; Jan. 22, 1997, 2 (letter). For two examples of Princeton's continued problems with race, see Lawrence Otis Graham, *Member of the Club: Reflections on Life in a Racially Polarized World* (New York, 1995), chap. 9, "The Underside of Paradise: Being Black at Princeton," and Melvin McCray '74 and Calvin Norman '77, producers, *Looking Back: Reflections of Black Princeton Alumni* (Princeton: video produced for the 250th Anniversary, 1996).

have them come and form a group apart would certainly be most undesirable." During his own presidency Wilson was ambitious in wishing Princeton to "draw its students from all over the *nation.*" He was simply not ready to enlist the university "in the Service of *All* Nations" as well.[17]

The final group of students whose presence Wilson would regret constitutes nearly half the student population today. Although he was happily married to a highly intelligent, artistically talented, and well-read woman and doted on three independent and able daughters, he simply was "not at all in sympathy with co-education." Indeed, although he taught for two years at the new women's college at Bryn Mawr and sent all three daughters to women's colleges, he may have been less than keen on higher education for the opposite sex in general. Lucy Salmon, one of his former graduate students at Bryn Mawr, was "quite sure that he never whole-heartedly believed in college education for women." With singular lack of tact, he once told her that "a woman who had married an intellectual, educated man"—as his wife Ellen had—"was often better educated than a woman who had had college training."[18] When he spoke at the graduation of his eldest daughter, Jessie, a Phi Beta Kappa from the Women's College of Baltimore (later Goucher College) in 1908, it was fully in character that he referred to "man" and "men" throughout and said not a word about women or their educational needs, capacities, or accomplishments. Unfortunately, he seems not to have evolved far from the young suitor who had once opined that "the question of higher education for women is certain to be settled in the affirmative . . . whether my sympathy be enlisted or not."[19]

Wilson's real objection was less to college for women than to college for men and women together. His objections were essentially

[17] *PWW*, 14:299 (Dec. 19, 1902; my emphases); 19:120–21 (Mar. 26, 1909).

[18] *PWW*, 7:616 (May 4, 1892); Louise Fargo Brown, *Apostle of Democracy: The Life of Lucy Maynard Salmon* (New York, 1943), 102. Professor Salmon (History, Vassar College) was also critical of Wilson's attitudes toward women in two letters to Baker dated Jan. 6 and 15, 1926: Baker Papers, container 115, reel 82. For Wilson's unhappy stint at Bryn Mawr, see Bragdon, *WW: Academic Years*, chap. 8; Mulder, *WW: Years of Preparation*, chap. 4; Arthur P. Dudden, "Woodrow Wilson at Bryn Mawr College," *Bryn Mawr* [Alumnae Bulletin] 26 (1955):6–7, 32–33.

[19] *PWW*, 3:499 (Nov. 30, 1884); 18:318–20 (June 4, 1908).

social. While he may have been convinced that women were "intellectually different from men" (perhaps mostly because the disenfranchised women of Bryn Mawr did not seem to share his intense interest in the history and principles of politics), he was more worried that coeducation would ruin something precious and mysterious about relations between the sexes. There was a good deal of Southern romanticism in his position, as well as some frank self-recognition. Now that "the first, experimental stage of college training for women" had passed, he worried as early as 1892, the driven, devoted pioneers were being replaced by women who go to college "of *course*, as young men have long done," not for the "missionary adventure" but for "the contacts, experiences, routine, enjoyment, and incidental profit of college life." In this new "period of danger," these "easy going and sociable" young women were prey to the lustful attentions of the male "scapegraces" in their midst. "It must be the riotous elements in my own blood," the passionate professor confessed to his wife, "that make me fear so keenly what even the most honorable young fellows might be tempted by mere beauty to do, where there is no restraint." "Such an exquisite flower is safest for a long time—during all the period of immaturity," he concluded, perhaps with his daughters in mind, "—in seclusion." One can only imagine how many of the more than three thousand female Tigers today share Wilson's feeling that coeducation is "demoralizing" and "fatal to the standards of delicacy" between men and women.[20]

If Wilson could survive the shock of seeing the polychromatic student population on parade, he might take some comfort from improvements in Princeton's warped "social organization" and in the balance of students' social and academic lives, despite the exponential growth of extracurricular "sideshows" to tickle every fancy. Given the historic increase in student qualifications, selectivity of admissions, and curricular demands from a hard-driving faculty of scholar-teachers, he would have less cause to worry that the extracur-

[20] Brown, *Apostle of Democracy*, 101; *PWW*, 7:444 (Feb. 21, 1892), 467 (Mar. 10, 1892); 8:583–84 (May 29, 1894). See also Virginia Kays Creesy, "Woodrow Wilson and the 'Demure Damsels,'" *PAW*, Mar. 4, 1975, 8; Apr. 29, 1975, 5 (letter); Judith Kaplan, "Woodrow Wilson and Women: The Formative Influences on Wilson's Attitudes toward Women," *New Jersey History* 104:1–2 (Spring–Summer 1986):23–35.

riculum constitutes for most students "absorbing occupations" rather than wholesome "diversions" from the strain of hard, intellectual work.[21] Yet two causes of legitimate concern remain: athletics and the eating clubs.

Wilson did not worry about the value of sports as such. He thought they were "in themselves wholesome," a "safety-valve for animal spirits" and teachers of fair play. Although he didn't play much himself, he was an ardent and often vocal fan of Princeton football and baseball, attending gridiron practices with half the student body and umpiring faculty baseball games. But as the head cheerleader for an intellectual awakening on campus, he did want to see sports subordinated to learning and the life of the mind.[22] To make his point, he even proposed to the alumni that honors students and members of Phi Beta Kappa "ought to wear the University P" since they were "the best players on our scholarship team." Wisely, he hastened to add that he wasn't trying to discredit the sports teams, only to "give the scholar as good a standing as the athlete."[23]

In his own day Wilson did not succeed in preventing the few sports that were played from being "absorbing occupations," for the players at least, if not for the student fans. Nor would he have seen much change in the sports scene today, except that so many students, male and female, play their own sports that student attendance at even the high-profile (male) sporting events is noticeably reduced and replaced, if at all, by alumni, parents, and local fans. He would regret that intercollegiate sports have become so specialized and intense that serious training often begins in grade school and is for many youngsters a year-round regimen of training and competition. Except in a few unusual sports such as fencing, rowing, and water polo, student-athletes are recruited by equally specialized coaching staffs to fill specific positions on teams; "walk-ons" and multiple-sport players are increasingly uncommon. The existence of the Ivy

[21] Woodrow Wilson, "My Ideal of the True University" (July 6, 1909), *PWW*, 19:300; Wilson, "What Is a College For?" (Aug. 18, 1909), *PWW*, 19:345.

[22] *PWW*, 8:450 (Feb. 2, 1894); 19:300, 345.

[23] *PWW*, 15:284; Woodrow Wilson, "The Revision of the Courses of Study" (June 14, 1904), *PWW*, 15:382–83; Wilson, "The Training of Intellect" (Mar. 18, 1908), *PWW*, 18:54.

League and the absence of athletic scholarships preserves some semblance of amateurism, but intercollegiate sports at modern Princeton have become as professionalized in their own way as many of the unregulated sports of Wilson's day.[24]

A bigger concern Wilson would share with one of his presidential successors, William G. Bowen, whose two longitudinal studies of elite college athletes between 1951 and 1998 for the Andrew W. Mellon Foundation (of which he was president) discovered alarming patterns of academic underperformance among Princeton and other Ivy-recruited athletes, male and, increasingly, female. On average, they had lower SAT scores and high school grades than their classmates; they underperformed in college, even worse than their grades and SATs predicted they would; they were more likely to rank in the bottom third of the class; they tended to socialize largely with other athletes, especially teammates; they participated in fewer extracurricular and cultural activities than other students; they majored in a narrow range of preprofessional social sciences; they were more conservative in their attitudes and values than their classmates; and when they graduated, they expressed less confidence in their intellectual abilities.[25] None of these findings would please Wilson, the national academic and athletic reformer.

[24] Craig Lambert, "The Professionalization of Ivy League Sports," *Harvard Magazine*, Sept.–Oct. 1997, 36–49, 96–98; James L. Shulman and William G. Bowen, *The Game of Life: College Sports and Educational Values* (Princeton, 2001), chaps. 2, 6; "The Culture and Value of Sports: A Roundtable Discussion," *PAW Online*, May 16, 2001 (http://www.princeton.edu/~paw/features/features_27.html); Bowen and Sarah A. Levin, *Reclaiming the Game: College Sports and Educational Values* (Princeton, 2003); Ronald A. Smith, *Sports and Freedom: The Rise of Big-Time College Athletics* (New York, 1988); John M. Murrin, "Rites of Dominion: Princeton, the Big Three, and the Rise of Intercollegiate Athletics," *PULC* 62:2 (Winter 2001):161–206; John Sayle Watterson, "Political Football: Theodore Roosevelt, Woodrow Wilson, and the Gridiron Reform Movement," *Presidential Studies Quarterly* 25:3 (Summer 1995):555–64; Watterson, *College Football: History, Spectacle, Controversy* (Baltimore, 2000).

[25] Nancy E. Cantor and Deborah A. Prentice, "The Life of the Modern-Day Student-Athlete: Opportunities Won and Lost," paper delivered at the Princeton Conference on Higher Education, Mar. 21, 1996 (based on the Mellon "College and Beyond" data for Princeton, Columbia, and Amherst); Shulman and Bowen, *The Game of Life* (based on the Mellon data for thirty-two institutions, including four Ivies: Penn, Columbia, Yale, and Princeton); Bowen and Levin, *Reclaiming the Game* (based on the Mellon data for thirty-three institutions, including all eight Ivies).

Another hangover from Wilson's day is the role of the eating clubs on Prospect Avenue, "The Street," but it has shown some improvement. The clubs began to proliferate in the 1890s and 1900s because the university failed to provide sufficient dining facilities for upperclassmen. As more sons of the Gilded Age flocked to the university with the "country club" reputation, they and their fathers built increasingly posh clubhouses for elegant dining and vigorous socializing. But unlike most fraternities elsewhere (which had been banned from Princeton in 1855 on John Maclean's watch and more permanently in 1875 by James McCosh), they did not house the members, except for a few club officers and alumni who returned for football games, reunions, and spring dances.[26] The sticking point for Wilson was not the opulence of the clubs, or even the bibulous behavior of their members, but their admissions procedures and total lack of "intellectual purposes or ideals."[27]

Even with fourteen clubs by 1910, only three-quarters of the upper classes could join; the rest were consigned to culinary and social purgatory. Some men were so crushed by rejection that they left college, and many who stayed were dispirited for their last two years, feeling cut off from their privileged classmates and *in* but not *of* the university. But the social damage, as Wilson saw it, ran deeper because of the way club members were chosen in the "bicker" process. In order to ensure election to specific clubs, sophomore groups formed small eating clubs in rented houses both to avoid the unpleasantries of Commons food and mass dining and to form "hat lines" (named for their distinctive colored hat bands) that made collective election to the upperclass clubs more certain. Despite administrative fiat, these sophomore groups were often recruited from similar freshman cliques, many of which in turn consisted of selective prep school cohorts. The individual, particularly a social late-bloomer or a bookish high schooler, therefore had little chance to make his mark and to be recognized by the clubmen, with whom he

[26] The large size and paneled poshness of the clubs were mandated—and bankrolled—by club alumni who sought not only to prepare undergraduates for city club life after graduation, but to provide themselves with another club in bucolic Princeton.

[27] *PWW*, 17:167 (c. May 30, 1907).

had virtually no academic and scant social contact (many freshmen were forced to live off campus for lack of space). Thus, not only did the upper classes foster a "sharp" and "distorted" social competition upon which a majority of the students "stake[d] their happiness," they failed to provide academic and moral leadership to the junior classes.[28]

The more Wilson was frustrated in his efforts to supplant the clubs with residential quads for all four classes, the more he came to regard the clubs as "distinctly and very seriously hostile to the spirit of study." He relished the results of a study that revealed that between 1903 and 1907 only 9 percent of the clubmen had won honors (the older, more prestigious clubs had the fewest) while 42 percent of the nonclubmen did. And as his losing battle with the club alumni anticipated and fueled his political shift toward progressivism, his academic rhetoric heralded the transition. By 1910 his speeches were studded with "democratic" talk and metaphors, targeting social exclusiveness and the unfair advantages of inherited wealth. "Learning," he argued, "knows no differences of social caste or privilege. The mind is a radical democrat."[29]

Today, however, Wilson would discover that the eating clubs, though still a distinctive feature of Princeton's extracurriculum, are no longer its exclusive center. Five of the ten clubs have open admissions on a first-come basis, and the five that are still selective are less prestigious than they once were and have relaxed their procedures, with sophomores now calling on the clubs instead of suffering the inanities and torment of bicker committees visiting them in their

[28] *PWW*, 16:519–25 (c. Dec. 13, 1906); 17:167 (c. May 30, 1907), 181–84 (c. June 6, 1907). On the club system, see William K. Selden, *Club Life at Princeton: An Historical Account of the Eating Clubs at Princeton University* (Princeton, 1996); Bragdon, *WW: Academic Years*, 272–74, 317–19; Mulder, *WW: Years of Preparation*, 187–202; Leitch, *Princeton Companion*, 146–49.

[29] *PWW*, 16:520, 523 (Dec. 13, 1906); 17:401–2 (Sept. 26, 1907); Woodrow Wilson, "The Country and the Colleges" (c. Feb. 24, 1910), *PWW*, 20:160. In the spring of 1908, the figures in the study of honors work were questioned by Wilson's close friend John Hibben and by a pro-club committee of trustees. The trustees concluded that the clubmen led a "cleanly, manly, and *fairly* studious life." Bragdon, *WW: Academic Years*, 332, 471n32, 473n53 (my emphasis).

rooms, as depicted so fatally by Geoffrey Wolff in *The Final Club*.[30] A number have increased opportunities for contact with faculty, and wired club libraries do more serious business after meals. Clubs even take pride in earning the best GPA on The Street as well as in hiring the best bands and throwing the best parties. Perhaps least of all from Wilson's standpoint, but a decided improvement nonetheless, the advent of female members promotes more normal relations with the opposite sex and reduces the importation and sexist treatment of women on bacchanalian weekends.

Yet for Wilson two weaknesses of the modern club system remain: it does little to promote the good influence of the upperclasses upon the more junior, and it makes only sporadic, token attempts to bring faculty and students together outside the classroom. Both of these flaws—and the club-induced decline of Princeton's "democratic spirit"—he thought could be remedied only in four-year residential colleges. In the late 1970s and early 1980s, long after Yale and Harvard had built their colleges and "houses" with Edward S. Harkness money, Princeton built or configured from existing facilities five colleges, only one of which—Rockefeller College in Holder Court—resembled a true enclosed quadrangle on the Oxford model Wilson had idealized. There can be no doubt that he would be disappointed that they house and feed only the freshman and sophomore classes. In 1907, after the board had rained on his full quad plan, he had expressed interest in the compromise suggestion of a friendly trustee that a truncated version would at least cultivate "a partial academic spirit in the two lower classes" and break up the nefarious "hat lines." But, reported the friend, "the essential idea of having all classes living on equality with the reflex of the more mature minds of the upper classes working on the lower seems to be his corner stone."[31]

On the other hand, Wilson would see that the advent of more qualified students and a more elective curriculum, which allows

[30] New York, 1990. See also "Bicker Week, 1974," by Edward D. Duffield II, '58, who underwent the bicker process again as a reporter: *PAW*, Feb. 4, 1975, 10–18.

[31] *PWW*, 17:380 (Sept. 10, 1907). Had Wilson lingered on the scene until today, he would take much comfort from the university's plan to use a new, sixth college on the south campus and four of the existing colleges (remodeled) to accommodate members from all four classes and graduate residence assistants: *PAW*, May 16, 2001, 12–13.

bright freshmen and sophomores to take any courses they can handle, throw the young and older undergraduates together early and often, as do sports teams and other extracurricular and service activities. He would also applaud the ubiquitous faculty presence in the colleges in the form of masters, fellows, guests, speakers, and seminar teachers. For half the student body at least, this is exactly the "community of constant, general, intimate contact" he had sought and failed to provide for his own Princeton. He told a Harvard audience in 1909 that scholar-teachers must mix socially and daily with students to "make thought a general contagion," but so far "the scholar is not in the game."[32] Today, he—and she—very much is and Wilson would applaud.

Although he might swallow hard before admitting it, the fullest realization of Wilson's idea of a residential quad is the beautiful Gothic Graduate College, dubbed in 1913 by some of its new denizens as "St. Andrew's-on-the-Links." Wilson had approved an early plan of it back in 1903. But in his last four years in office, he lost another battle to locate it in the center of the campus to promote the "organic" coordination of the university, although he did manage to reduce the administrative control of the Graduate *School* by "that arch-intriguer" Dean Andrew Fleming West. West had sided with Wilson for five years on every educational reform. But he crossed to the opposition when the president, after a behavior-altering arteriosclerotic incident in 1906, precipitously and without his usual careful consultation with faculty or trustees, pushed his quad plan ahead of the long-promised graduate college. In a speech to the faculty, even Wilson admitted that the quad plan was "nothing more or less" than West's idea of the Graduate College "adapted to the undergraduate life." That was the last straw for the impatient dean, who proceeded to raise funds on his own to build the college in splendid isolation, and—as it turned out—to drive Wilson from office in the bargain.[33]

[32] *PWW*, 16:214 (Nov. 9, 1905); Wilson, "The Spirit of Learning" (July 1, 1909), *PWW*, 19:284–85, 287.

[33] *PWW*, 17:424 (Oct. 7, 1907); 19:442 (Oct. 24, 1909). For the Wilson-West conflict, see Bragdon, *WW: Academic Years*, chaps. 16, 18; Mulder, *WW: Years of Preparation*, chap. 8; Thorp, *PGS*; James Axtell, "The Dilettante Dean and the Origins of the Princeton Graduate School," *PULC* 62:2 (Winter 2001):239–61.

Today, however, Wilson would have precious little reason to disapprove of Princeton's highly ranked graduate school. Until 2006, the graduate dean was physically and administratively tucked into Nassau Hall, and the Graduate College is presided over no longer by the ceremony-loving West or an august faculty master but by a young "residence life" professional.[34] The graduate faculty, all of whom teach undergraduates as Wilson had insisted his faculty should, is even more accomplished as a group than the double-handful of senior scholars he had wooed from Great Britain, the University of Chicago, and Penn and the fifty preceptors (many of whom soon taught graduate courses) from all over the country. Of more concern to Wilson, the Graduate College is no longer run on "dilettante ideals," and even its distance from the center of academic life has diminished somewhat with new roads, cars, and campus expansion. At the same time, although the Graduate School has been increasingly recognized by his successors as a major contributor to Princeton's national and international reputation, Wilson undoubtedly would be pleased that the much larger undergraduate college continues to dominate the life and memory of the new university.[35] Despite his university ideals and leadership, Wilson was at heart and in practice an undergraduate teacher, who had little interest in or time for graduate students.[36] He just wanted them to be intellectually the best they could be so they might "infect the place"—especially the undergraduates—"with the real spirit of scholarship."[37]

He also wanted them to be immersed in graduate extensions of the liberal arts, "pure"—as opposed to merely professional—"studies."

[34] In 2006 the graduate dean and his staff moved into a reconfigured Clio Hall, one of the two debating societies' Greek temples.

[35] *PWW*, 19:755 (Jan. 10, 1910); Thorp, *PGS*, chap. 10; James Axtell, "Rounding Out a Century: The Princeton Graduate School, 1969–2000," *PULC* 61:2 (Winter 2000):171–216.

[36] Bragdon interviews (WWC) with Edwin G. Conklin, Mar. 24, 1943, box 62, folder 21, p. 2; Oscar Veblen, June 9, 1939, box 63, folder 54; Robert McNutt McElroy, Nov. 20, 1940, box 63, folder 13, pp. 1–3; William F. Magie, June 12, 1939, box 63, folder 9, pp. 5, 9; Max Farrand, May 1, 1942, box 62, folder 37, pp. 1–3; Farrand, May 11, 1942, ibid., pp. 1–2; William Berryman Scott, June 9, 1939, box 63, folder 44; Luther Eisenhart, June 9, 1939, box 62, folder 35, p. 2.

[37] *PWW*, 14:158 (Oct. 21, 1902).

According to a senior scientist who knew him well, Wilson "hoped that Princeton would not undertake to develop technical or professional schools, but rather general subjects fundamental to the professions." In his own day, he declined the offer of a forestry school (actually a forest but no endowment) and linkage with a proprietary medical school in Philadelphia. A suggestion from trustee and ally Cyrus McCormick for "industrial training" such as Harvard's did not seem to Wilson "consistent with our system and purposes." Neither did an ordinary law school for practitioners, but he did favor a more philosophical "school of jurisprudence," a distinction he must have acquired during his own misapplied legal studies at the University of Virginia.[38]

Thus, Wilson would be gratified that Princeton, after a century, is still home to only three professional schools, all based on "fundamental" disciplines in the arts and sciences. It's equally safe to say that he would regard the Woodrow Wilson School of Public and International Affairs as a fair trade for a school of jurisprudence, particularly since the former is such a direct and apposite expression of "Princeton for the Nation's Service," the title of his inaugural address in 1902.[39]

Given Wilson's own superficial, non-lab education in science in the 1870s and his pronounced "literary" approach even to the social sciences he professed and wrote about, we might wonder how he would regard the high, Nobel-laden reputation Princeton enjoys in mathematics and science today. When he took office, the scientific side of the university had remained "relatively undeveloped" and the lab equipment was at least twenty-five years old. Unfortunately, Wilson himself was not much interested in or knowledgeable about developments in science, much less mathematics. But he knew, as he declared in his inaugural address, that "science has opened a new world of learning, as great as the old," and now belonged to "the true patriciate of learning," to the "fundamental studies" that every

[38] *PWW*, 10:69 (c. Dec. 2, 1896); 14:159 (Oct. 21, 1902); 19:76 (Mar. 3, 1909); Edwin Grant Conklin, "As a Scientist Saw Him," in Myers, ed., *WW: Princeton Memories*, 58; Bragdon interview with Conklin, Mar. 24, 1943, WWC, box 62, folder 21, p. 1.

[39] *PWW*, 14:170–85 (Oct. 25, 1902).

university worthy of the name had to promote and teach. So he leaned on the astute judgment of his dean of the faculty, Henry Fine, a first-class mathematician, to "build up a great graduate department in the sciences" to match those in "the literary and philosophical studies of the University." With Wilson's blessing and some trustees' bankrolling, Fine proceeded to hire some of the world's best in math and science and to design with their help and build the Palmer Laboratory for physics and Guyot Hall for biology, geology, and a museum of natural history. Like the new faculty, Wilson assured the Maryland alumni in 1910, the labs were "equal to any in the university world, whether in this country or abroad."[40]

Given that early head of steam, Wilson would not be surprised or displeased by Princeton's current fame as a powerhouse of math and science. Even the Institute for Advanced Study, Princeton's independent but closely allied neighbor, would not intimidate him—provided he was steered into the studies of the historians and social scientists rather than the theoretical physicists and other number-crunchers.

While scientists have their labs, humanists and social scientists need their own workshops in the university library. In Wilson's time, the Princeton library was "more than adequate" for a liberal arts college but not for the ever-growing research needs of a major university. In 1896, when then-Professor Wilson was trying to lure frontier historian Frederick Jackson Turner from Wisconsin, he had to admit that "the weakest part of Princeton is her library." Although a new library building had been funded and would be ready the following year, the collection held just over 100,000 titles, "little enough material for original work" with hit-or-miss coverage of major areas.[41] By the time Wilson stepped down in 1910, however, the library had made considerable progress. Wilson had yet to obtain the full half-million-dollar endowment he sought for it, but several special collections had "fairly rich" endowments. With more than 250,000 volumes, the library was considered by its discerning refer-

[40] *PWW*, 14:180 (Oct. 25, 1902); 17:39 (Feb. 15, 1907), 61–62 (Mar. 6, 1907); 20:232–33 (Mar. 11, 1910); Conklin in Myers, ed., *WW: Princeton Memories*, 57.

[41] *PWW*, 10:50–51 (Nov. 15, 1896).

ence librarian "large for the size of the student body and faculty," at least in the subject areas taught.[42]

Before the advent of the precept system in 1905, the library had been "very little used." After, there was a quickening of use, though mostly to gain access to assigned readings on reserve, often available in duplicate copies. Indeed, two former preceptors suggested that the intellectual revolution wrought by the precepts was incomplete. Political scientist Edward Corwin noted that "the minimum list of reading soon became for most students the maximum list," while his former colleague Charles McIlwain lamented that "there was less independent and original work than there should have been." Circulation statistics seem to bear them out. At the turn of the century, the average student had checked out just eighteen books a year, less than two per semester course; ten years later, the number had climbed only to twenty-three.[43] Wilson would be delighted to learn that today the students lug home nearly ninety books a year—as well as consult innumerable online Web sites and databases—for their research papers in most courses, junior papers, and senior theses. He would also take pleasure in the architectural continuity of Firestone Library with his beloved Gothic campus, its vast and accessible holdings, and its abundant quarters for study, research, and writing.

Princeton's art museum might not hold the former president's attention as much as the rare and special collections in Firestone and its satellites, but for the memory of his talented wife, Ellen, he would regard its collections, quality, and associated research library with favor. When he was courting Ellen Axson in 1884, he confessed that he knew "marvellously little about art." This was a somewhat daring—and challenging—admission because she had studied art privately and at a women's college in Georgia, had earned a living doing portraits, and was then an advanced student at the highly regarded

[42] *PWW*, 14:155–56 (Oct. 21, 1902); William Warner Bishop, "Reminiscences of Princeton: 1902–7," *PULC* 8:4 (June 1947):147–63, at 149–50.

[43] *PWW*, 16:513 (Dec. 13, 1906); 19:451 (Oct. 27, 1909); Bragdon interviews (WWC) with Harry Clemons, July 24, 1941, box 62, folder 19, pp. 1–2; Charles H. McIlwain, Jan. 2, 1940, box 63, folder 11, p. 2; Edward S. Corwin, "Departmental Colleague," in Myers, ed., *WW: Princeton Memories*, 22; Allen O. Whipple, Jr., "Undergraduates and the Library," *PAW*, Apr. 1, 1938, 577 (chart).

Art Students League in New York City. After marriage she continued his tardy aesthetic education. Their Princeton houses were filled with her work, which she continued to refine in annual stints at the Old Lyme [Connecticut] Summer School of Art, America's center of Impressionism. She and he took a grand tour of European art museums and architecture in 1903, which she supplemented the following year in Italy with just the girls. At home she copied important paintings in exhibitions that traveled to the burgeoning university art museum built in 1889. Although Wilson may have had "by nature" an affinity for good art, it was "Mrs. Wilson's influence," thought her knowledgeable brother Stockton, one of Wilson's closest friends, "which enabled him to discriminate and become so sure a judge of good painting."[44]

We have to be more tentative in divining Wilson's attitude toward the Princeton University Press today because he wrote—and perhaps thought—even less about it than he did about the art museum, and with good reason. Although the press was founded in 1905 to handle university-related printing jobs such as the *Princeton Alumni Weekly*, the *Daily Princetonian*, and various publications of the Princeton Theological Seminary, it was not incorporated until October 1910, as Wilson was leaving office. In 1911 publisher Charles Scribner built Gothic-style quarters for the new press on William Street, where it published its first two scholarly books the following year: President John Witherspoon's *Lectures on Moral Philosophy* to celebrate the past and Princeton Art Museum director Allan Marquand's *Della Robbias in America* to herald the new Princeton scholarship.[45]

In August 1907 Whitney Darrow, the young brain and energy behind the Press, sent Wilson a copy of the annual report to the

[44] *PWW*, 3:133 (Apr. 15, 1884); Frank J. Aucella, Patricia A. Piorkowski Hobbs, and Frances Wright Saunders, *Ellen Axson Wilson: First Lady–Artist* (Washington, D.C., and Staunton, Va., 1993); Frances Wright Saunders, *Ellen Axson Wilson: First Lady Between Two Worlds* (Chapel Hill, 1985), 16–17, 20, 47–54, 113, 147–56, 191–92, 196–97, 251–52, 256–59; Axson, "*Brother Woodrow*," 90–94 (quotation), 103.

[45] *PWW*, 17:351–52n2, 353–57 (Aug. 1, 1907); [Charles] Whitney Darrow, *Princeton University Press: An Informal Account . . .* (Princeton, 1951); *Letters from Charles Scribner, '75 to Whitney Darrow, '03 in the Early Days of Princeton University Press* (Princeton, 1968).

stockholders. Darrow was hopeful that future printing and "possibly" publishing work would come from New York and Philadelphia and particularly from "the growth of the Graduate School." In order to tie the Press and the university more closely, without losing the Press's independence, Darrow proposed three things. First, with the help of the English Department, he wanted to produce a "University Style" book to distribute to administrators and faculty, who might be persuaded to submit their manuscripts to the new press if it could show that it could "turn out work which is artistic and in good taste" and "suits the subject matter." Second, he needed an educated editor-in-chief, preferably from the faculty, to oversee the proofreading and quality control. And finally, he wanted the Press to share some of its profits with the university to help departments afford their various printing needs, which the Press would then meet at the most reasonable cost.[46]

Although this is the extent, ironically, of the Press's published paper trail through Wilson's presidency, it is difficult to imagine that the former professor, who loved reading, writing, and buying books more than most of his species, would not take pride in knowing that PUP's handsome, often artistic, and prize-winning books reach libraries and readers worldwide, spreading the university's name and augmenting its reputation in the process. The only publications that might give him pause are Arthur Link's uncompleted five-volume biography of Wilson and his immense *Papers of Woodrow Wilson*, which expose his every flaw and misstep to public scrutiny, along with his many strengths and accomplishments.[47]

Finally, the guesswork can stop as we come to the final two facets of Princeton's modern reputation. There can be no doubt whatever that Wilson would take pardonably personal pride in his university's ethos of distinctive excellence, and immense vicarious (if not envious) pleasure in the financial resources that make it realizable. No university president in full possession of his faculties would look askance at an endowment larger than the gross national product of many small countries. And only the most eccentric or inexperienced

[46] *PWW*, 17:354–57 (Aug. 1, 1907).

[47] Arthur S. Link, *Wilson: [various subtitles]*, 5 vols. (Princeton, 1947–1965).

executive would prefer an institution that settled for high adequacy or protean performance in a large range of centrifugal activities to one that strove for genuine excellence in a select number of centripetal endeavors.

Like most of his presidential peers, Wilson would have figuratively salivated at the thought of what he could have done with the 1900s' equivalent of eleven *billion* dollars. He could have built his Gothic quads over the objections of even the clubmen and Eastern alumni. He could have offered many scholarships to lower- and middle-class high school students to reduce the social impact of the sons of wealth. He could have financed fully the fifty preceptors and the expensive senior faculty stars he lured to Princeton. He could have built Dean West his graduate college but placed it where he, not the dean or some wealthy donor, thought it would best serve the university as a whole. He could have endowed his new science faculty and labs without going hat in hand to the Rockefellers. Perhaps he would have had enough left over to found a school of jurisprudence. In short, he could have lived without constant debt or indebtedness to a band of generous trustees and a Committee of Fifty devoted alumni whose annual gifts and subscriptions covered his worthy losses.[48]

The essential problem was that Princeton had to work with an endowment one-half or one-third the size of those of its natural competitors, "the largest and oldest Universities in the East." But Wilson had a dream, a "vision" as he said, and he was not about to let something as trivial as money stand in the way of realizing it. When he made his list of desiderata at the beginning of his term, he took it to alumni groups around the country. When he read the modest price-tag of the university's immediate needs, $2.25 million, he drew whistles from the audience; but when he finished painting his dream in full color and said it would cost them $*12.5* million, there was applause.[49] Perhaps they were stunned, or simply impressed by his silver-tongued bravado: Wilson always knew how to charm a crowd, the bigger the better. But either way, they failed to

[48] *PWW*, 17:61 (Mar. 6, 1907); 19:144–46 (Apr. 1, 1909), 166 (Apr. 19, 1909), 269n1, 320 (July 27, 1909).

[49] *PWW*, 14:271, 275 (Dec. 9, 1902); 16:4 (Feb. 18, 1905).

respond as generously as their new leader had hoped, particularly after he indirectly impugned their country-club degrees and eating-club snobberies. By the spring of 1909, ironically (and perhaps presciently), the Secretary of the Committee of Fifty was predicting that "in the near future, Princeton may depend upon her alumni for adequate financial support." This was the same prophet who had noted three years earlier, before Wilson raised the "quad" flag, that "the more closely in touch with Princeton a graduate is, the more readily he gives."[50]

What Wilson was forced to do, as Dean West and other "enemies" behind the scenes were doing, was to seek out individual alumni who could be persuaded to part with some of their fortunes to fund his soul-saving schemes for Old Nassau. Unfortunately, as his sister-in-law Margaret Axson closely observed during his troubles, "Woodrow was no earthly good at it. He insisted that the obligation of raising funds belonged properly to the trustees, while the president should be left free to run the college." Moreover, "he was temperamentally unfitted for the task of raising money. Normally a man of easy gracious manners, when confronted by a possible donor, he became shy, ill at ease, as embarrassed as though he were about to ask for money for himself."[51] Thus, while he would not have wanted to hit the endowment campaign trails as his successors have had to do, he would applaud the focused use of their hard-gotten gains and those of the Princeton Investment Corporation to sustain and embellish his dream.

That dream was nothing less than to make Princeton "the best and most distinguished institution *of its kind* in the world." This goal did not entail large size or trying to be all things to all men. "We can afford to be one of the lesser universities in number," he said, "if we are one of the foremost in power and quality," by which he meant

[50] *PWW*, 16:461 (Oct. 17, 1906); 19:146 (Apr. 1, 1909), quoting Harold Griffith Murray.

[51] Margaret Axson Elliott, *My Aunt Louisa and Woodrow Wilson* (Chapel Hill, 1944), 190–91. Margaret married Edward Elliott, Wilson's young dean of students, who may have corroborated her assessment of Wilson's fundraising disabilities. In 1904, Wilson remarked, in a fundraising letter to a Pittsburgh steel magnate, "To ask for money is unpalatable to any man's spirit, even though he ask, not for himself, but for the best cause in the world" (*PWW*, 15:221 [Mar. 30, 1904]).

only "*intellectual* distinction and *intellectual* primacy." He was, he confessed, "covetous of everything that would bring academic distinction" to Princeton because he believed that a university's "only object is intellect." He wanted every department to be "at the very front, not only in scholarship, but in influence and leadership." To accomplish that, he sought faculty "whom advanced students cannot afford not to study under, men who will themselves be the only kind of advertising that a University should condescend to." But he wanted Princeton's search for intellectual preeminence never to be a timid imitation of any other institution's. He wisely wanted its general purpose and defining pattern of characteristics to be "distinct to ourselves," the university "noticeable because of her individuality, because she stands for something different."[52]

If Princeton is one of the very best universities in the country, indeed the world, today, Wilson's articulate goals, disciplined focus on its distinctive character, unlimited faith in its potential, and enduringly persuasive rhetoric are largely, though of course not entirely, responsible. In his relatively short presidency, he was able only to begin the university's transformation and ascent to academic primacy. Six able successors and several generations of loyal Princetonians—students, faculty, administrators, staff, and alumni—have pursued the tasks he set in changing times and conditions. Though he might regard his most recent successor, as he regarded his former boss at Bryn Mawr, as a learned but misplaced woman, he would undoubtedly applaud Shirley Tilghman's courage and leadership abilities in furthering his dream in the new millennium. That she secured—from an undergraduate alumn*a*, no less—the gift of a sixth residential college to house (as he had wanted) members from all four classes, and some graduate students as well, would only compound his pleasure and surprise.

[52] *PWW*, 14:75 (Aug. 11, 1902), 385 (Mar. 8, 1903); 16:453 (Sept. 16, 1906, my emphasis); 17:117 (Apr. 24, 1907); 18:20 (Mar. 12, 1908), 55 (Mar. 18, 1908); Winthrop M. Daniels to Ray Stannard Baker, Baker Papers, container 104, reel 73, p. 49.

CHAPTER TWO

From Gentlemen to Scholars

Great individuals, not great organization men,
make a college or university great.

—Harold W. Dodds

The faculty is the indispensable mind and soul of a university. It is possible, after all, to have a collegiate institution without students—All Souls College, Oxford (founded in 1438), is still one—because a self-governing faculty can teach itself through research and scholarship.[1] On the other hand, an institution consisting solely of deans and vice-presidents would be superfluous and a college of students without teachers hugely ineffective.

But describing a university faculty is complicated by its compound nature. A faculty is, first of all, a collectivity, a collegiate body of professors, but a loose collection of distinctive and largely autonomous individuals. It is not uniform in age, rank, or quality. Its composition changes annually, though only slowly in new directions. A faculty recruits new, often young, members as it loses older members to mobility, retirement, and death, but by design or habit they often resemble their predecessors. Unlike the students, who are collectively ubiquitous nine months a year but who each acquire only a short, usually four-year, experience and memory, the faculty is a perdurable organism with a long-term investment in the institution and an equally long collective memory. Although a faculty is formed and framed largely by the academy, it is also responsive to the wider

[1] Sir C. Grant Robertson, *All Souls College* (Oxford, 1899). A. L. Rowse describes, in often lubricious detail, the dons' life in All Souls in *A Cornishman at Oxford: The Education of a Cornishman* (London, 1965) and *All Souls in My Time* (London, 1993).

society that supports higher education for both selfish, practical reasons and more idealistic, disinterested ones. Its mandate, therefore, is often seen by different constituencies as simple and straightforward, but in reality it is always intricate and subtly shifting.

The best description of Princeton's faculty in its quotidian variety and complexity is, ironically, a work of fiction. Carlos Baker's *A Friend in Power* (1958) describes the workings of a faculty presidential search committee at lightly disguised "Enfield University," whose camouflage colors are an unremarkable maroon and white.[2] During its writing, Baker was the Woodrow Wilson Professor of English Literature at Princeton and chairman of the English Department. He had written a book on Shelley and another on Hemingway's artistry, but had not yet begun his authorized biography of Hemingway, for which he is best known.[3] In 1956 he had served on a (nonfictional) committee to find a successor to President Harold W. Dodds, who had presided with conspicuous grace and resourcefulness through the Great Depression and World War II. Princeton's committee, like Enfield's, plucked from the local faculty a young humanist and decorated war veteran—Robert Goheen—for the top job.[4]

Despite several red-herring references to great teachers, the president, ample endowments, and football rivals at "Princeton," Enfield is unmistakably Baker's locus operandi.[5] Like Princeton, Enfield is old (founded in 1761), all-male, and located not far from Newark and the studios of WABC in New York. The town is small and dominated by the university; the "Inn" is centrally located on "Main Street," easily found by visiting lecturers. The university features an apparently all-male faculty, junior essays, senior theses, and a long street of "fraternity houses" that bear an uncanny resemblance to

[2] Carlos Baker, *A Friend in Power* (New York, 1958). For reasons that defy explanation, this quiet, unexciting book about American academe has been translated into several languages, including French, Punjabi, and Vietnamese.

[3] Carlos Baker, *Ernest Hemingway: A Life Story* (New York, 1969). See "Interview with Carlos Baker: Confessions of a Hemingway Biographer," *PAW*, Sept. 30, 1969, 8–12.

[4] "The New President," *PAW*, Jan. 18, 1957, 14–16.

[5] Even the Enfield president's parrot has been trained to say "Beat Princeton."

FIGURE 3. Carlos Baker, Professor of English, Hemingway biographer, and author of *A Friend in Power* (1958).

Prospect Avenue's eating clubs. The retiring president, a classical archaeologist (whose interest in antiquity echoes Goheen's), lives in a Greek Revival mansion known as "The Parthenon," little different in spirit from the Florentine Renaissance bulk of "Prospect," where the Princeton president lived until 1968. A lighted clock in a Georgian *chapel* bell-tower regulates classes, while the faculty meets in "Enfield Hall" in a venerable faculty room, with long polished pews facing each other across a central aisle and dark oil paintings of university worthies to proctor the proceedings, not unlike Nassau Hall's.

A tall "Phoenix" sundial is obviously meant to remind local readers of the Mather *pelican* sundial, a gift from Corpus Christi College, Oxford, in 1907, in the McCosh-Dickinson courtyard.[6]

Even fictional faculty resemble Princeton notables. One internal candidate is a well-known historian of the American Revolution commissioned to write Enfield's bicentennial history—a doppelgänger for colonialist Thomas Jefferson Wertenbaker, who published a truncated history of Princeton in 1946 in the university's two-hundredth year.[7] "A fifty-two-year-old sociological bad boy" (probably modeled on Princeton's Melvin Tumin) posits the antiquity of his discipline by referring to "the great Princeton professor's treatise" on Roman rule in Asia Minor, the exact title of classicist David Magie's two-volume opus published by Princeton University Press.[8] The novel's central figure, Edward Tyler, a teacher of eighteenth-century French literature and a scholar of Voltaire, seems to have borrowed his interests from Baker's eminent colleague in the French Department, Ira O. Wade, who published several books on Voltaire before 1958 and thereafter.[9]

In guiding the reader unhurriedly through Enfield's academic-year-long search for a new leader, Baker paints a surprisingly comprehensive picture of Princeton's faculty at work in the late 1950s.

[6] *PWW*, 17:462–66; photos between 354 and 355; Philip Pattenden, "Reading Mather's Sundial," *PAW*, June 15, 1981, cover, 10–12.

[7] Thomas Jefferson Wertenbaker, *Princeton, 1746–1896* (Princeton, 1946), reissued in 1996 with a preface by John M. Murrin. Wertenbaker's four typescript chapters carrying the story to 1946 are in his papers in the Department of Rare Books and Special Collections in Firestone Library.

[8] David Magie, *Roman Rule in Asia Minor to the End of the Third Century after Christ*, 2 vols. (Princeton, 1950). Magie's opus, all 1,661 pages of it, was "planned in my youth, begun in middle age and finally completed in my old age," the author wrote; it was for "nearly a quarter of a century . . . my hope and my despair" (vii). On Tumin, see Bernard Beck, "Melvin Marvin Tumin," in Marks, *Luminaries*, 328–35; Martha L. Lamar, "Faculty Portraits: Melvin Tumin," *PAW*, May 21, 1968, 14–15, 21.

[9] See Ronald C. Rosbottom, "Ira Owen Wade," in Marks, *Luminaries*, 351–57; Rosbottom, "Ira Wade's Enlightenment," *Studies in Burke and His Times*, 14:2 (Winter 1972–1973):133–54; Jean Macary, ed., *Essays on the Age of Enlightenment in Honor of Ira O. Wade* (Geneva: Librarie Droz, 1977). Wade's summation on Voltaire is *The Intellectual Development of Voltaire* (Princeton, 1969).

Ed Tyler's busy life as French professor and chairman of the Department of Modern Languages serves as the focus for most of Baker's inflected observations on his own university and colleagues. Part of Baker's goal in this most academic of academic novels, written during the anti-intellectual Eisenhower years, was obviously didactic, even mildly evangelical. As Tyler's good friend, biologist Cos Cobb, puts it, "The layman doesn't know what professoring really is." To which Tyler later adds, "The hardest job in the world is to be a good professor." *A Friend in Power* is, in no small measure, an effort to explain to a sizable lay audience just what professoring at an elite university really is and how hard it is to do well.

Since the book features no (overt) sex, murder (only a botched suicide), or greed (except a soupçon for benign power), its plot allows Baker to spend ample time and loving detail on the faculty's professional labors from October to June, one chapter to each month. Tyler aptly describes faculty life as a "three-ring circus" (recalling Wilson's metaphor), in which the faculty is expected and expects to perform consistently at a high level through a temporal cycle of autumn energy, winter doldrums, and spring depletion, capped by commencement hopes of summer renewal.

The three rings in Princeton's faculty performance were teaching, scholarship, and service to the university, profession, and nation. These were the areas in which every Princeton professor was—and still is—judged on a four-page "blue [now white] form" sent by department chairs to the dean of the faculty annually to justify retention, tenure, promotions, and raises.[10] The three criteria were not, Baker makes clear, of equal weight. As one of the Enfield trustees describes the ideal candidate for president, "he must be absolutely devoted to the two great tasks of the university: the education of young men and the extension of the boundaries of knowledge." Although a key item of the faculty uniform was a pocket-sized appointment book, Tyler and his Princeton contemporaries knew that even religious attendance at the meetings that filled its pages—a "top-

[10] The "blue form" was the "devilish concoction" of English professor Robert K. Root in his final year as dean of the faculty between 1933 and 1946 (Willard Thorp, "Making My Way at Princeton," *PULC* 54:2–3 [Winter–Spring 1993]: 178–87, at 184).

heavy schedule of ad hoc committees, standing committees, department committees, and outside committees"—did not lead to tenure or merit pay. Instead, they regarded committee work as "the price you pay for democratic government in a university." And long before the late 1950s, Princeton was known for its "genuinely collegial mode of operation."[11]

Teaching, of course, was the professor's first obligation, and Ed Tyler, like his Princeton creator, did it conscientiously, with pleasure, and well. At Enfield, teaching occurred in many guises and settings. Like most senior professors at coeval Princeton, Tyler teaches at all levels, from first-year to graduate. He reads freshman themes on La Fontaine's *Fables* and spends generous amounts of time going over his corrections and comments with the "boys" during office hours. In one of his eleven o'clock lectures, he probes "the multiple profundities of Montesquieu in the *Lettres persanes*." From dog-eared notes filled with "scribbled marginalia" and "interlineations," he hopes to craft not only an "urbane and finished product," but through "any verbal magic he could muster" to bring the French Enlightenment "alive into the heads (and if possible the hearts)" of his four dozen "yawning, alert, scratching, attentive, surreptitiously [newspaper-]reading, argumentative, girl-dreaming" undergraduate auditors. Over spring vacation, he plays catch-up by reading a pile of papers from his graduate seminar and a batch of "junior essays."

Like many Princeton professors, Tyler seems to take the greatest pleasure in watching and gently guiding the progress of a senior thesis, being researched and written by a C+/B- soccer player. Fenelosa began in October with the "crazy notion" that Voltaire was really a Christian. But after Tyler gave him a list of definitions to look up in the great skeptic's *Philosophical Dictionary*, the chastened young man disappeared for some time before deciding to compare Voltaire and Jefferson. After a February road-trip to Monticello, Fenelosa produced a seventy-two-page thesis that earned high marks from his advisor. At their initial encounter in the fall, Tyler had been

[11] William McCleery, *Conversations on the Character of Princeton* (Princeton: PU, Office of Communications/Publications, 1986), 9 (William G. Bowen); see also 15–16, 60–61, 69, 140.

prompted to think about ignorance, "the great foe of us all—and the collaborating friend. All year long," he apostrophized, "we will fight it, in all the forms it takes . . . this is our job, our private war, . . . as it is every fall, year in and year out and down the centuries." While the students might riot or generate other headlines, "the real events would happen inside: the bombshells, the hoisting petards, the hidden mines you didn't know were there and which, exploding in your consciousness, left you different from the man or boy you had been. Nothing exciting. Nothing special. Just a perpetual war perpetually renewed in all the classrooms and offices and laboratories."[12]

While teaching alone defines a college, Baker and his fictional colleagues emphasize that Princeton is a university with important scholarly duties to perform as well. One search committee member, a crusty chemist, tries to nix a local candidate from the English Department, a critic lately turned poet, with the confident assertion that "it might have been all right thirty, forty years ago, when this place was a college of liberal arts. But times have changed. This is a great university now." The committee needed no reminding, in part because the trustees had impressed upon them that the new president should be above all "a proven scholar. . . . One who has written books" or perhaps "made scientific discoveries."

Although Tyler is a full professor with tenure, he longs to escape with a Guggenheim Fellowship to France the following year to add a big volume on Voltaire to his personal "five-inch shelf of books." The university has offered a year's leave at half-pay to complement the Guggenheim which, his dean assures him, is "in the bag." Only in the spare interstices of his busy schedule, filled with classes and committees, can he find, "with luck, a couple of hours in the library" each week to read and make notes toward the new book. Even as he grouses that "no books were ever written . . . at a committee table. Correction: no good books," he recognizes the quality of the academic life: "Nothing to squawk about except the way your scholarly enterprises kept getting the short end of the stick." He agrees with his sage and comely wife Alice that "Professors are lucky. They can

[12] For Baker's views on teaching, see McCleery, *Conversations on Princeton*, 1–5; on his teaching, see A. Walton Litz, "Carlos Heard Baker," in Marks, *Luminaries*, 1–4.

write their own monuments and people will always read them." But he also knows first-hand the persistent challenge of writing books: "To avoid the rhetoric, to channel the idea, to harness the energy and direct it, to persevere until it was done and then to go through it again, and again, until it was perfect. No not perfect. Just not too imperfect, the monument not too lopsided."

By the same token, Tyler willingly enforces the university's "publish-or-perish" rules for tenure, as did Baker and other chairmen at Princeton. The year before, Tyler and the dean had to "can" an assistant professor of French. Although Don Drake is a good teacher, Tyler explains to a mutual friend, "he's such a perfectionist as a scholar that I doubt if he gets out a book until he's eighty. If that." Drake has ended up in a small sectarian college in the Midwest, but his appreciation of an occasional cocktail goes down wrong with his new employer and he is fired. When the college's irate dean accuses Tyler of deliberately omitting Drake's record for "habitual and chronic drunkenness" from his letter of recommendation, Tyler calmly ignores the insult and explains that "we failed to renew his contract simply because he had done no scholarly writing whatsoever. It seemed to us that his talents as a teacher could be best employed at some institution," he adds with an Ivy League jab, "where scholarly publications were not a necessary prerequisite to academic advancement."

When Baker's alter ego is not writing books or encouraging his junior faculty to do so, he engages in a number of other scholarly pursuits, all of which were well known to Princeton professors of modern languages. As chairman, Tyler attends the post-Christmas meetings of the MLA (Modern Language Association) to interview candidates for vacant positions in the department. Likewise, he vets article manuscripts for the *PMLA*, the association's house organ, the latest few on Diderot: "Contents to be judiciously appraised and returned to the editorial office." He faithfully attends *Le Cercle Français* to hear papers by ambitious young faculty and graduate students; the last on Gide's journals was "no more than fair. Wit, as usual, masqueraded as substance." He's a regular reader of the *Bulletin* of the American Association of University Professors, to which he belongs, and of the *New York Times*, especially the book review and education sections. And he's invited to lecture at other colleges. The most recent tour takes him to Georgia, four campuses in as many days, where he dispenses wit and wisdom in exchange for modest honoraria, fried chicken, and "Bourbon-and-branchwater."[13] Scientists similarly sold their services to industry and economists to Washington: Princeton in—and for—the Nation's Service, just as Woodrow Wilson had wanted.[14]

Although *A Friend in Power* offers a broad and nuanced picture of the Princeton faculty at work, a view that few students and alumni, much less "laymen," ever see, it is only a snapshot, taken at a single point in the middle of the university's fast-paced modern century. It does not and cannot show us the faculty's evolution to that point nor subsequently. Without the whole century-long story, we will fail to appreciate how Wilson began the decisive transformation of the Princeton faculty, from often amateur gentleman-teachers in a modest liberal arts college to professionalized scholar-teachers in a formidable and ambitious research university.

❁ ❁ ❁

A disturbing number of the faculty whom Wilson knew as an undergraduate in the late 1870s, joined in 1890, and even inherited as president in 1902 were ripe for reform or replacement. According to their younger colleagues, often fresh from the advanced graduate schools and laboratories of Europe, too many were "old" in learning, theological disposition, and academic ambition. While their numbers were not objectively large, their presence was magnified because the faculty was relatively small and the old-timers often taught large required courses. The majority had been recruited by President James McCosh between 1868 and 1888 and many of them were schooled at the small College of New Jersey, often called Princeton

[13] Baker took a nearly identical tour to Georgia during the week of Feb. 4–11, 1957, speaking at the University of Georgia, Emory, Agnes Scott College, and Georgia Tech. *PAW*, Mar. 1, 1957, 13.

[14] "Princeton in the Nation's Service" [Oct. 21, 1896], *PWW*, 10:11–31; "Princeton for the Nation's Service" [Oct. 25, 1902], *PWW*, 14:170–85; Theodore J. Ziolkowski, "Princeton in *Whose* Service?" *PAW*, Jan. 23, 1991, 11–16.

College. When McCosh arrived from Scotland and took office shortly after the Civil War, sixteen teachers (60 percent of them Princetonians) saw to the instruction of 264 unruly undergraduates, as much in "character," control, and Christianity as in intellectual pursuits; only three professors could claim any distinction as scholars. When he retired at the age of seventy-seven, his faculty of forty taught only 604 students—about the same 1:16 ratio—most but not all of them undergraduates.[15]

Beginning in the 1870s, McCosh encouraged a few "bright young men" (as he called them) to stay on for postgraduate work, and a number of the best with Princeton fellowships went on to doctorates from the new Johns Hopkins (founded in 1876) or European (largely German) universities, before returning to Princeton to teach. In 1877–1878 the college began to offer its own graduate courses, in eight subjects, and seven of its eight fellows stayed put rather than go abroad as they might have done previously.[16] At commencement in 1879, two of these home-scholars were awarded Ph.D.s when "Tommy" Wilson received his bachelor's degree. They were followed by ten more earned doctorates before McCosh stepped down; seven of them were Doctors of Science from the new John C. Green School of Science, established in 1873. Several other alumni favorites and graduates of comparable colleges, who had studied in Europe without taking a degree and had acquired some teaching experience, were given honorary doctorates; one recipient was Andrew Fleming West, the future dean of the Princeton Graduate School.[17] With a demonstrable gift for raising funds for buildings (thirteen) and endowed professorships (nine), McCosh longed to "make our teaching equal to our buildings."[18]

He might have succeeded better in raising the college to a new level had he been able to overcome three obstacles. The first was his

[15] J. David Hoeveler, Jr., *James McCosh and the Scottish Intellectual Tradition: From Glasgow to Princeton* (Princeton, 1981), 250–57, 335.

[16] Hoeveler, *James McCosh*, 285–90; Thorp, *PGS*, 23–25, 28.

[17] Hoeveler, *James McCosh*, 290; Thorp, *PGS*, 23–24, 32, 58–59. See James Axtell, "The Dilettante Dean and the Origins of the Princeton Graduate School," *PULC*, 62:2 (Winter 2001):286–319, and chapter 7, pp. 378–79, 389–90, below.

[18] Thorp, *PGS*, 19, 27.

board of trustees: half Presbyterian clergymen, all conservative, most "old dotards" (as he dubbed them) who would fall asleep in meetings when they were not questioning or thwarting his proposed reforms. The trustees jealously guarded their prerogative of appointing faculty members. At best, McCosh could send them two or three nominations, perhaps with a strong preference for one, but they chose in the end. Wisely, as he sought to raise the quality of his faculty, McCosh told the trustees, somewhat truthfully, that the ideal candidate was an alumnus, a "lively" teacher, and a "decided Christian," preferably Presbyterian. Although several of his inherited and acquired faculty were in fact alumni and Presbyterian clergymen, he did manage to get through the board twenty-three of thirty-six appointments who were not products of the college or the Princeton Theological Seminary, its cooperative but independent neighbor.[19]

Whatever their origins, many of his appointees were first-rate scholars. Charles A. Young ("Twinkle," as the students called him), a Dartmouth valedictorian at eighteen, put Princeton on the map as an international center of astronomy with his four major books on the sun, expeditions around the world to observe solar eclipses, and presidency of the American Association for the Advancement of Science.[20] McCosh collected valedictorians. William F. Magie, a Berlin Ph.D. and later long-time chairman of the Physics Department and dean of the faculty (1912–1925), was first in Wilson's talented class of 1879. Henry B. Fine, the class act of '80 in classics, earned a Leipzig Ph.D. before elevating the teaching of mathematics at Princeton and serving as President Wilson's indispensable dean of the faculty and president of the American Mathematical Society, which he helped found. Aristocratic and athletic Allan Marquand, head of '74, studied philosophy in Berlin before earning a doctorate at Johns Hopkins and teaching logic and Latin at Princeton. Self-educated in the history of art, he launched the Department of Art and Archaeology in

[19] Hoeveler, *James McCosh*, 239, 285, 295–96.

[20] Hoeveler, *James McCosh*, 244–45. On the day he died in 1908 in Hanover, N.H., there was a total eclipse of the sun. Alexander Leitch, *A Princeton Companion* (Princeton, 1978), 534–35.

1882 and published seminal works on the Della Robbias and on Greek architecture.[21]

McCosh's second obstacle was a disorganized curriculum, consisting largely of prescribed, year-long, but abbreviated (one or two hours a week) courses taught mostly in "recitations" (tedious drill sections), increasingly in large lectures, and rarely in hands-on labs. A few electives exposed upperclass students to new subjects, but classical languages, mathematics, science, and philosophy dominated the curriculum and religion suffused it. The burden on the faculty was as great as on the students. All professors taught too much for too little pay.[22] Many began their careers teaching subjects in which they had only minimal preparation or interest; others, even with seniority, taught a wide array of subjects, cursorily but not deeply. Heavy teaching loads, lack of research facilities, and the need to serve *in loco parentis* to obstreperous adolescents hampered their scholarship, as did "the insistence upon a certain standard quality of style in the publications of the Faculty, even upon quasi-technical subjects."[23]

The third obstacle to academic improvement was perhaps the most serious: the attitude and behavior of the students, who were on average a year or two younger than today's undergraduates and often underprepared for college work. In the tribal student cultures of the 1880s and 1890s, some of their members testified, "there was no strong intellectual curiosity, more a desire to attain a reasonably well-rounded equipment of cultural knowledge, 'when, if, and as' supplied by the faculty." A collective taboo also discouraged "absorption in or undue concentration upon intellectual effort": "scholastic honors were simply not among the idols of the tribe." Nearly forty years later, M'Cready Sykes '94 remembered with regret that his generation, like schoolboys, regarded the faculty as "natural enemies"

[21] Hoeveler, *James McCosh*, 289–91; Leitch, *Princeton Companion*, 177–80, 311–12, 314–16; Oswald Veblen, "Henry Burchard Fine—In Memoriam," *Bulletin of the American Mathematical Society* 35:5 (Sept.–Oct. 1929), 726–30.

[22] McCosh managed to raise the top salaries only $900, from $2,100 to $3,000 plus housing, in twenty years. Wertenbaker, *Princeton*, 300.

[23] Winthrop More Daniels, "Princeton Traditions and Tendencies," *The Critic* 766 (Oct. 24, 1896):239–41, at 240.

and "got away with murder." Between the canned tedium of recitations and the anonymity of large lectures, "real study was almost altogether optional."[24]

Unfortunately, too many faculty members were complicitous and cultivated a "take-it-or-leave-it" attitude. Professional standards were minimal. As long as the professor did "good work" in the classroom and had some knowledge of his subject, his position was secure. With a few, even popular, exceptions such as Young's astronomy, Fine's algebra, and Theodore "Granny" Hunt's English, most courses were "guts" or "snaps." A Princeton diploma could be gotten with "a preposterous paucity of anything approaching real scholarship."[25] "Razzing" the faculty instead was the students' favorite game. Professor Stillwell Schanck's outdated sophomore chemistry classes were "a riot all the time." If the students did not drown out his "droning, dull" lectures with swelling renditions of "Swing Low, Sweet Chariot," they hurled missiles and cat-calls about the room. The response of the former physician was to assert, "Well, gentlemen, I am here to teach you. If you won't listen, it's a matter of utter indifference to me."[26]

Although the students were "always ready for a row in any class," their mischief tended to erupt in the classes of notoriously weak or inept teachers. According to the shrewd analysis of Dean "Billy" Magie, the older underperformers on the pre-Wilsonian faculty seemed to outnumber the younger stars. In addition to "Bone" Schanck, some of the worst were:

Henry C. Cameron '47: Presbyterian minister and pedant with an "almost encyclopedic" knowledge of Greek grammar and vocabulary. Assuming that his students were ill-prepared for anything better, he made them "parse, and parse, and parse," line by tedious line, which

[24] Harrison B. Smith '86, "The 'Eighties—Unburdened by Complexes," *PAW*, Jan. 30, 1931, 395–97, at 395; M'Cready Sykes '94, "Gentlemen—The 'Nineties," *PAW*, Feb. 6, 1931, 419–21, 425, at 420, 421; Feb. 13, 1931, 439–41.

[25] Smith, "The 'Eighties," 395; Wertenbaker, *Princeton*, 366; Sykes, "The 'Nineties," 420.

[26] Henry W. Bragdon interview with William F. Magie, Aug. 6, 1940, p. 11; July 13, 1941, p. 14, WWC, box 63, folder 9; H. G. Murray '93, "Gentlemen-Scholars of 1890: No. 4—J. Stillwell Schanck '40," *PAW*, Nov. 2, 1934, 122.

FIGURE 4. An unflattering caricature of Professor of Greek Henry Clay Cameron, drawn by Wilson's classmate and close friend Robert Bridges '79 on the inside back cover of his freshman copy of Demosthenes' *Orations* (Boston, 1872).

naturally "killed any interest in Greek as literature." For which offense "disorder was rife in his classes" and the sophomores regularly destroyed his hat.[27]

George Macloskie: former student of McCosh at Queen's College, Belfast, Presbyterian minister in Ireland, and amateur naturalist

[27] Hoeveler, *James McCosh*, 241; Bragdon interview with W. F. Magie, Aug. 6, 1940, p. 10; July 13, 1941, p. 13, WWC, box 63, folder 9; Murray, "Gentlemen-Scholars of 1890: No. 5—Henry Clay Cameron '47," *PAW*, Nov. 9, 1934, 143. On the last day of class, the

when McCosh lured him to Princeton in 1874 after the trustees rejected his first choice. Years later he told Edwin Conklin, his successor as professor of biology, that he had been astonished at Princeton's offer and doubted his fitness for it. But he thought he might "learn enough natural history on the way over to keep ahead of the boys." Apparently he was wrong: Dean Magie thought "he could not conduct a course, was easily exasperated, and knew too little about his subject," for which he suffered "riotous classes."[28]

General (never Professor) *Joseph Kargé*: the "most colorful" member of the faculty in his day. A German-trained scholar, duelist, and veteran of the Polish Revolution of 1848, he fought for a New Jersey regiment in the Civil War. Professor of English Thomas Marc Parrott '88 recalled that "he spoke both French and German with an execrable accent, was irascible, played favorites, [and] was almost laughably incompetent to teach." He could be diverted from his elementary recitations for long periods by any question about military tactics, current events, or his adventurous life.[29]

❁ ❁ ❁

The election of Professor of Ethics Francis Landey Patton to succeed President McCosh in 1888 was a hopeful sign to the younger faculty who wanted to transform Princeton into a true university. Patton's personal appearance was not particularly auspicious. His "knit brow," penetrating eyes behind steel-rimmed glasses, long stringy side whiskers, mouth "set to the taste of vinegar," "pallor of a medieval monk," white lawn tie, and black high-buttoned frock coat suggested

---

students would steal his felt hat, cut it into pieces, and distribute them as souvenirs. Bragdon interview with Ralph Barton Perry, May 29, 1945, p. 2, WWC, box 13, folder 28. As a student, Wilson was particularly contemptuous of Cameron's recitations, "which [Cameron] made very stupid as usual" (*PWW*, 1:193; also 195, 199–200, 205).

[28] Thorp, *PGS*, 20; Edwin G. Conklin, "Biology at Princeton," *Bios* 19 (Oct. 1948):150–71, at 156–57; Bragdon interview with W. F. Magie, Aug. 6, 1940, p. 11; July 13, 1941, p. 14, WWC, box 63, folder 9.

[29] Murray, "Gentlemen-Scholars of 1890: No. 7—Joseph Kargé," *PAW*, Nov. 23, 1934, 189; Hoeveler, *James McCosh*, 241; Bragdon interview with T. M. Parrott, Sept. 15, 1942, p. 4, WWC, box 63, folder 25; Sykes, "The 'Nineties," 440.

the conservative Presbyterian minister he was.[30] But he was also a brilliant, witty, and compelling speaker and his inaugural address seemed to herald a golden age of institutional modernization and achievement.

Patton's approval of research and scholarship was perhaps the most encouraging theme the younger faculty heard. "The university is meant to be a place of research," he emphasized, and "the professor who has ceased to learn is unfit to teach. . . . There is no necessary antagonism between a man's work as a teacher and his work as an investigator. It is the man who is making contributions to his department whom the students wish to hear." But Princeton's professors were not able to pursue research as much as they should, he admitted, because they "as a rule are overworked in the classroom. We have not fully learned the difference between a professor and a pedagogue." The only sentence that may have given the faculty pause was his characterization of college administration as "a business in which Trustees are partners, professors the salesmen and students the customers."[31] If the customers were assumed to be right and the trustees sought to micromanage academic affairs, the roles of the president and faculty were in some doubt if not jeopardy. In fact, Patton's description boded ill for reform's prospects.

Although admirers and critics alike acknowledged that the president was "extraordinary . . . intellectually," he soon proved to be "a wonderfully poor administrator."[32] He was physically lazy, "extremely cautious" in the face of conservative trustees and alumni, and, in Wilson's opinion, "the worst correspondent in the United States," in part because he had no secretary until 1895 and wrote all correspondence, in duplicate, by hand, once he was moved to act.[33]

[30] *PWW*, 3:114 (Apr. 6, 1884); 7: between 326 and 327; 12: between 162 and 163 (photographs); Wertenbaker, *Princeton*, 344. The side whiskers remained until 1899. *PWW*, 11:240 (Sept. 15, 1899).

[31] Quoted in Wertenbaker, *Princeton*, 346.

[32] *PWW*, 7:62 (Nov. 3, 1890); Bragdon interview with Williamson U. Vreeland, Mar. 24, 1940, p. 1, WWC, box 63, folder 57.

[33] Murray, "Gentlemen-Scholars of 1890: No. 1—President Patton," *PAW*, Oct. 12, 1934, 57; *PWW*, 6:624 (May 5, 1890), 7:62–63 (Nov. 3, 1890); William Berryman Scott, *Some Memories of a Palaeontologist* (Princeton, 1939), 218; Leitch, *Princeton Companion*, 356.

Dean Magie, one of the self-styled "Faculty malcontents" at the time, diagnosed Patton's inertia as a "disinclination to be disagreeable" to anyone. Thomas Marc Parrott suggested that Patton's strict Presbyterian belief in predestination may have led him to "let things run themselves." Whatever the cause, Patton's indecisiveness manifested itself in a pervasive "slackness" of standards and lack of direction for the university. As Wilson complained in 1896, "Our president does not bother us by having a mistaken policy, he daunts us by having no will or policy at all."[34]

Patton's "policy of drift" did not prevent the college from growing. During his fourteen-year tenure, a dozen major buildings, including Pyne Library, were added to serve a student body that increased 89 percent to well over twelve hundred. Unfortunately, the jump in enrollments was caused mostly by low entrance standards and a reluctance to flunk any student out. The School of Science ended up with 37 percent of the undergraduates by dropping Greek as a requirement for admission.[35] Patton stated openly in faculty meetings that he had "no belief in discipline."[36] He was afraid that if standards were set too high, enrollments would drop and faculty salaries would have to be cut—a politically hazardous result. Wilson's rejoinder was that a lax Princeton "would not be a spot above Villanova or Lafayette," but he was certain that if Princeton did raise its standards, it would not only rank with Harvard and Yale but would in the long run attract *more* students, not fewer.[37]

The president's laissez-faire approach also resulted in a dramatic increase in faculty. By 1902 the faculty had grown 170 percent to 108,

[34] Bragdon interviews (WWC) with W. F. Magie, June 12, 1939, pp. 2, 2a; Aug. 5, 1940, p. 8, box 63, folder 9; and T. M. Parrott, Sept. 15, 1942, p. 1, box 63, folder 25; *PWW*, 10:78 (Dec. 15, 1896).

[35] Bragdon interview with G. C. Wintringer '94, July 12, 1941, p. 1, WWC, box 63, folder 65; Wertenbaker, *Princeton*, 365–66, 384–86.

[36] Patton has often been quoted out of context, but he did tell a meeting of New York alumni in his first speaking engagement after taking office: "I am not prepared to say that it is better to have gone and loafed than never to have gone at all, but I do believe in the *genius loci*" (Leitch, *Princeton Companion*, 355).

[37] Scott, *Some Memories*, 218; Bragdon interview with George McLean Harper, July 1, 1939, pp. 1–2, WWC, box 62, folder 56.

which dropped the student:faculty ratio to 12:1. But the appointment process was inconsistent and often marked by favoritism and "outrageous nepotism, with jobs given to sons, relatives, and friends of the right people."[38] This resulted in a fractured faculty of old guard and young Turks. Several of the Patton-era appointments were "brilliant investigators and teachers," Wilson among them.[39] These men immediately joined forces with the substantial cohort of McCosh's "bright young men," most in their thirties, who constituted the professionalizing wing of the faculty. In a timeless pattern of generational succession, the older, often clerical, moiety of professors was dismissed by their junior colleagues as "ossified," "fossilized," and "incompetent." When classicist Edward Capps was recruited from Chicago in 1907, he quickly learned that in Patton's day "the old faculty were largely Princeton graduates [68 percent] . . . and many of them were lazy. The place had become ingrown. There was little incentive, little ambition, because men inherited their jobs." Other newcomers felt that the older men on the scene resented them for "disturb[ing] them in their slumbers." Classicist Andrew West, an endowed chairholder since 1883 and the leader of Patton's disloyal opposition, lampooned the old guard in a wickedly witty poem on "The Three Snoozers."[40]

Although the young faction could claim a majority in faculty meetings by 1893, the old guard, "many of them trained in the tactics of Presbyterian General Assemblies," had enough skills to delay or circumvent many reform proposals. Patton's dilatory habits helped the old guard by slowing the movement toward more advanced graduate and professional studies. Several older members, such as

[38] In 1895–1896 Patton's son George '91, without a degree from the Princeton Theological Seminary after three years of study, was made secretary to his father and an assistant professor of biblical instruction. This prompted Mrs. Wilson to exclaim, "Truly it is a good and pleasant thing for a young scholar to have a fond father in the president's chair!" (*PWW*, 7:531n1, 9:206 [Feb. 18, 1895]).

[39] Bragdon interviews (WWC) with R. B. Perry, May 29, 1945, p. 1, box 63, folder 28; W. F. Magie, June 12, 1939, pp. 2, 2a; Aug. 5, 1940, p. 8, box 63, folder 9.

[40] Bragdon interviews (WWC) with Charles W. McIlwain, Jan. 2, 1940, p. 5, box 63, folder 11; G. C. Wintringer, July 12, 1941, p. 1, box 63, folder 65; Edward Capps, Mar. 23, 1943, p. 3, box 62, folder 16; Bliss Perry, *And Gladly Teach: Reminiscences* (Boston and New York, 1935), 155–56.

General Kargé, did not teach graduate courses for lack of knowledge or interest. They were therefore pleased when Patton dragged Princeton's feet on the establishment of a graduate school, West's pet project, and a law school, promised to Wilson.[41]

Only after the Sesquicentennial in 1896, when the college took on the name and responsibilities of a university and West, the event's impresario, raised $1.3 million for research and scholarship, did the younger faculty begin to effect major changes. In belated response to a faculty committee memorial of December 1896, the trustees approved a graduate school of arts and sciences four years later, with West as its dean. To sidestep any further Pattonesque stonewalling, West requested and received from the trustees the authority to choose his own faculty advisory committee and the privilege of reporting directly to the board rather than the president. The law school never even got to the drawing board, which so disturbed Wilson that only a substantial guaranteed salary supplement from a coalition of trustees and friends kept him from leaving Princeton.[42]

Such behind-the-scenes influence-peddling was the academic order of the day in America's nascent universities and established colleges. During the economic depression of the mid-1890s it was not unwelcomed by hard-pressed administrators and trustees, but it did erode their proper direction of institutional development and policy. While several members of Wilson's class of '79 effected his move from Wesleyan to a new chair of jurisprudence and political economy, other well-heeled alumni groups pushed their own favorites into Princeton seats.[43] In 1899 a number of prominent New York

[41] Perry, *And Gladly Teach*, 129, 144; Thorp, *PGS*, 34, 52.

[42] Thorp, *PGS*, 55–58, 62–68; Wertenbaker, *Princeton*, 377–83; *PWW*, 10:529–30 (Apr. 30, 1898).

[43] Henry Wilkinson Bragdon, *Woodrow Wilson: The Academic Years* (Cambridge, Mass., 1967), 185–87. As soon as Wilson secured his Princeton position, he urged his Johns Hopkins classmate Albert Shaw to have his friends "push you for all their influence is worth" for a Princeton chair in political economy (*PWW*, 6:625 [May 5, 1890]). Under Patton, as Dean Magie noticed, "influence counted most" (Bragdon interview with W. F. Magie, June 12, 1939, p. 2, WWC, box 63, folder 9). The practice of filling chairs with the choice of the endowers continued into Wilson's presidency, if former New York City mayor George B. McClellan, Jr., is to be credited. After leaving office, his friends allegedly secured the permission of Wilson and trustee Pyne to endow a chair of economic history for him. Before they could do so, Wilson left to begin his

alumni generously endowed a professorship in honor of James O. Murray, the late dean of the faculty and professor of English. But they did so "on condition that Dr. Henry van Dyke should be the first incumbent." It was no coincidence that Van Dyke '73 was the rector of the Brick Presbyterian Church in New York, the same church from which Murray had been plucked in 1875 and to which most of the donors belonged.[44]

The ingrown quality of Patton's faculty was also due to two other practices. One was that retiring chairs often selected their own successors. In 1893 Bliss Perry came to Princeton as professor of oratory and aesthetic criticism because his predecessor George L. Raymond recommended him. President Patton played very little part in the appointment. When Perry traveled to Princeton for an interview, Patton received him with "witty, indolent talk about things in general," but was "charmingly vague as to specific commitments and courses, and gave the impression of not taking either 'Oratory' or 'Aesthetic Criticism' very seriously."[45]

Perry was a Williams man, but most selections were Princeton alumni. That he flourished at Princeton was an exception to the

---

own political career and Dean Henry Fine "reneged," proposing only a university lectureship for McClellan. But the aging and absentee interim president, trustee John Stewart, allowed the former deal to go through and McClellan was installed in 1911. His admittedly "snap" course remained a student favorite for twenty years. *The Gentleman and the Tiger: The Autobiography of George B. McClellan, Jr.*, ed. Harold C. Syrett (Philadelphia and New York, 1956), 306–7.

[44] Thorp, *PGS*, 48–49; Thomas P. Roche, Jr., "The English Department in 1910," *PULC* 54:2–3 (Winter–Spring 1993):147–77, at 154, 156. Van Dyke was a prolific author—eighteen volumes in his collected works—but he remained fairly distant from the university and enjoyed a mixed reputation. Former president McCosh regarded him a "conceited little peacock" and another critic quipped that he was "the only man who could strut sitting down." In 1902 he was one of three unsuccessful candidates for the university presidency and four years later was a principled opponent of Wilson's quad plan. Bragdon interview with W. F. Magie, June 12, 1939, pp. 2, 2a, WWC, box 63, folder 9; Leitch, *Princeton Companion*, 488; Bragdon, *WW: Academic Years*, 277–79, 321–26; Roland Mushat Frye, "Henry van Dyke (1852–1933)," in Hugh T. Kerr, ed., *Sons of the Prophets: Leaders in Protestantism from Princeton Seminary* (Princeton, 1963), 148–60; Nathaniel Burt, "Henry van Dyke: Poet of Genteel Princeton," *Princeton History*, 7 (1988):1–10.

[45] Perry, *And Gladly Teach*, 121–23.

second practice that minimized outside influences and the healthy infusion of new blood and ideas. In the 1890s, Harvard philosopher Ralph Barton Perry '96 recalled, "men from other [American] colleges were not merely rare, they were viewed with suspicion. . . . Few men brought in from outside succeeded because the undergraduates generally found some reason for not liking them." A Harvard professor of German and a Yale engineer lasted only a year.[46]

In the end, particularly with the president's abdication in faculty development, the trustees were responsible for all appointments in fact as well as in law. Even after the alumni gained the right to elect five representatives in 1900, the conservative, largely clerical members of the board were capable of gathering enough allies to outvote the younger progressive members. The board also conducted faculty affairs in total secrecy, without any consultation with the whole faculty or even its professorial chairs. Thus, in March 1900 when the trustees promoted Arnold Guyot Cameron '86, son of the notorious classicist, from professor of French in the School of Science to the prestigious Woodhull Professor of French in the Academic Department, Wilson was fit to be tied. "How complete it all is," he fumed to his wife, "not a pound added to our working force; not a name added to our list, or prestige; money saved and second-rate men promoted!" He was disgusted, as were his young allies, with "the whole familiar process by which *choice* and *development* are avoided."[47]

If the students were "demoralized" by the curriculum, as a blue-ribbon faculty committee found in April 1902, the faculty was no less so by the state of the university, its direction, and its leadership. The time was clearly ripe for either major change or retrogression, for realizing its university aspirations or remaining a college in all but name and losing ground to its major rivals. Fortunately, the trustees, reconfigured with sixteen new, largely progressive, nonclerical members since 1896, saw their duty clear and persuaded Patton to resign with a hefty buyout. The reign of "King Log" and his policy of drift came to an end on June 9, 1902, when the

[46] Bragdon interview with R. B. Perry, May 29, 1945, p. 2, WWC, box 63, folder 28.

[47] Wertenbaker, *Princeton*, 376–77; *PWW*, 11:493–94 (Mar. 8, 1890).

faculty's floor manager, Woodrow Wilson, was elected to the presidency, the first lay president in Princeton's history and the very antithesis of slackness.[48]

❁ ❁ ❁

After twelve years of Patton's lax leadership, Wilson came to office with plenty of ideas for reform. As early as 1897 he had shared with brother-in-law Stockton Axson his plans for what he would do if he ever became "the autocrat of Princeton," a possibility he never entertained given Patton's relative youth. His main targets were the curriculum, the method of teaching, and the plan of college life, the first two of which required collateral changes in the faculty—its size, recruitment, and quality.[49]

Wilson carefully prepared the way for major reform by reordering key faculty committees, making important administrative appointments, and receiving—and taking—from the trustees effective authority over academic and faculty affairs. He chaired a new Committee on the Course of Study that after close collaboration with the whole faculty, melded the academic and scientific departments into a single faculty, rationalized and reduced the "hodgepodge" of upperclass courses into a system of departmental majors and "assisted electives," and raised—and enforced—standards for admission, continuation, honors, and graduation. The committee also reduced the number of courses a student took each term from seven to five and standardized the length of each course at three hours a week.[50] Wilson quickly appointed classmate "Billy" Magie, one of Patton's leading critics, as clerk of the faculty and in June 1903 installed Henry Fine, a keen judge of men and upholder of standards, as dean of the faculty in charge of student discipline, the curriculum, and faculty affairs.

[48] Report of the University Committee on Scholarship, Apr. 16, 1902, *PWW*, 12: 331–39; 10:52 ("King Log"); Scott, *Some Memories*, 255; Bragdon, *WW: Academic Years*, 277–79.

[49] Stockton Axson, *"Brother Woodrow": A Memoir of Woodrow Wilson*, ed. Arthur S. Link (Princeton, 1993), 115.

[50] Bragdon, *WW: Academic Years*, 293–94; *PWW*, 15:252–63; 277–92 (Editorial Note: The New Princeton Course of Study).

Of even greater moment for the faculty was Wilson's acquisition of unprecedented control over faculty affairs. This was troublesome for many faculty, old and young, slackers and actives alike, because Patton's hands-off administration had created habits of license and irresponsibility. In trying to recruit frontier historian Frederick Jackson Turner in 1896, a pampered Professor Wilson had put a good face on conditions by saying that he knew of no "greater academic freedom anywhere."[51] Without a system of professorial ranks (like the University of Chicago's) or even departments, he crowed, "each professor is master within the limits of his own chair." And since Patton did not "command or interfere," the "free play of individuality and independence" among the faculty was in no foreseeable danger, certainly not if the beneficiaries had their way.[52]

Once in office, however, Wilson saw that the faculty could no longer have their way if meaningful reform was to occur. In October 1902, to help rid the university of some of Patton's "dead wood," the trustees acceded to Wilson's request for unpublicized power to fire faculty, even tenured and chaired professors, "as he may deem for the best interest of the University."[53] A year later Wilson gathered

[51] Wilson taught only four class hours a week, on Monday and Tuesday, so he could write remunerative articles for national publications the rest of the week; he had permission to give a well-paid ($500) lecture course at Johns Hopkins for five weeks during term; he had absolute control of his department; he was chosen as the orator for the sesquicentennial celebration; and at $4,300 he was the highest-paid faculty member in the university. In short, said President Patton, "no other professor is as highly favored as he is" (*PWW*, 10:496–97 [Apr. 4, 1898]). A major reason for his privileged position was that he had been, and would continue to be, recruited for the presidency of several other universities, including the universities of Illinois, Nebraska, Texas, and Virginia (his law-school alma mater). *PWW*, 7:594, 598, 600, 608–9, 613; 9:285, 499–500; 10:95, 308, 485; 11:102; 12:35, 69.

[52] *PWW*, 10:52 (Nov. 15, 1896). See Wilbur Jacobs, "Wilson's First Battle at Princeton: The Chair for Turner," *Harvard Library Bulletin* 8:1 (Winter 1954):74–87.

[53] *PWW*, 14:162 (Oct. 21, 1902). The "secret" donation of this power was undoubtedly alarming to many faculty when it was eventually revealed. See Bragdon interviews (WWC) with Jacob Beam, Mar. 29, 1941, p. l, box 62, folder 9; W. F. Magie, June 12, 1939, p. 3, box 63, folder 9. In 1939 trustee Wilson Farrand speculated that public knowledge of Wilson's new power "may have contributed to his large majority in faculty votes," a surmise not borne out by the thoughtful independence of Wilson's whole faculty, pro and con (Bragdon interview with Farrand, Dec. 20, 1939, p. 2, WWC, box 62, folder 38).

even more authority in the president's office by appointing Harry A. Garfield, son of the U.S. president, lawyer, and municipal reformer of Cleveland, as professor of politics in late July 1903, without seeking prior approval of the trustees' curriculum committee and its "strict constructionist" clerical chairman. Wilson assured Garfield in early September, after the latter had rented a house in Princeton, that "of course the actual election of professors rests with the Board of Trustees," who would not meet until late October. "But the selection of men rests with the President, and in this case the thing is as good as done." Wilson's preemptive strike created a major precedent and a brief brouhaha, but the board as a whole simply acquiesced, augmenting the authority they had conferred on the president in June to create a system of academic departments and to appoint their chairmen.[54]

During his eight-year tenure, Wilson was not reluctant to exercise any of his new powers. Whether by hiring or firing, he sought to make Princeton "a place where the most brilliant teachers will feel they have got to teach."[55] But even one of his young faculty supporters later admitted that Wilson became "an autocrat up to the limit. [In appointments] he hardly left anything to the Faculty. He kept departments under his thumb; they were not consulted on what they now [in 1941] consider their most important right—to name their colleagues—to pick members of the highest grade."[56] This was not completely accurate, as we will see, but to faculty who had tasted the heady "academic freedom" of European universities or Patton's, it must have felt true enough.

The key to virtually all of Wilson's plans to rejuvenate Princeton and to give it "intellectual primacy" in the country was the faculty,

[54] *PWW*, 15:26 (Oct. 23, 1903), 556 (Sept. 1, 1903). Wilson had offered the chair to Garfield on June 11. *PWW*, 14:486–88. In 1904 Wilson also offered the Stuart Chair of Psychology to Frank Thilly, and Thilly had accepted, before the board met. On February 8, Wilson informed Thilly that the board would not convene until March 10 to officially approve his appointment. "I regard them as committed, but, of course, it is an imperative point of courtesy to do or say nothing that will make this matter public before they have taken formal action" (*PWW*, 15:163).

[55] *Chicago Chronicle*, Nov. 29, 1902, quoted in Bragdon, *WW: Academic Years*, 294.

[56] Bragdon interview with Jacob Beam, Mar. 29, 1941, p. 1, WWC, box 62, folder 9.

who, he told the trustees in his first report after taking office, were "overworked and underpaid." Unlike their European counterparts, they lacked equipment in almost every department, their teaching in the current distended curriculum was too much "obscure drudgery," and they had neither the income to secure a "natural place among gentlemen" nor the time for "independent study" that led to "scholarly reputation," the two reasons they entered the profession. "A true university," he reminded the board, "is a place for research as well as for instruction. It cannot keep alive without research; it cannot serve the country properly if it does not do its part in widening the boundaries of knowledge. . . ."[57]

Regrettably, Princeton had fallen out of—or never really made it onto—the list of great American universities because, while it had not kept up even with traditional rivals Harvard and Yale, upstarts such as Columbia, Johns Hopkins, and Chicago had "pressed in ahead." To simply catch up with the competition would require a major increase in endowment—$12.5 million—to expand and deepen library holdings; hire well-qualified "tutors" to jumpstart the curriculum; properly equip the School of Science; underwrite senior additions to the underweight departments of history, economics, and biology; build a museum of natural history; and establish the long-promised school of jurisprudence and a first-class graduate school of arts and sciences. The last item was no last-minute pipe dream. Wilson had been a member of a post-Sesquicentennial faculty committee in 1896 that sought to convince the trustees that a graduate school was not only "the proper completion of our Academic System," but a necessity if Princeton was to "maintain its place as one of the leading American Universities." It would, the committee argued, train faculty for college teaching, "promote intellectual seriousness in the undergraduate body as no other influence could," and do more than any other one thing to "increase Princeton's reputation in the world of learning." To increase faculty salaries even selectively and to hire new faculty at the junior and senior ranks would require additional endowments of more than $3.3 million, when the univer-

[57] *PWW*, 14:150–61, at 151–52 (Oct. 21, 1902); 18:20 (Mar. 12, 1908).

sity's current endowments, accumulated over 156 years, totaled only $3.8 million.[58]

Before building up the faculty to university strength, Wilson's first impulse was to clear out some of the underperforming faculty he had inherited. Young instructors on term appointments could always be "let go" for sufficient cause, but full professors and endowed chair-holders with "permanent status" (presumptive tenure for life) were altogether different. But not as different then as modern academics might think, because the American Association of University Professors (to which "Enfield's" Ed Tyler belonged in the late 1950s) had not yet been founded to set a national standard for faculty rights and responsibilities and especially to fight for academic freedom and the sanctity of tenure.[59] Wilson certainly understood, if he did not fully appreciate, the prescriptive power of custom in both political states and academe. But he also believed with characteristic certainty that he was acting for the greater good of the university when he set about cleaning house.

Even Wilson's friends who agreed that the faculty he inherited harbored "a good deal of dead wood" must have been surprised and in some awe when he actually asked for the resignations of three senior professors and an instructor. His request was the equivalent of firing, for "if the President asked a man to resign," said his faculty clerk, "he resigned."[60] The first to go was not asked to resign but summarily dismissed because he was a mere instructor of Latin. In April 1903, Charles W. L. Johnson was told by the president himself that he was unable to handle "the very skittish colts in our classes." To soften the blow, Wilson said he wished that Princeton teaching was "less peculiar and less exacting" (a kind fib) and offered to help Johnson find a new position.[61]

[58] *PWW*, 10:68–69 (c. Dec. 2, 1896); 14:154–60 (Oct. 21, 1902). On the founding of the Graduate School and the building of the Graduate College, see Thorp, *PGS*, chaps. 3–6; Axtell, "The Dilettante Dean;" and chapter 7, below.

[59] The AAUP was founded in 1915. See Richard Hofstadter and Walter P. Metzger, *The Development of Academic Freedom in the United States* (New York, 1955), chap. 10; Metzger, ed., *The American Concept of Academic Freedom in Formation: A Collection of Essays and Reports* (New York, 1977).

[60] Bragdon interview with W. F. Magie, June 12, 1939, p. 7, WWC, box 63, folder 9.

[61] Bragdon, *WW: Academic Years*, 295–96.

Johnson's dismissal was a warm-up for the next three, which required more executive backbone. Professor of French Edwin Seelye Lewis was asked to go in 1907 because, although reportedly "a research man from Hopkins" (which might have endeared him to the president), he was "a teaching failure." Future dean Magie found him "dull" and knew that "Wilson did not like him," having entertained him and his wife at obligatory "faculty dinings." Lewis's young chairman, Williamson Vreeland, described him as "a loafer who was intensely fond of playing bridge." Less forgivable was his penchant for "dismiss[ing] his classes after only half an hour."[62]

The force-out of Arthur Frothingham, Jr., longtime professor of archaeology and the history of art, had required even greater delicacy. Indeed, it was handled so deftly by both parties that the official record scarcely reveals its true origins. Were it not for the good memory of Wilson's close friend George McLean Harper, we could only surmise that Frothingham was asked to leave. The handwriting on the wall gained legibility in the spring of 1903 when the seniors sang the newest verses of the "Faculty Song" on the steps of Nassau Hall.[63] Ellen Wilson wrote to her absent husband that "the new verses . . . are all horrid except yours. This class must be peculiarly spiteful. The one on Frothingham *is* funny though. He has evidently taken a very *noticeable* brace." He needed to pull himself together for a fresh start after hearing:

> Here's to Frothy our latest find,
> He's gentle and easy to drive and kind.
> He had to make his courses hard
> Or he couldn't play in Woodrow's yard.

[62] Bragdon interviews (WWC) with G. M. Harper, July 1, 1939, p. 3, box 62, folder 56; W. F. Magie, June 12, 1939, p. 3, box 63, folder 9; W. U. Vreeland, Mar. 24, 1940, p. 1, box 63, folder 57; *PWW,* 15:155 (Feb. 3, 1904). Lewis's departure left no tracks in the official record. The trustees' minutes make no mention of it, nor did Wilson's annual report to the board, where he always described personnel changes at some length.

[63] The faculty song, sung to the Scottish tune of "The Muckin' o' Geordie's Byre," was borrowed from Trinity College (Hartford, Conn.) and introduced to Princeton by Andrew C. Imbrie '95 in his senior year. See Leitch, *Princeton Companion,* 173–74; Bragdon interview with Imbrie, July 28, 1940, WWC, box 62, folder 61.

By the end of Wilson's first year in office, it was—or should have been—obvious to the faculty, as it was to the students, that he had "put screws" to them and wanted them to "get to work to improve their courses."[64]

The next clue appeared the following March when Wilson recommended to the trustees a half year's leave at full pay for Frothingham, who planned to work in Rome on ancient Eastern archaeology. Since regular sabbaticals were not yet a faculty perquisite at Princeton, as they were at Harvard, Cornell, Columbia, and Brown, the leave might be seen as a token of Wilson's respect for Frothingham's scholarship, which was, he acknowledged, "so widely and so favorably known."[65] But it might also have been part of a generous buyout package, enabling Frothingham to exit gracefully and seemingly on his own terms. The second possibility gains credence after we learn that he stayed in Rome for the whole year before submitting his resignation in May 1905. After nineteen years on the Princeton faculty, Frothingham told Wilson and the board in separate letters that he was leaving to devote himself to his special calling. Both letters had a face-saving edge to them and were clearly shadowed by the heightened teaching standards that Wilson had imposed.[66]

"I feel," Frothingham wrote the board, "as if the original work which is my special province, and which I have been obliged for a number of years to abandon almost entirely on account of the increased requirements of teaching, can [only] with difficulty be carried on in connection with this University." For Wilson he drew an implied contrast between Princeton's overworked professors and the productive scholars he met at the international Archaeological Congress in Athens, who were "attached to institutions that leave them

[64] *PWW*, 14:441 (May 1, 1903); Bragdon interview with Charles Grosvenor Osgood, Apr. 14, 1939, p. 1, WWC, box 63, folder 24. See also William Starr Myers, ed., *Woodrow Wilson: Some Princeton Memories* (Princeton, 1946), 3, 55.

[65] Princeton instituted regular sabbatical leaves in 1911, the twenty-seventh college to do so. Harvard was first in 1880, Yale tagged along in 1907. Walter Crosby Eells, "The Origin and Early History of Sabbatical Leave," *Bulletin of the American Association of University Professors* 48 (Autumn 1962):253–56, at 254.

[66] *PWW*, 15:183 (Mar. 9, 1904), 16:246 (Dec. 14, 1905).

free to give no lectures at all or to lecture on what they happen at the time to be busy with for their own research work."[67]

Beneath the brave rhetoric can be sensed the real reason Frothingham was resigning: Wilson asked him to because his undergraduate courses were notorious "snaps" and, as George Harper testified from personal experience, he was "a fantastically dull lecturer," who could cast a pall over even "magnificent material" such as Trajan's tomb at Beneventum. There may have been a touch of irony in Wilson's cordial acceptance of Frothingham's resignation when he concluded that "there will be universal regret that it is necessary for you to break your long standing connection with the University." But Wilson was truly relieved that Frothingham had chosen not to make a fuss and promised to return to Princeton in the fall, "feeling as much at home as ever in the old atmosphere of friends and as much as ever a Princeton man." We can be certain that he sent Frothingham a copy of his fulsome notice to the board that celebrated, again in generous code, "the entire freedom afforded him by a release from exacting academic engagements."[68]

The third professor, and only endowed chairholder, Wilson removed accepted his fate neither willingly nor gently—characteristic behavior that contributed to his dismissal in the first place. Arnold Guyot Cameron, the Woodhull Professor of French whose promo-

[67] *PWW*, 16:93–94 (May 10, 1905). Two of the institutions he had in mind may have been Leipzig, where he earned his Ph.D., and Johns Hopkins, where he taught for three years before coming to Princeton. Thorp, *PGS*, 36.

[68] *PWW*, 16:103 (May 20, 1905), 246 (Dec. 14, 1905). This case must have been particularly hard for Wilson because his wife, Ellen, had once been befriended by Arthur Frothingham senior, a collector of prints and etchings, which he shared with the artistic Mrs. Wilson. But Frothingham junior had had some questionable dealings in Europe in the late 1890s, acting as a middleman (for commission) in various art purchases and playing the University of Pennsylvania Museum against Princeton. In 1896 he had been relieved of his editorship of the *American Journal of Archaeology* and Allan Marquand, his fellow professor of art, stopped paying his salary from his uncle's endowment. Dean Andrew Fleming West, Frothingham's champion, found funds for his salary from other sources. Wilson must have known of all these developments. *PWW*, 8:432, 456, 499; Betsy Rosasco, "The Teaching of Art and the Museum Tradition: Joseph Henry to Allan Marquand," in *An Art Museum for Princeton: The Early Years, The Record of the Art Museum, Princeton University*, 55:1–2 (1996), 32–41, 52n240.

tion to the chair in 1900 had seemed to the Wilsons nepotic and undeserved, was the son of Wilson's much-disliked professor of Greek, whom he regarded as equally unqualified for university-level work. A Princetonian for every degree, with only minimal experience in France, Guyot (as he was known) was a very popular undergraduate lecturer and a scholar whom the chairman of Cornell's French Department granted was "as well qualified as any man in the country."[69]

Wilson had no problem with his scholarship; he simply "did not believe his somewhat sensational classroom lectures were a healthy scholastic influence." Colleagues later supplied the details. One-time Professor of French George Harper remembered that Cameron "would not work with the department in organizing his courses; his lectures concerned everything, were rambling discourses on life in general," which accounted for much of their popularity. Williamson Vreeland, his chairman, found him "brilliant in some ways" but "impossible to get along with. His classes were amusing; he told stories, he talked about all sorts of topics, but he seldom taught any French." In short, said Dean Magie, he gave "nonsensical lectures."[70]

Cameron's pedagogical incompetence was cause enough for dismissal, but his conspicuous personality and "bizarre manner" compounded his offense in the eyes of socially conservative Princeton. Wilson declared him "a charlatan and a mountebank"—"a perfectly accurate description," said Magie—and deplored with his wife several "distasteful" features of the man, such as his strange "*walk* and conversation," that of "a poor, extravagant mimic man." Magie thought he went beyond mere eccentricity and was "nearly crazy and afflicted with a persecution complex."[71] His faculty photographs show a handsome narrow-eyed man with a full dark beard neatly trimmed, but sporting an ostentatious handlebar moustache and an

[69] *PWW*, 10:552n8; 15:52–54n1; Bragdon interview with W. Farrand, Dec. 20, 1939, p. 2, WWC, box 62, folder 38.

[70] Axson, "*Brother Woodrow*," 272; Bragdon interviews (WWC) with G. M. Harper, July 3, 1939, p. 3, box 62, folder 56; W. U. Vreeland, Mar. 27, 1940, box 63, folder 57; W. F. Magie, June 12, 1939, p. 3, box 63, folder 9.

[71] Bragdon interview with W. F. Magie, June 12, 1939, pp. 3, 3a, WWC, box 63, folder 9; *PWW*, 11:171 (July 16, 1899).

arrogant tilt of the head. He may have affected the look of a *boulevardier* among the staidly attired Protestants of Princeton; when editor-historian Arthur Link knew him in the 1940s, he still wore "a French-like flowing cape, beret, and moustache and was known for his flamboyance and exaggerated manners." While Wilson regarded both his character and his scholarship beyond reproach, he found him "so eccentric that he should not be retained in Princeton. It was all rather intangible," admitted Stockton Axson, but "nobody with less powerful convictions than President Wilson would have done anything. Certainly few college presidents would have acted with such honorable courage" to fire a tenured chairholder on the basis of "general disqualifications."[72]

Wilson thought of proceeding against Cameron as early as November 1903, but he waited until the following spring in order to take the pulse of the trustees.[73] At an interview in his Prospect living room, Wilson offered Cameron a terminal year to find another position, knowing that he had four young children and another on the way. But Cameron, insulted and incensed, literally popped a button (a pearl stud, which rolled under the sofa) and said some angry things he should not have said. Whereupon Wilson rescinded the year's grace and ordered him out of the house. This set off a minor storm of protest: the senior Camerons (he had retired when Wilson was elected), classmates, and friends fumed, gossiped, and petitioned for a reversal or clemency, but to no avail. Wilson would not reverse his decision, but, after an apology from Cameron and promise to "frame his method of teaching as to conform to a proper standard," he did restore the terminal year.[74]

[72] *PWW*, 11, 15: both between 292 and 293 (photographs); Axson, "*Brother Woodrow*," 271n12, 272n13.

[73] Wilson left a fragmentary draft letter addressed to Cameron that spoke of his "sincere desire . . . to do you full justice and take no step that might mortify you or put you into a false position such as might injure your prospects in your profession" (*PWW*, 15:52 [Nov. 18, 1903]). In March, Wilson told his wife that he had conferred with trustee John Cadwalader, who told him to "go ahead, a little row won't hurt when you are in the right and the matter can be explained to every one whose opinion is worth being concerned about" (*PWW*, 15:207 [Mar. 24, 1904]).

[74] Bragdon interviews (WWC) with W. F. Magie, June 13, 1939, p. 7, box 63, folder 9; W. Farrand, Dec. 20, 1939, p. 2, box 62, folder 38; *PWW*, 15:54n1, 362–64, 385–86, 463–

One reason Wilson did not give ground on the primary issue—teaching—was that he appears to have proceeded against all three professors because they were brought to his attention by his newly appointed department chairmen. Williamson Vreeland was only thirty-five when Wilson appointed him to run the four-man Department of Romance Languages, two of whose members were the problematical professors Lewis and Cameron. In 1940 Vreeland recalled that Wilson told him to "go ahead even if he were opposed by every one else" and that "he would back him up."[75] This suggests that, contrary to the legend of the faculty autocrat, Wilson delegated considerable authority to his department heads and expected them to enforce the higher new standards.

Even in his own Department of History, Politics, and Economics, where he played a strong personal role, he trusted chairman Winthrop Daniels to make the first move against those who failed to measure up. In the spring of 1909, Daniels informed three young instructors that they were being let go and gave each of them reasons why Wilson also disapproved of their performance. The next day Wilson wrote to thank Daniels: "I hate to ask anyone to share the burden with me," he said, "but it seems to me unless the initial steps at any rate are taken by the Heads of Departments, the departmental organization will lack something of its reality."[76]

---

66. After his forced resignation, Cameron remained unemployed for several years before working sporadically for the *Wall Street Journal* and other financial publications. Without independent means, he managed to put his sons through Yale, probably with scholarship help. It was reported that he never set foot on the Princeton campus again before he died in 1947, but that is a very difficult feat for any Princeton resident. *PWW*, 15:54n1.

[75] Bragdon interview with W. U. Vreeland, Mar. 27, 1940, WWC, box 63, folder 57. In 1927, Christian Gauss, one of Wilson's original preceptors, a distinguished professor of Romance languages, and dean of the college (1925–1946), thought that Wilson, although ignorant of "the conditions under which a department of modern languages must function, . . . was as positive [self-assured] in his dealing with a department about whose work he knew nothing as he was about departments in which he possessed a certain degree of competence." If Gauss was correct, Wilson certainly proved educable and willing to trust his chairmen and even whole departments. *The Papers of Christian Gauss*, ed. Katherine Gauss Jackson and Hiram Haydn (New York, 1957), 249 (Nov. 19, 1927).

[76] *PWW*, 19:77–78 (Mar. 2–3, 1909).

Wilson's dismissal of several faculty for inadequacy in the classroom was an acknowledgment that Princeton was a collegiate university with an equal, if not greater, responsibility to undergraduate teaching. Although Wilson strongly promoted faculty scholarship and advanced graduate studies, his first loyalty and obligation were to the undergraduate college, where he had made his own stellar reputation. From his day to this, Princeton has lived with that tension, in some periods more comfortably than others.

❁ ❁ ❁

Wilson, of course, not only fired faculty, he hired them, always with the active collaboration and often at the initiative of his department chairmen and his astute dean of the faculty, Henry Fine. Wilson enjoyed extraordinary success in attracting scholar-teachers to Princeton. He was as persuasive with senior scholars as he was with neophytes. Senior scholars, of course, could only come from other institutions, so "raiding" was a big part of Wilson's game as he sought to build Princeton's faculty to intellectual primacy.

His plan was deceptively simple, particularly since his annual budgets never matched his ambitions: by appointing sufficient numbers of "men who will themselves be the only kind of advertising that a University should condescend to," he would create a university of departments each of which would be "at the very front, not only in scholarship, but in influence and leadership."[77] This was especially important if Princeton wanted to make its graduate school as strong as its undergraduate college. Wilson also believed, for intellectual as well as economic reasons, that the college teaching faculty and the graduate research faculty should be one and the same, with the same dual loyalties, duties, and skills. As he reminded the trustees in his first report, "We none of us believe that the graduate and undergraduate work ought to be divorced."[78] A single faculty of scholar-teachers has been a Princeton hallmark ever since, though, again, not without inherent tensions.

[77] *PWW*, 17:117 (Apr. 24, 1907); 18:20 (Mar. 12, 1908).

[78] *PWW*, 14:158 (Oct. 21, 1902).

FIGURE 5. "Tommy" Wilson and Henry Fine's friendship began in 1877 on the staff of the (then fortnightly) *Princetonian*. Fine '80 (right) succeeded Wilson '79 (left) as managing editor in this yearbook photo from 1879.

Wilson's recruitment of senior professors provides a textbook model for academic raiding. Once Wilson, Fine, or a department head perceived a curricular need or, in more recent parlance, a "target of opportunity" who might be less than happy where he was or flattered by an outside offer, the president launched his personal, highly effective, yet genuine, charm offensive. He began by inviting the candidate to visit Princeton or offering to meet him in another city for an exploratory conversation. After an hour with Woodrow Wilson, listening to his verbal vision of Princeton's future and being subjected to his legendary eloquence, frankness, and intellectual force, few men were capable of saying no. When biologist Edwin Conklin, who had been lured from the University of Pennsylvania in 1908, first met classicist Edward Capps, purloined from the University of Chicago in the same year, Capps asked, "What brought you to Princeton?" Conklin replied, "Woodrow Wilson, and what brought you here?" "The same," he said.[79]

If the candidate managed to resist Wilson's initial persuasions, the president pursued him with frequent, flattering, and often handwritten notes and letters. When philosopher Frank Thilly returned from his Princeton interview to the University of Missouri, he had been home less than twelve days when Wilson dropped him a solicitous note that ended, "We feel that we *must* have you." Understandably, even though he took a cut in salary, Thilly moved to Princeton the following fall. Once the deal was sealed, Thilly thanked Wilson for the way he had been treated. "I have felt all along that I was dealing with human beings, with men of heart and soul, and not with dead things." The "introduction of the personal, human element," he said, had clinched his decision to come.[80]

Yet all the charisma in Christendom could not secure some of the best scholars in the English-speaking world if other, more material, offerings were not forthcoming as well. Most of the senior "stars" were offered Princeton's top salary of $5,000 plus moving expenses. When the budget had insufficient funds to cover another big salary, trustees dipped into their own pockets "long enough to tide us over the present time of stringency."[81] Some recruits got university housing. When trustee Moses Taylor Pyne offered to build a university house for Edwin Conklin and promised that he could occupy it as long as he remained in Princeton, Conklin "capitulated and agreed to accept a formal call to the chair of biology." Others got personal help, including on-site inspections, from Wilson and chairmen in

[79] Myers, ed., *WW: Princeton Memories*, 58–59; *PWW*, 15:134–35 (Jan. 16–18, 1904).

[80] *PWW*, 15:152 (Jan. 31, 1904), 156–57 (Feb. 4, 1904). Unfortunately for Princeton, Thilly left after only two years for Cornell, where he had taught briefly in the early 1890s. Wilson then applied his skills, while on a vacation in Scotland, to persuade a somewhat younger Norman Kemp Smith to leave the University of Glasgow for the university of Witherspoon and McCosh. Smith did so for a salary of only $4,000. *PWW*, 15:115n2; 16:454 (Sept. 16, 1906), 465 (Oct. 20, 1906), 507.

[81] *PWW*, 17:91, 117, 447, 597, 601.

finding houses to rent or purchase.[82] Scientists were promised lab equipment and assistants; Conklin also got to supervise the design and building of Guyot Hall, where he would work for the next forty-four years.[83] An annual subvention of $1,000 was found for Capps to move his journal *Classical Philology* from Chicago.[84]

Of most concern to top-flight research scholars (after salary) were—and still are—teaching loads and sabbaticals. Wilson knew well what kept him at Princeton in the 1890s, so he offered his senior prospects light teaching duties and more regular leaves than the rest of the faculty enjoyed. In his first year Frank Thilly taught only one course a semester, advanced psychology for juniors and a large required course in elementary psychology for sophomores.[85] Latin expert Frank Abbott, the second of Chicago's faculty losses, "made it practically a condition of his accepting the call to Princeton that the Graduate School be organized normally," by transferring from Dean West's hands control over teaching assignments and governance to an elected or presidentially appointed faculty committee.[86] To counter Penn's recent inducement to Conklin to stay, Wilson offered him a full year's leave at half-pay in his first year.[87] And when Edward Capps expressed some disappointment that Princeton had no "regular vacation [sabbatical] system, by which all permanent officers [faculty] enjoy relief from class-room work at fixed intervals in the interest of their own studies," Wilson promptly guaranteed him "six months' leave every three years from the start."[88]

If Wilson was successful in recruiting senior faculty in the face of inadequate budgets over eight years, he was even more so in attracting nearly fifty younger tutors, or "preceptors," in a single year. After consulting widely with department chairmen and working

[82] Myers, ed., *WW: Princeton Memories*, 58; *PWW*, 15:207, 245.

[83] *PWW*, 17:416–17, 471, 604–5; Bragdon interview with E. G. Conklin, Mar. 24, 1943, p. 1, WWC, box 62, folder 21.

[84] In the end, Chicago would not part with it. *PWW*, 17:116–17, 123–24, 173.

[85] *PWW*, 15:440 (Aug. 12, 1904).

[86] Bragdon interview with E. Capps, Mar. 23, 1943, p. 1, WWC, box 62, folder 16. See chapter 7, below.

[87] *PWW*, 17:438, 446, 448.

[88] *PWW*, 17:112 (Apr. 20, 1907); Bragdon interview with E. Capps, Mar. 23, 1943, p. 5, WWC, box 62, folder 16.

closely with the whole faculty to reform the curriculum in 1903–1904, Wilson sprang his "preceptorial" plan on the faculty the following year with much less ground-laying.[89] Yet opposition was almost nil, except from some trustees who wondered where to find the $2.5 million needed to endow an almost 50-percent increase in the size of the faculty virtually overnight. What Wilson proposed was, certainly for Princeton and indeed for most American colleges and universities, a revolutionary change in the educational process.

As colleges grew into universities and universities expanded to meet the nation's demand for professional training, "liberal culture," and the "collegiate experience," student enrollments outpaced faculty growth, class sizes inflated, and personal contact between teachers and learners declined.[90] The curricular emphasis was largely on teaching and little on learning, on courses and credits rather than subjects and mastery. Accordingly, the standard delivery system relied on passive, uninterrupted lectures and dispiriting recitative drills, both of which fostered sporadic cramming rather than "daily methodical study." According to Wilson, an excellent and hugely popular lecturer, "it is not the way to teach, this pouring of learning into empty pitchers."[91] He wanted a university in which the undergraduate's purpose, not unlike the graduate student's, is "to get and to take, not to receive," in which "he is not under a master, not being taught," but "is learning and . . . reading" on his own with friendly guidance. In this major reversal of educational emphasis, lectures and class work would only supplement the independent reading and writing of the students, who would now take the initiative for their own education.[92]

[89] Wilson had been thinking about the preceptorial plan since at least 1894. Woodrow Wilson, "University Training and Citizenship," *PWW*, 8:587–96, at 596 (c. June 20, 1894).

[90] Laurence R. Veysey, *The Emergence of the American University* (Chicago, 1965), chaps. 2–4, pp. 294–302.

[91] Woodrow Wilson, "The Princeton Preceptorial System," *PWW*, 16:107–9, at 108 (c. June 1, 1905); Bragdon interview with Harry A. Garfield, Feb. 14, 1940, p. 2, WWC, box 62, folder 46.

[92] Woodrow Wilson, "Statement on the Tutorial System," *PWW*, 16:6–7 (Feb. 18, 1905); Wilson, "The Preceptors," *PWW*, 16:84–85 (Apr. 28, 1905); Wilson, "Technical Education," *PWW*, 16:384–85, at 384 (May 4, 1906).

Wilson's solution was an American version of the Oxford tutorial system. Adopting the English word "preceptor" from the Inns of Court to avoid the American connotation of a hired remedial "tutor" or cram coach, Wilson wanted a major infusion of well-educated but personable, even "clubable," young men to make "reading men" of the students, especially in upperclass courses.[93] In relaxed weekly "conferences" of four to six students, usually in his own rooms or study, the preceptor would prompt an active conversation on the reading, not of canned textbooks but of serious books chosen by the course lecturer and himself to promote the investigation of a large, worthwhile subject. With the preceptor's guidance, the students also chose other books of interest, upon which they would present oral and written reports. Each conference was a class period taken from the traditional lecture course, the third of three hours each week, but the preceptor did not give grades, exams, or grief; he was meant to be the students' "guide, philosopher, and friend." His major task was to put "zest" into the students' work and to inculcate "the habit of talking about intellectual matters" outside as well as inside the precept.[94] In sum, the object of the preceptorial system, wrote Wilson, was to "give the undergraduate in a great university the advantage of the same sort of close and intimate contact and council with his instructors that the undergraduate of the small college enjoys."[95]

Where to get an instant supply of these scholarly paragons of personality was Wilson's next challenge. Well before the trustees approved their hiring and long before the endowment was in hand to pay their substantial salaries, Wilson gave each chairman of the

[93] Wilson told preceptor Hardin Craig that he had borrowed the name from certain tutors of law students at the Inns of Court in London. Hardin Craig, *Woodrow Wilson at Princeton* (Norman, 1960), 91.

[94] *PWW*, 16:62, 108; Hiram Bingham, "The 'Princeton System,' " *Yale Alumni Weekly*, Jan. 3, 1906, 257–58, at 257. See also Bragdon, *WW: Academic Years*, 304–8. The best description of the spirit of the preceptorial system is in Charles Grosvenor Osgood's chapter on Wilson in Willard Thorp, ed., *The Lives of Eighteen from Princeton* (Princeton, 1946), 291–97.

[95] Woodrow Wilson, "Statement of the Tutorial System," *PWW*, 16:6–7, at 6 (Feb. 18, 1905).

"reading" departments a quota and instructed them to find suitable candidates. One young chairman had no idea how to fill his quota and wisely consulted a publisher's "college rep" for suggestions of scholars doing interesting work. To find the right fifty, "hundreds were approached," but "many were kept from coming by the offer of higher salaries where they were." In just three months during the spring of 1905, the candidates were brought to campus for interviews with the various departments and with the president himself. A meal with the department was obligatory "to see what sort of human beings they were."[96] Some departments, such as English, voted as a whole; in others, the chairman and Wilson made the final decisions. With very few exceptions, those who were offered contracts from one to five years and salaries of $1,500 to $2,000 accepted with alacrity, drawn in part by the honor of sharing in a daring new experiment in American higher education.[97]

The preceptors' ideal qualifications were high but initially subject to some disagreement. Wilson, whose heart and experience belonged chiefly to the undergraduate college, tended to emphasize personality and pedagogical experience. In order to influence the privileged young men Princeton was admitting from East Coast prep schools, Wilson wanted "companionable . . . gentlemen;" "if their qualities as gentlemen and as scholars conflict," he told the student Press Club, "the former will win the place."[98] At the start of the search, Wilson even invited a few prep school teachers without advanced degrees or even much experience to apply, assuming that if masters of the nearby Lawrenceville School could prepare boys for Princeton,

[96] Bragdon interviews (WWC) with W. U. Vreeland, Mar. 24, 1940, p. 2, box 63, folder 57; Harry Clemons, July 24, 1941, p. 2, box 62, folder 19; T. M. Parrott, Sept. 15, 1942, pp. 1–2, box 63, folder 25; G. M. Harper, July 1, 1939, p. 2, box 62, folder 56.

[97] Robert K. Root, later Princeton's dean of the faculty, was happily teaching English at Yale when he was invited to an interview with Wilson, who had written him personally. "Before five minutes had passed," Root recalled in 1945, "I knew I was in the presence of a very great man. . . . Had Woodrow Wilson asked me to go with him and work under him while he inaugurated a new university in Kamchatka or Senegambia I would have said 'yes' without further question" (Robert K. Root, "Wilson and the Preceptors," in Myers, ed., *WW: Princeton Memories*, 13–18, at 14–15).

[98] *PWW*, 16:62 (Apr. 17, 1905).

they had the social standing and educational experience to guide their reading at higher levels.[99]

Dean Fine quickly disabused him of that notion and most department chairmen pressed ahead with a different emphasis, to which Wilson was soon persuaded. Since preceptors carried the rank and privileges of assistant professors, Fine believed that scholarly credentials and long-term promise were more important than native teaching ability. He insisted that "no man should be appointed a Preceptor who would not have a prospect of reaching professorial rank later." On the mathematics and scientific side, which Wilson entrusted to Fine, new appointments were made of "research men and productive scholars" to develop the faculty as "an intellectual body," sometimes, Dean Magie thought, "at the expense of undergraduate teaching."[100]

The emphasis on scholarly preparation and promise in all departments was appropriate because many preceptors were soon teaching graduate courses and precepting was a particularly demanding kind of teaching. T. J. Wertenbaker, a former preceptor in history and politics, argued that "in the lecture hall or class room the professor may conceal his shortcomings, but in the preceptorial conference, it is not possible. He must meet at close range an unending volley of questions, must take up every phase of his subject that may interest his preceptees." Even Wilson needed no reminding that "the man who is advancing in his chosen subject makes a better teacher than one who is standing still." It was he, after all, who had reminded the university community

[99] Bragdon interview with E. S. Corwin, June 9, 1939, WWC, box 62, folder 22; Jacob Beam to Bragdon, May 3, 1941, p. 4, WWC, box 62, folder 9; Bragdon, *WW: Academic Years*, 305–6. William Starr Myers was teaching history at the Gilman School in Baltimore when he was hired as a preceptor, but he had a Ph.D. from Johns Hopkins. Myers, ed., *WW: Princeton Memories*, 37–38; *PWW*, 16:309n1.

[100] Bragdon interviews (WWC) with J. Beam, Mar. 29, 1941, p. 2, box 62, folder 9; W. F. Magie, June 12, 1939, p. 2, box 63, folder 9; Oscar Veblen, June 9, 1939, box 63, folder 54; Veblen, "Henry Burchard Fine," 728–29 (see n. 21, above); Root, "Wilson and the Preceptors," in Myers, ed., *WW: Princeton Memories*, 13–14. The preceptors appointed in the science and mathematics departments were made assistant professors from the start and allowed to teach in more traditional ways, often in labs where teacher-student contact had always been close. Bragdon, *WW: Academic Years*, 306.

at the start of his presidency that "scholarship"—not teaching or service—"is our chief duty and our chief glory."[101]

Princeton's graduate school and faculty could not supply all or even most of the preceptors needed; even if they could, Wilson wanted to cast his net far and wide for the best young scholar-teachers he could find. This search contributed to a significant and intellectually important reduction in the parochial character of Princeton's faculty. Of the first 49 preceptors, 37 were hired away from 25 other institutions, while only 12 were promoted from within. And of the 37 preceptors who came with Ph.D.s, only 3 had received them from the Princeton Graduate School. Many contemporaries believed that the advent of these largely new outsiders "revolutionized Princeton [more] than the machinery of the preceptorial system" itself did. Wilson's pursuit of senior scholars without a Princeton connection had a similar effect. When he took office in 1902, the faculty was "dangerously inbred": 68 percent had Princeton degrees. When he left eight years later, Princeton graduates had dropped to 41 percent, and those below professorial rank to only 29 percent.[102]

Wilson's aggressive faculty-building reduced Princeton's parochialism in another way. His nationwide search for the best candidates required that Princeton become truly nonsectarian, without any religious tests for its faculty, to which he himself had been subject.[103] From his first months in office, Wilson made it clear that Princeton

[101] Thomas Jefferson Wertenbaker, "An Educational Need," *PAW*, May 26, 1920, 777–79, at 778; *PWW*, 14:132 (Sept. 18. 1902); 19:738 (Jan. 6, 1910).

[102] Bragdon, *WW: Academic Years*, 305–6, 361, 480n20; Bragdon interviews (WWC) with C. H. McIlwain, Jan. 2, 1940, p. 5, box 63, folder 11; William Kelly Prentice, June 6, 1939, p. 2, box 63, folder 31.

[103] When President Patton wrote Wilson in February 1890 to announce his unanimous appointment to the chair of political economy and jurisprudence, he noted that two or three trustees were nonetheless critical of Wilson's book, *The State*, because it "minimizes the supernatural" or "Divine Providence" in "the genesis of the State" and emphasized Roman law more than Christianity in the "regeneration of modern society." He put Wilson on notice that the trustees expected all chairholders to treat their subjects "under theistic and Christian suppositions" and "would not regard with favour such a conception of academic freedom or teaching as would leave in doubt the very direct bearing of historical Christianity as a revealed religion upon the great problems of civilization" (*PWW*, 6:526–27 [Feb. 18, 1890]).

was a "Presbyterian college" (as his clerical predecessors had boasted) only in the sense that "the Presbyterians of New Jersey were wise and progressive enough to found it." He reminded audiences that the founding charter of 1746 strictly prohibited "denominational distinctions" among any of its members. Unlike his unsuccessful bid as a faculty member to recruit Frederick Jackson Turner, a Unitarian, Wilson inadvertently but significantly brought to Princeton the first nonbeliever (philosopher Frank Thilly), the first Jew (English instructor Horace Kallen), and the first Roman Catholic (David McCabe, instructor in history, politics, and economics).[104] Following his lead, the trustees in 1906 officially declared the university nonsectarian, in part to make the faculty eligible for retirement pensions from the Carnegie Foundation for the Advancement of Teaching.[105]

The wholesale advent of the preceptors also dropped the student:faculty ratio to 7:1, where it remained for the rest of Wilson's term. This gave rise to some new verses of the 1906 faculty song:

Here's to those preceptor guys,
Fifty stiffs to make us wise;
Easy job and lots of pay,
Work the students night and day.[106]

The preceptors must have laughed at the contradiction between the third and fourth lines because they knew that "working the students" entailed even greater amounts of preparation on their part and, by research university standards, anything but an "easy job."

Before complaints chorused and adjustments in teaching assignments were made, most preceptors were burdened with onerous work loads, more demanding and various than those of the course lecturers and of other assistant professors in the "nonreading" departments. For the first couple of years, each preceptor handled conferences for both juniors and seniors in all of their departmental

[104] *PWW*, 10:134–35, 164 (Turner); 15:152–53 (Thilly), 375 (Kallen); 19:678 (McCabe).

[105] *New York Tribune*, Dec. 2, 1902, quoted in Mulder, *WW: Years of Preparation*, 177; *PWW*, 14:260–61 (Dec. 5, 1902); 16:468–69 (Oct. 20, 1906). See also Axson, "*Brother Woodrow*," 262–63n35.

[106] *Ten Years of Princeton University* [1896–1906] (New York, 1906), 40.

courses. In a still-undifferentiated department such as History, Politics, and Economics, preceptors might easily be assigned thirty-five students, whose work they were "to guide and to fructify" in six or eight subjects at once. In Edward Corwin's first year, he taught seventeen hours a week in seven subjects the first semester and sixteen hours in six subjects the second. Required to read 10,000–12,000 pages just to keep up with the students, the best face he could put on it was "at least I got an education." T. J. Wertenbaker had to precept in American History, Money and Banking, Jurisprudence, Constitutional History, City Government, and Finance. "It nearly broke my back," he complained, and the practice was "unfair to the preceptors."[107]

The preceptors were disadvantaged in several ways. They taught more hours a week than the lecturers in their courses; in 1909–1910, after several reforms had been made, the difference was still four hours.[108] If they had been content to remain preceptors for their whole academic lives, the extra load might have been borne. But most preceptors, like other junior professors with advanced degrees, were professionally ambitious and wanted to earn their own professorships and chairs. But the work load prevented all but the most workaholic and insomniac of them from pursuing their own research and the publication that would bring them to the notice of Dean Fine or other universities.

Research was also difficult because preceptors taught too many courses at a necessarily general level. They became "jack of all trades and masters of none" at a time in American higher education when "rising young scholars were specialists and wanted to teach their own specialties," preferably in their own lecture courses. This had two results. The preceptors who did manage to publish were often lured away by other universities or were promoted to Princeton professorships. Those who concentrated exclusively on their preceptorial du-

[107] Edward S. Corwin, "Departmental Colleague," in Myers, ed., *WW: Princeton Memories*, 22–23; Bragdon interview with T. J. Wertenbaker, Dec. 18, 1939, p. 2, WWC, box 63, folder 59. See also Bragdon interviews (WWC) with Robert McNutt McElroy, Nov. 20, 1940, p. 5, box 63, folder 13; Herbert Spencer Murch, n.d., p. 1, box 63, folder 18; Walter P. "Buzzer" Hall, "Memories of a Preceptor," *PAW*, Nov. 18, 1955, 10–12.

[108] *PWW*, 19:617–19, at 618 (Dec. 20, 1909).

ties for five years or more were often "stranded," Wertenbaker empathized, "for they could not be promoted when they were neither profound nor productive scholars, and they could not be kept on indefinitely as preceptors," particularly after 1913 when the rank was abolished and faculty precepted in no more than "two or three rather closely related subjects."[109]

Nonetheless, by nearly all accounts, the preceptorial system spawned a host of good results. The novelty and bold common sense of the plan garnered Princeton publicity that money could not buy. In North America, "probably nothing since the founding of Johns Hopkins University had attracted such far and wide attention to things purely educational." Abroad, media coverage reached as far as Constantinople, Syria, Tangier, and elsewhere in Africa.[110] Eventually, the plan was copied by other colleges and universities, but, as Yale's president complained good-naturedly, none could do so immediately because "Princeton had already got all the best preceptors in the country."[111]

On campus, both the method and the high quality of the men appointed to implement it led to a requickening of academic excitement and the "intellectual enfranchisement" of the undergraduates. Students who normally found the extracurricular sideshows more absorbing than the curricular big top were impelled, if not inspired, to read with more purpose, write with more clarity, and argue to greater effect. Many did acquire "the habit of talking about intellectual matters" in and out of class, even in the studiously unacademic eating clubs.[112] When polled, alumni from the classes of 1908 to 1915 declared that, for the first time in Princeton's history, they regarded

[109] Bragdon interviews (WWC) with T. J. Wertenbaker, Dec. 18, 1939, p. 2, box 63, folder 59; E. S. Corwin, June 9, 1939, p. 2, box 62, folder 22; Corwin, "Departmental Colleague," in Myers, ed., *WW: Princeton Memories*, 23; John D. Davies '41, "The Preceptors," *PAW*, Nov. 19, 1971, 6–8, at 8.

[110] Axson, "*Brother Woodrow*," 124; *PWW*, 16:460 (Oct. 17, 1906).

[111] Axson, "*Brother Woodrow*," 124; "The Preceptorial System," *Report of the President (1919)*, 15–16. By 1919, Bowdoin, Amherst, Rochester, General Theological Seminary, and the Rutgers Philosophy Department, among others, had adopted preceptorials.

[112] Root, "Wilson and the Preceptors," in Myers, ed., *WW: Princeton Memories*, 16; Bingham, "The 'Princeton System,'" *Yale Alumni Weekly*, Jan. 3, 1906, 257.

a Phi Beta Kappa key, not an athletic letter or captaincy, as the highest college honor. A majority admitted that they read more and had taken their work more seriously, without necessarily becoming "hard students." But they retained the "mental hunger" acquired from discussing good books and large ideas in their preceptors' homes and studies.[113]

In general, the precepts resulted in more work, fewer failures, better grades, and a gratifying increase in "the spirit of learning," Wilson's primary goal for the undergraduates.[114] Until the introduction of the four-course plan in 1923–1924 and the senior thesis soon after, the preceptorial system was thought by many to have given Princeton its "greatest advantage over every other college in America."[115]

❁ ❁ ❁

The abrupt and acrimonious end of Wilson's presidency in 1910—his forced resignation by the trustees as he ran for the governorship of New Jersey—could easily have slowed or reversed his curricular reforms and faculty development. His health-related failure to consult with the full university community before announcing his prescient but untimely quad plan of residential colleges and his unwill-

[113] V. L. Collins '92, "Twelve Years of the Preceptorial Method of Instruction," *PAW*, Apr. 18, 1917, 645–48, at 647; *Report of the President (1919)*, 21–23.

[114] Dean Fine to the Trustees' Committee on Morals and Discipline, *PWW*, 16:326–27 (Mar. 8, 1906); *PWW*, 17:68–69 (Mar. 14, 1907); Bragdon interview with H. Clemons, July 24, 1941, p. 2, WWC, box 62, folder 19; Craig, *WW at Princeton*, 111 (" 'B-grade' students tripled in numbers and proportion"); Woodrow Wilson, "The Spirit of Learning," *PWW*, 19:277–89 (July 1, 1909).

[115] *Report of the President (1919)*, 21. In "The Precept System: Myth and Reality of a Princeton Institution," *PULC* 64:3 (Winter 2003):467–503, Anthony Grafton charted the devolution of the precept "system" from its exciting, if structurally flawed, Wilsonian origins to today's larger, mostly graduate student–taught discussion "sections" of lecture courses, which are indistinguishable from those in most American universities. A brief version was published as "Precepting: Myth and Reality of a Princeton Institution" in *PAW*, Mar. 12, 2003, 16–19. In response to an Undergraduate Student Government "Report on the Status of the Princeton Precept System" (Apr. 2002), the dean of the college's office published a twenty-six-page booklet entitled *Inspired Conversation: The Princeton Precept* (Sept. 2003) for distribution to all students and preceptors.

ingness to compromise over the location of the Graduate College tarnished the bright beginnings of his tenure and divided the town and university into hostile camps. The saddest loss for Wilson, however, was his closest friend and advisor, Professor of Philosophy John Grier Hibben, who dared to oppose him in faculty meetings and on committees on both issues, Wilson thought out of expediency rather than principle.[116] Although they continued to speak and write to each other for a few years, Wilson never forgave his friend's "betrayal" and soon severed all ties with the couple with whom he and Mrs. Wilson shared Sunday dinner for years.[117]

Fatefully for Wilson, it was Hibben who was elected his successor after fifteen months of trustee stalemate. Hibben might easily have undermined the Wilsonian momentum out of spite, but he was not that sort of man. Until the broaching of the quad plan in 1906, he had shared all of Wilson's plans and philosophy. Wilson had leaned on him for advice so constantly and appointed him to so many faculty committees that some colleagues suspected him of being the president's "check-off" man or "personal representative."[118] He knew what mattered most to his old friend, but he refused to betray him or to impede Princeton's obvious progress. Several of Wilson's friends later had some hard words for Hibben—that he was "a second-class mind," inferior to his wife, "the real brains of the pair," a man of "no great vision" or initiative who had "nowhere near Wilson's capacity for leadership," someone better fitted to be "a first-rate headmaster of a boys' school." But every one of them acknowledged in the same breath that this gentle Presbyterian pastor was "a lovely person, absolutely square" (the seniors sang of "the

[116] Wilson's daughter Jessie recalled that her father began to break with Hibben when he discovered that Hibben did not deny the soundness of the quad plan, he only thought "it could not be brought to pass" (Ray Stannard Baker [RSB] interview with Mrs. Francis B. Sayre, Dec. 1, 1925, p. 5, Baker Papers, container 115, reel 82).

[117] Bragdon, *WW: Academic Years*, 302, 328, 333, 401n10; Mulder, *WW: Years of Preparation*, 197–99, 203, 211; Axson, "*Brother Woodrow*," 133–34, 145–46, 204–7, 281–82n5; Edwin A. Weinstein, *Woodrow Wilson: A Medical and Psychological Biography* (Princeton, 1981), 173–74, 180, 215–16.

[118] Bragdon interview with W. F. Magie, June 12, 1939, pp. 5, 5a, WWC, box 63, folder 9. See also Axson, "*Brother Woodrow*," 133, 145–46.

whitest man in all the fac"), "conciliatory and fair," "a just man" full of "genuine kindliness and courtesy." These qualities enabled him to heal a communal breach that "probably could have been healed by no one else."[119]

Hibben also saw to it that Princeton's progress was not interrupted after his unforgiving friend was gone from the scene. The strong and loyal faculty that Wilson had built was a major force for progressive continuity, but so was "the singularly happy choice" of "Jack" Hibben as his successor. According to Wilson's key lieutenant, Henry Fine, Hibben upon election called a meeting of Wilson's faculty leaders and begged them to join him in "continuing and furthering the great instructional and University work that Wilson had begun." Although Fine resigned the deanship of the faculty, Hibben persuaded him to become dean of the departments of science, a new post created solely for him. In 1925 Hibben appointed two of Wilson's former preceptors and allies—Luther Eisenhart and Christian Gauss—as his dean of the faculty and dean of the college, respectively. None of Wilson's friends or faculty ever had cause to complain that they were slighted or treated unfairly by the new president.[120]

The transition from Wilson to Hibben was so seamless that nearly everything that the faculty and the university accomplished academically during the presidencies of both Hibben (1912–1932) and Harold W. Dodds (1933–57) can be seen as "natural results" or "logical outcome[s]" of Wilsonian philosophies, policies, and trends.[121] Once

[119] Bragdon interviews (WWC) with C. G. Osgood, Apr. 14, 1939, p. 2, box 63, folder 24; W. M. Daniels, Mar. 30, 1940, p. 3, box 62, folder 28; Norman S. Mackie, Feb. 21–22, 1940, p. 1, box 63, folder 7; Dean Mathey, July 14, 1940, p. 3, box 63, folder 10; C. H. McIlwain, Jan. 2, 1940, p. 4, box 63, folder 4; McClellan, *The Gentleman and the Tiger*, 326. See also Scott, *Some Memories*, 297; Edmund Wilson, *A Prelude: Landscapes, Characters and Conversations from the Earlier Years of My Life* (New York, 1967), 120 ("by no means the worst of our mediocre American college presidents"); and, generally, Steven L. Buenning, "John Grier Hibben: A Biographical Study (1919–1932)" (Senior thesis, Dept. of History, PU, 1971).

[120] Henry Fine to RSB, Aug. 23, 1927, p. 8, Baker Papers, container 105, reel 74; Leitch, *Princeton Companion*, 155, 179, 207.

[121] Bragdon interview with C. G. Osgood, Apr. 14, 1939, p. 1, WWC, box 63, folder 24; *Report of the President (1925)*, 4; Harold W. Dodds, "Wilson the Educator," *PAW*, Oct. 12, 1956, 9–10.

the salient features of Wilson's program were carried out, in spirit if not in letter, by his two successors, we find ourselves re-viewing the familiar academic landscape of Carlos Baker and looking toward the Princeton of the present.

Although the campus and physical facilities grew prodigiously during Hibben's twenty years at the helm, Princeton continued Wilson's general policy of selective excellence.[122] The near-quadrupling of the endowment to more than $24 million went largely to triple the pool for faculty salaries and departmental expenses and to increase the number of books in the cramped library to 662,000 (up 136 percent). Of thirty new buildings, six were dedicated to research and instruction, including McCormick Hall for art, archaeology, and architecture (1922, expanded 1927), Frick Chemical Laboratory (1929), and Fine Memorial Hall for mathematics (1930). Significantly, the faculty grew only 73 percent to handle a 65 percent increase in the student body, which after 1922 was admitted selectively in both the college and the Graduate School.[123]

The faculty also continued to be reorganized to make more intellectual sense. Three professional schools—Architecture (1919), Engineering (1920), and Public and International Affairs (1930), the forerunner of the Woodrow Wilson School—were founded, each with a distinctly liberal arts and sciences cast to its vocational mission. As some departments came together to cooperate in the professional schools, others split into more coherent specialties: Psychology and Philosophy divorced and History, Politics, and Economics early split into two, and later three, departments.[124]

The curriculum was also rationalized and improved in step with Wilson's twin emphases on greater student initiative and independent study and on close faculty contact at all times. Freshmen were

[122] *Report of the President (1925)*, 2: "For many years past we have determined as a fundamental policy of the University that we will not seek extensive but rather intensive growth. . . . [We seek to] create a more widely pervading and powerful intellectual atmosphere in Princeton."

[123] *Report of the President (1932)*, 1, 10, 14; Leitch, *Princeton Companion*, 202, 254, 278, 300–1.

[124] *Report of the President (1932)*, 3, 4, 16, 19, 21, 22–26; " 'Princeton Was His Entire Life,' " *PAW*, May 26, 1933, 731–33, 737, at 731.

assigned faculty advisors, and preceptorials were extended downward to selected sophomore courses, though the faculty remained too few to offer small precepts in appropriate courses at every level. In 1918, proficiency in a classical language was dropped as a requirement for the B.A. and B.S. degrees, much to the chagrin of Dean of the Graduate School Andrew West and the nationally ranked Classics Department.[125]

The greatest curricular change occurred in 1923–1924 with the introduction of the "Upperclass Plan of Study" or, as the students named it, the "four-course plan." In place of a fifth course, upperclassmen (following their Harvard and Yale counterparts) were required to choose a departmental major and to take two courses each semester in it. They were also to devote the equivalent of the fifth course to independent study of a special topic within the major field, for which they were assigned a faculty advisor. At the end of the senior year, they had to pass a comprehensive examination on both their general and special fields with at least a "third group" grade (the "dead level of mediocrity" on the five-point grading scale then in use) to graduate. Almost immediately the preparation of the special topic led to the senior thesis, which virtually every student generation since has regarded as their single most valuable academic experience.[126]

The four-course plan—like the architectonic "New Plan" of 1945 with its divisional and distributional requirements—was seen by its

[125] *Report of the President (1932)*, 2–3. In Wilson's day, Princeton's Classics Department was the nation's best. By 1925 it had "slipped" to second place. West's 1917 defense, *The Value of the Classics*, came too late to turn the Princeton and national tide against mandatory classics. *PWW*, 18:12 (Mar. 9, 1908); Thorp, *PGS*, 192.

[126] *Report of the President (1923)*, 1–10; ibid. *(1924)*, 1–7; ibid. *(1932)*, 4–8; Luther P. Eisenhart, "The First Year of the New Plan of Upperclass Study," *PAW*, June 18, 1924, 794–95; John Grier Hibben, "The New Plan of Study," *PAW*, Oct. 29, 1924, 103–5; William F. Magie, "The New Plan of Study: Its Purposes and How It Is Working," *PAW*, Jan. 7, 1925, 293–94; Magie, "What the Faculty Think of the New Plan," *PAW*, June 17, 1925, 904–5; Struthers Burt '04, "Another Academic Milestone: The 'Four Course Plan' as a Supplement to the Preceptorial Method," *PAW*, Dec. 10, 17, 1926, Jan. 17, 1927, 339–43, 375–78, 425–29; Eisenhart, "The Plan of Undergraduate Study: Why the University Found It Necessary to Adopt the Present Method of Instruction," *PAW*, Jan. 16, 1931, 356–57. For more on the senior thesis, see chapter 4, pp. 187–97.

sponsors as a continuation of Wilson's desire to "intellectualize the undergraduates."[127] Hibben regarded the plan as "the natural and logical outgrowth of the preceptorial method of instruction," which gradually ceased to be the academic center of gravity. Like the preceptorial plan, its aim was to "put into the hands of our students a new instrument of power" and to "reveal to them the sources of intellectual pleasure."[128] Initially, the undergraduates, who now faced a hurdle at the end of their academic careers to match the one they had recently had to clear before they could start, were understandably concerned. The *Daily Princetonian* opened the plan's inaugural year by sharing "the feeling . . . abroad that Princeton is attempting to turn out intellectual super-men, caring nothing about men whose mental ability is only ordinary."[129] But soon they, like the alumni, began to take pride in the tough-loving alma mater that expected—and got—more from them than ever before.

The increase in curricular demands on the students had a parallel effect on the faculty. Being asked to teach large lecture courses, small precepts, upperclass specialties, and graduate seminars, while advising freshmen, departmental concentrators, and junior paper, senior thesis, and doctoral dissertation writers, put extraordinary demands on the Princeton faculty. To enable them to perform and to compensate them for these heavy duties, Hibben (and his successors) sought to give them maximum autonomy and competitive economic rewards. Wilson had given the faculty seven years of limited self-government in their new departments and in serious faculty meetings to reform the curriculum and launch the preceptorial program. Building on that experience, Hibben believed that the time was right to fully enfranchise the faculty.

At the first faculty meeting after he assumed office, Hibben "turned over to the Faculty the appointment of all its committees," Dean Fine applauded, "a thing wholly unprecedented and of the first

[127] RSB interview with H. B. Fine, June 18, 1925, p. 1, Baker Papers, container 105, reel 74. For the 1945 "New Plan," see Robert K. Root, "Teachers and Teaching," in Charles G. Osgood et al., *The Modern Princeton* (Princeton, 1947), 77–80; Donald A. Stauffer, *The Idea of a Princeton Education* (Princeton, 1946), 23–28.

[128] *Report of the President (1923)*, 5, 7; ibid. *(1925)*, 4.

[129] *DP*, Sept. 26, 1923, p. 3.

importance since the business of the Faculty is largely in the hands of these committees—this, though he knew that the great majority of the Faculty was made up of Wilson's old friends."[130] He did more. He created a faculty-elected advisory committee to meet regularly with the trustees' curriculum committee, to which he added his deans of the graduate school, faculty, and engineering school. He appointed three faculty each year to the trustees' honorary degrees committee to choose appropriate reflectors of Princeton's core values and philosophy. And most important of all, he established a Faculty Advisory Committee on Appointments and Advancement, whose three elected members, all full professors and often department chairmen, met with the president to decide all nominations for tenure, retention, and promotion. This hardworking, powerful "Committee of Three" (as it is still known after its voting faculty members grew to six and ex officio administrators to five) gave the faculty major authority over its own development as it dealt with departmental recommendations within the larger context of the long-range needs of the university. After witnessing Wilson's messy firing of Guyot Cameron, Hibben also saw the need to put in place new safeguards to protect "the rights of the individual in the case of dismissal from the faculty."[131]

Upon Hibben's retirement, the faculty gave him a beautiful leather-bound, engrossed, and illuminated address of appreciation. They selected two of his many accomplishments for special recognition. The first was that "under his guidance the intellectual distinction of the University has been enhanced by the addition to the faculty, or by the resolute retention in its ranks, of many scholars of high repute, and by the provision of greatly increased facilities for scholarly research." The second, and the more important in their eyes, was that "from the first he chose [unlike his predecessor, it did not have to be said] to be primus inter pares, taking the faculty into his confidence, entrusting to it a full measure of responsibility, steadily safeguarding its privileges and dignity."[132] In short, he had completed the founda-

[130] H. B. Fine to RSB, Aug. 23, 1927, p. 8, Baker Papers, container 105, reel 74.

[131] *Report of the President (1932)*, 12; " 'Princeton Was His Entire Life,' " *PAW*, May 26, 1933, 732.

[132] "A Tribute from the Faculty," *PAW*, May 6, 1932, 688–89, 704–5, at 704. Hibben was equally attentive to the economic needs of the faculty. During the prosperous 1920s,

tion of the modern Princeton faculty, a structure that would have been easily recognized by Carlos Baker and his colleagues and, after two significant additions of personnel and one decisive shift in emphasis, by President Tilghman's professoriate as well.

During the Hibben and early Dodds years, the faculty evolved "naturally" from Wilsonian precedents except in one regard: Hibben by choice and Dodds by necessity reverted to the pre-Wilsonian practice of favoring insiders for faculty appointments. By 1928, Hibben boasted to the alumni, 47 percent of the ranked faculty had either graduate or undergraduate degrees from Princeton; 100 alumni had been added since he took office in 1912. Even the outsiders, he thought, had become "thoroughly Princetonian." "That is a part of our policy: as rapidly as possible, wherever they are available, to add to the Faculty Princeton men in order to carry on, without any break in continuity, the Princeton tradition and the maintaining of the Princeton atmosphere."[133]

In 1937 Dodds lamented that during the past five years, "The higher ranks of the Faculty have not been strengthened by the occa-

---

he launched three successful endowment campaigns, largely to increase faculty salaries; his successor Harold Dodds campaigned to increase endowed chairs and research leaves in order to hold his best faculty who were tempted by outside offers. Hibben also regularized faculty pay scales by rank, establishing minimum and maximum salaries within each, and gave across-the-board as well as merit raises. To compensate for salaries that lagged behind those offered by academic rivals, Princeton offered generous fringe benefits in the form of retirement and insurance plans and subsidized faculty housing, which by 1952 were considered by the dean of the faculty to be worth 15–20 percent of any outside salary offers. *Report of the President (1923)*, 15; ibid. *(1932)*, 10–11; ibid. *(1937)*, 23–24; ibid. (1938), 16–17; Dean of the Faculty J. Douglas Brown, *Report to the President (1952–53)*, 14–15. In 2004 the university accommodated approximately 700 faculty, staff, and postdoctoral fellows in subsidized housing, at rents ranging from $670 to $4,500 a month. It also offered mortgages at 1 percent below the prevailing local rate, a program initiated by Dean Brown in the 1960s. Erik Linstrum, "University Offers Profs Subsidized Housing," *DP* (online), Apr. 27, 2004.

[133] John Grier Hibben, "How Faculty Promotions Are Effected," *PAW*, Oct. 5, 1928, 53–54, at 54. By 1932 a quarter of the faculty had degrees from the Princeton Graduate School. At the University of Chicago in 1929–1930, the inbreeding was much worse: 56 percent had advanced degrees from Chicago, and the same number had no experience elsewhere. Floyd W. Reeves et al., *The University Faculty*, The University of Chicago Survey, 12 vols. (Chicago, 1933), 3:34–35 (table 9).

sional addition of distinguished men from other universities as was done from time to time before the financial depression." In general, he said, it was Princeton's policy to develop its own senior faculty. But some outsiders were always needed to reduce parochialism and prevent complacency. He thus asked the board for "more professorships of great distinction, sufficiently endowed to constitute coveted prizes in the academic world, which will enable the University to retain in the face of calls elsewhere and to attract from the outside world leaders in the fields of the professorships."[134]

In that request lay a clue to one key trajectory of Princeton's future faculty.

❁ ❁ ❁

The first two changes in personnel were not yet visible in the socially and sexually homogeneous faculties of Carlos Baker's Princeton and "Enfield." In the late 1950s, women and people of color did not appear behind classroom lecterns, only behind typewriters, library check-out desks, and dining hall hot tables. With the advent of coeducation in 1969 and the civil rights movement, however, Princeton slowly realized that half the human race and virtually all of America's minorities were unrepresented, even in token numbers, in its faculty meetings and most of its course syllabi.

Female faculty members before coeducation were so rare that they could be counted on one hand. Sociologist Jessie Bernard of Penn State, the first female visiting professor, met with such a strong current of anti-feminism in her courses in 1959–1960 that she was moved to analyze it in the pages of the *Princeton Alumni Weekly*. She had met a "brilliant and talented" woman, "the first of her sex ever to serve as preceptor," who had faced the same sort of junior misogyny ten years earlier.[135] Suzanne Keller, a sociologist of the family, followed Bernard in 1966 and became the first tenured woman two years later, just ahead of coeducation. In 1972, the year women were first elected to the Board of Trustees, the faculty included forty-four

[134] *Report of the President (1937)*, 23–24.

[135] Jessie Bernard, " 'Breaking the Sex Barrier,' " *PAW*, Sept. 23, 1960, 3–7.

FIGURE 6. Ellen Chances, Ph.D. *72, teaching a seminar in Slavic Literature in 1978, the year she earned tenure.

women. When the alumni magazine sent a male reporter, Class of 1968, to interview five representatives, he discovered to his amazement that "women professors are just like men professors: they teach, they write, and they attend endless committee meetings. They are diverse, intense, and always busy."[136]

Eventually, some of these new professors came from Princeton's own graduate school. The first woman—just one—had been admitted in 1961 and the first Ph.D. awarded in 1964, but women were not encouraged to apply in significant numbers until the late 1960s. The first Graduate School alumna to earn tenure at Princeton (in 1978) was Ellen Chances, a 1972 Ph.D. in Slavic languages and literatures. Her mentor had been the exciting European émigré

[136] William McCleery, "Between Solitude and Society: A Conversation on the Meanings of Community with Suzanne Keller," *PAW*, Mar. 23, 1994, 12–17; Thomas Rawls, "The Second Sex Joins the Faculty," *PAW*, May 2, 1972, 8–12, at 8. One of those profiled was Nancy Weiss, assistant professor of history, since 1987 dean of the college.

writer Nina Berberova, one of the rare women on the faculty before coeducation.[137]

Even throughout the relatively flush recruiting years of the 1980s and early 1990s, deans of the faculty worried about Princeton's share of female professors. Academic stars such as Elaine Pagels (Religion), novelists Toni Morrison and Joyce Carol Oates, and literary critic Elaine Showalter were less difficult to attract than were sufficient numbers of promising junior women for the developmental pipeline.[138] Because of two-career families and residual Tiger chauvinism, it proved harder to recruit women than it did men. In Princeton's lean budget structure, spousal hires were rare. One of the most fortunate was the eminent senior historian of late antiquity, Peter Brown, who came from the University of California, Berkeley, in 1983 with his then-wife, Assistant Professor of Art History Patricia Fortini Brown.[139] At the end of Princeton's 250th year, after more than twenty-five years of institutional effort, Dean Amy Gutmann had to admit that women constituted less than 20 percent of the ranked faculty, only 14 percent of tenured faculty, but a rising 35 percent of assistant professors. All departments had at least one woman, though seven, largely in the sciences and engineering, lacked tenured women.[140] By 2004, 22 percent of the ranked faculty were

[137] Thorp, *PGS*, 285–89, 303–4, 327–29; *PAW*, Feb. 26, 1979, 21; Ellen Chances, "Nina Berberova," in Marks, *Luminaries*, 13–20. In 1974 Sylvia Molloy, Argentine-born professor of Romance languages, became the first woman to be tenured from the junior ranks. Dean of the Faculty Aaron Lemonick, *Reports to the President* (1988–1989), 1:16; *PAW*, May 2, 1972, 9; Nov. 22, 2000, 6.

[138] *PAW*, Nov. 16, 1981, 9 (Davis); Nov. 12, 1986, 18, 30 (Oates); July 12, 1989, 6 (Showalter); Nov. 10, 1993, 6–7 (Morrison).

[139] Ann Waldron, "Scholar of Late Antiquity Breaks Down Walls Between Disciplines," *Princeton Today* 0:1 (Prototype 1987):6; Waldron, "From Artist to Art Historian [Patricia Fortini Brown]," *PAW*, Oct. 27, 1993, 5.

[140] In 2001 President Tilghman appointed a Task Force on the Status of Women in the Natural Sciences and Engineering. It recommended that the university establish a $10 million endowment to "promote the recruitment, hiring, and retention of women faculty" in those fields. In 2002 the president appointed Maria Klawe as the dean of engineering and applied science. In 2003 Professor of Psychology Joan Girgus, a member of the task force, was named special assistant to the dean of the faculty to oversee gender-equity issues, which included more campus day care and spousal hiring. Robin Wilson, "Duke and Princeton Will Spend More to Make Female Professors Happy,"

women, but less than 15 percent were tenured. With women in five of the top administrative posts, those numbers were expected to rise.[141]

Black faculty were in even shorter supply. Although Princeton had established an African-American studies program in 1969, there were only fifteen blacks on the faculty by 1973; six were tenured but two of those were primarily administrators. The Graduate School went some way to increase the supply of minority professors for Princeton and other colleges and universities. Recruitment began slowly in the late 1960s but peaked in 1973 when seventy-nine blacks of both sexes enrolled. Unfortunately, as other universities began to compete heavily, Princeton's success rate dropped markedly through the early 1980s. But as black enrollments hit bottom in 1983 at only twenty-five, they were joined by thirty Hispanics and forty-five Asian-Americans, a trend that has continued.[142]

Yet very few black Ph.D.s, from the Graduate School or elsewhere, could be found to join the Princeton faculty. Nationally, about half of all black Ph.D.s teach at historically black colleges; since less than 4 percent of all doctorates (more than half in education) go to blacks, the competition for the best liberal artists and scientists by predominantly white, elite institutions is intense. In 2002 Princeton could offer only eighteen African-American role models and mentors (1.6 percent of its faculty of over eleven hundred) to the class of 2005, which was 9 percent black. Moreover, as Dean Robert Gunning warned in 1995, "retention of minority faculty members is as much a problem as their recruitment in the first place." He spoke

---

CHE, Oct. 10, 2003, A12; "Task Force on Women in the Natural Sciences and Engineering Issues Report: Princeton Has Made Progress, But There Is More Work to Be Done" (PU, press release, Sept. 29, 2003); Alyson Zureick, "Princeton's Women in Science Explain Task Force Finding of Gender Disparity," *DP* (online), Nov. 25, 2003.

[141] Dean of the Faculty Aaron Lemonick, *Reports to the President* (1982–1983), 1:74; Dean of the Faculty Amy Gutmann, ibid. (1996–1997), 1:11–12; Karen W. Arenson, "More Women Taking Leadership Roles at Colleges," *New York Times*, July 4, 2002, A1, A13; thanks to Associate Dean of the Faculty Toni Turano for the 2004 figures. Nationwide, 45 percent of assistant professors and 20 percent of full professors were women.

[142] Richard K. Rein '69, "Black Princeton," *PAW*, Mar. 6, 1973, 8–14; Thorp, *PGS*, 317–19, 329–32.

from experience because Professor of Religion Cornel West, a Princeton Ph.D., had just publicly decamped for Harvard to join Henry Louis Gates, Jr., in the premier African-American studies department in the country. When West returned to Princeton in 2002 after a public dust-up with Harvard's new president, Lawrence Summers, he was joined by Harvard colleague and philosopher Anthony Appiah. With similar additions at all ranks, and the retention of distinguished faculty, such as Professor of Medieval History William C. Jordan *73, Princeton's total minority faculty stood at 117 (15 percent), which put a very different face on higher learning than did Hibben's or Dodds's monochromatic dons.[143]

❁ ❁ ❁

Change in the spirit or emphasis of a university faculty is harder to detect than are more obvious alterations in number, color, and gender. The faculty themselves are keenly aware of tonal and normative changes because they largely initiate and wholly implement and exemplify them in their working lives. Students and alumni are somewhat slower to notice these shifts; when they do, they often react as if sacred tradition is being desecrated and destroyed for the worst reasons. A bellwether reaction to the most decisive but subtlest shift in emphasis by the Princeton faculty in the last century came in an essay in the *Alumni Weekly* in the summer of 1929. A new alumnus complained that "only those [faculty] who have done productive scholarship can win promotion. The result is that fine teaching is not rewarded and many fine teachers find it necessary to spend their time turning out pot-boilers to gain the position they deserve."[144]

[143] Eunice Kim, "Why Are There So Few African-American Professors on Campuses?" *DP* (online), Feb. 25, 2002; Dean of the Faculty Robert C. Gunning, *Reports to the President* (1994–1995), 1:18. Princeton has issued a standing invitation to Gates to complete the black hat-trick. Jacques Steinberg, "Princeton Embraces Scholar of Black Studies [Appiah]," *New York Times*, Jan. 27, 2002, 20; "African-American Studies Grows," *PAW*, Mar. 13, 2002, 9; "Cornel West *80 Leaves Harvard for Princeton," *PAW*, May 15, 2002, 10–11.

[144] Gerhard P. Van Arkel '29, "Princeton, More Old Than New" (third prize in the *PAW* essay contest on "How Thinks the Campus?"), *PAW*, July 2, 1929, 1134–35, at 1135.

It is hard to know what signs the young graduate was reading in the university's or faculty's behavior that inspired his now-familiar but then-novel lament. He must have missed President Hibben's October article in the same magazine, "How Faculty Promotions Are Effected." Explicitly mindful of how the alumni would vote on such matters, Hibben affirmed that he and the Committee of Three invariably gave the highest merit raises each year to men of "unquestionable *teaching* ability." His only allusions to scholarly research were general reminders that even college teachers had to keep up with the explosive new literature in their fields and that the faculty, as much as the students and alumni, had the "Princeton spirit" by seeking to "do everything they can . . . through their researches and their publications to bring credit and honor to the name of Princeton throughout the world."[145]

As if to calm the worst fears of the alumni, Hibben made abundantly clear in his final report to the Princeton community his stand on the growing debate over the proper balance of a university faculty's multiple duties. He began by quoting the 1748 college charter to emphasize that teaching was "our primary purpose and the very reason of Princeton's being." Then, in a hefty section on research, he reminded readers that "one of the essential functions of a university is to conserve and enlarge the field of human knowledge" and that "most of the best teachers . . . will not be attracted to an institution which does not give them the opportunity and stimulus for scholarly activity and research." But he quickly tempered that emphasis by saying that Princeton's development of research occurred "without in any degree lessening the importance and significance of the College within the University." In his conclusion he admitted that "the right adjustment of research activities of the Faculty to their *primary* responsibility as undergraduate teachers" was tricky, but claimed that Princeton had maintained a "finely poised balance" between the graduate and undergraduate interests and the research and teaching functions of the faculty, which were "naturally complementary." But he ended by counseling his successors that "Princeton College in distinction from Princeton University should never be relegated to

[145] *PAW*, Oct. 5, 1928, 53–54, at 54 (my emphasis).

the background or to a secondary place" and the faculty to make all of their growing knowledge from scholarship "*tributary* to [their] teaching."[146] The alumni, most of whom had attended a much smaller, less complex college, must have been largely mollified.

But not for long. During the tenure of Hibben's more worldly successor, Professor of Politics Harold Dodds, who had attended only the Graduate School for an M.A., Princeton unmistakably became a "real university" of major importance.[147] A great depression, a world war, and a postwar period of recovery and readjustment seem inauspicious times to move a highly regarded but relatively small "university-college" (Hibben's phrase) into the front ranks of national and even international universities. But Dodds managed to do it, without compromising Princeton's manageable size, dedication to teaching, or collegiate spirit. And in the process, the self- and institutional identity of the faculty shifted irrevocably from teacher-scholars to scholar-teachers, making them fully familiar and virtually identical in spirit to their successors, from Carlos Baker's day to the present.[148]

When Dodds stepped down in June 1957, the faculty told him at their last faculty meeting that "Princeton has grown, during your Presidency, in all the things which make a university—in intellectual eminence and in influence on our society. It is a better place for scholars to do their work than it was when you became President,

[146] *Report of the President (1932)*, 2, 12–13, 59 (my emphases).

[147] Joseph R. Strayer, "Harold Willis Dodds," in Leitch, *Princeton Companion*, 137–41, at 140.

[148] Hugh Stott Taylor, "A Community of Scholars," in Osgood et al., *The Modern Princeton*, 36–67, at 39: "The first fifty years of Princeton University, as successor to the College of New Jersey, can be characterized by [a] shift of emphasis from teacher to scholar-teacher." See also Dean of the Faculty J. Douglas Brown, *Reports to the President* (1963–1964), 1:289: "The historical rhythm in Princeton's pattern in faculty development has been emphasis on *teaching* until the early 1950s, shifting toward that on *scholarship* in more recent years. While, fortunately, the tradition of good teaching has continued in most departments, the pressure on senior men to attain leadership in their disciplines on a national basis has been reflected in their growing emphasis on scholarship and publication in selecting their younger colleagues. . . . It is a part of the climate of a national university."

and we are grateful."[149] What they were thinking of, no doubt, was the modest increase in labor-intensive undergraduates to 2,948 (28 percent), the substantial increase in faculty to 582 (78 percent), and the symbolically important increase in graduate students to 636 (117 percent)—all of which reduced the student:faculty ratio from a generous 8:1 to a luxurious 6:1. He also added thirty endowed professorships, almost doubling the number, and greatly increased the number of research leaves to more than thirty a year.[150] He raised salaries as quickly as he could, improved fringe benefits, and built more faculty housing. In 1941 the university acquired the Forrestal Campus across U.S. 1 to give engineering and nuclear physics elbow room.[151] On his watch new departments and programs were launched in music (1934), creative arts (1939), the humanities (1939), American civilization (1942), religion (1945), and Near Eastern studies (1947). Scientific research programs sponsored by the federal government and industry ballooned, requiring the addition of 237 professional staff to run the new facilities often inspired by war-time projects such as the development of the atomic bomb.[152] The greatest lift to teaching

[149] Leitch, *Princeton Companion*, 140.

[150] *Reports of the President (1952–1953)*, 15 (leaves). In 1948 chairman Joseph Strayer told President Dodds that "both morale and scholarship in the [History] Department were improved by the University's encouragement of research. The frequency with which leaves of absence and grants for travel and materials have been made has convinced members of the faculty that the University is interested in their work and conscious of their needs. As a result, the slump in thinking and writing which might have resulted from the overwork of the post-war years may well be averted" (*Reports to the President* [1947–1948], 191–92). Under President Nathan Pusey, Harvard also increased its endowed chairs, from 132 in 1953 to 212 a decade later (61 percent). Morton and Phyllis Keller, *Making Harvard Modern: The Rise of America's University* (New York, 2001), 212.

[151] J. I. Merritt '66, *Princeton's James Forrestal Campus: Fifty Years of Sponsored Research* (Princeton, 2002).

[152] William R. Bowen, *The Federal Government and Princeton University* (Princeton, Jan. 1962); Amy Sue Bix, " 'Backing into Sponsored Research': Physics and Engineering at Princeton University," *History of Higher Education Annual (1993)*, 9–52; Robert Kargon and Stuart Leslie, "Imagined Geographies: Princeton, Stanford, and the Boundaries of Useful Knowledge in Postwar America," *Minerva: A Review of Science, Learning, and Policy* 32:2 (Summer 1994):121–43. By 1957–1958 about fifty faculty were receiving half their salaries from sponsored research contracts. Dean of the Faculty J. Douglas

and research in the humanities and social sciences came from the long-postponed building in 1948 of the Harvey S. Firestone Memorial Library, an almost ideally functional product of faculty planning carefully adapted to Princeton's educational philosophy.[153]

The transition to unhyphenated university status did not occur overnight. After Dodds's election but before his inauguration, the *Alumni Weekly* conducted the first of several debates on whether Princeton was or should be a college or university. Both alumni participants—one an engineering graduate and architect of college buildings, the other a businessman with a B.A. and Ph.D. in economics—arrived at much the same conclusion, making several points, particularly about the faculty, that alumni were beginning to hear with some frequency in the *PAW*'s pages. "We are a college with a university faculty," said one. "In many fields our faculty has an outstanding national reputation," agreed the other, "and in several, particularly in the natural sciences, an international reputation." "The real issue," the second continued, "is between the scholarly teacher and the teacher without scholarly attainments." Precisely, said his genial opponent, "a faculty chosen only for teaching ability inevitably lacks prestige among the men who are to be taught, the one place where prestige is essential. . . . With the stimulation of men celebrated throughout the world (whether or not they be good classroom instructors) the young man can hardly fail to reach out for himself."[154]

Even President Dodds continued to speak of Princeton as a "university-college" before the war. In an article on the faculty, he reminded alumni that when the college changed its name in 1896, it assumed responsibilities and challenges unique to a university. But he also noted that "to meet its *teaching* responsibilities Princeton utilizes the facilities of a university in the form of a faculty of high standing in *scholarship* employing laboratories and libraries which

---

Brown, *Reports to the President* (1957–1958), 72. At Harvard, research appointments jumped from 107 in 1939–1940 to 815 in 1958–1959. Keller, *Making Harvard Modern*, 212.

[153] See chapter 7, below.

[154] Aymar Enbury II '00 and John F. Fennelly '20, "College or University—A Debate," *PAW*, Jan. 13, 1933, 319–21, at 320. Another debate on "Princeton—University or College?" seven years later was flatfooted and uninformed; two undergraduates from Whig-Clio conducted it. *PAW*, Jan. 12, 1941, 313–17.

only a university can provide." Moreover, he testified, contrary to the undergraduate-alumni myth, "many of our most distinguished scholars are likewise our best teachers."[155]

After the war, however, the self-identifying word from Nassau Hall was almost exclusively "university." The leading voice was that of J. Douglas Brown '19, *28, expert on industrial relations, consummate judge of talent, and Dodds's and Goheen's dean of the faculty (1946–1967) and simultaneously Princeton's first provost (1966–1967). Dropping the emotive hyphenate "-college," Brown spoke more and more frequently about Princeton as a "liberal university" and a "national university" and its faculty exclusively as "scholar-teachers" who had an obligation to "*lead*" in the search for new knowledge.[156]

This was especially true after Princeton's bicentennial observances in 1946–1947, when the university convened and its faculty chaired sixteen conferences of scholars and men of affairs to discuss the postwar world and its needs. The proceedings of each two-to-three-day conference were published as a pamphlet, which spread Princeton's name even farther. The final convocation in June featured a thousand-person procession, including President Truman, General Eisenhower, Admiral Nimitz, Albert Einstein, T. S. Eliot, and delegates from colleges and universities all over the United States and forty-three foreign countries. During the course of the year, at three other convocations, Princeton conferred honorary degrees on a hundred eminent persons, such as scholars and scientists Niels Bohr, Arnold Toynbee, Reinhold Niebuhr, and Jacques Maritain. All of these occasions reflected handsomely on Princeton's newly realized

[155] Harold W. Dodds, "Plan for Personnel: The Faculty and Its Relation to Princeton's Idea of a 'University-College,' " *PAW*, Apr. 7, 1941, 7–10, at 8. See also Dean Robert K. Root: "Our experience at Princeton has shown that the really great scholar is nearly always also a great teacher" (*PAW*, Dec. 16, 1938, 257–58).

[156] J. Douglas Brown, "The American Liberal University," *PAW*, May 6, 1955, 8–9; Brown, "Princeton as a National University," *PAW*, Feb. 4, 1964, 6–8. See also Dodds's address at the university's opening exercises in 1954, "The Nature of a University," *PAW*, Oct. 1, 1954, 6. After Brown retired, he adumbrated his Princeton-based philosophy in *The Liberal University: An Institutional Analysis* (New York, 1969), much as Dodds did in his post-retirement Carnegie study, *The Academic President: Educator or Caretaker?* (New York, 1962).

status as a world-class university. In particular, "the program of faculty conferences during the bicentennial year," Dodds remarked, "gave us new and objective testimony as to the quality of the Princeton faculty."[157]

After and even before the bicentennial, several signs and symbols of the faculty's decisive shift toward scholarship as the benchmark of academic quality were visible. The most prominent and earliest postwar manifestation of the new emphasis was Hugh Stott Taylor's official report to the faculty, *Princeton's Program of Scholarship and Research*, on July 2, 1945. Its importance was enhanced by Taylor's having succeeded to the deanship of the Graduate School the previous day. The report sought to address "the problem of the returning faculty member and his rehabilitation in scholarship and research," which was "intimately related to the character of graduate work" rather than undergraduate instruction. While the sciences and engineering had been fostered by the National Research Council and war work, the humanities and, to a lesser extent, the social sciences were lagging and experiencing "a real dearth of scholars in their forties and early fifties." Taylor called for more research leaves; increased research and travel funds; more technical and nontechnical assistance, particularly a new library; tougher standards for tenure and promotion; greater care and provision for scholarly publication; increased opportunities for younger faculty to teach graduate courses; and a program to recruit promising young instructors rather than hiring the immediately available men.[158]

The logic behind the last proposal gave rise to a local program of graduate student recruitment that soon grew into a long-term national program. Appropriately named the Woodrow Wilson Fellowship Program by its progenitor and first director, ex-Marine captain

[157] "Princeton Increases Faculty Salaries," *PAW*, Feb. 27, 1948, 4–5, at 4; Leitch, *Princeton Companion*, 51–52; Charles G. Osgood, *Lights in Nassau Hall: A Book of the Bicentennial: Princeton, 1746–1946* (Princeton, 1951). A decade earlier, Harvard had celebrated its tercentenary in similarly grand fashion. Keller, *Making Harvard Modern*, 3–10; *The Tercentenary of Harvard College* (Cambridge, Mass., 1937); David McCord, *In Sight of Sever: Essays from Harvard* (Cambridge, Mass., 1963), 41–107.

[158] [Hugh Stott Taylor], *Princeton's Program of Scholarship and Research: A Report to the University Faculty by the Dean of the Graduate School* (Princeton, July 1945), n.p.

and classicist Whitney J. Oates, it sought talented young men, most of them at first returning veterans, and later women, through faculty nominations and encouraged them with generous fellowships to attend or finish graduate school and to choose academic careers. Although 70 percent of the first three cohorts were Princetonians, the fellowships were not limited to Princeton graduates or to study at Princeton, but were designed to "provide a 'stockpile' of young scholars for the benefit of university education throughout the country." Among the first three veterans chosen was classicist Robert Goheen '40, one of the youngest lieutenant colonels in the U.S. Army who had ended his war service in the Luzon campaign. By 1947, the program had attracted several other graduate students who would soon join and bring distinction to the Princeton faculty, such as Edward T. Cone '39 (Music), John R. Martin (Art History), and Marius Jansen '44 (Far Eastern Studies). More than half of the fellows "would not have given a thought to the academic profession" without an invitation fellowship.[159]

If there was any doubt in the Princeton community that the postwar faculty was shifting its emphasis from teaching to scholarship, it was removed in May 1948 with the release of the University Research Committee's report on *Princeton and Scholarship*. The newly reconstituted twelve-man committee was chaired by Dean Taylor and included such prolific and hard-nosed scholars as Gerald Bentley (English), Gilbert Chinard (French), Gordon Craig and Joseph Strayer (History), and Jacob Viner (Economics). They minced no words. Declaring Princeton's teaching of a "high order," they confessed that "its role in scholarship has not been equally distinguished. The great contributions of brilliant men have been all too few, considering Princeton's position of prominence in the academic world." Dead wood was not a big problem. "In the University," they found, "there are few, if any, outstanding teachers who are not also scholars of

[159] *PAW*, Nov. 23, 1945, 3; Feb. 22, 1946, 3; Whitney J. Oates, "Recruiting for an Academic Career," *PAW*, Mar. 14, 1947, 5–7, at 7. After twenty-five years, about half of the eleven thousand fellows became academics while another quarter entered related fields, such as secondary or prep school teaching. Hans Rosenhaupt, "25 (Full) Years of Woodrow Wilson Fellowships," *PAW*, Mar. 18, 1969, 21–22, 39–42, at 21.

above average ability." But they were concerned that "as many as 10% of the [faculty] have had no significant scholarly achievements, are admittedly indifferent to scholarship, and do not propose to undertake research." Although Princeton was doing no worse than its postwar rivals, they predicted, it would "decline markedly in the next two decades if present conditions and tendencies persist."[160]

The main problem lay in the junior ranks, a larger proportion of whose members were judged below-average in scholarly capacity. Thus, the recent tendency to promote from within had to be abandoned for a broader, national search for the best scholar-teachers. The university was also urged to take several measures to increase its productivity and leadership in scholarship. The first necessity was that the faculty adopt "a militant belief in the intrinsic value of scholarship as a kind of categorical imperative and a way of life." Henceforth, academic rank should be governed solely by merit, and evaluations should be made annually. To enable the faculty to pursue their scholarship, they should teach no more than two courses a semester, be given leaves of absence "not as a unique privilege but as a regular right," and command "a first-rate level of salaries."[161]

That the university was serious about the new imperative for faculty scholarship was signaled by one of Robert K. Root's final acts as dean of the faculty in 1945–1946: his enlargement of the standard one-page form for faculty promotions to the "devilish" four-page "blue form" bemoaned by faculty and department chairs alike. Under "teaching," the department had to provide only an "estimate of probable effectiveness as a teacher of undergraduate and graduate students at Princeton" in various venues. Under "scholarship," on the other hand, the candidate had to include "significant contributions to the advancement of knowledge and originality; indications of continuing growth; evidence of recognition by scholars in the field," such as book reviews, and copies of his curriculum vitae. As Joyce Carol Oates once quipped, "in Princeton . . . a man is judged by the length of his bibliography."[162]

[160] "Princeton and Scholarship," *PAW*, May 7, 1948, 3, 7–9.

[161] "Princeton and Scholarship," *PAW*, May 7, 1948, 3, 7–9.

[162] *Conversations with Joyce Carol Oates*, ed. Lee Milezzo (Jackson, Miss., 1989), 171 (from a 1987 interview).

The immediate postwar and 1950s national booms in student enrollments combined with a shortage of qualified faculty to promote intercollegiate raids on faculty, particularly on places like Princeton that were publicly raising their standards and recruiting the best faculty they could find. Princeton reacted defensively by constantly improving its fringe benefits and its salaries, which the trustees uncapped at every rank in 1948 to give the administration greater flexibility in negotiations with raiders' targets. It increased its leave program (which by 1971 was regarded by the dean of the faculty as "the most generous . . . in the country"), and encouraged alumni and other donors to endow professorial chairs to attract and hold senior luminaries.[163] It also rewarded its most promising junior scholars with Bicentennial Preceptorships, "comparable in distinction to endowed chairs at the full professor level." During his three-year term, an assistant professor received annual research allowances of $500, a salary $500 above the rank average, and a year's leave at full pay. Although the award was named for a teaching program and could be used for course development, travel, or research, most "preceptors" felt compelled by the new university spirit to use the time for scholarship and publication.[164]

Once the junior faculty absorbed the university's new spirit of scholarship and shaped their own priorities accordingly, it was only a matter of time before the students recognized the shift. One sensitive barometer of student opinion was the seniors' faculty song, which after the war commented increasingly on the faculty's scholarship as well as their teaching and personal eccentricities.

[163] *PAW*, May 18, 1971, 5 (Dean Richard Lester). In 1963–1964 Princeton began to give a semester leave at full pay after every five semesters of teaching, partly to compensate for the relatively heavy demands created by Princeton's individualized mode of student contact. Dean of the Faculty J. Douglas Brown, *Reports to the President* (1966–1967), 1:401–2. Yale soon followed Princeton's lead. See Geoffrey Kabaservice, *The Guardians: Kingman Brewster, His Circle, and the Rise of the Liberal Establishment* (New York, 2004), 198.

[164] Leitch, *Princeton Companion*, 52; "Bicentennial Preceptors," *PAW*, Nov. 18, 1949, 5–6; Carla A. Sykes, "'The Bright Young Men': The Bicentennial Preceptors Have Paid Off," *PAW*, May 24, 1957, 10–12. The Bicentennial Preceptorships were quickly joined by several Procter and Gamble [Junior] Faculty Fellowships and, beginning in the late 1970s, by twenty-one University Preceptorships. PU, *Register, 2001–02*, 30–37.

Here's to Mason, Alpheus T.
Prophet of Democracy.
When he can't think of what to say
It's "Chapter Six in 'The Brandeis Way.' "

Meaner-spirited was their take on pre-decanal Hugh Taylor, wartime chemist.

H. S. Taylor is a noble scholar,
His grindings brought him many a dollar.
We know the guys who got the Prize,
But the boss won't have it when he dies.

Even the beloved creator of "Enfield University" was not exempt from ribbing:

Baker has the final say
About old Papa Hemingway;
On bullfights Ernie wrote a bit,
On Ernie, Carlos writes pure . . . wisdom.

Baker's colleague in philosophy, Walter Kaufmann, received a double dose of criticism, pedagogical and scholarly:

Kaufmann writes, and having writ
Moves on and writes still more of it.
We only wish that in his course
He would assign some other source.

By 1965, the students had even imbibed the "publish-or-perish" mentality of the research university Princeton had become:

English Department—it has blood
Dudley Johnson, he's the stud
St. Paul's, Princeton, Oxford school
Why the hell publish? He's no fool.[165]

[165] *Campus Songs* (1939), 18; (1942), 18; (1965), 14, 16, 18 (PUA). By 1965, fifty-four-year-old Edward Dudley Hume Johnson, a snappy dresser and excellent teacher, had published only one short monograph on Victorian poetry (1952) and a recent anthology of Victorian prose and poetry (1964). He later published two first-rate books on Dickens and British painting and edited an anthology of nature writing. Johnson Faculty File (PUA); Robert L. Patten, "Edward Dudley Hume Johnson," in Marks, *Luminaries*, 125–34.

Since the late 1950s, when Princeton accepted once and for all its status as a world-class research university and not, as President Goheen put it, "another Amherst," its faculty-reward structure has leaned heavily, decisively, on scholarship rather than teaching.[166] Princeton's greatest prizes, nearly two hundred endowed chairs, are invariably given to faculty who have published important, and usually numerous, works in their fields. Carlos Baker, "Mr. Hemingway," held the Woodrow Wilson Professorship of Literature from before he wrote *A Friend in Power* to his retirement in 1977. French historian Robert Darnton would not have become the Shelby Cullom Davis '30 Professor of European History in 1984 had he not published four major books, including *The Literary Underground of the Old Regime* (1983) and *The Great Cat Massacre* (1984). By the same token, Val Fitch's research on the unsymmetrical decay of subatomic particles elevated him from the Class of 1909 Professorship of Physics, which he received in 1969, to the Cyrus Fogg Brackett Chair of Physics in 1976 and, after winning a Nobel Prize in 1980, the new James S. McDonnell Distinguished University Professorship two years later. Best-selling novelist Toni Morrison was wooed to Princeton in 1989 partly by the honor of being the first incumbent of the Robert F. Goheen Professorship in the Humanities, endowed by the president's friends during A Campaign for Princeton in the mid-1980s.[167]

Although students and alumni with more collegiate views of the university sometimes object, Princeton's reward system is logical and justified. The university's claim on the world's attention and support is not based on its undergraduate athletic teams, whose records ebb and flow, nor on its teaching, which enjoys only a local reputation and is conducted largely behind closed doors. Princeton

[166] *PAW*, Feb. 13, 1968, 5. In December 2003 President Shirley Tilghman predictably aroused student alarm by publicly asserting that scholarship, not teaching, was the major criterion for faculty promotions and tenure. Erik Linstrum, "Balanced Budget Projected as Tenure System Defended," *DP* (online), Dec. 9, 2003.

[167] PU, *Register, 2001–02*, 17, 19, 20, 22–23; *The Quality of Teaching at Princeton: Twenty-two Professors Who Hold Endowed Chairs* (Princeton, 1992), n.p. (Darnton, Fitch, Morrison). The vast majority of faculty selected for inclusion in Marks, *Luminaries*, were known best for their books, research, and graduate teaching.

is known not only in New York, whose national media regard Princeton as an intellectual suburb, but in the wider world beyond the Hudson for its graduate school and the intellectual and scholarly eminence of its faculty.

Since 1930, Princeton has been associated in the public mind with the brainy theorists of the Institute for Advanced Study, particularly Albert Einstein, about whom the college seniors sang:

> The bright boys here all study Math
> And Albie Einstein points the path,
> Although he seldom takes the air,
> We wish to God he'd cut his hair

Although the Institute was endowed as an independent research center in "pure science and high scholarship," its mathematicians shared Fine Hall with Princeton's faculty until its own quarters were built in 1939 on grounds not far from the Graduate School. Some right-wing alumni even protested Einstein's "Communist" leanings because they assumed, erroneously, that he was a member of the faculty. The rest of the world simply associated the wild-haired Nobel Prize-winner with the university positively, as to a great extent it still does.[168] From Einstein's day to this, the fellows of the Institute have enjoyed full library privileges, sponsored colloquia, taught pro bono, and advised dissertations and even senior theses at the university. This close association has not only shed reflected luster on the university, but pushed its own faculty—some of whom become permanent or temporary fellows at the Institute—to continue to distinguish "the pretty good . . . from the best."[169]

It was less the Institute than President William G. Bowen (1972–1988) who led the Princeton faculty to a noticeably higher level of

[168] *Campus Songs* (1939), 21 (PUA); Leitch, *Princeton Companion*, 153–54, 271–72; "Our New Neighbor," *PAW*, Oct. 14, 1932, 83–84; Jamie Sayen, *Einstein in America: The Scientist's Conscience in the Age of Hitler and Hiroshima* (New York, 1985), 69–70. The 1994 Hollywood film *I.Q.*, starring Walter Matthau as Einstein and Meg Ryan as his fictional brainy niece, blithely conflated the university and the Institute. See Carolyn Moseley, "Einstein: The Movie," *PAW*, Sept. 14, 1994, 12–16.

[169] James Richardson, *Vectors: Aphorisms & Ten-Second Essays* (Keene, N.Y., 2001), 95. Richardson is a poet and member of the Princeton English Department.

FIGURE 7. Provost William Bowen answering questions at the 1972 news conference announcing his selection as Princeton's next president. President Robert Goheen smiles upon the trustees' choice of his successor.

professional achievement and scholarly strength. Regarded by many as "the smartest man on the faculty," Bowen sought to complement his predecessor's investment in buildings with an equally heavy investment in brainpower. In the face of double-digit inflation and red ink, he launched a "target-of-opportunity" plan in 1973 to make "a small number of absolutely outstanding appointments"—the intellectual leaders or future leaders of their fields—"without primary reference to fields of specialization."[170] Even after the plan succumbed to budgetary pressures in 1976, he and his deans somehow found the funds to hire faculty stars wherever they could be found. During his first four years alone, Princeton successfully raided Harvard, Yale, Columbia, MIT, UCLA, Berkeley, Johns Hopkins, Dartmouth, Northwestern, and the universities of London, Sydney, Chicago, Michigan, and Pennsylvania.[171] Not since Woodrow Wilson's search for preceptors had Princeton made such a dent in its rivals' ranks. The major difference was that Wilson sought gentlemanly *teacher*-scholars and Bowen wanted only the best *scholar*-teachers, regardless of gender or pedigree.

Like Wilson, Bowen played an unusually personal part in faculty-building, with the same winning combination of intensity, enthusiasm, and charm. When searches for luminaries began in the departments, chairs and faculty members "felt his enthusiastic support," which mattered. As negotiations progressed, Bowen often moved to the front lines of the recruitment effort. When Arnold Levine was being lured from SUNY-Stony Brook to create and lead the new Department of Molecular Biology, Bowen took him to a quiet, unpretentious lunch at the Great Wall Chinese Restaurant in the Princeton Shopping Center; dessert was a vigorous 2½-hour interview. Levine's colleague Thomas Shenk, who was being wooed at the same time, was impressed by the president's persuasiveness. "He had a clear vision of what he wanted to accomplish . . . and he placed top priority on quality. I found his ideas and standards irresistible." Again like Wilson, Bowen was concerned not only about what someone could add to the university, university counsel Thomas Wright '62 remembered, "but about finding jobs in the area for faculty spouses, about housing, and all the other things that are im-

[170] William G. Bowen, *Report of the President, 1982: A Campaign for Princeton*, 18; Bowen, *Report of the President, 1974: Faculty Recruitment and Advancement*, in *Ever the Teacher: William G. Bowen's Writings as President of Princeton* (1987), 318.

[171] William McCleery, "An Informal Talk with Princeton's President William G. Bowen on the Satisfactions of his Job; Education & Government; the Public State of Mind," *University: A Princeton Quarterly*, 69 (Summer 1976):18–24, at 18.

portant to someone thinking of coming to Princeton."[172] His meticulous attention to detail was famous.

Bowen did not hesitate, any more than Wilson did, to use the authority of his office to clinch a hire. When philosopher Saul Kripke resigned from Rockefeller University in the late spring of 1977 to accept Princeton's eager offer, he was understandably worried about declining the offers he had from UCLA and elsewhere before the trustees met in October to formally confirm his appointment. Bowen immediately grasped the situation and assured him that if the trustees rejected his recommendation, "there will be two of us looking for jobs."[173]

In addition to recruiting outside the university, Bowen sought to toughen the standards for tenure and promotion of existing faculty. As the most important and most persuasive (nonvoting) member of the Committee of Three, which simply advised the president, who made the final decisions, Bowen helped it set an enduring precedent for awarding half its tenure appointments to outsiders and rejecting a quarter of the departmental recommendations. He also approved the university's six-year "up-or-out" policy to avoid promoting junior faculty who were "quite good" or even "very good" but not "absolutely outstanding." On his watch, the ratio of assistant professors receiving tenure remained at 20 percent, down from 50 percent in the 1950s and 33 percent in the late 1960s, when he joined the Committee of Three as provost.[174]

[172] David Williamson, "The Bowen Legacy," *PAW*, Dec. 23, 1987, 9–15, at 11; Thomas Shenk (e-mail), Oct. 21, 2002.

[173] Bowen (e-mail), Oct. 4, 2002; Paul Benacerraf (e-mail), Oct. 4, 2002.

[174] Bowen, *Report of the President, 1984: Junior Faculty at Princeton*, in *Ever the Teacher*, 319–21, 349–51, 353, 366. In 2004 it was still difficult for young faculty to gain tenure. In the world-class Math Department, only two assistant professors had received tenure in the past eighteen years. The situation was little different throughout the Ivy universities. Sanhita Sen, "In Math Dept., Tenure an Elusive Achievement," *DP* (online), Oct. 11, 2004; Piper Fogg, "Hello . . . I Must Be Going," *CHE*, June 18, 2004, A10–A12. Even winners of the President's Distinguished Teaching Award, such as historian Andrew Isenberg, were not tenured if their scholarship was thought to be less than truly excellent. Although recommended by the History Department, he was denied tenure by the powerful Committee of Three, which advises the President. Julie

When Bowen stepped down in 1988 he had increased the faculty 11 percent, two-thirds of them in tenured positions. In fifteen years, the academic infrastructure had grown from 30 departments and 17 programs to 33 departments and 23 programs. He had also overseen the construction of five new buildings and the renovation and expansion of many others, including three residential colleges and the striking Thomas Laboratory for the new molecular biologists. But he regarded faculty recruitment as the "single most satisfying set of activities that I have been involved in." To enable and encourage his successor to pursue the same goal, he sought and received ample funds from A Campaign for Princeton (whose prospectus he wrote) to reinstate his "target-of-opportunity" plan and to endow thirty-eight distinguished professorships. Most of these were used to recognize and retain outstanding faculty who regularly received outside offers, such as mathematician Charles Fefferman, medieval literary scholar John Fleming, Sinologist Denis Twichett, and, fortuitously, molecular biologist Shirley Tilghman.[175]

❁ ❁ ❁

When universities or graduate schools are ranked, either by popular media such as *U.S. News & World Report* or by academic bodies such as the National Research Council, the assessments depend heavily on the scholarly, not pedagogical, reputation of the institution's faculty and departments. Since 1966, Princeton's graduate school and faculty (which by design is synonymous with its undergraduate faculty) has been ranked sixth or seventh best in the country in four

---

Kestenman, "Students Protest Isenberg's Tenure Denial," *DP* (online), Apr. 23, 2003; Sam J. Cooper, "Students Give Tilghman Isenberg Tenure Petition," ibid., May 1, 2003; Kestenman, "Isenberg Files Appeal to Reverse University Tenure Decision," ibid., Sept. 26, 2003; Chanakya Sethi, "Appeal Denied, Isenberg Goes to Temple U," ibid., Mar. 2, 2004; Sethi, "Isenberg Case Reveals Discord, Controversy," ibid., Mar. 29, 2004.

[175] Bowen, *Report, 1982: A Campaign for Princeton*, 18–19; William McCleery, *The Story of A Campaign for Princeton* (Princeton, 1987), 16, 118–19. Thanks to Prof. Judith Walzer of The New School, Bowen's former academic assistant, for her memories of his modus operandi.

national assessments. Princeton would undoubtedly rank much higher—as it does in the *U.S. News* overall ranking of research universities, placing or tying for first many times since 1996—but for its lack of a medical school to drive and give public visibility to scientific research, its relatively small graduate population compared to its undergraduate enrollment (about 40 percent), and its tenth-place position among the top research universities in terms of federal research and development grants. When the Princeton faculty was compared with its peers in 1997 on a per capita index of research productivity based on awards, grants, and scholarly publications, it ranked second only to Stanford and UC-Berkeley.[176]

Much of a university's academic reputation is built on the newsworthy prizes its faculty wins. The Swedish Academy's Nobels are the headliners and Princeton has captured more than its share—nine since 1977—particularly considering its size. Nineteen-ninety-three was a banner year when three Princetonians—Toni Morrison (for literature), and Joseph Taylor and Russell Hulse (for physics)—answered the early-morning calls from Stockholm. The following year, senior research mathematician John Nash took home the economics prize for his early work on game theory. His miraculous recovery from paranoid schizophrenia, which destroyed his academic career at its early height, was featured in Sylvia Nasar's *A Beautiful Mind* (1998) and Ron Howard's Academy Award–winning film of the same title (2001). Speaking of Princeton's Nobel Prize–winning ways, Provost Stephen Goldfeld said, "It helps in recruiting undergraduates, it helps in recruiting graduate students, it helps in recruiting professors and keeping them, it helps in fundraising, it helps politically."[177]

[176] See chapter 7, pp. 431–32.

[177] "Three Princetonians Win Nobels," *PAW*, Nov. 10, 1993, 6–8, at 7; "Nash Wins Nobel in Economics," *PAW*, Nov. 9, 1994, 4–5; Sylvia Nasar, "Lost Years of a Laureate," *PAW*, Mar. 22, 1995, 16–22 (reprinted from the *New York Times*, Nov. 13, 1994, sec. 3, pp. 1, 8). By comparison, Harvard won twenty-six Nobels in science between 1945 and 1990; eight went to medical school faculty, four other awards were in medicine and physiology. Keller, *Making Harvard Modern*, 391. The latest Princeton laureate is psychologist Daniel Kahnemann, who won the prize in economics in 2002 even though he had never taken a course in economics. Daniel Altman, "A Nobel Prize Bridges Economics and Psychology," *New York Times*, Oct. 10, 2002, C1, C6; Joshua Tanberer, "Kahnemann Wins Nobel Prize in Economics for Behavioral Study," *DP* (online), Oct.

Nearly as eye-catching are the MacArthur Foundation's so-called genius grants. Between 1981 and 2003, twenty-three Princeton faculty received the surprise largesse of no-strings salaries and benefits for five years; five more scholars joined the faculty soon after winning.[178] A recent winner was Andrew Wiles, whose solution of Fermat's 350-year-old theorem in 1993 led to headlines around the world, the $100,000 Wolf Prize, a special Fields Prize (the mathematical equivalent of the Nobel), and a musical on Broadway called *Fermat's Last Tango*, starring a much less diffident "Professor Wiles" in his ascetic "Princeton" setting.[179]

Surprisingly for a university located in a still-small New Jersey town, Princeton's intellectual reach is literally global. In 2004, international students comprised 40 percent of graduate enrollments. Most of their predecessors waved the Princeton colors when they returned home and spread the word about the published faculty with whom they had worked. The scholarly reputations of many Princeton faculty in area studies have independently earned them recognition from foreign governments and learned societies. Fritz Machlup, prolific economist, excellent skier and fencer, and joyful workaholic ("Sleeping is for sissies," he liked to say), was offered the governorship

---

10, 2002. In January 2004 physicist James Peebles and astronomer James Gunn were awarded, with Cambridge astronomer Sir Martin Rees, the $500,000 Crafoord Prize by the Royal Swedish Academy of Sciences. The prize was established in 1980 to honor work in sciences not considered by the Nobel Prize. Astronomers are honored every four years. In 2004 Peebles also won the Shaw Prize in Astronomy, $1 million given by the Shaw Foundation of Hong Kong. Boris Spiwak, "Physicists Peebles and Gunn win Crafoord Prize," *DP* (online), Feb. 3, 2005; "Wiles Selected to Receive Shaw Prize," PU, press release, June 7, 2005.

[178] PU, *Profile, 2002–03*, 4.

[179] Gina Kolata, "Wily Math Whiz," *PAW*, Sept. 15, 1993, 10–13; *PAW*, Jan. 24, 1996, 13; Oct. 21, 1998, 7; Oct. 25, 2000, 16; Wilborn Hampton, "Yep, You Can Sing That in X, Y and Z," *New York Times*, Dec. 13, 2000, B3; Lindsey White, "History Professor Grafton Awarded Prestigious Balzan Prize for Study," *DP* (online), Sept. 12, 2002. In 2005 Wiles also won the Shaw Prize in Mathematical Sciences. "Wiles Selected to Receive Shaw Prize." In 2002 hydrologist Ignacio Rodriguez-Iturbe (Civil and Environmental Engineering) received the $150,000 Stockholm Water Prize, known informally as "the Nobel Prize of water" (Steven Schutz, "Princeton Hydrologist Wins the 'Nobel Prize of Water,' " *PWB* [online], Apr. 1, 2002.)

of the National Bank of Austria in the mid-1960s because of his scholarly command of international economics. In 1978 Professor of Near Eastern Studies Bernard Lewis received a $35,000 prize from the Israel Institute of Technology for his "profound insight into the life and mores of the peoples of the Middle East through his writings." Both André Maman, professor of Romance languages, and historian Robert Darnton received France's highest decoration when they were made *Chevaliers de la Légion d'Honneur* in 1976 and 2000, respectively; Maman also received the *Ordre des Palmes Académiques* seven years later. Similarly, the Federal Republic of Germany bestowed its Order of Merit (First Class) in 2000 on Professor of Germanic Languages and Literatures Theodore Ziolkowski for acquainting "countless young Americans with Germany, her language, history, and culture." In 2002 Renaissance historian Anthony Grafton received the Balzan Prize in history (worth one million Swiss francs), as his colleague Charles Gillispie had several years earlier.[180]

In the long run, the sporadic glitter of international renown does less to reflect the sustained quality of faculty thinking and research at contemporary Princeton than does the university's day-to-day presence in the national media, serious and popular. Academe's own national newspaper of record, the weekly *Chronicle of Higher Education*, pays frequent attention to Princeton faculty, as did the now-defunct chronicle of high gossip and intellectual trends, *Lingua Franca* (1990–2001). Since the turn of the millennium, for example, the *Chronicle* has published Professor of History Nell Irvin Painter's essay on "Black Studies, Black Professors, and the Struggles of Perception." It has also profiled classicist and former associate provost Georgia Nugent, who oversaw Princeton's educational technology and distance-learning programs, and Grafton, whose dazzling array of books on Renaissance and early modern Europe earned him the headline "The Alchemist of Erudition." In 2002 Woodrow Wilson School professor Stanley Katz, former president of the American

[180] Fritz Machlup Faculty File (PUA); Burton G. Malkiel, "Fritz Machlup," in Marks, *Luminaries*, 182–89; "Lewis Honored," *PAW*, June 5, 1978, 21; "Maman Made Officer in *Légion d'Honneur*," *PAW*, Oct. 14, 1987, 22; "A French Kiss [for Darnton]," *PAW*, Feb. 9, 2000, 12; *PAW*, Oct. 25, 2000, 16 (Ziolkowski).

Council of Learned Societies, published two critiques of the modern research university.[181] In its September 1998 issue, *Lingua Franca* showcased a lively article entitled "Who's Afraid of Elaine Showalter?" Readers were informed that Showalter, professor of English and president-elect of the Modern Language Association, was the author not only of *Hystories*, a controversial new history of "hysterical disorders," but of a year's worth of critic's columns in *TV Guide*.[182]

Other print media of a less academic but still serious nature are drawn to Princeton faculty for their outstanding scholarship or expertise. The *Washington Post* placed an appreciation of the colorful and prize-winning work of practicing Professor of Architecture and designer Michael Graves in its well-read "Style" section. Before becoming editor of the *New Yorker*, David Remnick '81 wrote a memorable profile of Professor of Religion Elaine Pagels, MacArthur Fellow and authority on the early Christian Church. She was moved to examine *The Origin of Satan* (1995) after her six-year-old son died of a respiratory ailment and her husband was killed in a mountain-climbing accident a year later.[183] In a Sunday column on the difficulty

[181] *CHE*, Dec. 15, 2000, B7–B9 (Painter); Andrea L. Foster, "How a Princeton Classicist Leads in Information Technology," *CHE*, June 29, 2001, A28–A29; Scott McLemee, "The Alchemist of Erudition," *CHE*, July 5, 2002, A12–A14; Stanley N. Katz, "Choosing Justice over Excellence," *CHE*, May 17, 2002, B7–B9; Katz, "The Pathbreaking, Fractionalized, Uncertain World of Knowledge," *CHE*, Sept. 20, 2002, B7–B9. Three years later, Katz also published "Liberal Education on the Ropes," *CHE*, Apr. 1, 2005, B6–B9, followed by an online "Colloquy in Print," *CHE*, Apr. 22, 2005, B16.

[182] Emily Eakin, "Who's Afraid of Elaine Showalter? The MLA President Incites Mass Hysteria," *Lingua Franca: The Review of Academic Life*, Sept. 1998, 28–36.

[183] Benjamin Forgey, "Michael Graves, Postmodern Man," *Washington Post*, Feb. 17, 2001, C1, C5; also Julie V. Iovine, "An Architect's World Turned Upside Down," *New York Times*, June 12, 2003, D1, D9; David Remnick, "States of Mind: The Devil Problem," *New Yorker*, Apr. 3, 1995, 54–65. In 2003 Pagels's *Beyond Faith: The Secret Gospel of Thomas* (New York, 2003) became a surprising bestseller, in part because of her accessible blend of personal experience and scholarship. Dinitia Smith, "The Heresy That Saved a Skeptic," *New York Times*, June 14, 2003, A17, A19; Jennifer Greenstein Altmann, "Book on Religious Roots Resonates with Lay Readers," *PWB* (online), Feb. 9, 2004. See also Karen W. Arenson, "Princeton's Star Power," *New York Times Education Life*, Apr. 25, 2004, 24.

of weeding out his personal library, *Washington Post Book World* reviewer Michael Dirda dropped two Princeton names that apparently were—or he thought should have been—known to educated readers. "I love the great, majestic works of scholarship, summas," he declared, and mentioned D. W. Robertson's *A Preface to Chaucer*.[184] "In another life or if I'd been a lot smarter in this one," he continued, "I would have been . . . Peter Brown, the vastly learned authority on late antiquity."[185] The *New York Times* gave a fillip to Princeton's scientific reputation with profiles of two "Scientist[s] at Work," theoretical astrophysicist Bohdan Paczynski, a refugee from Communist Poland, and ninety-year-old quantum physicist John Archibald Wheeler. The *New York Times* has also featured Professor of Economics Alan Krueger, who at thirty-two became the chief economist at the U.S. Department of Labor while teaching at Princeton. His colleague Paul Krugman writes a twice-weekly column of opinion for the *New York Times* "Op-Ed" page and occasional feature articles for the Sunday *Magazine*.[186]

[184] Michael Dirda, "Readings," *Washington Post Book World*, Oct. 8, 2000, 15; D. W. Robertson, Jr., *A Preface to Chaucer: Studies in Medieval Perspectives* (Princeton, 1962). See Lynn Staley, "Durant Waite Robertson, Jr.," in Marks, *Luminaries*, 228–34; Robin Cathy Herman '73, "Princeton Portrait: Durant W. Robertson," *PAW*, Mar. 7, 1972, 7.

[185] Among Brown's many influential books are *Augustine of Hippo* (London and Berkeley, 1967), *The World of Late Antiquity: From Marcus Aurelius to Muhammed* (Cambridge, Mass., 1971), and *The Rise of Western Christendom: Triumph and Diversity, AD 200–1000* (Cambridge, Mass., 1997). In 2001 Brown was one of five scholars (another was Princeton philosopher Alexander Nehamas) to receive the first Andrew F. Mellon Foundation Distinguished Achievement Awards for scholars in the humanities. The three-year awards, for as much as $1.5 million each, provide the recipients and their universities with "enlarged opportunities to deepen and extend humanistic research" (Andrew W. Mellon Foundation press release, Nov. 7, 2001). In November 2002 Near Eastern Studies professor Michael Cook received the same award, as did historian Anthony Grafton in 2003. Daniel Lipsky-Karasz, "NES Professor Cook Awarded $1.5m. in Mellon Research Grant," *DP* (online), Nov. 26, 2002; "Grafton Chosen for Mellon Distinguished Achievement Award" (PU, press release, Dec. 16, 2003).

[186] James Glanz, "Bohdan Paczynski: Finding Opportunity Where Others See Impossibility," *New York Times*, Jan. 12, 1999, D3; Dennis Overbye, "John Archibald Wheeler: Peering Through the Gates of Time," *New York Times*, "Science Times," Mar. 12, 2002, 1, 5; Louis Uchitelle, "A Real-World Economist: Krueger and the Empiricists Challenge the Theorists," *New York Times*, Apr. 20, 1999, C1, C10; Howard Kurtz, "Professor Ahab [Krugman]," *Washington Post*, Jan. 22, 2003, C1, C4.

In nearly every major venue where books and ideas are sold and talked about, Princeton faculty seem to be represented out of all proportion to their numbers. Even after she retired in 1999, the playful English accent of classicist Elaine Fantham could be heard on Saturday mornings as host Scott Simon called upon her to comment on ancient Roman and Greek customs and culture for the listeners of National Public Radio's "Weekend Edition."[187] The Princeton presence is perhaps most conspicuous in the pages of the leading English-speaking book reviews. The intellectuals' opinion-making *New York Review of Books* turns to Princeton faculty more frequently than those of any other university, with the possible exception of Oxford, for its extensive essay-reviews. Michael Wood (English and Comparative Literature), Robert Darnton, Anthony Grafton, Peter Brown, James McPherson (all History), and Joyce Carol Oates (Humanities) contribute regularly, as did their predecessors Lawrence Stone (History) and historian John H. Elliott (the separate but symbiotic Institute) in previous years. Alexander Nehamas (Philosophy) and Elaine Showalter (English) similarly grace the pages of the *Times Literary Supplement* and the *London Review of Books*, read by many American academics as faithfully as the New York reviews.

❋ ❋ ❋

Despite Princeton's growing emphasis on research since World War II, teaching continued to be a high priority and a distinctive strength of its faculty. In 1947 Dean Robert K. Root boasted that a hallmark of modern Princeton was its devotion to undergraduate as well as graduate teaching. With a single faculty of scholar-teachers and an extremely low student:faculty ratio (8:1 at the time), the university offered "exceptional opportunities for close personal contact of the teacher and the taught. . . . It would not be easy," he claimed, "to find any other institution of higher learning where scholars of wide distinction are so accessible to the rank and file of undergraduates." Indeed, "some of Princeton's most productive scholars insist on hav-

[187] Dinitia Smith, "A Lesson on Iraq from a Classicist," *New York Times*, Feb. 8, 2003, A19, A21.

ing frequent opportunity to teach freshmen."[188] His remarks are as true of Princeton today as they were more than half a century ago.

Like McCosh and Wilson before them, all of Princeton's presidents since William Bowen have taught an undergraduate, usually an introductory or freshman, course while in office. That example speaks more eloquently about the seriousness of the university's dual priority than any number of *pronunciamentos* issued from Nassau Hall ever could. Emblematic of Princeton's reputation as a serious place for teaching was the E. Harris Harbison Award, given annually in the 1960s and 1970s to ten or twelve of the nation's best teachers by the Danforth Foundation. The award was named for Princeton's European historian, "Jinx" Harbison, a superb classroom teacher as well as a formidable and graceful scholar. Two early winners of the $10,000 award were Professor of Religion Malcolm Diamond and A. Walton Litz of English.[189] Princeton professors continue to win awards for teaching excellence. In 1995–1996, liberal artist and engineer David Billington and ecological biologist James Gould were back-to-back winners of the New Jersey Professor of the Year award given by the Carnegie Foundation for the Advancement of Teaching. Five years earlier, Billington had also received a $50,000 award from the Charles A. Dana Foundation for his innovative development of curricula, texts, and materials that integrate the study of engineering with the liberal arts.[190]

When Harold Shapiro came from the University of Michigan to assume the Princeton presidency in 1988, he brought a legitimate Big Ten concern that the shift from teaching to scholarship had gone too far, even in the more humanly scaled Ivy League. This worry was sharpened by a small but noisy chorus of often intemperate and misdirected complaints about the American professoriate by pre-

[188] Root, "Teachers and Teaching," in Osgood et al., *Modern Princeton*, 68–69.

[189] Jerrold E. Seigel, "Elmore Harris Harbison," in Marks, *Luminaries*, 113–18; "Jinx Harbison's Memorial" and "Last Lecture," *PAW*, Nov. 3, 1964, 6–9, 16–19; *PAW*, Jan. 20, 1970, 9 (Diamond); Sept. 26, 1972, 10 (Litz).

[190] *PAW*, Nov. 21, 1990, 29; Jan. 24, 1996, 13 (Billington); Dec. 11, 1996, 10 (Gould). For Billington's approach to research and teaching, see Bruce Cole, "Discipline and Play: A Conversation with David Billington," *Humanities*, March–April 2005, 6–10, 50–54.

dominantly conservative critics and commentators.[191] So he undertook a series of initiatives throughout the 1990s to restore some balance to the faculty's priorities and duties, but with renewed emphasis on teaching to promote *learning*, as well as continued respect for the contextual constraints under which Princeton and all research universities had to function at the turn of the twenty-first century.

Before abandoning the substantial annual reports on various academic themes that President Bowen had issued, Shapiro devoted his 1991 report to *Teaching at Princeton*, primarily of undergraduates. The report concluded with a series of faculty reflections on the pedagogical side of their work. John Fleming, medievalist, printer, and professor of English and comparative literature, testified that "Princeton is one of the few places where one constantly runs into colleagues talking or thinking about teaching." Professor of Politics Amy Gutmann pointed to the strains involved in working at a university where scholarship and teaching are both "infinitely demanding pursuits" and "one always falls some significant degree short of perfection." Sociologist Suzanne Keller, like her "Enfield" colleague Edward Tyler, spoke candidly of how serious teaching during the semester necessarily impinges on one's scholarly research and writing. Being a professor at Princeton, she said, is a constant struggle "between work, reputation, teaching obligations, colleagueship." Yet all made it clear that teaching was not only a persistent concern long after tenure but a major aspect of Princeton's distinction and distinctiveness.[192]

Shapiro reinforced those messages the following year by publishing a glossy album, *The Quality of Teaching at Princeton*, subtitled "Twenty-two Professors Who Hold Endowed Chairs." The chairholders had all been chosen for their scholarly excellence and productivity, but here they emphasized their strong commitment to the classroom and the synergy of discovery and discussion. Charles Fef-

[191] James Axtell, *The Pleasures of Academe: A Celebration & Defense of Higher Education* (Lincoln, 1998), 210–50.

[192] *Report of the President (1991)*: *Teaching at Princeton*, 17, 19, 21. President Bowen devoted two major reports to the faculty, one in 1974 on the whole faculty and one in 1984 on the junior faculty; both emphasized the importance of teaching and Princeton's distinctive preference for balanced scholar-teachers.

at twenty-four became the youngest full professor in istory and is now "one of the greatest mathematicians ntury," taught (and still teaches) introductory calculus anced graduate courses in his several esoteric specialties. Likewise, Nobel laureate Val Fitch taught introductory physics. Like many other faculty stars, both men had chosen not to leave for universities with much lighter teaching loads. For reasons that remain inexplicable to many of their friends and rivals elsewhere, Princeton professors prefer a university where, as Dean Brown once held, "the title 'research professor' is an inappropriate title . . . in the same way that 'teaching professor' would be." Dean Joseph Taylor reemphasized the point in the pages of the *Alumni Weekly*, assuring concerned readers that "virtually all of our faculty (no matter how 'elite' they may be, both individually and as a group) are regularly involved with teaching undergraduates as well as graduate students. Potential faculty members with other aspirations need not apply, and that fact is well known among academics."[193]

Presidential words on behalf of teaching seldom alter the scholarly priorities and rewards of faculty at major research universities, but Shapiro sought to pay more than lip service. In 1991, with an endowment provided by trustees Lloyd Cotsen '50 and John J. F. Sherrard '52, he established four President's Awards for Distinguished Teaching, normally two for senior faculty and two for junior. The honorees receive substantial checks, as do their department libraries in their name. These awards were initially presented at the academic year's opening exercises, but in 1994 they were shifted to Commencement to emphasize their importance.[194] The Cotsen family also established

[193] *The Quality of Teaching at Princeton*, n.p. (Fefferman, Fitch); J. Douglas Brown, *The Commonplace Book of an Academic Dean* (Princeton: Princeton University, Industrial Relations Section, 1978), 45; *PAW*, Nov. 21, 2001, 6 (Taylor). In his final report to the president in 1967, after twenty-one years as dean of the faculty, Brown cautioned that in hiring outsiders "care should be taken to avoid special deals in respect to teaching loads, excessive research opportunities or facilities, or relief of the normal burden of departmental responsibilities. . . . Princeton has profitted far more in adding team-players over the years than by adding 'prima donnas' that tend to disrupt morale" (*Reports to the President [1966–1967]*, 1:390).

[194] Four New Jersey school teachers are also honored at Commencement. These prizes were established in 1959 by an anonymous donor. "Teaching Prizes," *PAW*, May 15, 1959, 15.

the Cotsen Faculty Fellowship Program. Faculty largely in the humanities and social sciences who are recognized as outstanding teachers of undergraduates receive a generous research fund and summer salary for three years; their departments receive book funds, and two advanced graduate students in each department receive tuition, full summer support, and the stipend of assistants-in-instruction (AIs) for working with the fellow to develop new undergraduate courses or other improvements in the teaching program.

In 1996, with endowments from the hugely successful bicenquinquagenary campaign, Shapiro launched a program of Presidential Teaching Initiatives, an idea he had adumbrated in a strategic-planning document three years earlier. The initiatives came in three parts: a 250th Anniversary Fund for Innovation in Undergraduate Education, which underwrote seventy-four proposals in its first year alone; four Visiting Professorships for Distinguished Teaching; and a Center for Teaching and Learning, located in the new Frist Campus Center and directed by master teacher Georgia Nugent.[195] In July 2000 the university also brought online an Educational Technologies Center, designed to introduce faculty to the possibilities of multimedia for revising existing courses and creating new ones for students raised on PCs, DVDs, and video games.[196] Together, these initiatives have transformed the Princeton classroom, putting chalk and blackboards on the defensive, while sustaining the university's long tradition of excellent teaching begun by Woodrow Wilson.

Despite the continuing (though much diminished) presence of "snap" courses and professors who honor their research more than their students, Princeton students receive teaching from faculty and

[195] "New Awards for Good Teaching," *PAW*, Oct. 23, 1991, 8; Harold T. Shapiro, "Presidential Teaching Initiatives [PTI]," *PAW*, Mar. 6, 1996, 56; Shapiro, "Innovation in Undergraduate Education: Language On Line," *PAW*, Oct. 23, 1996, 49; Shapiro, "PTI: Knowing, Learning, and Making Decisions," *PAW*, Dec. 11, 1996, 57; Shapiro, "The 250th Anniversary Fund for Innovations in Undergraduate Education," *PAW*, May 7, 1997, 65; Shapiro, "Venture Capital for Our Teaching Enterprise," *PAW*, Dec. 3, 1997, 57; Shapiro, "The Center for Teaching and Learning," *PAW*, Dec. 17, 1997, 41. Deborah A. Kaple, "Medievalist Enchants His Students," *PAW*, Apr. 8, 1998, 7, profiled visiting distinguished teacher Teofilo Ruiz *74, Cuban refugee, Spanish historian, and the Carnegie Foundation's "Outstanding Professor of the Year" in 1994.

[196] Caroline Moseley, "Beyond the Blackboard," *PAW*, Apr. 18, 2001, 20–23.

opportunities for learning equal to any in the country, indeed the world. At Princeton, Carlos Baker said after guest-teaching at colleges and universities across the country, "the concept of the scholar-teacher is better realized . . . than at any other place I know of." From the intellectual architect of "Enfield University," that was high praise indeed.

CHAPTER THREE

Getting In

The quality of a university is measured more by the kind of student it turns out than the kind it takes in.

—ROBERT J. KIBBEE

AS AN EDUCATIONAL SPECIES, undergraduates are chameleons with a four-year life span. They evolve quickly and change their looks and minds with great but unpredictable frequency. Capturing their essence and charting their evolution over several generations is made difficult by their complex social make-up and their ready adaptation to local habitat. Although their traditional activities, curricular and extracurricular, provide them with considerable historical continuity, college students are also subject to generational fashions in personal appearance, attitudes, campus customs, pastimes, and lingo. And over the long term they respond to changes in the larger society of which they are a part, sometimes creatively, always with alacrity.

Like most of their collegiate cohorts, Princeton students were given to frequent revision because they were stranded in adolescent limbo, newly freed from most of childhood's constraints but still shy of true adult responsibility and independence. Although their four years on campus constituted only 5 or 6 percent of their normal life-spans, they were decisive years that allowed and encouraged personal exploration, reinvention, and a certain amount of rebellion if need be. President Wilson, after all, suggested that a college education should "make a person as unlike one's father as possible."[1]

But for much of the twentieth century, the student search for individuality was usually conducted en masse, in gregarious crowds of equally insecure seekers. "When a freshman arrives," noted a Prince-

[1] *PWW*, 19:31, 47, 99, 714, 741.

ton senior early in the century, "he wonders what he is up against and he tries hard to be a part of something that he does not really understand. . . . The sophomore lives and acts as though college life were going to last forever," which makes him look "so foolish"—sophomoric. But the senior "knows what he's here for," having caught "whiffs from the world outside." In short, he concluded, "it takes two years to make a college student" and "two more to let him make of himself a college graduate." Small wonder, then, that "the collective temper of a college," as longtime dean Christian Gauss observed, "is more mercurial than the temper of an equal body of older and less responsive persons."[2]

Since a college has its students for such a short time, what it can do to or for them depends importantly on the matriculants' previous lives—their parentage and socioeconomic upbringing and their intellectual, moral, and academic preparation. College faculties, no matter how learned, dedicated, or charismatic they are, can only do so much with the far-from-raw material they are given by the admissions office. Just how much they can accomplish in four abbreviated years also depends on the students' future goals and their immediate reasons for, and attitudes toward, going to college, all of which are famously subject to change during the process.

❁ ❁ ❁

Princeton, like most private elite colleges before World War I, demanded a good deal from its all-male applicants. First, after Wilson's reforms in 1904, they had to pass a reinforced battery of Princeton entrance exams in English, Latin, mathematics (through plain geometry), Greek, and French or German. Those seeking the newly fortified Bachelor of Science (B.S.) or the new Bachelor of Letters (Litt.B.) degrees could substitute for Greek (and a good bit of ancient history) proficiency in advanced math (trigonometry and solid geometry) and *either* physics and more of the first modern language *or* the second language.[3] The exams were given in Princeton and a

[2] Christian Gauss, *Through College on Nothing a Year, Literally Recorded from a Student's Story* (New York, 1915), 152–53, 162; Gauss, *Life in College* (New York, 1930), 110–11.

[3] *PWW*, 15:252–53 (Apr. 16, 1904), 277–78.

growing number of cities and prep schools around the country for a fee of five dollars, no small sum in 1905 (about $100 in 2004 values) when it was instituted to weed out weak or casual applicants. By 1906 Wilson could report that the number of well-prepared applicants was steadily increasing. "Formerly," he noted, "a large number of ill-prepared and unstudious boys came to Princeton from the secondary schools, particularly the private schools," because "our exams were often less difficult or our standards less rigidly maintained than those of other universities of the same rank and reputation."[4] Higher entrance standards also led to fewer failures in the first-year exams and a noticeable decline in the formerly high rate of freshman dismissals.[5]

Despite the rigor of Princeton's admission requirements, many freshmen were admitted with one or more "conditions" or weaknesses in subject preparation as detected by low or failing entrance-exam scores. Only 23 percent of those who entered in the fall of 1904 did so unconditionally. After the Wilsonian reforms their numbers rose quickly, but throughout his tenure six in ten freshmen needed some sort of remediation.[6] Some of these conditional admits were graduates of public high schools that did not offer classes in all of the required subjects (such as Greek) or at a sufficiently advanced level (such as solid geometry) to satisfy the Princeton faculty. Others simply failed to apply themselves in fully staffed private schools, knowing that traditionally (before Wilson) Princeton had accepted a large proportion of their schoolmates who had swotted the books no harder than they had.

If the former group could fill their scholastic gaps with extra coursework or paid sessions at "Johnny" Hun's Tutoring School, and the latter group could disabuse themselves of the notion that "an hour or two of study a day was quite enough for a 'university man'

[4] *PWW*, 16:264 (Dec. 14, 1905), 516–17 (Dec. 13, 1906).

[5] The annual flunk-out rate dropped from 16 percent in 1904–1905 to 11 percent in just two years. The introduction of the preceptorial system in 1905 also taught the freshmen the virtue and necessity of consistent application throughout the term rather than cramming for final exams, as was their predecessors' wont. *PWW*, 16:24, 200, 325–27, 466–67; 17:69, 438.

[6] *PWW*, 15:555 (Dec. 8, 1904); 16:467 (Oct. 20, 1906); 17:559 (Dec. 13, 1907); 18:585 (Jan. 1, 1909); 19:684 (Jan. 1, 1910).

to do," they stood a good chance of earning a degree. Only 3 to 4 percent of upperclassmen flunked out. One reason, thought Wilson's academic enforcer, Dean Henry Fine, was that "our standards are not excessively high. Any student who possesses ordinary ability," as he put it, "and who will consent to be reasonably diligent can easily reach them."[7]

If the Princeton applicant got over the admissions hurdle, he faced another challenge: the bursar's bills for tuition, room, and board. Although as late as World War II Princeton was regarded by some as a college "in the country," the early gentrification of the town did not make for a cheap education.[8] In the 1890s and particularly after the college's sesquicentennial celebrations, the small, simple college town slowly but unmistakably became a "fashionable suburb" of New York and Philadelphia, between which it sits half-way. Wealthy alumni returned to Princeton and bought, refurbished, or built country mansions on ample antebellum estates. In 1897 former U.S. President Grover Cleveland reinforced the trend by retiring to a commodious house on Hodge Road. Society gradually took on the look and tone of the *monde*, which often put the underpaid faculty at some disadvantage. Smart-looking horses, carriages, and automobiles soon left bicycling professors—and college presidents—literally in the dust. Silver-spooned sons also matriculated in greater numbers. Although their campus dress did not differ from the "extravagantly ordinary" garb—the black sweaters and corduroy trousers—of their classmates, the advent of saddle horses, roadsters, and club-worthy tuxedos heralded a fissure in Princeton's famous class "democracy." As a result of this broad transformation, life in Princeton became more expensive for all its denizens, not least for those operating and attending the newly dubbed university.[9]

In 1908, for example, the college catalogue estimated the basic expenses of an academic year to be between $382 and $730, which

[7] *PWW*, 16:24–26 (Mar. 9, 1905), 326 (Mar. 8, 1906).

[8] Christian Gauss, "Life on the Campus," in Charles G. Osgood et al., *The Modern Princeton* (Princeton, 1947), 12.

[9] Stockton Axson, *"Brother Woodrow": A Memoir of Woodrow Wilson*, ed. Arthur S. Link (Princeton, 1993), 112–14; Bliss Perry, *And Gladly Teach: Reminiscences* (Boston and New York, 1935), 133–34.

did not include the substantial cost of books, debating hall dues, clothes, room furnishings, incidentals, travel, and vacations. The family investment in a Princeton degree, therefore, could have purchased a small fleet of Model T Fords, which sold for $850 apiece.[10] Nor, unlike in most private institutions today, was the Princeton price discounted.[11] Financial aid was in its infancy, and freshmen were not eligible in any event. In 1908 Princeton awarded only forty scholarships to its more than twelve hundred undergraduates: ten at $150—for Bachelor of Arts (A.B.) candidates only—who made "first-group" standing the previous year, and thirty at $125 for those who made second-group marks.[12] The same high-ranking A.B.s were also eligible for up to $50 remissions of tuition each semester, but these were interest-free loans rather than bona fide discounts. A few students worked to pay part of their way through, but a Bureau of Self-Help was not established until 1911 to assist them in finding jobs.[13]

The result of Princeton's lofty admissions standards and its relatively high cost was a "constant increase in the number of boys entering Princeton from families of wealth," particularly from equally expensive "college preparatory schools." The situation worried both Wilson and Dean Fine, who felt strongly that there should be "a

[10] According to the senior poll in 1902, actual expenditures rose from $794.09 in their freshman year to $942.33 in their final year, an annual average of $861.21. *Nassau Herald* (1902), 114.

[11] William G. Bowen and David W. Breneman, "Student Aid: Price Discount or Educational Investment?" *Brookings Review* (Winter 1993):28–31; Michael S. McPherson and Morton Owen Shapiro, *The Student Aid Game: Meeting Need and Rewarding Talent in American Higher Education* (Princeton, 1998); Elizabeth A. Duffy and Idana Goldberg, *Crafting a Class: College Admissions and Financial Aid, 1955–1994* (Princeton, 1998).

[12] In 1908 Dean Fine estimated, on the basis of the first term's records, that only twenty-five students would be eligible for scholarships the following year. *PWW*, 18:246–47 (Apr. 9, 1908). The first group (of five) comprised the top 10 percent of the class, the second group the next 20 percent. Edwin E. Slosson, *Great American Universities* (New York, 1910), 94.

[13] *Catalogue of Princeton University, 1908–1909* (Princeton, 1908), 321–22, 348–50; Gauss, "Life on the Campus," 27. The interest from four small funds was reserved for deserving poor students or those preparing for the ministry.

corresponding increase in the number coming from families of moderate means" to "keep the tone of the place healthy and democratic." They also knew, as did their Big Three counterparts, that the graduates of large city high schools, often from families of "limited means," on average outperformed their prep school classmates in the college classroom. But Princeton could not attract more of these serious-minded achievers because few public schools offered Greek, which was required for A.B. candidacy. This, in turn, forced them to enroll in the B.S. and Litt.B. programs, where they had to pay full tuition, without any possibility of remissions or scholarships. Fine's concerns were obviously shared, for when he urged the trustees to equalize the opportunities for financial aid across the three programs, they complied with alacrity.[14]

Although the Princeton entrance exams were finally dropped in 1916 in favor of those given by the College Entrance Examination Board (CEEB), Greek was no longer required for admission after 1919, and the number of scholarships jumped to nearly three hundred by 1921, yet the social profiles of Princeton's classes remained remarkably similar until after World War II.[15] They did so in the face of growing enrollments. Like most colleges and universities, Princeton felt obliged in the 1910s and 1920s to respond to the accelerated demand for the college experience among the nation's increasingly prosperous middle and upper classes.[16] (It also preferred, as always, not to fall too far behind Harvard and Yale.) By 1920, after military

[14] *PWW*, 18:246–47 (Apr. 9, 1908).

[15] Marcia Graham Synnott, *The Half-Opened Door: Discrimination and Admissions at Harvard, Yale, and Princeton, 1900–1970* (Westport, Conn., 1979), 6–7, 13; Jerome Karabel, *The Chosen: The Hidden History of Admission and Exclusion at Harvard, Yale, and Princeton* (Boston, 2005). (Thanks to Professor Karabel for advance copies of his chapters on Princeton.)

[16] In 1900 only 4 percent of the eighteen–twenty-one-year-olds attended college. Between 1890 and 1925, however, the increase in college enrollments was nearly five times the increase in the national population. U.S. Bureau of the Census, *Historical Statistics of the United States: Colonial Times to 1957* (Washington, D.C., 1960), 210–11; Lester William Bartlett, *State Control of Private Incorporated Institutions of Higher Education* (New York, 1926), 2; David O. Levine, *The American College and the Culture of Aspiration, 1915–1940* (Ithaca, 1986), 19, 38–40, 68.

demobilization, Princeton enrolled over eighteen hundred undergraduates; within three years nearly twenty-two hundred competed for space in Princeton's paucity of dorms and rented rooms. But rather than diversify the college, the larger new classes were carefully crafted in the image of their smaller predecessors, whose social outlines had emerged largely from the academic requirements and economic exigencies of the Wilson years.

In 1910, in his *Great American Universities*, Dr. Edwin Slosson characterized Princeton's aim as "homogeneity," as contrasted with Harvard's search for "diversity" in its student body and curriculum. Princeton, he observed, "practically offers one particular kind of college training to one rather limited social class of the United States." Not only did the university show no interest in women, blacks, or foreign students, its "high, narrow" entrance requirements, "tuition fees and expensiveness," lack of professional schools, and particularly its "rules and customs, its life, traditions, and atmosphere, shut out or fail[ed] to attract the vast majority of potential students."[17] Remarkably, Slosson's assessment of the Wilsonian college held true for Princeton until new social forces released by World War II began to transform its student demography and culture. When growing enrollments in the early 1920s opened Princeton's gates to a potentially diverse student body, moreover, the university narrowed the entrance again to maintain the status quo with an innocent-sounding but in fact prejudicial policy of "selective admissions."

The one social class that Slosson saw at Princeton was, of course, the upper class, which included the higher reaches of the aspiring middle class. For a college with a popular reputation as "the pleasantest country club in America" (in F. Scott Fitzgerald's indelible words), an upper-crust membership was apropos. From Wilson's day to World War II, its students came predominantly from contiguous regions, elite prep schools, well-to-do, educated families, and mainline Protestant churches. And they made the task of the admission office easier by targeting Princeton and then accepting its offer with quick thanks but little surprise.

[17] Slosson, *Great American Universities*, 104–5. Slosson's chapters originally appeared in the *Independent* in 1909.

Unlike Harvard and Yale, Princeton before 1945 was less a national than an intersectional university.[18] In 1908, for example, more than two-thirds of its undergraduates came from New Jersey, New York, and Pennsylvania, largely within a 125-mile radius. A mere 5 percent came from the Southeast, from which Princeton had drawn large numbers before and even after the Civil War. In all, the students hailed from forty-six states, but most states could claim only one or a small handful of young Tigers. Seven more had prepared in foreign countries, most of those English-speaking. By 1939, thanks in part to the Great Depression and reduced scholarships, more than three-quarters of the entering students traveled short distances from homes in the Middle Atlantic states. Not until the establishment in 1948 of a nationwide Regional Scholarship program did Princeton make an earnest effort to draw the best students, regardless of family circumstances, from every region of the country.[19]

The circle of schools from which Princeton's freshmen were drawn was equally circumscribed. From 1900 through the 1940s, between 70 and 90 percent of the new arrivals had prepared at private day or boarding schools. In 1908, as in 1928 and 1938, more than eight in ten freshmen were "preppies," and the Depression only increased their numbers as the middle class took a proportionally bigger hit than the rich and hard times forced public schools more so than prep

[18] Harvard inaugurated a National Scholarship program in 1934 and in six years made 161 awards, mostly to sons of modest families from the "provinces." Yale had begun a more modest program of University Regional Scholarships in 1928. Between 1930 and 1944, however, it drew only 223 freshmen (an average of 15 a year) to New Haven from six major regions. Morton and Phyllis Keller, *Making Harvard Modern: The Rise of America's University* (New York, 2001), 33–34; George Wilson Pierson, *Yale: The University College, 1921–1937* (New Haven, 1955), 489–91, 684 (table G); Jerome Karabel, "Status-Group Struggle, Organizational Interests, and the Limits of Institutional Autonomy: The Transformation of Harvard, Yale, and Princeton, 1918–1940," *Theory and Society* 13:1 (Jan. 1984):1–40, at 23. See also Richard Farnum, "Elite College Discrimination and the Limits of Conflict Theory," *Harvard Educational Review* 67:3 (Fall 1997):507–30, for an alternative explanation of Karabel's data.

[19] *Catalogue of Princeton University, 1908–1909*, 420; *PAW*, Apr. 14, 1939, 581. By the early 1960s, by contrast, fewer than half of the student body had come from the surrounding three states. Only a third had in 1998. E. Alden Dunham, "A Look at Princeton Admissions," *PAW*, Jan. 19, 1965, 6–9, 14–15, at 9; *Report of the Undergraduate Admission Study Group* (Oct. 5, 1998). For the Regional Scholarships, see p. 145.

schools to reduce their faculties and standards.[20] In 1927 F. Scott Fitzgerald, harking back to his own entering class in 1914, accurately described the scholastic origins of Princeton's "clientele." "An average class," he wrote, "is composed of three dozen boys from such Midas academies as St. Paul's, St. Mark's, St. George's, Pomfret and Groton, a hundred and fifty more from Lawrenceville, Hotchkiss, Exeter, Andover and Hill, and perhaps another two hundred from less widely known preparatory schools. The remaining twenty per cent enter from the high schools." And like Wilson and Dean Fine before him, the avatar of the Roaring Twenties noted that the gritty high schools, not the "gilded" prep schools, furnished the larger proportion of eventual campus leaders. "For them," he admired, "the business of getting to Princeton has been more arduous, financially as well as scholastically. They are trained and eager for the fray."[21]

Although the relative proportions of successful high schoolers, prep schoolers, and elite prep schoolers did not change at all before World War II, the range of schools from which would-be freshmen applied grew noticeably, portending a major shift in Princeton's scholastic demography after the war. In 1911, for instance, entering freshmen had prepared at 55 high schools and 91 prep schools; 10 came from Trenton High School and 55 from Lawrenceville, Princeton's major "feeder" just five miles down the road. Thirty years later, the successful applicants hailed from only 64 more schools; but in 1955, with somewhat larger classes and much more "democracy," equal numbers of freshmen had attended 270 public schools and 126 private academies.[22]

[20] *PWW*, 18:488 (Nov. 6, 1908); Synnott, *Half-Opened Door*, 5, 194. In the 1930s, at Yale and especially Harvard (which took commuters), entering classes had substantially more high schoolers. Karabel, "Status-Group Struggle," 20.

[21] According to Fitzgerald's rough estimate, the top ten prep schools provided 38 percent of a typical class. In 1930 and 1940, the top dozen schools sent between 30 and 33 percent of the freshman classes. Karabel, "Status-Group Struggle," 22 (table 3).

[22] *PAW*, Dec. 13, 1911, 184, quoted in *Best of PAW*, 75; Bill Edwards, "The Admissions Problem," *PAW*, Nov. 4, 1955, 8–10, at 10. In 1956, 51.5 percent of Harvard's freshmen came from public schools; Princeton admitted more high schoolers than prep schoolers in 1953, but the yield maintained the prep school dominance until 1958. Penny Hollander Feldman, *Recruiting an Elite: Admission to Harvard College* (New York, 1988 [originally 1975 Harvard University Ph.D. diss.]), 66 (table 3.5); Karabel, *The Chosen*, 237, 242, 355.

Princeton's homogeneity also encompassed religion. Nearly two-thirds of its pre-war classes claimed membership in Presbyterian or Episcopal churches. As Wilson was leaving the presidency in the fall of 1910, the entering class consisted of 109 Presbyterians, 109 Episcopalians, a scattering of other Protestants, 16 Roman Catholics, and only 6 "Hebrews" (as Jewish students were known). Student Presbyterians, religious descendants of Princeton's founders, were in the process of losing ground to Episcopalians, whose prosperous, higher-church families in New York, Philadelphia, and elsewhere were remaking the social demography of the college. By the 1920s, Episcopalians clearly outnumbered the adherents of any other faith. Catholics had also gained steadily, if slowly; almost all were Irish and many were athletes. But Jews somehow remained scarce, no more than two dozen (3 percent) in any class. None were immigrants, few were poor, and most were of Northern European ancestry.[23]

If all these signs suggested that most members of Princeton's classes had been raised in well-to-do families, they were not misleading. Throughout the prosperous 1920s and the more straitened 1930s, at least nine of ten freshmen had been sired by white-collar fathers at or near the top of the economic totem pole. Even more than Harvard fathers, Princeton paters were in the professions or business, usually in executive offices. Only a handful were salesmen, farmers, or blue-collar workers; Harvard had nearly twice as many sons of the modestly incomed, reflecting its greater resources and more national outreach.[24]

Predictably, Big Three fathers—and increasingly mothers—tended to be well educated, the more so as time went on. In 1913, the fathers of 30 percent of Princeton freshmen were college graduates. In the ten classes between 1924 and 1933, 85 percent of the matriculants could claim that one or both parents had attended college. (The mothers came mostly from Smith, Wellesley, and Bryn Mawr, where Princetonians found their favorite prom dates). In the middle

[23] Synnott, *Half-Opened Door*, 176–78, 194–95 (table 6.3).

[24] Karabel, "Status-Group Struggle," 25–26; "The Roots of the Tree," *PAW*, Nov. 17, 1933, 191–92.

of the Depression, nearly seven in ten fathers had not only graduated from college, 38 percent had also gone to an Ivy League school; nearly a quarter were old Tigers.[25]

Privately endowed colleges have always depended on the loyalty, traditionalism, and eventual generosity of alumni children or "legacies," and Princeton was no exception. In fact, it was a pace-setter. Except for Yale, Princeton accepted more legacies before and well after World War II than did any of its major rivals. And when admissions became more selective in the 1920s, these members of the Princeton "family" were welcomed at greater rates than other applicants, even those with higher academic qualifications. On the eve of World War I, only 9 or 10 percent of the freshman classes were Tiger cubs. By 1929, at both Yale and Princeton, one in six freshmen was a legacy, and the percentage kept rising throughout the Depression as prep school graduates increased their presence on campus. In 1939, although Yale took the prize for admitting a class that was nearly one-third legacies, a full quarter of Princeton's student body were alumni sons.[26] Both schools were forced by the Depression to accept nearly all applicants, but they had also assured their alumni during the more selective 1920s that none of their sons who met the entrance requirements would be denied entry. This assurance came to be seen by most alumni as a "right" even after selectivity was restored to handle postwar application booms, understandably when three-fourths of Princeton's legacy applicants were successful throughout the 1940s and 1950s.[27]

❁ ❁ ❁

[25] *Report of the President (1913)*, 34; Karabel, "Status-Group Struggle," 25–26; *PAW*, Nov. 17, 1933, 191–92.

[26] Thurston J. Davies, "Another Freshman Class," *PAW*, Sept. 16, 1930, 3–5, at 4; Synnott, *Half-Opened Door*, 157; Peter A. Schwartz, "Chip Off the Old Block," *PAW*, Dec. 15, 1939, 277–79, at 277; Brooks Mather Kelley, *Yale: A History* (New Haven, 1974), 406.

[27] Karabel, "Status-Group Struggle," 17; S. Georgia Nugent, "Changing Faces: The Princeton Student of the Twentieth Century," *PULC* 62:2 (Winter 2001):207–37, at 218; *PAW*, June 6, 1947, 7; Oct. 2, 1959, 13.

The creation of a homogeneous Princeton before World War II was only partly a function of high entrance requirements and costs. It was more the result of university leaders—President Hibben, trustees, and administrators—who deliberately chose not to risk alienating their traditional clients and patrons by educating too many new rivals for their secure spots in America's socioeconomic hierarchy. Instead of establishing a substantial number of scholarships to attract academically talented high schoolers from across the country, for example, Princeton chose to build seven Gothic dormitories during the 1920s to reinforce its residential ideal and image by moving freshmen from local rooming houses onto the campus.[28] This public emphasis on "bricks over brains," in turn, reinforced the student culture's satisfaction with the "gentleman's C" and its eager pursuit of social grace ("smoothness") and extracurricular "sideshows."

To confirm and consolidate its genteel traditionalism, Princeton relied largely on a new policy of "selective" or restrictive admissions and a powerful new gatekeeper. In January 1922, the trustees decided to limit future undergraduate enrollments to about two thousand to preserve the residential experience and close faculty attention that had long been advertised as essential features of a Princeton education.[29] This initially entailed admitting 600–625 freshmen from some 1,200 applicants because 20 percent regularly flunked or dropped out within the first two years and a third by the end of junior year.[30]

[28] In 1926–1927, 1,702 students lived in dorms, 36 in clubs, 17 at home, 7 in town working for rent, and 539 (23 percent) in rented rooms. By 1931, after the dorms were built, the residential ideal was still not realized. In July the university controller decreed that the university would no longer collect rents from a long list of off-campus rooming houses. In 1934, 35 percent of the freshmen lived off campus; about 50 upperclassmen lived in the eating clubs. Edward D. Duffield to G. C. Wintringer, Nov. 13, 1926; Wintringer, notice, July 21, 1931, Historical Subject Files, #A-109 (vertical files), "Dormitories—thru 1952," PUA; William K. Selden, *Princeton—The Best Old Place of All: Vignettes of Princeton University, 1884, 1934, 1984* (Princeton: privately printed, 1987), 39.

[29] As of December 1920, Princeton could accommodate only 1,275–1,350 students in its present dorms and another 400 when planned dorms were built. The dining halls could feed only 1,200 students. Enrollment stood at 1,814. Synnott, *Half-Opened Door*, 189.

[30] *PAW*, Apr. 22, 1925, 682; Nov. 30, 1962, 4. In 1920, Princeton is said to have turned away 1,500 applicants. In this Princeton was somewhat unusual on a national scale. In that year only thirteen of forty top colleges and universities were at all selective. Harvard

FIGURE 8. Dean of Admission Radcliffe Heermance determining the fate of another applicant, after hours.

To implement the new policy, the trustees appointed a director of admission to head a new Committee on Admissions comprised of four members of the faculty, which had always guarded its exclusive prerogative of deciding who they would teach. Partly to disarm any faculty opposition, the trustees chose longtime Assistant Professor of English Radcliffe Heermance for the job, promoting him to full professor in the process despite his lack of a Ph.D.[31]

The rufous-moustached, barrel-chested Heermance was an apposite choice to lead Princeton's effort at status maintenance. A

rejected only 229 applicants and Yale took everyone who fulfilled its basic entrance requirements. Charles E. Widmayer, *Hopkins of Dartmouth* (Hanover, N.H., 1977), 63; Levine, *The American College*, 139.

[31] Synnott, *Half-Opened Door*, 188–92; H. Alexander Smith, "Entering College and Remaining There Under the New Programme," *PAW*, Apr. 22, 1925, 681–83.

Williams College graduate in 1904, he taught at Lawrenceville for three years while somehow collecting M.A.s from his alma mater, Harvard, and Princeton, where he enjoyed Dean West's hospitality at Merwick.[32] In 1909 he joined the Princeton faculty as an instructor in English and soon became one of the students' favorite preceptors and lecturers. A short spell in the stateside ROTC infantry during World War I earned him a major's star, which was replaced by the "chicken wings" of a lieutenant-colonel in 1923. This gave him the rank as well as the look of a "Prussian colonel." Two years later he had added to his duties the deanship of freshmen, a new post that gave him major authority over Princeton's neophytes. In 1926 the *Princeton Tiger* celebrated his ascendancy with the lines (accompanying a cartoon bust): "Heermance, whose eclectic urge / with countenance supinely frozen / seeks to stem the swarming surge, / For many are called but few are chosen."[33]

To select Princeton's newly limited classes, Heermance devised three application forms: a personnel form, on which the applicant explained his reasons for wanting to go to college and especially Princeton; a recommendation form for each of three witnesses to the applicant's "character and promise"; and, most important, a "head master's" form, for the applicant's grades and the master's assessment of the pupil's attitude toward his work and contributions to the school, as well as "whether he was a good sportsman, if he was a player." These six thousand forms the director alone read before the applicants took the College Board exams in June. He sorted them into four classes according to scholastic potential but also "character," as measured by Princeton's "high ideals." "Class 4," he told the alumni, "consisted of all those whose character did not come up to our standards, and who could not enter Princeton, no matter how many points they passed on examination." In 1923, the first year of the new program, only five men were excluded for character flaws, but the door was opened for abuses as well as legitimate uses of directorial discretion in subsequent years.[34]

[32] For Merwick, see chapter 7, pp. 386–88, below.

[33] "Radcliffe Heermance," *PAW*, June 10, 1932, 801–2, 807; *Princeton Tiger*, 36 (1926–1927), 29 (PUA).

[34] Synnott, *Half-Opened Door*, 192–93; Radcliffe Heermance, "The Operation of the Plan of Selective Admission," *PAW*, Apr. 9, 1924, 549–51.

When the word went out that Princeton was limiting enrollment, university officials rushed to disabuse anxious parents and alumni of the notion that only "exceptional scholastic standing or some sort of a 'pull' " could guarantee admission. The assurance they gave on the first point must have been particularly comforting. One traditional avenue of access *was* cut off: "back-door" admission by transfer from other, weaker colleges was reduced to just twenty-nine upperclassmen the first year and even fewer thereafter.[35] But otherwise the admissions committee did not raise the academic bar any higher.[36] Indeed, by attaching considerable new weight to the applicant's character and "the part he has played as a member of the school community," it may have, in effect, lowered it. As Heermance assured alumni, "there never was a time, in the history of Princeton, when the average student, with a good school record . . . stood a better chance of gaining admission."[37]

Strong evidence that he was not understating the new "not so high" standards for the sake of his audience is that a failure or two on the College Board subject exams would not bar the way to Old Nassau. Moreover, instead of beginning the freshman year with "conditions," the new class of failures—147 in the first year—simply had their conditions written off. "We do not believe any more," announced the university's executive secretary, "in handicapping the boy who has had difficulty with his entrance requirements." (He hastened to add that Harvard had adopted the same policy, as if to assuage guilt by association.)[38]

[35] In 1923, 728 men applied for transfer. "Is It Difficult to Enter Princeton?" *PAW*, Oct. 1, 1924, 6; Heermance, "Operation of the Plan," 549. Today Princeton is unusual in accepting no transfers; in 2000 Yale took in 36 (5 percent of all transfers who applied) and Cornell 754 (38 percent). *Washington Post*, Feb. 11, 2003, A6 (chart).

[36] In 1924 the editor of *PAW* assured readers that "whatever the limitation of enrollment may have accomplished, it has not changed the [CEEB] examinations in the least degree, nor raised the passing mark. . . . What limitation *has* done is to say quite frankly that Princeton no longer admits all applicants merely because of their scholastic success. But it hasn't made that success any harder to achieve" ("Is It Difficult to Enter Princeton?" 6).

[37] *PAW*, Oct. 1, 1924, 5; "Is It Difficult to Enter Princeton?" 6.

[38] Heermance, "Operation of the Plan," 550–51; Smith, "Entering College and Remaining There," 682.

The kind of class that Heermance consistently sought to fashion until he retired in 1950 made little room for diversity, intellectual or social. In 1924 the alumni were told not only that "the superior student is not now guaranteed admission" but that "the more evenly developed boy, the 'all-around' boy, stands a better chance than he ever did." Twenty-four years later, the director affirmed that "there has been no significant change of admission policy" since he took office. Princeton, he said, was still seeking "the well-rounded young man who has participated actively in the best things of school life and who may be expected to contribute his interest and accept his responsibility as a citizen on the campus."[39] In other words, rather than crafting a well-rounded *class* from a collection of spiky individualists and specialists, Heermance—and therefore Princeton—chose a homogeneous class of well-rounded *individuals*, each of whom was at least moderately good at all three aspects of college life—academic, social, and extracurricular. In this undifferentiated mix, the mere "brain" or "grind" had little or no place and mediocrity was more common than true excellence.

The wide discretion conferred upon Princeton and several other elite institutions by the popular demand for a college experience, if not education, allowed their admission officers to hand-pick classes with a combination of new and old methods that did little to threaten their traditional clients and contributors. They could do this because their admission officers, like Heermance, were products of the same social and academic classes as those from which they were recruiting. Left to their own devices, they were unlikely to commit class treason or to conduct experiments in social engineering by choosing radically different classes of freshmen.

❁ ❁ ❁

At the beginning of the new admissions regime in the 1920s, officials sought to convince parents and alumni—and perhaps themselves—that "we do not really reject. We *select* from the material offered."[40]

[39] "Is It Difficult to Enter Princeton?" 6; Nugent, "Changing Faces," 221, 222.

[40] Smith, "Entering College and Remaining There," 683. Robert N. Corwin, the chairman of Yale's Board of Admissions from 1920 to 1933, sought to avoid Harvard's reputation for anti-Semitic admissions policies. He suggested that "it would give us

But one group of applicants saw through Princeton's verbal mist because they felt the sting of deliberate, albeit covert, rejection. From early in the century, applicants from Jewish families were admitted in very small numbers. This trend, in turn, discouraged others from applying altogether. Although the number of Jewish acceptances quadrupled between 1906 and 1922 (from six to twenty-five), they never constituted more than one in twenty freshmen.[41] As early as 1909, Princeton's climate of discrimination was notable. "Anti-Semitic feeling" seemed to Edwin Slosson "more dominant at Princeton than at any of the other [thirteen top] universities" he visited. "If the Jews once got in," he was told, presumably by a university official, "they would ruin Princeton as they have Columbia and Pennsylvania."[42]

Princeton's prejudice against Jewish students was founded on neither their potentially "ruinous" numbers nor their religion per se, but on ambient anti-Semitism at three levels. First, America in the 1910s and "tribal '20s" was in the throes of one of its sporadic spasms of nativism and isolationist xenophobia. Since the 1880s, when Czarist Russia launched pogroms against its Jewish population, emigration to the United States had accelerated. The displacement of Eastern European Jews and particularly Jewish university students by World War I and its revolutionary aftermath only added to the surge. The influx of mostly poor, strangely accented aliens worried the descendants of America's earlier immigrants and seemed to threaten their hold on the nation's economic and political life. Armed with spuriously scientific theories of "race," "100-Percent Americans" of largely Anglo-Saxon ancestry and Protestant faith responded by persuading Congress to pass immigration quotas in 1921, 1924, and 1929 to restrict the "new immigration," particularly from Eastern and Southern Europe. Needless to say, the Jewish elements in those

---

better publicity if we should speak of *selection* and of the rigid enforcement of high standards rather than of the limitation of numbers," which had "come to connote a special kind of limitation" (Corwin, "Limitation of Numbers," Jan. 9, 1923, Yale University Archives, quoted in Karabel, *The Chosen*, 113).

[41] Karabel, "Status-Group Struggle," 10 (table 1). Inexplicably, Karabel's table contradicts his assertion that the number "almost doubled" between 1906 and 1922.

[42] Slosson, *Great American Universities*, 105.

emigrant populations faced the strongest prejudice from the insecure nativists.[43]

On an intermediate level, Princeton shared anti-Semitic prejudices with a number of northeastern colleges and universities, with whom it cooperated and traded intelligence. By the late 1910s, many of these elite schools perceived that they had a "Jewish problem." Urban institutions felt the most pressure because the great majority of Jewish immigrants settled in New York and other cities in the northeastern corridor. By 1920, New York City's population was 30 percent Jewish and its nine largest educational institutions were nearly 40 percent Jewish; Columbia's Jewish enrollment had reached 40 percent before it instituted a selective admission policy in 1921. The "problem" was that university officials believed that "excessive" numbers of unacculturated Eastern European Jews would drive their more "refined" WASP students and supporters into flight, as they had done to some degree at Columbia and seemed poised to do at Harvard and Yale.[44]

In concert with the national mood, the elite universities, especially the Big Three, settled on admission quotas as their solution to the "Jewish problem." At a Princeton meeting of the Association of New England Deans in 1918, members worried that "more and more the foreign element is creeping in" and wondered how they could "get

[43] John Higham, *Strangers in the Land: Patterns of American Nativism, 1860–1925* (New Brunswick, N.J., 1955; New York, 1968); Higham, *Send These to Me: Jews and Other Immigrants in Urban America* (New York, 1975); E. Digby Baltzell, *The Protestant Establishment: Aristocracy & Caste in America* (New York, 1966); Marcia Graham Synnott, "Anti-Semitism and American Universities: Did Quotas Follow the Jews?" in David A. Gerber, ed., *Anti-Semitism in American History* (Urbana and Chicago, 1986), 233–71, at 239; Synnott, "The Admission and Assimilation of Minority Students at Harvard, Yale, and Princeton, 1900–1970," *History of Education Quarterly* 19 (Fall 1979): 285–304, at 286–87; Harold S. Wechsler, "The Rationale for Restriction: Ethnicity and College Admission in America, 1910–1980," *American Quarterly* 36:5 (Winter 1984):643–67.

[44] Stephen Steinberg, *The Academic Melting Pot: Catholics and Jews in American Higher Education*, Carnegie Commission on Higher Education Report (New York, 1974), chap. 1; Harold S. Wechsler, *The Qualified Student: A History of Selective College Admission in America* (New York, 1977), chap. 7, at 173–74; Synnott, "Anti-Semitism and American Universities," 235–36; Robert A. McCaughey, *Stand, Columbia: A History of Columbia University in the City of New York, 1754–2004* (New York, 2003), chap. 9.

the boys of American parentage to come to college." Dean Frederick Jones of Yale summed up the proceedings when he urged his colleagues to "change our views in regard to the Jewish element. . . . We must put a ban on the Jews."[45]

Within the next few years, the Big Three and several peer schools installed carefully camouflaged quotas on their Jewish applicants, usually under the guise of "limited enrollment" or "selective admission" plans. Columbia's comfort level was 15 to 20 percent (though it actually admitted 8–10 percent), Harvard's between 10 and 15 percent. Despite Dean Jones's early alarm, Yale's Jewish population, largely Russian Jews from Connecticut high schools, did not exceed 10 percent until 1925. Thereafter Yale did its best to keep its ethnic Elis in the 8–12-percent range. Princeton, with the smallest "problem" of all (a high of twenty-five matriculants in 1922), decided two years later to limit "Hebrew" freshmen to under 3 percent, the Jewish segment of the national population. By 1925, Jews numbered only eleven in a class of 641. Their numbers did not exceed twenty until after World War II. Even in the depths of the Depression, when Dean Heermance accepted 79–85 percent of all applicants in a desperate search for "paying guests," fewer than one in five Jewish applicants made the cut.[46]

The third level upon which Princeton played out its anti-Semitic prejudices was local, but the results there fed the university's reputation in the academic world at large. Limiting enrollments alone gave Princeton and other elite institutions added cachet by virtue of supply and demand. But reducing socially "undesirable" elements in the student body endeared them to their blue-blooded constituents for making qualitative as well as quantitative efforts to prolong their dominance. Creating social homogeneity on the Princeton campus

[45] Synnott, "Admission and Assimilation of Minority Students," 289; Karabel, "Status-Group Struggle," 9.

[46] Levine, *The American College*, 149; Synnott, *Half-Opened Door*, 143 (table 5.3), 158 (table 5.9), 182 (table 6.2); McCaughey, *Stand, Columbia*, 272; Dan A. Oren, *Joining the Club: A History of Jews and Yale* (New Haven, 1985), chap. 3, 320–21 (app. 5); Synnott, "Admission and Assimilation of Minority Students," 291; Nugent, "Changing Faces," 218 (quoting psychologist Carl Bingham). Woodsy Dartmouth did not experience a "Jewish problem" serious enough to warrant a quota until 1931, when it sought a 5 percent ceiling. Levine, *The American College*, 151–53.

was not what Wilson had in mind. True democracy, he argued, was made up of "unchosen experiences," and Princeton's narrow, preselected social life had little room for either. He would have agreed with Columbia dean Frederick Keppel, who thought that "College 'democracy' is overrated. . . . When students say democracy, they very often mean oligarchy," particularly when "a boy of impeccable breeding is ignored socially because he happens to be a Jew."[47]

But those in favor of excluding Jews argued—or assumed—that the majority of Jewish applicants were *not* of "impeccable breeding," and from their blinkered point of view they were not wrong. As first- or second-generation newcomers in a hurry to assimilate, most Jews came to college with more intellectual talent and ambition than social graces. Most lacked the "right" clothes, addresses, luggage, pedigrees, manners, friends, schooling, and points of reference. Moreover, the "gentleman's C" and the extracurricular culture of the pre–World War II campus held little charm for them, for whom a college education was less a status symbol than the route to social mobility. If gauche "grinding" and academic success were the social price they had to pay, many were content to pay it.[48]

But Princeton thought that the price entailed additional costs, which *it* was not willing to pay. An editorial in the *Nation* spoke for Princeton and other guardians of the "genteel tradition" when it predicted that "the infiltration of a mass of pushing young men with a foreign accent, accustomed to overcome discrimination by self-assertion, would obviously change the character of undergraduate life at any of these institutions and lessen its *social prestige*."[49] Loathe to risk losing face with its elite constituents, Princeton joined some of the nation's best universities in reinforcing the worst social prejudices, anti-intellectualism, and fears of an anxious American society.[50]

[47] Levine, *The American College*, 145–46; "The Country and the Colleges," c. Feb. 24, 1910 (draft), *PWW*, 20:157–72, at 161; Frederick P. Keppel, *The Undergraduate and His College* (Boston and New York, 1917), 121–22.

[48] Steinberg, *Academic Melting Pot*, 13, 19; Oren, *Joining the Club*, 39, 43, 52, 56.

[49] "May Jews Go to College? *Nation*, 114 (June 14, 1922), 708 (my emphasis).

[50] Levine, *The American College*, 156, 161. Julie A. Reuben suggests that the selective policies of the elite colleges were "not simply a cover for anti-Semitism; they were part of a broader agenda aimed at shaping the community life of students. . . . [T]he value that educators placed on a cohesive student community supported social prejudice" (*The*

The need to implement covert quotas on Jewish admissions spurred Princeton and other selective institutions to invent an imaginative array of tools of exclusion. The most popular and least open to attack was the emphasis on "character" and the assumption that character was "non-randomly distributed by ethnic group."[51] Since scholarship alone (even the new Scholastic Aptitude Test [SAT] of 1926) was no longer capable of reducing the number of Jewish freshmen, the intangible nature of "character" gave admission officers maximum discretion in choosing classes. Unlike scholastic aptitude, character was best found outside the classroom, on the playing fields, editorial boards of student publications, and the stage, as it was in England's "public" (i.e., private) schools, which served as models for most American prep schools.[52] Schoolmasters and, if possible, alumni interviewers were now asked to rate potential Tigers on such qualities as "manhood" ("sense of honor, fearlessness, forcefulness"), "leadership" ("personality" and "popularity"), and "participation in athletics" ("feats performed" and "sportsmanship"), as well as "home environment and companions" and "religious belief and attitude toward religious activities."[53]

While these tests could be applied disingenuously to Protestant and even Catholic boys, they were also encoded to draw upon nega-

---

Making of the Modern University: Intellectual Transformation and the Marginalization of Morality [Chicago, 1996], 264, 344n87).

[51] Karabel, "Status-Group Struggle," 12, 15, 16, 33n48.

[52] James McLachlan, *American Boarding Schools: A Historical Study* (New York, 1970).

[53] Steinberg, *Academic Melting Pot*, 20; Synnott, *Half-Opened Door*, 190; Nugent, "Changing Faces," 216–17. Princeton was especially influenced by the Rhodes Scholarships as it instituted its "selective" admissions policy. President Hibben acknowledged in his annual report for 1920–1921 that "the Rhodes Scholarship requirements present an excellent precedent" (*PAW*, Feb. 9, 1921, 381). It was no coincidence that Princeton's criteria for "character" mirrored those of the Rhodes application. During its first thirty-nine years (1904–1939), Princeton seniors won more Rhodes (61) than any other American university or college; Harvard (46) and Yale (43) trailed well behind. Karabel, *The Chosen*, 120–22, 131–32, 133–32, 133; Frank Aydelotte, *The American Rhodes Scholarships: A Review of the First Forty Years* (Princeton, 1946). Princeton still held a wide lead throughout the 1950s, but by 1970 it had slipped to third behind Harvard and Yale, where it remains today. *PAW*, Jan. 17, 1958, 14; Feb. 10, 1970, 5; Thomas J. Schaeper and Kathleen Schaeper, *Cowboys into Gentlemen: Rhodes Scholars, Oxford, and the Creation of an American Elite* (New York and Oxford, 1998), 228.

tive Jewish stereotypes. Jewish males were widely thought to be aggressive or "pushy," interested in self-advancement more than in their classmates, and "unmanly," satisfied with intellectual rather than athletic or social success. In an era when "school spirit" was supposed to be universally shared and expressed, the stereotype of the selfish Jewish grind was especially damaging.[54] A WASPish letter to the *Nation* in 1923 claimed that "the Hebrew . . . takes all and gives nothing . . . to college. He will not go out for activities. He will not be a member of the cheering section at athletic contests." Fifteen years later, Dean Heermance declared at a meeting of the Committee on Admission that in his experience Jews were "unable to be loyal" to anything. Neither critic stopped to consider, as a Columbia dean had, that Jewish students "might contribute more than their share" if they were not "embittered and rendered intellectually sulky by bad treatment."[55] The cruel irony that Jewish students were often excluded from extracurricular activities and then blamed for their lack of participation was equally lost on both men.

Other tactics and tools devised to detect and exclude Jewish applicants were more transparent than "character" assessment. Obtrusive questions about the applicant's religious preference and his parents' ethnicity, nationality, birthplaces, and religion became regular features of college applications, as did required photographs. At Prince-

[54] In 1932, researchers asked 100 Princeton students to check words that described various ethnic groups. The top four vote-getters for "Jews" were *shrewd* (79 percent checked it), *mercenary* (49 percent), *industrious* (48 percent), and *grasping* (34 percent). When 333 Princetonians took the same test in 1950, their top responses were *shrewd* (47 percent), *intelligent* (37 percent), *industrious* (29 percent), and a tie between *ambitious* and *mercenary* (28 percent). G. M. Gilbert, "Stereotype Persistence and Change among College Students," *Journal of Abnormal and Social Psychology* 46 (1951):245–54, at 248 (table 1). Postwar Princeton experienced a slow but significant increase in Jewish students: 54 matriculated in 1948, 41 more in 1949; by 1959, 15 percent of the undergraduates were Jewish. This had the effect of humanizing and reducing the stereotyping of "Jews" in general. Synnott, *Half-Opened Door*, 222 (table 7.2); Lawrence Bloomgarden, "Our Changing Elite Colleges," *Commentary* 29:2 (Feb. 1960):150–54, at 153.

[55] Nugent, "Changing Faces," 217; William C. Greene, Jr., letter to the *Nation*, 116 (May 16, 1923), 573; Minutes of the Committee on Admissions, Jan. 25, 1938, quoted in George E. Tomberlin, Jr., "Trends in Princeton Admissions" (Senior thesis, Dept. of Sociology, PU, 1971), 134; Keppel, *The Undergraduate and His College*, 210.

ton, mandatory residency, which excluded urban commuters, and the virtual ban on transfer students cut off two sources of Jewish applicants. The Big Three's awakened interest in regional representation and scholarships, while it promoted their status as national universities, also served to transfer freshman slots from the heavily Jewish Northeast to more "American" towns and suburbs in the West, Midwest, and South.[56] Although required chapel attendance at Princeton was officially nondenominational, it subjected Jewish students to a relentlessly Christian program and value system. As a supplement to the (culturally biased) College Board exams, psychological tests to assess "native intelligence" enjoyed brief popularity. When Jewish students displayed a disconcerting habit of scoring as well as those of Anglo-Saxon ancestry, the tests were dropped in favor of the SATs that resulted from them.[57] When Jewish applicants did manage to squeeze through the cracks, they were put on malleable waiting lists (as a less suspicious alternative to direct rejection) or denied the scholarship help that many of them needed. If they had adequate means to attend, many of their places were taken by a rising tide of alumni sons.[58]

Princeton's exclusionary tool kit worked well. The number of Jewish freshmen dropped 56 percent between 1922, the year selective

[56] Karabel, "Status-Group Struggle," 14; Steinberg, *Academic Melting Pot*, 30. Columbia College under Yale-educated Dean Herbert Hawkes adopted the intrusive application form with photo, the personal interview, and a policy that preferred candidates from outside New York City, preferably from prep schools. McCaughey, *Stand, Columbia*, 267–69.

[57] Princeton psychologist Carl C. Bingham was the chief architect of such exams and later a valued staff member of the College Board. For his role in developing the SATs, he was the "Chief Advisor" to Dean Heermance and the Princeton admissions office. As an assistant professor and ardent eugenicist, Bingham first administered a psychological exam to all Princeton freshmen in 1922. Nugent, "Changing Faces," 212–14; Carl C. Bingham, "Psychological Tests at Princeton," *PAW*, Nov. 28, 1923, 185–87; Wechsler, *The Qualified Student*, 158–61, 163, 247–48; Nicholas Lemann, *The Big Test: The Secret History of the American Meritocracy* (New York, 1999), 29–35, 38–41.

[58] Synnott, *Half-Opened Door*, 151, 155, 156, 159; Synnott, "Admission and Assimilation of Minority Students," 289–90; Synnott, "Anti-Semitism and American Universities," 250; Karabel, "Status-Group Struggle," 16, 23, 25, 34n66, 35n71, 38n110; Levine, *The American College*, 152–53; "May Jews Go to College?" 708.

admissions was installed, and 1924, when the 3 percent class quota went into effect. But no one in the administration rushed forward to claim credit for it. On the contrary, in 1948, when the admission office was in the process of admitting a record fifty-four Jews, Dean Heermance told the *Daily Princetonian* that "we have *never* discriminated on any basis whatever. We abhor quota systems whether racial, school, or geographical."[59]

That's not how his contemporaries understood the situation at Princeton. In the early 1930s, President Hibben had also denied the existence of a Jewish quota during a discussion with University of Chicago President Robert M. Hutchins. Whereupon Hibben's bright and feisty wife, Jennie, protested: "Jack Hibben, I don't see how you can sit there and lie to this young man. You know very well that you and Dean Eisenhart get together every year and fix the quota."[60] Even earlier testimony documented discrimination if not the quota itself. In 1922, when the Big Three were coordinating solutions to the "Jewish problem," Heermance's Yale counterpart, Robert Corwin, observed that Princeton's unique first line of defense was to discourage Jewish applications altogether by making known the opposition of "undergraduate sentiment" and the eating clubs, which instinctively refused "social honors" to any Hebrews who slipped through the elaborate "selective admissions" apparatus.[61]

Equally strong evidence that Heermance either had a poor memory or sought to rewrite history came from Varnum Lansing Collins,

[59] "Dean Heermance Denies Claim That Quota System Used Here," *DP*, Mar. 24, 1948, 1 (my emphasis). Heermance made the same claim in June 1939 when he tried to explain to Bruce M. Wright, the son of a black father and white mother, why he had first been accepted by Princeton in 1936 but asked to leave when he arrived to register in the fall. Karen W. Arenson, "Princeton Honors Judge It Once Turned Away for His Race," *New York Times*, June 5, 2001, A22; Donald L. Maggin '48, "Smashing Princeton's Color Bar: Racism Stymied by 1940s Students," *The Independent: A Journal of Ideas from Princeton* (Spring 2004):28–29 and continuation on http://princetonindependent.com. See n. 78 below for more on the handling of Wright's case.

[60] Steven L. Buenning, "John Grier Hibben: A Biographical Study (1919–1932)" (Senior thesis, Dept. of History, PU, 1971), 60.

[61] "Limitation of Numbers," Freshman Office Records, Committee on Limitation of Numbers 1922, Yale University Archives, Sterling Memorial Library, quoted in Synnott, *Half-Opened Door*, 197.

a member of the Committee on Admissions and Secretary of the University in 1922. In a letter to an alumnus fundraiser, he wrote, "I hope the Alumni will tip us off to any Hebrew candidates," knowing full well that older alumni would favor boys who reminded them of their own younger selves. But then he remembered that "our strongest barrier is our club system. If the graduate members of the clubs will ram the idea home on the undergraduate bicker committees and make the admission of a Hebrew to a club the rarest sort of a thing, I do not think the Hebrew question will become serious."[62] Only at Princeton, with its dominant ethos of "clubability," did the student body exercise such effective, quasi-official power over the fate of university applicants. As Wilson had learned the hard way during his quad fight, the eating-club tail was perfectly capable of wagging the university Tiger.

The harsh absurdity of Princeton's social system for the young Jewish men who did matriculate is reflected in one set of numbers and two lives. Between 1930 and 1939, eighty-nine self-identified Jewish seniors revealed in the *Nassau Herald*, the student yearbook of record, a spare and often isolated existence during their years on campus. Over half lived alone all four years, largely in the same few dorms that were clearly segregated by religion, ostensibly for the social comfort of the faithful. Two-thirds participated in two or fewer extracurricular activities. A half-dozen men inhabited single rooms the whole time and enjoyed no campus activities. Most Princeton students, of course, shared quarters with multiple roommates and were encouraged to engage in numerous activities outside the classroom.[63]

[62] Varnum Lansing Collins to Henry M. Canby, Nov. 23, 1922, quoted in Synnott, *Half-Opened Door*, 160.

[63] Jordan Roth, "The Real Robert Cohns: The Exclusion of Jewish Students at Princeton University in the 1920s and 1930s" (Paper for Freshman Seminar 124, "The Aims of Education," Spring 1994), 15, in Hist. Subj. Files (vertical), #A-109, "Anti-Semitism" (PUA). Even after the war, parents also contributed to the anti-Semitic housing situation. In his first semester at Princeton, Lawrenceville graduate James Greenwald '54 returned from Thanksgiving break to find that his roommate, with whom he had studied and gotten along very well, had moved out because his parents "refused to pay his tuition if he roomed with a Jew" (Roy Heath, *Princeton Retrospectives: Twenty-Fifth-Year Reflections on a College Education* [Princeton: Class of 1954, 1979], 183).

Figure 9. The allegedly Semitic looks of Richard Holzman Demuth '31, which barred the all-around salutatorian of his class from eating-club life.

The lives of Jewish students, however well bred they were or accomplished they became, were tarnished by Princeton's pervasive anti-Semitism, particularly in the clubs. Richard Holzman Demuth '31, son of a retired New York manufacturer and product of the prestigious Horace Mann School, was, according to DeWitt Clinton Poole, the director of the School of Public and International Affairs, "one of the most brilliant, and . . . most substantial students in the University," a young man possessed of "an unusual degree of dignity." At graduation he was recognized as the class salutatorian and a junior-year member of Phi Beta Kappa. But he was no mere grind. Along the way he had also won several oratorical prizes, been a mainstay of the debating team, played in the university orchestra and the banjo club, carried away the prestigious McLean Prize and the *New York Times* current events contest in his junior year, and garnered a scholarship for European travel and research toward his senior thesis.

But Demuth had also lived alone for four years and was never invited to join an eating club. It was "generally understood," he remembered, that "Jewish students were not encouraged to engage in bicker."[64] Although Director Poole could never detect any of what he called "the objectionable qualities which are sometimes attributed to his race," he admitted that "Demuth's difficulty is that he is a Jew, not by religion . . . but strikingly so in appearance." He was also a professed Liberal on a Republican campus, but that seems not to have blighted his social prospects as much as being regarded, even by friendly advisors, as a physiognomical representative of a (seldom-)chosen people.[65]

Henry Morgenthau III had nothing but a well-publicized surname to suggest Jewish ancestry. Yet he, too, came to grief on Princeton's social shoals, even while his father served as Franklin Roosevelt's Secretary of the Treasury. After a toney upbringing in New York City, he graduated from Deerfield Academy in 1935 after his father had assumed the second-highest cabinet post and the second ever held by a Jew. Neither at egalitarian Deerfield nor in Washington's "barrier-free social whirl" had "Hank" experienced any detectable discrimination. Nor did he expect any at Princeton. After his great-grandfather emigrated from southern Germany for business reasons in 1866 and his grandfather had served Wilson as ambassador to Turkey, the Morgenthaus, like many German-Jewish families, be-

[64] Some Jewish students, mostly athletes, did manage during the 1930s to join eating clubs, albeit largely the five youngest and least prestigious. Several Jewish club members clearly neglected to declare their religion or ethnicity and "passed."

[65] *Nassau Herald* (1931), 120; Roth, "The Real Robert Cohns," 7, 10–11. Fortunately, Demuth's treatment at Princeton did not prevent him from graduating from Harvard Law School, having a distinguished career in international finance, and serving for nine years on the advisory committee of the Woodrow Wilson School. *Who's Who in America*, 37th ed. (1972–1973). In 1922, "the St. Paul School crowd" in Colonial Club tried to blackball senior Malcolm S. Davis "because of his 'Ginsberg' beak." They were stopped by the joint persuasions of the club president and treasurer. *The Colonial Club of Princeton University, 1891–1991* (Princeton, 1991), 48 (thanks to Willis M. Rivinus, the compiler and editor, for a copy).

came so thoroughly assimilated that they had "lost all positive sense of Jewish identity," celebrating Christmas and Easter American-style and never attending temple. But when others discovered their Jewish identity for them, the young Princetonian later realized, "we had nothing to fall back on."[66]

He needed support when the "polite, sadomasochistic experience" called bicker came around in his sophomore year. Like most of his classmates, he sat night after night in his Campbell Hall room during the critical weeks, waiting for club "callers" to knock. "Some nights there were none. Sometimes they approached and passed on. Then they would stop; there was a knock on another door, an exchange of muffled voices, a door clicking shut, and silence." Finally, it dawned on him that he was not going to receive a bid, not even from Court, Gateway, or Dial Lodge, the newer, less choosey clubs "at the bottom of the pecking order."[67]

In retrospect, he attributed his failure to a kind of "arrogant optimism," which assumed that joining a Princeton club was no different from becoming a part of the Washington social scene. In the capital, a Jew was treated as an "honorary Aryan" if his father was high in the administration. So "with no cultivation and cementing of appropriate friendships, no leveraging of family and alumni connections," he "lined up for the slaughter." Of a dozen Jewish classmates, five joined no club; most of the rest were taken by Court and Gateway, who also made some "awkward, uncomfortable maneuvers" toward Hank after the original bids had gone out.[68]

"At Princeton," Morgenthau remembered, "I began to learn in a negative way about Jewishness and anti-Semitism." Despite his tweedy, patrician looks, his distinguished family (which won him an invitation to visit Einstein at home), his cross-country "P," his visibility on the editorial boards of the *Nassau Literary Magazine* and the *Daily Princetonian*, and his work at the Princeton Summer Camp

[66] Henry Morgenthau III, *Mostly Morgenthaus: A Family History* (New York, 1991), 278, 279. The first inkling of trouble came during his first week on campus, when he found under his door a note that said, "Despite your ham-eating propensity, you have something you cannot conceal" (Van Wallach, " 'A Community to Turn To': The Center for Jewish Life . . . ," *PAW*, Apr. 19, 1995, 12–18, at 16).

[67] Morgenthau, *Mostly Morgenthaus*, 279–80.

[68] Morgenthau, *Mostly Morgenthaus*, 279–80.

for inner-city boys, he was declared unfit to eat with by more than three-quarters of the two upper classes. When the pain subsided, he recalled more than half a century later, "a new numbness set in. From then on, I was a social paraplegic." This "emasculating experience" left him feeling "less than a Princeton man" and "frustrated by the knowledge that no act of self-mutilation would enable me to succeed." Only later would he take some comfort from his cousin Barbara Tuchman, who six years earlier had discovered, as a freshman at Swarthmore, that its sororities did not pledge Jews. In hindsight, they agreed that what happened to them both was less "traumatic" than "idiotic." But "cuts suffered at Princeton never ceased to bleed."[69]

Too late for those denied admission and those who were not, Princeton's discrimination against Jews began to subside during World War II. Confronting the Final Solution to the "Jewish problem" in Europe caused many Americans to recognize the moral smallness and danger of their own temporary solutions at home. On campus, *Daily Princetonian* chairman Frank Broderick '43 reminded Princeton in a series of hard-hitting editorials that its discriminatory admission practices implicitly perpetuated "a racial theory more characteristic of our enemies than of an American university."[70] And students who had shared K-rations, foxholes, and deadly enemies with Americans of other faiths, backgrounds, and colors were much less likely to blackball them for frivolous reasons when they returned to Princeton on the G.I. Bill.

Jewish students began to emerge from their cautious low profile in 1946 when their numbers began to increase substantially and they formed a Student Hebrew Association, which evolved into Hillel three years later. A campus rabbi's salary was paid by B'nai B'rith,

[69] Howard Simons, *Jewish Times: Voices of the American Jewish Experience* (Boston, 1988), 53; Morgenthau, *Mostly Morgenthaus*, 279–81; *Nassau Herald* (1939), 383; Geoffrey Wolff, *The Final Club* (New York, 1990), 143.

[70] Dan Klein, "Ahead of His Time: Frank Broderick '43 Pushed for an Integrated Princeton," *PAW*, Dec. 20, 1995, 39–40, at 40; also in *Best of PAW*, 205–6. Editorial co-chairman Phillip Quigg '43 was equally responsible for the *Prince* editorials pushing for integration. Letter to the editor from Alan W. Horton '43, *PAW*, Feb. 7, 1996, 2. According to Quigg, he wrote the second editorial of three. Maggin, "Smashing Princeton's Color Bar" (online version), 6–8.

and Friday night services in Murray-Dodge Hall satisfied the Sunday chapel requirement. In 1950 the university removed all religious questions from its applications, and seven years later New Jersey outlawed mandatory photographs as well. Measures such as these did much to diversify Princeton's classes. When biology professor William Jacobs arrived in Princeton soon after the war, he was shocked at the sight of his first class: "It was like looking at a roomfull of siblings." By 1960, 15 percent of the undergraduates were Jewish; that figure reached 20 percent by the late 1970s. In 1961 Orthodox students could eat kosher meals at Yavneh House on Olden Street. Ten years later, a kosher kitchen for all Jewish students opened in Stevenson Hall on Prospect Street among the clubs. In 1972 the university began to offer classes in modern Hebrew. A decade later the faculty, now distinguished by hundreds of Jewish scholar-teachers, established an interdisciplinary Committee for Jewish Studies to oversee some twenty-one courses and the writing of senior theses in Jewish history, culture, literature, and religion.[71]

The full integration of Jewish students and Judaism was perhaps best symbolized by the Opening Exercises in September 1981. At two o'clock in the afternoon instead of during the regular Sunday morning worship service, new and returning students convened in the Gothic splendor of the University Chapel before an altar holding only a chalice and a menorah, the cross having been screened off for the occasion. Frederick Borsch, the Christian dean of the chapel, officiated the religious portion of the proceedings, but the campus rabbi read the litany. For the same reason, the baccalaureate service at Commencement was moved to Sunday afternoon, and speakers from a variety of faiths were invited to speak. One of the most mem-

[71] In time the committee metamorphosed into the Program of Jewish Studies (now the Program in Judaic Studies), which offers an undergraduate certificate of completion. Seth Akabas, "Friends of Hillel," *PAW*, Feb. 9, 1983, 28; Wallach, "A Community to Turn To," 17–18; Synnott, *Half-Opened Door*, 222–23; William P. Jacobs, "Need More Diversity," *PAW*, Feb. 7, 1958, 11–12, at 11; Bloomgarden, "Our Changing Elite Colleges," 153; David Zielenziger, "First Hebrew Classes Begin," *DP*, Sept. 20, 1972, 6; "Jewish Studies," *PAW*, Mar. 22, 1982, 11; Mark J. Sherman, "On the Campus: Jewish Life Today," *PAW*, Oct. 19, 1981, 9. In 1988 Harold Shapiro became the first Jewish president of Princeton.

orable interdenominational talks was delivered by Gerson Cohen, then chancellor of the Jewish Theological Seminary in New York and parent of a graduating senior.[72] Throughout the academic year, regular services were held in various locations for each of the three Jewish congregations (Reform, Orthodox, and Conservative) and the university asked faculty to be sensitive to students who might be absent for the calendar of Jewish holidays. The establishment in 1993 of a $4.85 million Center for Jewish Life on the site of the old Jewish-friendly Prospect Club sealed Princeton's institutional commitment to leave behind the unhappy days of exclusionary quotas and religious discrimination.[73]

Despite the steady progress that official Princeton made in living down its past, its reputation for prejudice died hard. The selectivity of the clubs instead of admissions was often the object of suspicion, and national notoriety surrounding the "Dirty Bicker" of 1958 did nothing to allay it. After several years in which 100 percent of the sophomore class received at least one bid to a club, the class of 1960 at the end of bicker had twenty-three men without one: fifteen were Jewish and five were National Merit Scholars. The problem was not anti-Semitism pure and simple: each of the seventeen clubs had Jewish members, although several clubs applied clandestine quotas of their own. As Steven Rockefeller '58, chairman of the Undergraduate Inter-Club Committee, fairly observed, it was "the present system of club selectivity with no acceptable alternative [provided by the university] plus 100 percent" that led to trouble, particularly as Princeton's enrollment grew steadily throughout the 1950s and 1960s. But as classmate Myron Margolin, president of Prospect Club, which had gone nonselective in December 1957, also recognized, "The selective basis of the club system did lead to abuses, among them institutional anti-Semitism."[74]

[72] The moving force behind both of these inclusive innovations was charter trustee John Coburn, Episcopal Bishop of Massachusetts at the time. William G. Bowen to author, Apr. 14, 2003.

[73] Sherman, "Jewish Life Today," 9; Wallach, "A Community to Turn To."

[74] Frederick C. Rich, *The First Hundred Years of the Ivy Club, 1879–1979* (Princeton, 1979), 195–97, 200; William K. Selden, *Club Life at Princeton: An Historical Account of the Eating Clubs at Princeton University* (Princeton, 1996), 50–51; Wolff, *The Final Club*, 96–104; Myron H. Margolin, letter to the editor, *PAW*, Dec. 1, 1981, 7.

The unfortunate legacy of 1958 and its pre-war antecedents continued to shadow the university. When high school senior and future history professor Anthony Grafton was looking at colleges in the mid-1960s, "Princeton had a particularly anti-Semitic reputation." He chose the University of Chicago, which had a larger and more acceptably intellectual Jewish presence. As late as 1981, when Princeton had sixty volunteer Jewish resident advisors to "mother" its hundreds of Jewish students, the outside Jewish community still viewed Princeton as "a den of anti-Semitism." Even reassurance by the campus rabbi could not remove all doubts.[75]

❁ ❁ ❁

Before World War II ended, signs appeared that American higher education in general and Princeton in particular were about to change in major new directions. The most telling was the G.I. Bill of Rights of 1944. To everyone who had served in the armed forces for at least ninety days after September 1940, the federal government offered to pay for education or training in any approved institution "in which he chooses to enroll." Anyone who had served three years was eligible

[75] Michelle Woollen and Gwendolen Jones, "The Colors of Old Nassau: The Changing Hue of Princeton Charlie," in *The Orange & Black in Black & White: A Century of Princeton Through the Eyes of* The Daily Princetonian (Princeton, 1992), 63 (Grafton); Sherman, "Jewish Life Today," 9. For an overview, see Marianne Sanua, "Stages in the Development of Jewish Life at Princeton University," *American Jewish History* 76:4 (June 1987):391–415. For Jewish life and anti-Semitism at Harvard, see Nitza Rosovsky, *The Jewish Experience at Harvard and Radcliffe* (Cambridge, Mass., 1986). When the percentage of Jewish students at Princeton dropped noticeably in the 1990s (as had Jewish applicants as a percentage of students applying to colleges nationally), several Jewish faculty and students were understandably quick to wonder if West College had reinstated the bad old "selective admissions" from the 1920s and 1930s. Princeton's Jewish population was only half of Harvard's and Yale's, according to imprecise Hillel estimates. "Notebook," *CHE*, May 7, 1999, A49; Ben Gose, "Princeton Tries to Explain a Drop in Jewish Enrollment," *CHE*, May 14, 1999, A47. In 2002, ironically, several predominantly Christian universities made news by actively recruiting high-scoring Jewish students to raise their rankings in *U.S. News & World Report*'s college issue and the like. Daniel Golden, "Colleges Court Jewish Students In Effort to Raise Rankings," *Wall Street Journal*, Apr. 29, 2002, A1, A8.

for four years of support, which increased if he was married. This heralded not only the return of most of the 777,000 male students who had left college to enlist or to answer the draft, but applications from imposing numbers of the two million high school graduates who had also served, all of whom now had independent means to attend any obliging college or university in the land. By the fall of 1946, 2,484 veterans were on the tranquil Princeton campus, many still in khaki trousers and flight jackets or pea coats. The following year, 3,100 intellectually hungry vets crowded into classrooms next to 500 awed youngsters fresh from school. In 1948 Dean Heermance received more than 5,000 applications for only 725 spaces, giving new meaning to the old policy of selective admissions.[76]

Two other appearances on the wartime campus also pointed the way toward Princeton's future, although not until the 1960s. One was the advent of twenty-three civilian women sent by the Army Air Corps to study photogrammetry (mapmaking from aerial photographs) in the Engineering School. Uniformed WACs—members of the Women's Army Corps—also bunked in the hitherto monastic Graduate College as students in the Army Post Exchange School. When an illustrated feature article on the distaff mapmakers appeared in a Newark newspaper, President Dodds was quoted as saying, "While Princeton University did not necessarily believe that women's place was in the home, it certainly did believe that women's place was not in Princeton's classrooms." The "girls," he explained, were there only because Washington had outlawed discrimination in all federal wartime programs.[77]

Under the same auspices, Princeton's first black undergraduates in the twentieth century initially appeared as members of the Navy's

[76] I. L. Kandel, *The Impact of the War upon American Education* (Chapel Hill, 1949; repr. Westport, Conn., 1974), 243–44, 246–48; Nugent, "Changing Faces," 221–22. See also Keith W. Olson, *The G.I. Bill, the Veterans, and the Colleges* (Lexington, Ky., 1974) and Michael J. Bennett, *When Dreams Came True: The G.I. Bill and the Making of Modern America* (Washington, D.C., 1996).

[77] Richard D. Challener, "Princeton and Pearl Harbor: Town and Gown," *Princeton History*, no. 11 (1992):28–65, esp. 51–53, 55. See also Robert K. Root, "The Princeton Campus in World War II" (1950), rev. by Jeremiah Finch (1978), typescript (PUA).

V-12 program in 1945.[78] The V-12 program sent young inductees deemed to have potential to perform advanced technical jobs to college for special training, rather than directly to war. Significantly, the plan, part of the wider Navy College Training Program, was intended to "permit selection of the country's best qualified young men on a broad democratic basis, without regard to financial resources."[79] Of the four African-American sailors who earned a spot in Princeton classes, two stayed on to graduate from the university in 1947: John Howard (who had transferred from Columbia) and Arthur Jewell Wilson '48 (who took an accelerated degree).[80] All four were apparent answers to Frank Broderick's editorial pleas to end "White Supremacy" at Princeton. At least temporarily and in small measure, Princeton was no longer "the last of the leading institutions outside the deep south which still adheres to this faith in racial superiority."[81]

[78] Bruce M. Wright, the first (half-)black undergraduate since 1792, was admitted by mistake in 1936. When he arrived on campus to register, authorities noticed his color and asked him to leave. When he summoned the courage three years later to ask Dean Heermance for an explanation, the dean drew attention to the number of Southern students at the college and suggested that "a member of your race might feel very much alone." Even Robert Wicks, the dean of the Chapel to whom he was sent next, dismissed him brusquely with the warning that "the race problem is beyond solution in America. Don't waste your time fighting the system here. You are butting your head against a stone wall." Probably only the track coach was sorry to see him go: Wright was the New Jersey champion in the mile. Arenson, "Princeton Honors Judge It Once Turned Away;" Maggin, "Smashing Princeton's Color Bar" (online version), 2–5. In 1915 Princeton had also turned down Paul Robeson, the son of the town's former black Presbyterian minister and a star student and athlete, solely because a Negro would not be "happy" at the all-white college. Robert V. Keeley, ed., *Reminiscences of Times Past: The Princeton University of 1947–1951 as Recalled by Members of the Class of 1951 for Their 50th Reunion* (Hagerstown, Md., 2000), 2.

[79] Lemann, *The Big Test*, 55; Kandel, *The Impact of the War*, 153.

[80] Challener, "Princeton and Pearl Harbor," 57; Francis James Dallett (former university archivist), letter to the editor, *PAW*, Nov. 28, 1972, 5. Nugent, "Changing Faces," 224, and Karabel, *The Chosen*, 236, err in dating Wilson's degree to 1948.

[81] "White Supremacy at Princeton," *DP*, Sept. 29, 30, 1942. In 1946 a number of veterans founded the Liberal Union to combat discrimination of all kinds on campus. In 1947 it began a two-year campaign of letter writing and phone calls to encourage blacks and other minorities to apply. Their efforts paid off when three black students enrolled in the fall of 1949, to the chagrin of Dean Heermance. John H. Bunzel '46,

In winning the war against totalitarianism abroad, America was also made to face the incompleteness and inconsistencies of its own democracy. In no area were these more evident than in higher education, especially at places like Princeton. In 1947 a blue-ribbon commission appointed by President Harry S. Truman published a sobering six-volume report entitled *Higher Education for American Democracy.* Citing numerous barriers such as economic disparities, restrictive curricula, and religious and racial discrimination, the commission underlined the urgent need to expand and to equalize educational opportunity to equip Americans for the brave new technocratic world ahead and to realize the national promise of democracy. In boldface the report emphasized that "one of the gravest charges to which American society is subject is that of failing to provide a reasonable equality of educational opportunity for its youth."[82]

As if in direct response to the commission's charge, Princeton instituted a program of Regional Scholarships the following year. "The admissions policy of a great university . . . ," explained Minot Morgan, the director of financial aid, "should be the acceptance of the most likely candidates in terms of their potential contribution as world citizens twenty years after graduation," regardless of address or financial circumstance. One four-year scholarship worth $800–$1,200 a year (depending on the winner's distance from Princeton) was awarded to each of twenty national regions, including parts of Canada. When tuition was only $600 and room, board, and fees between $690 and $775, the scholarships were relatively generous in sum if not number. In the program's second year, only 16 of 744 freshmen were selected for the honor; 13 had attended public high schools. By 1950, as word circulated through alumni and secondary school networks, over a thousand boys competed.[83]

"When Change Began," *PAW,* Mar. 24, 2004, 18, 44; Keeley, ed., *Reminiscences of Times Past,* 2; Maggin, "Smashing Princeton's Color Bar."

[82] President's Commission on Higher Education, *Higher Education for American Democracy,* 6 vols. (Washington, D.C., 1947), 1:27. See also Levine, *The American College,* 215–18; David D. Henry, *Challenges Past, Challenges Present: An Analysis of Higher Education since 1930* (San Francisco, 1975), 55–68.

[83] Minot C. Morgan, "Regional Scholarships Established," *PAW,* Nov. 14, 1947, 8; "Regional Scholarships," *PAW,* Nov. 4, 1949, 6; "Regional Scholars," *PAW,* Oct. 19, 1951, 5–6.

FIGURE 10. Arthur Jewell (Pete) Wilson, Jr., '48 in his Navy uniform as part of the V-12 program. After captaining the basketball team, he completed an accelerated program of study and graduated in 1947.

Despite appearances, Princeton's democratic ambitions were stoked less by federal exhortation than by traditional competition. Princeton had finally assumed the full obligations of a university "in the Nation's Service" during its bicentennial in 1946–1947.[84] The launching of the $20.1-million Third Century Fund, largely to restore to competitiveness badly eroded faculty salaries and support, was also aimed at a million-dollar endowment to enlarge the scholarship pool.[85] The main target of these scholarships was talented high school graduates outside the East, whom Harvard and Yale had begun to recruit in earnest fourteen–twenty years earlier. All three universities were not only seeking national eminence, but acting decisively on a half-century of experience that demonstrated that public school graduates as a group worked harder and performed better than their prep school classmates.

Predicting and selecting the top academic performers had been made easier by major revisions in the College Board exams in 1942. These quickly became the standard instruments for college admissions as well as the awarding of scholarships when, to accommodate mass military use, the SATs went exclusively to multiple-choice questions designed to measure general or "developed" aptitude. At the same time, the Achievement tests ceased to be based on fixed syllabi, favored and followed largely by eastern prep schools, and were redesigned to evaluate broader mastery of subjects and their principles. All of these changes allowed high school students nationwide to shine in open and fair competition. This, in turn, promoted social mobility on an unprecedented scale among the aspiring middle class by enabling their children to attend elite colleges and universities, once the monopoly of the hereditary upper class.[86] From then on, American higher education, particularly its private four-year institutions such as Princeton, would quickly assume the look and

[84] See chapter 2, pp. 88–89.

[85] "Princeton Proposes A Third Century Fund," *PAW*, Nov. 15, 1946, 8–9.

[86] Dunham, "A Look at Princeton Admissions," *PAW*, Jan. 19, 1965, 14; idem, "A Revolution in Admissions," *PAW*, Nov. 15, 1966, 6–7, at 6. After 1954 the National Merit Scholarship Program, financed by corporate sponsors, administered its own test and awarded portable scholarships to thousands of deserving students. Lemann, *The Big Test*, 97–100.

characteristics with which brave applicants and proud alumni are so familiar today.

❁ ❁ ❁

In profile, Princeton's entering class of 2006 reflected the logical development of the university's goals and admission policies that had emerged by the early 1960s. In September 2002, 1,166 freshmen arrived with their formidable cargoes of computers, sound systems, mountain bikes, and anxious parents. Almost half of them were women, nearly a third American racial minorities, 8 percent from abroad. They represented all fifty states (with heavy concentrations from New Jersey, New York, and California) and forty-six foreign countries. Fully half of them, including international students for the first time, had received financial aid, not surprisingly given the $38,000 price tag for the first year. Nine percent of them were the first in their families to attend college. Most of all, they were astonishingly bright: 45 percent of the class were "Academic Ones," those with the strongest academic credentials, in admission office parlance; 149 were National Merit Scholars. A substantial majority had been educated in public high schools. "Tagged" or recruited athletes for Princeton's thirty-eight intercollegiate sports teams comprised nearly one-fifth of the class; 11 percent were legacies. And all were lucky to be there. Fred Hargadon, the dean of admission, had sent fat letters of acceptance (which began, "Yes!") to only one in nine applicants. He could have admitted, he said, two complete classes of identical quality. Given that, and Princeton's number-one placement in *U. S. News & World Report*'s college rankings for three of the previous four years, it is small wonder that nearly three-quarters accepted the university's offer.[87]

[87] Ruth Stevens, "Malkiel: Princeton Has 'Another Extraordinary Year' in Admissions, Financial Aid," *PWB*, Oct. 7, 2002; National Merit Scholarship Corporation, *Annual Report, 2002* (Evanston, Ill., 2003); Marjorie Censer, "Edwards Challenges the Legacy Preference," *DP*, Feb. 3, 2003, 3; "Trustee Committee Recommends Increasing Size of Undergraduate Body," PU, press release, Jan. 31, 2000, 2; PU, *Profile, 2002–2003* (Princeton: Office of Communications, 2002), 8–9.

Princeton's post–World War II emphasis on intellectual firepower in its faculty and graduate students applied increasingly to its undergraduates as well. Spurred on by Cold War competition, the launching of Sputnik into outer space, and the resulting national interest in developing "gifted and talented" baby-boomers, Princeton began to place greater emphasis on an applicant's academic prowess and real excellence in extracurricular activities than on his inchoate and hard-to-read "character." This meant that after 1962, when thirty-year-old E. Alden Dunham, Phi Beta Kappa '53 became dean of admission, Princeton's goals were "diversity" and well-rounded *classes* of pointy achievers, most of whom would remain (in the words of a later dean) "well rounded at a very high level." Diversity—of backgrounds, points of view, and vocational interests—was essential because "there is no need in a residential college to bring together people who are alike." And the development of intellectual talent was a great university's raison d'être, even if many Princeton students thought that Dunham was trying to "out-wonk Harvard." Their fear was largely unwarranted because "Academic Ones" comprised only 12 percent of the classes of 1967 and 1968; nearly as many entered with *non*academic one credentials, such as gifted athletes, journalists, and musicians.[88] But the trend toward brighter and more creative freshmen was discernible, and inexorable, as Princeton's stock rose in the national college market.

In backing Dunham's priorities, a university trustee asserted, perhaps for the first time since Woodrow Wilson stepped down, that "the direction of Princeton's admissions policy must be similar to the direction of the nation."[89] He was referring to—and approving—two signal changes in Princeton's direction. One was a trend away from prep school students, who since 1958 had been outnumbered by high school products.[90] A reduction in prep school numbers was not of

[88] "Special Issue: Admissions at Princeton," *DP*, Oct. 29, 1964, 1, 4–5; Margaret M. Keenan, "Dean Wickenden '61 Looks Back," *PAW*, June 1, 1983, 26–27, at 26. See also Dunham, "A Look at Princeton Admissions," 6–9, 14–15, and "A Revolution in Admissions," 6–7.

[89] "Admissions at Princeton," 5.

[90] Harvard experienced a similar shift to public school students in 1953; Yale remained prep (nonpublic) school heavy until 1963. Penny Hollander Feldman, *Recruiting an*

much consequence because sons of often well-heeled alumni still constituted about 20 percent of the entering classes and a major fundraising campaign had just ended in 1962 that garnered over $59 million, a fair portion of it earmarked for financial aid. This enabled Princeton to put admission decisions on a "need-blind" basis and to take more middle-class high schoolers without fear of future economic consequences.[91]

The trustees, the faculty, and particularly President Robert Goheen (who initiated the idea) were also behind Dunham's recruitment of qualified "Negroes," believing that America's diversity needed to be reflected in Princeton's classes and dorms and that black Americans as well as white should be educated as leaders by elite institutions like Princeton. But attracting black applicants, even without regard for family income, was no easy matter. Princeton had several strikes against it. First, as the "northernmost of the southern colleges" only fifty miles above the Mason-Dixon line, Princeton had an enduring reputation for hostility to blacks, which eating-club behavior and Confederate flags on dorm-room walls did nothing to alleviate. Those who were admitted were more likely to choose "the more liberal atmosphere of the Ivy League colleges farther to the North."[92] Princeton's racist reputation was reinforced in the black community by bitter memories of President Wilson's discouragement of black applicants and, worse, his perpetuation of segregation

---

Elite: Admission to Harvard College (New York, 1988), 70 (which is contradicted by table 3.5 on p. 66); George W. Pierson, *A Yale Book of Numbers: Historical Statistics of the College and University, 1701–1976* (New Haven, 1983), 97–98.

[91] "Admissions at Princeton," 5; Thomas J. Bray, "Admissions Troubles," *PAW*, Apr. 26, 1963, 4; *PAW*, Feb. 23, 1962, 7; Dunham, "A Look at Princeton Admissions," 7. Yale did not move to need-blind admissions until 1966. Geoffrey Kabaservice, *The Guardians: Kingman Brewster, His Circle, and the Rise of the Liberal Establishment* (New York, 2004), 264.

[92] Interview with former president Robert Goheen, in *Looking Back: Reflections of Black Princeton Alumni*, video produced by Melvin McCray '74 and Calvin Norman '77 (Princeton: Association of Black Princeton Alumni, Alumni Council, and Office of the 250th Anniversary, 1997); "Admissions at Princeton," 5, 6; Bray, "Admissions Troubles," 4; Martin Mayer, "How to Get into Princeton," *PAW*, Sept. 28, 1962, 6–9, 14–17, at 9.

and discrimination in the federal government.[93] Moreover, the university was located in a residentially segregated small town, and most of the blacks who Princeton and the other Ivies recruited were city-born and bred.[94] Since underfunded and often segregated inner-city schools were unpromising incubators of scholastic talent, the few stars they produced were fought for by the same socially conscious elite colleges, but faced the daunting prospect of having to play "Jackie Robinson" on the smaller, all-white campuses like Princeton. Finally, recruitment was made all the more difficult because photographs were not allowed on applications, and alumni interviewers were newly sensitized not to use language, even coded, that might suggest racial or ethnic prejudice.

Before President Goheen committed Princeton to meaningful integration in 1963, the admission office received about twenty applications from blacks a year; only a handful of those admitted actually

[93] Charles Puttkammer '58, letter to the editor, *PAW*, Jan. 28, 1964, 3; George Coleman Osborn, "The Problem of the Negro in Government, 1913," *The Historian* 23 (May 1961):330–47; Henry Blumenthal, "Woodrow Wilson and the Race Question," *Journal of Negro History*, 48:1 (Jan. 1963):1–21; Nancy J. Weiss, "The Negro and the New Freedom: Fighting Wilsonian Segregation," *Political Science Quarterly* 84:1 (Mar. 1969):61–79. Growing up in Hampton Roads, Virginia, in the 1910s and early 1920s, longtime Howard University English professor Arthur P. Davis listened to his father's tirade against Wilson while reading the daily newspaper at the family dinner table. "All Negroes of my generation were taught to dislike Woodrow Wilson. It was Wilson, we were told, who turned Princeton back into an all-white school. And, of course, when he became president he put in certain discriminations here [Washington, D.C.]. . . . I have considered it ironic that my father's grandson should be Princeton's first black professor" ("A Washington Life—by Arthur P. Davis, as told to Jill Nelson," *Washington Post Magazine*, July 5, 1987, 26–29, at 29). Of course, there was nothing to "turn back." Only one black had taken a degree, an M.A., before Wilson's presidency, and another did the same in 1906 during it. *PAW*, Nov. 28, 1972, 5. But Davis was right about the irony of Charles Twitchell Davis becoming the first black professor at Princeton: he was appointed an assistant professor of English in 1955 and remained so until 1961, when he moved to Penn State. Charles Twitchell Davis, Faculty File (PUA).

[94] Jessica Ellen Lautin, "That Side of Paradise: A Story of Princeton: The University, the Town, and the African American Community" (Senior thesis, Dept. of History, PU, 2003); Jack Washington, *The Long Journey Home: A Bicentennial History of the Black Community of Princeton, New Jersey, 1776–1976* (Trenton, 2005).

came to brave the social isolation, and a quarter of those left in the first year. Two black freshmen had entered in 1956, only one in 1961. Ten had been persuaded to come in both 1962 and 1963, but by the following year only twelve blacks remained on campus.[95] The arrival in 1964 of Dr. Carl Fields from Teachers College, Columbia, helped turn the situation around. Fields was a product of New York's mean streets, a track star at St. John's University, within walking distance from his Brooklyn home, a decorated Pacific war veteran, and an experienced counselor. As the first black administrator ever hired by Princeton, initially in the Bureau of Student Aid and then as Assistant Dean of the College, he negotiated Princeton's civil, liberal, but tough-minded bureaucracy with tact and forceful conviction to ease the difficult transition of its black recruits and to increase their feeling of belonging to and ownership of the university.

One of his first acts was to stop the well-intentioned assignment of black freshmen to single rooms, which had only increased their isolation. He brought the estranged black town and gown together by establishing a Family Sponsor program to provide each black student with a supportive local black family, who may have known the university only as a low-wage employer and its students only as stereotypical superior rich kids. He convinced the admission office to broaden its qualifying criteria to include the "work experience" of surviving difficult environments and racism. In 1967 he helped forty of Princeton's forty-five black undergraduates to form an Association of Black Collegians (ABC) for mutual support in retaining black identities while meeting Princeton's high academic demands and social pressures. That year the group sponsored a conference on "The Future of the Black Undergraduate," which drew participants from forty-one colleges and universities; the following year, to honor the memory of Martin Luther King, Jr., representatives from fifty institutions attended a conference on "Black Awareness," whose

[95] In 1964 Princeton had fifteen black undergraduates sponsored by the African Scholarship Program for African Students; ten majored in engineering and most of the rest in the physical sciences. They were as culturally strange to the African Americans as the inner-city blacks were to them. Donald L. Fitzhugh, Jr., "The Africans Speak," *PAW*, Feb. 11, 1964, 8–11, 14.

twenty-eight ABC-led seminars did much to educate white Princetonians about America's second-oldest problem. Subsequently, Fields enlisted the ABC to conduct a special orientation for all minority students each September to familiarize them with Princeton's distinctive features, ethos, and expectations. He also persuaded the university to establish a Frederick Douglass Award for outstanding service to the university by a graduating black senior and to present it on Class Day before Commencement. And before Fields left for another path-breaking post at the University of Zambia in 1971, he witnessed the founding of an Afro-American Studies Program and oversaw the establishment of a Third World Center (now appropriately renamed the Carl A. Fields Center for Equality and Cultural Understanding) in a converted field house as a gathering place for Princeton's growing minority population.[96]

❁ ❁ ❁

Another cardinal direction in which American society was headed during the 1960s was toward women's rights, and Princeton re-

[96] Carl A. Fields, "One University's Response to Today's Negro Student," *PAW*, Mar. 12, 1968, 26–31; idem, "The Black Arrival at Princeton," *PAW*, Apr. 18, 1977, 11–19; idem, "A Time of Adjustment," *PAW*, Apr. 25, 1977, 15–20; "Princeton Portrait: Carl A. Fields," *PAW*, Oct. 21, 1969, 9; "ABC's Ministry," *PAW*, Apr. 30, 1968, 13–15, 18. When sufficient numbers of qualified black students could not be found or developed quickly enough, Ivy League admissions officers turned to other underrepresented American minority groups. Increased immigration from Southeast Asia in the 1970s and 1980s brought an increase in applications from second-generation Asian-Americans. By 1985, when Princeton admitted 193, some questioned whether Asians were being discriminated against in the admissions process, not unlike Jews in the 1920s and 1930s. A study at Princeton showed that Asians were admitted at a rate slightly below that of all applicants, largely because they tended to lack nonacademic breadth and the vast majority intended to major in math, science, or engineering. But if the category of "special preferences" (legacies, athletes, and blacks), in which Asians were underrepresented, was discounted, Asian-Americans were admitted at a higher rate than that of the remaining whites in the applicant pool. The issue persists. In 2004 only 15 percent of American undergraduates were of Asian descent; 3 of 40 trustees were Asian-American. Michael Winerip, "Asian-Americans Question Ivy League's Entry Policies," *New York Times*, May 30, 1985, B1, B4; "Admissions Policies Unfair to Asians," *DP* (online), Nov. 29, 2004.

sponded at the same time it began to address the civil rights and educational needs of black Americans. President Goheen, the husband of a Vassar graduate and father of four young daughters (and one son), took the lead also in moving Princeton toward the education of women. As late as 1964, however, he had thought that "Princeton doesn't have any social problems coeducation would cure."[97] But the times would not hold still and evidence of both social and academic problems at Princeton mounted. In January 1965, for example, the *Daily Princetonian* devoted a feature article and an editorial to documenting "the profound unhealthiness of the Princeton undergraduate's social life with women," restricted as it was to superficial, orgiastic weekends.[98] During the rest of the week, the editors complained, monastic study was his primary "business" (as the president liked to call it), which led to "abstention, frustration, and unhappiness." Coeducation, they were certain, was "the solution for Princeton's social illness," as arch-rival Yale had come to realize already.[99]

[97] Robert F. Goheen, quoted in *Time*, Jan. 15, 1965, 36. Within a month Goheen admitted that "coeducation would solve some problems, but it would also create many" ("Dr. Goheen Rejects Coeds at Princeton in Spite of Pleas," *New York Times*, Feb. 8, 1965, 27).

[98] Daniel N. White '65 reminded his classmates about "Lust and Love at Pre-Coed Princeton" in their 25th-reunion book and *PAW*, May 15, 1991, 63–64; reprinted in *Best of PAW*, 281–83.

[99] "Commitment to Coeducation," *DP*, Jan. 8, 1965, 3; reprinted in *The Prince Remembers: One Hundred Years of* The Daily Princetonian, ed. Judy Piper Schmitt (Princeton, 1977), 145–46. To put its money where its mouth was, the *Princetonian* board soon offered $500 toward coeducation. To which Goheen's response was, "the university's first responsibility lies in educating men; taking in a thousand women would use up classroom seats that should be filled by men" (Dorrit Ann Cowan, "Single-Sex to Coeducation at Princeton and Yale: Two Case Studies" [Ed.D. diss., Teachers College, Columbia University, 1982], 88; "The Princetonian Gives $500 for Coeducation," *New York Times*, Mar. 10, 1965, 43). See also Marcia Synott, "A Friendly Rivalry: Yale and Princeton Pursue Parallel Paths to Coeducation," in Leslie Miller-Bernal and Susan L. Poulson, eds., *Going Coed: Women's Experiences in Formerly Men's Colleges and Universities, 1950–2000* (Nashville, 2004), 111–50. Undergraduate dissatisfaction with Princeton's social life was not a recent phenomenon. From 1902 on, the *Nassau Herald* senior poll asked "If you ran Princeton. . . . " Consistently, the graduates' favorite answer by far was "Make it co-ed." See, for example, *Nassau Herald*s for 1902 (122), 1916 (366), 1942 (607), and 1950 (n. p.). By 1967 half of the student body said they wanted coeducation so badly that they were willing to see Princeton divert funds from existing projects or

The university's adults concurred, though for different reasons. Although Princeton got its share of the top students in the country, the dean of admission and the faculty were unhappy that perhaps only half of each class were "absolutely first-rate" and that a third of those admitted chose rival colleges. "These students," Dean Dunham testified, "all too often are the very people we want most. There is no doubt whatsoever in my mind," he concluded, "that coeducation is very much a factor in their decision not to attend Princeton." Three-quarters of the faculty, especially its younger members, were likewise convinced that coeds would help attract the best-qualified male students and would enhance the intellectual life of the university for all.[100]

By 1966, Nassau Hall began to give coeducation in some form "high priority amid many other concerns." At that juncture, Goheen thought that a coordinate women's college across Lake Carnegie would suit Princeton best, if a hefty eight-figure gift would materialize.[101] A quiet and mismatched courtship of Sarah Lawrence, the once-"progressive" women's college in Bronxville, New York, began the following spring. But by June the college had dismissed Princeton's overtures (as Vassar was about to spurn Yale) in favor of retaining its own identity and preventing its 550 women from being swallowed up by 4,050 hungry Tigers.[102]

---

admit fewer males. John V. Dippel, "On the Campus: The Coeducation Study," *PAW*, Dec. 5, 1967, 6, 11–12, at 12.

[100] "The Education of Women at Princeton: A Special Report," *PAW*, Sept. 24, 1968, 8, 12.

[101] Nugent, "Changing Faces," 230–31; William McCleery, "An Informal Call on Princeton's Robert F. Goheen in His 10th Year as President," *University: A Princeton Quarterly*, no. 31 (Winter 1966–67):6–14, at 7–8; also in *PAW*, Dec. 6, 1966, 18–26, at 19–20; "Vassar to Yale?" *PAW*, Jan. 17, 1967, 4. At different times $80 million and $40 million were mentioned, without any firm basis. Inflation was always a factor. In an April Fool's issue in 1927, the *Daily Princetonian* ran an article entitled "Princeton Gets $20,000,000 to Become Co-Educational." The bequest of "Nettie Green" was to have built Gothic-style dorms "southeast of the Baker Memorial Rink" for four hundred women. Cowan, "Single-Sex to Coeducation at Princeton," 91, 125.

[102] Merrill Folsom, "Sarah Lawrence Declines Merger," *New York Times*, June 3, 1967, 33; Barbara A. Foote (former Vassar trustee), "A Royal Marriage," *Vassar: The Alumnae/i Quarterly* (Winter 2004), Extras (http://www.aavc.vassar.edu/vq/winter 2004/extras_foote.html).

Apparently Princeton had forgotten that it once had an "affiliated" college for women just down Nassau Street. From 1887 to 1897, Evelyn College borrowed faculty, trustees, libraries, labs, museums, curricula, exams, and standards from Princeton. Its three or four dozen students were largely the daughters of Princeton and Seminary faculty and the sisters of Princeton undergraduates, and its standards were acknowledged to be as high as Barnard's or Radcliffe's. Although the traditional education it gave was virtually a carbon copy of its male neighbor's, Princeton would not award the young women a Princeton degree until its endowment and future were more secure, which they never were. But Goheen might have taken counsel from a female supporter of Evelyn who wrote in *Harper's Bazaar* that "it is possible and probable that coeducation will be the system of the future" and that an affiliated college was but a temporary substitute for the real thing.[103]

In May 1967, in the midst of his unpublicized pursuit of Sarah Lawrence, Goheen surprised the campus by announcing in the student paper that "It is inevitable that, at some point in the future, Princeton is going to move into the education of women. The only questions now are those of strategy, priority, and timing." The decision was made, he later recalled, "not because we [in Nassau Hall] felt pressure from the *Daily Princetonian*, nor the students, nor faculty, but because of our assessment that American society had changed and was changing" and that it was simply "anachronistic that Princeton limited itself only to the education of men." Princeton could no longer "ignore the educational needs of one half of the human race." The main consideration, he told the *Princetonian*—the *Prince*—was not the amelioration of the undergraduates' "warped" social life, but "what Princeton could offer to women in

[103] Adaline W. Sterling, "Evelyn College," *Harper's Bazaar* 29 (Sept. 26, 1896):806–7; Francis P. Healy, "Notes on Evelyn College," *PULC*, 52:1 (Autumn 1990):139–45; Healy, "A History of Evelyn College for Women, Princeton, New Jersey, 1887 to 1897" (Ph.D. diss., Ohio State University, 1967); Molly Murdoch, "Evelyn College Was State's First for Women," *Princeton Recollector* 1:8 (Feb. 1976):17–19; Catherine Keyser '01, *Transforming the Tiger: A Celebration of Undergraduate Women at Princeton University* (Princeton, 2001), 1–6.

higher educational opportunity and what women could bring to the intellectual and the entire life of Princeton."[104]

Having taken the plunge in womanly waters, Goheen appointed a faculty-administration committee under the chairmanship of economist Gardner Patterson to study the strategy, timing, and costs of going coed. This Princeton blueprint, completed in July 1968, was so thorough and competent that other universities contemplating coeducation, especially Yale, used it to speed up the process. But everyone knew that Princeton's alumni would provide the most resistance to the introduction of the opposite sex to their halcyon-dazed alma mater. So the administration published the full Patterson Report in the alumni magazine in September and dispatched administrators, faculty, and students to meet alumni groups in twenty-six locations across the country throughout the fall. In the meantime, at the end of November, the faculty voted overwhelmingly for coeducation, and John Davies '41, the colorful editor of the *Alumni Weekly*, devoted his first editorial in fourteen years to "Coeducation—A Self-Evident Conclusion." "A hangover from the Victorian era," he gibed, "all-male education now appears a sort of dinosaur or dodo, irrelevant to the interests of modern life. . . . Perhaps a few 'Gothic' non-coeducational institutions will live on, but like zombies they will be dead but not know it."[105]

[104] Robert Durkee, "Goheen: 'Coeducation is Inevitable,' " *DP*, May 17, 1967, 1; "A President Recalls Coeducation," *DP*, Apr. 13, 1989, 1; Luther Munford, "Anatomy of a Decision," *PAW*, Nov. 11, 1969, 8–12, 18; a longer version appeared as "Coeducation at Princeton: The Struggle of an Idea at a University in Transition," *DP*, Oct. 21, 1969, 5–14. Goheen was also not unmindful that as Princeton received more research funding from the federal government, federal regulation would very likely mandate equal opportunity for women and minorities. Only a year after Princeton went coed, federal guidelines did just that. In 1972 Title IX of the Education Amendment came down even harder on sex discrimination. Cowan, "Single-Sex to Coeducation at Princeton," 121–23; Albert A. Logan, Jr., "Federal Guidelines: Universities Told They Must Grant Equal Opportunity to Women," *CHE*, July 6, 1970, 5; Margaret C. Dunkle and Bernice Sandler, *Sex Discrimination Against Students: Implications of Title IX on the Education Amendments of 1972* (Washington, D.C., 1974).

[105] "The Education of Women at Princeton;" "Trustees' Statement on Coeducation [Jan. 12, 1969]," *PAW*, Jan. 21, 1969, 12–13; "Coeducation Endorsed," *PAW*, Nov. 26, 1968, 7; "Coeducation—A Self-evident Conclusion," *PAW*, Nov. 26, 1968, 11.

The following January, the trustees made what they described as "the largest single decision that has faced Princeton in this century," committing the university to full coeducation. They were persuaded, they said, by the faculty and by alumni who worked in education that "the educational experience is improved and serves better to prepare students for the late 20th century world when it is carried out in mixed, rather than single-sex circumstances." They had also noticed that "all over the world higher education has moved away from the older, mono-sexual lines of evolution." And although never mentioned, it was not lost on the board that their Yale counterparts had declared for coeducation two months earlier.[106]

Yet the crucial question of when coeducation would actually begin had not been settled. To exert some pressure on the administration and to get a small taste of academic women during the week, the undergraduates organized a "Coed Week" in early February, again following Yale precedent. When nearly eight hundred women from thirty colleges descended on Princeton to occupy rooms chivalrously vacated by their male occupants, they were met by a seven-inch snowstorm, flowered toilet paper in the johns, and a packed schedule of classes, parties, and educational entertainment. Campus reactions to the experiment were predictably favorable. The *Daily Princetonian* observed that "for one week Princeton was a more humane place to go to school. . . . The whole campus seemed more natural." One of the organizers predicted that "Princeton will be the greatest school in the country once it is coeducational." Neil Rudenstine, the dean of students, thought the experiment was a great success, but scratched his head over the female need for full-length mirrors.[107]

One group of women viewed the proceedings with a mixture of amusement and anticipation.[108] Sixteen exceptional young women from a variety of liberal arts colleges were spending their junior year at Princeton in a Cold War–inspired, Carnegie Corporation–funded

[106] "Trustees' Statement on Coeducation," 12–13; Munford, "Anatomy of a Decision," 12.

[107] Keyser, *Transforming the Tiger*, 21–25.

[108] Holly Hoffmeister, "Princeton's Longest Mixer: Critters Laugh While Coeds Take Over," *DP*, Feb. 13, 1969, 1.

FIGURE 11. A bedtime portrait of the Critical Language coeds of 1967–68, in their Victorian residence on Library Place.

Cooperative Undergraduate Program for Critical Languages. They were there to learn the languages (and associated histories and cultures) of "critical" parts of the globe that America needed to know and Princeton had special competence to teach, such as Chinese, Russian, Arabic, Turkish, and Persian. Along with several male counterparts, female "Critters" (as they were affectionately known) had been a small but steady presence on the Princeton campus since 1963, when the first five made their well-publicized appearance. While the men roomed in Wilcox Hall, where the whole group ate, the women biked or hiked from a large Victorian house near the seminary until the last few classes moved into the new Graduate College quadrangle even farther from campus.

Too few to foment a social revolution, the female linguists did enjoy full weekends with undergraduates who were lucky or brazen enough to preempt the competition. They also earned their way into several extracurricular activities. Sue Jean Lee '70 became the first member of a Triangle Club cast who did not have to cross-dress to play a female role. Others wrote humor for the *Tiger* and features for the *Prince*, hosted a radio show on WPRB, represented off-campus residents in the student assembly, and played club hockey with the men. A few integrated eating clubs before blacks did, though Judy Corrente '70, who, ironically, had helped plan Coed Week, lost a bid to Quadrangle by two votes. Despite a 214-to-1 demographic disadvantage, the Critters constituted for Princeton what the university band called "an annual concession to inevitability" and others regarded hopefully as the "Trojan Horse" of full coeducation. If they gave the egregiously male campus only a small taste of what it was like to live and learn with smart women full-time, it was a flavor that lasted.[109]

As word spread that Princeton was going coed in the near but indefinite future, applications from women poured into the admission office. (Based on much less hope, male applications dropped below the previous year's total, when Princeton was the only Ivy League school to show a decline.)[110] Over five hundred eager young women applied, unsolicited, without interviews, and with no guarantee that any women would be admitted or, if they were, that coed classes would begin in the fall. But they were and they did after the trustees voted on April 21 to accelerate the process, which news prompted the campus radio station to play the "Hallelujah Chorus" at full volume. Their 24–8 vote was prompted by an anonymous $4 million gift from trustee Laurance S. Rockefeller '32 and the purchase of the largely university-owned Princeton Inn for use as a dorm to help absorb the 171 first-year women and their more numerous successors.[111]

Princeton's newest class of coeds was impressive by any measure. They consisted of 101 freshmen (chosen from 505 applicants), 49 upperclass transfers, and 21 former and current Critters. Among them

[109] Dale Lasater, "Five Girls Break Sacred All-Male Tradition," *DP*, Sept. 23, 1963, 1, 3; Martha L. Lamar, "Problems of Critical Languages," *PAW*, Nov. 16, 1965, 10–12; "With the Ladies," *PAW*, Oct. 17, 1967, 7, 15; Jane Steinberg, "214 to 1: Junior Year at Princeton . . . ," *Mademoiselle* 68 (Apr. 1969):232–33, 295–98; Cowan, "Single-Sex to Coeducation at Princeton," 80–84.

[110] "Coeducation Issue," *PAW*, Feb. 4, 1969, 4. With the definite advent of women, male applications shot up 13 percent in 1970. William G. Bowen, *Report of the President: Coeducation at Princeton* (1980), 6; also in *PAW*, Apr. 21, 1980.

[111] "Plans for Coeducation," *PAW*, May 6, 1969, 8–10, 15.

were 22 legacies, 1 Asian American, and 6 African Americans, most of whom had to be recruited late in the process. Forty-nine were given financial aid, some of which came from a new scholarship fund for women endowed by a family whose sophomore son had recently died in a fall. The brains and talent of these pioneers ran deep. Their verbal SATs were forty-six points higher than the men's, their Achievements fifteen points. And they brought the same daunting array of athletic, community, and extracurricular accomplishments as the men. Even New Jersey's Miss Bikini was a straight-A student, recipient of a National Merit commendation, editor of her school literary magazine, president of the drama club, and a finalist in a state oratorical contest.[112]

Not only Princeton men awaited the large-scale advent of undergraduate women. From their Gothic aerie overlooking the golf course, 123 female graduate students had cheered and been cheered by the admission news; more than 200 were in residence as the junior coeds moved into Pyne Hall in the glare of national media coverage. But Princeton's graduate women were themselves relative newcomers. The first—and only—woman admitted in 1961 was regarded by the Graduate School as an exception, not a precedent, and she was indeed different from most graduate students. Sabra Meservy, Phi Beta Kappa graduate of Barnard, Columbia M.A., faculty wife, and mother of three, taught at Douglass College, Rutgers's women's college, after spending three years in Turkey. Her dissertation on Turkish history earned her a Ph.D. in 1966, two years after T'sai-ying Cheng of China took home Princeton's first female doctorate for her work in biochemistry.[113] Yet once the female foot was in the door, it could not be dislodged without a betrayal of principle and a public relations disaster.

Princeton risked neither in the fall of 1969 when it opened its arms, if not soul, to 171 women undergraduates.[114] While Yale was

[112] Keyser, *Transforming the Tiger*, 27–28; "Plans for Coeducation," 10; "Scholarship for Women," *PAW*, June 10, 1969, 5; *PAW*, Sept. 23, 1969, 3 (Miss Bikini), 4 (Class of '73).

[113] Cowan, "Single-Sex to Coeducation at Princeton," 84; Thorp, *PGS*, 286–89, 303–5, 327–29; chapter 7, p. 420.

[114] Jane Leifer '73, "Trials of the Coed 100," *PAW*, May 29, 1973, 8–11, at 9.

preparing to stage its own coed reception, Princeton did its gallant best to welcome the first female members of the classes of 1970 to 1973. The administration installed thirty-one-year-old Halcyone Bohen (Smith B.A., Radcliffe M.A.T.) as Assistant Dean of Students to oversee the transition, security locks on Pyne Hall, more lights on walkways, and doors on toilet stalls. They replaced seven-foot male-sized beds with six-foot daybeds, moved in extra wardrobes, and furnished every room with matching bedspreads, curtains, and bolsters (which earned mixed reviews). Little could be done initially about the spring-loaded toilet seats, but manly efforts were made to outfit more ladies' rooms around campus, particularly in the library, and to find locker rooms, uniforms, and practice times for athletes and suitable classes in physical education.[115] The warmest welcome, however, came during the opening freshman assembly in Alexander Hall. A local alumnus who had originally opposed coeducation gave each woman a chrysanthemum and had a poem read in their honor. Most of the recipients were delighted; a few resented it because it marked them as different when all they wanted was to be themselves, "Princeton students, not Princeton phenomena."[116]

Becoming just Princeton students was a slow but steady process for the next four years and beyond. It was helped along the following year when the women fled their Pyne Hall "ghetto," settled into thirteen different dorms alongside the men, and were reinforced by

[115] "Princeton Portrait: Halcyone H. Bohen," *PAW*, Sept. 30, 1969, 7; "Altering Pyne," *PAW*, Sept. 23, 1969, 4; Mary L. Azoy '71, "Notes on Coeducation: A Princeton Woman's Impressions," *PAW*, Oct. 14, 1969, 10–13; Leifer, "Trials of the Coed 100," 8–9; Kirsten Bibbins, Anne Chiang, and Heather Stephenson, eds., *Women Reflect About Princeton* (Princeton: Office of Communications/Publications, 1989), 16, 19, 27, 50. Although modern dance had been available for physical education credit before coeducation, the advent of women gave it a major boost. In 1969 the dynamic Israeli-born, Julliard-trained dancer Ze'eva Cohen joined the Creative Arts Program and put modern dance on the Princeton curricular map for both men and women. In response to the first call for those interested in a dance program, ten women and fifty men appeared. Sydney T. Neuwirth, "Dance, Dance, Dance . . . ," *PAW*, Oct. 22, 1974, 10–11; Caroline Moseley, "Mind, Body, Spirit: On the Boards with Choreographer Ze'eva Cohen," *PAW*, May 11, 1994, 16–23; "Dancing into Life," *Princeton: With One Accord* (Spring 1997):8.

[116] Azoy, "Notes on Coeducation," 11; Leifer, "Trials of the Coed 100," 9.

nearly three hundred more sisters. When the trustees removed their modest female quota and instituted an "equal access" policy in 1974, true parity was at least possible. When all but three eating clubs opened their doors and tables, the women could detect a large crack in Princeton's masculine carapace.[117] But women may have won the struggle for acceptance not in the classroom (where as a group they continued to outperform the men) but on the playing fields of intercollegiate athletics.

Claiming the Pyne Prize for outstanding senior in 1973 and valedictorian and salutatorian honors in 1975 was proof positive of women's academic capacity.[118] But the Ivy League and NCAA titles they won during the next few years melted many a flinty alumnus heart and captured the attention of more than a few male classmates. After only four years on campus, Princeton women had fielded undefeated teams in tennis, squash, and swimming, and women's crew had set a national record in winning the Eastern championship. Margie Gengler '73, captain of the undefeated tennis team, never dropped a set in her intercollegiate career. In 1974, the basketball team won the Ivies, the swimmers and the tennis team took the Easterns, and the sailing and squash teams were national champions. Juniors Carol Brown and Janet Youngholm took home the national crown in pairs rowing. Two slim dynamos, Emily Goodfellow '76 and Amie Knox '77, were the first Princeton athletes to win twelve varsity letters.[119]

[117] By 1973, 17 percent of the women belonged to eating clubs. Leifer, "Trials of the Coed 100," 10, 11; John M. Fenton, "Coeducation: An Interim Report," *PAW*, Nov. 24, 1970, 6–9, at 7.

[118] Keyser, *Transforming the Tiger*, 31, 37–38; Bowen, *Report of the President (1980)*, 10. In 1973 Princeton's first four-year coed class graduated 93 members of Phi Beta Kappa; 30 (32 percent) were women, who constituted only 18 percent of the class. *PAW*, July 3, 1973, 8.

[119] Alexander Leitch, *A Princeton Companion* (Princeton, 1978), 530; Leifer, "Trials of the Coed 100," 11; Leslie Aldridge Westoff, "U.S. Women Excel in Sports (Especially at Princeton)," *University: A Princeton Quarterly*, no. 63 (Winter 1975):20–24, also in *PAW*, Feb. 25, 1975, and *Best of PAW*, 361–64; Keyser, *Transforming the Tiger*, 65–70; Dan White, "A White Sweater for Ms. Gengler," *PAW*, May 1, 1973, 20–22; Cathy Wolf, "The 12-Letter Winner," *PAW*, May 17, 1976, 14; Stephen R. Dujack, "Amie Knox, 12-Letter Winner," *PAW*, May 30, 1977, 14. For women's athletic performances before 1980, see Bowen, *Report of the President (1980)*, 23–24.

Despite the prominence of their academic and athletic successes, some Princeton women believed that they were asked to "fit into the existing culture," as one pioneer said, "and there was nothing that changed to accommodate them." The expectation, another added, was that women could simply be added to the traditional university and nothing essential about Princeton would have to change.[120] But Princeton did change, and in ways that not only accommodated the special needs of women but improved the whole university.

As the Patterson Report had predicted, women initially tended toward majors in the humanities and "softer" social sciences, such as history and psychology. This concentration had the salutary effect of balancing the academic divisions, which had developed a top-heavy prominence in the sciences and engineering. Women in the classroom not only showed no reticence about speaking up, they increased "the variety of viewpoints expressed" and "the methods of attacking problems." "Their skepticism about the received wisdom, their quest for clarity, their advocacy of a more generous moral vision," sociologist Marvin Bressler testified, "have introduced a welcome dimension . . . which was less prominent before the advent of coeducation." In the considered opinion of the faculty, "*overall* academic performance has been improved through the addition of women."[121]

Consonant with the expansion of women's roles and importance in American society, women students and faculty demanded greater attention to the issues of both male and female gender and sex roles, past and present, not only in specialized "women's studies" courses but in disciplines virtually across the curriculum, including the "objective" sciences. In 1976 an interdisciplinary Faculty Committee on Women's Studies was formed to promote the study of these larger questions and to develop curricular offerings. Six years later, a formal Women's Studies Program was formed under the direction of anthropologist Kay Warren *74. By that time more than two hundred senior theses on women-related themes had been written, giving credence and some urgency to the ongoing need for (but cautiously

[120] Bibbins, Chiang, and Stephenson, *Women Reflect About Princeton*, 160, 162.

[121] Bowen, *Report of the President (1980)*, 11–15 (Patterson), 19 (Bressler); Karen Sullivan, "Are Princeton's Women Afraid of Economics?" *PAW*, May 8, 1973, 12–13; Keyser, *Transforming the Tiger*, 41 (my emphasis).

slow hiring and tenure of) more female faculty. Research materials were not hard to find. Firestone Library's card catalogue alone had nine drawers devoted to "woman" or "women." And the 1979 acquisition of the Miriam Y. Holden Collection on Women's History brought six thousand additional volumes and related photographs, clippings, periodicals, and manuscripts, making Princeton one of the four richest repositories for women's history in the country.[122]

All these developments took place as feminism and "sexual politics" were agitating boardrooms, bedrooms, and faculty meetings across the country. The activists' goal (and not all women at Princeton or elsewhere were activists by any means) was not patronizing tokens or gestures, but wholesale adjustments of male attitudes and full parity of opportunity, power, and pay. On the Princeton campus, two innovations in 1971 signaled the administration's readiness to address women's issues and grievances. The first was the addition of two alumni daughters and wives to the historically all-male Board of Trustees, followed two years later by Marsha H. Levy '73, Pyne Prize–winner and first alumna trustee.[123] The creation of a Women's Center, initially in Green Hall Annex, created a space where graduates and undergraduates could meet to articulate a different vision of what a coeducational university could be, however discomfiting it might be to some adolescent males and tradition-bound alumni. Women met largely to heighten male and female sensitivity to sexist attitudes and behavior and to lobby the administration for improved female services at the health center, including birth control and abortion, and for increased safety on campus. In December 1981 Center activists organized the first "Take Back the Night" march to highlight the dangers to women on a male-majority campus, particularly rape and sexual harassment.[124]

[122] Margaret M. Keenan, "The Controversy over Women's Studies," *PAW*, Apr. 21, 1980, 12–15, 17–18; Keyser, *Transforming the Tiger*, 45–48; Bibbins, Chiang, and Stephenson, *Women Reflect About Princeton*, 97–108; Ann Waldron, "The Holden Collection on Women's History," *PAW*, Apr. 21, 1980, 16; Bowen, *Report of the President (1980)*, 18.

[123] Leitch, *Princeton Companion*, 482, 530; Bowen, *Report of the President (1980)*, 30.

[124] Bibbins, Chiang, and Stephenson, *Women Reflect About Princeton*, 109–24; Keyser, *Transforming the Tiger*, 57–64, 73–74; Marc Fisher '80, "On the Campus: SECHual Politics," *PAW*, Nov. 5, 1979, 18; brief version in *Best of PAW*, 311–12.

Although Princeton attended to the wants and needs of its women students as well and as fast as it could, given a host of counterpressures and constraints, it had few doubts that coeducation was an institutional blessing. In the tenth anniversary year of coeducation, President William Bowen devoted his annual report to a lucid assessment of the changes wrought. Graduate and undergraduate women were still outnumbered by their male classmates, but the gaps were narrowing and women had achieved virtual parity in leadership, scholarship, and athletics. Bowen vouched for the "near universal agreement that coeducation has led to a dramatic improvement in the general quality of academic life at Princeton." Speaking for the faculty, Albert Sonnenfeld, chairman of Romance Languages and Literatures and former master of Princeton Inn (now Forbes) College, held that "coeducation has not only been a positive influence on all aspects of Princeton University life, it has been the essential factor in making Princeton the most attractive place in the country not only for students but for faculty." Historian Charles Gillispie was even more positive. He had no doubt that coeducation was "the best thing that has happened to Princeton since [its founding in] 1746."[125]

Of course, there were alumni who disagreed; Princeton women felt then and still feel now the heavy hand of "tradition."[126] But as early as 1980, Bowen was among many for whom Princeton was "not so much an all-male institution that has become coeducational, as a coeducational institution that once was all-male." Perhaps that change in outlook had no better expression than that of a female

[125] Bowen, *Report of the President (1980)*, 3, 18, 22–23.

[126] Kruti Trivedi '00, "Muscling Aside the Men," *PAW*, Mar. 10, 1999, 9. In 1934, University of Chicago president Robert Maynard Hutchins maintained that "all alumni are dangerous. They see their Alma Mater through a rosy haze that gets thicker with the years. They do not know what the college was really like. They do not want to know what it is like now. They want to imagine that it is like what they think it was like in their time. Therefore they oppose all change. . . . The more sentimental an alumnus is, the more dangerous he is" (Hutchins, "The Sentimental Alumnus," in *No Friendly Voice* [Chicago, 1936], 87–94, at 87). Largely because of the frequent publication of the *PAW* (27 issues a year in 1977, 21 in 1980, 17 in 1988, 16 of late), Princeton alumni may be better informed and less dangerous. *Best of PAW*, vii.

member of the class of 1974. When asked by a preceptor for "the coed's point of view" on a point of discussion, she responded coolly and without pause, "Why look at me? We're all coeds now."[127]

❁ ❁ ❁

Once the racial and gender composition of Princeton's entering classes began to resemble the national population as a whole, the university could only strive to increase their overall quality. With only minor pauses, it has drawn ever more highly qualified classes since the 1960s, so steadily that many alumni are haunted by the proud but disturbing thought that they might no longer be admitted to alma mater. Because of its statistical odds (about one in ten today), the new version of selective admissions is even more daunting than the first. And because the Committee on Admissions continues to make individual choices based on human judgment, the process is no more transparent. Although the admission office eschews "quotas" per se, even benevolent ones, it does select classes with a number of agreed needs and goals in mind.

In 1979, Dean James Wickenden, Jr., '61 reminded alumni (as his predecessor had in 1965) that "the Admission Committee could—if there were marked changes in policy—build a qualified class quite dissimilar to the one that now enters Princeton." Every year the committee must somehow balance the institution's desire for academic stars, extracurricular talent, competitive athletes for nearly forty teams, ethnic and racial diversity, engineers, and legacies whose "personal attachments . . . to Princeton's history and traditions" can benefit their classmates (and later the university's endowment fund).[128] In the last quarter-century, it has largely maintained the same balance, making only small adjustments mostly to augment the number of women and minorities and to satisfy the faculty's call for more academically gifted students to elevate their classes.

[127] Bowen, *Report of the President (1980)*, 3; Keyser, *Transforming the Tiger*, 33, quoting the 1974 *Bric-a-Brac*.

[128] "To: All Princeton Alumni, From: James W. Wickenden, Jr. '61, Director of Admissions, October 1979," four-page insert in *PAW*, Oct. 5, 1979, between 18 and 19, p. 3; Dunham, "A Look at Princeton Admissions," *PAW*, Jan. 19, 1965, 7.

The task of the admission office has also shifted subtly from passive selection to active recruitment. As high school seniors have applied to more and more colleges to hedge their bets against falling acceptance rates (caused in part by those multiple applications) at most elite institutions, Princeton has had to rev up its traditionally competitive drive to recruit the best students not only nationally but globally and to devise ways to increase its "yield" of applicants, particularly Academic Ones, who have been accepted by both Princeton and its major rivals. Princeton's geographical reach is evident in the falling percentage of freshmen drawn from the surrounding three-state region and the increase in international students. In the early 1970s, half of the entering classes haled from the immediate region. By 1998, only a third did; Pennsylvania had been supplanted by California as the third-highest contributor and the five westernmost states (including Alaska and Hawaii) sent over 11 percent of the class. Foreign students, only thirteen of whom had matriculated in 1955, contributed between 8 and 9 percent of much larger classes from the late 1990s on.[129]

Recruiting literally around the world, Princeton has increased the quality of its freshman classes significantly since the late 1950s. Its acceptance rate—which suggests just how choosy the university can be in its search for talent—fell from 41 percent to 24 percent by 1965, seven more points by 1985, to 11.3 percent in its 250th year.[130] As just one measure of the entering classes' growing quality, their average SAT scores went from a combined 1198 in 1950 to 1316 in just ten years.[131] By 1978 they had slipped (as scores had nationally) to 1307,

[129] *Report of the Undergraduate Admission Study Group* (1998), 2–3 (see also Wes Tooke '98, "Study Group Looks at Admissions," *PAW*, Nov. 18, 1998, 4–6); *PAW*, Oct. 9, 1996, 6; Sept. 9, 1998, 64; Oct. 11, 2000, 9; *Facts about Princeton* (Princeton: Dept. of Public Information, Sept. 15, 1955); Stevens, "Malkiel," *PWB*, Oct. 7, 2002.

[130] PU, *A Report Prepared for the Middle States Association of Colleges and Secondary Schools Commission on Institutions of Higher Education* (1961), 20, Hist. Subj. Files, #A-109, box 200 (PUA); Dunham, "A Look at Princeton Admissions," 9; *PAW*, Oct. 9, 1985, 22; Oct. 9, 1996, 6.

[131] Even after pronounced improvement, a visiting member of the Middle States Association accrediting team in 1961 declared that "three-fourths of the students admitted are excellent; the other quarter are no better than average" (*Report of the Middle States Association* [*of Colleges and Secondary Schools*] *Visiting Group to Princeton University*

but rebounded thirty-six points by 1988, when 251 freshmen scored over 750 on the verbal portion (only 13 had in 1960). The last entering class of the century averaged 1490, second in the country only to California Institute of Technology, a much smaller school.[132]

A better, though still imperfect, measure of Princeton's ability to attract the best students is its yield of accepted applicants.[133] In the mid-1960s, before the social malaise caused by lack of coeducation seriously afflicted the student body, Princeton snagged more than two of every three admittees. But even with the advent of women, the university's yield dipped disappointingly to little more than half throughout the 1970s and 1980s. Not only did Yale go coed simultaneously and Harvard and Radcliffe combine forces, but Princeton's social system continued to dissuade potential students, especially the most academically gifted. The incomplete residential college plan for underclassmen, the lack of a campus or student center, and the selective eating clubs (which Dean Wickenden regarded as "an albatross around our necks") sent many could-be Princetonians to Harvard, Yale, MIT, and Stanford and did little to seduce their top choices.[134] In 1970, a well-publicized year after coeducation began,

---

on the Conferences Held There with Members of its Administration and Faculty from November 26 through November 29, 1961, 3 [President's Office, PU]). See also Karabel, *The Chosen*, pp. 294, 310–13, 316–20.

[132] Heath, *Princeton Retrospectives*, 5; Fred Hargadon, "Chances for Admission, Then [1960] and Now," *PAW*, Dec. 20, 1989, inside front cover; Christopher Avery, Andrew Fairbanks, and Richard Zeckhauser, *The Early Admissions Game: Joining the Elite* (Cambridge, Mass., 2003), 297–304 (app. A), based on the College Board's database for 1999–2000. In 1995 the SATs were "recentered," which thereafter added about fifty points to each test score, math and verbal.

[133] Former president William Bowen argues that universities should de-emphasize admission "yields" because only the *quality* of the matriculants, not the mere percentage of those admitted who come, matters. William G. Bowen and Sarah A. Levin, *Reclaiming the Game: College Sports and Educational Values (II)* (Princeton, 2003), 274, 423n21.

[134] Robert K. Durkee '69, "On the Campus: Admissions," *PAW*, Mar. 4, 1969, 4; Keenan, "Dean Wickenden '61 Looks Back," 27; "Who Goes to Princeton?" *PAW*, Oct. 13, 1970, 4. By the late 1990s, Princeton's alcohol-dominated social life and minority discomfort were added to its limited dining and social arrangements as reasons for admitted applicants to go elsewhere. *Report of the Undergraduate Admission Study Group* (1998), 9–10.

Princeton lost 380 of its top candidates to Harvard-Radcliffe and Yale and could persuade only 153 of theirs to come to New Jersey. Only after 1994, when Princeton faculty won three Nobel Prizes, mathematician Andrew Wiles solved Fermat's last theorem, and Princeton began to tie or oust Harvard regularly from *U.S. News & World Report*'s top college ranking, did Princeton's yield begin a steady climb out of the 50-percent range to a record postwar high of nearly 74 percent in 2002.[135]

Although the rise in overall yield rates was gratifying, Princeton made the most progress in recruiting Academic Ones, roughly those who had A averages in school and scored above 725 (now 750) on both SAT and Achievement tests. In 1963–1964, when the current applicant-rating system was begun, only 12 percent of the first two classes admitted were Academic Ones. Twenty years later, the percentage had nearly doubled. Part of the increase was due to the influence of history professor Lawrence Stone upon the Faculty Committee on Admissions, which was persuaded to add 5 percent more Academic Ones (50–75 students) to the "foundation group" that was admitted first and to reduce the number of "special" admits, particularly athletes.[136] In the entering class of 2008, over 50 percent were drawn from the most promising students in the country, indeed the world.[137]

Yet Princeton was frustrated that it could not take more. In 1998 a twelve-person, largely faculty, study group recommended—and the trustees approved after a full examination by its own subcommittee

135 "Who Goes to Princeton?" 4; "One in Seven," *PAW*, May 11, 1994, 10; Stevens, "Malkiel," *PWB*, Oct. 7, 2002. In 1983, although Princeton's overall yield was only 55 percent, it shared dual offers evenly with Yale and MIT; Harvard took three-fourths of those offered admission to both universities. In 2004 Princeton, Yale, and MIT had yields over 70 percent, but they all trailed Harvard. *PAW*, Nov. 16, 1983, 13; Chanyaka Sethi, "Yield Declines to Five-Year Low," *DP* (online), Oct. 7, 2004.

136 "Admissions at Princeton," *DP*, Oct. 29, 1964, 1; "New Dean of Admission," *PAW*, Apr. 6, 1983, 19; Keenan, "Dean Wickenden '61 Looks Back," 26–27; *PAW*, Dec. 14, 1984, 1–2; Feb. 27, 1985, 1–2.

137 Dean Nancy Malkiel's report to the faculty on Sept. 13, 2004, in Daniel Lipsky-Karasz, "Faculty: Grad School Fellowships Debated," *DP* (online), Sept. 14, 2004; The Trustees of PU, *Report of the Wythes Committee* [Paul M. Wythes '55, Chair] (Jan. 29, 2000).

chaired by Paul M. Wythes '55—the addition of 125–150 students of exceptional intellectual and performing-artistic talent to four consecutive classes beginning in 2006, while holding the number of recruited athletes steady. The added enrollments would be housed in at least one new four-year residential college (eventually the $30-million gift of eBay CEO Margaret "Meg" Whitman '77 and several other donors).[138] The prospect of enticing these young stars to Princeton was enhanced by the start of a twice-revised, extremely generous financial-aid policy, one of the happy results of the university's $1.14-billion Anniversary Campaign.[139]

The only successful applicants whose numbers fell from their postwar heydays were athletes and children of alumni. Princeton deans of admission, like their peers elsewhere, worry that "the alumni parents of rejected children will stop giving" to the university's "unending fundraising campaigns." Fred Hargadon (1988–2003) once joked that he probably cost Princeton "several million dollars

[138] By 2002 the plan had been revised: three four-year colleges were planned, two newly configured from the existing Butler and Mathey colleges. Each of the remaining three two-year colleges would be paired with one of the four-year colleges. With a new ellipse dormitory near Poe Field, the build-up in class size leading to 5,200 undergraduates began in the fall of 2005. "Committee Proposes Program for Four-Year Residential Colleges," PU, press release, Sept. 20, 2002; *Report of the Four-Year College Program Planning Committee,* Aug. 20, 2002; Ruth Stevens, "Construction Pace Picks Up with New Buildings, Renovations," *PWB* (online), Apr. 4, 2004.

[139] *Report of the Undergraduate Admission Study Group* (1998); "Trustee Committee Recommends Increasing Size of Undergraduate Body," PU, press release, Jan. 31, 2000; "Rockefeller, Forbes, Wilson, now Whitman," *PAW,* Mar. 13, 2002, 8; "Anniversary Campaign Raises Record $1.14 Billion for Princeton," PU, press release, July 19, 2000. In 1998 the university abolished or reduced loans in favor of outright scholarships for low- and middle-income families, reduced the contribution required from the family, and reduced or eliminated the value of home equity in the calculation of the family's contribution for all those receiving financial aid. In 2001 Princeton abolished all loans in favor of outright grants and admitted all international students on a need-blind basis. Ben Gose, "Princeton Plans Major Increase in Aid for Middle- and Low-Income Students," *CHE,* Jan. 30, 1998, A35–36; "University Lowers Price Tag for Some Students," *PAW,* Feb. 25, 1998, 4, 6; Florence Olsen and Kit Lively, "Princeton Increases Endowment Spending to Replace Students' Loans With Grants," *CHE,* Feb. 9, 2001, A32; Andrew Brownstein, "Upping the Ante for Student Aid," *CHE,* Feb. 16, 2001, A47–49; Eric Quiñones, "In Tight Economy, Princeton Remains Committed to Aid," *PWB,* May 5, 2003.

each year by not admitting kids on the list sent to him by the development office." But one of his predecessors, James Wickenden (1978–1983), noted that "people whose children are denied admission are initially upset, and maybe for a year or two their interest in the university wanes. But typically they come back around when they see that what happened was best for the kids." When he rejected two sons of a Princeton trustee involved in a $420-million fund-raising project and the child of a board member who managed the university's then-$2 billion endowment, there were "no apparent ill effect[s]."[140]

Legacies, however, do have the advantage of "an assumption of welcome." As they are at Harvard and other elite schools, their applications are read personally by the dean of admissions, and—"all other things being equal" (that is, if they are in the top half of the applicant pool)—they are often given the nod in the final round.[141] Accordingly, and because they have usually enjoyed educational advantages of school and family, they have always been admitted at rates twice or three times higher than those who have never attended a P-rade or Reunion. In 1970, for instance, two of every five Princeton sons and daughters were accepted, while only one in five in the whole applicant pool was. When the general acceptance rate dropped to 11 percent in 2002, legacy acceptances dipped to 35 percent, the lowest since 1954 when more than eight in ten were admitted. This preferential treatment, however, has not precluded a calculated reduction in their numbers. From the mid-1970s to the mid-1980s, legacies numbered around 250 and comprised about 17 percent of each class; in the class of 2006, they were down to 130, or 11 percent, in good measure through self-selection. In reading their parents' *PAW*s, they

[140] John Larew, "Why Are Droves of Unqualified, Unprepared Kids Getting into Our Top Colleges? Because Their Dads Were Alumni," *Washington Monthly*, 23 (June 1991):10–14, at 13; Bill Paul '70, "Getting In: An Inside Look at Admissions and Its Dean, Fred Hargadon," *PAW*, Nov. 22, 1995, 11–19, at 17, and *Getting In: Inside the College Admissions Process* (Reading, Mass., 1995), 194.

[141] Wolff, *The Final Club*, 319; Daniel Golden, "Family Ties: Preference for Alumni Children in College Admission Draws Fire," *Wall Street Journal*, Jan. 15, 2003, A1; "To: All Princeton Alumni," *PAW*, Oct. 5, 1979, insert, p. 3. In 2003 newly appointed Dean of Admission Janet Rapelye instituted a committee system for reading *all* applications.

cannot have failed to recognize the growing odds against their getting in. Even as Princeton's entering classes grew, twenty fewer legacies applied in 2002 than in 1970. Since the mid-1990s, Ivy legacies in general have brought SAT scores and earned grade-point averages slightly higher than those of their classmates.[142]

Because Princeton has since 1970 fielded an unusually large number of varsity teams, recruited athletes have enjoyed a tremendous admissions advantage, even though their scholastic credentials in general have been significantly lower than those of their nonathletic peers. By the late 1990s, nearly one in five students, male and female, played on Princeton's thirty-eight intercollegiate teams.[143] About 70 percent of them were recruited by Princeton's coaches and admitted as such; the rest were "walk-ons," largely in the lower profile sports such as crew, fencing, and track. Historically, the admissions office rejected only 30–40 percent of the athletes on the coaches' wish lists, though sometimes to the coaches' chagrin. Pete Carril, Princeton's longtime basketball coach and philosopher, used to refer to West College, the home of the admission office, as "Heartbreak Hotel." "One of the things that has helped me at Princeton," he said, "is that I have no desire to be famous, because Admissions has turned down guys who would have made me famous."[144]

[142] "Who Goes to Princeton?" 4; PU, *Profile, 2002–2003*, 9; *PAW*, Nov. 19, 1954, 9; Feb. 27, 1985, 2. See also Debra Thomas and Terry Shepard, "Legacy Admissions Are Defensible, Because the Process Can't Be 'Fair,' " *CHE*, Mar. 14, 2003, B15. From 1981 to 1988, 36 percent of Harvard's legacy applicants were admitted; 43 percent of Yale's made the cut between 1982 and 1991 (both at more than twice the rate of their peers). John D. Lamb, "The Real Affirmative Action Babies: Legacy Preferences at Harvard and Yale," *Columbia Journal of Law and Social Problems* 26:3 (Spring 1993):491–521, at 503 (table 1) and 505 (table 3).

[143] According to Princeton's official Equity in Athletics Disclosure Act report for 1997–1998, 20 percent (942 of 4,600 undergraduates) were varsity athletes. James Shulman and William G. Bowen, *The Game of Life: College Sports and Educational Values* (Princeton, 2001), 366. Director of Athletics Gary Walters put the figure between 18 and 19 percent, due to duplication of names caused by multiple-sport participation. "The Culture and Value of Sports: A Roundtable Discussion," *PAW* (online), May 18, 2001, 4–5.

[144] "The Culture and Value of Sports," 5; Paul, *Getting In*, 206–13, at 209; Dan White, "Pete Carril vs. 'Heartbreak Hotel,' " *PAW*, May 8, 1978, 42–44, at 42. See also John W. Fischer '65, "Spring Sports: Recruiting Athletes," *PAW*, May 4, 1965, 14–15; Shulman

When sports fan Fred Hargadon became West's concierge in 1988, ironically, he began to reduce the number of recruited athletes in each class by shortening the coaches' wish lists. Forced to make tough choices, the coaches realized they stood a better chance of getting their top six-to-eight picks if those students stood higher on Princeton's Academic Index than many of their previous picks had. (The Index was designed in the mid-1980s by the Ivy League presidents to establish bands of SAT scores and high school grades, appropriate to their particular student bodies, within which athletes had to qualify.)[145] Hargadon's policy of "fewer but better" was also the product of his re-education after coming from PAC-10 Stanford. He had learned that without athletic scholarships, Princeton had traditionally admitted about 400 athletes because 200 might come and 175 might stay with their sport all four years. By 2001 he had halved the number of recruited jocks, without any discernible effect on Princeton's ability to win games or championships.[146]

Yet Princeton had struck a Faustian bargain. In return for admitting marginally better qualified students, West College rewarded coaches with more of the choices on their truncated lists. But these recruits tended to be more vested in their sports, more likely to play all four years, and, unfortunately, more likely to underperform in the classroom. So the student-athletic dilemma continues, as it probably will as long as elite colleges and universities decide that athletics,

---

and Bowen, *The Game of Life*, chap. 2; Bowen and Levin, *Reclaiming the Game*, chaps. 2–3. At Harvard in the 1980s, 49 percent of recruited athletes were admitted, with consistently lower scores than those of nonathletic, nonlegacy applicants. Lamb, "The Real Affirmative Action Babies," 503–4.

145 Shulman and Bowen, *The Game of Life*, 13–14, 46; Emily Weiss, "Varsity Blues: Athletics and the Modern University," *Nassau Weekly*, Apr. 1, 1999.

146 "The Changing Face of West College: An Interview with Fred Hargadon, the New Dean of Admission," *PAW*, Nov. 9, 1988, 18–22; Paul, *Getting In*, 206–13; "The Culture and Value of Sports," 6. By 1997 recruited athletes comprised only 16.4 percent of the entering class, down four points from 1988. In 2003, Hargadon's last entering class, the percentage was down to 14 percent, where it remained under new dean Janet Rapelye. *Report of the Undergraduate Admission Study Group* (1998), 2; Tooke, "Study Group Looks at Admissions," 4 (graph); Anne Lineback, "Admission Dean Rapelye Gets Passing Grade from Coaches," *DP* (online), Apr. 28, 2004.

especially the winning kind, are a vital part of students' extracurricular development and school spirit.

At the beginning of the twenty-first century, it became increasingly clear that admission to America's elite colleges was a high-stakes game as well as a meritocratic search for "the brightest and the best." Although "the big secret in college admissions," Dean Hargadon assured anxious applicants and parents, "is that there is no big secret," there were several small secrets revealed and, in some cases, reviled. In addition to the substantial "unfair" advantage enjoyed by minorities, athletes, and legacies, it was discovered by a trio of researchers that those who applied for early decision at elite colleges, *particularly* Princeton, increased their chances of admission two or three times over those who applied during the regular process in the second semester of their senior year. They found that 55 percent of Princeton's early applicants were admitted, compared to only 19 percent of the regular applicants, which increased the early birds' chances some 58 percent, or the equivalent of well over an extra hundred points on the SATs. And contrary to Dean Hargadon's assertion that the early pools of applicants were stronger and therefore merited a higher rate of acceptance, Princeton's successful early applicants had SAT scores and other qualifications slightly *below* those of the regular applicants, partly because most recruited athletes are encouraged to apply early.[147]

Perhaps early admission advantages would have been less troubling had they not given an additional boost to already privileged applicants. Most early applicants were white or Asian, came from well-to-do families, and attended select high schools or prep schools, whose counselors knew the rules of the admissions game. Wealthier families also had the resources to make numerous college

[147] Avery, Fairbanks, and Zeckhauser, *The Early Admissions Game*, 1 (quote), 9, 137, 140, 147–49, 154, 156, 158–59. Legacies, athletes, and minorities were excluded from the admissions office statistics (138). Forty-nine percent of the class of 2008 was admitted early; 32 percent of those who applied early were accepted, in a year when the overall acceptance rate was under 13 percent. Chanakya Sethi, "University Admits Half of '08 Early," *DP* (online), Jan. 7, 2004.

visits to allow their children to narrow their choices on an informed basis. They also did not have to wait until the spring notification date (April 15) to compare financial aid offers from different colleges, although this was of less concern at Princeton where, after 1998 and especially 2001, financial aid was perhaps the most generous in the nation.[148]

The competition among Ivy League and other elite colleges created and perpetuated the early admissions game, particularly after the enrollment boom of the early 1960s. As applications increased and acceptance rates fell, more seniors applied to multiple colleges as "safeties" or "back-ups." This prompted Yale and Princeton to initiate National Scholar programs in 1966–1967, by which all top applicants were informed of their admission likelihood. The goal, in part, was to reduce the number of regular applications and to spread the admission office workload over the year. In 1973, the Big Three informed all applicants in January whether they were "likely, possible, or unlikely" to be admitted in April. Since the scheduling of this plan was problematic, the Ivies all moved in 1976–1977 to early admission plans, which gave decisions by December so that the unsuccessful could apply to other colleges in January. The Big Three and Brown chose "early action," in which the college decided early but allowed the student to apply to other schools at the same time. The rest of the Ivies went to "early decision," which allowed only one early application and obligated the admittee (at least morally) to attend that school unless its financial aid offer was insufficient. As rivals shifted plans and positions to gain temporary advantage, Princeton shifted to early decision in 1995–1996, along with Yale. The effect was minimal: Princeton continued to get the students who wanted badly to go there and lost those who were playing the game or wanted greater flexibility in their college planning.[149]

Only two things are certain about the future of admissions: Princeton will continue to compete aggressively for the best seniors in the country and, to some extent, the world (though the definition

[148] Avery, Fairbanks, and Zeckhauser, *The Early Admissions Game*, 13–14, 30, 58–60.

[149] Avery, Fairbanks, and Zeckhauser, *The Early Admissions Game*, 25–31, 36–37.

of "best" will evolve); and the state of play will depend as much on the moves of Princeton's chief competitors as on its own strategies. Whether these maneuvers result in "fairer" admission procedures or in "better," more "diverse" classes, only time will tell.[150]

[150] In 2003 Janet Lavin Rapelye, the dean of admission at Wellesley College, became Princeton's first female dean of admission. She had previously worked at Bowdoin, Williams (from which she graduated, like her predecessor Radcliffe Heermance, in 1981), and Stanford (from which Hargadon had come fifteen years earlier). In her first year she installed a committee system of decision making; restored relations with the Alumni Schools Committee; increased faculty involvement in recruiting; increased applications and admissions to the School of Engineering; redesigned the college "viewbook"; reached into earlier grades of secondary schools with information; agreed to use the Common Application beginning with the class of 2009; admitted 3 percent more legacies than Hargadon had; and scrapped his famous "Yes!" letter of acceptance. Zachary A. Goldfarb, "Wellesley Dean of Admission to Replace Hargadon in July," *DP*, Mar. 28, 2003, 1; "Janet Lavin Rapelye Named Dean of Admission at Princeton," PU, press release, Mar. 27, 2003; Ruth Stevens, "Rapelye Looks Forward to Representing Princeton," *PWB*, Apr. 7, 2003; Ruth Stevens, "Rapelye: Class of 2008 'The Very Best,' " *PWB*, Sept. 5, 2004, 1; PU, press release, "Princeton Welcomes New Students, Classes Begin Sept. 9" (Sept. 3, 2004).

CHAPTER FOUR

In Class

What really matters is not what is taught,
but what is learned.

—Harold T. Shapiro

Historically, college students have at least one thing in common: they must submit themselves to a faculty-made curriculum and do a certain amount of studious work to retain their privileged status as students. From twelfth-century Paris to present-day Princeton, this has given the collegiate species considerable continuity, an essential marker by which they may be known. But they seldom confine themselves to study or to the official curriculum. Understandably, a steady regimen of study is too sedentary, solitary, and focused for healthy, gregarious, and curious young people in search of stable identities and hormonal relief. And no matter how well-designed the curriculum, it cannot prepare them for postgraduate or "real" life in all the ways they would like or imagine they will need. So they create or resort to an *extra*curriculum to supplement, or in some cases supplant, the prefabricated curriculum they have been offered. In time—and more quickly since the 1960s—many subjects of student interest migrate from the extracurriculum to the course catalogue.[1]

Since Woodrow Wilson's day, neither faculty nor students have allowed the Princeton curriculum to remain unchanged for long. During their brief residencies, students often chafe under the illu-

[1] Frederick Rudolph, "The Neglect of Students as an Historical Tradition," in Lawrence E. Dennis and Joseph F. Kauffman, eds., *The College and the Student* (Washington, D.C., 1966), 47–58; Helen Lefkowitz Horowitz, *Campus Life: Undergraduate Cultures from the End of the Eighteenth Century to the Present* (Chicago, 1987), 4, 12–16, 20–21.

sion of a static and the burden of a required curriculum. Without a long view, they seldom see the constant tinkering and often major overhauls that curricula receive from intellectually alert, socially conscious, and student-responsive faculties. Although Princeton lost its appetite and rationale in the 1960s for standing *in loco parentis* in the students' social lives, the faculty relinquished none of its authority over the curriculum, but responded positively to the intellectual needs and interests of students as well as their own. This resulted in a steady growth of courses offered, refinement of teaching techniques, and reliance on student initiative and responsibility for their own learning.

Yet even as the faculty reduced the students' course load and hours in the classroom, they adjusted their standards and expectations to the rising academic capacity of the entering classes. The ratcheting up of academic standards, in turn, not only produced counterintuitive inflation and compression of grades; in some students it reduced extracurricular involvement by sublimating or obviating their need for it. Yet in others it increased their intensity and commitment as they applied the same standards to creative and performing arts that had been encouraged by the admissions process and recognized increasingly in the curriculum.

❁ ❁ ❁

Before the implementation of the four-course plan for upperclassmen in 1923–24, and even afterward until the Great Depression, most Princeton students displayed no great love for or eager involvement in the curriculum. Wilson's preceptorials had their day as an experiment in pedagogy, but even they lost their novel appeal with the loss of the preceptor rank in 1913 and the increased specialization and research orientation of the faculty.[2] The quickening pulse and "intellectualization" of the campus that Wilson's and Dean Fine's

[2] Anthony Grafton [Professor of History], "Precepting: Myth and Reality of a Princeton Institution," *PAW*, Mar. 12, 2003, 16–19; Grafton, "The Precept System: Myth and Reality of a Princeton Institution," *PULC*, 64:3 (Winter 2003):467–503.

reforms produced had receded by the inauguration of President Hibben in 1912.

The proliferation of the paraphernalia of scholarship might have given a different impression. The precept-driven increase in reading apparently led to a pronounced upswing in the need for glasses. In 1902, 28 percent of the graduating class wore them. By 1915, 42 percent did; nearly a quarter of the class got their first pair in college. Typewriters advertised their way into dorm-room décor. "Typewrite Your Notes," enjoined L. C. Smith, "Now is the Time to Start Right." The Hammond people hit the keys even harder. "Students! You Need a Typewriter . . . Help you to get better marks," they promised, and offered to rent one for $10 a year or $6 for five months.[3] In 1924 the loose-leaf spiral notebook made its debut to bring some order to the chaos of lecture notes.

But other signs suggest that all was not well in academe. Perhaps the most convincing evidence is the frank testimony of unrepentant but not boastful student spokesmen. A mild version was the *Daily Princetonian*'s lament in 1926 that "study in too enthusiastic a form has been 'bad form' " and "is still surrounded with unattractive associations in the minds of many. Too constant attendance at the Library is likely to lead to derogatory classification." Six years later, senior R. G. Burlingham celebrated an increase in "sporadic but genuinely interested attempts at scholarship" and Princeton's "gradual emergence from the intellectual doldrums of collegiatism," thanks to the administration's ban on automobiles in 1927 and the four-course plan. But he contrasted the recent renaissance with the previous decade when formal education was "merely tolerated" and the students' attitude toward the faculty was either indifferent or patronizing. The motto of the typical Tiger in the 1920s, he said, was "educate me if you can catch me." As Yale professor Henry Seidel Canby had noted not long before, students at elite colleges received instruction "as the Eskimo receives the arts of the white man—politely, but with some suspicion and not a little contempt."[4]

[3] *Nassau Herald* (1902), 119; *PAW*, Apr. 28, 1915, 706–7; *Princeton Pictorial Review*, June 12, 1915.

[4] "Good Form," *DP*, Mar. 22, 1926, 2; R. G. Burlingham '32, "The State of Culture at Princeton," *PAW*, Mar. 25, 1932, 549, 551 (reprinted from the *Nassau Literary Magazine*

Despite the substantial reforms of the Wilson era, the subsequent two decades saw a partial return to the student attitudes of the lazy Patton years.[5] Ernest Poole, who graduated in 1902 just before Wilson, his favorite professor and friend, was sworn in, later described Princeton's student ethos in two autobiographical novels. In *The Bridge* (1940), he confessed matter-of-factly that "the classrooms of my day were mainly places of genial ease or utter boredom, until exams, when the desperate cramming came." Twenty-five years earlier, in *The Harbor*, Poole had drawn a fuller but no less dispiriting picture of academic life. "What a desert of knowledge it was back there," he exclaimed. "Together with my companions I assumed a genial tolerance toward all those poor dry devils known to us as 'profs.' " The faculty demanded little of the students and the students responded accordingly: "It was a case of live and let live." "Our placid tolerance of the profs included the books they gave us" because the main idea in all courses was to "do what you had to but no more."[6]

Another sign of trouble became more apparent in 1925 when the advent of senior comprehensives put even greater emphasis on the results of examinations.[7] The majority of pre-Depression students, armed with up to thirty allowable cuts a term, sought to beat the system by paying only passing attention to classes and cramming for finals. For those who used their cuts liberally, tutoring schools offered their services until they were outlawed by the administration in 1942. John Gale Hun's famous school used the pages of the *Tiger*

90:4 [Apr. 1932]: 5–16); Henry Seidel Canby, *College Sons and College Fathers* (New York, 1915), 31.

[5] See chapter 2, pp. 38–41, 43.

[6] Ernest Poole, *The Bridge* (New York, 1940), 63; Poole, *The Harbor* (New York, 1915), 51–53.

[7] Comprehensive exams of some sort were first required in all departments in 1914. But by 1921 a special faculty committee deemed it "inadvisable to attempt the establishment of comprehensive examinations in Princeton at the present time" because of the expense. Two years later a different committee decided otherwise, following the lead of Harvard and Oxford. Harold T. Shapiro, "The President's Page: The Senior Thesis—Origins," *PAW*, Mar. 23, 1994, 49; Anne Elizabeth Ruderman, "In Partial Fulfillment: A Study of the Princeton University History Department Senior Theses" (Senior thesis, Dept. of History, PU, 2001), 9; Larry Zygmunt '92, "Hurdling Comps: Seniors Face Unexpected Obstacles on the Road to Commencement," *PAW*, June 3, 1992, 11.

to sell its wares throughout the 1910s and 1920s, promising in its motto that "We tutor but do not cram." A Princeton Tutors' Association promised to perform similar miracles in a building on Nassau Street. Another remedy for spasmodic class attendance was sets of lecture notes, offered for sale by enterprising student agencies until they, too, were closed down in 1923. When British student John Benn spent a year at Princeton in 1922–1923, he was offered "a quite embarrassing selection of typescripts." One service charged $4 a course, a rival gave six for $20, while a third "prided itself on a very specialized summary which would be limited—a sort of *edition de luxe*!" In 1915 a *Tiger* joke asked, "What is the most popular dance at Princeton?" and the insider's knowing answer was "The Latin trot," yet another shortcut to scholastic survival.[8]

In the prevailing campus culture, no amount of last-minute study aids could prevent an unseemly number of academic casualties. During Wilson's presidency, between 11 and 16 percent of the freshmen flunked out and were sent home to ponder their delinquencies. Most were given a second chance, which, to judge by their senior records, they did not always use wisely. In the much-improved class of 1910, one in four had been summoned before the faculty for various offenses, an average of five times each; more than 10 percent had been sent home, nearly half had been "conditioned" (about three times each), more than a quarter had received "pensums," or extra class work, for unexcused class absences (one lad had twenty hours' worth), and 15 percent—35 men—had been arrested by the local constabulary. As late as 1927, after selective admissions and the four-course plan had begun to separate the student wheat from the chaff, 61 seniors admitted that they had been suspended and 214 that they had failed at least one course during their career; 39 had flunked between four and seven courses and still managed to graduate. Presumably, these fellows were not among the 60 percent of their class who respected a Phi Beta Kappa key more than a sports "P." They may have taken their cue from the *Daily Princetonian* in their sopho-

8 "The Diary of a Freshman," *PAW*, Oct. 7, 1914, 47–48 (also in *Best of PAW*, Feb. 8, 1995, 4, 30 [PTA]); *Princeton Tiger*, Jan. 1915, 11; Dec. 5, 1919; 1926–27 passim; John A. Benn, *Columbus—Undergraduate* (Philadelphia, 1928), 86–87.

more year when it opined, perhaps defensively, that the gold key was not worth the sacrifice of keeping one's "nose to the educational grindstone."[9]

The university resorted to several tactics to induce the undergraduates to take the curriculum as seriously as they took their other interests. In (vain) hopes of mobilizing public opinion against the slacker set, the registrar posted grades at the end of each semester on wooden easels in the reception gallery of Alexander Hall for all to see. "There was no hiding," wrote Howard MacAyeal, well after world events had given student seriousness a decided boost. But he doubted that anyone cared. "No one else does care, who you are or what you got. You had to walk around and search [your grades] out, nervously; and it was only truly embarrassing if you fell over and fainted from the horrible shock of a really bad grade."[10]

If peer pressure didn't work, the threat of extra work was held over the laggard's head. When F. Scott Fitzgerald's alter-ego, Amory Blaine, exceeded his quota of class cuts in his sophomore year, he was obliged to take "an additional course the following year."[11] And when the extra course load—or his acquired indifference—resulted in a failure in conic sections, Amory was forced to resort to a tutoring school before classes began the following September, four hours a day boning up, largely in the company of bone-headed athletes.

[9] *PWW*, 16:24, 200, 325–27, 466; 17:69, 438; 20:355–56; *Nassau Herald* (1910), 78; (1927), 643, 649; "Outside Activities," *DP*, Jan. 24, 1925, 2. In Edmund Wilson's day (1912–1916), even "PBK had no prestige, was considered, in fact, rather second-rate." Unlike at earnest Yale, Wilson thought, at Princeton students "had no incentive to excel in any [intellectual or literary] pursuit" (*A Prelude: Landscapes, Characters and Conversations from the Earlier Years of My Life* [New York, 1967], 117).

[10] H. S. MacAyeal, *Tiger! Tiger!* (London: Minerva Press, 1996), 268 (thanks to Howard MacAyeal for a copy of his fascinating and scarce book); Roy Heath, *Princeton Retrospectives: Twenty-Fifth-Year Reflections on a College Education* (Princeton: Class of 1954, 1979), 267, 268.

[11] F. Scott Fitzgerald, *This Side of Paradise* (New York, 1920; 1977), 86. In 1927 the faculty decided that seniors, with their new responsibilities under the four-course plan, could have unlimited cuts. Juniors were exempted some time later. But it took until 1959 for Princeton to realize that monitoring cuts for the underclasses was time ill-spent. Christian Gauss, *Life in College* (New York, 1930), 113; Donald W. Kramer '60, "On the Campus: Cuts Recording," *PAW*, Sept. 25, 1959, 7.

Later delinquents were required to attend "the dreaded summer session," which Princeton sponsored until World War II, to erase their conditions.[12]

But the university's most effective weapon in the war against minimal effort was more carrot than stick. Observing the gusto with which students pursued their extracurricular interests, the faculty decreed (in the words of short-story writer Day Edgar) that "any student who wants to ride one of his hobbies must keep his marks above a specified minimum grade." When Amory Blaine flunked his make-up exam in conic sections, he was dropped from the *Prince*'s editorial board, which effectively squashed any chance he had for election to the august Senior Council.[13] The nonfictional faculty, at least, hoped for better results from its methods.

With the onset of the Great Depression, and certainly during the war that followed, the faculty obtained better results with less effort on their part. As in many other colleges around the country, the students themselves took a serious turn and decided that education and the curriculum were not irrelevant to their futures after all. If boredom with the mass conformity and "standardized vulgarity" of excessive "collegiatism" had not wrought a major change in student attitudes, the gravity of world affairs would have. The once-blasé "Princeton man" of the 1920s, cloaked in "self-conscious, pseudo-sophisticated diffidence," could no longer hold the pose while staring into the face of unemployment or death on the battlefield.[14]

[12] Fitzgerald, *This Side of Paradise*, 99–101; Edmund Wilson, "Harvard, Princeton, and Yale," *Forum* 70:2 (Sept. 1923):1871–79, at 1873; Day Edgar, *In Princeton Town* (New York, 1929), 225, 273; PU, *A Report Prepared for the Middle States Association of Colleges and Secondary Schools Commission on Institutions of Higher Education* (1961), 55, Historical Subject Files, #A-109, box 200 (PUA). Unlike summer schools in many other universities, Princeton's summer session was as long and as demanding as regular term courses. Classes met six days a week for 6 weeks. About 120 students attended throughout the 1930s, most of them freshmen and sophomores. Professor Robert Albion, director of the summer school, in Harold W. Dodds, *Report of the President (1938)*, 30–31.

[13] Edgar, *In Princeton Town*, 227–28; Fitzgerald, *This Side of Paradise*, 101–2.

[14] Alfred Monroe Wade '30, "Princeton's Collegiate Tendencies," *PAW*, July 2, 1929, 1135–36; Burlingham, "The State of Culture at Princeton," *PAW*, Mar. 25, 1932, 549; Joseph V. Quarles, Jr. '29, "A New Phase of Collegiateness," *PAW*, Sept. 27, 1929, 9.

By the early 1930s, Princeton was fast losing its country-club reputation and becoming known for its rising standards and student interest in "things intellectual." If it was not yet a "poler's paradise" or "scholar's university," a growing number of undergraduates who were "interested in their work . . . and willing to spend time on it" was giving loafers "no ground to stand upon." Although the students themselves played a key role in "setting the standards and setting them . . . higher," the major impetus for reform came from the faculty, which was undergoing its own renaissance, particularly in math and science.[15] Under the leadership of mathematician Luther Eisenhart, chairman of the committee that drafted the four-course plan and after 1925 dean of the faculty, the faculty led the university through a series of major curricular changes, most of which quickly won the approval and cooperation of the undergraduates.

The most important and most lasting reform was the four-course plan itself.[16] Its major provision—independent study (with course relief) for juniors and seniors—is still the key feature of undergraduate life. (Its other provision—the senior comprehensive exam—in time has become less imposing and less important.) As a logical extension of the preceptorial method, the plan sought to substitute active for passive learning, and self-discovery for force-feeding and mindless memorization. This proved enormously appealing, if initially daunting, to students who found little challenge or engagement in the formal curriculum and therefore sought both outside the classroom. At a national meeting of alumni in 1928, senior Joseph V. Quarles, chairman of the Undergraduate Council, explained why the contemporary undergraduate was "more mature, less collegiate, and more interested in his academic work." The main reasons, he argued, were "a greater amount of independent work" and "a more interesting Faculty," both of which led to a "better valuation" of the importance of outside activities and a decline in "charm-hunting or going out for activities simply for the prestige involved." The four-course

[15] Paul S. Havens '25, "Is Princeton Too Hard?" *PAW*, May 8, 1931, 751; Gerhard P. Van Arkel '29, "All the Sad Old Men," *PAW*, Apr. 1, 1932, 568–69.

[16] See chapter 2, pp. 75–76.

plan, the major engine of change, "not only makes men take it seriously because of its difficulty, but it gives many a concentrated field of study, which, rightly or wrongly, they feel will be of value in their life work."[17]

Seven months later, four prize-winners in the *Alumni Weekly*'s essay contest on "How Thinks the Campus?" reinforced their leader's reading of the campus ethos. William Milligan Sloane III '29, no great fan of the new plan, acknowledged that "the increased burden of departmental work, particularly in the number and length of the required essays, results in lessened emphasis on other activities." He and classmate Gerhard Van Arkel described the reduced interest in athletics, publications, and other extracurricular activities. Mass spectating at team games and athletic hero-worship were giving way to widespread participation in individual sports such as tennis and golf and in intramural contests for "fun and exercise." Likewise, many competitors for slots on the editorial board of the *Prince* withdrew "because of studies," although the length and difficulty of the competitions had been "nearly halved in the last three years." Even the venerable customs of weeknight movies and postprandial socializing at the clubs were down, all due to the press of academic duties. Unlike the alumnus who greeted the four-course plan with "they're trying to make a damned educational institution out of the place," Van Arkel boasted that that aim had "already been attained in large measure."[18]

As upperclassmen, the four essayists wrote from a privileged perspective. They took only four courses a semester, pursued special subjects and reading lists of interest suggested by their major departments, and wrote long research papers on topics they themselves had chosen. But the plan did little to redeem the freshman and sophomore years from what a recent graduate called "their dreary prep-

[17] "Senior Cites Campus Trends," *PAW*, Nov. 23, 1928, 266–67. The National Alumni Association met in Columbus, Ohio, on November 2–3.

[18] William Milligan Sloane III '29, "Present Day Trends at Princeton," *PAW*, July 2, 1929, 1131–32; Otis B. Bosworth '30, "The New Campus Philosophy," *PAW*, July 2, 1929, 1132–34; Gerhard P. Van Arkel '29, "Princeton More Old Than New," *PAW*, July 2, 1929, 1134–35; Wade, "Princeton's Collegiate Tendencies," *PAW*, July 2, 1929, 1135–36.

school extension atmosphere."[19] Accordingly, the faculty soon sought to upgrade and enliven the underclass curriculum. They transferred certain junior-year courses to the sophomore year; by 1927–1928 all the departments except Astronomy offered at least one course to give underclassmen a taste of the disciplinary pleasures and challenges that majors might expect. In 1930–1931 the B.S. degree, which had no Latin prerequisites, was abolished to put more emphasis on the work done *in* college than on the preparation the student brought *to* college. A modern language (French or German) and math, Latin, or Greek were the only courses required by the end of sophomore year. This reversed the usual pattern in American colleges, in which studies in the first two years were largely prescribed and largely elective in the last two. Freshmen who ranked at admission in the top third of the entering class could elect one or two sophomore courses, and none of the courses in the underclass years were familiar (and sometimes boring) surveys but specialized courses on important topics likely to engage serious students.[20]

❁ ❁ ❁

The most innovative and enduring feature of the four-course plan—the senior thesis—was not even mentioned in the initial proposal. The thesis grew out of the independent-study provisions at the request of a few departments. Rather than a steady diet of largely directed reading to prepare for comprehensive exams, English, Economics, and Biology—one department from each division, by chance—suggested in 1925 that a major research and writing project of the student's choosing would do much to develop active self-learning. By 1931 virtually every department required a senior thesis as well as shorter junior papers by way of preparation. In both years

[19] Everett N. Case '22, "Undergraduate Life at Cambridge and Princeton," *PAW*, Mar. 26, 1924, 510–11, at 511.

[20] Luther P. Eisenhart (dean of the faculty), Report (1925–33), in Dodds, *Report of the President (1933)*, 10–16, at 13–14; PU, *Catalogue, 1930–1931*, 52–53; Robert Greenhalgh Albion, "Curriculum Changes at Princeton," *Journal of Higher Education* 3:2 (Feb. 1932):59–62.

the written exercises and the year-end exams received a single grade that determined departmental honors at graduation.[21]

The still-unique feature of Princeton's thesis requirement is that all seniors write one as members of a 100 percent honors program, not a special program limited to the best students. No other major university in the country has the low faculty-to-student ratio that makes such a requirement possible, or as dedicated a research faculty willing to commit as much time and effort to one-on-one thesis-advising in addition to their regular responsibilities. Harvard and Yale require theses only of majors in certain departments or of those who seek to graduate with honors.[22] And no other university planned and built a major research library with a locked carrel for nearly every senior in the humanities and social sciences (the scientists have lab space) to pursue their research and do their writing in relative peace.[23] The senior thesis was the product of an unusual moment in Princeton's development, when economic prosperity, faculty improvement, selective admissions, a turn in student ethos, and an enduring Wilsonian philosophy converged to foster a daring experiment in higher education. As other colleges have discovered, Princeton's moment was virtually unique. If Princeton had waited to establish the thesis requirement today, says Dean of the College Nancy Weiss Malkiel, "there isn't a way in the world that we could."[24]

For Princeton seniors, the prospect of having to produce a hundred-page thesis remains as daunting today as it did seventy or eighty

[21] William F. Magie [dean of the faculty], "What the Faculty Thinks of the New Plan," *PAW*, June 17, 1925, 904–5; Luther P. Eisenhart [dean of the faculty], "The Plan of Undergraduate Study," *PAW*, Jan. 16, 1931, 356–57, at 357; Dodds, *Report of the President (1933)*, 10.

[22] Callen Bair, "Thesis Requirement Still a Unique Princeton Endeavor," *DP*, Apr. 8, 2003, 1, 4; John Lurz, "Making Advisor Relations Work," *DP*, Mar. 25, 2003, 1; William McCleery, *Conversations on the Character of Princeton*, rev. ed. (Princeton: Office of Communications/Publications, 1986, 1990), 22, 29, 41–42, 47, 83, 99, 105, 132–33. Yale required all students to take departmental comprehensive exams in 1937 and to write independent essays or theses in 1941, but later backed away from the thesis for everyone. George Wilson Pierson, *Yale: The University College, 1921–1937* (New Haven, 1955), chaps. 16–17, esp. 349–53.

[23] See chapter 8, p. 465. See Callen Bair, "Carrel Culture Brings Levity to Seniors' Thesis Deadline," *DP*, Apr. 24, 2003, 1, 2.

[24] Quoted in Ruderman, "In Partial Fulfillment," 16.

years ago. But for the great majority of alumni, the thesis defines the quintessential and single most valuable academic experience in their college careers.[25] Socially, it unites the senior class in a way that nothing else can. The process of thesis-writing can be seen as a classic rite of passage, little different in its stages and functions from a coming-of-age ceremony among the Iroquois or the Trobriand Islanders. Every classmate goes through roughly the same anticipation, separation (into carrels), self-doubt, a lengthy liminal period of testing, and reincorporation upon completion. To signal their bond in recent years, everyone tries to include in his or her thesis a short "senior quote," chosen for its aphoristic humor, wisdom, or abstruseness.[26] And long after they leave Princeton, many alumni have nightmares that "this is the day my thesis is due and I have forgotten even to start." Having heard about the thesis from the time they first stepped on campus, Princetonians are imbued with thesis legend and lore long before they undergo their own trials-by-fire.[27]

Given the inherent difficulty of the task, it is small wonder that not every senior emerges a confirmed believer in its worth. Among the first few classes of thesis-writers were several skeptics. One alumnus from the late 1920s worried that "not all students are capable of producing a good piece of work" (a thought secretly shared by most faculty from time to time).[28] Another believed that "all the

[25] When asked to name their most valuable academic experience, 42 percent of 1,052 alumni from the classes of 1954, 1964, and 1969 chose the senior thesis; the second most popular answer was "courses," with only 7 percent. Peter C. Wendell '72, " 'If You Had It to Do Over Again . . . ,' " *PAW*, Mar. 4, 1975, 9–12, at 9; Heath, *Princeton Retrospectives*, 57–63, 138, 173, 198, 239, 266, 270; *The Thesis: Quintessentially Princeton* (Princeton: Office of the Dean of the College, 2002), which contains thirty-one paired accounts of the thesis process by seniors and their advisors.

[26] The Colonial Club "section" of 1982–1983 takes credit for originating the "Thesis Phrase." The first was "Bourbon is our friend," the inspiration of a tipsy female member. *The Colonial Club of Princeton University, 1891–1991* (Princeton, 1991), 112.

[27] Kelly Lynn Ehrhart, "Ritual and Interpretation of the Princeton Senior Thesis: Rite of Passage for a College Community" (Senior thesis, Dept. of Anthropology, PU, 1997), 89.

[28] Emeritus Professor of History Lawrence Stone, an Oxford product, created a furor in 1991 when he dared to suggest in the pages of the *PAW* that theses should be optional for all students but required only for honors graduates. Those who did not write them would profit more, he argued, from senior seminars in which somewhat shorter research papers based on primary sources would be written. He withdrew his suggestion when

theses written since the [Four-Course] Plan was inaugurated could be used for an excellent conflagration after the next Yale defeat and the world would continue to revolve on its axis." Both men missed the point. Of course, not every senior rises to the challenge. Some don't take it seriously, others choose too ambitious a topic, many begin too late, many more procrastinate, and a few (perhaps 2 percent) panic and never finish in time to graduate with their class.[29]

But the faculty believes that everyone admitted to Princeton is capable of such work, and that the *process* of self-education that it demands is more important than the finished product. "The theses may not be world-shaking in themselves," English professor Donald Stauffer reminded prospective students in a postwar booklet entitled *The Idea of a Princeton Education.* "The point is that they educate the men who write them," even if the results are somewhat disappointing. Looking back twenty-five years to his senior year, a 1954 alumnus and private school teacher admitted that "I didn't do too good a job on my thesis . . . on Edward Arlington Robinson. . . . I took a giant topic without knowing its limits, but it was a great experience. . . . The slap on the wrist for not doing enough was a positive thing. I've even used my thesis comments when teaching Robinson to students. They enjoy my embarrassment."[30]

More often, the thesis process gives "confidence and competence to ordinary and gifted students alike." In a 1931 appraisal of the new plan, the Graduate Council (forerunner of the Alumni Council) discovered that in the last six classes, those that began to write senior theses, 167 men who had received fourth-group grades and 17 who

---

a barrage of letters to the editor defended the thesis process, whatever the quality of the product. Lawrence Stone, "Is the Mandatory Thesis Necessary? A Proposal from a Former Professor," *PAW*, Mar. 20, 1991, 40–41; letters, *PAW*, Apr. 17, 1991, 3; May 15, 1991, 6–8, 10; July 10, 1991, 5.

[29] *The Upperclass Plan of Study at Princeton: An Analysis of the Experiences and Opinions of Graduates, 1925–1929* (Princeton, 1931), c-36, c-114, also quoted in Ehrhart, "Ritual and Interpretation," 57–58; Shapiro, "The Senior Thesis—Origins," *PAW*, Mar. 23, 1994, 49.

[30] Donald A. Stauffer, *The Idea of a Princeton Education* (Princeton, 1947), 14; Heath, *Princeton Retrospectives*, 158–59 (for less edifying examples of imperfection, see 143, 162, 184, 223, 237).

I was born in New York City of wealthy parents who gave me every advantage. I attended Buckley and drilled with the Knickerbocker Greys, after which I was enrolled at an ancient and respected New England preparatory school, where I was at the head of my class and elected president of the senior council. At Princeton I busied myself with innumerable undergraduate activities. My future seemed secure. One evening, shortly before I was to have graduated, I passed my advisor. "Adam," he said, "when are you handing in your senior thesis?" "Thesis?" I replied, "What senior thesis?"

Figure 12. Since the late 1920s, every Tiger's nightmare, as depicted by *Princeton Tiger* cartoonist William F. Brown '50.

had made only fifth-group grades (of seven) in their sophomore year won honors in their departments upon graduation. This may help to explain why only 16 percent of the two thousand men in those classes registered any dissatisfaction with the plan and its results. And the faculty discovers "again and again [that] a mediocre student does really competent work" and "a good student surprises himself and his classmates and teachers by producing a brilliant job."[31]

Although the purpose of the thesis, President Dodds emphasized, was not necessarily to make "original contributions to knowledge," an impressive number of theses have made contributions and others have been original enough to become books and articles, to take their place beside the scholarship or art of their faculty advisors.[32] In October 1931, for example, the *Journal of Negro History* published in full the thesis of Leo Hirsch, Jr., "The Negro and New York, 1783–1865," which was not only one of the earliest Princeton theses devoted to African-American history, but had been completed only six months earlier; it barely had time to receive a plain 35-cent binding at the library. Three years later, the History Department produced at least two theses worthy of publication. The resident medievalists, Gray Boyce and Joseph Strayer, recommended that Victor Roberts's thesis, "A Century of Latin Missions: The Friar Travelers in the East, 1245–1369," be published by the university press. Thinking the subject too narrow for its readers' interests, the Press opted to publish instead William Sheldon's "Populism in the Old Dominion: Virginia Farm Politics, 1885–1900"—solidly researched but no page-turner—the following year. In the sciences, numerous articles resulted from senior work in Princeton labs. In the early 1930s chemistry students were especially inventive, contributing to the *Journal of the American Chemical Society* on a regular basis. In 1956 four theses in biology led to journal articles.[33]

[31] Walter L. Johnson '97, "Princeton's Educational Program," *PAW*, June 5, 1931, 860–61, at 860; Stauffer, *Idea of a Princeton Education*, 14.

[32] Harold W. Dodds, "The Four-Course Plan in Review," *PAW*, Nov. 24, 1939, 209–11, at 210.

[33] "Noteworthy Senior Theses," *PAW*, Feb. 12, 1932, 417; "The Senior Thesis," *PAW*, June 8, 1934, 785; "Letters to the Editor," *PAW*, Dec. 4, 1978, 4–5 (Victor J. Roberts); Dodds, *Report of the President (1955–1956)*, 22.

Most theses fall in the 75–100-page range, too long for a normal article and too short for a book.[34] But many Creative Writing theses are produced in lengths publishable in their genres—poetry books being shorter, and novels and short-story collections longer—than the average thesis in other subjects. Student poems are also published individually in periodicals such as *Shenandoah*, as were several by a recent graduate in 1984, next to a number by a fellow poet on the faculty. In 1960 Scribner (New York) and Gollancz (London) bought Lauren Stevens's 70,000-word thesis on a fictional Maine family when his typewriter was barely cool. It was published the following year as *The Double Axe*. Maria Katzenbach's novel *The Grab* received even warmer reviews from the critics when it appeared soon after serving "in partial fulfillment" of the requirements for her B.A. in 1976.[35]

One of the most highly evolved—and most successful—theses was A. Scott Berg's 1971 study of legendary editor Maxwell Perkins's discovery and development of Fitzgerald, Hemingway, and Thomas Wolfe in the 1920s and 1930s. It began with Berg's teenage obsession with Fitzgerald, for whom he was named by his mother who gorged on Fitzgerald's novels while pregnant. For the California boy who slept with *This Side of Paradise* under his pillow for two years, there was no doubt that he would go to Princeton and join Fitzgerald's eating club, Cottage. By his second day on campus, he began to

[34] The record for the longest thesis may be held by Jeanne Faust '76 for "Francis Scott Key Fitzgerald '17: A Collection of Short Stories" (English) at 756 pages; but see also n. 41, below, for Peter Joseph's original three-volume thesis at 706 pages. The shortest so far is Gianluca Tempesti '89's three-pager on "Opto-Electronic Integrated Circuits" (Electrical Engineering). "By the Numbers: Senior Theses," *PWB*, Apr. 21, 2003.

[35] William G. Bowen, *Report of the President, 1985: The Creative Arts at Princeton*, 10, 27; Lauren F. Stevens, *The Double Axe* (New York and London, 1961); Maria Katzenbach, *The Grab* (New York: William Morrow, 1977). Although Ian Caldwell '98 and Dustin Thomason's best-selling *The Rule of Four* (New York, 2004) did not originate as a senior thesis, it features an unusual Princeton thesis and has done much to publicize Princeton's rare requirement. Professor of History Anthony Grafton's long review of the book in the *New York Review of Books* ("Big Book on Campus," Sept. 23, 2004, 66–69) further underscored its Princeton provenance, some of it in his course on Renaissance magic and science that co-author Caldwell took.

explore the extensive literary archives in Firestone Library deposited by Charles Scribner's Sons. By the end of his freshman year, he had gone through all the Fitzgerald material and had become curious about Perkins. When he became an early (sophomore) concentrator in English, he was wisely assigned to Carlos Baker, Hemingway's biographer. Baker put Berg onto Wolfe, about whom he wrote two junior papers. For a third paper he compared the literary styles of Fitzgerald and Hemingway, proving to himself, at least, that the Princetonian was better than "Papa." All of this preparation led naturally to his senior thesis, "Three to Get Ready," which addressed Perkins's handling of his talented but troublesome trio.

Berg's research in the Scribner papers was thoroughly engrossing, so much so that a month before theses were due he had yet to write a word. With a healthy nudge from his advisor, Berg sat down and churned out ten pages a day. When he had finished, with no time to spare, his manuscript topped 250 pages, for which he had to get special dispensation from the English Department. Undismayed by its length, the department's two readers agreed that it was an A+, which in turn earned it the department's prize for best thesis.

The day after commencement, Berg dove back into Firestone in search of Perkins's "second echelon" authors, such as Fitzgerald's friend Edmund Wilson '16 and Struthers Burt '04, whose long, evenhanded appraisal of the four-course plan for the *Alumni Weekly* helped win the plan—and the senior thesis—widespread approval among the alumni.[36] But following Carlos Baker's sage advice that "people die, papers don't," he also launched interviews with more than a hundred people who had known Perkins or his authors. His first draft of *Max Perkins: Editor of Genius*, fashioned from 5,000 color-coded 5″ x 8″ notecards, ran to 3,000 typescript pages and needed a decisive editorial hand as much as Wolfe's bloated manuscripts did. When it was published (after four rewrites) by E. P. Dutton in 1978, it was a lean, sculpted 500 pages. Dedicated in part to his Princeton mentor Carlos Baker, the book was a critical and

[36] Struthers Burt, "Another Academic Milestone: The 'Four Course Plan' as a Supplement to the Preceptorial Method," *PAW*, Dec. 10, 1926, 339–43; Dec. 17, 1926, 375–78; Jan. 14, 1927, 425–29.

commercial success, becoming a Literary Guild selection and winning a National Book Award. Berg went on to write even longer and more successful biographies of movie mogul Samuel Goldwyn and Charles Lindbergh, to become a Princeton alumni trustee in 1999, and—appropriately—to underwrite a $3,500 scholarship for English majors wishing to use the summer, as he once had, for research or writing "in connection with their Princeton independent or course work."[37]

The topics chosen for theses are sensitive measures of students' personal values, backgrounds, and even futures.[38] Douglas Parsons

[37] Robert Dahlin, "Story Behind the Book: 'Max Perkins: Editor of Genius,' " *Publisher's Weekly*, May 22, 1978, 218; Charles L. Creesy, "From Senior Thesis to Best-Selling Biography," *PAW*, Oct. 23, 1978, 14; Lisa See, "PW Interview: A. Scott Berg," *Publisher's Weekly*, Mar. 24, 1989, 49–50; J. I. Merritt, "Berg Does Lindbergh," *PAW*, Nov. 18, 1998, 10–15, at 15; A. Scott Berg, "Three to Get Ready" (Senior thesis, Dept. of English, PU, 1971); Berg, "The Writing Life: Slices of Americana," *Washington Post Book World*, Nov. 1, 1998, 1, 10–11; "Six Join Board of Trustees," *PAW*, Sept. 8, 1999, 11; "Sophomore Named First A. Scott Berg '71 Scholar," PU, press release, Apr. 30, 2001; Jessica Hafkin, "Stories of 20th Century Heroes: Biographer A. Scott Berg '71," *DP*, Apr. 24, 2001, 3; Lindsay McGregor, "Three Awarded A. Scott Berg '71 English Research Scholarships," *DP*, Apr. 15, 2003, 1, 4; Sam J. Cooper, "Berg '71 Writes Bestseller on Hepburn's Life, Career," *DP* (online), Sept. 25, 2003. Princeton students, especially senior-thesis writers, enjoy generous funds for summer research, much of it involving extensive travel. In 1980 a member of the class of 1942 gave $100,000 for thesis research, a sum that was tripled the following year when a '55 gave $200,000. In 1992 former Secretary of State George P. Schultz '42 gave $1 million to support senior research in public policy in the Woodrow Wilson School; the previous year he had vigorously defended the senior thesis when Professor Lawrence Stone proposed to make it less than mandatory (see n. 27 above). Ryann Manning, "Theses from Afar," *DP*, Apr. 17, 2000, 3; PAW, Oct. 6, 1980, 19; Dec. 14, 1981, 10; May 15, 1991, 6; Apr. 1, 1992, 4. In 2002–2003, funds for student research approached $250,000 (thanks to Associate Dean of the College Richard G. Williams for this estimate). Miriam Bocarsly, "Senior Thesis Funding Applications Rise, Funding Availability Lags," *DP*, Dec. 2, 2002, 1, 4. See also Katherine Reilly '05, "Thesis Research on a Global Scale," *PAW Web Exclusives: On the Campus*, Nov. 3, 2004.

[38] Erwin Panofsky, "In Defense of the Ivory Tower," *Centennial Review of Arts and Science* 1:2 (Spring 1957):111–22, argues that tower-dwellers have the advantage of height, which enables them to "see things in a perspective rather different from that in which [things] present themselves when swirling around [observers] on ground level." If they are prevented by their location from acting, they can at least warn those below of impending danger and folly.

'38 would not have written "Horace Greeley—Neo-Jeffersonian," he confessed, "if I had not gone to the Horace Greeley School" in Chappaqua, New York, for two years. Likewise, Katherine Boisture's interest in the slave ship *Amistad* and the Africans' time in Farmington, Connecticut, began when "I was a 14-year-old eighth grader doing a report on these men and their abolitionist allies, visiting the Africans' home, their school, their church and the place where one of them is buried, all within a few blocks of my own house." The prescience of former Senator Bill Bradley's 1965 thesis on Harry S. Truman's fight for the Missouri senatorship in 1940 was even more uncanny than "Coverage of the Boer War in the New York Newspapers" by *Daily Princetonian* editorial editor and later *New York Times* senior editor John Oakes '34.[39]

Senior theses also register changes being rung around the world. As Anne Ruderman '01 discovered in her thesis on the history of history theses, the students' own day influences the topics they choose from the past and how they interpret their findings. Moreover, she found, "the student reaction to the outside world is quicker (and shorter lived) than its absorption in academic trends" (something most faculty, to their chagrin, already knew). Newspaper headlines were and still are metaphorically "no sooner dried on newsprint than they are wet again in thesis type." In the 1930s the Great Depression, fascism, and Nazism commanded Tigers' attention. Arthur Hess '39, a politics major, traveled to Germany in the summer of 1938 to work in German archives and to interview Nazi officials for his thesis, "The Philosophy and General Aims of National Socialist Foreign Policy." His classmate Norman Gill also spent seven weeks

[39] Douglas van ness Parsons, "Horace Greeley—Neo-Jeffersonian" (Senior thesis, Dept. of History, PU, 1938), preface; Katherine Boisture, "Friends and Neighbors: Abolitionists in Farmington, Connecticut and the *Amistad* Africans" (Senior thesis, Dept. of History, PU, 2000), preface; William J. Bradley, " 'On the Record I Stand': Harry S. Truman's Fight for the Senatorship in 1940" (Senior thesis, Dept. of History, PU, 1965); Ruderman, "In Partial Fulfillment," 20–21. See also "Noted Alumni and Their Thesis Topics: Sometimes a Great Match," *Features Digest* [PU, Office of Communications], Feb.–Mar. 1980; Eunice Kim, "Students Use Senior Theses to Explore Personal Journeys, Past Experiences," *DP*, Apr. 16, 2002; "By the Numbers: Senior Theses," *PWB*, Apr. 21, 2003.

there, collecting material for his "objective historical" take on the Anschluss, Germany's illegal annexation of Austria on March 11.[40]

Three decades later, student interest in the civil rights and women's movements and in the Sixties counterculture found expression in numerous theses. Typical was Bruce Wasser's report, "Robert Kennedy and Black America: 1961–68," submitted to the History Department in 1971, three years after Kennedy's televised assassination by a lone gunman. With the advent of coeducation, the study of women, families, and feminism took a leap forward. In 1971, after taking Eric Goldman's famous course on modern America and reading Studs Terkel's *Hard Times* on the 1930s, Peter Joseph '72, a superkinetic senior in the Woodrow Wilson School, decided to collect and write an oral history of the whole turbulent decade just ended. On earnings from a variety of student agencies that he ran, he traveled 15,000 miles and interviewed 250 Americans great and small, from reclusive novelist Ken Kesey and expansive Edward Kennedy to McDonald's flippers and California strippers. The thesis he produced, "Good Times," was a collage of encounters with the characters and crises of the 1960s, from "sex, drugs, and rock 'n roll" to ghetto riots, the Cuban missile crisis, and the student power movement. By the turn of the twenty-first century, theses were being written on the AIDS epidemic in South Africa, the year 2000 computer problem, and the military doctrine of "first strike."[41] Given the engaging thinness of the present between past and future, the topicality of thesis subjects will undoubtedly continue, in history as in every other room of the ivory tower.

❁ ❁ ❁

[40] Ruderman, "In Partial Fulfillment," 25–28, at 26; H. Gardner Ainsworth '39, "No-Course Plan," *PAW*, May 12, 1939, 667–70, at 668.

[41] Ruderman, "In Partial Fulfillment," 46–52; Michael Rodemeyer '72, "Good Times," *PAW*, Mar. 21, 1972, 8–9; Peter T. Joseph, "Good Times: An Oral History of the 1960's," 3 vols. (Senior thesis, Woodrow Wilson School and Dept. of History, PU, 1972); Caroline Moseley, "Senior Thesis Can Be Capstone of Four Years," *PWB*, Apr. 3, 2000, 1. Most departments publish commencement programs listing the senior theses for the year.

years (1925–1933), the four-course plan was regarded
uccess. According to its chief architect and overseer,
the seniors who failed to meet departmental re-
raduation fell from a high of forty-three to only
n 3 percent of the class. Honors graduates dropped
from generous percentages in the high 40s and stabilized in the mid-30s as the demanding senior thesis became universal. University Store trade-book sales and library circulation shot up to accommodate the independent study habits of the upperclassmen. The new work ethic also extended into the underclass years, particularly among the sophomores, who had to maintain a respectable average to be eligible for eating-club membership. College-wide, those who couldn't make the grade and were asked to leave fell from 142 to 62.[42] Before his retirement and death in an automobile accident in 1933, President Hibben had realized his initial hopes that the new plan of study would enable the undergraduates to acquire "habits of independent thinking," "new knowledge of their own seeking" and making, and the "inspiration" of "great subjects."[43]

What the new plan did not do, as time would reveal, was to acquaint Princeton students with the major divisions of knowledge, as the faculty saw them. Nor did it link the largely elective underclass years with the upperclass years of specialization and independent study in an intellectually coherent whole. World War II also raised troubling questions about the efficacy and quality of American education in general. Too many Americans, including college graduates, did not seem to know why they were fighting and what they were defending. As they had after World War I and would again after Vietnam, preludes of economic distress and spiritual uncertainty caused by wholesale death and destruction spawned widespread, if short-lived, movements in America for "general education" in both secondary schools and higher education. The advocates of general

[42] Dodds, *Report of the President (1933)*, 13, 15; Albion, "Curriculum Changes at Princeton," 59; Carrick, "Sophistication on the Campus," *PAW*, Nov. 16, 1928, 232.

[43] Hibben, *Report of the President (1923)*, 2; (1924), 6–7. Later classes were no less positive about the plan. When seniors in 1934 were asked "What Would You Do If You Ran the University?" only twelve said they would "Make the Four-Course Plan optional." In 1950 only seventeen in a much larger class wished to "Abolish Theses" (*Nassau Herald* [1934], 600; [1950], senior poll, n. p.).

education trotted out a long list of alleged benefits. It would, they argued, "train citizens for public responsibility, remind them of their common heritage, promote 'self-realization,' and introduce nonscientists to the world of science." In addition, it would, by reaffirming the central values of Western civilization, fortify Americans for the ideological and spiritual battles of the Cold War with "world communism," rooted in the Soviet Union.[44]

In the fall of 1947, Princeton implemented its own version of general education in the form of distribution requirements and a pyramidal progression of studies from general to specialized. In an effort to cure the "sophomore slump" and to redress what emeritus dean of the faculty Robert Root called "the growing anarchy of uncontrolled election in underclass years," the latest "new plan"—in a fit of postwar optimism—sought to "knit the four years into a single, coherent whole, each year closely articulated with the next." In the first two years, students would consolidate their hold on basic mathematical and linguistic tools, acquired in school and required for advanced studies. Into their five-course load they would also fit two semester courses in each of four "divisions" of knowledge: natural science, social studies, arts and letters, and an unusual fourth group consisting of history, philosophy, and religion.[45] This group was thought to be synoptic, to encompass the other three. By taking two of its courses, it was hoped, the student would acquire some sense of "the essential unity of all knowledge" and the habit of "organizing and systematizing all his intellectual activities"—both of them utopian goals for late-teenagers aching to be free of secondary-school demands and older veterans in search of intellectual freedom.[46]

[44] Ernest L. Boyer and Arthur Levine, *A Quest for Common Learning: The Aims of General Education*, Carnegie Foundation Essay (Princeton, 1981), 15, 55–56 (app. A), 59–61 (chart 1); Russell Thomas, *The Search for a Common Learning: General Education, 1800–1960* (New York, 1962), chap. 4; Frederick Rudolph, *Curriculum: A History of the American Undergraduate Course of Study Since 1636* (San Francisco, 1977), 252–64.

[45] By 1947, the faculty had prepared thirty-three new or revised courses to serve as distributional choices. E. Harris Harbison, "The Distributional Requirements," *PAW*, Feb. 21, 1947, 6–7.

[46] Osgood et al., *Modern Princeton*, 76–80; Stauffer, *Idea of a Princeton Education*, 23–28; "University's New Plan of Study" with "President Dodds's Comments," *PAW*, Dec. 7, 1945, 7–8.

Although the course requirements themselves may not have felt particularly onerous to freshmen who knew nothing of Princeton's pre-war elective freedom (returning veterans were another matter), the heart of the new plan—divisional requirements—was a direct challenge to the century's inexorable trend toward specialization. In the sophomore and junior years, the student had to elect one of three divisions—sciences, social studies, or humanities—and take "coordinated" work in several of its departments. One benefit of this provision was that it gave sophomores a temporary "intellectual home" until they chose a major for the last two years. At the end of his junior year the student would write a general divisional exam rather than the existing general exam in his major department, increasingly with the ball-point pen that had appeared in 1944.[47]

For upperclassmen, the four-course plan remained in effect in all other regards, except that the senior thesis-writer could take only three courses and choose from a range of special seminars for majors. "At no point in the program is any one particular course required," Princeton emphasized, to distinguish itself from Harvard, which popularized "core courses" in its famous "Redbook," *General Education in a Free Society*.[48] Since Princeton believed as much in "the diversity of human beings" as in "the unity of knowledge," said President Dodds, it sought to give its students as much choice as possible within an "organic" (one of Wilson's favorite words) program of study.[49]

Postwar undergraduates coped with, profited from, and maneuvered around this elaborate curriculum for exactly nine years, a short shelf-life for college curricula. If they found it problematic or objectionable, they might throw themselves into the revived extracurriculum or an active social life, much of it away from the campus at friendly women's colleges. But they invariably participated in a "hid-

[47] Osgood et al., *Modern Princeton*, 79; Stauffer, *Idea of a Princeton Education*, 24–26; "The New Plan of Study," *PAW*, Nov. 21, 1947, 5.

[48] *General Education in a Free Society* (Cambridge, Mass., 1945); Morton and Phyllis Keller, *Making Harvard Modern: The Rise of America's University* (New York, 2001), 42–46; Phyllis Keller, *Getting at the Core* (Cambridge, Mass., 1982).

[49] "Freshmen Begin Distributional Courses," *PAW*, Oct. 3, 1947, 5; "President Dodds's Comments," 7; Osgood et al., *Modern Princeton*, 76.

den curriculum" to relieve their anxiety, a semiprivate agenda in which they read clues about the faculty, other students, and the social context and made a game of calculating what the faculty actually expected as opposed to what they formally required. Every college generation plays a similar game. But it is played more competitively, with more intellectual and emotional consequences, when formal requirements are either too many or too rigid, leaving students little space to exercise individual learning styles or little time to complete even engrossing work to their own highest standards.[50] Throughout the late 1940s and 1950s some Princeton students played the game—indeed, all games—hard. But most seem to have adapted to the prescribed course of study without serious complaint, impressed by the polished lectures in their distribution courses and suitably challenged by their general exams and independent research as upperclassmen.[51]

By 1955–1956, however, the faculty began to tinker again with the curriculum during its meetings in Nassau Hall. Some changes, especially during the 1960s, were made in response to a new, less docile generation of undergraduates; most originated in the increasingly specialized faculty and their professionalized departments. The first change, which took effect in 1956–1957, abolished the divisional requirements as too restrictive of both student and department autonomy. While the eight-course distribution requirements remained, the general divisional exam was removed from the juniors' worry-list, though the seniors returned to a four-course load.[52] With the juniors' four-course load, this revision created a graduation requirement of thirty-six courses, lighter than most universities but still heavier than Harvard's four-course norm for all four years.

In the fast-moving, bumptious Sixties, curricular changes were moved and approved by the faculty one after the other. The decade opened with a series of reforms that signaled the triumph of departmental autonomy and student independence. Some alarm was voiced

[50] Benson R. Snyder, *The Hidden Curriculum* (New York, 1971). Snyder was a psychiatrist at MIT, whose class of 1965 provided the basis of his research over four years.

[51] For a typical 1950s class (1954) and their views on their Princeton experience twenty-five years later, see Heath, *Princeton Retrospectives*.

[52] The change in requirements is most visible in the undergraduate course catalogues between 1955–1956 and 1956–1957.

in the fall of 1961 when a few extra-large lecture courses, such as Eric Goldman's "Modern America," with 444 students, moved to three lectures a week and scrapped their numerous (and costly) precepts. Officials hastened to explain that this was not an abandonment of Princeton's hallowed preceptorials (which remained part of 700 other courses, an increase of 250 since the war), but a pedagogical experiment. To make the lecture experience more clear-eyed if not clear-headed (and to save money on repainting and repairs), they also banned smoking from lecture halls, four years before the U.S. Surgeon General issued his famous health warning; preceptors and preceptees were still free to fumigate themselves.[53]

More uniformly favorable was the students' reaction to four other changes. Two-week reading periods were inserted in the academic calendar to give more time for independent reading and the unrushed completion of lengthy research papers before final exams, which in the first semester occurred, and still occur, after the winter break.[54] A similar experiment had been tried in 1939, but the accelerated curriculum of the war years scuttled it prematurely. To the same end, seniors were given the "option" of taking only three courses during the spring semester while they wrote their theses. And to fill the chancy sophomore gap left by the removal of the divisional requirements, the university allowed early concentration in the second semester by those who had earned at least a (modest) 3.3 group average as freshmen. This concession to specialization, like the others, was made in part to help the admission office divert more of the top high school brains from Harvard and to continue the reconfiguration of Princeton's public profile from country club to intellectual

[53] Rhys Evans '62, "A Year of Change," *PAW*, June 2, 1961, 5–7, at 7; Mark Rose '61, "On the Campus," *PAW*, Dec. 9, 1960, 20. In the fall of 2005 smoking was banned from all undergraduate dormitories because of the dangers of second-hand smoke. "Health Concerns Prompt Smoking Ban in Undergraduate Dormitories," *PWB* (online), Feb. 21, 2005.

[54] Eric Herschthal, "Academic Calendar to Remain Despite Harvard Reforms," *DP*, Oct. 3, 2003; Renata Stepanov, "For Princeton, New Years Bring Exams, Dean's Date, Anxiety," *DP*, Jan. 15, 2003, 1: "The tradition of administering finals after winter break is only shared with Harvard University." Most colleges switched to preholiday exams in the mid-1970s.

powerhouse. So, too, was a new University Scholar Program, which allowed up to fifty super-bright freshmen to concentrate right away, exempt from distribution requirements and free to take graduate courses as soon as they were able. To the faculty's relief, the young scholars exhibited, in addition to pronounced "professionalism and purposefulness," a reassuring diversity of interests and no "extreme flouting of the normal curriculum."[55]

As civil rights, anti-war, and countercultural issues and protests increasingly agitated America's campuses, the Princeton student body turned most of its energies toward securing coeducation and winning more social and academic freedoms. In 1965–1966, the faculty not only rejected a committee proposal to increase the distribution requirements, it allowed them to be fulfilled over all four years instead of the first two. The following year it also allowed the students to take four nonconcentration courses Pass/Fail, to encourage more intellectual exploration without concern for résumé-building grade-point averages. On the other hand, to prevent students from loading up on departmental courses in hopes of impressing graduate or professional schools, the faculty permitted them to take no more than twenty-two courses in one division and to count only twelve departmental courses toward the degree. Beginning with the class of 1970, all students also had to acquire some mastery of a modern foreign language; this was an abrupt change from the previous year's decision that they could choose either advanced math or a language and from a postwar requirement that they acquire only a reading knowledge of French or German. Needless to say, conversational Vietnamese was not the most popular elective.[56]

Before the decade ended, however, the students had secured unprecedented freedoms. Not only did coeducation arrive in 1969 to stay, but a year earlier members of the opposite sex won an extension

[55] Evans, "A Year of Change," 5–7; "New Program," *PAW*, Apr. 29, 1960, 9; "Reading Periods," *PAW*, Oct. 21, 1960, 13; Thomas P. Roche, Jr., "The University Scholar Program," *PAW*, Mar. 2, 1965, 6–8.

[56] Edward H. Tenner '65, "On the Campus: Curriculum Proposals," *PAW*, Mar. 2, 1965, 4; J. Merrill Knapp [dean of the college], "The Undergraduate Curriculum," *PAW*, Jan. 18, 1966, 8–11, 16; PU, *Undergraduate Announcement, 1966–1967*, 35–36; PU, *Catalogue, 1946–1947*, 107.

of the right to visit dorm rooms—for study or other purposes—to ten o'clock on weeknights and two a.m. on weekends. Perhaps of wider interest was the 1967 reduction in the course load of underclassmen to four—equal to the juniors'—and of seniors to three in the first semester to match the second. In explaining the 17 percent drop in course—not work—load, new Dean of the College Edward Sullivan pointed to Harvard's "long time" four-course curriculum and concluded memorably that "courses are not everything." The increased quantity and quality of work expected in most Princeton courses and in junior papers and senior theses, he maintained, warranted the reduction, as did the decanal desire to foster intellectual exchange in less formal settings.[57]

Two other innovations were greeted with student approval. In the fall of 1969 the university shifted from the "group" system of grading to the more universal alphabetical ladder; Princeton's single ordinals were not used in American schools. Since each of the groups had acquired pluses and minuses in 1965, the A–F system (with pluses and minuses) was equally calibrated for fine professorial distinctions.[58] The mere shift to the familiar academic alphabet narrowed the range of grades available from seven to five. Moreover, increasingly qualified entering classes effectively persuaded the faculty, by their vocal expectations and classroom performances, to issue only the upper two letter grades. A principled or soft-hearted desire by the faculty to ensure academic deferments from the Vietnam draft for their male students also contributed to the twin phenomena known as *grade inflation* (an increase in the average grade awarded) and *grade compression* (a narrowing of the range within which grades are assigned).[59]

[57] "Princeton Extends Hours for Women in Dormitories," *New York Times*, Apr. 22, 1968, 51; John R. Alexander '67, "On the Campus: Reduce Work Load?" *PAW*, Nov. 15, 1966, 4; Peter Sandman '67, "Princeton Portraits: Edward D. Sullivan," *PAW*, Feb. 28, 1967, 10–11, 14. In one of his cartoons in *Tiger! Tiger!: Princeton in Caricature* (New York, 1950), William F. Brown '50 depicts a young woman leaving home with a suitcase for the weekend. She assures the worried parent behind her, "It's perfectly all right, Father. Princeton men have no sex after six."

[58] "Grading System (pre-1968)," Hist. Subj. Files (vertical), #A-109 (PUA).

[59] Greg Phillips '93, "On the Campus: Fatty Transcripts," *PAW*, Feb. 24, 1993, 8; Randal C. Archibold, "Just Because the Grades Are Up, Are Princeton Students

Following a national trend, Princeton experienced two major periods of grade inflation and administrative—never student—concern. The first was between 1969 and 1975, when A's on undergraduate transcripts rose from 17 to 30 percent of all marks, D's and F's dropped to 5 percent, and the "Gentleman's C" gave way to the "Lady's and Gentleman's B" (45 percent) as the lowest acceptable grade. The second period began in 1989 and continued into the new millennium with vigor. At its height in 1997–1998, 84 percent of Princeton's (usually) hard-working students were pulling down A's and B's, only 8 percent had to endure the mortification of C's, and D's and F's had all but vanished.[60]

In the absence of the draft, the causes suggested by faculty and administrators for the second spurt of inflation and compression included "aggressive" student lobbying for higher grades with which to impress graduate and professional schools, student acculturation of new faculty to "the Princeton way," parental demands for "their money's worth," and faculty reluctance to stick out as "tough graders," which might jeopardize their course enrollments and elicit retribution from student course evaluations. Registrar Anthony Broh offered two additional explanations. One was that fewer students were taking Pass/D/Fail courses (changed from simple Pass/Fail and extended to six courses in 1989–1990) for fear of presenting "lightweight" transcripts to graduate and professional schools; they thus took regular courses and expected high grades for their efforts.[61]

Smarter?" *New York Times*, Feb. 18, 1998, A1, B8; "Are Students Getting Smarter?" *PAW*, Mar. 6, 1996, 10, 12; "A's and B's Are the Norm," *PAW*, Mar. 25, 1998, 5.

[60] "Grade Inflation," *PAW*, Apr. 17, 1973, 6; PU, *The Report of the Commission on the Future of the College* [Marvin Bressler, chairman] (1973), 234, table 6.16; Phillips, "Fatty Transcripts," 8; Faculty Committee on Examinations and Standing [FCES], *Grading Patterns at Princeton: Report III* (PU: Office of the Dean of the College, Sept. 30, 1999), 9–10, tables I, III, IV. In order to track inflation and related problems, the dean of the college has issued an annual report on grading patterns since 1998.

[61] "Are Students Getting Smarter?" 10, 12; Archibold, "Just Because the Grades Are Up," B8; Carlos Ramos-Mrosovsky '04, "Grade Deflation: The Real Threat," *DP*, Nov. 27, 2001, 6; Eric Harkleroad '03, "Giving Credit Where Credit Is Due," *DP*, Nov. 27, 2001, 6; Jennifer Hafkin, "Grading at Princeton: Part 1," *DP*, Nov. 5, 2001, 3; "Grading at Princeton: Part 2," *DP*, Nov. 12, 2001, 3; FCES, *Grading Patterns at Princeton* (Feb. 5, 1998), 3; PU, *Undergraduate Announcement, 1989–1990*, 38–39.

The registrar's second explanation, one shared by most students and not a few faculty, was that Princeton students were simply getting smarter, more motivated, and harder-working. In the words of a young *Prince* columnist, "Grades have risen because Princeton students are better than they used to be. This is not arrogance, but statistics." Princeton's generous financial-aid policy that greatly broadened the pool of superior applicants, its stingy admission rate, and its rising "yield" of scholastic stars suggest that he was on the right track. So did the fact that the average grade-point average at Princeton was "virtually indistinguishable" from the average at five Ivy peers and Stanford.[62]

Even if much of Princeton's grading pattern could be explained by the rising quality and performance of its students, the administration felt strongly that "the faculty owes students a more fine-tuned assessment of their performance" and the world beyond the university "some means of identifying qualitative differences among the students Princeton graduates." Recognizing that change could only be incremental and slow, the college dean's office issued a twenty-five-page *Guide to Good Grading Practices* to all faculty in the fall of 2000. Among its many sage suggestions to professors were: "Articulate what your expectations are for particular grades," "Employ the full spectrum of the grading range," and "Do not alter grades simply because students ask or implore you."[63]

While making minor adjustments in their grading practices, most Princeton professors are unlikely to begin handing out scads of C's to some of "the best [students] in the world" (as a recent president of the student government put it), who invariably arrive on campus trailing clouds of high school A's, median SATs near 1500, and other

[62] "Are Students Getting Smarter?" 12; Ramos-Mrosovsky, "Grade Deflation;" FCES, *Grading Patterns at Princeton* (Feb. 5, 1998), 4. Henry Rosovsky (former dean of the faculty at Harvard) and Matthew Hartley argued in 2002 that inflation of both grades and letters of recommendation was "rampant and systemic . . . across undergraduate institutions and disciplines," especially in the Ivies. *Evaluation and the Academy: Are We Doing the Right Thing? Grade Inflation and Letters of Recommendation*, Occasional Paper (Cambridge, Mass.: American Academy of Arts and Sciences, 2002).

[63] FCES, *Grading Patterns at Princeton* (Feb. 5, 1998), 4–5; PU, *Guide to Good Grading Practices* (Office of the Dean of the College, Sept. 2000), 8–9.

extraordinary talents. While they might try to decompress their class grades minimally, they are unlikely to deflate them radically because most believe, with former provost and dean of the faculty (and now President of Penn) Amy Gutmann, that "there is no problem as long as grades reflect the quality of work done" and not merely the effort put into it.[64]

Faculty also recognize that students do better when they have more responsibility for and control over their academic work. Like their peers elsewhere, Princeton students earn higher grades in concentration electives than in lower-level distribution courses, in courses with final papers than those with exams, in small interdisciplinary programs than in large, less personal departments, and on junior papers and senior theses than in faculty-dominated courses. It is no coincidence that as Princeton has put more of the curriculum into the hands of its students, their grades have escalated.[65]

In the fall of 1968 the undergraduates welcomed another curricular innovation as warmly as they would receive the university's shift to alphabetical grading (with its gradual inflation of honors) the following year. Acceding to student demand, the faculty allowed students to initiate seminars in or across various departments on topics not covered in existing courses. Each seminar proposed had to have a qualified faculty member to guide it, required reading and writing assignments, and a sufficient number of students committed to take it. In the first year, ten seminars were offered each semester. By 1974 enthusiasts had clambered to get into a total of 132 courses; many were oversubscribed and some metamorphosed into larger classes to accommodate the supplicants. The seminars' popularity stemmed

[64] Archibold, "Just Because the Grades Are Up," B8 (quoting David Ascher '99, president of the Undergraduate Student Government); "Are Students Getting Smarter?" 12 (quoting Gutmann). In 1999, after receiving some critical feedback, the FCES recommended that the A+ (formerly with a 4.3 numerical value) receive only 4.0. In May 2000 the faculty approved. FCES, *Grading Patterns at Princeton: Report III*, 10; Kathryn Federici Greenwood, "Should Princeton Abolish the A-Plus?" *PAW*, Nov. 17, 1999, 6; FCES, *Grading Patterns at Princeton: Report IV* (Sept. 29, 2000), 2–3.

[65] FCES, *Grading Patterns at Princeton: Report III* (Sept. 30, 1999), 9, tables II–IV. See also Valen E. Johnson, *Grade Inflation: A Crisis in College Education* (New York, 2003).

not only from their relatively small size and student inspiration (which in an agitated period of "student power" was no small victory), but from the intriguing topics they treated, albeit in a familiar academic fashion. Many subjects eventually, some soon, made their way into the regular curriculum, such as artificial intelligence, Afro-American music, gothic fiction, and Eastern European politics. Others took advantage of temporary interests and talents. "Poetry and Printing" paired two related arts seldom studied in tandem, both of which had distinguished practitioners in contemporary Princeton. "Documentary Film Editing" capitalized on the visit of French filmmaker Marcel Ophuls (*The Sorrow and the Pity*), who put the class to work on his raw footage for a documentary on the Nuremberg trials.[66]

The student-initiated seminars were—and still are—usually devoted to advanced topics suitable for upperclassmen, who were also eligible or required to take seminars in their major departments.[67] They were also three-hour courses, unlike the one-hour precepts attached to larger lecture courses, in which research papers replaced final exams. As sites of enhanced student motivation and intense, disciplined discussion, they had long been thought by faculty and educational psychologists to promote learning better and with more lasting results than other class formats. Understandably, the university sought, in time, to extend their benefits to the underclasses, particularly freshmen.

In 1986–1987, with support from the Ford Foundation, each of the five residential colleges sponsored a seminar for freshmen each semester. By 2002–2003, sixty-four seminars offered 850 freshmen—more than two-thirds of the class—such intellectual fare as "Historical and Contemporary Issues in Bioethics," taught by Harold Shapiro, former Princeton president and former chair of the National Bioethics Advisory Commission, "The Tragic, the Comic, and the

[66] Susan Williams '74, "On the Campus: Student-Initiated Seminars," *PAW*, Feb. 12, 1974, 7; "The University," *PAW*, Nov. 19, 1974, 6.

[67] In recent years, as the curriculum has grown, only one or two student-initiated seminars a year have been necessary to satisfy student demand for relevant or engaging courses.

Political" (Professor of Religion Cornel West), "Poems and Experience" (Neil Rudenstine, former Princeton dean and provost and former president of Harvard), and "Walden in Our Time" (William Howarth, professor of English and former editor of the multivolume *Writings of Henry D. Thoreau*). In 1997 ten freshmen read the *Iliad* and the *Odyssey* with Robert Fagles, the premier translator of both epics. He regarded "reading the oldest poems in the West with the youngest people at the University" as "one of the most heartening experiences I have had in more than thirty-five years at Princeton," so much so that he repeated the course on "Homer" in Mathey College in the fall of 2001. One of the most durable seminars, "Active Geological Processes," was first offered in 1989 by seismologist Robert Phinney and Jason Morgan, one of the founders of the theory of plate tectonics. It featured an arduous, week-long field trip to the Sierra Nevada Mountains in California during fall break. Between camping, trekking, and eating professor-cooked food, the students kept notebooks in which they wrote up and drew what they saw before returning to campus to work on final papers.[68]

One of the major values of the freshman seminars to the university is that they have served as supplements to and partial substitutes for precepts, which are much shorter and less frequently led by senior faculty. The seminar program, said faculty director John Fleming, "seeks to institutionalize and make mandatory the experience on which Princeton prides itself." As precept instruction has gradually been given over to advanced graduate students and young instructors, freshmen in seminars have had opportunities to engage topics of absorbing interest with many of the university's leading scholar-

[68] Harold T. Shapiro, "The Freshman Seminar Program," *PAW*, Mar. 18, 1992, 41; Jennifer Greenstein Altmann, "West Spends First Fall Back on Campus with First-Year Students," *PWB*, Nov. 4, 2002, 1, 6 (the same issue included stories on sociologist Suzanne Keller's seminar on leadership and morality and on Visiting Professor of Engineering Christopher Rogers's class on robots); *PAW*, Apr. 16, 1997, 3 (Fagles); Steven Schultz, "Field Experience 'Rocks' for Freshmen in Geology Seminar," *PWB*, Dec. 10, 2001, 1, 7. See PU, *The Program of Freshman Seminars in the Residential Colleges, 2004–05* and previous editions for seminar descriptions. For more on Fagles, see Ann Waldron, "Homeric Vision," *PAW*, Jan. 26, 1994, 12–18; Chris Hedges, "A Bridge Between the Classics and the Masses," *New York Times*, Apr. 13, 2004, A25.

teachers in a close, informal setting.[69] This has put a new face on Wilson's ideal of inspiring and empowering the young through personal contact and discussion with their elders, but it has done nothing to alter its essential spirit. He would also be pleased to learn that students "form their most enduring intellectual friendships with fellow students in the seminar."[70]

The latest use of seminars may not generate as many warm memories among the freshmen. Since 2002 a new one has been required to cure their pesky writing problems brought from secondary school. The problems are of long standing. Since the 1960s freshmen were required to take a regular English course with a "w" following the number to indicate "writing intensive." Taught by regular faculty, these courses understandably put more emphasis on reading comprehension and content than on writing. In the late 1980s, courses outside English were eligible to satisfy the requirement, all of which could also satisfy a distribution requirement at the same time. But the influx of freshmen from an increasingly broader pool of secondary schools, public and private, also brought more variable writing skills than in the past. After internal and external reviews of the writing program, Princeton revamped it completely.

Beginning in the fall of 2002, every freshman was required to take a writing seminar, which increased the B.A. graduation requirements to thirty-one courses (the engineering minimum remained at thirty-six) and no longer counted toward distribution credit. Limited to twelve students each and meeting twice a week for eighty minutes, these seminars were based on topics from all disciplines but required less reading and more attention to the development of writing skills.

[69] A lengthy *Report on the Status of the Princeton Precept System* by a committee of the Undergraduate Student Government in Apr. 2002 pointed to widespread dissatisfaction among students. In response, the Office of the Dean of the College prepared a booklet of suggestions for improvements entitled *Inspired Conversations: The Princeton Precept* (2003).

[70] Grafton, "Precepting," *PAW*, Mar. 12, 2003, 19; Deborah Arotsky, "Do Freshman Seminars Bring Students and Faculty Closer Together?" *DP*, Apr. 1, 2002, 3 (quoting John Fleming); "Seminars Introduce Freshmen to 'the Adventure of Learning,' " *PWB*, Nov. 4, 2002, 1 (quoting Associate Dean of the College Howard Dobin).

While absorbing something about Dracula, DNA, or "Bandits in Myth and History," students learned the techniques and strategies that distinguish good high school prose from the best college writing. To teach the hundred new seminars each year, Princeton turned not only to regular Princeton faculty, postdoctoral scholars, and advanced graduate students, but to a new cadre of twenty full-time lecturers with academic Ph.D.s and writing or editing experience.

This costly addition of faculty and small seminars enabled each freshman to benefit from frequent writing assignments that progress in length and complexity, opportunities for revision, frequent one-on-one conferences with the instructor, peer review, and oral presentations, all of which are regarded as hallmarks of effective writing pedagogy. Although students responded more favorably to the new seminars than had their predecessors to the "w" courses, because the classes are required and extra and entail a great deal of criticism (always potentially ego-bruising) and steady effort, they will probably never top the undergraduate list of favorite academic experiences.[71]

❁ ❁ ❁

Although the faculty in its curriculum-making role seems to have been preoccupied with responding to student *demands* since the 1960s, it has been equally or more concerned with fine-tuning its offerings to satisfy the changing educational *needs* of new generations. Sometimes deletion prevailed over accretion, the usual mode of curriculum-fashioning. Two pieces of silliness on the nonintellectual side of the curriculum were disposed of with the sincere if quiet

[71] Ruth Stevens, "Writing Program Revamped," *PWB*, Jan. 8, 2001; "Expansive New Writing Program Launched," *Princeton: With One Accord* (Fall 2001), 1, 7. Thomas Bartlett, "Why Johnny Can't Write, Even Though He Went to Princeton," *CHE*, Jan. 3, 2003, A39–40; Katherine Reilly '05, "The Failings of Writing Requirements," *DP*, Feb. 4, 2002, 8; Emily Stolzenberg, "Learn to Write Despite Writing Seminar," *DP* (online), Feb. 8, 2005. To assist students at all levels with writing problems or questions, an expanded Writing Center operates in Wilcox Hall. For a list of courses offered each semester, see the Princeton Writing Program Web site: http://web.princeton.edu/sites/writing.

gratitude of the students (and former students). In 1990 Princeton dropped both the mandatory swimming test and the two-semester physical education requirement that had plagued or embarrassed freshmen since 1911. Responding to a new generation of health and fitness buffs, the faculty decided that being able to float for ten minutes was no longer an essential mark of an educated Tiger. In earlier tests, always performed in the nude before coeducation, the freshmen were obliged to swim 220 yards, with both breast and back strokes, and to make a "fair dive" (not, mercifully, from the high board) to qualify for graduation. Yet no one in administrative memory had ever been denied a diploma for failing the test, so the inconsistency was finally expunged.[72]

Affecting only two classes but affecting them strongly, another exercise in gratuitous nudity was halted in 1966, partly through pressure from the *Daily Princetonian*. In 1948 and 1966, each member of the entering class was summoned to McCosh Infirmary, told to undress, and then photographed front, side, and rear without fig leaf or explanation. The purpose was to forward the "scientific" research of W. H. Sheldon, a closet eugenicist and Columbia-based expert in "somato-typing" who sought to establish the relationship between one's combination of body types (ectomorph, mesomorph, and endomorph) and intelligence, temperament, and "moral worth." This prurient nonsense occurred at Ivy League and Seven Sister colleges (and other institutions across the country) from the 1940s through the 1960s. When his work was discredited amid new assertions of student privacy, too late to save the "face" of thousands of self-conscious teenagers, most of the pictures were destroyed by the colleges, but 27,000 negatives ended up in the National Anthropological Archives at the Smithsonian. The potential for embarrassment—or blackmail—that lay in photos of now-famous alumni of Yale and Vassar, Princeton and Wellesley, prompted "The Nation's Attic" to take the unprecedented step of macerating and burning its scandalous holdings. In March 1995, Princeton's Archivist Ben Primer man-

[72] "Faculty Drops Swimming Test, Physical-Education Requirement," *PAW*, July 18, 1990, 7; "University Plunges into New Era, Abolishes Time-Honored Swim Test," *DP*, Sept. 14, 1990, 1, 12.

fully tossed a total of 1,319 photos into a giant shredder. The only pictorial evidence that remains of the Adonises of '52 and '70 resides in a small plastic bag of paper crumbs in Mudd Library.[73]

The faculty performed a more positive tune-up in the spring of 1995 when it redefined the nature of the distribution requirement, which students had met, without undue protest, since 1947. Under that requirement (with its 1965–1966 revision), every A.B. candidate had to take two courses in each of four "divisions" at any time during his or her four years. The requirement was premised on the assumption, or hope, that taking eight miscellaneous courses in four-to-eight disparate departments would provide a Princeton graduate with a sound general education in the liberal arts and sciences, regardless of what those courses taught or how they taught it. This assumption became hopelessly outdated as the course book swelled, departments ceased to offer a single methodological product, and the production of knowledge grew increasingly interfiliated and cross-disciplinary.[74]

A backdrop to reform was the largely conservative attack on America's universities, particularly elite ones, their faculties, and their curricula in the late 1980s and 1990s. Vociferous critics, most of them nonacademics, charged that American higher education, "all coherence gone," produced students whose ignorance, particularly of Western history and culture and the "canon" of "great" (i.e., Western male) literature, was nothing less than a national scandal and the primary cause of *The Closing of the American Mind* (as the University

[73] "Princeton's Posture Photos Shredded," *PAW*, Apr. 19, 1995, 8, 10; Ron Rosenbaum, "The Great Ivy League Nude Posture Photo Scandal," *New York Times Magazine*, Jan. 15, 1995, 26–31, 40, 46, 55; "Naked Freshman Photos Classify Body Structures," *DP*, Sept. 19, 1966, 5; Editorial, *DP*, Sept. 20, 1966, 2; "Posture Photographs," Hist. Subj. Files (vertical), #A-109 (PUA). The bag, and the archivist's ear-plugs from the noisy occasion, are in the Memorabilia Collection, Box Z-7 (PUA). Some of Vassar's photos were macerated in the same operation; Princeton and Vassar split the $64 cost.

[74] Faculty Committee on the Course of Study, *Proposed Changes in Undergraduate Degree Requirements* (Office of the Dean of the College, Oct. 28, 1994), 2–4. President Shapiro's strategic-planning document, *Princeton University—Continuing to Look Ahead* (Nov. 1993), put in motion a re-examination of the distribution requirements by the faculty.

of Chicago's Allan Bloom called it in his bestseller). Implicated in the conservative indictments were three-plus decades of curricular additions and adjustments to recognize the historical and continuing importance of racial and ethnic minorities, civil rights and wrongs, women, gender and sexuality, and non-Western countries and continents for students' understanding of America and the modern world. And just below (if not on) the surface was fear of the intellectual and moral dangers thought to be inherent in various Continental imports of neologistic theory, collectively dismissed as "postmodernism."[75]

Thoroughly attuned to the uses and abuses of theory, yet conscious of the need to introduce students to the major methodologies of the key divisions of contemporary knowledge, the Princeton faculty redefined courses for the purpose of distribution and added two requirements for a total of ten. Courses were now categorized in the catalogue by intellectual aim and approach, regardless of department or subject matter. Beginning in the fall of 1996, A.B. candidates had to take one course in each of four categories: Epistemology and Cognition (EC), Ethical Thought and Moral Values (EM), Historical Analysis (HA), and Quantitative Reasoning (QR). Two courses were required in Literature and the Arts (LA), Social Analysis (SA), and Science and Technology, with a lab (ST). Because of the complex development of knowledge in the late twentieth century, many departments offered courses that could satisfy as many as five different requirements; most satisfied more than one.[76] With the addition of a Freshman Writing Seminar and the continuation of the foreign language requirement, which might take as many as four semesters

[75] James Axtell, *The Pleasures of Academe: A Celebration & Defense of Higher Education* (Lincoln, 1998), 210–50; Francis Oakley, *Community of Learning: The American College and the Liberal Arts Tradition* (New York, 1992), chaps. 4–5; W. B. Carnochan, *The Battleground of the Curriculum: Liberal Education and the American Experience* (Stanford, 1993); Lawrence W. Levine, *The Opening of the American Mind: Canons, Culture, and History* (Boston, 1996).

[76] In 2002–2003, for example, the Politics Department offered several courses in political theory that qualified as EM, two analytical courses as QR, and most as SA. Religion courses satisfied requirements for EC, HA, EM, SA, and LA. PU, *Undergraduate Announcement, 2002–03*, 302–8, 323–27. For the teaching of ethics in various guises, see the special issue of *PAW* devoted to "Exploring Ethics" (Jan. 26, 2005).

to complete, the Princeton graduate in the new millennium was obliged by the faculty to devote twelve to fifteen of his or her thirty-one courses (39–48 percent) to laying a liberal foundation for future life and adaptive learning.[77]

❁ ❁ ❁

Few of the curricular changes in the past half-century met with unqualified support, or even the acquiescence, of Princeton alumni, the most conservative constituency of the college community. As if by some kind of natural law, alumni tend to regard their own college days as the gold standard, though they seldom do at the time. Yet (to reprise the somewhat jaundiced words of University of Chicago President Robert M. Hutchins), "They do not know what the college was really like. They do not want to know what it is like now. They want to imagine that it is like what they think it was like in their time. Therefore they oppose all change."[78] Like their counterparts elsewhere, Princeton alumni from time to time have expressed their strong misgivings not only about the current administration and faculty, but about the general "softening" of standards and "coddling" of students.

The first group to raise alarms was the "Alumni Committee To Involve Ourselves Now" (ACTION), which organized early in 1969 under the leadership of Jere Patterson '38, Rhodes Scholar, Princeton parent, and New York advertising executive.[79] Concerned that recent political events on campus and the advent of coeducation spelled deep trouble for alma mater, they conducted a poll that summer of some 1,325 randomly selected alumni. Unsurprisingly, the older the alumni, the more they favored a tougher response to campus disruptions, the continuation of ROTC, and a faculty that taught more

[77] "Requirements for AB and BSE Revised," *PAW*, Oct. 25, 1995, 8. Yale began to move its distribution requirements in a similar direction only in 2003. Una Au, "Reconstructing the Yale education," *Yale Herald* (online), Apr. 4, 2003, 1–6.

[78] Robert Maynard Hutchins, "The Sentimental Alumnus" (1934), in *No Friendly Voice* (Chicago, 1936), 87–94, at 87.

[79] "Thunder on the Right: An Interview with Jere Patterson '38, Chairman of ACTION," *PAW*, Oct. 20, 1970, 10–13.

and published less. A generational fault-line also ran through their answers to questions about the desirability of more student involvement in university governance and admission of racial minorities. But when it came to the curriculum, the alumni consulted were "overwhelmingly opposed to the radical changes demanded by some student activists: abolition of exams and grades, unrestricted choice of courses, and programs of Afro-American studies directed and taught only by Negroes."[80]

Less than three years later, as Provost William Bowen assumed the presidency, the disgruntlement expressed by ACTION grew into a larger, noisier, and more persistent organization known as CAP, "Concerned Alumni of Princeton." For its first three years, the group was led by Asa Bushnell '21, former commissioner of the Eastern Collegiate Athletic Conference, and Shelby Cullom Davis '30, U.S. ambassador to Switzerland and donor in 1964 of $5.3 million to endow two chairs in American and European history. In November 1972 CAP launched *Prospect*, then a monthly publication sent free to some 13,000 alumni who might wish to share in CAP's "constructive criticism" of the university and its leaders.

Like its conservative predecessor, CAP liked precious little about America in the 1960s and early 1970s and even less about developments at Princeton. Their list of complaints was long: left-leaning, brainwashing faculty; misguided admission policies that admitted too many women, blacks, high schoolers, and Harvardian "geniuses"; compromising, weak-kneed presidents who ignored the alumni except at fundraising time; and curricular changes that abandoned the coherent structure and confident teaching of their own days for educational "agnosticism" and craven kowtowing to shaggy, pot-smoking students whose goal was as much personal freedom ("license") as

[80] "ACTION Poll," *PAW*, Nov. 11, 1969, 4–5. When President Goheen was invited to respond, he noted that the poll's questions were "loaded" with hot-button words ("incite," "turmoil," "manipulate") and calculated either to confuse issues or to elicit negative responses. Student "activists," for example, did not seek or secure the abolition of exams (or other instruments of evaluation) when they advocated and received from the faculty a minimal number of Pass/Fail courses. *PAW*, Nov. 11, 1969, 5.

they could get or get away with, if not social and political revolution. Through the orange journalism of *Prospect* and persistent hectoring of President Bowen through letters and memos, CAP sought to turn the educational clock back to a golden age of "well-rounded" collegiatism, before Princeton became a modern research university forced to live in a political world not of its own making.[81]

It was a measure of CAP's largely political agenda that the only *Prospect* article devoted solely to the curriculum did not appear until September 1975. The article's ostensible target was the Bressler Report on the future of the college, which had appeared two-and-a-half years earlier and had been summarized at length in the *Alumni Weekly* at the time.[82] The *Prospect* article focused on the report's admission that, in the intellectual and educational climate of the 1970s, the Princeton faculty no longer agreed that it was possible to "identify what it means to be an 'educated' man or woman, and to teach these materials and subjects." Thus CAP concluded that "educational anarchy" prevailed because the faculty would not "define what a [student] should learn," beyond a handful of distribution courses chosen largely at random by the student from 721 offerings. Blaming Presidents Goheen and Bowen for pusillanimity and complicity, CAP argued that "with the faculty intent on research, in control of the University, and unable to agree on the components of general education anyway," it was simply easier "to allow the gradual dissolution of a structured curriculum, giving in to student demands for more and more freedom in choosing their courses and continued

[81] "A New Magazine," *PAW*, Nov. 14, 1972, 6; " 'Prospect,' "*PAW*, Jan. 23, 1973, 8; "Interview with Shelby Cullom Davis '30," *PAW*, Nov. 5, 1974, 9–11; E. J. Kahn, Jr., "Annals of Higher Education: A Tiger by the Tail," *New Yorker*, May 23, 1977, 88, 90–94, 96–108. For an even-handed examination of the question, "Are Princeton's Students Being Brainwashed?" see Robert Segal [graduate student in Religion] in *PAW*, Feb. 20, 1973, 10–13; Feb. 27, 1973, 12–13. See also Letters to the Editor, *PAW*, Mar. 13, 1973, 5; Donald W. Light [assistant professor of sociology], "The Faculty & Politics: Dispelling the Myths," *PAW*, May 22, 1973, 8–9; William G. Bowen, *Report of the President (1974), Part II: The Politics of the Faculty* (reprinted in Bowen, *Ever the Teacher*, 323–36).

[82] An eight-page "Highlights from *The Report of the Commission on the Future of the College*" was inserted in *PAW*, May 15, 1973, between pp. 14 and 15.

relaxation of standards and requirements." Nearly full-page profiles of the "Great Books" curriculum at St. John's College and the University of Chicago's "Common Core" program, which "counters the forces of specialization with a sound and unshakeable background in Western culture," revealed CAP's educational assumptions. For them, higher education was largely the collective absorption of preselected course content, a *product* to be tested on examinations, not, as Princeton and most elite universities had decided long before the "licentious" Sixties, a *process* of discovery and acquisition of intellectual skills and methods, most effectively through personal choice and independent study.[83]

Although CAP continued its stand-still assaults on ever-evolving Princeton well into the 1980s, it was left to others to level another kind of criticism at the curriculum. In the spring of 1978, Oregon attorney Donald H. Burnett '52 sent a report to President Bowen and the Board of Trustees questioning the educational costs of shortening the instructional year through reading periods in 1960–1961 and the reduction in course requirements seven years later. He had been prompted by his twenty-fifth reunion the previous year, he said, to think about the work load his class carried compared to that of the Class of '77. Even before his study was published in *PAW*, the Class of '78 publicized it by including a numerical chart comparing the work loads of its two predecessors in the *Nassau Herald*.[84] Burnett might have served a useful, less controversial purpose had he stopped after showing that class days had decreased by 37 (22 percent) and class hours by 602 (36 percent). But he went on to assign arbitrary "work points" to exams and papers and discovered a 23 percent de-

[83] "A Princeton Education: Looking at the Curriculum," *Prospect* 4:5 (Sept. 15, 1975):15–22. Not only was CAP operating with the usual "golden-age" myopia of alumni, it failed to notice that most of the Bressler Report *affirmed* Princeton's traditional philosophy and curriculum and, as *PAW* had reported a year earlier, that its most "imaginative" suggestions for curricular change were quickly rejected by the allegedly "radical" faculty. "Bressler Commission," *PAW*, Oct. 8, 1974, 8. I am grateful to then vice-president for public affairs Robert Durkee for a lengthy e-mail regarding the history and philosophy of ACTION and CAP (May 15, 2003).

[84] Donald H. Burnett '52, "Weighing the Work Load," *PAW*, Oct. 9, 1978, 21–25; *Nassau Herald* (1978), 74.

crease. Unfortunately, he omitted from his calculations both reading periods, when a great deal of work was (and is) done, and all independent written work in the junior and senior years, which had (and has) increased since the early 1950s.

Princeton's collective answer to Burnett's and similar, more recent, accusations was what he dismissed as the "fewer-but-deeper" defense. Echoing President Bowen and a number of faculty Burnett had dismayingly consulted for his study, four deans, two professors, and a *Prince* columnist explained in *PAW*, "The Demands Are Different Now." They argued that student achievement was less the result of hours or days spent in the classroom than of "habits, climate, total institutional milieu, quality of student body and faculty, student and faculty expectations, self-imposed standards, outside pressure from graduate schools or from society as a whole." They emphasized that much material previously covered in college was now taught in high school and graduate material was now covered in undergraduate courses. Thus Princeton students operate at a "higher level of intellectual sophistication than previously" and are capable of much more, and better, independent research and writing. Dean Robert Jahn (Engineering), Dean Donald Stokes (Woodrow Wilson School), and English Department chairman A. Walton Litz, Jr., all of whom graduated from Princeton the year before Burnett did, testified that in their long experience, "Today's students are . . . more dedicated to their work and produce work of the higher quality." Rather than the "fewer-but-deeper" explanation, Dean Jahn argued, "less rote, more creativity" more accurately described the "evolutionary changes" of the past quarter-century.[85]

[85] Joan S. Girgus [dean of the college] and Aaron Lemonick *54 [dean of the faculty], "The Demands Are Different Now," *PAW*, Oct. 9, 1978, 26–30. In 2001–2002 Alan J. Schlesinger '68 p'04 and C. Webster Wheelock '60 *67 p'93 renewed Burnett's criticisms of Princeton's "light" work load. Both drew attention to the Saturday morning classes and five-course loads of earlier classes. Wheelock estimated that he and his classmates in the humanities "did about 60 percent more course work to graduate than do today's Princetonians" (Letters to the Editor, *PAW*, Nov. 7, 2001, 4 [Schlesinger]; Feb. 27, 2002, 4–5 [Wheelock]; *PAWPlus* (online), "Letter Box," Apr. 8, 2002 [Alexander D. Feldman '01]; Sept. 1, 2002 [Wheelock]). In 2002–2003, Princeton had only 120 teaching days, compared to Chicago's 165. Kate Swearengen '04, "On the Campus: Winter to Winter," *PAW* (online), Mar. 12, 2003.

❁ ❁ ❁

Although faculty, administrators, and alumni had their say on the curriculum, the Princeton constituency with the biggest stake in it was its student consumers. More than anyone but a few deans, they viewed it as a whole and experienced it directly, and they did not—do not—hesitate to judge it with the exuberant frankness of youth. Student evaluations have been around since there were students, since the medieval universities.[86] In the twentieth century, Princeton students have assessed the evolving curriculum through senior polls and songs about the faculty, formal and informal course critiques, and voting with their feet, and as alumni in later memories. Overall and through time, they have given most of their professors and courses high marks.

A traditional but unrefined measure of curricular quality is the popularity of courses and their professors. This is a somewhat dull instrument because students choose both for many different reasons—all personal, most reasonable, some regrettable. Still, with liberal add/drop "shopping" periods, a course that did not satisfy or meet expectations could be abandoned. So popularity has some value as an index of student judgment, particularly among strong students of intelligence and discernment.

In the mid-1920s the most popular majors were Economics, English, and History, followed at some distance by Philosophy and Politics. Within a decade, in the middle of the Great Depression, the students had shifted their academic interests decisively from the humanities to the more "relevant" or career-oriented social sciences; English and Philosophy lost 52 majors while Politics, Economics, and History gained 151. Throughout the 1960s, 1970s, and 1980s, the "hot," star-studded History Department held the top spot, followed

[86] Bologna's students wielded the most clout by hiring and firing their professors. Students elsewhere in Europe simply moved to another university if they were dissatisfied. As in President Patton's day, unpopular professors received the students' "loud laughter, whistling and disorder," even thrown stones. Charles Homer Haskins, *The Rise of Universities* (New York, 1923), 14–15; Lynn Thorndike, ed., *University Records and Life in the Middle Ages* (New York, 1944), 33, 237, 299–301, 392; Alan B. Cobban, "Medieval Student Power," *Past & Present*, no. 53 (1971):28–66.

consistently by English and Politics.[87] In 1997, at the height of the stock market bubble, Economics jumped to the top, but quickly fell back to its customary fourth place when the bubble burst. Of thirty A.B. departments in 2002–2003, 55 percent of the junior class chose to concentrate in only five, creating staffing and space problems for those happy few but underutilizing the potential of smaller, more sequential, and equally strong departments and programs in the sciences and foreign languages.[88]

Popular majors usually entailed several large courses, most of which owed their size more to the popularity of their lecturers than to concentration requirements. As World War II wound down in 1945–1946, the most popular course with Princeton's 1,588 civilian students and 480 naval trainees was Walter P. Hall's History 109 on Western civilization and the contemporary crisis. Nicknamed "Buzzer" for the noise made by his hearing aid and famous for his bold vests and bulldog companion, the Wilson-appointed preceptor-turned-Dodge Professor of History drew 618 auditors, nearly a third of the student body. Second to Hall's numbers were the postwar enrollments in "Introduction to Psychology" (457), Shakespeare (368), and the English Romantic Movement (272).[89]

As times and students changed, the largest courses in the fall of 1994 had a different look and feel. The leader, Economics 101—"The

[87] Mark Silk, "The Hot History Department: Princeton's Influential Faculty," *New York Times Magazine*, Apr. 19, 1987, 44–47, 50, 56, 62–63.

[88] John Grier Hibben, *Report of the President (1923)*, 10; "Trend Away from the Humanities" (chart), *PAW*, Jan. 31, 1936, 369; "By the Numbers: The Most Popular Majors" (chart), *PAW*, Dec. 17, 1997, 4; Marjorie Censer, "University Investigates Major Trends, Seeks Boost in Smaller Departments," *DP*, Jan. 17, 2003, 1, 2; Callen Bair, "Small Certificate Programs Attract Varied Students," *DP*, Apr. 21, 2003, 3; "By the Numbers: Undergraduate Concentration Patterns [2002–2003]," *PWB*, Nov. 3, 2003. In October 2004 the Office of the Dean of the College published a 72-page booklet on the various *Major Choices* made by successful alumni in smaller departments. Karin Dienst, "New Book Promotes Choice of Majors," *PWB* (online), Oct. 18, 2004; Ruth Stevens, "Initiative Under Way to Educate Students About Range of Majors," *PWB* (online), Mar. 1, 2004.

[89] "Courses," *PAW*, Apr. 12, 1946, 5. On Hall's reputation as a spellbinding lecturer, see "Buzzer's Garibaldi," *PAW*, Dec. 7, 1951, 12; "The Faculty," *PAW*, Feb. 15, 1952, 8; Geoffrey L. Tickner '52, "On the Campus," *PAW*, June 6, 1952, 15; "A Memorial to Walter P. 'Buzzer' Hall," *PAW*, Sept. 28, 1962, 3–4.

FIGURE 13. Professor Walter P. (Buzzer) Hall conducting a history precept with his usual animation.

National Economy"—with 392 students, capitalized on the undergraduates' entrepreneurial ambitions during the prosperous Clinton years. On the other hand, Victor Brombert's urbane, French-accented lectures on "Modern European Writers" drew most of the 349 auditors to Literature 141, a writing-intensive course.[90] (General) Physics 103, (Organic) Chemistry 303, and Molecular Biology 211 enjoyed high enrollments thanks to science and engineering majors and pre-medical students as well as to legendary instructors such as Maitland Jones, the "Orgo Master."[91] The 237 enrollees in "The American Civil War and Reconstruction" (History 376) elected to be there to hear James McPherson's articulate and evocative lectures

[90] Annual Giving advertisement featuring Brombert, *PAW*, Mar. 24, 1980, 35; Kathryn F. Greenwood, "Class Act: Exploring the Human Condition in Great Works," *PAW*, Nov. 6, 1996, 7, 9. Brombert explores his European upbringing and wartime adventures in *Trains of Thought: Memories of a Stateless Youth* (New York, 2002).

[91] Samantha L. Miller '95, "Orgo Master," *PAW*, Dec. 22, 1993, 9–12.

and to read his best-selling, Pulitzer–Prize-winning text, *Battle Cry of Freedom*.[92]

When the inevitable rosy haze forms over alumni memories of their academic experiences, they tend to remember best the outstanding senior professors who lectured in their introductory or distribution courses. The older the alumni, the less they tend to recall the actual content of their courses or even the words of their professors. But they can frequently remember with warm exactness the impression those teachers made upon their younger, impressionable selves. The most memorable performances, perhaps, were set-piece lectures on historical or literary characters that attracted extra auditors from all over campus by word-of-mouth advertising. "Buzzer" Hall's final declamatory masterpiece on Garibaldi, which was co-sponsored by the Whig-Clio debating society and the heavily Italian Princeton Janitors' Union, not only drew more than seven hundred fans to McCosh 50 but was broadcast on the campus radio station.[93]

Likewise, medievalist Durant "Robbie" Robertson's ribald re-telling of the Wife of Bath story from *The Canterbury Tales* was not to be missed, nor were actor and English professor Thomas Roche's "brilliant, must-see lectures" on Hamlet and Lear, which drew many who were not registered for his Shakespeare course. E. H. "Jinx" Harbison's last lecture in "Renaissance and Reformation" history, featuring sharp dialogue between all the major figures of the period, was so instructive and well-constructed that the *Alumni Weekly* published it whole beside the department's memorial to their Erasmian colleague. But the students who got the biggest bang for their buck were in Hubert Alyea's chemistry courses. The impish "Dr. Boom," who inspired Disney's film "The Absent-Minded Professor," was notorious for transforming his classes into pyrotechnic displays of chemical reactions and principles.[94]

[92] "Jefferson Lecturer James M. McPherson" issue, *Humanities* [NEH], 21:2 (Mar./Apr. 2000); "By the Numbers: Top Enrollments This Fall," *PAW*, Dec. 7, 1994, 6.

[93] "Buzzer's Garibaldi," *PAW*, Dec. 7, 1951, 12.

[94] Alice Fahs '73 in Mimi Chubb, "University Alters Curriculum to Reflect New Events, Technology," *DP*, Nov. 18, 2002, 3 (on Robertson and Roche); Robin Cathy Herman '73, "Princeton Portrait: Durant W. Robertson," *PAW*, Mar. 7, 1972, 7; Lynn Staley, "Durant Waite Robertson, Jr.," in Marks, *Luminaries*, 228–34 (also in *PAW*, Oct. 21, 1998, 47–48); "Jinx Harbison's Memorial," *PAW*, Nov. 3, 1963, 6, 16; E. H. Harbison '28, "Last Lecture," *PAW*, Nov. 3, 1963, 7–9, 16–19; "Bang! The A-Bomb Story," *PAW*,

When the Class of 1954 was planning their twenty-fifth reunion, they decided to invite psychologist Roy Heath to interview sixty-four members for a serious retrospective on what Princeton meant to them as undergraduates and since. Half of the members chosen had been Heath's advisees in a special Carnegie Corporation-funded project in which he met with and interviewed them individually and in small groups at least three times a semester for their first two years. The other thirty-two men had been in Heath's weekly preceptorials in psychology. Both groups were representative samples of their class in terms of SATs, majors, honors, and later careers. In largely unguided, one-hour interviews, each alumnus was asked to speak about the significant, growth-provoking people and experiences in their lives at Princeton. Besides friends and roommates, the people who stood out most in their memories were some fifty teachers (out of some five hundred) whose lectures and precepts made an indelible impression. Philosopher and former Far Eastern civil servant Walter Stace, art historian John Martin, Spanish émigré and Cervantes expert Américo Castro, Voltaire scholar and lookalike Ira Wade, sociologist "bad-boy" Melvin Tumin, chain-smoking Shakespearean Donald Stauffer, actor-turned-physicist Eric Rogers, whose lecture on Copernicus left nary a dry eye in the hall—these and other men were remembered for their commanding intellectual presence and passion, their high standards, and for embodying "the possibility of achieving distinction in the context of the burdens of life." Of the sixty-four men interviewed, only ten failed to mention a specific teacher or course, either favorably or unfavorably; four of them had left Princeton prematurely.[95]

Nov. 17, 1961, 7–9; Daniel White '65, "The Amazing Dr. Boom," *PAW*, May 16, 1972, 10–13; "In Memoriam: Princeton's 'Dr. Boom,'" *PAW*, Nov. 27, 1996, 6.

[95] Heath, *Princeton Retrospectives*, 3–8, 11–19. See also Heath, *The Reasonable Adventurer: A Study of the Development of Thirty-Six Undergraduates at Princeton* (Pittsburgh, 1964), in which he divided freshmen into three psychological types—Non-Committers, Hustlers, and Plungers—and followed their psychological development through graduation. The Heath Project is described and updated with additional memories in Walter Mott '54, "S. Roy Heath and the Class of 1954 Advisee Project," *Lives of '54: After Fifty Out*, ed. Alan E. Mayers '54 (Hagerstown, Md. 2004), 600–26 (I am grateful to Alan Mayers and Russell Marks '54 for a copy).

Courses and professors recollected in distant tranquillity often earned similar ratings from alumni when they were still students, experiencing the quotidian goads, demands, and grades of undergraduate class work. Throughout the Wilsonian century, Princeton students—graduating seniors, especially—have exercised their timeless right and propensity to assess their teachers and courses publicly. The steps of Nassau Hall, where for two-thirds of the century seniors gathered in the late spring to sing old favorites and the latest verses of the faculty song, was perhaps the most daring venue. There they good-naturedly, though sometimes sharply, called the faculty to account. In 1903 they sang:

Here's to Paul Renass van Dyke
Who rants and raves and rides a bike
If he keeps on we'll have to strike
Oh, here's to Paul Renass van Dyke.

Here's to Allen Art Marquand
An easier Prof. has not been found.
The men elect him for a mark
Because he lectures in the dark.

By 1922 they added:

Here's to Master Warner Fite,
He knows what's wrong; he knows what's right.
No end of knowledge seems to lurk
Behind his academic smirk.

Here's to Harper, Shakespeare's peer,
He gives his gut-course half a year;
Spouts out verses by the yard,
Has it in for Bill the Bard.

By the 1930s, the seniors, in doggerel that seldom scanned, wished to discard faculty dead-wood along with the Great Depression:

Frank MacDonald, grand old gent,
His heart is filled with sentiment.
His lectures never seem inspired
For Frank MacDonald is too tired.

Murch's writing coterie
Meets with him in '03.
Tired Herbie lies a-bed,
Discussing stories he's not read.

Ten years later, they thought they had the History Halls' numbers:

Here's to foaming Buzzer Hall
In History he found his call.
His hats and ties are made with care
From "Garibaldi's" underwear.

Oratorical Beppo Hall
Tries to make liberals of us all.
But though he thinks he's done his best
We're liberal just for the hour test.

In the fractious mid-1960s, the about-to-be graduates made no secret of their political leanings:

Arno Mayer's got a 'cept
Of which there is no secret kept.
The line that Arno always barks
Sounds suspiciously like Marx.[96]

Eric Goldman's not been seen
In fifty miles of Cannon Green.
But still he draws his weekly pay
While feeding 'cepts to L.B.J.[97]

Yet they could also admire the scholars of the deep past, who took them away, at least temporarily, from their own tempestuous times:

[96] Mayer was one of CAP's favorite *bêtes noires*. See "Arno Mayer: A Demonstrator's Friend," *Prospect* 2:9 (Oct. 8, 1973), 23; "Three Top Professors And What They Teach," *Prospect* 4:4 (June 1, 1975):14–15; T. John Jamieson, "Perverse Persistence," [review of Arno J. Mayer, *The Persistence of the Old Regime: Europe to the Great War* (New York, 1981)], *Prospect* 11:2 (Spring 1982):6–7 (reprinted from *American Spectator* [Jan. 1982]).

[97] See "On the Cover," *PAW*, Jan. 28, 1964, 5; Eric F. Goldman, "*The Tragedy of Lyndon Johnson*: A History Professor Becomes White House 'Intellectual In Residence,' " *PAW*, Jan. 21, 1969, 8–11; Daniel J. Kevles, "Eric Frederick Goldman," in Marks, *Luminaries*, 86–108, esp. 104–6.

Robertson doth pointe the waye
To what olde Chaucer hadde to saye,
When he reedes from Chaucer's pages,
You think you're in the Middle Ages.[98]

How far the faculty-song verses expressed the opinions of the whole senior class is impossible to tell; probably a few versifiers—presumably not English majors—pinned their favorite and unfavorite faculty to the page. A somewhat more reliable index of senior sentiment was the poll conducted annually by the *Nassau Herald*, one of the two student yearbooks. From Wilson's day to midcentury, the seniors answered a changing variety of questions about their teachers and courses. The Class of 1902's "most popular professor" was Wilson himself. By 1910 he had been supplanted by Murray Professor of English Literature Henry van Dyke, "ranting" Paul's literary brother. Among Wilson's fifty "preceptor guys," William Starr Myers (Politics) and Hardin Craig (English) were regarded as the best. Throughout most of the super-collegiate 1910s and 1920s, the seniors' favorite professor was George B. McClellan, former mayor of New York, whose large lecture course on "European Economic Problems" was frequently voted the "easiest" and "most popular," seldom the "most valuable." At the same time, "Buzzer" Hall was beginning his ascent in student affection. In 1916 he was the seniors' favorite preceptor by a large margin; by the late 1920s he had added "most interesting lecturer" and "most inspiring teacher" to his list of kudos.[99]

Graduating seniors were also free to hand out less glowing judgments, frequently on the "hardest," "dullest," and "most useless" courses. Before 1950, Physics, Economics 201 (Money and Banking), and various introductory History courses vied for "hardest." The "dullest" category claimed new "winners" nearly every year, but

[98] *Campus Songs*, Princeton Music Collection, AC#56 (PUA), (1903), 10; (1922), 17, 21; (1932), 23; (1939), 20; (1942), 12, 15; (1965), 15, 17 (PUA).

[99] *Nassau Herald* (1902), 120; (1910), 79; (1916), 362, 363, 365; (1927), 645; Roland Mushat Frye, "Henry van Dyke (1852–1933): Many-Sided Litterateur," in *Sons of the Prophets: Leaders in Protestantism from Princeton Seminary*, ed. Hugh T. Kerr (Princeton, 1963), 148–60; Nathaniel Burt, "Henry van Dyke: Poet of Genteel Princeton," *Princeton History*, no. 7 (1988):1–10; *The Gentleman and the Tiger: The Autobiography of George B. McClellan, Jr.*, ed. Harold C. Syrett (Philadelphia and New York, 1956), 328–29.

Econ. 201 and sophomore Psychology and Philosophy, especially Logic and Metaphysics, often got the nod. In 1927 the "most useless" prize went to Hygiene, with Astronomy and Econ. 201 close behind. As soon as the Great Depression broke, "Money and Banking" moved into first, presumably because it was unable to explain (away) the Crash of 1929. By 1942, it was not only regarded as the dullest course, but the second-hardest (behind Politics 301) and the second-most valuable (after History 201).[100]

After the war, however, the seniors no longer needed to answer curricular questions for the *Herald* because they had other venues for expressing their opinions. It is unlikely that many professors or deans took much, if any, account of the seniors' yearbook ratings before the war. But the influx of mature, serious-minded veterans on the G.I. Bill cast student opinion in a new light. When the illustrated magazine *Nassau Sovereign*, supported by the Undergraduate Council, began systematically to collect and analyze student evaluations of all courses in late 1946, the administration and faculty paid more attention, not all of it positive.[101] Drawing on returns from some 70 percent of the undergraduates, the *Sovereign* surveys sought to put the wartime faculty's dead wood on notice and to encourage departments to add new materials to "old duds." In a "Black Market Catalogue Issue" (February 1948), which included a spoof replica of the official undergraduate catalogue, faculty members were ranked in four tiers according to their accumulated scores on the first four *Sovereign* course evaluations. The bottom tier was labeled "Specialists in Writing and Research."[102]

When the *Sovereign* went out of business at midcentury, the *Daily Princetonian* assumed the survey role. In 1952 the *Prince* published

[100] *Nassau Herald* (1916), 365; (1927), 649; (1942), 607; (1950), n. p.; "The Seniors: What They Think of Each Other and of Life in General," *PAW*, May 30, 1930, 868.

[101] The first "Course Evaluation Survey," which included the results of a preliminary survey of summer school courses, appeared in the *Nassau Herald* in December 1946. The last *Sovereign* survey was conducted in the spring of 1949. In the winter of 1935 the *Daily Princetonian* had run a series of departmental profiles by senior concentrators, but they were statistically unreliable. *PAW* reprinted a few on Feb. 1 and 8, 1935.

[102] *Nassau Sovereign* 6:4 (Dec. 1946):14–18; *Unofficial Register of Princeton University*, 7:5 (Feb. 10, 1948), *The Undergraduate Catalogue Issue for 1947–1948*, 9, 11, 13, 15, 17–18.

and sold out two editions devoted to course evaluations, one for each semester. Following the *Sovereign* format, each course received a set of numerical grades for readings, lectures, and precepts or labs (fewer than half of the registered students responded) and a write-up based upon only ten questionnaires from a representative sample of class members in all grade groups. In addition, each department or program was given a written evaluation on the basis of questionnaires distributed to the senior class. Before the decade ended, the *Prince* prepared three more evaluation issues. But a "steady stream of [faculty] vituperation," directed at their amateur methodology, broad-brush questions, and unhelpful, often contradictory, assessments, followed every issue and eventually forced the paper to discontinue the practice.[103]

By the mid-1960s, however, the national expansion of higher education, greater emphasis on faculty research, and larger classes contributed to widespread student dissatisfaction with their lot and a demand for greater accountability in the classroom. Following other universities, particularly Harvard and Yale, senior Steven Grossman '66 published an irreverent *Guide to Undergraduate Courses*. Its unrepresentative student write-ups of fewer than a hundred courses found few fans among the faculty, who usually found themselves in a no-win situation among contradictory comments directed at their class organization, teaching performance, and reading assignments. Even *PAW*'s campus reporter (and later editor) Landon Jones '66 recognized the patent unfairness of the results.[104]

Responding to the national malaise over undergraduate education and to a less obvious but assumed need at Princeton, a seven-man "Joint [Faculty-Student] Committee of Inquiry on Undergraduate

[103] *DP*, Apr. 19, 1952, 1–8; Nov. 10, 1959, 1; John Angus McPhee '53, "On the Campus: Course Evaluation," *PAW*, May 8, 1953, 9; Donald W. Kramer '60, "On the Campus," *PAW*, Nov. 20, 1959, 12; Peter M. Sandman '67, "Student Evaluation of Teaching?" *PAW*, Oct. 11, 1966, 15–16, 20, at 16.

[104] Landon Y. Jones, Jr. '66, "On the Campus: Guide to Courses," *PAW*, May 10, 1966, 4. Professor of Economics Harvey Rosen's playful responses to contradictory evaluations of his teaching of Economics 102 in the fall of 1998 were published in "The Last Word: On Course Evaluations," *PAW*, Mar. 24, 1999, 5, having first appeared in the *Daily Princetonian*.

Instruction," appointed by President Goheen in November 1965, advocated the need for a set of four questionnaires to promote better undergraduate teaching and more discriminating feedback to students selecting courses and to administrators responsible for faculty promotions, raises, and tenure. With Carnegie Corporation support, the committee implemented a three-year pilot study to refine the questionnaires and to give them trial runs in a few departments. In the spring of 1969 the university began to distribute evaluations that were, according to Professor of English Gerald Bentley, "much more elaborate than anything being done anywhere else," including Yale and Berkeley, whose reform proposals the committee had studied.

The first questionnaire was given to sophomores to assess their academic experience during their first two years. The second went to seniors to evaluate their concentration work. The third was mailed to graduates by their first year out to elicit impressions on their whole Princeton experience. But the most useful instrument for all concerned was the evaluation form given to every student in every course at its conclusion. Seeking to avoid blanket "approve/disapprove" responses, this form asked precise questions about specific features of the various components of the course, as the *Prince* polls had done less skillfully a decade earlier. All of these ratings—on a one-to-five scale—were then crunched in the university's mainframe computer and the results distributed to the relevant parties. Faculty used them to refine or reform their courses; deans and chairmen used them to make personnel and curricular decisions; and students used them not only to select courses on a more informed basis, but to publish under the aegis of the Undergraduate Student Government their own course guides with more personal written comments.[105] So well de-

[105] *Report of the Joint Committee of Inquiry on Undergraduate Instruction* [Professor of History Charles C. Gillispie, Chairman] (May 5, 1966), in Hist. Subj. Files (vertical), #A-109 (PUA); "Student Course Evaluation," *PAW*, Jan. 21, 1969, 7; Laurie Lynn Strasser, "Student Catalog Determines If Courses at PU Pass or Fail," *Princeton Packet*, Dec. 9, 1994, 1A, 12A; Strasser, "Guide Reveals Best Bets, Regrets," *Princeton Packet*, Dec. 9, 1994 (also in "Student Life, 1980—", Hist. Subj. Files [vertical], #A-109, [PUA]). In 1976 the 300-page USG guide was entitled *An Above-Ground Guide to Princeton Academia* and sold for $1.50. It was based on only four thousand returns (an average of fewer than five per course) of a questionnaire like that in use at Columbia; two hundred volunteers wrote the course critiques. By the new millennium, the USG guide was

signed and so useful were the questionnaires that all but the third are still being administered today.

For those who continued to worry that Princeton's high-powered faculty were neglecting their teaching for research, foreign junkets, and tennis, the university's course evaluations should have been reassuring. On a five-point scale in which 5=excellent, 4=good, and 3= fair, the faculty's overall teaching performance in the fall of 1981 was 4.1. Ten and twenty years later it was 4.2. In only one area—"papers, reports, problem sets, exams"—did the score decline, from 4.1 to 4.0. By the fall of 2001 the quality of lectures had risen to 4.2, precepts/classes to 4.1, and readings to 4.0. The best performance was turned in by seminars, which rose from an impressive 4.3 to an outstanding 4.5. Even labs, the least popular of teaching venues, improved steadily to 3.8.[106]

Hardened skeptics might object that, just as the faculty had given in to grade inflation and compression, the grateful students had reciprocated in their grading of faculty and courses. Two inconvenient facts suggest otherwise. First, the college dean's office has found no correlation between grades earned in a course and student ratings of the course.[107] And second, while Princeton's grade inflation leveled off and actually declined (minimally) by 1998, student ratings continued to rise by 2001 for lectures, seminars, and precepts/classes. Several departments saw significant improvements in their scores. English and History, both filled with first-rate, hard-nosed scholar-teachers, jumped from 4.3 to 4.5 in a decade; their scores for lecturing and teaching of seminars rose precipitously. Physics, a department never given to easy grades, also rose in student esteem to 4.1, despite suffering a sharp fall in lab scores to 3.2.

It would appear that as Princeton students improved in academic preparation and intellectual sophistication, they were matched step for step by qualitative improvements in the faculty, particularly in

---

published only on-line. Peter Gentile '78, "On the Campus: Consumer Reports," *PAW*, Nov. 29, 1976, 7.

[106] PU, *Student Evaluation of Undergraduate Instruction*, Master Tabulation, Fall 1981; Summary of All University Courses, Fall 1991, Fall 2001 (Registrar's Office).

[107] E-mail from Dean Nancy Malkiel, June 2, 2003. The literature on student evaluations supports Princeton's findings.

pedagogical prowess. With more and better preparation in graduate school and further guidance at Princeton from the McGraw Center for Teaching and Learning and related facilities, Princeton's faculty had developed teaching techniques equal to their intellectual passion, power, and imagination.

❁ ❁ ❁

In the century since Woodrow Wilson reformed the curriculum and raised standards, the academic lives of Princeton students have undergone a long series of adjustments and transformations. Few of these changes were apparent to them as individuals or classes because they took place slowly, incrementally, rather than in sudden, radical bursts, and the life span of an undergraduate is only four years. One way to gauge the spirit of the changes taking place is to compare the academic accoutrements and activities of a typical Princeton student before World War II with one on Princeton's brave new campus at the beginning of the twenty-first century.

The academic equipment of a pre-war student was minimal. His reading assignments tended to be in hefty, hardback textbooks, which covered the material for the whole semester. He took notes in class and wrote exams with a pencil or fountain pen. He finished his written assignments on a clunky manual typewriter, making copies on onionskin paper with fly-away sheets of carbon paper. Between frequent and numerous classes, even on Saturday morning at 7:40, and en route to the library, he carried his books and notebooks at his side cradled in one cramped hand, rain or shine. All the documents for his independent research, however extensive, he transcribed by hand, unless he could afford the delay and high cost of obtaining photostats. If he wanted to pursue research at another institution or library, he conducted a slow, formal exchange of correspondence via the mails for permission, usually involving letters of introduction from university officials or senior faculty. If the archives he wanted to consult were outside the United States, he traveled by sea during the summer, with plenty of time for preparatory or leisure reading aboard ship.

The Princeton undergraduate in the new millennium is outfitted for academic life in a much different and more complete way. She (to reflect the reality of coeducation) has reading assignments mostly in numerous and once-cheap but increasingly expensive paperback books and in journal articles; the latter are available on individualized course Web sites or in electronic journal repositories such as JSTOR (which former president Bowen was instrumental in establishing through the Andrew F. Mellon Foundation, which he headed after stepping down from Princeton). She organizes her work by leaving notes to herself or by page-marking books and materials with yellow adhesive "post-its." She takes notes with sleek, felt-tip pens the old-fashioned way or, increasingly, on a laptop computer, which runs on its own battery or can be plugged into special outlets liberally distributed throughout classrooms, dorms, and libraries. If she doesn't have her own laptop, the library will lend her one, like a reserve book, for two hours; in addition, banks of desktop computers are scattered through the stacks and catalogue rooms. She does most of her writing on the computer—first drafts tend to be rougher but much easier to correct and redraft than in yesteryears—and then prints off clean, automatically spell-checked copies on a personal or university laser printer. If she wants additional copies or copies of research materials, she resorts to a copy machine with her credit-laden university identity card.

Between campus venues she hauls everything around in a formidable backpack, looking as if she were on a weeklong trek in the Adirondacks. Besides a bottle of spring water (for survival hydration between buildings), she totes an all-purpose video cell phone (to coordinate her hectic schedule and keep in touch with friends and family) and a portable CD player or iPod with earphones (for study-time "white noise"). On any given day she might also pack a set of paint brushes, sheets of music, or a pair of ballet slippers, because the curriculum has long (well before coeducation) included popular courses and programs in the creative arts.[108]

[108] In addition to certificate programs in Creative Writing, Theater and Dance, and the Visual Arts, the university offers courses in the arts in the departments of Art and Archaeology, Music, and Architecture. Since 1966 many of the creative arts programs

Despite appearances, the modern undergraduate does share some essential activities with her pre-war predecessor. She still goes to classes (admittedly fewer, never on Saturday, and hardly on Friday) and reads assignments. She crams for and takes exams, monitored only by a venerable student-wrought and -run Honor Code.[109] She does problem sets in math and writes lab reports in science. And, quintessentially, she writes final papers, junior papers, and senior theses. What has changed the most is the way she pursues the research for those papers.

---

have been housed in 185 Nassau Street, a converted public school that writer and faculty member John McPhee '53 once attended. The Creative Arts program began officially in 1939 with a few courses in writing; it was greatly expanded in 1966 when Princeton was still all-male. Edmund L. Keeley '48, "The Creative Arts Program," *PAW*, Nov. 7, 1967, 8–13; R. Bruce Beckner '71, "The Flourishing State of the Arts," *PAW*, May 4, 1971, 8–12; Michael J. Beahan, "Teaching the Visual Arts," *PAW*, June 11, 1979, 16–20; Elizabeth D. Morrison '74, "Theater and Dance," *PAW*, Oct. 6, 1982, 28–30; Elizabeth Burr '86, "On the Campus: Choosing a Creative Thesis," *PAW*, Apr. 24, 1985, 14; Margaret M. Keenan, "Working in the Creative Arts," *PAW*, Apr. 24, 1985, 15–20; William G. Bowen, *Report of the President, 1985: The Creative Arts at Princeton* (also included in *PAW*, Apr. 24, 1985, between pp. 20 and 21); Harold T. Shapiro, "The President's Page: 185 Nassau Street—the Visual and Creative Arts," *PAW*, June 1, 1994, 49; Deborah A. Kaple *91, "Toni Morrison's *Atelier*," *PAW*, Sept. 10, 1997, 12–17; "Then & Now: Princeton's Creative Writing Program," *Princeton: With One Accord* (Spring 1998), 8; Adaku Ibekwe, "The Visual Arts Program, a Major Less Traveled," *DP*, Feb. 10, 2003, 3; Jennifer Epstein, "Creative Writing Program Produces Aspiring Writers," *DP* (online), Dec. 6, 2004; Anthony Dudney, "What's in a Prose? Creative Writing at Princeton," *DP* (online), Mar. 10, 2005; Karin Dienst, "[James] Seawright Helps Students Shape Experiences into Artwork," *PWB* (online), Apr. 25, 2005.

[109] The Honor Code was initiated by a group of students, some from the South, in 1893. The code pertains only to examinations and quizzes (which are unproctored), not lab work or papers, which fall under the jurisdiction of a joint student-faculty Committee on Discipline. The Honor Code's greatest weakness is that a majority (c. 60 percent) of students would not report a close friend they caught cheating, and only the same number would turn in a stranger. "Test of Honor," *PAW*, Dec. 1, 1989, 19; "Commitment to Honor Code Tenets Shaky," *PAW*, Dec. 11, 1996, 9. For an explanation and the constitution of the code, see the annual PU, *Undergraduate Announcement*. On the origins of the code, see Jeremiah S. Finch, "The Honor System," in Alexander Leitch, *A Princeton Companion* (Princeton, 1978), 260–61; James J. Elliott '96, "Birth of the Honor System," *PAW*, June 16, 1944, 4; Edward Tenner '65, "The Honor Code Through Wilson's Spectacles," *PULC* 64:3 (Winter 2003):425–44.

She certainly resorts to Firestone Library and its satellites: books, journals, and manuscripts still constitute the fundaments of scholarly research, and creaky microfilm readers still grant access to essential sources. But the library is a very different place from what it was when it opened in 1948. Many of its holdings are now available online, and literally all of its catalogue and finding aids are. Moreover, its holdings now include huge databases of statistics and collections of photographs and texts, which are instantly available online. And thanks to computer technology and the World Wide Web, its "holdings" are no longer exclusively its own: the library Web site is now a giant portal leading to a universe of links, sites, and repositories equally bountiful, so that the laptop researcher in her carrel or on her bed virtually has the twin worlds of information and knowledge at her fingertips.[110]

Just as she can choose her courses from nearly thirteen hundred offerings, only her imagination limits her selection of topics for her research papers and senior thesis. If travel is required in person, she can e-mail her research destination that she is coming, charge a plane ticket on her credit card (applying for reimbursement from generous university accounts), and, with her ubiquitous backpack, hop a flight even during fall or spring break. If she needs more time and access, she can take a semester or two for formal study abroad.[111]

❋ ❋ ❋

[110] See chapter 8, pp. 483–85.

[111] Although other colleges and universities had initiated junior-year abroad programs in the 1920s and 1930s, Princeton did not allow its students to join them until 1950, and then only if the programs met strict criteria of quality and the students had 2.0 group averages overall and in their sophomore language course (French, German, or Spanish, initially). Despite recent university encouragement, relatively few Tigers (c. 160) chose to leave their friends and the Princeton social scene for a semester or year; nearly two hundred students attend summer programs abroad instead. World events after Sept. 11, 2001, put a damper on some study-abroad programs. D. William Alden [assistant professor of French], "The Junior Year Abroad," *PAW*, Apr. 21, 1950, 6–7; Dave Itzkoff '98, "On the Campus" Should I stay or Should I go . . . ," *PAW*, Nov. 5, 1997, 15; Letters to the Editor: "Study Abroad," *PAW*, Jan. 28, 1998, 2 (Assistant Dean of the College Nancy A. Kanach); Harold T. Shapiro, "The President's Page: Study Abroad," *PAW*, Sept. 8, 1998, 73; "Princeton Pushes Study Abroad," *PAW*, Dec. 1, 1999, 8–9.

Today as yesterday, young men and women come to Princeton with more than academics on their minds. They expect to make new friends, to have formative, life-changing experiences, to make contacts for later careers, to have a good time. But they also expect to stretch and grow intellectually, to profit from a smart faculty and a rich curriculum. Since the late 1910s, Princeton seniors have valued a Phi Beta Kappa key much more than a varsity "P," a seat on the Senior Council, or any other form of "Extra-curricular Wheeldom."[112] Different generations have expressed their valuation of, and engagement in, the "life of the mind" (a phrase they would eschew as too grandiose) in different ways. Perhaps two expressions from different eras reveal the respect most Princetonians have felt for their curricular opportunities and encounters.

Addressing the Class of 1954 at their senior banquet, Adlai Stevenson '22, former middling student, governor, and presidential candidate, urged them to carry away "the wise serenity, the unhurried objectivity which is the atmosphere of Princeton." Although on that emotional evening they knew they would soon leave with "old, good friends," Stevenson, the product of a university with a flapper reputation, counseled them, in a happy phrase well used by campus speakers ever since, "Don't forget when you leave, why you came." By which he meant, as he had explained earlier in his talk, the intellectual life. "Your greatest satisfactions, your greatest rewards," he reminded them from his own experience, "resulted from the free interplay of ideas. You know that your most penetrating insights resulted from the exchange and the interchange and clash of ideas," in class and out. It was language the '54s understood and appreciated with a standing ovation.[113]

Forty years later, in the pages of the *Nassau Herald*, an anonymous senior spoke to the same intellectual pulses and impulses, but in words that resonated with a different generation of hyper-busy, competitive "Organization Kids" (as social critic and columnist David

[112] Senior poll, *Nassau Herald* (1950), n.p.

[113] Heath, *Princeton Retrospectives*, 1–2; Chris Berger, '06, " 'Interplay of Ideas' Is the Best Reason to Attend Princeton," *DP*, May 7, 2003, 6.

Brooks dubbed them).[114] To a question asking for a characteristic phrase most reminiscent of their Princeton years, the most serious—and fitting—answer was: "Trying to get an education at Princeton is like trying to get a drink of water from a fire hydrant."[115] The difference in tone from Stevenson's evocation is unmistakable, but so is the latent pride and sense of purpose they share.

[114] David Brooks, "The Organization Kid," *Atlantic Monthly*, Apr. 2001, 40–46, 48–54.

[115] *Nassau Herald* (1994), 43.

CHAPTER FIVE

Beyond the Classroom

The greatest part of what a man learns at college
is not in the classroom.

—Woodrow Wilson

When Princeton students were not drinking deep from curricular springs, they were neither idle nor disengaged from college life: they were creating it in their own image. From the early nineteenth century on, the undergraduates designed, built, and maintained an extracurriculum that rivaled the official course of studies for popularity, attention, and presumed profit. Like those that sprang up on every other American campus, it identified "their enthusiasms, their understanding of what a college should be, their preferences." It revealed their attitude toward the curriculum and registered its demands, or lack thereof. And it often responded more quickly than the curriculum to key movements in the off-campus world and to society's shifting expectations of college graduates. It was, in short, the most sensitive barometer of what was going on at the college.[1]

The "guild of students"—as a Brown University professor called it after medieval Bologna's power brokers—founded this alternative system of education for three primary reasons: to provide facilities and opportunities that the colleges did not, to make colleges less like monastic retreats and more like the world from which the students

[1] Frederick Rudolph, "Neglect of Students as a Historical Tradition," in Lawrence E. Dennis and Joseph F. Kauffman, eds., *The College and the Student* (Washington, D.C., 1966), 47–58, at 53. On the development of the extracurriculum, see Helen Lefkowitz Horowitz, *Campus Life: Undergraduate Cultures from the End of the Eighteenth Century to the Present* (Chicago, 1987); Frederick Rudolph, *The American College and University: A History* (New York, 1962), chap. 7; David O. Levine, *The American College and the Culture of Aspiration, 1915–1940* (Ithaca, 1986), chap. 6.

had come and to which they would soon return, and to provide outlets for their competitive spirits, creative imaginations, and need to serve as well as belong. The college life they created was "a sort of miniature world," separate from the academic structure imposed by the administration and faculty and much more like the world beyond the college gates. And because the world to be served was ever-changing, the extracurriculum changed with it, registering its barometric oscillations most clearly in the pages of the student yearbook.[2]

When Woodrow Wilson was promoted to the Princeton presidency in 1902, he inherited an extracurriculum even richer and more energetically pursued than the one he had participated in as a student in the late 1870s. The football and baseball teams he had managed, the *Daily Princetonian* he had edited, and the American Whig Society in which he had spoken and argued were still drawing men away from their studies.[3] But they were now joined by a plethora of "social, athletic, dramatic, musical, literary, religious, and professional organizations of every kind, besides many organized for mere amusement." The "peculiarity" of America's universities, including Princeton, Wilson lamented in 1909, was that "the sideshows have swallowed up the circus." College life organized by the students had come to absorb their "whole interest and attention and energy," and "those who perform in the main tent must often whistle for their audiences, discouraged and humiliated." The extracurriculum, in a word, had "thrust the truest, deepest, most important objects of college work and association into the background." Undergraduates tolerated their formal studies only to gain access to four pleasurable years of college life.[4]

[2] Wilbur C. Abbott, "The Guild of Students," *Atlantic Monthly* 128 (Nov. 1921):618–25; WW, "What Is a College For?" (Aug. 18, 1909), *PWW*, 19:335; WW, "Address at the Inauguration of Henry Harbaugh Apple as President of Franklin and Marshall College" (Jan. 7, 1910), *PWW*, 19:742; WW, "The Country and the Colleges" (c. Feb. 24, 1910), *PWW*, 20:158–59.

[3] Henry Wilkinson Bragdon, *Woodrow Wilson: The Academic Years* (Cambridge, Mass., 1967), 15–46; John M. Mulder, *Woodrow Wilson: The Years of Preparation* (Princeton, 1978), 51–54.

[4] WW, "Address to the Presbyterian Union of Baltimore" (Feb. 19, 1909), *PWW*, 19:57–58; WW, "The Spirit of Learning" (July 1, 1909), *PWW*, 19:286; 19:341, 344 (Aug. 18, 1909); 20:162 (c. Feb. 24, 1910).

To Wilson's mind, the trouble was not with the extracurriculum per se, most of whose organizations and activities were "quite innocent and legitimate" and "thoroughly worthwhile." They were "wholesome means of stimulation," which kept young men from "going stale and turning to things that demoralize[d]." The problem was two-fold. First, most of these "extremely absorbing" enterprises were "irrelevant to study," indeed "subtly antagonistic to it." The few activities that were not antagonistic to the curriculum were only "*semi*-intellectual" in character. And second, although nine out of ten undergraduates regarded the extracurriculum as the real gist of college life, that majority included the *best* students, "most of the finest, most spirited, most gifted youngsters in the undergraduate body," the very men the faculty "most desires to get hold of and to enlist in some enterprise of the mind." It was these men, "whose training would count for most in leadership outside of college, in the country at large," who were receiving "too trivial a preparation" in the unreal "mimic world" of the extracurriculum.[5]

Changes in the college-going population inflected Wilson's concerns. In the 1870s most undergraduates at Princeton and other elite colleges were preparing for learned professions—law, college teaching, the ministry—in which books and continued study would be staples. This endowed the official curriculum with considerable relevance for the students, even if they wished for more practical or up-to-date courses and readings to keep pace with the evolving professions they sought or imagined. But by the 1890s a growing majority of undergraduates were sons of inherited wealth or middle-class ambition, whose future goals were business and "material achievement." These young men, the president knew, wanted to be "made men of, not scholars," and they turned to the extracurriculum to achieve their goals. "Manliness, *esprit de corps*, a release of their social gifts, a training in give and take, a catholic taste in men, and the standards of true sportsmen" were admirable in themselves, he acknowledged, but they were not what a college, especially Princeton, should give them.[6]

[5] *PWW*, 19:287 (July 1, 1909), 341, 344, 345 (Aug. 18, 1909), 742 (Jan. 7, 1910); 20:162 (c. Feb. 24, 1910).

[6] *PWW*, 19:281, 285 (July 1, 1909); 20:160 (c. Feb. 24, 1910).

Many students, parents, and alumni regarded the college extracurriculum as the most effective training ground for careers in business and the social life they entailed. When they were not pushing the faculty for courses of more immediate vocational usefulness, such as "Money and Banking" and "Industrial Psychology," they repeated the extracurricular mantra, "Don't let your studies get in the way of your education." The "spirit of learning" was supplanted by the "spirit of material achievement," which showed itself in "effective organization for success in competitive athletics, in the elaborate undergraduate undertakings into which money pours from indulgent fathers and sympathetic alumni, in the reproduction in college life of those social ambitions and means of success which so disturb and distract, which even threaten to displace, the course of study." In the miniature world of the extracurriculum, the students did what the rest of the world was doing, thought Wilson—"*except* its business." Soliciting ads for college publications, putting on theatrical tours, and even managing sports teams Wilson (an expert in political economy) dismissed as "make-believe business," not subject to real-world competition and failure. The students' "immoderate addiction" to these small, "unimportant" things prevented them from gaining the "intellectual discipline and moral enlightenment" that America required of its leaders and only colleges could provide.[7]

Wilson's solution to this national and local problem was elegantly simple to state but, in his own time and for nearly two decades thereafter, impossible to effect. "The sideshows," he allowed, "need not be abolished. They need not be cast out or even discredited." But he insisted that they be "subordinated. They must be put in their natural place as diversions, and ousted from their present dignity and preeminence as occupations." At Princeton, Wilson sought to do this by reforming the curriculum, reinvigorating the faculty with young preceptors and senior "stars," and reducing the importance of the eating clubs, most effectively, he hoped, by building in the future four-year residential colleges where students and faculty could meet

[7] *PWW*, 19:279 (July 1, 1909), 335, 346 (Aug. 18, 1909), 742 (Jan. 7, 1910); 20:160 (c. Feb. 24, 1910).

regularly, naturally, to spread the "contagion" of learning and to concentrate their life and studies upon "the essentials."[8]

In the first half of his presidency, he made substantial progress in reanimating Princeton's intellectual life. But during the last four years, when he tried to push through his quad plan, he discovered the truth that many college presidents and deans before and since learned the hard way: unless the students themselves—abetted by parents, alumni, and society itself—alter their educational priorities, the college will be powerless to subordinate the extracurriculum to higher concerns. Perhaps, despite the power of his ideals and oratory, he should have known better.

Like most academic reformers, he overestimated the attractions of the intellectual life for adolescents in the turmoil of self-fashioning. As a sincere Christian, he understood better the desire of some to serve or uplift others, even from mixed motives. But for all his own extracurricular involvement as a student, the fifty-two-year-old professor-turned-president underestimated—or simply forgot—the undergraduates' need for physical release, their social need to belong, and their need for competition to help define their personal values, identity, and place in the world. His analysis of the extracurricular conundrum was more astute and eloquent than that of any of his academic peers and successors, but he failed to reckon fully with the youth and psychology of the collegiate population and the social ambience in which they operated. Until the four-course plan unleashed and enlisted their academic initiative and the Great Depression and World War II concentrated their minds on serious things, Princeton students remained addicted to the extracurricular world of their own making.

❁ ❁ ❁

A revealing glimpse into the pleasures and pains, profits and costs, of student involvement in Princeton's absorbing sideshows comes from the letters of Richard Halliburton '21 to his parents in Memphis, Tennessee. The future world traveler, star lecturer, and best-

[8] *PWW*, 19:288–89 (July 1, 1909), 345 (Aug. 18, 1909); 20:160 (c. Feb. 24, 1910).

selling author of adult and children's adventure tales was immersed largely in college publications—the *Daily Princetonian* and the *Princeton Pictorial Magazine* (the *Pic*), a vehicle for essays written and photographic. He came by these interests naturally: he loved to write, "believing in originality at the sacrifice of almost all else," and he had edited the Lawrenceville School paper while preparing for Princeton. At Lawrenceville, which usually sent about fifty boys a year to Princeton, he also acquired a coterie of close friends, four of whom became his roommates in college. A Lawrenceville clique of sixteen sought membership in the same eating club, Cap and Gown.[9]

In mid-March 1919 he announced to his father that "for some reason I've taken the responsibility of my crowd onto my shoulders. I'm going to get us into the best club on Prospect Street or bust. . . . Sometimes, I ardently wish I were one of the phlegmatic kind of students that stick to their books regularly and don't strain over anything and are too insensitive to worry over lack of position or influence. Often they leave college," he admitted, "with a better mental capacity to handle life and business." But he went "dashing around expending all my energy on things that count for nothing after I leave Princeton. What good is it going to do me," he asked, "if I make a club I'm after and have to lose interest in my books and too much sleep?" A month later he apparently answered his own question with the proud news that, although the club wanted some of his and some of another group of five, his stuck together and was elected at the expense of the smaller coterie. After the welcoming banquet, he exclaimed, "I was never so happy. Princeton is really

[9] *Richard Halliburton: His Story of His Life's Adventure, As Told in Letters to His Mother and Father* (Indianapolis and New York, 1940), 8, 14, 16 (Apr. 16, 1919), 77 (Apr. 17, 1921) (hereafter Halliburton, *Letters*); Chip Deffaa '73, "On the Trail of Richard Halliburton '21," *PAW*, May 13, 1975, 8–13; Jonathan Root, *Halliburton: The Magnificent Myth—A Biography* (New York, 1965), 41–42, 44. Deffaa collected the research for a biography of Halliburton but apparently never wrote it. By comparing the original letters in Firestone Library with the letters published by his father in 1940, he discovered that the senior Halliburton "doctored" many letters, particularly those written after Princeton. "Lines were changed, deleted, added," especially those concerning his son's longtime male companion, Paul Mooney, who died with him on a reconstructed Chinese junk in the Pacific in 1939.

opening up [socially]. The clubs cement the friendships one has made during his first two years, and coming not until a fellow is almost a junior, the influence cannot harm."[10]

He had not needed the prestige of club membership to secure his first editorial position, on the *Prince*, earlier in his sophomore year. Of the eight candidates competing for the board, he was selected for the quantity, quality, and fitness of the news stories he submitted. In April he wrote home that he would soon "start in on the *Prince* and 'make up' [lay out the paper] twice a week till commencement. It's hard work," he confessed, "but great training"—for what he did not say and his parents did not ask. This was in answer to his own question a month earlier, "Is the *Prince* board with its grinding demands worth while?" By early May, however, he had revised though not discarded his public stance on the daily. "The *Prince* is a real pleasure," he wrote, "whereas I dreaded it before I took hold. I'm through by one o'clock—two nights a week. Things hum in the office. It's the only activity in college that has a business-like air about it," he assured his father, a civil engineer and real estate agent. "I've begun to think 'Editor-in-Chief' of course, but I'm quite sure I don't want it. I know too much about it. The three men that run the paper are so many slaves. I'd rather be editor of one of the less important magazines," which published much less frequently, he did not have to say, and presumably required much less slavish devotion.[11]

Five days later, he casually reported that he had been elected to the editorial board of the *Pic*, two copies of which he sent home. "I'm not terribly puffed up over the honor," he assured his folks, "but it helps to fill up the 'what I've done' space under my picture in the yearbook and gives me another bangle to put on my watch chain. I don't see what's to keep me from becoming editor—I'm in the right club 'n everything." In less than a month, one extracurricular prize lent its influence to securing another, just as savvy young Dick had

[10] Halliburton, *Letters*, 15 (Mar. 10, 1919), 16 (Apr. 16, 1919). Root suggests, after interviews with Halliburton's roommates, that "nonconformist" Dick was carried into Cap and Gown by his classmates rather than vice versa. As a freshman, he had "queered" his reputation by refusing to wear the traditional black "dink" and to stay off certain lawns forbidden to first-year students. Root, *Halliburton*, 45.

[11] Halliburton, *Letters*, 14, 15 (Mar. 10, 1919), 16 (Apr. 16, 1919), 17 (May 8, 1919).

FIGURE 14. Richard Halliburton '21 (front center), editor-in-chief of the *Princeton Pictorial*, poses gravely for the 1921 *Nassau Herald*.

calculated. His roommates and close friends were no less busy plotting their nonacademic college careers. "Our crowd," he reported proudly, "is all *doing* something." Shorty Seiberling won the basketball managership and was acting and debating. Three others were seeking to manage the swimming, track, and rowing teams. Larry Keyes was "doing all the athletics for the bunch," while he took care of "the writing." "And we will all get *somewhere someday*," he predicted.[12]

Dick's plans for the following summer and fall semester came as a surprise to his parents. Foreshadowing his future as a globe-trotter, he stole off to New Orleans in July, joined the International Workers of the World, and hired on as a crewman of a cargo ship headed for Europe. When he wrote his mother from New Orleans to announce his intentions, he revealed that he had been very restless his freshman

[12] Halliburton, *Letters*, 15 (Mar. 10, 1919), 17 (May 13, 1919).

year and would have gone the following summer had mandatory army camp not prevented him from joining the navy. He came "very near going" in the middle of his sophomore year, but Europe was still "inhospitable" at the end of the Great War. Moreover, it was "his last chance at the *Prince*" and "a wonderful chance to get through all my required courses at Princeton, and get founded in general."[13]

Absorbing the cultural sights of Europe, including the Gothic architecture of Oxford (which understandably reminded him of Princeton), temporarily slaked his thirst for adventure. In late January 1920, he returned to Old Nassau for the second term, assured that his formal studies of French in Paris and other cultural experiences qualified him in the registrar's eyes to proceed with his class toward graduation. After Easter vacation, he also learned that he had been elected editor-in-chief of the *Pictorial*, an honor not without a downside, as he quickly learned.[14]

After a late-summer outing on horseback into the Rockies with three friends and two picturesque Indian guides, he returned for his senior year, ready like most seniors to rule the roost. An early letter to his parents floated up a summer metaphor. In describing the start of the new year, he wrote that "it seemed I was drifting along calmly in a canoe at home and all of a sudden go dashing over some roaring falls which are Princeton." (Overwhelming torrents of water apparently came readily to Princeton students seeking metaphors for their college experience.) After lobbying professors to get into their popular courses and getting a gym locker, he "moved *Pic* furniture, saw all *Pic* men back, [and] had posters printed. . . . I'm up to my neck in my subscription campaign," he groused happily, "to get at the students before the *Tiger* [the campus humor magazine] and *Prince*. Last year we had 300 subscriptions among the students; I'll not stop under *1000* this time."[15]

Within days his ambition was somewhat dampened when, after three nights of aggressive salesmanship, the board managed to solicit only 300 subscriptions. "How I detest soliciting!" he protested. "It's

[13] Halliburton, *Letters*, 21–22 (July 19, 1919).

[14] Halliburton, *Letters*, 19–56, 58.

[15] Halliburton, *Letters*, 61–62 (Sept. 27, 1920).

so far beneath the dignity of a senior, and head of the paper, but every ounce of our strength is necessary to meet competition." Continued effort paid off. By mid-October "our subscription has passed 525 on the campus and we ought to glean 250 more." Home football games were a major bonus. At one game with 10,000 spectators he hoped to sell 500 issues, though the night-time printing required cost double and he "had to cut five classes" to prepare the layout. The big Yale game in early November drew 50,000 fans and "we hope to sell 4000 copies," at 50 cents because "everybody will be in a holiday mood and will pay" it. They had just raised the regular price from 25 to 30 cents, which did nothing to curtail sales. "My despair of 1000 paid subscriptions was groundless," he boasted. "We oversold our last edition and had to steal or buy the issues out of the dormitory rooms to cover outside subscriptions," largely to alumni. Small wonder that he and his staff regarded it as "the best *Pic* since its beginning" in 1913, if not "the *best* pictorial published by any college in America, and thus the world." But for "the lack of organization, the escaped steam and inefficiency and general irresponsibility" the editor-in-chief might have actually believed the latter claim.[16]

Even after the mad rush of the football publishing season, the editor could not take a breather. "I've been utterly *consumed* by the *Pic* all week," he groaned in early December. "Sometimes I think I *hate* it all, and yet when I once plunge in I forget all else but the joy of production—producing something live and worthy and readable. That's the only motive." This prompted a thoughtful confession. "Funny, in college we fight literally for honors and opportunities to work ourselves to death. We get no honor, certainly no reward in money, we risk our friendships and club life and grades in lifting the *self-imposed* burden—and if we are not lifting, feel self-reproachful. . . . The trouble is I'm interested only in the *Pic* and all else here is incidental. But," he added, as if to drive home Wilson's point, "everyone else is the same way."[17]

Young Halliburton knew himself well enough to know that he craved "action and freedom," not safety, routine, and predictability.

[16] Halliburton, *Letters*, 62 (Sept. 30, 1920), 63 (Oct. 10, 1920), 64 (Oct. 19, 1920), 65 (Nov. 2, 1920).

[17] Halliburton, *Letters*, 67 (Dec. 6, 1920).

By his own accounting, his extracurricular work for the *Prince* and the *Pic* gave him both—but at a price, which he also recognized clearly. Throughout his senior year he dared to reckon up some of those costs for his parents. He was certainly prompted by the sudden resignation in mid-October of his photographic manager after an all-night layout session before Monday classes. When asked for an explanation, the photo man said that "for three years he had slaved, sat up nights, neglected his studies, read not a line, drifted from his friends, grown thin and developed a worry habit." In his last year, he was "going to try to be free and live his own life. . . . Now he gets eight hours' sleep and two hours' exercise—can read, visit, write and be free of 'wrinkled care.' I understood his position so well," said the bag-holder, "I could not be very angry at him. He figured out it didn't pay in the long run. I wonder if it does! . . . Life is short—especially youth—it seems a shame that it makes so many of us draft horses" (however willingly).[18]

Within weeks Dick began his own list of costs—personal, academic, even moral. In a bold confession to one's parents, he announced, "I've snitched pictures, and lied for the *Pic* and torn up valuable books—done anything to put out the best possible issue—not to be prevented by any little consideration for personal property." More disappointing, to him at least, were his academic failings. In the face of a heavy fall schedule of Shakespeare, Public Speaking, Money and Banking, Oriental Literature, French, and Nineteenth-Century Poetry, he studied "only by snatches, interrupted, hurriedly, and as for steady, concentrated grind, where one *gets* an idea and holds it, not at all." By contrast, two of his roommates exasperated him, "for every evening they see their friends for an hour after dinner, study from 8 till 11:30, do their work well and consistently and go to bed just as I'm coming in from the *Pic* office for an hour's work only, so as to get to bed by 12:30." When he confessed that he had failed his Money and Banking midterm with a 20, the only test he had ever botched, he brushed it off with "I've not the time to bother. I'll never be a banker" (though his lavish lifestyle would present big

[18] Halliburton, *Letters*, 63–64 (Oct. 19, 1920), 77 (Apr. 17, 1921).

money problems later in life). The challenge, he said in December, was "to get through on wits and not wisdom."[19]

As his final semester hove into view, the self-described "human dynamo" looked forward to an easy, restful time when his editorial duties at the *Prince* and *Pic* would come to an end after April 1. To prepare for that unimaginable day, he turned down invitations to form a Southern Club for the Undergraduate Schools Committee, to edit the senior class book, to go on speaking tours for the YMCA, and to stand for class odist. He also chose very carefully "five easy, pleasant, cultural, informative courses," calmly sidestepping "anything that smelled of work and essays." When the dean saw his schedule, he asked sarcastically, "Aren't you afraid you are going to be overworked?" But when the day came to lay down his editorial burdens, he found himself surprisingly and "utterly lost with nothing to do." "In fact," he said, "I really don't like it."[20]

His enforced leisure, however, did give him time to assess his college career and how much advantage—or how little—he had taken of his opportunities. With unflinching honesty, he concluded that he had missed much. Indeed, his cool assessment had begun in early March as he prepared to perform in his Advanced Public Speaking course. "I shall speak on our lost academic spirit in college—which I bewail," he told his parents, "but am a cause of as much as anyone. Our interest is every place but on our books. Princeton and other universities, therefore, turn out business men of culture, men who will lead in the material world, but few great college presidents, writers, diplomats, philosophers, professors, research students, in comparison with old [European] universities, where academic training was of first importance."[21]

A month later, after his *Pictorial* release and the fragrant arrival of spring, he mused that one day he would like to live in Princeton, with its "academic, cultured, social atmosphere" and its "unequaled

[19] Halliburton, *Letters*, 63 (Sept. 30, 1920), 65 (Nov. 2, 1920), 66 (Nov. 8, 1920), 67 (Nov. 30, Dec. 6, 1920).

[20] Halliburton, *Letters*, 68 (Dec. 6, 1920), 71–72 (Jan. 22, 1921), 72–73 (Feb. 9, 1921), 75 (Apr. 9, 1921).

[21] Halliburton, *Letters*, 73 (Mar. 6, 1921).

group of educational authorities," who were then "too close to be appreciated." "With all this dazzling mass and source of inspiration and wisdom," he confessed, "I have spent my two years of discretion—with *Pic*. Am I a better man for it or has it been a waste? I've taken and know no biology, no geology, little math, little philosophy, no astronomy, no architecture, no chemistry, no foreign language but French." Basically, after three-and-a-half years at one of America's best universities, he knew only a little French (mostly from his Paris study), how to speak in public, a little modern painting, some European and American history, and "English, English, and more English." Even before the four-course plan and distribution requirements, it was no consolation that he was not alone.[22]

Clearly, he was not pleased with the results. Eight days later, he continued his uncomfortable introspection in a letter home. "Among the students of every college there are always a group of men who think more clearly, speak more intelligently, seem to be more developed mentally and socially than the great mass of their fellow students. They are mostly Phi Beta Kappas, influential speakers, serious students. In which class is included none of my close friends or I," he admitted ruefully. "In other words, I see myself satisfied with less than the best, choosing something other than the highest development Princeton can give me." The best he could claim was the rating for "most original" in the senior class poll, thanks in large part to block voting by his clubmates in Cap and Gown.[23]

❋ ❋ ❋

In the student hierarchy of extracurricular activities, major athletics often stood at the top during the first few decades of the twentieth century. But even then, sports (especially football) stars and captains had to compete with editorial board members of the *Daily Princetonian* for undergraduate regard, as measured by senior polls and college fiction. Amory Blaine, F. Scott Fitzgerald's alter ego, quickly figured out that "writing for the *Nassau Literary Magazine* would get him nothing [socially], but that being on the board of the *Daily*

[22] Halliburton, *Letters*, 75 (Apr. 9, 1921).

[23] Halliburton, *Letters*, 71 (Jan. 22, 1921), 76–77 (Apr. 17, 1921); *Nassau Herald* (1921).

Princetonian would get any one a great deal," including membership in the best eating clubs. When he flunked the re-take of the conic sections exam, he knew he would be dropped from the *Prince* and his "short career" as a college somebody was over.[24]

The *Prince* counted highly for several reasons. First, it was one of the largest student-run activities on campus, employing from fifty to a hundred-plus students. Founded in 1876 as a biweekly, it had kept a daily eye on the campus world and often the world beyond since 1895. Second, it was the dominant opinion-maker on campus as well as virtually the only source of (mostly reliable) information.[25] Until the advent of e-mail, even the administration was forced to use its pages to inform the student body of policy or personnel changes quickly and inexpensively. In its sheer utility, said former chairman Richard J. Kluger '56, it was "the least toylike of extracurricular activities."[26] Third, its professional demands were known to be the heaviest on campus, particularly for board members. While athletes and musicians might practice and play 20 hours a week, *Prince* staffers committed as much time and major editors put in 45–50-hour weeks, often at considerable risk to their academic standing.[27] In the 1950s the paper lost five chairmen in eight years to academic underperformance.[28] Although the board serves only one year and steps down at

[24] Alexander Leitch, *A Princeton Companion* (Princeton, 1978), 383; F. Scott Fitzgerald, *This Side of Paradise* (New York, 1920, 1977), 52, 102. The senior polls reported in the *Nassau Herald* consistently rated the *Prince* as the most or second-most highly regarded extracurricular activity.

[25] In the opening years of the twentieth century, before Wilson took office, Ernest Poole '02 noted that the *Daily Princetonian* sought "not the trivial news of the faculty's dull, puny plans for the development of our minds, but the real vital news of our college life, news of the things we were here for, the things by which a man got on, news of all the athletic teams, of the glee, mandolin and banjo clubs, of 'proms,' of class and fraternity elections, mass meetings and parades" (*The Harbor* [New York, 1915], 51).

[26] Richard J. Kluger '56, "The Golden Age: The 'Prince' in the 1950s," in *The Orange & Black in Black & White: A Century of Princeton Through the Eyes of* The Daily Princetonian (Princeton, 1992), 112–14, at 112.

[27] Richard Just '01 did not begin serious work on his senior thesis in the Woodrow Wilson School until January because he was editor-in-chief of the *Prince*, "a job that consumed about 80 hours a week" (*The Thesis: Quintessentially Princeton* [PU: Office of the Dean of the College, 2002], 57).

[28] One of the casualties was chairman R. W. Apple '57, who flunked out twice. He later graduated from Columbia magna cum laude. Calvin Trillin, "Profiles: News-

the end of the first semester of senior year, many members find that late January is too late to do justice to the indispensable senior thesis. This kind of sacrifice for the college community does not go unnoticed or unrewarded by their classmates.

Prince leaders also earn respect because of the intense competition they undergo to earn their often well-paid positions. After managing editor Woodrow Wilson introduced competition for board positions in 1879, getting to the top entailed a rigorous, sometimes "internecine," process of natural selection. Hamilton Fish Armstrong '16, editor of *Foreign Affairs*, remembered the half-dozen surviving "heelers" his freshman year: "We were exhausted, suspicious, eating little, sleeping little, barely hanging on to passing grades in our academic work, bleary-eyed, pimply, scavaging for bits of news to supplement the stories assigned to us, fighting in every way possible, fair or foul, to add to our lineage in the paper." In 1976 Donald C. Stuart '35, former managing editor, could still recall the trauma of his very first day as a candidate. It lasted eleven hours—4 p.m. to 3 a.m.—because he was assigned the "copy" chores, preparing all notices (which he "bungled badly, hence no time for supper"), "gophering" to the *Princeton Herald* print shop on Witherspoon Street with sticks of type, and doing occasional personal errands for the night editors. Still, when he returned to his room for a short hour of German, he realized "through the exhaustion that newspaper work was for me."[29]

---

hound," *New Yorker*, Sept. 29, 2003, 70–81, at 72, 76; Genevieve M. Muinzer '76, "Alumni Profile: Political Reporter R. W. Apple Jr. '57," *PAW*, Oct. 18, 1976, 12–13; Reeve Parker '58, "Extracurricular Decline: Woodrow Wilson's Dream Has Come True But Nobody's Very Happy about It," *PAW*, Apr. 25, 1958, 3–7, at 5. Another academic cost is course selection. Board members must often choose only morning classes (to be free for afternoons and evenings at the *Prince* offices) and relegate their study time largely to "Friday and Saturday marathon library sessions." Obviously, their involvement in other extracurricular activities is severely limited; even club dinners have to be skipped regularly. Christine B. Whelan '99, "All the News that Fits the Prince," *PAW*, Oct. 6, 1999, 64.

[29] Grenville Garside '51, "The Daily Princetonian: 75th Anniversary Banquet This Week Marks 'Diamond Jubilee' of Campus Publication," *PAW*, Feb. 2, 1951, 7–9, at 7 (Wilson); Leitch, *Princeton Companion*, 383 (Armstrong); Judy Piper Schmitt '76, ed., *The* Prince *Remembers: One Hundred Years of* The Daily Princetonian, *1876–1976* (Princeton. 1977), 175 (Stuart). When Adlai Stevenson '22 was heeling the *Prince* in the spring of 1919, he spent "7–8 hours a day" for several weeks. *The Papers of Adlai E. Stevenson*, ed. Walter Johnson, 8 vols. (Boston, 1972–79), 1:76 (May 25, 1919).

FIGURE 15. Four busy-looking staffers prepare another issue of the *Daily Princetonian*, sometime in the 1940s.

Like many heelers before and since, Stuart discovered that "putting out a newspaper becomes addictive," as even Wilson, who produced issues only fortnightly, understood all too well. Editor-in-chief Christine Whelan '99 stood in a long line of Tigers who believed, "at least for a year, that the *Prince* was the center of the universe." "Leashed to the paper by pager," modern editors realize that "there is no such thing as time off," not even for the wholehearted, if not single-minded, academic work they originally were admitted and came to do. A half-century earlier, one of her male predecessors acknowledged that the *Prince* "became more a part of our lives . . . than our studies, our clubs, or our girlfriends."[30]

Many generations of staffers have joked about majoring in the *Prince* and attending to their academic studies as extracurricular activities.[31] The humor has a serious side to it because, of all the myriad

[30] Whelan, "All the News that Fits the Prince," 64; Kluger, "The Golden Age," 112.

[31] Charles L. Creesy '65 [former *Prince* Editor-in-Chief], "The Daily Princetonian at 100," *PAW*, Jan. 31, 1977, 12.

activities available to the Princeton undergraduate in the past century, the *Daily Princetonian* consistently provided the most direct and best vocational training to the greatest number. Many Princeton journalists discovered that what engaged them (extra)curricularly became a lifelong calling and career. The roll call of former *Prince* editors who have made their mark on the national journalistic stage is long and well known and contributes to the paper's campus reputation as a signal preparation for the business of "real life."[32]

Through the first seven decades of the twentieth century, the *Prince* drew devotees as much for its inky mystique as for its central role and visibility on campus: late nights (with cookies, Cokes, and pizzas) in the newsroom and at the printing plant, ego-bruising staff competitions, "the roguish pleasure of interviewing deans on a basis of near-equality," fierce battles for the chairmanship, touch football games with the *Yale Daily News* (*the* oldest college daily, as it likes to remind the second-oldest), and sumptuous annual banquets with distinguished speakers. Until 1972, when the *Prince* finally went to photo-offset composition (and in 1988 to Apple computers), the ink and type-fonts were a nightly reality in the *Herald* print shop. Since high school journalists had no experience in producing a daily newspaper, the *Prince* had to rely on an experienced craftsman to show each new generation the ropes, to do the actual composing on a creaky, temperamental, hot-lead linotype machine, and from midnight to six a.m. to print the issues on a hand-fed, flat-bed letterpress, made in 1896 when the College of New Jersey declared itself Princeton University.[33]

[32] John S. Martin '23 and José Ferrer III '61 (*Time*), John B. Oakes '34 and R. W. "Johnny" Apple '57 (*New York Times*), Donald Oberdorfer '52, T. R. Reid '66, and Joel Achenbach '82 (*Washington Post*), Frank Deford '61 (*Sports Illustrated*), John Stossel '69 (*ABC-TV*), William H. Greider '58 (*Rolling Stone*), James F. Ridgeway '59 (*New Republic* and *Village Voice*), and Richard J. Kluger '56 (*New York Herald Tribune*) are only a few *Prince* alumni.

[33] Donald J. Sterling, Jr. '48, "The Daily Princetonian," *PAW*, Mar. 12, 1948, 6–7; Virginia Kays Creesy, "The *Princetonian*'s First Century," *PAW*, Jan. 31, 1977, 13–15; John W. Reading '67, "Hand Set and Stone Proof: The Hot Lead Years," in *The* Prince *Remembers*, 132–35; Andy Schneider '87, "On the Campus: A Day in the Life," *PAW*, Feb. 11, 1987, 34, 63; Aaron Kornblum '93, "From Hot Lead to Photo-Offset: How the 'Prince' Makes It to Your Doorstep," in *The Orange & Black in Black & White*, 103–5.

From the end of World War II until his retirement in 1987, the gruff, indispensable presence behind the *Prince* operation was Larry DuPraz, a flat-topped, cigar-smoking townie, high school graduate, and volunteer fireman. In the minds of thousands of his student-fans, this stubby veteran with a bite as sharp as his bark was "one of the toughest professors at Princeton." At his ink-stained, no-nonsense hands, generations of would-be journalists were educated in "craft, fidelity, dedication, perseverance, [and] excellence—qualities that not even an [umpteen]-thousand-dollar education can buy." His most serious students thought they had attended—though probably not graduated with any honors from—the "Larry DuPraz School of Journalism, one of Princeton's most successful colleges," or "the University of DuPraz."[34]

In late-night commentaries over layouts or in caustic comments at any juncture, "Professor" DuPraz taught two main lessons. One was absolute quality: he was devastatingly "scornful of error and sloppiness," to which harried student-editors with undone homework on their minds were often prone. The other lesson was humility. He taught his bookish acolytes not to "overestimate degrees and titles," but, more pointedly, that "snot-nosed college kids were not as smart as they think they are." Although many Princelings never realized it, "beneath that gruff exterior," testifed Thomas Bray '63, former *Prince* chairman and later president of the board of the paper's corporation, "was a gruff interior." Yet most learned to love being "abused by him—which he did with great precision—partly because Larry was from the real world, outside the Gothic romance of the campus, and his sarcasm punctured our pretensions." Their other professors were bred—and taught—in a kinder, gentler school and often had a harder time earning their respect and attention. Few of them hosted their own "class" reunions after each P-rade, at which

[34] Whelan, "All the News that Fits the Prince," 64; "The Man Behind the *Prince*," *PAW*, Feb. 11, 1987, 35–41, at 40 (adapted from a special insert in the Jan. 21 *Daily Princetonian*, the last issue put out by the "Professor"). In 1999, after fifty-two years, Larry was still an afternoon presence in the *Prince* newsroom, deriding the latest "crap" and dispensing stories of hot-lead presses, scandalous editorial boards past, and world-class student pranks.

they recalled with deadly precision, as Larry did, each name, face, and former foible.[35]

The competition, compensation, professional experience, and byline gratification was even greater for a much smaller cohort of student journalists who comprised the Press Club, the first college organization of its kind in the country. In 1900, fifteen student "stringers" for some sixty daily newspapers across the country organized to "promote the proper publication of news which will be of benefit to Princeton and most of all to prevent the circulation of news which would be detrimental to the interests of the university." Being a campus reporter for a big city paper or international wire service was potentially lucrative. Interview-shy ex-President Grover Cleveland, now retired to Princeton, always granted an audience to Press Club members because, he said, "it may mean five or ten dollars for the boy, and that would pay his board for a week." After World War II "you could earn a good part of your college costs," particularly if one did the work of all twelve members over the summer; this brought in $100 a week, or three times what Jeremy Main '50 made after graduation when he started with International News Service in Washington, D.C.[36]

But access to these sums was strictly limited, much more so than at the *Prince*. Initially, each stringer's position was regarded as private property and was sold to the highest bidder, who might or might not know how to write the "inverted-pyramid" stories required by

[35] "The Man Behind the *Prince*," 39, 40. Since 1957 the university has also enhanced the skills of student journalists by offering a number of Ferris/McGraw courses in journalism and "The Literature of Fact," taught by John McPhee '53 and a visiting roster of first-rate journalists. Jessica Lautin, "Above the Fold: Alumni Leaders in Journalism," *DP*, Apr. 17, 2001, 3.

[36] In the 1970s, working for large papers, an experienced hand could earn $100–200 a month. There were other compensations. After the car ban in 1927, Press Club reporters were allowed to keep cars on campus for their "work"—and, confessed James Barnett '31, "to go into Philadelphia to see girls and go to parties." Sheryl Beaver '77, "On the Campus: Trial by Writing," *PAW*, Nov. 22, 1976, 7; Leitch, *Princeton Companion*, 377–78, at 377; *One Hundred Years of the Press Club* (Princeton, 2000), 7, 15, 22, 31 (thanks to Suzanne Hagedorn '89 for a copy). See also Robert S. Brooke, "Professional Journalism at Princeton: 105 Years of the University Press Club" (Senior thesis, Dept. of History, PU, 2005).

newspapers. In 1915 Professor Christian Gauss, the club advisor, instituted reforms. The old auction system was replaced by a rigorous eight-week competition for freshmen and first-semester sophomores, in which, typically, only three or four candidates are selected for three-year sinecures. Over the trial period, each candidate must write twenty stories—news, sports, features, and investigative. For the straight news and sports pieces, they are given the cooperative club's standard "dope sheets" containing the basic facts and quotations, from which each member crafts his or her own dispatch. For the other stories, they do their own interviewing. At the end of each two-week period, candidates are dropped so that by the final week only eight or ten hopefuls remain. According to many successful alumni, this kind of boot camp, and subsequent on-the-job training, made the club "the best school of journalism anywhere."[37]

Most of the news reported by Princeton's own was, of course, university-related. Sports news was always in demand. So was notice of major new buildings (the Chapel, Firestone Library), the opinions of famous residents (Einstein, Thomas Mann, Robert Oppenheimer), presidential successions (particularly from the first Jewish president to the first woman), and various student movements (the strike against the Vietnam War, coeducation, and the ever-popular Nude Olympics). Some of these stories came from working closely with the university's public relations director (PRD), such as Dan Dunn Coyle '39, who was memorialized in the 1946 faculty song:

> Here's to Coyle of PRD,
> Better known as DDC.
> He'd hang his mother with a loop
> Just to get another scoop.

Others stories were the products of luck and hard work. Scoops such as the kidnapping of the Lindbergh baby, Einstein's death,

[37] Leitch, *Princeton Companion*, 377; Beaver, "Trial by Writing," 7; *One Hundred Years of the Press Club*, 31. Some of the club's best-known alumni are David Lawrence '10, founder of *U.S. News & World Report*, Clinton press secretary Mike McCurry '76, *New Yorker* Editor and Pulitzer Prize-winner David Remnick '81 (who was passed over in the freshman competition), and Wendy Kopp '89, founder of Teach for America.

and the "invasion from Mars" that allegedly landed just north of Princeton Junction (the figment of Orson Welles's famous 1938 radio drama "War of the Worlds") earned many student reporters big bylines and paychecks, as well as invaluable experience in "the honorable profession which they [were] studying incidentally to their curriculum."[38]

As a former student editor and practicing belletrist, President Wilson probably would have regarded only two student publications as "semi-intellectual"—the *Prince* and the older *Nassau Literary Magazine* (the *Lit*). The *Lit* had been founded in 1842 (six years after Yale's) "to afford a medium," its first editor said, "through which young writers might publish incognito their first lucubrations to the world." By the 1890s and no longer in disguise, the likes of Jesse Lynch Williams '92, the author three years later of the much reprinted *Princeton Stories*, and Booth Tarkington '93, Indianapolis's best-selling novelist and playwright, both got their start at the *Lit* before graduating to Scribner's magazine and publishing house. Ever since, it has published—and sometimes rejected—the early work of some of America's most creative talent, including Edmund Wilson '16, F. Scott Fitzgerald '17, poet W. S. Merwin '48, John McPhee '53, and artist Frank Stella '58. Today, the renamed *Review* continues to solicit poems, stories, photographs, and art from anyone in Princeton's creative community and twice a year publishes what a small band of editors considers worthy.[39]

Less worthy and much less intellectually redeeming in Wilson's eyes was the *Princeton Tiger*, which wobbled into existence in 1882 but after nine issues disappeared for seven years. Originally a monthly and soon supported by ads for swish New York clothiers and hotels and national brands of cigarettes and "spirits," the magazine sought to "keep alive the flame of humor," said *Tiger* Trustee Edward Strauss '72, and to "remind people not to take themselves too seriously." The *Tiger*'s fortunes flowed and mostly ebbed with changing national moods and its own inability to avoid humor that

[38] *One Hundred Years of the Press Club*, 8, 15, 26, 29; Leitch, *Princeton Companion*, 378.

[39] Leitch, *Princeton Companion*, 333–36.

was lame, tame, or profane.[40] When its faculty or administrative targets felt too sharp a sting, it was forced to tuck tail and withdraw from the field for a time. During its heyday between 1914 and 1930, the magazine enjoyed 10,000 subscribers in "both hemispheres." Flush with success, it appealed to freshmen to join the staff the better to develop "initiative, originality, and business sense." The "wide circle of friends" to be gained on the job was an additional bonus because "these are the men you will have to do business with after you leave."

After World War II, college humor lost much of its appeal and *Tiger* subscriptions dropped precipitously, as did national advertisers and the size and number of issues. Although the magazine still manages to poke its finger in the eye of the world four times a year, its brand of smutty satire and sophomoric humor appeals to relatively few students and even fewer adults. A (frequently re-elected) board of twelve attracts fluctuating staffs of two to twenty.[41]

❋ ❋ ❋

[40] In 1935 F. Scott Fitzgerald thought the *Tiger*, for which he had written for three years, inferior to the Yale *Record*, the Harvard *Lampoon*, and the Cornell *Widow*, largely because "most of the local wit was concentrated on producing the hullabaloo of the Triangle show, and lately the [Theater] 'Intime' reviews" (*Correspondence of F. Scott Fitzgerald*, ed. Matthew J. Bruccoli and Margaret M. Duggan [New York, 1980], 409).

[41] Leitch, *Princeton Companion*, 388–89; John Avon Nevins, "Campus Organizations: The Tiger," *Nassau Sovereign* 1:4 (Feb. 1939):20–22, 26; Herbert Davis, "The Tiger," *Nassau Sovereign*, 6:3 (Nov. 1946):16–17; *Roaring at One Hundred:* The Princeton Tiger Magazine *Centennial Album* (Princeton, 1983); "Celebrating a Century of College Humor," *PAW*, Dec. 1, 1982, 21–25, 35; Edward Tenner '65, "Opinion: The Sad Truth About College Humor," *PAW*, Dec. 1, 1982, 26–27, 34. In 1952 the *New York Times Magazine* hosted a literary debate between John McPhee, managing editor of the *Tiger*, and Richard C. Lemon, chairman of the Yale *Record*, on the state of college humor. McPhee declared it dead, killed largely by "the spreading availability of professional entertainment." Lemon found it flourishing, everywhere "except possibly at Princeton." "It's Collegiate—But Is It Humor?" *New York Times Magazine*, May 25, 1952, 17, 58, 59. The debate goes on: see Carlin Romano, "Knock, Knock. Who's Not There? College Humor," *CHE*, Mar. 5, 2004, B15. For anthologies of the best work from 65 and 95 college humor magazines, respectively, see *Max Shulman's Guided Tour of Campus Humor* (Garden City, N.Y., 1955) and Dan Carlinsky, ed., *A Century of College Humor* (New York, 1971).

By 1902 young Princetonians, like their peers elsewhere, came to college with an extracurricular urge to express themselves not only in writing but in song. Wilson understood perfectly. Possessed of a rich tenor voice, he loved to sing and even joined the Johns Hopkins Glee Club as a graduate student.[42] Even before his presidency, seniors gathered on the steps of Nassau Hall on spring evenings to sing new and old verses of the faculty song. Vocalizing students of all classes discovered the acoustical qualities of the arches in the many new Gothic buildings on campus, especially Blair Hall's.

Until the beginning of World War II, the only formal outlet for musical expression was the Glee Club, initially only thirteen members who specialized in college songs. The group was founded in 1874 in response to an editorial plea in the *Nassau Lit* by senior Andrew Fleming West, future professor of classics and dean of the Graduate School. In addition to campus concerts, often accompanied by the banjo and mandolin clubs, the Glee Club soon performed on spring and Christmas tours around the country.[43] At football games, much to Wilson's delight, its members sat together in order to lead student singing at half time, a practice interrupted in 1919 by the advent of the University Band.[44]

In the 1930s, after music had gained a firm place in the university curriculum, the Glee Club was trained and directed by the music faculty. Now considerably enlarged and accompanied by chamber or full orchestras instead of banjos, it performed, as it has ever since,

[42] Bragdon, *WW: Academic Years*, 108, photo opposite p. 99 (Bragdon is incorrect that Wilson helped found the group; see *PWW*, 2:524–25n1, also 2:608, 3:4–5, 29, 45, 100, 117).

[43] Jesse Lynch Williams described a joint tour of the South in the 1890s that "travelled in a special train of private cars lent by the parents of some of the members." The trip had been a success "both in the money and the fine impression the clubs had made, which latter would advertise the college . . . the object of this enterprise" (*Princeton Stories* [New York, 1895], 141).

[44] In 1994 the once-sedate but now whacky and sometimes offensive band celebrated its seventy-fifth anniversary, much to the chagrin of many alumni who have witnessed its half-time escapades. Peter Doskoch '87, "Music, Marching, and Mirth," *PAW*, Oct. 27, 1993, 7–12.

in major concert halls and opera houses in Europe and Latin America as well as North America.[45] The highlight of the 1973 trip to Mexico was singing "Old Nassau" atop the Pyramid of the Sun at Teotihuacán. The following year, the now-coed ensemble of a hundred singers celebrated its centennial with concerts in Alexander Hall at home and Carnegie Hall in New York.[46]

In 1941, on the eve of America's entry in World War II, the first of nine major close-harmony *a cappella* singing groups was born. The Nassoons had emerged two years earlier during a Glee Club concert in New Haven after the Yale football game, when an octet sang "Perfidia" in five-part swing voicings to a surprising ovation and became overnight rivals of Yale's famous Whiffenpoofs. The 'Soons were joined in friendly rivalry back home the year after the war by the Tigertones, who inaugurated one of the major attractions for group members—tours of island resorts, women's colleges, and southern spring-break vacation spots. These stints grew with the popularity of the groups so that European and world tours are now commonplace for the oldest and best.

Although the early groups were also vehicles to escape the all-male campus and to meet women, the arrival of coeducation did not kill the men-only groupings. Indeed, it spawned a trio of all-female and a trio of coed ensembles. The Tigerlilies debuted in the fall of 1971 when eight friends sang "How High the Moon" under the 1879 Hall arch. The desire of one 'Lil to harmonize with her Nassoon boyfriend gave birth to the first Ivy League coed group, the Katzenjammers, two years later.

[45] After nominal beginnings in 1886, the University Orchestra was formally organized after World War I. Since 1935 its directors have been provided by the Music Department. As curricular opportunities for music study have grown, the size and quality of the orchestra have grown appreciably. Today, it gives seven concerts a year, including one at Reunions, traditionally in Richardson Auditorium in Alexander Hall. It also tours Europe during the intercession; in January 2005 the hundred-person ensemble performed in three locations in Portugal. Rehearsal time is advertised on the PUO Web site as being "considerably less than that of an athletic team." Leitch, *Princeton Companion*, 347; Desiree Fowler, "A Taste of Portugal for the University Orchestra," *DP* (online), Feb. 3, 2005.

[46] Leitch, *Princeton Companion*, 216–17.

By 1992 these nine vocal groups, involving a total of 110 to 130 members, had performed during more than a hundred national tours and released more than seventy albums. Their crowd-pleasing repertoires, ranging from Big Band harmonies, Beatles, and Beach Boys to rock, rhythm, and blues, and their witty performances have made them "some of Princeton's most conspicuous ambassadors to the wider world and probably some of its best recruiting assets," noted former Nassoon David Mehnert '87, " . . . farther-flung than the Triangle Club, and more broadly appealing than any sports team." The intense bonds that develop between members, who practice 6–8 hours a week and tour 3–6 weeks a year, and the unique cultures and styles that emerge breed deep loyalties among group alumni. When they reassemble at reunions or chat online, they forget the difficulties of "arranging music," the "tedium of learning the repertoire," the "drudge work of selling albums," and the misadventures of travel and transportation. They remember only that they made good music together, pleased hundreds of audiences great and small, and did not endanger their academic standing with excessive participation. First tenor Wilson would regard those all worthy results.[47]

Since acting is a close cousin to singing, Princeton undergraduates early developed venues for their theatrical talents. Before World War I, the English Dramatic Association provided an extracurricular home for traditional-minded actors, as have the Theatre Intime (which also does original plays by students) since 1919 and the Princeton Shakespeare Company since 1994. But the Triangle Club, which emerged in 1893 from an earlier drama group, hit on a winning combination of music, dance, and comedy to become the university's most visible and popular theatrical troupe. Entirely student-written, -choreographed, -performed, and -financed, Triangle's annual

[47] Leitch, *Princeton Companion*, 217–18; Charles B. Saunders, "The Nassoons," *Nassau Sovereign* 6:7 (Apr. 1947):8–9, 30–31; David Mehnert '87, "Arch Singers," *PAW*, May 6, 1992, 21–24, at 21, 24. At least four groups have come and gone, the oldest of which, the coed Madrigals, lasted from 1976 to 1991. Each of the current groups has a well-illustrated Web site, which lists the members, concert dates, tour news, albums for sale, and repertoire of songs.

productions were first performed on campus in a flimsy building called the Casino. After it burned in 1924, the club found permanent quarters in the new McCarter Theater, toward whose completion in 1930 it contributed $100,000.[48]

The club's largesse flowed from its own sizable box office returns, mostly from its annual Christmas tours around the country. The tours were aimed largely at alumni, who remembered the clever lyrics, memorable tunes, and hairy-legged, all-male kickline that characterized the typical Triangle show. What tour audiences did not hear were the "off-color remarks, purple puns, and double entendres," mostly at the expense of the faculty and administration, that were presented in student-only performances before the adult public saw the show.[49]

Triangle shows were elaborate enterprises, "great, seething anthills," lyricist and one-time "actress" F. Scott Fitzgerald called them. After the writers and lyricists produced a script during the previous spring and summer, the club put out a call in the fall for singing actors, musicians, and technicians. "The club itself was the most influential of institutions," Fitzgerald wrote, "over three hundred men competing for it every year." In 1931, 120 tried out for the chorus alone; 28 made the cut but only 24 would take the Christmas trip. The year Fitzgerald wrote some of the lyrics for "Fie! Fie! Fi-Fi!" (which he called "Ha-Ha Hortense!" in *This Side of Paradise*), the show traveled—with full "cast, chorus, orchestra, and scenery all through Christmas vacation"—to eight cities, including Louisville, Memphis, Chicago, and Baltimore.[50]

[48] Leitch, *Princeton Companion*, 476–80; Donald Marsden '64, *The Long Kickline: A History of the Princeton Triangle Club* (Princeton, 1968); H. Lee Stern, "Campus Organizations: The Triangle Club," *Nassau Sovereign* 6:2 (Sept. 1946):8–9, 22–23.

[49] Christian Gauss, "Life on the Campus," in Charles G. Osgood et al., *The Modern Princeton* (Princeton, 1947), 12–35, at 24–25; "Triangle Turns 100!" *PAW*, May 15, 1991, 27–29, at 28; "1909 Alumni Recall Campus in Wilson's Day," *Princeton Recollector* 4:8 (June 1979):1, 10–15, at 13. In its first fifty years, the club visited fifty cities in twenty-six states and grossed as much as $40–50,000 a year. Malcolm S. Forbes, "Campus Organizations: The Triangle Club," *Nassau Sovereign* 1:2 (Nov. 1938):18–20, 28, 30.

[50] Later tours went to as many as twelve cities in thirteen days. In 1960 and 1962 the club performed at U.S. Army bases in France and Germany during summer tours

Figure 16. Billed as "the most beautiful showgirl" in the cast, F. Scott Fitzgerald '17 also wrote the lyrics for the Triangle Club's musical of 1915–16, *The Evil Eye*.

The cast rode in the Pullman comfort of three railroad cars, one—the "animal car"—reserved for "the spectacled wind-jammers of the orchestra." At every stop, tuxedos were de rigueur for the late-night, post-show parties at their hotel. Debonair Princetonians were the local debutantes' seasonal catch and "everyone fell in love," particularly after "a proper consumption of strong waters" and advanced "petting," a still-new social phenomenon unknown to pre-war parents. All this despite the oversight of "chaperone" Benjamin Franklin

sponsored by the USO. *PAW*, Dec. 1, 1982, 18; Clark Gesner '60, in *Going Back: An Oral History of Princeton* (Princeton: Princetoniana Committee of the Alumni Council, 1996), 28–30.

Bunn '07, "Uncle Ben," the club's graduate treasurer who accompanied some forty-five tours until he was nearly ninety.[51]

"How a Triangle show ever got off was a mystery," Fitzgerald marveled, "but it was a riotous mystery, anyway, whether or not one did enough service to wear a little gold Triangle on his watch-charm." As early as 1910, before the shows began to elaborate and to mimic or satirize big Broadway musicals, fellow students noticed that the club "absorbed a very large amount of undergraduate time and effort." Late-fall rehearsals in Fitzgerald's day commonly lasted "from two in the afternoon until eight in the morning, sustained by dark and powerful coffee, and sleeping in lectures through the interim."[52] Understandably, the typical show featured a star who invariably "got expelled or sick or something just before the trip." But as Jesse Lynch Williams argued in his 1895 *Princeton Stories*, "These trips are not only good fun, they are part of one's education."[53] Although Wilson resorted to vaudeville musicals to relieve the stress of his national presidency, it is less certain that the university president would have recognized the educational value he sought for Princeton students in one of their most consuming sideshows.[54]

Much closer to the president's thinking—and heart—were the venerable literary and debating societies or "halls," Whig and Clio.

[51] Fitzgerald, *This Side of Paradise*, 52, 62–65; *PAW*, Nov. 6, 1931, 140; Leitch, *Princeton Companion*, 479–80; "Triangle Turns 100!" 29. Today the touring company travels by bus and truck.

[52] In 2004 rehearsals lasted "three hours a day Monday through Thursday and five or six hours on Sundays" (Jessica Gross, "Learning the 'Hoppity Hop' Before Opening Night," *DP* [online], Nov. 11, 2004).

[53] Fitzgerald, *This Side of Paradise*, 63; Allen Goodrich Shenstone, "Princeton, 1910–1914," *PULC* 44:1 (Autumn 1982):25–41, at 36; Osgood, *Modern Princeton*, 24–25 (Gauss); Williams, *Princeton Stories*, 145.

[54] Eleanor Wilson McAdoo, *The Woodrow Wilsons* (New York, 1937), 233. In 1917 Dean Frederick Keppel of Columbia lamented "the awful banality of the average college show," but declared that "the best are on the average those of Princeton, Pennsylvania, and the Massachusetts Institute of Technology." In general, he held, "the value of these shows is in the social good times at rehearsal more than in the public performance." He also urged the troupes to exploit "the wealth of local color which the students could find all around them in their college life" (*The Undergraduate and His College* [Boston and New York, 1917], 134–35).

Founded as the American Whig Society in 1769 and the Cliosophic Society the following year, these groups sought to train future leaders in public speaking, debate, literary expression, and parliamentary procedure. In the nineteenth century, virtually every undergraduate belonged to one society or the other. Hall rivalry was keen for members, prizes, and medals, and the coveted positions of commencement orators. Until the twentieth century, Princeton diplomas were decorated with ribbons in the colors of the graduate's hall—blue for Whigs, pink for Clios.[55] Hall members signed an oath never to reveal their proceedings or to admit nonmembers to the society buildings, Ionic Greek temples (with combination locks) in midcampus behind Nassau Hall and Cannon Green.[56]

As the only secret societies allowed on campus, the halls served as substitutes for fraternities, which President McCosh had banned in 1875. But more important, they were apt expressions of the students' desire to augment the official curriculum and to exercise self-discipline. In the 1850s the hall libraries together held nearly as many books—especially up-to-date books on literature, history, politics, and current events—as the college library, which was open only two hours a week. Equally appealing, they also received a steady supply of newspapers and magazines, which were also lacking in the college

[55] Professor of Physics Allen Shenstone, a student between 1910 and 1914, recalled hall initiations in which new members drank "a liquid that resulted in a Whig member urinating blue and a Clio member pink, the colors of the ribbons on their respective diplomas" ("Princeton, 1910–1914," 30). Adlai Stevenson '22 reported to his mother his two-hour initiation into Whig in January 1919: "They put black bags over our heads and we had to go thru the whole thing crawling on our stomachs. They certainly did paddle us and we had to crawl thru a long winding passage under the foundations of the hall." When it was over, President John Grier Hibben spoke to them about the hall's history, including the role of his predecessor and former friend Woodrow Wilson. *Papers of Stevenson*, 1:71 (Jan. 12, 1919).

[56] Leitch, *Princeton Companion*, 504–6; J. Jefferson Looney, *Nurseries of Letters and Republicanism: A Brief History of the American Whig-Cliosophic Society and Its Predecessors, 1765–1941* (Princeton: American Whig-Cliosophic Society, 1996); Looney, "Useful Without Attracting Attention: The Cliosophic and American Whig Societies of the College of New Jersey, 1765–1896," *PULC* 64:3 (Spring 2003):389–423; Jacob N. Beam, *The American Whig Society of Princeton University* (Princeton: American Whig Society, 1933).

library. The written essays and orations the halls promoted weekly allowed the students to explore more modern themes and to treat them more imaginatively than did the classical curriculum.[57]

Woodrow Wilson was an ardent member of Whig Hall as an undergraduate. Although he did not excel in the declamatory set speeches employed in competitions, he was elected Speaker, the presiding officer, because of his superiority in extemporary debate and his efficient conduct of meetings. His model of persuasive oratory was the British House of Commons, where public speaking was, he argued in the *Daily Princetonian*, spontaneous, passionate, and forceful. In his junior year, he founded a Liberal Debating Club to practice the parliamentary style of oratory and political maneuver. There and in the wood-paneled, blue-trimmed chamber of Whig Hall, he honed the verbal skills that soon made him Princeton's best lecturer and one of the most eloquent and persuasive speakers of the twentieth century.[58]

When Wilson became president of Princeton and sought to raise it to new intellectual heights, he reminded the undergraduates that extracurricular activities were for their "leisure hours," served only to "limber" up their mental faculties, and simply did not "count for very much" in the real world. But, as he told the assembled freshmen in his last month in office before running for governor, one of the very few activities that were not "temporary" and slight in value was public speaking. Throughout his tenure, he had presided over the annual fall mass meeting to promote Whig and Clio Halls, telling the audience that, as a hall alumnus and president of the university, he strongly recommended that freshmen "take up work in the Halls." He clearly supported the faculty chosen to speak about the benefits

[57] James Buchanan Henry and Christian Henry Scharff, *College As It Is, or, The Collegian's Manual in 1853*, ed. J. Jefferson Looney (Princeton: Princeton University Libraries, 1996), 78–82, 89–91, 97; James McLachlan, "The *Choice of Hercules*: American Student Societies in the Early 19th Century," in Lawrence Stone, ed., *The University in Society*, 2 vols. (Princeton, 1974), 2:449–94; Thomas S. Harding, *College Literary Societies: Their Contribution to Higher Education in the United States, 1815–1876* (New York, 1971).

[58] Bragdon, *WW: Academic Years*, 30–34; Beam, *American Whig Society*, chap. 13; Robert Alexander Kraig, *Woodrow Wilson and the Lost World of the Oratorical Statesman* (College Station, Tex., 2004), chap. 1, esp. p. 24.

of membership, which included proficiency in debating and extemporary speaking and knowledge of parliamentary law.[59]

The new president lent the halls more than verbal support, however, because they sorely needed it. Since their apogee in the 1880s, they had seen their utility, popularity, and memberships decline. Although they raised two new expensive marble temples in 1893, their star was fading. With expanded undergraduate enrollments, a smaller proportion of the student body could be accommodated in the halls. The rise of the eating clubs and college sports deflected much of the student desire for belonging and competition. Students of a literary bent found more outlets in student publications than in stilted hall exercises. The once-inadequate college library grew and improved markedly, relegating the hall libraries to the status of reading rooms for periodicals and novels. Improved train service contributed to student "weekending," which took hall members away from their regular Friday night meetings. And the curriculum itself began to offer more current and creative courses, which further cut into the halls' raison d'être.[60]

While trying to dampen the student passion for sideshows in general, Wilson threw his weight behind the halls and the cause of public speaking. In 1906 he very much approved—if he did not initiate—a special trustee committee recommendation to "put the fixed fees of the Halls" on the college bills and to "supply the Halls with training in public speaking and debate" by holding special English classes in those subjects for freshman members in their respective buildings.[61] But this was as far as Wilson wanted to go in "connecting the required work of the University with the voluntary action of the literary societies, whose strength and vitality," he said, "really consist in their independence."[62]

[59] *PWW*, 14:138–39 (Oct. 2, 1902); 21:169–71, at 170 (Sept. 26, 1910).

[60] Looney, *Nurseries of Letters*, viii, 46–49, 51, 52; Leitch, *Princeton Companion*, 505; Jesse Lynch Williams, "Princeton University," in Joshua F. Chamberlain, ed., *Universities and Their Sons*, 5 vols. (Boston, 1898), 1:536–70, at 568, 570.

[61] In 1919 Adlai Stevenson joined Whig as an "active member" in order to take "Hall English which is a course," he explained to his mother, "you can take in place of regular Freshman English. It is mostly the science of oratory, argument etc." (*Papers of Stevenson*, 1:71 [Jan. 12, 1919]).

[62] *PWW*, 16:325 (Mar. 7, 1906); 18:583 (Jan. 1, 1909).

He also participated actively in the coaching and encouragement of Princeton's intercollegiate debate teams. In the 1890s, as a new faculty member, he had joined history colleague Winthrop Daniels and Bliss Perry of the English Department in training the Tiger debaters for their championship matches with Harvard and Yale.[63] Later, Hardin Craig, who was assigned to Whig Hall to teach the new English course and to revive the lost verbal arts, praised the busy university president for visiting often and expressing to the students "his faith in debating as a developmental force in education." Wilson also reminisced about "exciting or amusing debates in which he had taken part or which he had heard" when he was a student member. And "he rarely failed to reveal his keen interest in the maneuvering subtleties of parliamentary practice." As his hesitation over further university involvement suggested, Craig noted, "his interest rested on his faith in self-directed, spontaneous *intellectual* activity on the part of the students themselves."[64]

Yet even Wilson's powerful enthusiasm could not compensate for the loss of the students' interest. In 1910 hall meetings dropped from weekly to monthly; secrecy was abandoned three years later and the hall constitutions were simplified. Well before the physical merger of Whig and Clio in 1928, they had abandoned literary exercises to concentrate on sponsoring outside speakers. Whig Hall remained a center of undergraduate training in debate and public speaking, taught formally by a debating coach and a professor of public speak-

[63] Winthrop M. Daniels, *Recollections of Woodrow Wilson* (New Haven, 1944), 19–21; Bliss Perry, *And Gladly Teach: Reminiscences* (Boston and New York, 1935), 135; Kraig, *Woodrow Wilson and the Lost World*, 80–81; Dayton David McKean, "Woodrow Wilson as a Debate Coach," *Quarterly Journal of Speech* 16 (Nov. 1930):458–63. When Christian Gauss joined the faculty in 1905, Big Three debating was big sport. From 1909 each university prepared two teams, one to present the negative, say at home, and the other the affirmative away. To await news of the outcome of the away match via telegraph, most of the undergraduates and faculty filled Alexander Hall, where they were entertained by a Glee Club quartet. If Princeton won the dual match, "cheers like those celebrating a winning touchdown broke from the crowd and the undergraduates started their midnight P-rade" (Osgood, *Modern Princeton*, 23). See Roberta J. Park, "Muscle, Mind and *Agon*: Intercollegiate Debating and Athletics at Harvard and Yale, 1892–1909," *Journal of Sport History* 14:3 (Winter 1987):263–85, esp. 279–82.

[64] Hardin Craig, *Woodrow Wilson at Princeton* (Norman, 1960), 7–8 (my emphasis).

ing and informally by upperclassmen. But in 1941 the assets of the two groups were transferred to the university and the American Whig-Cliosophic Society was christened, with a legitimate claim to fame as "the nation's oldest political, debating, & literary society." By 1975, when it elected its first female president, it was again the largest extracurricular activity on campus, enjoying more than a thousand members. At the beginning of the new millennium, it still attracts to revived weekly meetings students with interests in the debate team, a Model UN, and a Model Congress.[65]

❁ ❁ ❁

Despite Wilson's efforts to reduce the relative importance of the sideshows, they continued to proliferate faster than enrollments. By the outbreak of World War I, Princeton's fewer than 1,400 students could choose from 17 intercollegiate and intramural sports and 50 organizations. The variety of interest groups was not great. Thirty clubs were based on state, sectional, or prep school origins; only five were activity- or future profession–driven. Five musical groups, two theater troupes, and Whig and Clio appealed to the most vocal students. The Philadelphian Society, the campus equivalent of the YMCA, fought for the student soul against three predominantly drinking clubs; the seventeen upperclass eating clubs claimed even more converts.[66]

By 1947 the end of the serious business of war turned many returning veterans and new students to long-postponed enjoyments of a nonbookish sort. President Dodds noted the appeal of 55 pre-war groups and 25 new ones, not counting athletics or the eating clubs,

[65] Looney, *Nurseries of Letters*, viii–xii, 53–59; Leitch, *Princeton Companion*, 505–6; Beam, *American Whig Society*, chap. 14; Harold C. Buckminster '48, "Whig-Clio: 1947 Style," *PAW*, Nov. 28, 1947, 6–7.

[66] Shenstone, "Princeton, 1910–1914," 35–36. On the Philadelphian Society at Princeton (1825–1929), see P. C. Kemeny, *Princeton in the Nation's Service: Religious Ideals and Educational Practice, 1868–1928* (New York, 1998), 54–56, 106–9, 160–64, 186–88, 200–17; Matthew Morey Coburn, "The Philadelphian Society: An Investigation into the Demise of an Evangelical Student Christian Organization at Princeton University in the 1920s" (Senior thesis, Dept. of Religion, PU, 1991).

which also resumed full schedules after wartime hiatuses. Within forty years, the extracurricular pickings nearly doubled, to 147, for a studious student body of over 4,500. An even more academically assiduous population of 4,600 in 2002–2003 turned to 203 amazingly varied organizations, 11 eating clubs, 38 intercollegiate sports teams, 35 club sports, and nearly 600 intramural teams to develop their other talents and interests, which the admissions office had once recognized and rewarded. If a student could not find an interest served by any of the 18 music, 9 theater, 10 dance, 13 political, 41 multicultural, 18 service, 3 environmental, 16 religious, 25 media, 6 career, and 23 special interest groups on campus, he or she could form a group of the like-minded. This was obviously the route taken by the founders of Flamenco Puro, the Arab Society, Mariachi Princípe, *Tory* magazine, Random Acts of Kindness, Baha'i Club, Princeton Juggling, and the Mime Company.[67]

But numbers alone cannot tell the whole story of extracurricular involvement. The spirit in which the bulk of the students pursued their nonacademic interests is the key to deciding whether the side-shows were regarded as "diversions" or as "occupations." Before the late 1920s, mass college chauvinism and "charm-hunting"—the pursuit of extra-curricular activities to demonstrate one's "college spirit" and to collect gold charms to wear on one's watch chain—were the order of the day. British student John Benn '26 noted that "the American student who shows no desire to achieve some 'extra-curriculum' position is at a disadvantage socially . . . unless, of course, obvious athletic or intellectual prowess renders extra adornment unnecessary." Many students defended Princeton's honor in athletic venues, and most of the rest spectated with spirit. Even transfer students were quickly won to the prevailing campus culture. When 101 of them were asked in 1922 if there was too much interest at Princeton in football and in the extracurriculum, 90 percent said no, arguing that the latter provided "excellent training for a man's work outside [college]."[68]

[67] *PAW*, Nov. 28, 1947, 6; Mar. 12, 1986, 13; PU, *Student Guide to Princeton, 2002–2003* (Princeton: Office of the Dean of Undergraduate Students, 2002), 58–62.

[68] John A. Benn, *Columbus—Undergraduate* (Philadelphia, 1928), 73; *Princeton Pictorial*, Feb. 6, 1922, 206–8, at 207.

The advent of the four-course plan, economic depression, another world war, and Sputnik, rather than presidential persuasion, brought about a decisive and largely permanent shift in student priorities. By the early 1930s, a general revolt against "that mythical something known as 'college spirit' " had overtaken the campus, and the typical undergraduate had concluded that "it isn't a matter of life and death whether Princeton defeats Yale, or, in fact, whether Princeton defeats anybody." After a brief extracurricular renaissance after the war, a student columnist in 1958 declared that "Woodrow Wilson's Dream Has Come True" and "extracurricular activities in general are in a state of decline," due largely to greater academic demands.[69] In a new "spirit of anti-doism," student convention frowned on showing too much enthusiasm (an alleged Yale trait) or identifying too closely with non-academic activities. In their senior year, a third of the class of '58 engaged in no extracurricular activities whatever, saving their free time for Firestone Library or post-dinner relaxation in the clubs.[70]

After the student activism and culture wars of the 1960s and early 1970s, individualism became even more noticeably a Princeton trait. Students chose or created extracurricular activities for personal rather than collegial reasons. After some temporary résumé-loading in the ambitious 1980s and early 1990s, Princeton's increasingly challenged and busy undergraduates chose fewer activities and tended to specialize in those of particular interest. When the graduating class of 2002 was asked how they would spend their time if they could "do" Princeton all over again, 54 percent said they would spend more time on their studies and 62 percent in extracurricular pursuits. But 70 percent of the hard-charging "Organization Kids" thought they would spend more time socializing with friends, to take a breather from both studies and sideshows.[71] In short, they wanted it all and even more.

[69] As early as 1917 Dean Keppel of Columbia noted that "when a passing mark is all that the faculty seems interested in, students will rush into too many undergraduate activities" (Keppel, *The Undergraduate and His College*, 206).

[70] Parker, "Extracurricular Decline," *PAW*, Apr. 25, 1958, 3–7. According to Parker, even drinking was down. "Undergraduate Drinking: Creeping Asceticism Drives Student Consumption to All-Princeton Low," *PAW*, Oct. 2, 1959, 3–5.

[71] *Nassau Herald* (2002), 23. The Bressler Commission asked a similar question of 1,052 alumni from the classes of 1954, 1964, and 1969. Sixteen percent said they would study harder; 21 percent would participate in more athletic and extracurricular activities.

❁ ❁ ❁

Whether Princeton students committed more or less time to the extracurriculum, two activities—one social, the other physical—held a firm claim on the majority's attention throughout the twentieth century and into the next. The first was the eating clubs, that peculiarly Princetonian invention. The second was athletics, as it was in virtually all American colleges and universities attended by high-spirited, energetic young adults. The attraction was understandable. In seeking excellence, philosopher Paul Weiss reminded us, humans "like to be perfected physically and mentally." By nature, however, young people do not yet possess the full means to excel intellectually or to contribute meaningfully to society and culture. But they can more nearly—and without waiting—achieve *physical* perfection. Even if "they all cannot exhibit what man at his best can do, they can all make evident the kind of work that must be done if excellence is to be achieved." Thus they gravitate to athletics because "it offers them the most promising means for becoming excellent" in the all-important present.[72]

For a university of large academic ambitions and attainments, Princeton has enjoyed an unusually robust reputation for athletic prowess since the last third of the nineteenth century. Although Ivy-scale, "medium-time" sports since the early 1930s have been increasingly overshadowed by the semiprofessional teams of our behemoth state universities, Princeton (and its Big Three rivals) once dominated the intercollegiate sports scene in America.[73] Moreover, since 1985, Princeton has not only dominated the Ivy League overall, it is the only school without athletic scholarships—and one of the

---

With their eye on the "main tent," 21 percent said they would choose a different major. These were the three most popular responses. Peter C. Wendell '72, " 'If You Had It to Do Over Again . . . ,' " *PAW*, Mar. 4, 1975, 9–12, at 11 (table 5).

[72] Paul Weiss, *Sport: A Philosophic Inquiry* (Carbondale, Ill., 1969), 17, 19, 21.

[73] Ronald A. Smith, *Sports and Freedom: The Rise of Big-Time College Athletics* (New York, 1988); John M. Murrin, "Rites of Domination: Princeton, the Big Three, and the Rise of Intercollegiate Athletics," *PULC* 62:2 (Winter 2001):161–206; George B. Kirsch, "Payoffs, Ringers, and Riots: Princeton and the Rise of Intercollegiate Football, 1880–1895," *PAW*, Sept. 11, 1991, 12–17.

smallest—to rank among the twenty-five most successful sports programs in the country, winning several national championships to secure its place.[74]

It is easily forgotten, for example, that now–Ivy League teams dominated college football in the late nineteenth and early twentieth century, that four of them played in the Rose Bowl, that three of their players won the Heisman Trophy—named for an Ivy coach—as the nation's best player, and that fight songs, marching bands, and sports pages grew largely from ivied soil. Few also remember that the Ivies, particularly the Big Three, invented the All-America team and filled most of the early ones, produced the first coaches, arranged the basic rules, conceived many of the strategies, devised much of the equipment, and even named the positions. Not surprisingly but even less known, the Ivy universities once experienced all of the scandals that currently plague big-time college sports. "There is nothing wrong in this world that we didn't invent," admitted former Princeton professor and Ivy League Executive Director James Litvack. Fortunately, they had the courage and good sense to fix the problems by articulating and adopting the amateur principles of the Ivy League between the end of World War II and 1954.[75]

At the turn of the last century and well into the 1920s, games at Princeton "played a very large part in a student's life even if he was only a spectator." College tradition and pride took most of the student body on a daily pilgrimage in the fall, rain or shine, to watch

[74] In 2002–2003 Princeton was the runaway winner of the league's unofficial all-points championship for the seventeenth straight year; it had won the points race in 24 of the previous 27 years. In 2001–2002 it also placed twenty-first in the Sears' Directors' Cup for overall athletic success, the fourth time it had placed in the top 25. In 1997 *Sports Illustrated* rated Princeton the tenth-best "Jock School" in the nation on the strength of its team successes, abundance of club sports, and new facilities. Three years later, *Sports Illustrated for Women* put Princeton at ninth for female athletes. *Princeton Athletics, 2002–2003: At the Head of the Class* (Princeton: Dept. of Athletics, 2002), [1]; *Princeton Athletics: The Tradition Continues [2003–04]* (Princeton: Dept. of Athletics, 2003), [1]; Doug Lederman '84, "Tigers on Top," *PAW*, Nov. 6, 1996, 13–22, at 13; *PAW*, June 4, 1997, 25; *PAW*, Oct. 11, 2000, 14.

[75] Leitch, *Princeton Companion*, 274–75; Mark F. Bernstein, *Football: The Ivy League Origins of an American Obsession* (Philadelphia, 2001), ix–x.

football practice. For the same reasons, virtually the whole university, faculty included, traveled to New York City on Thanksgiving Day to watch the last big game of the season, usually against formidable Yale. At home, remembered Allen Shenstone '14, "the popularity of football was so great that the Pennsylvania Railroad maintained at least a dozen tracks for parking special trains that brought thousands from New York and Philadelphia and even from New Haven, Boston, and Washington. . . . Undergraduate attendance at major football games probably exceeded 75 percent." Basketball was coming into its own as a spectator sport, but hockey was still considered the premier winter sport. Unfortunately, Princeton lacked a rink until 1923, so relatively few students witnessed the improbable feats of rover "Hobey" Baker '14, "probably the greatest hockey player ever produced in the United States."[76] The team had to practice in New York and played most of its games in icy New England and Canada. In the spring, baseball drew large numbers of candidates for the freshman and varsity teams, but also for class teams, which played a regular series of well-attended intramural games.[77]

By the late 1920s, however, student attitudes toward sports began to change noticeably. Three upperclass essayists in the alumni magazine's "How Thinks the Campus" contest noted a definite trend away from major sports teams toward "self-development," engagement in activities "for what [the individual] can get out of them." This led to a depletion of the "spectator class" and a turn toward individual and intramural sports for "fun and exercise." Tennis, squash, and golf gained in popularity while interest in football waned, even when Princeton beat Yale. "Football hysteria may exist in other colleges," observed one senior, "but certainly not here, even among the members of the team." A classmate conceded that although membership on a major sport team remained a "distinct social and popular asset," there was "no blind hero-worship of athletics." "Large bands of the

[76] John D. Davies, *The Legend of Hobey Baker* (Boston, 1966); excerpted in *PAW*, Sept. 27, 1966, 10–12, 16–17; Emil R. Salvini, *Hobey Baker: American Legend* (St. Paul, Minn., 2005).

[77] Williams, "Princeton University," in *Universities and Their Sons*, 1:557; Shenstone, "Princeton, 1910–1914," 33, 38. See also Nelson R. Burr '27, "Remembering Princeton in the '20s," *PAW*, May 9, 1977, 9–14, at 13.

faithful" no longer "traveled to University Field for each practice" because the current undergraduate lacked a "*philosophy* of loyalty which makes it necessary for him to 'root for the team.' "[78]

Throughout the middle third of the century, official Princeton adumbrated a philosophy of sports that emphasized "recreational competition" and the balanced development of the "whole man" rather than the "glorification of the individual," the "prestige or profit of the college," or "public spectacle."[79] In tune with this message, the undergraduates continued their shift from organized team sports and spectating to participation in individual and especially intramural sports. In 1937–1938 over 4,100 men (including duplications) played in nearly 1,100 intramural contests—touch football, basketball, softball, and hockey being the most popular. Eleven years later, intercollegiate teams enjoyed a brief surge in participation after the deprivations of the war, but several junior varsity teams were disbanded for lack of recruits; 57 percent of the students played intramurals. By 1958, when extracurricular activities in general were declared to be in serious decline, 75 percent of the student body still took part in some form of athletics (down from an estimated 90 percent in 1932). Yet the undermanned JV football team was abolished, other coaches complained that many nonstarters "exhibited considerable reluctance to ride the varsity benches," and many fewer men played three sports than they had in the past.[80]

During the 1950s and 1960s, Princetonians had plenty to cheer about. The gridiron success of Princeton's baffling single-wing offense and the derring-do of such stars as Heisman-winner Dick Kaz-

[78] William Milligan Sloane III '29, "Present Day Trends at Princeton," *PAW*, July 2, 1929, 1131–32; Otis B. Bosworth '30, "The New Campus Philosophy," *PAW*, July 2, 1929, 1132–34; Gerhard P. Van Arkel '29, "Princeton, More Old Than New," 1134–35.

[79] "Football Agreement," *PAW*, Nov. 30, 1945, 3–5; "A Forum on Princeton Athletics," *PAW*, Nov. 25, 1949, 11–14; Harold W. Dodds, "The Princeton Philosophy of Athletics," *PAW*, Mar. 1, 1957, 6–11; W. Raymond Ollwerther '71, "Sports: An Interview with President Goheen," *PAW*, May 18, 1971, 10–11.

[80] "Intra-Mural Athletics on the Increase," *PAW*, Dec. 7, 1938, 237; "Forum on Princeton Athletics," 11–13; Parker, "Extracurricular Decline," 4; Gerhard P. VanArkel '29, "All the Sad Old Men," *PAW*, Apr. 1, 1932, 568–69.

maier '52, Cosmo Iacavazzi '65, and soccer-style place-kicker Charlie Gogolak '66, as well as the winning ways of the basketball squad and the scoring magic of three-time All-American Bill Bradley '65, the country's leading player, kept the seats filled and local chauvinism elevated.[81] But the captious energy of the late 1960s and early 1970s led to a "general de-emphasis of athletics" on the nation's campuses, including Princeton. A quarter of the male students (and a growing number of the newly arrived women) still played intercollegiate sports, but fewer tried out, a third quit, and their classmates showed less support for teams and less respect for "P" wearers. Those who did play did so less for "school spirit" than for love of the sport and a search for personal excellence. They continued to value the time-discipline and camaraderie of sports, and coaches thought they worked as hard as ever, but they expected coaches to be less military and rule-bound, particularly about players' hair length and what they smoked after practice.[82]

The Athletic Department hoped that the late Sixties were an aberration, and they were not disappointed. Indeed, Princeton played sports with the same intensity it devoted to its search for intellectual excellence and academic competitiveness under President (and former college tennis star) William Bowen. The advent of high-powered women, newly liberated by feminism and Title IX to seek their own place in the athletic sun, gave an obvious push to the university's rising goals. So did healthy endowments and the building of top-of-the-line athletic facilities. But intercollegiate and Ivy athletics were heading inexorably in a new direction, virtually heedless of institutional wishes or worries. Thrilled by the competition, Princeton responded willingly to the new conditions and challenges, and over the next quarter-century compiled a record unmatched by any of its Ivy League rivals. But well before the century ended, the university

[81] Leitch, *Princeton Companion*, 42–45, 192–94; "Princeton's All-Century [Football] Team, 1900–99," *PAW*, Dec. 15, 1999, 16–17.

[82] William F. Highberger '72, "The Changing Student Athlete," *PAW*, Feb. 2, 1971, 9–11. Following an Ivy League trend, Princeton's five home football games lost more than 6,200 spectators between 1969 and 1970. Chris Connell '71, "Sports: The Question of Recruiting," *PAW*, Feb. 9, 1971, 14–15.

realized that it was paying a substantial social and academic price for its athletic success and instituted reforms to restore the balance.

The one aspect of the Sixties that did not go away with Vietnam and student protests was the shift from spectating to participation. Although certain star performers and winning records could still attract students to some teams and contests, even in women's or minor sports, spectatorship in general has steadily declined. In the bellwether sport of football, the fan base has fallen dramatically since the mid-1960s. Palmer Stadium, built in 1914 to seat 45,000, had drawn an average of 39,000 fans in the mid-1930s and a still-healthy 20,000 as late as 1965. By 1980, however, the stadium was barely one-quarter full, an understandable response, perhaps, to the team's decadal record of 53 losses, 4 ties, and only 33 wins. Three winning seasons in the early 1980s brought attendance only up to 16,450. When dangerously decaying Palmer was replaced in 1998 by Rafael Viñoly's stylishly contemporary horseshoe, the seats were trimmed to a more realistic 27,800. In its first three years, 18,000 (64 percent) of them were filled, largely with nonstudents. By 2003 the Tigers drew an average of only 13,270 fans to their five home games, which led the Athletic Department to aim its marketing at the alumni and the community rather than the students.[83]

The decline in football followers has several causes and is not necessarily a cause for lament. In the Ivy League in particular, football is no longer the exclusive focus of intercollegiate athletics. Like basketball at Penn and soccer at Columbia, for example, Princeton lacrosse (men's and women's), having won nine national titles since 1992, has a large fan base, and the new Princeton Stadium has hosted

[83] Scott C. Oostdyk '82, "Where Have All the Fans Gone?" *PAW*, Dec. 15, 1982, 16–17, 20; "New Football Stadium Nears Completion," *PAW*, June 10, 1998, 6; Stephen R. Dujack '76, "Back to the Future," *PAW*, Oct. 7, 1998, 14–19; *Student Guide to Princeton, 2002–2003*, 68; David Baumgarten, "Princeton Stadium: Plenty of Quality Seats Left," *DP* (online), Sept. 16, 2004. Ivy League football in general suffered a similar decline in attendance. In the mid-1960s the eight teams averaged 20,000; by the mid-1990s the average had been cut in half. Bernstein, *Football*, 264; Austin Starkweather and Michelle Leutzinger, "Dwindling Fan Support Means Fewer Cheers for Old Nassau at Sports Events" (part two of ten-part series on "Princeton Athletics: Beyond the Game"), *DP* (online), Nov. 12, 2002.

NCAA tournament games.[84] The proliferation of professional teams, the proximity of the Meadowlands sports complex, and saturation coverage of college and pro football games on television certainly took a toll, as did the abandonment of the single wing and the advent of coeducation in 1969. With women on campus, "football weekends" lost their logic. Before coeducation, students bought 2,800–3,000 tickets per game, by 1981, only 900. The fall-semester break instituted in 1970 also drained students from the campus for two weekends. Yet when they are there, having the shortest academic calendar among their peers and some of the heaviest demands impels many students to devote Saturday afternoons to class reading, paper writing, or musical practice. The gargoyle over the Campus Club entrance may aptly symbolize the new situation on campus: it pictures a begowned and mortarboarded professor administering a fierce tackle to a leather-helmeted footballer.[85]

But the major reason for the decline in football watching is that Princeton fields so many varsity (38), club (30–35), and intramural (c. 600) teams, besides offering some 150 physical education classes for recreation, that most students are simply too busy with their own physical exertions to devote much time to those of their classmates.[86] They apparently agree with "Teddy" Roosevelt, who argued in 1907 that "it is of far more importance that a man shall play something himself, even if he does it badly, than that he shall go with hundreds of companions to see someone else play well."[87] Since winning team-

[84] Philippe de Pontet '93, "After Years in the Desert, Laxmen Reach The Promised Land: A National Title," *PAW*, July 8, 1992, 16–18; David Marcus '92, "Turnabout Artist: Coach Bill Tierney Restored Lacrosse's Winning Tradition—and Created a Juggernaut," *PAW*, May 20, 1998, 18–21; Marcus, "National Champs Again! Men's Lacrosse Wins Its Sixth Title in 10 Years," *PAW*, July 4, 2001, 34–35; Lindsay Kramer, "Double Take: Women's Lax Wins Second-Straight National Title," *PAW*, July 2, 2003, 29.

[85] Oostdyk, "Where Have All the Fans Gone?" 16–17, 20; *PAW*, Nov. 22, 1957, cover, 7.

[86] At Princeton an intercollegiate club sport differs from a varsity sport in having a part-time coach, no special support in the admission process, and modest funding from the university.

[87] *Student Guide to Princeton, 2002–2003*, 69; Theodore Roosevelt, address at Harvard University, Feb. 23, 1907, quoted in Bernstein, *Football*, 264.

records (and associated spectatorship) have no positive correlation with alumni giving at Princeton (or the other Ivies)—indeed, often the *reverse*—the university can take comfort in knowing that the institutional pride of its current and past students derives more from their intellectual than their athletic experiences.[88]

The academic prowess of the athletes themselves is another matter altogether. Since its founding in 1954, the Ivy League (or Group, as it is officially designated) has insisted that the academic programs of its members are "paramount," that "student athletes should be generally [the 1945 football agreement said "truly"] representative of their class," and that they "should be held accountable to the same academic standards as other students."[89] The Ivy presidents' concerns, including Princeton's, have deep historical roots.

Periodically, the classroom performance of Tiger athletes has been a burning issue since the Civil War, when intercollegiate athletics caught fire. In 1867 President John Maclean warned the trustees, "I have my fears, that the evidently increasing devotion to such sports as base-ball, which seems to pervade the whole country, and more especially, the youths of Academies and Colleges, will interfere seriously with study and with serious thought." His fears were not unfounded. By 1885 his successor James McCosh was complaining that the campus heroes were men "who devote as little time as possible to their studies. The president of the Athletic Association and the captain of the Foot Ball [team] lately elected stand at the very foot of their classes." It was worse than that. Two years earlier, a record check had discovered that only 7 of the 27 members of the football and baseball teams were in the top halves of their classes; 15 were in the lowest two groups. From 1875 to 1885 nearly all Princeton athletes graduated, but in 1895—after an influx of "special students" and other

[88] James L. Shulman and William G. Bowen, *The Game of Life: College Sports and Educational Values* (Princeton, 2001), chap. 10; Sarah E. Turner, Lauren A. Meserve, and William G. Bowen, "Winning and Giving: Football Results and Alumni Giving at Selective Private Colleges and Universities," *Social Science Quarterly* 82:4 (Dec. 2001):812–26; Jennifer Jacobson, "Winning Sports Teams Have Little Effect on Colleges, Report Says," *CHE*, Sept. 17, 2004, A35.

[89] "Football Agreement," 4; Council of Ivy Group Presidents, Statement of Principles (1954, as amended 1979) [www.ivysports.com].

ringers—only 68 percent of the football team eventually earned a degree. Even the football-mad *Prince* conceded that "a high measure of physical activity tends to postpone the period of mental maturity, and that the youths much given to field sports . . . are apt to be behind their fellows in intellectual development."[90]

The *Prince* lent a hand in 1922 when coach Bill Roper's highly successful football team was, he lamented, "literally shot to pieces by failure of the men to meet scholastic requirements." In a drastic move, he urged his brighter players to tutor their dimmer teammates, but the daily's editors trumped his plea by urging "all Phi Beta Kappa men and others of high standing" to volunteer to assist "members of the first squad that are back in their studies" (the second-string was apparently on its own). The hard-bitten editors of the *New York Times*, who caught wind of the story, declared the "naivete" of their junior counterparts "charming."[91]

The leading Tiger sportsmen of the next decade did little more to cover themselves with academic glory. A comparison of ninety leaders of nine major extracurricular activities in the classes of 1930–1939 found that the captains of football, baseball, and track and the football manager had the lowest averages, significantly below the all-student average of 2.57 (on a 5-group scale). Only the Triangle Club impresario ranked as low. This news from the dean's office must have altered the impression given to the alumni in 1938 in an article on twenty-three *legacy* sons who had won "honors in both athletics and scholarship," including *second*-group averages in single subjects. Significantly, only three played more than one sport, which then occupied a single season.[92]

When the Ivy universities exchanged academic information on their athletes in 1951–1952, Princeton reported that the basketball team had performed beyond expectations. Of its 19 members, 6

[90] Minutes of the Trustee Council, PU (College of New Jersey), ser. 1, vol. 4, p. 430; vol. 6, pp. 599–600 (PUA), quoted in Murrin, "Rites of Domination," 166, 174, 194n44; also 193; Kirsch, "Payoffs, Ringers, and Riots," 14.

[91] "Coach Roper Plans Drastic Measures," *New York Times*, Mar. 30, 1922, 24; "Scholarship, Then, Does Suffer!" *New York Times*, Mar. 31, 1922, 16.

[92] "PBK and/or Varsity 'P,' " *PAW*, Mar. 29, 1940, 575; "Some Noteworthy Scholar-Athletes Who Are Sons of Princeton Alumni," *PAW*, Oct. 14, 1938, 54–55.

stood in the first quintile of grades, 6 in the second, and none in the bottom fifth. The classroom performance of the 38 varsity football players was also surprising, but for slightly different reasons. Only 1 man ranked in the first quintile ("fewer . . . than in recent years"), 8 in the second, while a dozen made only the fourth slot and 4 brought up the rear. At least it could be said that 15 were majoring in history, engineering, and English, "held to be among the most difficult in the University."[93]

The underperformance of Princeton athletes, particularly those recruited for the "major" or high-profile sports, has continued to be a problem. But it is only one of several problems associated with sports that have confronted university officials since midcentury. Many stem from the dramatically altered landscape of scholastic and intercollegiate athletics in America in the past thirty-five or forty years. Sports at all levels have not only expanded exponentially to include girls and women, they have become much more specialized and professionalized. The skill level of high school and college athletes in many sports has risen so sharply that preparation and training must often begin in primary or secondary school, with hearty (and expensive) supplements of camps, clubs, coaches, and conditioning.

At the college level, this has led to fierce competition for the best athletes, a contest that Princeton and the other Ivies must wage without oxymoronic "athletic scholarships" and "letters of intent," which differ little from professional contracts. Most athletes now play only one sport, but devote the whole year to conditioning and competition.[94] They also expect first-rate facilities—fields, courts, and pools, boat houses, locker rooms, fitness centers—and full-time coaching, which leads coaches themselves to specialize in only one sport.

[93] "Here and There: Students First," *PAW*, May 23, 1952, 5.

[94] In 1995 only 6–7 percent of Ivy League athletes played more than one sport; in 1951, 16 percent did. William G. Bowen and Sarah A. Levin, *Reclaiming the Game: College Sports and Educational Values* (Princeton, 2003), 101–5, esp. figs. 4.10, 4.11. At Princeton, football star Dick Kazmaier '52 also played basketball, for which he had been initially recruited; Bill Bradley '65, the most highly recruited basketball player in 1960–1961, played some baseball as well. The last twelve-letter winners were women: see chapter 3, p. 163.

When coaches are not on the road recruiting, they are leading their teams through expanded schedules, often into traditionally sacrosanct exam periods and holidays. Competitive recruiting, in turn, means that many fewer "walk-ons"—students with some experience, skill, and desire who try out for a team when they arrive at college or after—can find places, except in "minor" or lower-profile sports that are not played in most high schools, such as squash, water polo, or crew. For economic and other reasons, most colleges have phased out JV and freshman teams, which raises the bar still higher for high school athletes hoping to make the jump to college competition.[95] As a consequence of all these developments, many young people who devote so much time, effort, and concentration to their sport understandably come to fashion identities primarily as "jocks," who, even if they are intellectually gifted, tend to discount or credit less that side of themselves.[96]

Although all colleges and universities have been subject to these national forces, Princeton and its Ivy League rivals have felt the inevitable tension between the twin drives for excellence of mind and body more acutely than most of their bigger Division I-A counterparts. At Princeton the tensions became more palpable and public as its national reputation rose in step with its students' qualifications and faculty quality. Contributing to these tensions were the growing size and prominence of the Graduate School, with its historical distance from undergraduate life, and the substantial influx of international faculty and students, who do not share the peculiarly American faith in the compatibility of game playing and higher education. The result was that many voices in the faculty and administration sought to put a premium on Princeton's academic identity and questioned the extent and expense of the university's commitment to athletics.

[95] Craig Lambert, "The Professionalization of Ivy League Sports," *Harvard Magazine* 100:1 (Sept.–Oct. 1997):36–49, 96–98; Shulman and Bowen, *The Game of Life*, 23–27; Bowen and Levin, *Reclaiming the Game*, 43–49.

[96] See James Axtell, "The Making of a Scholar-Athlete," *Virginia Quarterly Review* 67:1 (Winter 1991):71–90 (also Axtell, *The Pleasures of Academe: A Celebration & Defense of Higher Education* [Lincoln, 1998], chap. 7) on the difficulties of identity formation for young athletes.

These voices came to be heard loud and clear in the 1990s, as Princeton's athletic aspirations took on national targets, such as NCAA championships and Sears Cup rankings, as well as continued domination of the Ivies. In 1991–1992 a joint faculty-administration Strategic Planning Committee on Undergraduate Education looked at athletics in its larger consideration of the size and composition of the student body. Their concerns prompted a fuller study of athletic-academic relations by the Trustee Committee on Student Life, Health, and Athletics in 1993–1994. Between 1994 and 1997 the Andrew W. Mellon Foundation, led by former Princeton president William Bowen, assembled a database ("College and Beyond") of the admissions, academic, and extracurricular records of 93,660 full-time students who entered thirty-four elite colleges and universities (including Princeton) in the fall of 1951, 1976, and 1989. This was used by Bowen and his Mellon colleague James Shulman to write *The Game of Life: College Sports and Educational Values*, published in 2001. Reactions to the book prompted the foundation to expand the database to include all eight Ivy League universities (only four, including Princeton, had been part of the original database) and to add information on the entering cohort of 1995, in order to probe more deeply the subtleties and growth of an "academic-athletic divide" in a variety of elite institutions. Bowen's second book, *Reclaiming the Game*, written with colleague Sarah Levin (All-American sailor and the daughter of Yale President Richard Levin), not only incorporated more information on Princeton athletes than the previous internal probes had produced, but contextualized them nationally. If Princeton had "jock" problems, it was certainly not alone, although some had a distinctly orange flavor.[97]

The university's own studies found Princeton's athletic programs and philosophy to be appropriate and in good health. They acknowledged that athletics were "part of, and an important contributor to,

[97] The "College and Beyond" database is described in William G. Bowen and Derek Bok, *The Shape of the River: Long-Term Consequences of Considering Race in College and University Admissions* (Princeton, 1998), app. A, the first book to result from its use. See also Shulman and Bowen, *The Game of Life*, xxv–xxxi; Bowen and Levin, *Reclaiming the Game*, chap. 1, esp. 15–19. The Yale situation is similar: see Mac Caplan, "Athletics at Yale: A Fragile Balance," *Yale Herald* (online), Sept. 12, 2003.

Princeton's broad mission of education and personal growth." At their best, they believed, "competitive athletics can encourage a desire for excellence, respect for colleagues, fair play, teamwork, leadership, perseverance, and integrity." Sports can also "teach students to deal with both winning and losing and to understand the rewards that come from dedication to a larger purpose." Thus, the university remained "fully committed to a first-rate athletic program within the context of its primary academic mission."[98]

Despite a generally healthy diagnosis, all four studies detected imbalances and causes for institutional concern. The most basic problem was demographic. Because Princeton's student body is the third smallest of the Ivies, and because Princeton chooses to support one of the largest arrays of intercollegiate sports (varsity and club) in the country, the *proportion* of athletes, especially recruited athletes, was (and still is) significantly greater than at peer schools and much higher than at the better-known Division I-A "jock factories," such as Michigan and Oklahoma, which offer many fewer sports opportunities (except spectating) to much larger student populations. In the early 1990s, recruited athletes comprised about 20 percent of each entering class (down from 24 percent in the 1980s). When "walk-ons" and players of club sports were added, over 40 percent of Princeton undergraduates participated in intercollegiate athletics—as they still do, though the recruits have dropped to 14 percent and the club rosters have grown.[99]

The location, persuasion, admission, and retention of so many prime athletes who are capable of holding their own in Princeton classrooms is obviously fraught with difficulties. The first is that every Ivy athlete must qualify for admission according to an Academic Index (AI) specific to each institution.[100] The smarter the stu-

[98] PU, Trustee Committee on Student Life, Health, and Athletics, *Report on Princeton Athletics* (Nov. 30, 1994), 1, 18. See also [Thomas H. Wright, university vice-president and secretary], *Intercollegiate Athletics at Princeton in the 1990's* (Spring 1992), 1–2.

[99] *Intercollegiate Athletics at Princeton in the 1990's*, 3, app. A, B; *Report on Princeton Athletics* (1994), 4–5n2, 10–11.

[100] Created in 1981 by League director James Litvack and the eight presidents, largely to monitor the recruits in the high-profile men's sports (football, basketball, and hockey), the AI establishes a band width of entering SAT and Achievement scores and high school rank based on the mean results of all matriculants. In general, athletes must

dent body, the smarter the "representative" athletes must be. Another difficulty is that, without athletic scholarships to bind them, over half of Princeton's recruits drop their sport by the end of junior year.[101] Although some "walk-ons" take their places, the university must admit nearly two athletes for every team position. This, of course, reduces the number of gifted mathematicians and musicians, painters and poets, actors and journalists who can be admitted to add to the richness and diversity of the undergraduate experience.

The issue of admissions "inefficiency" is complicated by one of admissions "inequity." Once athletic applicants are "tagged" as priorities on coaches' "wish lists" and are found to measure up to Princeton's lofty AI, they have a chance of being admitted more than four times greater than the rest of the applicant pool, much higher even than alumni children or minorities, who also receive extra consideration. Since many athletes, especially the most desirable, are encouraged by coaches to apply for early admission, their chances increase still further, to six times greater.[102] In 1994 Dean of Admission Fred Hargadon asserted that "in none of the Ivy schools are athletes truly academically representative of the student body." To prove his point for Princeton, he offered the ratings those in the class of 1997 received from the Committee on Admissions. While almost twice as many nonathletes (92 percent) received academic ratings of 1–3 as did athletes (55 percent), nearly six times as many players (45 percent) entered with 4's and 5's as did nonplayers (8 percent). Understand-

---

score within one standard deviation of the mean to be eligible for admission. Football players are subject to a somewhat more elaborate calibration. See Shulman and Bowen, *The Game of Life*, 13–14, 46, and Bowen and Levin, *Reclaiming the Game*, 176, 263, 268, 343n7, 387, nn. 9, 11, for its operation and problems.

[101] Both *Intercollegiate Athletics at Princeton in the 1990's*, 5–6, app. C, and *Report on Princeton Athletics* (1994), 14, speak of a 40 percent drop. But in the classes of 1989–1993, 55 percent dropped out before senior year. Trustee "Athletic Study: Summary Draft" (Spring 1994), tables 2–3 (I am grateful to Taylor Reveley, chairman of the trustee committee that undertook the 1993–1994 study of athletics, for a copy of this document and others relating to the inquiry.)

[102] Shulman and Bowen, *The Game of Life*, chap. 2; Bowen and Levin, *Reclaiming the Game*, chap. 3; Christopher Avery, Andrew Fairbanks, and Richard Zeckhauser, *The Early Admissions Game: Joining the Elite* (Cambridge, Mass., 2003), 60–62, 238–40.

ably, the dean's wish was for more applicants with both academic and athletic 2's.[103]

He was not likely to get them as long as Princeton's athletes continued to enter with SATs 100–115 points below the rest of the class. Given the height of the average matriculant's SATs, this difference is not very large and clearly falls within Princeton's AI. Moreover, in a *national* context, sporting Tigers are an impressively brainy lot. In 1994 the average SATs of Princeton's football players was 165 points higher than the *highest* average for Division I-A football players (Stanford's) *and* higher than the average SATs for the *student bodies* at all but four Division I-A schools (Rice, Northwestern, Stanford, and Duke).[104]

Nevertheless, the *relatively* weaker entering qualifications of athletes quickly translates into lower performances in the classroom and often breeds a number of academic and social problems, which are seldom shared by students who participate in other time-consuming extracurricular activities. Even in elite universities, of course, every class will have a bottom half in academic standing. But at Princeton (and the other Ivies), recruited athletes, particularly those in high-profile sports, have a strong tendency to overpopulate the academy's lower floors, a trend that has accelerated since the 1950s.[105] For instance, in the classes of 1991–1993, when "grade inflation" had long been the rule, the grade-point average of recruited male athletes was 2.9 (on a 4-point scale); all other students averaged 3.3. Many of the high-profile athletes fared much worse; the football and swimming teams brought up the rear with 2.7. While 38 percent of their classmates earned A's, only 10 percent of the athletes did so; 23 percent

[103] *Report on Princeton Athletics* (1994), 11; Fred Hargadon, "Notes for Trustee Session on Athletics" (Jan. 14, 1994), 1, 4.

[104] Hargadon, "Notes for Trustee Session," 2; "Athletic Study: Summary Draft" (1994), table 15 (registrar's report on the classes of 1991–1993). Bowen and Levin, *Reclaiming the Game*, 89–90, reported that in the Ivy League entering cohort of 1995, recruited male athletes in high-profile sports had SATs 165 points lower than those of the students at large; those in lower-profile sports lagged 100 points. Sportswomen were only 65 points behind.

[105] Shulman and Bowen, *The Game of Life*, chaps. 3, 7, esp. pp. 261–62; Bowen and Levin, *Reclaiming the Game*, chap. 5.

of the sportsmen received C's or less, compared to only 6 percent of the rest. At commencements in 1985–1989, after senior theses were written and graded, the results had been no better: 70 percent of the men in the most populous sports graduated in the bottom 30 percent of the class or, very rarely, did not graduate at all.[106]

Even more worrisome to Princeton faculty and administrators is that recruited athletes, like their Ivy counterparts, largely *under*perform academically, that is, they do less well than their entering credentials predict they will. Students involved in other extracurricular activities, however, do *better* than predicted.[107] One partial explanation is that athletes spend *at least* twenty hours a week on their sport, more than double what the average extracurricular "active" spends. But the athletes underperform even when they are not playing, out of season, or after they have quit the team altogether. Nor does a prototypical "athletic culture" explain the problem. "Walk-ons" share the same athletic culture, but underperform only minimally, if at all.

The most compelling explanation is that *recruited* athletes, as Associate Dean of the College Richard Williams noted, "are given a strong message that they are wanted at the school, but specifically in the capacity of athletes." They are selected for their exceptional dedication to their sport and, in part, their willingness to subordinate all other demands, including academic study, to it. Small wonder that they carry the same focus and priorities to college.[108]

[106] "Athletic Study: Summary Draft" (1994), table 17; *Intercollegiate Athletics at Princeton in the 1990's*, app. D. Female athletes (with an average 3.1 GPA) came closer to the all-student average of 3.25 and tended to bunch their team averages. Despite the athletes' standing in the classroom, very few failed to graduate. In 1991 Princeton led the Ivy League in the percentage of its athletes who graduated in five years (97.4); in 2003 it still did. "Princeton Athletes Lead Ivies in Graduation Rates," *PAW*, May 15, 1991, 38–39.

[107] Shulman and Bowen, *The Game of Life*, 65–68, 146–50; Bowen and Levin, *Reclaiming the Game*, chap. 6. Because of grade inflation and grade compression, underperformance is best stated in terms of class rank rather than GPA. Recruited male athletes in high-profile Ivy League sports tend to rank nineteen points lower at graduation than their entering qualifications predicted. As the proportion of Academic Ones in each Princeton class increases, of course, a significant number of nonathletes will also underperform, at least statistically. Doug Lederman '84, "What Price Victory?" *PAW*, Dec. 17, 2003, 22–29.

[108] Bowen and Levin, *Reclaiming the Game*, 164–67, at 166.

They also fail to take full advantage of Princeton's intellectual and cultural richness by cleaving to their teammates—after practice and socially—an inordinate amount of the time. Only half participate in activities beyond their sport, and few attend concerts, debates, or other offerings. They also tend to congregate in three social science majors (Economics, History, and Politics), a trend that has also accelerated since the 1950s. In shying away from the more demanding sciences and engineering and from the "softer" humanities, they give the appearance of choosing "jock majors." Their heavy presence, often marked by team apparel and seating patterns, and their often less prepared or even attentive performances reinforces negative faculty and student stereotypes of all athletes, even though "walk-ons" and women (both of whom major across the curriculum and do better work) usually do not deserve to be included. This is doubly sad because by their sophomore year the athletes themselves have a lower opinion of their intellectual capabilities than they had coming to college, and lower than those of students who spend as much time in groups of comparable social cohesiveness, such as minority associations, religious fellowships, and eating clubs.[109]

For all the academic costs of playing intercollegiate sports at a high level, it may well be that the physical, social, and emotional benefits to the individual justify them; certainly, most of the athletes who continue to play sports think they do. But as a private elite institution of higher education, Princeton has decided that the costs and benefits are somewhat out of line. So it has implemented measures to balance the ledger. The Ivy Group presidents have helped by reducing the number of football recruits in each class from 35 to 25 and requiring each member school to raise its AI floor. In 2003 they also applied the Index to all Ivy sports, not just the three high-profile male sports, and mandated 49 days during the academic year when teams may not engage in any organized work-

[109] Nancy E. Cantor and Deborah A. Prentice, "The Life of the Modern-Day Student-Athlete: Opportunities Won and Lost" (paper presented at the Princeton Conference on Higher Education, Mar. 21–23, 1996); *Intercollegiate Athletics at Princeton in the 1990's*, 7–8; "Athletic Study: Summary Draft" (1994), tables 18–19 (majors); Shulman and Bowen, *The Game of Life*, 74–75; Bowen and Levin, *Reclaiming the Game*, 117–25, 421 (app. table 5.1).

outs under a coach.[110] On campus, the admission office under Fred Hargadon, whose philosophy in the new climate became "fewer but better," cut the percentage of recruited athletes in the entering class to seventeen; by 2003 the number had dropped to fourteen. In return, however, it accepted more of the "tagged" names on the coaches' shorter "wish lists," which understandably included the most dedicated athletes who might play all four years, but whose academic interests and credentials were not necessarily any higher than those of their predecessors.

The trustees' report on athletics in 1994 included a short manifesto that emphasized more than once that Princeton is a university whose "paramount commitment is to *academic* excellence and the *academic* and personal growth of its students." They applauded the recent reorganization of the duties of the Dean of Student Life, intended in part to "integrate better the Department of Athletics . . . in a more coordinated approach to campus life," and the efforts of the residential colleges to incorporate coaches into the life of the colleges.[111]

A more promising effort to shrink the athletic-academic disparity was the creation of a Faculty Academic-Athletic Fellows program in 1999. Inspired by the close relationship that sociologist Marvin Bressler had developed with Pete Carril's basketball teams over the years, Director of Athletics Gary Walters '67 instituted the program to break down stereotypes on both sides by personalizing the educational process. Every men's and women's varsity team now has at least one faculty fellow (many have several) who support the players in their demanding dual pursuits. By becoming not only "trusted advisors but confidants and friends" of the coaches and players, more than sixty faculty, such as Elizabeth Bogan (Economics), Sean Wilentz (History), and Jeffrey Stout (Religion), have gained added respect for the complicated role that student-athletes—must play at a high-power Ivy university. A hopeful decrease in the pernicious stereotypes of "dumb jock" and "aloof egghead" has been one result of the program.[112]

[110] Welch Suggs, "Ivy League Votes to Raise Academic Standards for Athletes," *CHE* (online), June 19, 2003.

[111] *Report on Princeton Athletics* (1994), 1–2, 4, 15–16 (my emphasis).

[112] Matt Golden '94, "Profs and Jocks Crossing the Great Divide," *PAW*, Oct. 11, 2000, 20–21; Paul Steinbach, "Good Fellows," *Athletic Business Magazine* (Aug. 2001),

Princeton's essential problems—the unrepresentative academic qualifications and the underperformance of its recruited athletes—however, will not be solved by palliative manifestos or measures. But their impact may be diluted by the increase in undergraduate enrollment approved by the trustees in 2000. They recommended that Princeton add 125–50 students in each of four years and that a sixth residential college be built to accommodate the increase. Although the addition of talented scholars, artists, legacies, minorities, international, and perhaps transfer, students was projected, the one group that is definitely not slated to grow is recruited athletes, whose numbers are largely determined by the number and size of varsity teams.[113]

❁ ❁ ❁

Although four of every ten Princeton undergraduates today play varsity or club sports, the most popular extracurricular activity since Wilson's day has been eating. College students have always eaten with gusto, but only Princetonians turned eating into a contact sport. Their competitive juices were stimulated—to a degree unusual in the history of American higher education—not by *what* they ate, but by *where* and *with whom*. In the process, they created a social system that did much to diminish Princeton's vaunted democracy and to retard its growth as a truly meritocratic institution of higher learning.

When the college and then the university after the Civil War failed to provide enough, or good enough, dining facilities for all of its students, the students, with the help of well-heeled parents, provided their own. At first, members of all four classes formed small, temporary, eating clubs in local boarding houses. "Tommy" Wilson belonged to the "Alligators," while other contemporaries dined as "Knights of the Round Table," "Nimrods," and "*Nunquam Plenus* (Never Full)." Then, beginning in 1879, "selective associa-

---

25–27; Danielle Ponzio, "Question and Answer with Elizabeth Bogan," *DP*, Oct. 15, 2003, 3.

[113] Royce Flippin '80, "And Then There Were 5,100: Wythes Committee Recommends 10-Percent Enrollment Increase," *PAW*, Mar. 8, 2000, 20–21; The Trustees of PU, *Report of the Wythes Committee* (Jan. 29, 2000), 10.

tions" of upperclassmen rented commodious houses around town and later built luxurious mansions along Prospect Avenue, where they could take three square meals a day and socialize with chosen companions. When Commons was opened in University Hall (a converted hotel) in 1906 for the freshmen and two years later for the sophomores, the upperclassmen consolidated their hold on the proliferating eating clubs and their composition.[114] By 1907, 75 percent of the upperclassmen belonged to a club, an increase of over 25 percent since Wilson assumed the presidency five years earlier.[115] It is small wonder that he was alarmed by the social stratification, non-intellectualism, and ostentation of the clubs and sought to submerge or eliminate them in his all-class residential quad plan.[116]

But the clubs were there to stay. What did change over the next century were their numbers, memberships, and methods of admission. Until the late 1960s, the number of clubs held steady at sixteen or seventeen. But the way they selected their "sections" annually began to change with the democratizing influx of veterans after World War II. Sporadic protests, revolts, and boycotts since World War I had questioned the operative values and human costs of "bicker," the process by which the clubs sought to recruit new members (preferably the class's movers and shakers) and the sophomores sought invitations (preferably from the changing roster of most prestigious clubs). In the aftermath of war, in which Americans of all regions, races, and ethnicities had fought side by side, however, the clubs began a long string of "100 Percent" bickers in which no sophomore who wanted to join a club was left out. This trend was rudely interrupted by the "Dirty Bicker" of 1958, when 23 "undesirables" remained unchosen; at least 15 were Jewish, and 5 were National Merit Scholars.[117] Full bickers continued into the 1960s, but only

[114] Leitch, *Princeton Companion*, 146–47; William K. Selden, *Club Life at Princeton: An Historical Account of the Eating Clubs at Princeton University* (Princeton: Princeton Prospect Foundation, [1996]), 1, 4, 6–15; Dean A. Allen, "History of the Undergraduate Social Clubs at Princeton," *Social Problems* 2:3 (Jan. 1955):160–65.

[115] Frederic C. Rich '77, *The First Hundred Years of the Ivy Club, 1879–1979* (Princeton: The Ivy Club, 1979), 88; *PWW*, 17:42 (Feb. 18, 1907).

[116] See chapter 1, above.

[117] Rich, *Ivy Club*, 194–200; David Spitz, "Quiet Quotas: Airing Bicker's Dirty Laundry," *Nassau Weekly* 19:13 (Feb. 5, 1998):6–7; Selden, *Club Life at Princeton*, 50–51; Geoffrey Wolff, *The Final Club* (New York, 1990), chap. 4; Walter Goodman, "Bicker

under protest by club leaders who condemned the university's continued failure to provide alternative social and dining facilities and reasserted that admission to the university did not guarantee admission to a club.[118]

The egalitarian advent of the "Age of Aquarius," civil rights, and coeducation in the late 1960s finally brought needed reforms to the club system. Hirsute students in tie-dye and bell bottoms who took politics and war personally and demanded a greater voice in university and national governance found that the culinary coteries on Prospect Avenue mattered much less than they had in the past. By 1971–1972, fewer than half of the juniors and seniors ate in the clubs, which brought several clubs to their financial knees. By 1975 only eleven clubs remained, some the result of amalgamations. Most of the rest went coed and nonselective, from self-preservation and/or principle. Meals served by black waiters on china and white linen gave way to cafeteria self-service or student waiters—"rate men"—who worked for reduced board fees. The rest of their classmates chose their food and company from an expanded list of alternatives, such as Adlai Stevenson Hall, the Madison Society, and the four-year Woodrow Wilson College.[119]

---

at Princeton: The Eating Clubs Again," *Commentary* 25:5 (May 1958):406–15; Jerome Karabel, *The Chosen: The Hidden History of Admission and Exclusion at Harvard, Yale, and Princeton* (Boston, 2005), 304–10.

118 Selden, *Club Life at Princeton*, 46.

119 Leitch, *Princeton Companion*, 409–10; Selden, *Club Life at Princeton*, 49, 52–53. The heterogeneous, some would say healthier, social system of the early 1970s was dealt a blow in 1979 by the adoption of the CURL (Committee on Undergraduate Residential Life) plan to provide residential colleges only for freshmen and sophomores. This effectively forced most upperclasspersons to return to the eating clubs, which grew in number and social importance. The raising of the legal drinking age in New Jersey from eighteen to twenty-one in January 1983 also promoted the semi-private clubs and their free-flowing taprooms. *PAW*, Mar. 26, 1986, 9. Since 1982 the growing popularity of unofficial, nonresidential, underclass fraternities and sororities, outlawed in 1875, has also contributed to club resilience. Many of these semi-clandestine organizations serve as "feeders" to specific eating clubs—a revival of the "hat lines" that Wilson disliked and abolished in 1906–1908. In 1993, eighteen fraternal and sororal organizations claimed about 15 percent of the student body; the same percentage belonged ten years later. In the summer of 2004 Princeton sent a letter to parents and guardians of the Class of 2008, "strongly discourag[ing]" their freshmen from joining Greek organizations, in order "to expand their circles of acquaintances and experiences, not prematurely narrow

In the opening years of the new millennium, three-quarters of the upperclasses took their meals in eleven clubs, six of which were open to all on a sign-in, first-come-first-served, basis; five were selective.[120] The bicker clubs accepted only 50–70 percent of their "bickerees," and even the sign-in clubs quickly filled up, leaving many to seek sustenance and society elsewhere. "The underlying problem with the eating club system," the *Prince* diagnosed, "is that there is simply too much demand for the supply. Each club has a physical limit to the number of people it can seat, and when that number is reached" the doors must be closed.[121] The availability of the Frist Campus Center, the kosher Center for Jewish Life, dorm kitchens, and co-ops, while they met the alimentary needs of the remaining quarter of the upperclasses, did little to satisfy their social desires. For better or worse, the clubs remained the focus of Princeton's undergraduate weekend life, and those who did not belong to "The Street" often felt the loss.

Princeton's eating clubs were certainly satisfying for most of those who joined. Save for potentially long walks to and down Prospect

---

them." Matthew T. Henshon '91, "Fraternities and Sororities Explode in Popularity," *PAW*, Mar. 21, 1990, 12–13; D. Allan Drummond '95, "On the Campus: The Greek Society," *PAW*, Dec. 22, 1993, 7–8; "Editorial: Our Big Fat Greek School," *DP* (online), Sept. 15, 2003; Sam J. Cooper, "Black Sororities Divide University, Administration Wary of Greek Life," *DP* (online), Nov. 7, 2003; Andrew Romano '04, "On the Campus Online: Keeping It Social: Members Only," *PAW Online*, Dec. 17, 2003; Catherine Stevenson, "Frosh Cautioned Against Going Greek," *DP* (online), Sept. 16, 2004; Christian Burset, "University Confronts Greek Life," *DP* (online), May 9, 2005.

[120] After Campus remained open for nearly thirty years, its graduate directors decided in 2003 to return the club to a bicker system, in an effort to attract more applicants by enhancing its "reputation" through exclusion. Two years later, it switched back, just before closing its doors in August due to low membership. Sam J. Cooper, "Campus Club Will Switch to Bicker System," *DP* (online), May 12, 2003; David Robinson, "Editor's Notebook: Club's Choice Reflects Our Drive to Exclude," *DP* (online), May 14, 2003; Jennifer Epstein, "Campus Club to Return to Sign-in," *DP* (online), Jan. 17, 2005; Epstein, "Campus Club Closes, Future Uncertain," *DP* (online), Aug. 18, 2005.

[121] Daniel Lipsky-Karasz, "Tower Heavily Bickered as Most Sign-In Clubs Fill Up," *DP* (online), Feb. 10, 2003; David Sillers, "A Personal Defense of the Bicker Process," *DP* (online), Feb. 12, 2003; Angela Ricci, "Bicker and Sign-In Eating Clubs Have Equal Support," *DP* (online), Nov. 10, 2003. Ironically, three of the most selective clubs also conducted fall bickers to give juniors and seniors another chance to join. Alison Eng, "Clubs Conclude Fall Bicker, Welcome New Members," *DP* (online), Sept. 30, 2003.

Avenue for every meal, rain or shine, club members enjoyed several perquisites. Over the course of two years, they shared meals, table talk, and club activities with friends and familiars from three classes. They had congenial, even posh, places to dance, drink, and date and comfortable homelike settings (virtually the only ones on campus) to entertain family and other visitors. A few members on financial aid received room and board for managing the clubhouses. From the early 1970s, refurbished, newly carreled, and Web-wired club libraries served as quiet oases of postprandial study for some. And not least, the chosen had the satisfaction of belonging to exclusive organizations with long and sometimes distinguished bloodlines, which often led to valuable alumni contacts and future memberships in strikingly similar city clubs.[122]

For all their real and continuing advantages for student members, the clubs have drawn fire from a long list of observers, inside and outside the system. President Wilson was only the first to regard the clubs as a serious problem for the university. Two years after Wilson stepped down, Owen Johnson (Yale '00), the author of the classic *Stover at Yale*, published an equally astute analysis of "The Social Usurpation of Our Colleges" in *Collier's Magazine*. Princeton's club system, he thought, was relatively open and benign in the early stages of its evolution, unlike Harvard's closed and secret senior societies and Yale's new fraternities. But he worried that in time the "grave" potential dangers of the club system would be realized and do irreparable damage to the class unity and "democratic association" that set Princeton apart from its rivals. Princeton, he said, is "an example of a bad theory, democratically administered." And it would take very little for it to succumb—in clubhouses easily mistaken for "the homes of millionaires"—to "snobbery, luxuriousness," and "entrenched privilege" through a "competitive system prone to form disintegrating and jealous sets."[123]

[122] Peter Parrott Blanchard, Jr. (president of the Class of 1935), "A Substitute for the Club System," *Princeton Pictorial*, Feb. 5, 1936; Selden, *Club Life at Princeton*, 68, 83; Evarts Ziegler '38, "Prospect Not Always Pleasing," *PAW*, Feb. 16, 1940, 429–32, at 430–31; "Bicker Business," *Nassau Sovereign* 7:3 (Dec. 1947):28–31, at 29.

[123] Owen Johnson, "The Social Usurpation of Our Colleges. IV-Princeton," *Collier's Magazine*, June 15, 1912, 17–18, 24.

Johnson prophesied only too well. Over the next three decades, the club system developed its least attractive features, some of which not even war or student revolution could remedy. Because the clubs are privately owned and operated by incorporated alumni and therefore largely outside its control, "the University would like nothing better than to forget [them]," an attitude reinforced by the fact that only one president (Robert Goheen) ever belonged to a club as an undergraduate. From the perspective of admissions, former dean Fred Hargadon declared the club system "Princeton's Achilles heel."[124] At his fiftieth reunion, Nelson Burr remembered that for the Class of 1927, as for so many others, "the club problem was the ghost that would not leave the banquet." And shortly before he died while reading his beloved alumni magazine, even Cottage Club alumnus F. Scott Fitzgerald '17 pronounced his malediction on "a lousy cruel system," whose "ragged squabble of club elections with its scars of snobbishness and adolescent heartbreak" he would gladly abolish.[125]

Criticisms of the club system from the beginning have revolved around three major themes: cost, nonacademic emphasis, and bicker. For (sometimes) better food and quieter and more intimate dining environments, club members have always paid considerably more than those who ate in university dining halls. In the 1920s and 1930s the club tab was double. By 1940, club meals cost an average $14 a

[124] Alfred S. Dashiell '23, "The Princeton Clubs Today," *PAW*, June 8, 1928, 1075–91, at 1090; David P. Brog, "Residential Colleges Redux," *Nassau Weekly*, Feb. 27, 1992, 10 (quoting Hargadon). In the first prospective-student "viewbook" prepared under new dean of admission Janet Rapelye, the eating clubs were not pictured at all and mentioned—briefly—only twice: once to say that "the historic eating clubs where many junior and senior men and women dine," along with dorms and campus organizations, host "a busy calendar of activities," again to mention "intramural sports" as one of those activities. *Princeton University, 2003–04* (Princeton: Admission Office and Office of Communications, 2003), 4, 30. The lack of coverage was not unnoticed.

[125] Nelson R. Burr '27, "Remembering Princeton in the '20s," *PAW*, May 9, 1977, 9–14, at 13; F. Scott Fitzgerald, *Letters to His Daughter*, ed. Andrew Turnbull (New York, 1965), 107 (Mar. 18, 1940); F. Scott Fitzgerald, *Afternoon of an Author: A Selection of Uncollected Stories and Essays*, ed. Arthur Mizener (Princeton: PUL, 1957; New York, 1958), 70 (Dec. 1927); *The Letters of F. Scott Fitzgerald*, ed. Andrew Turnbull (New York and London, 1964), 445 (Nov. 13, 1939).

week, compared to only $8 in the Yale colleges and $10 in the Harvard houses. By the late 1960s and early 1970s, the difference between Princeton meal plans was still $300–400 a year. In 2002–2003, students on financial aid were allowed $3,930 for meals. Since the clubs charged between $5,200 and $5,550, those who wished to join a club had to take out student loans to cover the $2,540–3,240 difference over two years. Predictably, poorer students often dropped out of clubs or did not attempt to join in the first place, which reinforced an economic cleavage between students as well as a social one.[126]

Faculty and administrators have worried more about the non-academic, even anti-intellectual, nature of the club experience. President Wilson sought to make the students' avid extracurriculum less "extra" by liberating "leisure and study" from the "air-tight compartments" they occupied. He was convinced that the students' out-of-class pursuits, while delightful and harmless in themselves, were "exclusively social" and devoid of "serious content." The clubs were the worst offenders: they were "distinctly and very seriously hostile to the spirit of study, incompatible with the principles of a true republic of letters and of learning." Armed with data that documented the academic underperformance of club members compared to non-members, he settled on quads or Oxford-style colleges as the best way to "coordinate" the students' social life with "the intellectual impulses which have brought us to the brink of real achievement."[127]

After the still-avid graduate clubmen of the East killed his quad plan, Wilson's diagnosis of the club problem was sustained by students and faculty alike. Even in the 1920s and 1930s, the heyday of "selective admissions" and major curricular reform, former dean

[126] Selden, *Club Life at Princeton*, 37; Blanchard, "Substitute for the Club System," [2–3]; J. Sterling Hutcheson, "A Survey of Club Finances," *Nassau Sovereign* 2:5 (Feb. 1940):10–13, 32; John Stutesman, "From a Broader Point of View," *Nassau Sovereign* 2:8 (May 1940):10–11, 23, 34, at 11; Ziegler, "Prospect Not Always Pleasing," 432; Adam Frankel, "Clubs and Financial Aid: A Tale of Two Princetons," *DP* (online), Feb. 3, 2003.

[127] *PWW*, 16:523 (c. Dec. 13, 1906); 17:167 (c. May 30, 1907), 177 (c. June 6, 1907), 401–2 (Sept. 26, 1907). In the "liabilities" column of his 1928 assessment of club life, Alfred Dashiell noted that "the bonds of interest [in the clubs] are purely social, with little reference to the intellectual" ("The Princeton Clubs Today," 1091).

of the college Howard McClenahan was persuaded that "the clubs stifle the intellectual life of Princeton."[128] In 1961, senior *PAW* columnist William S. Rukeyser teasingly asked if "Creeping Intellectualism" was invading Prospect Avenue. He first pointed to a few tentative faculty talks and dinner guests in some of the clubs and a more concerted effort at academic rapprochement in the aptly named Woodrow Wilson Society, "the social system's mental gymnasium," in Wilcox Hall. But he concluded that there were "few real indications that Washington Road is losing its status as the Gaza Strip between scholastic pursuits and mindless recreation." The best measure of The Street's intellectual health, he noted, was "the frequency with which the average student—without the prompting of a faculty member's presence—finds himself discussing ideas over dinner or at the card table." By that index, the current respect for ideas, "as in the 1930's," was "a lamentably rare commodity in the Princeton social system."[129]

Six years later, in 1967, the faculty weighed in on the club problem. Responding to a lengthy student report on bicker, a faculty committee concluded that the clubs, with the possible exception of Tower, were a "decided hindrance" to "a more complete integration of intellectual and social life." "There are few organized intellectual activities in the clubs, and they are not available equitably to all upperclassmen. The practice of appointing faculty fellows in the clubs, holding precepts or seminars regularly or occasionally there, or conducting symposia . . . is not widespread." To overcome this and a number of related problems, the committee recommended that the university build four-year colleges (Wilson's quads), go coed, and, in the meantime, push for the replacement of bicker with a "preferential assignment" or sign-in system of club admission.[130]

Within three years, the university did admit women and create the first two of five residential colleges (though after 1982 only for

[128] Blanchard, "Substitute for the Club System," [3].

[129] William S. Rukeyser '61, "Creeping Intellectualism Invades Prospect Street," *PAW*, Oct. 27, 1961, 3–5. Walter Goodman argued that, during the Dirty Bicker of 1958, the bias was "as much an expression of anti-intellectualism as of anti-Jewishness" ("Bicker at Princeton," 414).

[130] PU, Minutes of the University Faculty, May 1, 1967, [1–2, 5], PUA.

freshmen and sophomores). And several clubs did shift to open admissions as well as welcome women to their ranks.[131] All of these changes did much to improve the club scene and even to narrow somewhat the gap between leisure and study. But because five clubs retained their selective admissions procedures, the clubs' thorniest and most persistent problem remained unsolved.

In the words of the faculty report and the opinion of most critics, "the least desirable features of club life are enforced by Bicker." Despite sporadic attempts in past decades to allow sophomores to exercise some control over admission by applying in groups of friends in various numbers, bicker continued to guarantee the upper hand to current club members. As club memberships and entering classes grew and the classes became more talented and diverse, however, the bicker process lost most of its efficiency and rationale. As the student authors of the 1967 report observed, bicker exaggerated the importance of conformity and consensus in club life. It often resulted in "overly homogeneous groups" apt to confirm current members' "predispositions" and in "sheltering [students] from learning situations . . . conducive to intellectual and emotional growth." The faculty committee agreed. "During Bicker," they lamented, "imagination, intellectual vitality, and serious scholarly proclivities are generally underrated while facades of sociability assume undue importance. Exclusiveness, status considerations, and concern that the individual 'fit in' with a particular group take precedence over respect for the differences among people." Moreover, bicker often "breaks up or strains friendships that were formed during underclass years."[132] And

[131] The move to coed clubs was initially swift: by 1971–1972, only three of thirteen clubs remained all-male. But they remained so until Sally Frank '80 filed a sex-discrimination complaint against the clubs and the university with the New Jersey Civil Rights Division in February 1979. Cottage Club capitulated and settled with Frank in 1986, but Ivy and Tiger Inn went to the mat only in 1990 when the New Jersey Supreme Court ruled against them. In July 1990 New York law professor Frank received Princeton's Alumni Service Award, partial recompense for the often rough treatment she received from club members and alumni during her eleven-year battle for equality and well after (in letters to *PAW*). Robert Earle '72, "On the Campus: The Clubs & Coeducation," *PAW*, Dec. 7, 1971, 5; *PAW*, Sept. 12, 1990, 8, 10; July 18, 1990, 12.

[132] In the 1920s, Day Edgar noted, the *Daily Princetonian* recommended that bickerees stick with friends in making their club decisions. "And," he wrote, "nine out of

Figure 17. The conformity generated by the eating clubs' bicker process was captured in this cartoon by P. Gregory Schwed '73 for the *Daily Princetonian.*

for too many students, "Bicker encourages the inference that intellectual values do not and should not have any bearing on social relationships." Accordingly, the professors concluded, "Bicker has no place in modern Princeton."[133]

Yet bicker persists, burdened with many of its traditional drawbacks. In addition to separating friends when club bids are made, bicker has always exerted pressure—always subtle, often heavy—upon the behavior of the two lower classes. In 2002 as in 1902, freshmen and sophomores became "club conscious" early and were afraid to develop "individuality" for fear of not being regarded as good "club material." Until the late 1960s, this kind of self-squelching too often led to "a barren conformity." "The life of the

every ten sophomores, unconsciously imitating their predecessors of many years, joined the most enviable club within their reach and allowed the matter of friendship to adjust itself to new patterns of life" (*In Princeton Town* [New York, 1929], 307). A survey of sophomores in 1939 by the *Nassau Sovereign* revealed that the greatest reason for dissatisfaction with the clubs (at 54 percent) was that respondents were "not in club with closest friends" ("Sophomore Opinion of the Clubs," *PAW,* May 12, 1939, 677). See also "A Vital Indictment," *Nassau Sovereign,* 2:7 (Apr. 1940), 9–11; Donald T. Williams, "Princeton's Club System," *Nassau Sovereign,* 6:3 (Nov. 1946):14–15; Natasha Degen, "Eating Clubs: Bicker Process Evolves as University Grows," *DP* (online), Feb. 6, 2004.

[133] PU, Minutes of the University Faculty, May 1, 1967, [5–6] (PUA). Most of these criticisms had been made in 1936 by Peter Blanchard, the class president of '35, in "Substitute for the Club System," [2–3].

underclassman is tempered word and deed," said the *Prince* in 1926, "by the prospect of a day of reckoning when any peculiarities he may have will be paraded against him in the secret councils of the most high." "Any extreme in habiliment, pleasures or opinions is apt to be characterized as 'running it out,' " explained John Peale Bishop '17, "and to 'run it out' is to lose all chance of social distinction. Talking too loudly in Commons, an undue concern for the souls of unconverted Chinese, drinking more liquor than can be held quietly and steadily, dressing too dowdily or too flamboyantly . . . all these are 'running it out' and wooing damnation."[134]

This kind of pressure only increased in the spring of sophomore year when Bicker Week—once an official university holiday of *two* weeks—arrived.[135] For much of the past century, the sophomores were given little or no opportunity to visit the various clubs and were ordered to stay in their rooms every evening from seven to ten during the week to receive delegations from the clubs that were interested in one or more roommates. By interclub law (broken frequently by nervous parties on both sides), "matters bearing directly upon club membership" were not to be discussed except during the Bicker Week calls.[136]

[134] Blanchard, "Substitute for the Club System," [2]; *DP*, Dec. 8, 1926, 3; John Peale Bishop, "Princeton," *The Smart Set* (Nov. 1921), in *The Collected Essays of John Peale Bishop*, ed. Edmund Wilson (New York and London, 1948), 391–400, at 395; also *PWW*, 17:233 (June 27, 1907), 18:28 (Mar. 12, 1908); Wolff, *The Final Club*, 341; PU, *The Report of the Commission on the Future of the College* (Princeton, Apr. 1973), 43–44. Peale's classmate and close friend F. Scott Fitzgerald defined "running it out" as "anything which brought an under classman into too glaring a light." "Being personally conspicuous was not tolerated, and the influential man was the non-committal man" (*This Side of Paradise*, 51–52). Geoffrey Wolff borrowed the phrase to describe similar put-downs in the 1950s. *The Final Club*, 87–88.

[135] In the mid-1950s, bicker was a two-week affair. Wolff, *The Final Club*, 95; Edward Said, *Out of Place: A Memoir* (New York, 1999), 274.

[136] *Now That You Are Eligible . . .* (Princeton: Undergraduate Interclub Committee, 1947), 10. In recent decades, open-house visits to the clubs for interviews and "challenges" or "games" (which can result in crudities akin to fraternity hazing) replaced room visitations. Justin Mikolay GS, "Bicker 501: How to Sneak a Grad Student into Cap & Gown," *DP*, Mar. 13, 2002, 3; Kate Swearengen '04, "A Losing Proposition? Eating Clubs Bring Out the Best and Worst," *PAW Web Exclusive* (online), Mar. 13, 2002; Sillers, "A Personal Defense of the Bicker Process," *DP* (online), Feb. 12, 2003.

By all accounts, these club visits (and others during the late-winter orientation period) were strained and strange, their suspense heightened by waiting for telltale steps on the stairs and the anticipated knock. If not all the roommates were equally desirable, the club might send a "small-talk specialist, called a 'dump-artist' " to distract the unwanted. This could lead to inane or insulting questions such as "What's your favorite kitchen utensil?" or "What flower would you most like to be if you were a flower?" Indeed, the whole procedure struck many, perhaps most, candidates as arcane—or silly. "Bicker's rules of decorum were as runic as the rules of court tennis . . . the scoring was Byzantine. . . . All was inference. . . . It was nothing at all to go wrong," remembered Geoffrey Wolff '59, "you just had to take your eye off the ball for an instant." The rules were especially mysterious to those who had not been socially baptized in an Eastern prep school.[137] Wearing the wrong-colored shirt or an unmodish jacket, being near-sighted or bow-legged, or having "too much pull in heaven" could result in disbarment from the club *monde*. Worse yet, bearing a Jewish surname, a dark skin, or a strange accent (other than genteel Southern) was often grounds for exclusion.[138] The silliness of this procedure may have been captured

[137] Until the 1950s the majority of eating clubs took a preponderance of prep school graduates. Ivy, the oldest and most prestigious club, took its *first* high school member only in 1951. Selden, *Club Life at Princeton*, 37; Rich, *Ivy Club*, 112, 144–45, 176–77; Karabel, *The Chosen*, 301–2.

[138] Wolff, *The Final Club*, 87, 88, 91, 92, 93; Bishop, *Collected Essays*, ed. Wilson, 395; Fitzgerald, *This Side of Paradise*, 78; Rich, *Ivy Club*, 159, 206–7; Said, *Out of Place*, 274–75; Lawrence Otis Graham, *Member of the Club: Reflections on Life in a Racially Polarized World* (New York, 1995), 185–90, 211, 218–19. When the *Harvard Crimson* sent reporter John E. McNees in 1958 to investigate what he called "The Quest at Princeton for the Cocktail Soul," he found several forms of "the stigmata, the brand, the taint: . . . the error of wearing white bucks for so solemn an evening, the misdemeanor of a soft, stammering voice, the felony of too loud and sure a tone, the atrocity of a blue suit, . . . slanted eyes and yellow skin. . . . " (McNees and Elizabeth W. McCarthy, "100 Per Cent on Prospect St.," *Harvard Crimson Online*, Apr. 21, 1981, 1, 4). To counteract nonsense of this sort, a 2002 spoof in the *Prince* announced a plan to hold the first day of bicker at the clubs in the nude. The Interclub Council president allegedly said that "a lot of people are really nervous at Bicker . . . and have a difficult time acting like themselves. The idea will really let us see who these people are. It is going to make the Bicker process real" (Michael Jenkins, "Sophomore Class Finds Nude Olympics Alternative" *DP* [online], Jan. 18, 2002).

best by Triangle songwriter Clark Gesner '60, who reminded his classmates of their sophomore year at Class Day Exercises:

> Then Bicker appeared, and our lives were re-geared
> To the pace of the French Inquisition;
> And through ten-minute trials and hysterical smiles,
> We discovered our social position.[139]

The clubmen had their own vocabularies of rejection, which were almost as harsh and supercilious as some of their blackball judgments.[140] In the 1910s and 1920s a "sad bird" or "wet smack" was a "pronounced individualist" who did not readily conform to group or college life. In one of Day Edgar's Princeton stories, the club chances of a self-help student are dismissed by his rich, preppy cousin because he is a "wet smack"—"a fellow who hasn't any dope on himself, and doesn't dress the way we do, and doesn't go out for the things we go out for."[141] Bicker committees in the equally conformist 1950s and even into the 1970s focused their disdain on "weenies," "wonks" (from "know" spelled backwards), "wombats," "bananas," and "lunchers." Some were "out to lunch (OTL) all 3 meals" or "All-Americans," so out of it they made everyone's cut list. "Aeoli" (asshole) and "fleg-neg" (a score of 7: flagrant neglect, in the contemporary group-grading system) were reserved for the bottom of the social heap. Together, these undesirables might be dismissed

[139] Cynthia Penney '83, interview with Clark Gesner '60, Apr. 18, 1995, Oral History Project of the Princetoniana Committee, Princeton Alumni Council (transcript), 52 (PUA).

[140] In some clubs, actual black and white balls dropped into a wooden ballot box were used to conduct referenda on candidates. According to Ivy Club historian Frederick Rich, even legendary Ivy in its earliest days required *two* black balls to veto a bickeree. Subsequent elections were conducted by consensus and, more rarely, by majority vote. *Ivy Club*, 208. In the 1940s Colonial Club switched from black and white balls to ballots and votes. *The Colonial Club of Princeton University, 1891–1991* (Princeton, 1991), 68. By the 1980s, admission to Cottage, the second-oldest club, required a two-thirds vote. Graham, *Member of the Club*, 188. For photographs of a club ballot box, see Don Oberdorfer, *Princeton University: The First 250 Years* (Princeton, 1995), 141 (in color); *PAW*, Feb. 24, 1993, 10 (in black and white).

[141] Christian Gauss, *Life in College* (New York, 1930), 36, 70–71; J. Woodford Howard, Jr. *59, "Judge Medina's School Days," *PAW*, June 5, 1988, 22–25, at 23; Edgar, *In Princeton Town*, 297–98.

as "100 Percenters."[142] By the 1980s, failing to be elected to a club was to be "hosed," a term still in use twenty years later.[143]

What the clubmen, heady with power and absorbed by their exclusionary task, rarely considered was the psychic and emotional toll their rejection took on their fellow students. Young men—and later women—who were smart and talented enough to be admitted to increasingly meritocratic Princeton were declared unfit to eat with, an indictment whose pain more than a few carried to their graves; "cuts suffered at Princeton never ceased to bleed." Some became embittered and left the university prematurely; many were "seriously hurt" and felt like "pariahs" or "outcasts," socially marooned as "the bottom dropped out of [their] college life."[144] Most were rendered defiant or defensive by the realization that they had been "held to judgment" by their peers and "found wanting" in some essential way. As the protagonist in Geoffrey Wolff's *The Final Club* concluded with deliberate understatement, "Bicker was not an interesting use of a great institution," particularly when it was and continues to be used to choose a mere "aristocracy of the stomach."[145] Most

[142] Roy Heath, *Princeton Retrospectives: Twenty-Fifth-Year Reflections on a College Education* (Princeton: Class of 1954, 1979), 38–39; James M. Markham '65, "On the Campus: The Princeton Idiom," *PAW*, Nov. 19, 1963, 4, 16; Peter G. Brown '70, "Keycepts on Yooney Slang," *PAW*, Feb. 24, 1970, 12–13, 15; Wolff, *The Final Club*, 66; Wolff, *The Duke of Deception: Memories of My Father* (New York, 1979), 212; Said, *Out of Place*, 275. In his senior-class poll, John Gregory Dunne '54 received three votes in a category called "Summa Cum Luncheon" (*Harp* [New York, 1989], 141). For two bicker chairmen who realized that they had to apply superficial social standards, against their own better judgments, see Otto Butz, ed., *The Unsilent Generation: An Anonymous Symposium in Which Eleven [Princeton] College Seniors Look at Themselves and Their World* (New York, 1958), 70; Heath, *Princeton Retrospectives*, 230.

[143] Graham, *Member of the Club*, 188; "A Bitter End to Bicker," *DP* (online), Feb. 5, 2004.

[144] Howard, "Judge Medina's School Days," 23; Wolff, *The Final Club*, 143; Dewitt C. Jones, Jr. '13, "Class Spirit," *PAW*, Oct. 21, 1960, 18; "1909 Alumni Recall Campus in Wilson's Day," *Princeton Recollector* 4:8 (June 1979):11; Ernest Poole, *The Bridge* (New York, 1940), 61; *PWW*, 17:182 (c. June 6, 1907), 222–23 (c. June 25, 1907), 392–93 (Sept. 19, 1907).

[145] George F. Kennan, *Memoirs, 1925–1950* (Boston, 1967), 11–12; Wolff, *The Final Club*, 339; *PWW*, 17:230 (June 26, 1907).

alumni, including those who enjoyed club life while on campus, seem to agree.[146]

The university bears ultimate responsibility for the creation and perpetuation of the clubs by not providing sufficient and attractive dining and social facilities for the upperclasses and by winking at some of the worst features of the club system, particularly bicker. But from the beginning of club dominance during Wilson's presidency, the human costs of bicker have been actively defended by club members as the perhaps unfortunate but tolerable price to be paid for maintaining the clubs' essential right of free association. Even when physical limitations rather than lack of will prevented the clubs from satisfying 100 percent of the demand for membership, clubmen have been quick to excuse bicker's exclusivity by resorting to an analogy with the "real," noncollegiate, world, where "natural selection" in an almost Darwinian sense is thought to prevail.[147] In his 1912 analysis of Princeton's emerging social system, Owen Johnson characterized the clubmen as "a rather elastic autocracy, self-convinced that the same laws that divide society in the outer world inevitably must form social divisions in college." Opposed to their thinking

[146] When asked to name Princeton's three greatest assets, alumni invariably put the faculty and curriculum at the top; the clubs anchor the bottom. "The 'Weekly' Surveys . . . ," *PAW*, Feb. 24, 1941, 14; Heath, *Princeton Retrospectives*, *passim*. In 1939, when 90 percent of the upperclassmen belonged to clubs, a sophomore poll found 59 percent who thought the club system "in need of improvement," 28 percent who sought "fundamental changes," and 8 percent who favored abolition and a completely new system; only 5 percent were thoroughly satisfied. "Sophomore Opinion of the Clubs," *PAW*, May 12, 1939, 677. When the Commission on the Future of the College (chaired by Professor of Sociology Marvin Bressler) asked the classes of 1954, 1964, and 1969 to name their single most valuable or useful extracurricular activity or aspect of social life, only 3–5 percent said bicker; 25 percent each deemed bicker and club life particularly useless or harmful. Wendell, " 'If You Had It to Do Over Again . . . ,' " *PAW*, Mar. 4, 1975, 9–12, at 10–11 (tables 3–4).

[147] When the 1953 bicker achieved 100 percent for the fourth consecutive year only with much gnashing of teeth and applied pressure, the chairman of the Interclub Committee spoke of the hallowed "Princeton club tradition of *natural* selection" and argued that it was "infinitely more cruel and inhuman to place these unfortunates [men unchosen at the end of "natural" bicker] in a club when it is a known fact that they are not wanted" (John Angus McPhee '53, "On the Campus," *PAW*, Mar. 13, 1953, 10).

was an "aggressive democracy," led by President Wilson, who "insisted that the university should exist independently of worldly cleavages, preserve its social autonomy, by self-sufficient standards of unrestricted intercourse."[148]

At Geoffrey Wolff's semifictional Princeton, the pro-bicker position was elaborated in the 1950s by a university booklet presumptuously entitled *Now That You're Ready for Bicker*, which listed ten reasons why the club-selection process mimics the "real world" of choice and consequence, of "discrimination, in its most benign sense."[149] But former club members may give franker expression to the hard-nosed philosophy of breakfast table autocracy. One alumnus told the Bressler Commission that bicker was "the closest experience to the reality of life that Princeton offers. It has all the prejudices, stupidity, and human strain under pressure that business and life in general possess." He, for one, found it "very educational."[150]

Twelve-letter-sportswoman Emily Goodfellow '76 had little time to socialize at Cap and Gown during her upperclass years in the mid-1970s, but she honored the whole process of bicker as a valuable part of her practical education. "People slam bicker for the inequities and the unfairness," she testified twenty years later, "but in a lot of ways it is like the real world. People make decisions based on how you speak, the color of your skin, what you look like, the fact that you are a woman—decisions that aren't fair and that sometimes don't make sense. The University spends a lot of time telling you how special and gifted and wonderful you are . . . and many students start believing it. Bicker brings you back down and shows you that things aren't always fair."[151]

148 Johnson, "The Social Usurpation of Our Colleges," 17.

149 Quoted in Wolff, *The Final Club*, 82. Wolff was probably remembering from his own day *Now That You Are Eligible*, which the university distributed from 1942 to 1957. It does not contain a ten-point list. A later booklet, *The Upperclass Choice, 1965–1966*, does suggest that "the Bicker process is obviously only as perfect as human nature itself" (4).

150 Wendell, " 'If I Had It to Do Over Again . . . ,' " 11.

151 *Going Back: An Oral History of Princeton* (Princeton: Princetoniana Committee of the Alumni Council, 1996), 27. See also Tom Hale, "Selectivity of Bicker Mirrors the Real World," *DP* (online), Feb. 4, 2004.

But Woodrow Wilson saw no reason why a university had to mimic the imperfect ways of the world, why it should not set a *higher* example of toleration, intelligence, and fairness. As he told his faculty, "an American college is not a place for exclusiveness" if it is to provide "the best training for citizenship [and leadership] in a democratic country." He also believed in the educational value of "unchosen contacts" with people of diverse minds and values. He would have agreed with Supreme Court Justice Lewis Powell who argued in the famous Bakke case (1978) that "people do not learn very much when they are surrounded only by the likes of themselves."[152]

Yet the division of social opinion that Wilson acutely felt in 1910 and Owen Johnson detected two years later is alive and well at modern Princeton. For every club member who touts the tough realism of bicker, another student counters that the inherited "culture of exclusion" is not only "hurtful and wrong" but can be deconstructed. "Selection does happen everywhere," admitted *Prince* editor David Robinson '04, "but what happens on this campus is a distorted caricature of the real world's selectivity."[153]

Unhappily, bicker and the club system too often characterize Princeton in the minds of applicants, undergraduates, graduate students, and the popular media.[154] When a reporter from the *Harvard Crimson* visited Princeton during bicker in 1981, she concluded, as

[152] WW, Notes for Faculty Meeting Speech, Oct. 7, 1907, *PWW,* 17:420; WW, Speech at *Daily Princetonian* Annual Banquet, May 1, 1909, *PWW,* 19:179; WW, Address to Princeton Alumni Association of New England, Boston, Nov. 13, 1909, *PWW,* 19:497. Justice Powell owed his remark to President William Bowen's essay on "Admissions and the Relevance of Race" (*PAW,* Sept. 26, 1977, 7–13; also in *Ever the Teacher: William G. Bowen's Writings as President of Princeton* (Princeton, 1987), 422–36). Bowen, in turn, attributes the expression to Eugene Y. Lowe, who wrote it for an Honor System convocation at Princeton. Bowen to author, Jan. 26, 2004.

[153] David Robinson, "Editor's Notebook: Club's Choice Reflects Our Drive to Exclude," *DP* (online), May 14, 2003; Stephanie Greenberg, "Rethinking Bicker from the Inside," *DP* (online), May 12, 2004.

[154] Typical of the media coverage are two articles: one in *Time* (Mar. 23, 1953) called "A Matter of Background," which criticized bicker for snobbery and making too much of candidates' social pedigrees, the other in the *New York Times* (Oct. 13, 2002) entitled "The Halls of Ivy, The Smell of Beer: At Princeton, Its Storied Eating Clubs Are the Target of a Crackdown on Drinking" (sec. 14, pp. 1, 8).

many have since, that "an outsider observing Bicker finds it difficult to take the whole thing seriously. The enormous anxieties generated in every member of the sophomore class, the superficiality and downright silliness of its standards and ceremonies, the blatant injustices of the values and principles the system inculcates—all would seem ludicrous in any civilized community, but they are doubly comic when set in one of the nation's greatest universities."[155] University officials, trustees, and faculty hope this will change in the near future as Princeton begins to realize Wilson's residential-college plan for all four classes. In the experience of both Harvard and Yale, quads have solved the main problems associated with the eating clubs, culinary and social, and have avoided the worst—exclusion.[156] This time around, the Tiger alumni appear to be behind the plan.

In the meantime, the Princeton community can best try to maintain perspective by heeding two former clubmen. Four years after graduating in 1917, John Peale Bishop argued that the trouble with the clubs was not so much that they were undemocratic, snobbish, or luxurious. "No," he said, "the trouble with the clubs is that, once in them, they matter so little after having seemed to matter so much." Princeton English professor Thomas Riggs '37 likened bicker to a tribal initiation rite, but with a key distinction: the tribesman was preparing "to be worthy of a vision of the supernatural; the Princetonian is preparing himself to be worthy of eating three meals a day."

[155] McNees and McCarthy, "100 Per Cent on Prospect St.," 5. Even club officers admit the difficulty of defending the system outside Princeton. In 2004 Ivy Club vice-president Sabrina Mallick '04 confessed, "I feel like our social system is weird and unique . . . and when you try to describe it to someone on the outside, it's hard not to sound like some sort of jerk" (Molly Senger, "Prospect Avenue: Life on the Street: Eating Club Officers Reveal the Perks of Mansion-Living,"*DP* [online], Mar. 24, 2004).

[156] Even in the 1930s, Harvard's final clubs attracted only 11–12 percent of the upper three classes; after World War II their cachet declined even further. Yale's senior societies tapped only 10 percent of the graduating class. Unlike at Princeton, where a large majority of the three upper classes belong to the eating clubs, "the many thems," as one of Geoffrey Wolff's fictional clubmen put it, "at least had the solace of their own great society." Only Princeton had "100 Percenters." Synnott, *The Half-Opened Door*, 112; Wolff, *The Final Club*, 74; Karabel, *The Chosen*, 239, 310–11.

Bicker, he reminded *Prince* readers, was essentially "a religious frenzy over the choice of a restaurant."[157]

❁ ❁ ❁

President Wilson would undoubtedly be alarmed by the proliferation of extracurricular activities available to Princeton students today. At the same time, he would be pleased by, if somewhat wary of, the university's long domination of Ivy League athletics, and equally dismayed by the persistence of the eating clubs and bicker. But he would also regard with due admiration the extraordinary range and depth of the extra-academic talents its students bring to Princeton and develop while there. Although he might be worried by the time commitment and devotion some give to their favorite activities, he would realize that the academic big top is in little danger of being swallowed up by the sideshows.

In light of the major and minor curricular reforms—virtually all in the spirit of his own—put in place since his time, he would know that Princeton's academic requirements cannot be taken lightly, and that the faculty no longer has to whistle to get the students' attention or to engage them in the primary intellectual business of the university. Perhaps more surprising still, he could see that the "spirit of learning" he had worked so hard to spread throughout the curriculum has seeped into many of the myriad activities the students pursue between classes. For the academic reformer who also understood that "the greatest part of what a man learns at college is not in the classroom," that might be the most welcome discovery of all.[158]

[157] Bishop, *Collected Essays*, ed. Wilson, 394; Riggs quoted in McPhee, "On the Campus," *PAW*, Apr. 17, 1953, 13.

[158] WW, Talk at the Baltimore Presbyterian Union, Dec. 5, 1902, *PWW*, 14:261.

CHAPTER SIX

A Charming Turbulence

If [the students] change, nothing can
stop the college from changing.

—JAMES McCOSH

RUNNING between and beneath the Princeton curriculum and extracurriculum was a sturdy but fluid student culture, a tribal tradition and code that sought to make sense of the "bewildering episode" that college was and is. As on other campuses, Princeton's student culture was at once general and local. In its "intense conventionalism," it closely followed the fashions of the country at large, "sometimes distorting them, but always obeying herd dictates." Yet each campus fashions its own variations on the prevailing youth and national cultures. In their newfound and often daunting freedom from family and school, Princeton freshmen conformed with alacrity to the campus culture inherited from and reshaped by short-lived generations of upperclassmen and, later, women. But their acculturation was usually "an attempt to be *original* in a mass movement," to express gregariously their independence.[1] This constant tension between stylish conformity and acceptable originality defined student cultural expression at Princeton long before Wilson's presidency and has ever since.

If we approach Princeton's student culture over the past century as a kind of tribal culture, we would do well to apply the perspective

[1] Clayton Sedgwick Cooper, "The American Undergraduate," *Century Magazine* 83:4 (Feb. 1912): 514–23, at 516; Frederick P. Keppel, *The Undergraduate and His College* (Boston and New York, 1917), 92; "Youth in College," *Fortune* 13, pt. 2 (June 1936): 101; Alfred Monroe Wade '30, "Princeton's Collegiate Tendencies," *PAW*, July 2, 1929, 1135–36, at 1135 (my emphasis).

and tools of ethnohistory, a common-law marriage of anthropology and history.[2] Like anthropologists, we should look at the campus culture holistically, at all its defining parts and aspects, and ethnographically, at the distinctive ways in which its student members lived and thought about their lives, the codes and values they shared to give meaning, direction, and order to them. But in seeking what made Princeton students sui generis and different from Harvard or Yale or Amherst students, we will also need the historian's close attention to chronology and to change over time. For while the student culture persisted, it constantly changed shape, tone, and emphasis. As E. B. White noted in 1965, when Princeton students were clamoring for coeducation (which his Cornell classmates had opposed in the 1920s), "the one constant in the academic picture is that students are always undergoing a charming turbulence of mind and body."[3]

Tiger Rags

A key aspect of student culture that changed with some frequency was personal appearance. Like their college peers elsewhere, young Princetonians were keenly responsive to national fashion trends for both youth and adults, particularly those emanating from New York clothiers, from which many of their fathers took their sartorial cues. But for the first six decades of the last century they also tried to fashion a recognizable "Princeton style," whose distinctiveness some popular magazines were all too ready to certify. In most aspects,

[2] James Axtell, "The Ethnohistory of Native America," in *Natives and Newcomers: The Cultural Origins of North America* (New York, 2001), 1–12. For two exemplary ethnographies of campus culture, see Michael Moffatt, *Coming of Age in New Jersey: College and American Culture* (New Brunswick, N.J., 1989) and Lucia Nixon, "Rituals and Power: The Anthropology of Homecoming at Queen's," *Queen's Quarterly* 94 (Summer 1987): 312–31. Professor of Anthropology Lawrence Rosen and some of his students have pursued Princeton's culture ethnographically. Eric Quiñones, "Making Connections: Rosen Sees Changes in Muslim Culture Up Close," *PWB*, Feb. 24, 2003. See also David Berreby, "It Takes a Tribe," *New York Times Education Life*, Aug. 1, 2004, 22–23, 36.

[3] "The Talk of the Town," *New Yorker*, Jan. 23, 1965, 25.

however, these various expressions of Tiger fashion were widely shared with—if not borrowed from—other eastern colleges, especially their Big Three competitors in all things. The "Princeton Look" was in reality an "Ivy Look," which in turn was largely traceable to an eastern prep school template. Only when Princeton diversified its student body, when the numerical and social dominance of prep schoolers declined substantially in the 1960s and the attendant "cultural revolution" took adolescent fashion in strange new directions, did Princeton dress drift away from a single stereotype. A partial return to "preppiness" in the late 1970s could not prevent the new-millennial "Princeton Look" from resembling ever so strongly the sartorial heterogeneity of most American campuses.

When Wilson assumed the presidency and long after he left, the only class of Princetonians who might have been easily identifiable as such was freshmen. By not-very-old "tradition" and the dictates of the all-powerful Senior Council, freshmen were obliged to wear a standard uniform designed to tame their coltish exuberance, develop class spirit, and honor the seniority of all upperclassmen, particularly the sophomores, who were delegated the duties of campus-cultural enforcement. Within days if not hours after arriving, the "newies" learned to abase themselves properly by wearing nothing but black: turtleneck jerseys, corduroy trousers, garters, socks, shoes, and, when it rained, oilskin slickers and rubber hats. The chief token of class identity and humility was a small peaked beanie called a "dink," which could be laid aside when accompanying visitors or attending a Yale football or baseball game. Fancy vests, derby hats, colored caps, anything orange, and yellow slickers were *verboten*. Only on Sunday could regular clothes—of a sober sort—be worn.[4]

[4] In 1914 a new freshman was so excited by a Sunday dinner invitation that he got out of his black "freshman clothes" and "sported a loud tie, socks and hat." He even went so far as to replace his black garters with "pale pink ones" ("The Diary of a Freshman," *PAW*, Oct. 7, 1914, 48; also in *Best of PAW*, 129–30). For the freshman uniform, see "1909 Alumni Recall Campus in Wilson's Day," *Princeton Recollector* 4:8 (June 1979): 10; Allen Goodrich Shenstone, "Princeton 1910–1914," *PULC* 44:1 (Autumn 1982): 25–41, at 29; John Peale Bishop '17, "Princeton" [1931], in *The Collected Essays of John Peale Bishop*, ed. Edmund Wilson (New York, 1948), 391–400, at 397; John A. Benn, *Columbus—Undergraduate* (Philadelphia, 1928), 21.

During and after the Great War, in which many Princeton students risked their lives, freshman dress restrictions were gradually eased until all but the dink disappeared. In 1916, for example, the Senior Council allowed freshmen to wear soft collars and to cuff their trousers. The *Prince* tut-tutted and a student columnist in the alumni magazine worried that if the seniors could be persuaded that dinks could be replaced by woolen toques in cold weather, (*outré*) mackinaw jackets would surely appear next. Soon the freshman (below his bean) was free to emulate his campus superiors, particularly the sophomore "birds of much gaudier feather," who had been privileged to wear yellow slickers, "the badge of all [their] tribe."[5]

The exuberant and prosperous postwar decade made it difficult to dampen any undergraduate flamboyance in dress or behavior, especially in the presence of pace-setting "Slickers." According to F. Scott Fitzgerald, who sought to become one, the Slicker—unlike the prep school Big Man—wore his hair short, parted in the middle, and slicked back with water or tonic "as the current of fashion dictated." He dressed carefully and well, pretending that "dress is superficial" but knowing that "it isn't." He affected white flannels, Livingston collars, dark ties, and more. Several longtime Princeton clothiers remembered the introduction in the 1920s of sporty knickerbockers, belted Norfolk sport coats, Harris tweeds, regimental striped and wool challis ties, and white bucks from England, Scottish argyle socks, and the quintessentially collegiate raccoon coat, all of which had their day and some of which became classics, like the older blue blazer.[6]

In the midst of a period of competitive conformity and fads, some campus sages wanted to believe that conservatism was—or should be—the keynote of the Princeton undergraduate "in everything from neckties to ideas." Like so many of their elders at home and in the admission office, who were equally uncomfortable with the world's

[5] Henry T. Dunn '17, "The Undergraduate Week," *PAW*, Oct. 18, 1916, 63–64; also in *Best of PAW*, 112; Christian Gauss, *Through College on Nothing a Year* (New York, 1915), 104; Gauss, "Life on the Campus," in Charles G. Osgood et al., *The Modern Princeton* (Princeton, 1947), 16.

[6] F. Scott Fitzgerald, *This Side of Paradise* (New York, 1920, 1977), 42–43, 44; "Topics of the Town: A Look Back," *Town Topics* [Princeton], Apr. 7–13, 1957, 14, 16.

new tensions and America's new faces, these young WASPs instinctively reached for an ethnic scapegoat. One essayist lamented that "'Collegiate' clothes . . . are not the product of college imaginations . . . the way slang is. The clothes that we are dictated to wear are the things that Louis Kaplan, Browning King, Rosenthal-Maretz, *and the rest* have decided that they want to sell to us. . . . [T]he tailoring world has invented them, and the college world takes them without murmur and without question." After living through a decade of "selective" admissions and immigration quotas, he was conditioned to take strong issue with the *Prince*'s editorial position, which five years earlier was that Princeton men did "not bother about the latest dictates of fashion which emanate from the *semitic* sartorial salons of New York and New Haven."[7] He was apparently also oblivious to another *PAW* article eight months earlier by an alumnus eight years out, who noted that, contrary to the notion of haberdasher hegemony, "style experts are now sent by leading clothiers to observe the minutest detail what the young college man is wearing in his cloistered retreat." Old jerseys, dirty white flannels, yesterday's rumpled suits, corduroys, and caps had given way, he approved, to a "self-consciousness" and "sophistication" in dress.[8]

Despite the Great Depression, undergraduates who could afford Princeton's tuition continued to dress with some style throughout the 1930s. When blue jeans became popular with juniors early in the decade, the Undergraduate Council (which had replaced the Senior Council) ordered local clothiers not to carry them and bought up their unsold stock! More to the taste of fashion arbiters were tab collars, which *Tiger* ads in 1933 declared "the style hit of the season." The Princeton ideal was known as the "Smoothie," a sprightlier version of the Slicker. When the *Tiger* featured Dean Gauss in its 1932

[7] William Milligan Sloane III, '29, "Present Day Trends at Princeton," *PAW*, July 2, 1929, 1131; Alfred Monro Wade '30, "Princeton's Collegiate Tendencies," *PAW*, July 2, 1929, 1136 (my emphasis); *DP*, Mar. 11, 1924, quoted in Paula Fass, *The Damned and the Beautiful: American Youth in the 1920's* (New York, 1977), 441n4 (my emphasis).

[8] Lynn Carrick '20, "Sophistication on the Campus," *PAW*, Nov. 16, 1928, 231. According to *Life*, "tailors and haberdashers" in 1938 were still watching Princeton students closely because the latter were acknowledged "style leaders" who were "apt to dress on the flashy side" ("Princeton Boys Dress in a Uniform," *Life*, June 6, 1938, 31).

"Smoothie Number," he sported argyle socks (clearly visible beneath his high-water pants), a plaid vest, a figured tie, and a pocket hanky.[9]

Self-help students with fewer funds, on the other hand, made do with a "blue serge suit in which there was no fashionable surplus of cloth" and/or "sloppy gray flannel bags and a tweed coat," all "guaranteed to last for four years." This hatless and hapless wardrobe, costing no more than $45 in 1936, was demeaned by some as a "depression fashion of imitating the proletariat."[10] According to *Life*, it was far from typical of the Princeton man's investment in self-presentation. The average well-dressed Tiger allegedly spent about $400 *a year* to buy 3 suits, 12 shirts, 18 ties, 20 pairs of socks, and a topcoat in the latest modes. A more accurate survey by the *Nassau Sovereign* put the Tiger tab at just over $150, for only half as many articles. Despite the editors' glee over being able to tarnish the college's "country club" image, their survey was still an impressive demonstration of student wealth and devotion to dress. Whatever his budget, the average Princetonian was able and apt to wear "the 'collegiate uniform' of the season" by "following the crowd in form, but expressing his individualism in specific material and design of cloth."[11]

The one conspicuous exception to the young Tigers' fashion sense before World War II was the popular senior "beer suit," consisting of white denim bib overalls and painter's jacket. Tradition has it that the outfit had its origins in 1912 when some seniors adopted it to protect their dark suits from the suds produced "while quaffing beer

[9] *PAW*, June 11, 1937, 765; *Princeton Tiger* 42:11 (Feb. 17, 1933), back cover; *Princeton Tiger* 42:3 (May 19, 1932), 13. The jeans were called "applejacks."

[10] Day Edgar, *In Princeton Town* (New York, 1929), 281; "Youth in College," 101.

[11] "Princeton Boys Dress in a Uniform," 31; "Sovereign's Scientific Survey," *Nassau Sovereign* 1:3 (Dec. 1938): 12; Sterling Hutcheson, "On the Average Princetonian," *Nassau Sovereign* 1:4 (Feb. 1939): 17. In 1957 a senior member of Princeton's "unsilent generation" also believed that "adherence to the Ivy League norm in clothes (which regardless of popular misconceptions, leaves very considerable leeway for the expression of individual preferences) is . . . a Lilliputian threat to meaningful individualism, if it is a threat at all" (Otto Butz, ed., *The Unsilent Generation: An Anonymous Symposium in Which Eleven [Princeton] College Seniors Look at Themselves and Their World* [New York, 1958], 173–74).

FIGURE 18. Senior beer suits lost some of their proletarian authenticity in 1932 when worn over Oxford-cloth shirts, ties, and lamb's wool sweaters.

and carving their initials on the tables of the old Nassau Inn." Within a few years every senior wore one, particularly in the spring semester, for *Pictorial* and yearbook photos and to claim the class privileges of sitting around the Mather Sundial in McCosh courtyard and singing on the steps of Nassau Hall. The Class of '18 is credited with first emblazoning on the back of the jacket a distinctive class design, appropriately a foaming glass of beer.

Until coeducation, subsequent designs featured some combination of tigers, women, beer, and current events, local or national. According to one proud owner, the '37 suit featured a "wheelbarrow logo with a partially deflated football for a wheel (indicating only semi-success on the gridiron our senior year), a sketch of 'the Nass' being carried away (the old Nassau Inn was about to be torn down to make way for Palmer Square), a quart milk bottle labelled with the University seal (signifying our alleged favorite beverage), and a dangling dumb-bell (a good-humored hint that we might not have been the brightest of Princeton classes)."[12]

From one perspective, the beer suits might be seen as a symbolic expression of solidarity with America's economic underclass and as a way to camouflage some of the differences in wealth and wardrobe on campus. But since they could not be worn alone, their owners had several ways to individualize their appearance and to proclaim their socioeconomic status and taste. Precious few workingmen wore their rumpled white denims with Princeton letter sweaters, white Oxford cloth button-down shirts and silk ties, imported argyle socks, and shiny cordovans, brown-and-white saddle shoes, or clean white bucks. Moreover, as a *Life* photographer showed the world in 1938, the Princeton "uniform" for all classes (social and academic) was a natural-shoulder, three-button tweed jacket and darker *un*-baggy flannel slacks.[13]

World War II brought several new uniforms to campus, none of them "tweedy" but some of them quite "smooth" in the eyes of the women's colleges. The posting of Army and Navy detachments to Princeton for training and the increased popularity of ROTC put a temporary hold on the student search for sartorial distinction. But as soon as the war ended and veterans streamed back to campus, the hunger for civilian normalcy led to a strong revival of the "Princeton Look." The conservative tweed-and-flannel standard that dominated the late 1930s again captured the undergraduate fancy until the cultural and sartorial revolutions of the late 1960s and early 1970s broke its grip.[14]

[12] Along more academic lines, the '25 logo depicted a tiger crushed by four heavy tomes, symbolizing the burden imposed by the new four-course plan. Alexander Leitch, *A Princeton Companion* (Princeton, 1978), 48; "Princeton Beer Jackets: History and Lore," Princetoniana Committee Home Page (www.alumni.princeton.edu/~ptoniana/projects.asp) ; Caroline Moseley, "Colorful Class Jackets Continue 77-Year-Old Tradition," *PWB*, May 29, 1989, 3; Jane Martin, "Under the Ivy," *PAW Web Exclusives*, Apr. 21, 2004; Robert L. Edwards '37, *My Moment in History: An Autobiography* (Hartford, Conn., 1999), 75; Ann Waldron, "A Bevy of Beer Jackets," *PAW*, May 16, 1990, 23–25.

[13] "Princeton Beer Jackets" (Class of 1922 photo); *Nassau Herald* (1927), 643–50; (1934), 596–600; "Princeton Boys Dress in a Uniform," 31.

[14] In 1950 an anonymous student complained in a letter to the *Prince* of Princeton's extreme "clothing conformity." "Must a Princeton man," he asked, "always look like a Princeton man?" (*DP*, Feb. 25, 1950, 3).

The revived "uniform," however, had a few variations, largely the product of the war and the democratization of intellect fostered by the G.I. Bill and Princeton's search for a more national student body. One was the great popularity of tan chino or khaki trousers, cheaper and less formal than dress slacks but capable of holding a crease. These, like fur-collared flight jackets, navy peacoats, double-breasted trench coats, high-laced brogans, and a variety of battle fatigues, stormed the campus on both their wartime wearers and students too young but sorry not to have served.[15] Another variation was button-down shirts in more casual blue (and later yellow and pink) Oxford cloth. And in a gesture of egalitarian understatement, *dirty* white bucks, frayed collars (if need be, artificially), conservative colors and patterns, and much smaller wardrobes became the order of the day.[16]

The postwar relaxation of dress also took other forms. In the cooler months, Shetland sweaters (crew and V-neck) and tan, plaid-lined golf jackets often replaced sport coats, which were also worn sans tie. In warmer weather, especially during Houseparties and other spring weekends, Bermuda shorts (Madras and plain) exposed winter-white legs to the New Jersey sun.[17] Bass Weejuns, classic brown "penny" loafers often worn with white athletic socks, made their appearance in the early 1950s and soon replaced the excessively

[15] In a 1947 *Nassau Sovereign* survey, more than a third of the students said they "usually" wore ex-military garb and nearly half did "sometimes." In Carlos Baker's *A Friend in Power*, students and faculty in the mid-1950s were still wearing ex-military clothing. "The Sovereign Survey," *Nassau Sovereign* 6:8 (May 1947): 22–23; Baker, *A Friend in Power* (New York, 1958), 73, 103, 184, 221, 224, 232; H. S. MacAyeal, *Tiger! Tiger!* (London, 1996), 82.

[16] "The Sovereign Survey," *Nassau Sovereign* 6:8 (May 1947): 22–23. In his sophomore year, Edward W. Said '57, a product of Mount Hermon prep school, watched in "astonishment as two classmates in an adjoining suite applied sandpaper to a pair of new blue button-down shirts, trying in a matter of minutes to produce the effect of the worn-out aristocratic shirt that might get them into a better club" (*Out of Place: A Memoir* [New York, 1999], 275).

[17] In 1939 *PAW* reported that "an epidemic of shorts has struck the campus," in all colors and lengths, including cut-off beer suits hemmed at the U-Store for 25 cents. Eleven years later, a feature article on Princeton in *Holiday* showed plenty of student (and date) leg in photos of Houseparties weekend. Frederic E. Fox '39, "On the Campus," *PAW*, June 9, 1939, 772; John Brooks, "Princeton," *Holiday* 8:4 (Oct. 1950): 102–3.

sportif saddle shoe as the favorite alternative to dirty bucks. Student informality on the postwar campus was a decided departure from the dressier standard raised after World War I. Donald W. Griffin '23 could not remember anyone in his day going to classes or club "without coat and tie. They looked like young businessmen going to New York."[18]

For tweedy, pipe-smoking "Bill" Lippincott, Princeton student from 1937 to 1941 and dean of students from 1955 to 1968, the campus trend toward informality was regrettable. In 1963 he told a *Prince* reporter that the "marked change" in dress since World War II had lowered Princeton standards too far. Without resorting to administrative edict (which he knew would not succeed in the face of cultural custom), he hoped that someday coats and ties would be worn to all classes and meals. They were then not required for classes and only for Sunday lunch in Commons and a few meals at some clubs. He no doubt knew what he was up against because the Undergraduate Council the previous year had roundly rejected an administrative proposal to require coats and ties at all Commons dinners.[19] It may also have rankled the dean that Yale still required coats and ties for both lunch and dinner in its ten residential colleges and therefore that many Yalies wore them to class from sheer convenience.

But sartorial change was "blowin' in the wind" and few could forecast it, not even *PAW*'s campus correspondent, senior Edward Tenner. In his final column in June 1965, he deconstructed several tropes of student attire. As his title, "Tweeds Classified," suggested, three levels of "Tweeds" dominated the scene. An understandable minority of "Tigers" (who alternated beer jackets year-round with outdoorsy flannel and down), "High School Harrys" (sports shirts under Princeton-insignia wear), "Grubs" (sockless sneakers and colored T-shirts), and "Beats" (Grubs in blue work shirts and slightly longer hair) provided background color to a familiar campus dress code.[20] The following year, however, the advent of five-inch-wide

[18] "Griffin Recalls Campus Change," *Princeton Recollector* 1:2 (June 1975): 14.

[19] Mel M. Masuda, "Dean Discusses Changes in Undergraduate Dress," *DP*, Dec. 13, 1963, 1. On Lippincott, see "The Days of a Dean," *PAW*, Feb. 29, 1972, 6–9.

[20] Edward H. Tenner '65, "On the Campus: Tweeds Classified," *PAW*, June 1, 1965, 6.

FIGURE 19. Tower Club's portrait in the 1974 *Nassau Herald* suggests that the sartorial trends of the countercultural Sixties were gradually returning to the more collegiate fashions of the early 1960s, without the formality.

ties, often in garish colors and patterns, heralded a revolution in student appearance.

As "sex, drugs, rock-'n-roll," and political protest hit America's campuses, the Princeton "uniform" went into eclipse, except on a few die-hard conservatives. It was replaced by randomized costumes, not wardrobes, of tie-dye, polyester, bell-bottoms, plaid flannel, and proletarian protest wear, guaranteed to annoy parents, alumni, and the tweedy gents in Nassau Hall. To judge by club, class, and candid photos in the two yearbooks—the *Nassau Herald* and the *Bric-a-Brac*—until the mid-1970s even coeducation could not halt the sartorial slide into eclecticism. Women in love beads, combat boots, "granny" dresses, and braids did nothing to push their male classmates back into ties and tweeds.[21]

[21] The changes in style are best documented in the *Nassau Herald* and the *Bric-a-Brac* from the mid-1960s to the mid-1970s. Complete runs of each can be found in the reference room of Mudd Library (PUA).

Nor would these brainy Delilahs ask the men to cut their hair. In 1936 *Fortune* declared that "the short crew cut is the symbol of aristocracy" on Big Three campuses; those with long hair were called "queeries."[22] Not so by the late 1960s, when college-town barbershops went into deep recession. Princeton's alumni magazine kept careful score of student hirsutism. Between 1950 and 1966, senior classes sitting for their yearbook pictures sported a maximum of 4 moustaches and 3 beards a year, usually none at all. By 1969, facial cover had been cultivated on 76 upper lips and 25 chins, and head hair concealed many ears and necks. When the magazine stopped counting in 1972, the tally had jumped to 106 "soup-strainers" and 79 full or semi-beards. Valedictorian Hal White spoke at commencement against the Vietnam War in black bushy beard and nape-long hair.[23]

After the sartorial confusion of the long Sixties, student "turbulence" did not regain its charm until the late 1970s and early 1980s. Political agitation over the war in Southeast Asia and the university's investments in South Africa receded slowly but surely by the early 1980s. So did hair length, facial flora, and runaway sideburns that soon embarrassed every senior who was caught by the camera wearing them. Of the 646 male seniors pictured in the 1983 *Nassau Herald*, only 41, mostly whites, sported full or partial beards; 81, a disproportionate number of blacks and Hispanics, went for moustaches. Long and unkempt hair was rare, but most styles were fuller, covering the tops of the ears; long sideburns were mercifully a thing of the past.

Student dress took less time to lose its countercultural edge. Contradicting a *New York Times* profile of "The New Princeton," senior Alan Tonelson assured the alumni in the fall of 1973 that "little bits and pieces of The Old Princeton" were making a comeback. Jeans were getting "stiff competition from chinos and Farah slacks." While flannel shirts were still in, work shirts were out. "Tweeds, corduroys and elbow patches" abounded. In the mid-1970s, Topsiders, the prep set's sailing shoe and "a numinous symbol of Prince-

[22] "Youth in College," 161.

[23] Craig Conderacci '71, "Not a Laughing Matter," *PAW*, Nov. 17, 1970, 6; *PAW*, Oct. 26, 1971, 4; *PAW*, June 27, 1972, 4, 5.

ton," also gave work boots, clogs, Earth Shoes, and Wallabees a run for their money.[24]

By the early 1980s Lisa Birnbach's *Official Preppy Handbook* had made "preppy" and "Lacoste" dirty words on campus, according to former *PAW* editor and Hotchkiss product John D. Davies '41. Not only did high schoolers outnumber prep schoolers three to two, the preps had largely capitulated to the dominant high school style. Unlike "the old Princetonian dressed in a costume as ritualized as the Kwakiutl Indian's," the new Tiger in his ("her" was not in Davies's picture) "casual undress" resembled "nothing so much as a walking army-surplus store." The situation was rife with irony. In the 1950s many "hereditary tweeds," as a senior essayist dubbed them, "the boys who were born with Black Watch plaid diapers on," took "cynical pleasure" in watching newly arrived high schoolers scramble and fumble to adopt the preppy Princeton "uniform." Now the tables were turned and the high schoolers, had they cared to, might have relished the sartorial "surrender of the preppies" to a much looser dress code shared by college-age young people across the country.[25]

On the Princeton campus today, if some students did not wear Princeton insignia and colors, the student body would be, to outsiders, virtually indistinguishable from the clothed cohorts crossing any other American campus. Not even freshmen are recognizable. After a brief revival of the (reconfigured) dink in 1947, and a few bloody skirmishes in the 1950s in which frosh tried to hold onto their hats (to prevent rioting sophs from shaving their heads), the dink went the way of the dodo, unmourned except by alumni with selective memories.[26]

[24] Alan Tonelson '74, "On the Campus," *PAW*, Oct. 2, 1973, 7; Rich Stengel '77, "On the Campus: By Their Shoes Shall You Know Them," *PAW*, Mar. 1, 1976, 9.

[25] Lisa Birnbach, *The Official Preppy Handbook* (New York, 1980); Butz, ed., *The Unsilent Generation*, 173; John D. Davies '41, "Opinion: The Surrender of the Preppies," *PAW*, Oct. 19, 1981, 13–15.

[26] MacAyeal, *Tiger! Tiger!*, 235, suggested that no-nonsense veterans in the postwar classes were largely responsible for the dink's demise. The Class of '51 agreed. The administration outlawed the head-shaving wars in 1958 after some serious accidents with scissors. "New Frosh to Don Dinks, Ties in Fall," *DP*, May 23, 1947, 1; Robert V. Keeley, ed., *Reminiscences of Times Past: The Princeton University of 1947–1951 as Recalled by Members of the Class of 1951 for Their 50th Reunion* (Hagerstown, Md., 2000), 24–25,

Princeton Patois

If members of the Tiger tribe could not easily be recognized off campus by their appearance, they only had to break into their coded speech to be tagged as Princetonians. References to unique Princeton sites, institutions, and characters were and always will be infallible clues to true natives of Nassau. Two otherwise anonymous persons overheard talking about cane sprees, the Dinky, precepts, the 'Soons, Woodie Woo, bicker, and Dean's Date would instantly be identified by a third student or alumnus as fellow tribesmen; an outsider would simply be nonplused.[27] Somewhat harder to recognize would be the distinctive student slang that also distinguishes Princeton's culture from that of other colleges. While many Princeton people, practices, and places persist over relatively long periods, student patois tends to evolve rather quickly on the inventive tongues of short-lived campus generations. To each of those generations, their special slang is a code meant to bind its members to each other and the university, as well as to prevent outsiders from penetrating their charmed circle. That it often shares elements with the slang of other, often widely flung campuses diminishes only somewhat the difficulty of parsing its exclusionary references and meanings.

College slang has been around since students gathered in the medieval universities. The first serious effort to document it in America was Harvard senior Benjamin H. Hall's *A Collection of College Words and Customs*, published in 1851. In an enlarged edition five years later,

---

38, 88, 100–101; "On the Campus," *PAW*, Oct. 6, 1950, 9; John Angus McPhee '53, "On the Campus," *PAW*, Oct. 10, 1952, 11.

[27] For cane sprees, see 362–65, below. The Dinky is the (usually) one-car shuttle train that makes the 2.7-mile, four-minute run between Princeton and Princeton Junction, where commuters connect with Amtrak and NJ Transit trains. Classes before the 1980s knew it as the PJ&B (Princeton Junction and Back). Lawrence Biemiller, "Where the Only Station Stop Is Princeton," *CHE*, May 16, 2003, A48; David McIlroy, "The Dinky: Decades of History and Lore," *DP* (online), Apr. 29, 2004; John A. Wilmot, "The Princeton Branch: From Camden & Amboy to NJ Transit," *Trains* 47:8 (June 1987): 44–51. The 'Soons were the Nassoons *a capella* singing group. Woodie Woo is the Woodrow Wilson School of Public and International Affairs. Dean's Date is the last day that course papers will be accepted each semester; see p. 372n131, below.

Hall drew on the argot of thirty-four American colleges, including Princeton.[28] But he missed many slang words and phrases in use around Nassau Hall, as two Princeton seniors, James B. Henry and Christian H. Scharff, demonstrated in their book-length guide to Princeton life in 1853. Since they sought to describe the college culture for future students, they felt obliged to offer a glossary of "cant phrases, odd expressions and fantastic abuse of words" currently in use. "These words," they noted, "insinuate themselves in every conversation, between two or more students; and even in the vacation when College life happens to be the topic of conversation." Some of their "classical Jargon" is perfectly understandable to Princeton students today. A *boot-lick* got no sympathy, nor did a *bore* or a sanctimonious *relig*. More sympathy went to a student who *fizzled* in recitation and ended up *probationed*. To *stump* a professor's question by making no effort to answer was worse than *fizzling*. To *splurge* on clothes was acceptable, but to *skunk* the tailor by ignoring the bill was not. To produce a *funk* in chemistry class put one in an equally bad odor, almost as much as one who in gab sessions *gassed* away without sense or surcease.[29]

In the twentieth century, every generation of students felt a similar urge to "coin its own slang to describe its own college experiences and campus types." Exercising youth's "natural delight in languagemaking" (as H. L. Mencken called it), Princeton students not only appropriated terms from the national slang pool, but continued to fashion "pungent novelties" for their exclusive consumption. These verbal equivalents of secret fraternal handshakes took several forms.[30] "Clipping" the ends of words, fore but mostly aft, yielded the most familiar terms: *dip*[loma], *frat*, *prof*, *Y*[MCA], *gym*, *dorm*, [pre]*'cept*, *prom*[enade], and Wilson's downfall, *quad*. "Blending" was not as

[28] Benjamin H. Hall, *A Collection of College Words and Customs*, rev. and enl. ed. (Cambridge, Mass., 1856; Detroit, 1968).

[29] James Buchanan Henry and Christian Henry Scharff, *College As It Is; or, The Collegian's Manual in 1853*, ed. J. Jefferson Looney (Princeton: PU Libraries, 1996), 27–38.

[30] James M. Markham '65, "On the Campus: The Princeton Idiom," *PAW*, Nov. 19, 1963, 4; H. L. Mencken, *The American Language: An Inquiry into the Development of English in the United States*, 4th rev. ed. (New York, 1947), 558–59, 569; Peter G. Brown '70, "Keycepts on Yooney Slang," *PAW*, Feb. 24, 1970, 12–13, 15.

common, such as *boot-lick*, *goose-egg* (0 in score), *honey man* (repeater of other people's jokes, often an old alumnus), *polycon* (political economy), and *sour-ball* (a chronic grumbler), all from c. 1900.[31]

Changing the part of speech or meaning of a familiar word also produced many slang standards. In the late 1920s *wet* was a generally opprobrious adjective no one wanted applied to himself. A *gut* was a notoriously easy course, one that *gut-hoppers* habitually chose. *Shooting the bull* was a perennial pastime of dorm life when one needed a break from *pounding* or *hitting the books*. *Wolfing* (poaching) your *wife*'s (roommate's) date was to *stick out your neck* (commit an unpardonable error). In 1970 to *snow* your own date was not to precipitate on her but to impress her. Having too much to drink might cause one to *ralph* (vomit) on her, which would *not* snow her. And *skating* away from the clean-up only added insult to injury. She was very likely to *flush* (reject) you if you dared to call again.[32]

The biggest contributor to campus slang has been what the linguists call figurativeness, "the picturesque substitute for the 'real' word." From the mouths of judgmental collegians, "good slang is never fair. It distorts, ridicules, lampoons." It uses novel and often racy synonyms and phrases to "jar the hearer into fresh recognition of an object." Understandably, the most daring or challenging aspects of Princeton life provide the most powerful inspirations—girls, eating clubs, and drinking.[33]

Male Princeton's adolescent names for the opposite sex were legion and often vaguely insulting. In 1900 the only term that wasn't shared with the rest of the college world was *fairy*. By the flapper-filled 1920s, when Princeton slang in general "flourished like a bay

[31] Markham, "The Princeton Idiom," 4; E. H. Babbitt, "College Words and Phrases," *Dialect Notes* 2, pt. 1 (1900), 1–70 at 24, 38, 41, 50, 63.

[32] "In the Vernacular," *PAW*, May 18, 1928, 947–48; "Keeping Up with Joe Gish," *PAW*, May 24, 1929, 981–82; Edmund Wilson, *A Prelude: Landscape, Characters and Conversations from the Earlier Years of My Life* (New York, 1967), 125; Brown, "Keycepts on Yooney Slang," 12–13, 15.

[33] Brown, "Keycepts on Yooney Slang," 12, 13; H. H. Rightor '32, "Current Undergraduate Slang," *PAW*, May 22, 1931, 798. Women undoubtedly have their own slang, but I have found no evidence of the feminine (or feminist) variety at Princeton. They surely have a full set of terms for men, though they may share much of the male-invented campus idiom.

tree," woman-words came largely from the national checklist. *Babe* was the favorite, sending *bim*[bo?] into obsolescence; *a plenty nutsy babe* couldn't be topped. At a minimum, *witch*, *flooze*, and *quiff* rounded out the line-up. By the end of the more subdued and sophisticated 1930s, the young Princetonian, especially if he was a *red-hot* seeking female companionship, spoke of *fires*, *spooks*, *queens* or *queen-bees*, and, if desperate, *bags*.[34]

Twenty-five years later, the argot was totally different: *choan* (origin unknown), *honey*, and *squeeze* were generics; *tough*, *fine*, and *sof-fine* were high markers. Women who did not *turn on* their dates, particularly at *cattle drives* (mixers), were dismissed as *losers*, *zombies*, or *scary* (incomprehensibly intellectual).[35] With coeducation, the trade in gender terms may have equalized but definitely dropped off the alumni magazine's radar, to the chagrin of the campus cultural historian. The annual "Official Princeton Dictionary," sent by the *Prince* to all entering freshmen since 1957, could hardly perpetuate the objectification (or worse) of women once they joined the paper's staff and editorial board in goodly numbers. "Townie" still referred to local girls, but "import" applied equally to male dates from other colleges: "With the advent of women's liberation female students have awakened to the fact that they are not required to sit around and wait for the Princeton males to ask them out." One term that appeared in 1985—"JAP" (abbreviation for Jewish American Princess), "a prissy, jewelry-laden nymphet from Long Island (pronounced Lawn Geyland) who comes to Princeton to find a nice Jewish boy, and finds Elm Club instead"—was a sad revival of Princeton's old anti-Semitism mixed with adolescent misogyny. Fortunately, it was dropped from the next edition.[36]

[34] Babbitt, "College Words and Phrases," 34; Burr, "Princeton in the Twenties," 11; "In the Vernacular," 947; "Keeping Up with Joe Gish," 982; Rightor, "Current Undergraduate Slang," 798. For more jargon from c. 1900, see "Letters from a Self-Made Son to His Mother: Being a Slang History of the Undergraduate Life of One Princetonian," *Princeton Tiger* 15, no. 1, p. 13 (Feb. 25, 1901), no. 2, pp. 11–12 (Apr. 15, 1901), no. 3, p. 10 (Oct. 2, 1901), no. 4, pp. 10–11 (Oct. 26, 1901); no. 6, p. 15 (Apr. 6, 1902).

[35] Hutcheson, "On the Average Princetonian," 17; "Our Mother Tongue?" *PAW*, Oct. 10, 1941, 7–8; Brown, "Keycepts on Yooney Slang," 13.

[36] *DP*, July 25, 1977 (Sec. II: Dictionary), 4, 7; July 27, 1981, 3, 7; July 29, 1985, 2, 3, 4.

Student stereotyping and put-downs are perennial features of college life at the best of times, particularly at a competitive place like Princeton, but they had their widest application during the run-up to eating-club selections. The character assessments (and assassinations) of bicker force-fed the invention of demeaning and dismissive terms for applicants and often sadistically enjoyable terms for the process of rejection. In 1900 *chumps* (queer fellows), *muckers* (mean, tricky fellows), *prunes* (slow-witted fellows), *Rubes* (oafish boors), and *yaps* (contemptible persons) made the local list of distinctive put-downs. In the 1920s *smooth*, *Brooksey* fellows lorded it over *dopeless* (clueless) *wet smacks*, *sad* or *queer birds*, and creative, do-gooding *softies* who let their studies interfere with their education.[37] A decade later, *boobs*, *meat-balls*, *grinds*, *goons*, and *A.K.*s (ass-kissers) all *sucked*, were not *on the ball*, and usually *missed the boat* and were *axed*. By the 1960s *weenies*, *wonks*, *toads*, and *lunche(r)s* were likely to be *swassed* (eliminated) from bicker, while *nice guys* and *jocks* (including *gorillas* and *moose*) and even *face-men* and *shallow tweeds* were likely to *hum right in*. The Class of '83 added to the list *dweebs*, *pencil-neck geeks*, and *space patrol leaders*, who were invariably *hosed* by the bicker committees.[38]

Whether conducted in a club, a dorm room, or the Nassau Inn's once-stag taproom, drinking has been a venerable tradition at Princeton, as on most campuses. Because the consumption of alcohol, usually to excess, has been an all-American sport since the colonies were founded by bibulous Europeans, the campus vocabulary of drinking borrows heavily from an enormous and inventive national glossary, so much so that originality on any one campus is suspect. But each campus generation chooses favorites from the array of

[37] Babbitt, "College Words and Phrases," 27, 46, 52, 56, 70; Fass, *The Damned and the Beautiful*, 229–30 (quoting the *DP*, Dec. 1, 1924); Wade, "Princeton's Collegiate Tendencies," 1136; Christian Gauss, *Life in College* (New York, 1930), 36. The dull plumage of *sad birds* (and *birdies*) was recognizable in the early 1900s as well. "Letters from a Self-Made Son," no. 3, p. 10; no. 4, p. 10.

[38] Rightor, "Current Undergraduate Slang," 798; Hutcheson, "On the Average Princetonian," 17, 35; Markham, "The Princeton Idiom," 4; Brown, "Keycepts on Yooney Slang," 13, 15; "A Princeton Lexicon," *PAW*, Sept. 26, 1972, 11; *Nassau Herald* (1983), 34. For more terms of rejection, see chapter 5, pp. 303–4.

words and phrases available to endow its own culture with verbal liquidity, if not originality. At the turn of the last century, the only two drink-related terms at Princeton that caught the dialectician's eye were a *sponge* (a person with a large capacity for drink) and *to put* (vomit) when he literally couldn't hold his liquor. On a clandestine visit to Trenton, a freshman encountered a local burgher *dippy with the grog*. Edmund Wilson '16 remembered *pass out cold* and *the champagne kind o' got to him* as useful Princeton colloquialisms.[39]

Given the existence of bootleggers and speakeasies, Prohibition (1919–1933) posed no impediments to vivid verbalization about the forbidden article and its effects. In 1931 junior H. H. Rightor testified that "at the present moment the act of drinking is *touching it* or *polishing off a few*; a drink is a *quick one*, a *snort*, or a *hooker*; and when *the lid is off* one gets *rosy*, *on the ball*, *high*, *stinking*, and maybe *passes out*." A *Nassau Sovereign* survey in 1940 revealed that of the 43 percent of undergraduates who planned to get drunk after final exams in May, 54 percent intended to be *happy*, 30 percent *roaring*, and 16 percent *blotto*.[40]

The postwar growth of campus tippling led to an efflorescence of slang nationwide, much of it considered unfit for publication in alumni magazines. Princeton's was no exception. In 1963 one student columnist provided an unremarkable list of terms for inebriation: *plowed*, *smashed*, *tanked*, *gilled*, *blind*, *stoned*, *looped*, or simply *blotto*. Once the desired state was attained, the imbiber would likely *fade*, *flake out*, or *pass out*. "At Yale," our expert noted, "we find much the same use of the terms, therefore refuting [the] theory that these are solely 'rural idioms.'" One of his successors made a small addition to the "effects" vocabulary by noting that the 1957 "Official Princeton Dictionary" entries *barf*, *York*, *put the bird*, and *heave* were gone by 1960, to be replaced ten years later by *ralph* or *blow lunch*.[41] Fortu-

[39] Babbitt, "College Words and Phrases," 53, 63; "Letters from a Self-Made Son," no. 1, p. 13; Wilson, *A Prelude*, 125.

[40] Rightor, "Current Undergraduate Slang," 798; "Sovereign's Scientific Survey," *Nassau Sovereign* 2:8 (May 1940): 16.

[41] Robert K. Heimann, "Alcoholics Not So Anonymous," *Nassau Sovereign* 7:6 (Mar. 1948): 12–15; Markham, "The Princeton Idiom," 4; Brown, "Keycepts on Yooney Slang," 12–13.

nately for readers of *PAW*, the inside scoop on student mishandling of alcohol took a sociological turn in the 1980s and 1990s as national and local trends in binge drinking claimed headlines across the country.[42] The campus slang didn't die—it never will as long as students drink—but the glorification of it in print did.

God Boxes and Tribal Faiths

At the beginning of the last century, religion was a powerful bond among Princeton's undergraduates. Raised in just a handful of Protestant denominations, they worshiped the same patriarchal deity and used nearly the same vocabulary to speak of their relationship with Him. Seniors voted the Bible their favorite book. To support their steadfastness in the faith, the university required them to attend daily and Sunday worship services in an impressive university chapel. It also sanctioned and supported the Philadelphian Society, the campus branch of the Young Men's Christian Association (YMCA), which enlisted a majority of the students in its promotion of personal piety and collective good works.

But as American society, the university, and the student body changed during the twentieth century, religion lost its adhesive quality and much of its campus-cultural utility. As society secularized, higher education specialized, and religion pluralized, students could no longer find in their faith common ground, a way to define themselves as Princetonians by testaments of beliefs or even habits of assembly. Though many did deepen their faith while in college, most undergraduates had to look elsewhere for cultural commonalities to define their tribal membership.

[42] See, for example, David Williamson '84, "Drinking: A Sobering Look at an Enduring Princeton Pastime," *PAW*, Mar. 21, 1990, 14–19; D. W. Miller '89, "Saying When: Princeton Faces Its Drinking Problem," *PAW*, Nov. 25, 1992, 6–10; Wes Tooke '98, "Confronting the Beast: Princeton Once Again Looks for Solutions to Its Alcohol Problem,"*PAW*, Mar. 24, 1999, 12–15; Jill P. Capuzzo, "The Halls of Ivy, The Smell of Beer," *New York Times*, Oct. 13, 2002, sec. 14 (New Jersey), 1, 8; Alexandra Silver, "Students Skeptical about Effect of [Trustees'] Alcohol Initiative on Drinking," *DP* (online), Nov. 29, 2004.

Prophetic changes began as soon as the century opened. Woodrow Wilson, the first lay president but the son and son-in-law of Presbyterian ministers, initiated a series of reforms that alarmed conservative alumni and outsiders but pleased the student body. In 1906 he persuaded the trustees to declare the university officially nonsectarian and to reduce the number of clerics on the board from twelve to eight, having declared upon taking office that Princeton was a Presbyterian college "only because the Presbyterians of New Jersey were wise and progressive enough to found it."[43] This statement may have surprised the Presbyterian half of the student body, but it was a heartening signal to the rising tide of Episcopalians, the significant numbers of other Protestants, Roman Catholics, and undeclared, and the less numerous "Hebrews" who had matriculated.[44]

In 1902 he also abolished the Department of Biblical Literature and its required courses, mostly to rid the university of theological conservative George Patton, the former president's nepotically appointed son. But he reinstated the teaching of biblical history and literature three years later by appointing liberal theologian Lucius H. Miller '97, former member of Cap and Gown eating club and recent graduate of Union Theological Seminary in New York, who attracted large enrollments to his now elective classes. Alert to the dangers of creating doubt in young students "by ramming dogma down the throat," the president retained mandatory daily chapel but allowed a generous number of unexcused absences or "cuts" and reduced each service from twenty minutes to fifteen and then, at the nonparticipating faculty's suggestion, to ten. In 1905 he persuaded the trustees to abolish altogether the Sunday evening worship service, a time that could be and was quickly used for voluntary prayer

[43] Wilson also stopped the award of free tuition to the sons of Presbyterian ministers (which he had received as an undergraduate) and to preministerial candidates and loosened connections between the university and the Princeton Theological Seminary. "Wilson and Patton Differ," *New York Tribune*, Dec. 2, 1902, 4; *PWW*, 16:468–69 (Oct. 20, 1906); P. C. Kemeny, *Princeton in the Nation's Service: Religious Ideals and Educational Practice, 1868–1928* (New York, 1998), 142, 143–45, 147.

[44] *PWW*, 16:467 (Oct. 20, 1906); 18:586 (Jan. 1, 1909); Kemeny, *Princeton in the Nation's Service*, 166.

meetings and Bible study conducted by the Philadelphian Society. A year later the students were equally pleased to be excused from half of the morning services. Their major reservation pertained to the administration of attendance: each student had a small "prayer card" with his name on it that he turned in at the chapel door to have his presence recorded. His accumulated cuts appeared on his report card for parents to see.[45]

Yet Wilson, whose driving Christian faith made his own life (he said) "worth living," often led daily prayers and gave eloquent sermons on Sunday, where his sober piety was easily mistaken for that of a bona fide minister. He also supported and frequently addressed the Philadelphian Society, whose membership grew from five hundred to over eight hundred during his tenure. Although he did not believe that overtly religious courses for undergraduates were necessary, he sought to sacralize the whole liberal arts curriculum. As he told a baccalaureate audience in 1905, he could not envision "the spirit of learning," with its ennobling, elevating idealism, "separated or divorced from the spirit of religion." And although he moved the university toward a more liberal brand of Protestantism than his predecessors had espoused, he retained Princeton's historical Christian character by adapting its semi-official faith and practice to modern society and to the rising intellectual demands of a research university. In the process, he won the approval of the students by blending liberal Protestantism with liberal democracy to create a civic religion not only for Princeton but for the nation, which he expected them to lead.[46]

The irenic John Grier Hibben, an ordained Presbyterian minister as well as professor of philosophy, made no radical departures from Wilson's religious initiatives. Indeed, responding to steady complaint from the students and an alteration in their religious profile,

[45] Kemeny, *Princeton in the Nation's Service*, 148–52, 158–59, 291n144; Deane Edwards '06 scrapbook, PUA.

[46] Kemeny, *Princeton in the Nation's Service*, 128–29, 145, 150, 151, 161; Baccalaureate Address, June 11, 1905, *PWW*, 16:126. See also John M. Mulder, *Woodrow Wilson: The Years of Preparation* (Princeton, 1978), 178–82.

Hibben saw to it in 1915 that daily chapel became voluntary. As the college expanded and became more socially desirable, entering freshmen from Episcopal families outnumbered Presbyterian sons; in the fall of 1910 their numbers were equal for the last time.[47]

No matter what their religious background, even the most devout students resented being compelled to attend worship services. For freshmen newly freed from restrictive prep school environments, chapel twice a week and every other Sunday might not have seemed an onerous obligation.[48] But their seniors quickly developed more expansive visions of personal autonomy befitting their advanced age and status. While voluntary participation in the Philadelphian Society and other social-service organizations was brisk, senior polls and the *Prince* hammered away at the inherent contradiction between the intellectual freedom of the classroom and the constraints placed on the search for religious truth. Year after year, seniors, when asked by yearbook pollsters what they would do if they ran the university, gave as their number one answer "Abolish [compulsory] chapel." ("Make it coed" was a distant second.)[49] On March 10, 1914, the captive chapel audience issued a strong vocal protest by erupting in an "epidemic" of coughing during a lengthy prayer. The following fall a *Prince* poll found that 960 students opposed compulsory daily chapel and only 199 had no objection; on the question of Sunday services they were evenly split.[50]

But not for long. As soon as the students secured one concession from the administration they immediately sought another until they achieved full freedom to seek meaning and perhaps salvation in their own distinctive ways and time. Their search for that freedom occu-

[47] Kemeny, *Princeton in the Nation's Service*, 184; PU, *Annual Report of the President (1910)*, 15.

[48] In 1914 one freshman regarded the Princeton requirements as "a 'pipe' after many years of chapel every day and twice on Sunday at 'prep' "("The Diary of a Freshman," *PAW*, Oct. 7, 1914, 47; also in *Best of PAW*, 129).

[49] *Nassau Herald* (1902), 122; (1910), 81; Weir Stuart, "The Undergraduate Week," *PAW*, Apr. 28, 1915, 707.

[50] Kemeny, *Princeton in the Nation's Service*, 183, 298n39 (*Prince* editorials); "Princeton Chapel Revolt," *New York Times*, Mar. 11, 1914, 1; Leitch, *Princeton Companion*, 86; "Compulsory Daily Chapel Opposed by Big Majority," *DP*, Nov. 4, 1914, 1.

pied nearly a half-century of substantial change, on their part and the university's. One event that accelerated their demands was the accidental burning of the stylistically eclectic but handsome and well-loved Marquand Chapel during Houseparties weekend in May 1920. The student body had outgrown the chapel's seating capacity by 1898, when two services had to be offered each Sunday. But when university services had to be moved to Alexander Hall, which some likened to a "locomotive roundhouse," the students found yet another reason to resent being forced to attend.[51]

If Marquand was too small, Alexander was too large and uninspiring. According to the *New York Times*, it offered "little atmosphere of worship because of its association with mass meetings and entertainment." President Hibben in his academic robe usually presided, seated on the stage in a canopied throne called "the buggy" by student wags. During the febrile, skeptical 1920s, when "campuses generally were not very devout" and H. L. Mencken and his *American Mercury* assailed the old pieties, "puritanism," and the Bible Belt, required chapel did not call forth the most worshipful behavior from Princeton's undergraduates. Late-risers appeared in "various states of dishabille," some dozed, and others read. Those who couldn't tolerate the aridities of Alexander fled to various town churches. But even there they had to have a card signed to certify to the dean's office their compliance with the attendance requirements. "Some called it the 'God ticket' and resented it."[52]

The prescribed displeasures of Alexander Hall came to an end in 1928 when a beautiful new chapel was dedicated on the site of the former chapel. Designed by the university's supervising architect, Ralph Adams Cram, the majestic fourteenth-century English Gothic–style edifice was at the time the largest collegiate chapel in the country, second in the world only to the Chapel at King's College, Cambridge. An eighty-yard nave and a seventy-six-foot vaulted ceiling created ample room for two thousand worshipers and a visual

[51] Sara E. Bush and P. C. Kemeny, "The Princeton University Chapels: An Architectural and Religious History," *PULC* 60:3 (Spring 1999): 317–52, at 339, 340 (photo); Nelson R. Burr '27, "Princeton in the Twenties," *PAW*, May 9, 1977, 9–14, at 13.

[52] *New York Times*, Feb. 8, 1926, 7; Burr, "Princeton in the Twenties," 13.

feast of images and allusions in its forty-five stained-glass windows.[53] To its High Church Episcopal architect, the Chapel implied and enforced "spiritual values without which education, no matter how efficient, fails of its essential purpose." Many students could agree, but cynicism ran deep in that era of intellectual disillusionment and skepticism. Campus jokesters called the Chapel "The Great White Whale," suggesting its use as a bowling alley, and the "Two Million Dollar God Box," an ironical "protest against materialism." The loudspeaker they dubbed the "speak-easy."[54]

Along with the awe-inspiring Chapel came a series of reforms meant to draw student worshipers. Replacing the president in the pulpit was Robert T. Wicks, a forty-six-year-old Congregational chaplain from Mount Holyoke College and a graduate of Hamilton College and Union Theological Seminary. At the suggestion of a trustee subcommittee, the new Dean of the Chapel, whose previous experience had been with family congregations and the well-behaved Holyoke women, instituted some changes designed with Princeton's restless males in mind. The Sunday service music program was improved, visiting preachers twice a month chose topics from student suggestions, and sermons were limited to twenty-five minutes because, as the *Prince* had once noted, the students would not tolerate services longer than an hour: "this is their religion." Another trustee suggestion—that voluntary attendance would improve the students' attitudes and conduct—went unheeded for many more years. The students' mood was not improved by their knowing that Harvard had not required chapel since 1886 and Yale had done away with its requirement two years before Wicks arrived.[55]

[53] The Chapel and its iconography are described thoroughly and expertly by former professor of the history of architecture Richard Stillwell in *The Chapel of Princeton University* (Princeton, 1971). See also Raymond P. Rhinehart, *The Campus Guide: Princeton University* (New York, 1999), 49–53; Bush and Kemeny, "The Princeton University Chapels," 343–49.

[54] Ralph Adams Cram and Frank Ferguson, "The Architects' Description of the Chapel Designs," *PAW*, Nov. 23, 1921, 179–81, at 179; Harold C. Buckminster, "Old Nassau and Heaven Too," *Nassau Sovereign* 6:7 (Apr. 1947): 18–19, at 18; Burr, "Princeton in the Twenties," 13.

[55] Buckminster, "Old Nassau and Heaven Too," 18–19; Bush and Kemeny, "The Princeton University Chapels," 349; Kemeny, *Princeton in the Nation's Service*, 4, 218; Leitch, *Princeton Companion*, 86.

Although Dean Wicks quickly earned the students' personal affection, partly by his good-natured but histrionic attacks on "SEX," "HOLLYWOOD QUEENS," "MAMMON," and students in the balcony making toast, he swam upstream against a strong current of indifference and doubt. A 1927 *Prince* poll of student religious attitudes found that when given a choice between theism and atheism, belief won out, 973 to 101. But when asked to decide between theism and agnosticism, the doubting Thomases won by a margin of 573 to 525.[56]

In 1929–1930 two events symbolized the prevailing mood on campus. First, the Philadelphian Society folded for lack of interest and because its volunteer activities were now assumed by the Student Christian Association, which was run out of the Chapel Dean's office in Murray-Dodge Hall. Second, a well-known statue of "The Christian Student," which stood near Pyne Library, was initially gilded by a sophomore and later toppled by some tippling members of '29 who were celebrating their commencement as mature adults. The life-size bronze by Daniel Chester French, who also did John Harvard in Cambridge and, more forgivably, Lincoln for the memorial in Washington, depicted a handsome if somewhat smug undergraduate in football uniform, an academic gown slung casually over his shoulder, and a pile of books tucked in his left arm like a pigskin. Rioters from a football rally pulled it over again the following year, clueless or uncaring that it had been commissioned and donated by Cleveland H. Dodge '79, close Wilson friend, major donor, trustee, and international president of the YMCA, to honor his brother Earl, also '79, football captain, honor student, and a founder of the Philadelphian Society on campus.[57]

[56] "Students Feeling Divided on Problem of Personal Deity," *DP*, Mar. 3, 1927, 1; Kemeny, *Princeton in the Nation's Service*, 200–202.

[57] Kemeny, *Princeton in the Nation's Service*, 217; Matthew M. Coburn, "The Philadelphian Society: An Investigation into the Demise of an Evangelical Student Christian Organization at Princeton University in the 1920s" (Senior thesis, Dept. of History, PU, 1991); Otis B. Bosworth '30, "The New Campus Philosophy," *PAW*, July 2, 1929, 1132–34; Leitch, *Princeton Companion*, 96–97; Clifton R. Read '29, "Revisiting the Christian Student," *PAW*, May 4, 1981, 27–29; also in *Best of PAW*, 157–60. After the second incident, the university moved the statue into storage for thirty-five years before placing it on loan at the French Museum in Stockbridge, Mass. In 1987 the "Student" was returned without incident to the lobby of Jadwin Gymnasium.

Figure 20. Daniel Chester French's lifesize statue of *The Christian Student* (1913) as it stood near Pyne Library.

The students did not stop with vandalism in their campaign to persuade the powers-that-be to free them from compulsory religion. The 1929 faculty song subtly conveyed the message:

> Here's to Reverend Bobby Wicks,
> Who came to us our souls to fix;
> Two million dollars for his house;
> To fill it up—he turns to Gauss.

(The last line is a sly reference to aptly named Christian Gauss, the dean of the college who enforced chapel attendance.)[58]

One of the regular student criticisms of the Sunday chapel requirement throughout the 1920s was that it seemed to be designed to curtail the students' weekending in New York and at the eastern women's colleges. When the university banned the student use of cars in 1927 (after a spate of fatal accidents), student suspicion only increased. To defuse it, Dean Wicks reinstituted a regular Sunday evening service as a concession to what one unsympathetic student called "the week-enders and men too lazy to get up [at eleven] for an hour morning service."[59] The unhappy students, however, realized that the dean's gesture did not address the real issue, so they upped the ante. In 1935 the *Prince* sent a Leica cameraman into the Chapel to document the quality of "worship" at a typical Sunday morning service. What he found were students "half asleep, some tying shoes and neckties, some reading the New York *Herald Tribune*, some playing Salvo, some doing lessons, and some simply gawking at the rafters." As *Fortune* magazine noted, "it clinched the case against chapel with the Board of Trustees."[60]

But not totally: only *upper*classmen were free to choose to attend or not. In keeping with its reputation for cautious (some would say glacial) responsiveness to social change, Princeton did not allow

[58] Sloane, "Present Day Trends at Princeton," 1132.

[59] Alfred S. Seshiell, "The Undergraduate Week," *PAW*, Mar. 14, 1923, 470–71, at 470; also in *Best of PAW*, 120–21 (citing the new *Prince* editorial board's screed, "Religion and the Ramrod"); "Student Life: Automobile Regulations thru 1954," Historical Subject Files (vertical), #A-109, PUA; Burr, "Princeton in the Twenties," 13 (car ban); "If I Were Running Princeton," *PAW*, May 16, 1930, 827; also in *Best of PAW*, 128.

[60] "Youth in College," 101.

sophomores to skip church until 1960 and freshmen until 1964. Although the trustees (sounding very Sixties) said they made their final decision "in the best interests of a freer, more honest, creative expression of religion," it was perhaps no coincidence that they made it just as the first class matriculated that might well have staged a sit-*out* of the Chapel to protest the last vestige of religious paternalism.[61]

The gradual abolition of chapel requirements had a predictable initial effect on attendance but less so on subsequent belief and practice, which fluctuated with national moods and student religious demography. Unlike World War I, America's "good war" in Europe and the Pacific produced few cheap cynics or "foxhole converts" among Princeton's wartime students or returning veterans. The graduating class of 1942 confessed that only 165 members had attended the university chapel at any time during their senior year, and 215 had not.[62] A *Nassau Sovereign* survey of the whole student body in 1946 elicited a more nuanced and detailed response. Only 5 percent claimed to believe in no god, and 18 percent were agnostics. Another 21 percent believed in a personal God but were not active members of any church; more than twice as many *were* active members. At the same time, nearly three-quarters thought it was not necessary to go to church to be a good Christian. If left to their own devices, only 7 percent said they would never attend church; twice that number would go every Sunday. The rest were evenly split between those who would go "seldom" and those who would attend "fairly often." And although 63 percent did not believe in miracles, equal numbers rejected the notions that modern science made Christianity "irrational and outmoded" and that "man was completely controlled by his environment and heredity."[63]

Within two years, the Chapel's new dean, Donald B. Aldrich, could report Sunday congregations of fifteen hundred, half of whom

[61] Leitch, *Princeton Companion*, 87.

[62] *Nassau Herald* (1942), 608. In 1962 a *Prince* survey found that only half of the seniors had not darkened the Chapel's doors. Landon Y. Jones '66, "On the Campus: God & Man at Princeton," *PAW*, Oct. 5, 1965, 6.

[63] "The Sovereign Survey," *Nassau Sovereign* 6:3 (Nov. 1946): 20–22, at 21.

were "volunteers."[64] Seven hundred students were members of the Chapel Fellowship, fifty preministerial students conducted daily services throughout the year, and the Student Christian Association actively pursued good works, such as helping at YMCAs and state homes for boys and conducting clothing and book drives for war-torn European countries. One of the Chapel's main draws was its eighty-voice choir under Carl Weinrich, master organist and maestro. A *Prince* critic called the chapel choir "Princeton's most distinguished musical organization . . . without question." Their singing, he said, was "comparable to a weekly opening of the Library Treasure Room."[65]

By the mid-1950s Dean of the Chapel Ernest Gordon, dauntless survivor of the River Kwai death march, was suggesting in his Scottish burr that about 40 percent of Princeton's "silent generation" were "interested" in religion and another 20 percent were perhaps "on the fringe." Yet daily chapel was confined to some fifteen "lads" and early morning communion services had been discontinued for lack of takers. A decade later, although "among Eastern collegians church-going [was] still not the 'in' thing," Sunday attendance had rebounded from the temporary loss of 400–500 newly liberated freshmen to nearly 1,000 a week, except when it shot up to 1,600 on major dating weekends. According to a *Prince* poll, the older the student, the more he read the Bible, believed in a personal deity, and attended church. Most students, however, put their religious or ethical instincts to work in secular social service, such as the Blairstown summer camp and the Trenton tutorial project. Although "phonyness" and "revivalism" were definitely out, "openness" and

[64] To put the dean's figures in perspective, many attendees were the families of faculty and townspeople. Moreover, a year later, only 20 percent of upperclassmen said their church attendance was "regular." Twice as many said it was "nonexistent," although some 80 percent of them had attended church regularly at home or school before coming to Princeton. Peter Cartwright, "Compulsory Chapel," *Nassau Sovereign* 8:8 (May 1949): 18, 26.

[65] Donald B. Aldrich, "Religion on the Princeton Campus," *PAW*, Oct. 22, 1948, 7–9; Charles Garside, Jr. '48, "The Chapel Choir—Princeton's Most Distinguished Musical Organization," *PAW*, Oct. 22, 1948, 9.

"willingness to become involved" were definitely 'in,' as the late 1960s and early 1970s demonstrated.[66]

By the end of the 1970s, however, the twin forces of secularization and religious pluralism had reduced weekly chapel attendance to only 2–3 percent of the undergraduates and limited all forms of organized religious participation to about a third of them, a figure that stood at century's end as well. It was now, a student reporter assured the alumni in 1979, "socially acceptable to profess no creed" at all; a hundred freshmen (c. 11 percent) left their religious preference cards blank. Symbolizing the new climate was President William Bowen, the first non-minister who was not descended from one. Upon taking office, he and the trustees agreed that he would not attend weekly chapel services, as all of his predecessors had done. Although he continued to support the chapel and religious life on campus, as long as they were voluntary, the secular university had arrived.[67]

One major reason for the students' low chapel involvement was the increasing diversity of their religious backgrounds. As Princeton's entering classes more closely resembled the American population, so, too, did their religious heritages and preferences. Once overwhelmingly Protestant, Princetonians were now a majority of other faiths. Catholics (c. 800) and Jews (850–900) together outnumbered Protestants (c. 875); 200–300 evangelicals and 150 Southern Baptists rubbed shoulders and minds with Eastern Orthodox, Quaker, Unitarian, and Christian Science classmates, as they would later with Muslims, Buddhists, Hindus, Mormons, and Baha'is. Needless to say, not all of these seekers were comfortable in the university's imposing cruciform cathedral. They gathered instead in Murray-Dodge Hall (where each group had an office and usually an affiliated

[66] "A Talk with Ernest Gordon," *PAW*, June 1, 1956, 15–16; Jones, "God & Man at Princeton," 6, 16; "The Religious Scene: Now Chapel Attendance Is Back Up," *PAW*, Feb. 6, 1968, 6–9.

[67] Nicholas A. Ulanov '79, "Defining the Chapel's Mission," *PAW*, Mar. 26, 1979, 15–20. In 1970, 28 percent of Princeton's freshmen had declared no religious affiliation in a national American Council of Education survey; only 13 percent of their peers at thirty-two other private universities had done so. "A Summary of Princeton Freshmen," *PAW*, Feb. 23, 1971, 7.

chaplain or part-time coordinator), in the Center for Jewish Life and its predecessors, or in town congregations, as they do today.[68]

The tribalizing of Princeton's religious identity in the past quarter century was not of great concern to the deans of the chapel (and, more recently, deans of religious life), except on the four official interfaith occasions when the Chapel played host to the whole university. The large cross behind the altar was merely the main reminder of the Christian origins and continuing spirit of the Chapel. In September 1981, at the strong suggestion of faculty and trustee committees, Princeton held its first truly ecumenical service to open the academic year. The cross was screened off and a Jewish menorah and prayer books and scriptures of several religions, including a Muslim Koran, joined a Christian chalice on the communion table. Lessons from the Old and New Testaments were read by a variety of clerics and laypersons, and the prayers and greetings were familiar to both Jews and Christians, as were the Bach and Handel anthems. From that day to this, Opening Exercises, the Service of Commemoration, the Service of Remembrance, and Baccalaureate have been celebrated in a similar fashion to welcome Princetonians of all faiths and none.[69]

If two-thirds of Princeton's students showed no interest in organized religious activities, it cannot be assumed that they were indifferent to the religious questions that perplex most people their age. As some of America's academic adepts, they exhibited intellectual

[68] Ulanov, "Defining the Chapel's Mission," 15–17, 19; A. Melissa Kiser '75, "The New Pluralism," *PAW*, Mar. 26, 1979, 20–23, 26; Kathryn F. Greenwood, "Searching for God: Students Follow Diverse Spiritual Paths to the Source of Their Beings," *PAW*, June 5, 1996, 15–21; PU, *Student Guide to Princeton, 2002–2003* (Princeton, 2002), 56–57. Yale students have followed a similar pattern. Jennifer Kaylin, "Gods & Man at Yale," *Yale Alumni Magazine*, May/June 2005, 32–41.

[69] *Report of the Faculty Committee on the Chapel* (May 1979), 8-pp. insert in *PAW*, June 25, 1979; *Report of the Trustees' Advisory Committee on the Roles of the Chapel and the Dean of the Chapel* (Nov. 1979), 8-pp. insert in *PAW*, Nov. 19, 1979; Dean Frederick H. Borsch '57, "From the Chapel: Worshipping Together in the University," *PAW*, Feb. 8, 1981, 7–9; William McCleery, "A Conversation with Joseph Williamson, Dean of the Chapel," *PAW*, May 16, 1990, 26–27.

hunger for the integrity of the search as much as for answers. Before World War II, the official curriculum offered them little help. But occasional lecture series on religious themes often drew large undergraduate audiences. In 1915, for example, during a university-sponsored "Religious Education Week," four lectures by Albert P. Fitch, president of Andover Theological Seminary, drew crowds of nine hundred to Alexander Hall. His reassuring description of a "clubable faith" compatible with modern science appealed much more than the rantings of Iowa revivalist Billy Sunday, who was denied permission to preach to the Princeton sinners. In the fall of 1922 three Princeton scientists and a Seminary expert on the Old Testament drew similar crowds to sixteen Sunday-night lectures on "Evidences of Christianity." The events, sponsored by the Philadelphian Society, had to be moved from Murray-Dodge to Alexander Hall to accommodate the interest.[70]

In 1940 the university appointed George Thomas professor of religious thought to initiate the teaching of religion as one of the liberal arts, not as proselytism.[71] At the end of the war, after Hiroshima and Auschwitz made it clear that science had much to answer for and no longer had all the answers, Princeton established a Department of Religion to facilitate a troubled generation's inquiries into the nature, history, and literature of all the world's religions, not just Christianity. By the spring of 1948, 450 undergraduates were enrolled in religion courses, which now also counted toward the distribution requirements in the New Plan of Study. In the 1960s and 1970s, when

[70] Kemeny, *Princeton in the Nation's Service*, 189, 207. In 1915 the seniors in their yearbook poll said that they would "make religion . . . more vital" if they ran the university, pointing to the "Fitch meetings" as an example of vitality. Stewart, "The Undergraduate Week," 706.

[71] In 1928 Dean of the Chapel Robert Wicks had proposed to teach a course to the freshmen to provide them with "religious conviction," but the faculty vetoed the idea. In the 1980s Dean Frederick H. Borsch '57, educated at Princeton, Oxford, and General Theological Seminary and author of four books, did teach a popular course in the Religion Department, which his successor, Joseph C. Williamson, a Harvard Ph.D., continued. Kemeny, *Princeton in the Nation's Service*, 217; Craig A. Canine '81, "New Man in the Pulpit," *PAW*, Feb. 9, 1981, 10; "New Dean of the Chapel Named," *PAW*, Feb. 8, 1989, 10; McCleery, "Conversation with Joseph Williamson," 26.

activism was all the campus rage, enrollments of 1,200–1,300 pointed to a search for religious and moral fundaments.[72]

The postwar "openness to see if religion has anything to offer" has persisted, but more as intellectual inquiry and service activity than as churchgoing. As a student columnist informed the alumni in 1965, "the Princeton student would rather find out about religion in the classroom than involve himself on Sunday." Robust enrollments in religion courses suggest that for many, perhaps most, students, religious study is still more accessible than religious experience. Lacking most of the major life-altering experiences—marriage, childbirth, aging, death—that fuel religious needs, the students understandably turn to the intellectual resources they are taught and encouraged to use in their academic "Citadel of Reason."[73] If reason and reading

[72] Carla A. Sykes, "Religious Scholarship," *PAW*, Feb. 28, 1958, 8–11; Leitch, *Princeton Companion*, 403–4. Laurance S. Rockefeller '32 was perhaps typical in searching for intellectual ballast for his fundamentalist Baptist inheritance. Arriving in Princeton with a long list of "don'ts," he came to believe that standards and values were guidelines, not absolutes. He threw himself into good works—the Student Christian Movement (of which he was president), the Philadelphian Society, and the Princeton Summer Camp (where he became a student director)—but also took every course that the Philosophy Department offered. In declaring a philosophy major, he wrote his father that "I am of the opinion that the appreciation and the desire for what is good takes more study and insight than does the understanding and taste for the best music and art." His senior thesis, "The Concept of Value and Its Relationship to Ethics," concluded that "ultimately the validity of . . . intuitions must rest on metaphysical grounds, and so are a matter of faith. It is at this dropping off place of values and facts that the basic religious experience is found" (Robin W. Winks, *Laurance S. Rockefeller: Catalyst for Conservation* [Washington, D.C. and Covelo, Calif., 1997], 31–33).

[73] Aldrich, "Religion on the Princeton Campus," 7; Jones, "God & Man at Princeton," 6; Timothy B. Cogan, "A Campus Chaplain's Views on Student Religious Attitudes," *University: A Princeton Quarterly*, no. 70 (Fall 1976): 12–16, at 12; also insert in *PAW*, Jan. 31, 1977. As American society becomes more or less religious, college freshmen can be expected to follow. A survey of 112,232 freshmen in the fall of 2004 found that most believe in God and 69 percent say their beliefs provide guidance. But fewer than half follow religious teaching in their daily lives and as many describe themselves as "doubting," "seeking," or "conflicted." Thomas Bartlett, "College Students Mix Doubt and Belief in Their Spiritual and Religious Views, Study Finds," *CHE* (online), Apr. 14, 2005. An evangelical group of Ivy League alumni, some veterans of the Campus Crusade for Christ, founded the Christian Union in 2002 seeking to "reclaim the Ivy League for Christ." By 2005 it had bought and established evangelical student centers

alone do not feed their souls and humanity full, they can join their numerous classmates who seek nourishment from a profusion of faiths, prayers, and practices.

The Intrusive World

For most American students, college historically has been a four-year moratorium on "real life," a socially sanctioned time-out for learning about the world to prepare for mature engagement with it. And for the most part, real life has kept its distance, allowing for quiet, often theoretical, contemplation of its features and foibles. But occasionally the world has intruded on the campus to confront its denizens' theories with practical challenges. Wars at home or abroad have been the usual uninvited guests, but other political or moral crises have also disrupted the normally calm campus scene. On those occasions, Princeton students, like their peers elsewhere, resorted to political action, partly to experience the first flush of adult engagement and power, partly to make a difference in the larger world, and partly to expel the intruders in order to resume their studies.

The political strategies and tactics they deployed they also learned on campus. High school or prep school politics seldom provided adequate training; student government typically lacked autonomy, budget, or consequence. Quotidian college politics offered not much more. When the world intruded, ad hoc forms of organization and response had to be forged, sometimes with the help of the faculty and administration, often by borrowing from historical predecessors or contemporary peers. Being young and inexperienced, some students—a small minority—resorted to tactics that were neither productive nor consonant with the university's fundamental frame of reason and dialogue. Yet in the end, Princeton escaped the fates of Berkeley, Columbia, and Harvard, Kent State and Jackson State in the 1970s, and emerged a much stronger, better place.

---

on or near the campuses of Cornell, Brown, and Princeton and planned others for the rest of the Ivies. Laurie Goldstein and David D. Kirkpatrick, "On a Christian Mission to the Top" (fourth article in a series on "Class Matters"), *New York Times*, May 22, 2005, 1, 22–23.

According to Princeton students, as for Americans in general, there were good wars and bad. The two world wars were considered by most students worth fighting and their causes even worth dying for. Young Tigers such as hockey star "Hobey" Baker and "Slicker" F. Scott Fitzgerald were eager to join the first fray to "make the world safe for democracy," as President and former Princeton president Wilson urged them to. They prepared patriotically in upperclass ROTC units, classes, and summer camp. Because America entered the war late, however, the disruption to campus life was relatively short-lived. Student opposition to the war was minimal before America signed on in the spring of 1917; after, it vanished.[74]

In the decade that followed, by contrast, most students at Princeton and elsewhere were politically apathetic. They worried more about personal freedom and cultural style—Prohibition, birth control, and the Bible—than socioeconomic conditions or growing international tensions. Dismayed by the ravages and human waste of World War I, they retreated into political conservatism, religious pacifism, and capitalist complacency. "Between the horror of the next war and our disgust with the last," one spokesman wrote in *Scribner's* magazine, "most of us have come not to think about war at all." Despite the faculty, *Prince* editors, and even staunchly Republican President Hibben who backed Democratic candidate John W. Davis in 1924, Princeton students (straw-)voted with their fathers for Calvin Coolidge two-to-one. But they also organized important intercollegiate conferences on disarmament and a world court and founded the National Student Federation of America, which soon expanded into a world federation.[75]

Princeton's political quiescence lasted until the middle of the Great Depression, when the growth of ROTC, social-scientific study of the "isms," and awareness of economic realities and reactionary fascism at home and abroad altered the student mood. One

[74] Willis Rudy, *The Campus and a Nation in Crisis: From the American Revolution to Vietnam* (Madison, N.J., 1996), chap. 3; *Best of PAW*, 109–10, 111, 112, 113–18.

[75] Fass, *The Damned and the Beautiful*, chap. 8, at 333, 345; *Best of PAW*, 121; Burr, "Remembering Princeton in the '20s," 13 (also in *Best of PAW*, 136); Calvin B. T. Lee, *The Campus Scene, 1900–1970: Changing Styles in Undergraduate Life* (New York, 1970), chap. 2.

goad was the prediction of Princeton graduate student Arthur French in an article in the national *Student Review* in April 1934 that "Fascism will find a readier home in Princeton than in any other university in the country." Yet the *Bric-a-Brac* that year and the next documented a proliferation of political clubs for every taste, from the right-minded American Liberty League to the left-leaning League for Industrial Democracy. Moreover, on April 12, 1935, a thousand Princetonians left their classes to show their support for a national student protest of growing militarism, arms build-ups, and fascistic nationalism. The editor of the alumni magazine was grateful that Princeton students had not yet copied "the more advanced form of the 'demonstration' . . . popular at urban universities" or bred leaders equal to their "contemporaries in Latin America." But many alumni expressed alarm when some students took the American equivalent of the Oxford Pledge—not "to fight for King and country in *any* war"—and hissed their ROTC classmates at commencement.[76]

The Princeton Anti-War Society and several religious groups opposed to war did a brisk business until Pearl Harbor was attacked on December 7, 1941, and America suddenly found itself in another "good" war, allegedly "the war to end all wars."[77] Despite President Dodds's advice to stay in school until they were called up, hundreds of Princetonians enlisted in the armed services. Among them were Terrace Clubbers Urban Rushton and Lewis Gorin, Jr., who as se-

[76] James Wechsler, *Revolt on the Campus* (New York, 1935; repr. Seattle, 1973), 428, 433; *Best of PAW*, 179–80, 181, at 180; Lee, *The Campus Scene*, chap. 3. See also Eileen Eagan, *Class, Culture, and Classroom: The Student Peace Movement of the 1930s* (Philadelphia, 1981): Robby Cohen, *When the Old Left Was Young: Student Radicals and America's First Mass Student Movement, 1929–1941* (New York, 1993).

[77] In February 1939 a *Nassau Sovereign* survey found that 75 percent of Princeton undergraduates would fight if drafted for war on foreign soil; nearly 25 percent said they would go to jail as conscientious objectors. *Nassau Sovereign* 1:4 (Feb. 1939): 16. By October, a *Yale Daily News* poll of c. 1,500 Yale undergraduates revealed that while 96 percent said they "would fight in defense of the United States proper," 95 percent were "against our entrance into conflict at this time" ("Huge Majority Votes against Joining War," *Yale Daily News*, Oct. 4, 1939, 1). See also Geoffrey Kabaservice. *The Guardians: Kingman Brewster, His Circle, and the Rise of the Liberal Establishment* (New York, 2004), 70–85.

niors in the spring of 1936 had inadvertently launched a national campaign against the "imminent" next war on the back of a malt-shop napkin. Dismayed by Congress's recent allocation of a $2 billion bonus to World War I veterans after intense pressure from the American Legion, the inventive pair formed the Veterans of *Future* Wars, whose symbol was the Statue of Liberty with her palm extended. The platform of the whimsical organization was a demand to Congress for a $1,000 bonus to all men eighteen–thirty-six who would inevitably serve in the next war, many of whom would not live to benefit from it when it fell due in June 1965. When friends in the Press Club gained the upstart VFW national attention, students around the country rushed to join. Within weeks, nearly six hundred college "posts" had been founded. Extensive media coverage and endorsements emboldened Princeton's "National Council" (other Terrace members) to issue a new plank, that before declaring war outside the United States, Congress must obtain the popular vote of at least three-fourths of the states. Few outsiders saw the humor in the eating-club confection. The National Commander of the original Veterans of *Foreign* Wars called the Tiger cubs "a bunch of insolent puppies" who were "too yellow to go to war." Another veteran simply shrugged them off with "Aw, hell, what can one expect, Woodrow Wilson came from there."[78]

In 1945, after four long years in military theaters around the globe, America's student-soldiers sought to resume their peacetime lives and studies. Again, isolationism and "privatism" settled over the Cold War nation's campuses, including Princeton. The "Silent Generation" sought other, homebound, adventures, in eating-club tap rooms, on playing fields, and at women's colleges, even in classes and senior theses. Without a large draft and with plenty of exemptions, the Korean War hardly exercised college campuses, particularly in the face of governmental Red-baiting, CIA front-funding, loyalty oaths, and Congressional witch-hunts. It was not a particularly good war, except perhaps in Washington eyes, but it was also

[78] Richard D. Challener '44, "VFW," *PAW*, Oct. 19, 1956, 13–16, at 14; Penn T. Kimball II '37, "The Veterans of Future Wars," *PAW*, Apr. 19, 1966, 12–13, 17, at 13.

not worth the risk of conspicuous protest and attention-drawing demonstrations.[79]

Vietnam was another war altogether. Not only was it a losing proposition from the outset, it was for most young Americans "the wrong war, in the wrong place, at the wrong time." The operations of the politicized Selective Service made this bad war only worse and hardened the anti-war position of most college men, particularly those on elite campuses. In the mid-1960s Gen. Lewis B. Hershey, the reviled head of Selective Service, ordered local draft boards to reclassify campus anti-war activists for immediate induction into the army, a provocative move that drew public rebuke from the Ivy League presidents and many others. After March 1966, draft deferments were reserved for full-time students who ranked in the upper half of their freshman class and even higher if upperclassmen; worse yet, the colleges were expected to furnish the class rankings. As draft calls climbed between 1966 and 1968, all graduate students and members of previously shielded occupations became suddenly vulnerable.[80] As a result, hundreds of thousands of young men, many of them on college campuses, resorted to active draft resistance and, more effectively, draft evasion, often with the help of college-funded draft-counseling centers. The installation in late 1969 of a new draft lottery system, which reduced freshman vulnerability to less than 10 percent, and the switch to an all-volunteer army as President Nixon pulled back from the unwinnable ground war the following year, restored a measure of predictability to young peoples' lives.[81]

Early in 1968, Institute fellow and former diplomat George F. Kennan had predicted that "an abandonment of the draft would alone cure a large part of the troubles of the present generation of students."[82] About those on many campuses and at Princeton in par-

[79] Rudy, *The Campus and a Nation*, 150; Lee, *The Campus Scene*, chap. 5.

[80] The National Security Council quickly reversed the Selective Service rule change and continued deferments for graduate students in engineering, mathematics, and the natural sciences. Students headed for teaching and theology also received favorable treatment. Rudy, *The Campus and a Nation*, 173, 178.

[81] Rudy, *The Campus and a Nation*, 171–81, at 171.

[82] George F. Kennan, *Democracy and the Student Left* (Boston, 1968), 161; the text was originally delivered at the dedication of a new library at Swarthmore College and

ticular, he was only partly right because the war was only one of several sources of student discontent in the long Sixties. Distrust of the "immoral" Washington "war machine" was certainly key at Princeton as elsewhere. But a variety of war-related and unrelated issues came together to raise up a small minority of radical agitators, spearheaded after 1962 (after 1965 at Princeton) by the Students for a Democratic Society (SDS), and to mobilize at times a sizable majority of students.

While America was embroiled and increasingly stymied in the jungles of Vietnam, battles were being fought at home over racism and civil rights for blacks and other minorities, equal rights for women, and the environment. From another part of the world, apartheid in South Africa claimed attention, particularly of students who sought to use their colleges' endowments—through disinvestment—to leverage their moral outrage at the behavior of a foreign government. Fueling these student passions over national and global concerns were several hot-button local issues. While fearing a call from their draft boards, many Princetonians verbally and sometimes physically protested the insulting disparity between the draftable age to kill (eighteen) and the legal age to vote and drink (twenty-one). As freshmen were being declared adults by the federal government for geopolitical purposes, college officials denied them coed classmates, female visitors in their dorms after absurdly early hours, and the right to drive and park in Princeton proper. As the language of "rights" filled the political air, students, too, sought and increasingly fought for their own freedoms from paternalistic oversight. As their world seemed to spin further out of their control, they understandably sought more input in the decisions that immediately affected their lives. The growing need to keep "alienation" at bay, the search for moral certainty (which often led to moral absolutism and intolerance), and the drive to shake loose and seize any reins of power they could made for several years of tension and often volatility on college campuses, including Princeton's.

---

published as "Rebels Without a Program" in the *New York Times Magazine* on January 21, 1968.

In the carefree spring of 1963, before John Kennedy, Martin Luther King Jr., and Robert Kennedy were assassinated, student power at Princeton was applied primarily to lifting Volkswagens, breaking windows on the "PJ&B" train, and tearing down the iron fence around the president's home at Prospect.[83] By the fall of 1967, however, undergraduate (and occasionally graduate) energies discovered the perfect local symbol of the "military-industrial complex's" ability to "pollute" even the wells of academe. The Institute for Defense Analyses (IDA), a nonprofit think tank for the Defense Department sponsored and manned by twelve major research universities, had been housed since 1962 in a rented university building near the Engineering Quad. Because of Princeton's membership, President Goheen sat on the Institute's board.

When the SDS chapter learned that the IDA was writing research reports for the Pentagon on such topics as "Tactical Nuclear Weapons" and "Interdiction of Trucks from the Air at Night," they launched a pamphlet and petition offensive and, over the next few years, led several demonstrations against the facility in attempts to drive it off campus, if not out of business. Since the Institute was only leased from the university, its own unarmed guards and local police handled the protests, almost always without violence. One of the few casualties was the youthful university dean of students, Neil Rudenstine, who was accidentally decked by a frustrated staff member in an entrance-way mêlée. Until Princeton canceled its membership in IDA and Goheen managed to effect an early cancellation of its lease, many students earned their "radical" stripes on the IDA barricades.[84]

[83] Since Princeton was not yet coed, panties had to be "liberated" from the local Choir School. "Spring Riot," *DP*, May 7, 1963, 1, 4.

[84] Seema Anita Misva '92, "End of Innocence: Student Empowerment in the '60s," in *The Orange & Black in Black & White: A Century of Princeton Through the Eyes of* The Daily Princetonian (Princeton: DP, 1992), 89–91; Richard K. Rein '69, "The Rise of Student Power," *PAW*, May 23, 1972, 8–9, 13–14; John V. Dippel '68, "On the Campus," *PAW*, Oct. 31, 1967, 4; Edward R. Weidlein III '68, "On the Campus," *PAW*, Nov. 7, 1967, 6; "University News," *PAW*, Oct. 22, 1968, 7; Robert K. Durkee '69, "On the Campus," *PAW*, May 13, 1969, 6, 16; Chris Connell '71, "On the Campus," *PAW*, May

If the SDS sometimes led Princeton's largely middle-of-the-road-to-liberal students in protest, Presidents Johnson and Nixon did more to agitate them into mass action. As the United States became hopelessly mired in Southeast Asia and the military body count soared in the late 1960s, teach-ins, faculty and student protest votes, and noisy but relatively modest student demonstrations against the war punctuated academic routine. The demonstrators often lumped local with international concerns, which diffused their focus and reduced their staying power. Black students, now being admitted in greater numbers, had their own issues and sought to keep the white SDS radicals at arm's length.[85]

Frequently, these various demonstrations congregated in front of Nassau Hall in hopes of gaining an audience or leverage with university officers or the assembled trustees within. When the powers-that-were could or would not grant the crowd its wishes off the cuff and on the spot, the impatient students on a few occasions swarmed into the marble vestibule, the sacrosanct Faculty Room, or a dean's office and plopped themselves down for an increasingly predictable sit-in. Much to Princeton's credit, these invariably ended with a decanal reading of university rules and sanctions and a thoughtful clean-up of the premises by the withdrawing occupiers.[86] When an SDS protest leader ruefully admitted that "we don't believe anyone can radicalize Princeton," he predicted well. Unlike schools such as Co-

---

26, 1970, 6–7; "IDA Must Stay," *PAW*, Jan. 26, 1971, 4; "New Home for IDA," *PAW*, Dec. 7, 1971, 4; Susan Williams '74, "On the Campus," *PAW*, May 23, 1972, 7.

[85] On a wintry March 11, 1969, the Association of Black Collegians led a peaceful takeover of administrative and financial offices in the New South highrise on the South Campus to protest the university's refusal to disinvest in corporations doing business in South Africa. When a few SDS supporters came inside, partly to escape the cold, the moderate black leadership invited them to leave, which they did. As Jerome Davis '71, ABC's coordinator, characterized his group's stance toward SDS-style confrontation and threat, "This is Princeton, not Dodge City" (Durkee, "The Black Culture," *PAW*, June 3, 1969, 8–11, 16, at 16; W. H. Earle II '69, "On the Campus," *PAW*, Apr. 22, 1969, 6, 18).

[86] Weidlein, "On the Campus," *PAW*, May 21, 1968, 20–21; *PAW*, Apr. 18, 1972, 4; Robert Earle '72, "On the Campus," *PAW*, May 9, 1972, 8–9.

lumbia, Harvard, and Kent State, which were "seriously wounded" by resort to force and violence, Princeton never called—and never had cause to call—the local or state police, much less the National Guard, to quell its student unrest.[87]

Princeton survived the febrile Sixties through a delicate combination of reasonable compromise, firm principle, and astute leadership at all levels that earned the trust of a student body "too reasonable and too fair-minded" to be led "around by the nose" by "the genuinely Yahoo elements on the student left."[88] Even the anguish and outrage provoked by Nixon's extension of the war into Cambodia did not close the university or lead to mayhem. Unlike many universities that participated in the resulting national strike against the war, Princeton remained open and hosted a series of mass community assemblies in the Chapel and Dillon Gymnasium to allow a thorough venting of issues, positions, and psychic steam.[89]

Princeton also provided a "constructive alternative to violence" by launching a faculty-inspired grassroots "Movement for a New Congress" to support anti-war and other reform-minded candidates. To avoid the suspicion of the IRS, the university itself merely rented rooms in the basement of Palmer Hall (now the Frist Campus Center) to the MNC's student volunteers who coordinated the activities of some 36 regional and 400 local offices around the country.[90] But

[87] Dippel, "Student Power," *PAW*, Feb. 6, 1968, 10–12, 15, at 11; Interview with Dean Neil Rudenstine "On Student Activism," *PAW*, Nov. 18, 1969, 8–9, 15, at 9. On Ivy League universities less fortunate, see Robert A. McCaughey, *Stand, Columbia: A History of Columbia University in the City of New York, 1754–2004* (New York, 2003), chaps. 15–17; Roger Rosenblatt, *Coming Apart: A Memoir of the Harvard Wars of 1969* (Boston, 1997): Kabaservice, *The Guardians*, chaps. 9–10.

[88] Robert Earle, "On the Campus," *PAW*, May 9, 1972, 9.

[89] Connell, "On the Campus," *PAW*, Oct. 21, 1969, 8–9; Peter G. Brown '70, "On the Campus," *PAW*, Oct. 28, 1969, 5, 8–9; "Princeton Vietnam Assembly," *PAW*, Nov. 25, 1969, 10–11; Brown, "On the Campus," *PAW*, May 19, 1970, 6–7; Landon Y. Jones, "The Events of May," *PAW*, May 19, 1970, 8–13; Robert Earle, "On the Campus," *PAW*, May 9, 1972, 8–9.

[90] Jones, "The Events of May," *PAW*, May 19, 1970, 11; Brown, "Movement for a New Congress," *PAW*, May 26, 1970, 12–13; Luther T. Munford '71, "On the Campus," *PAW*, Oct. 6, 1970, 5; S. Frederick Starr, "The Princeton Plan," *PAW*, Oct. 13, 1970, 6–7 (a

with faculty approval, the administration also inserted in the venerable academic calendar a two-week fall break—soon reduced to one—before the fall elections to enable politically concerned students to work in campaigns at home or in New Jersey.[91]

Princeton took two other unprecedented steps in the angry spring of 1970 that earned the students' trust and helped to moderate their passions. First, the faculty, for the first time in its history, voted on a national political issue, 261–12 against the war, because they believed that America's military recklessness abroad threatened fundamental liberties and the fabric of civil society at home, which were essential to the proper functioning of colleges and universities. Apart from this single exception, Professor of History Lawrence Stone noted, Princeton preserved "the political neutrality of the university as an institution . . . with great care."[92] Many students were disappointed that they couldn't enlist the institution more fully in their partisan causes, but most came to respect the consistency and integrity of the university's position.

The faculty and, more reluctantly, the trustees also voted for the future withdrawal of ROTC from campus. President Goheen preferred the faculty position of March 1969: no academic credit for ROTC courses, no ROTC grades used to determine academic standing, ROTC staff designated as visiting lecturers rather than professors, and the ROTC departments reduced to programs. The air force and the navy found even these conditions unacceptable and voluntarily withdrew in 1971 and 1972, respectively. After a thorough vetting of student opinion and reconsideration, the trustees again voted in favor of retaining the army program, largely for the sake of

---

shorter version appeared in the *New York Times*); Joseph L. Lincoln '70, "Princeton Plan Analyzed," *PAW*, Nov. 17, 1970, 7, 15.

[91] In 1973 the national voting age was dropped to eighteen, so virtually all undergraduates were enfranchised. The New Jersey drinking age also dropped to eighteen in the same year.

[92] In the previous fall, the faculty had voted 371–19 against in an informal poll. *PAW*, June 9, 1970, 11; Lawrence Stone, "Princeton in the Nation's Service," *PAW*, June 30, 1970, 1–6, at 6 (the essay appeared originally in the *New York Review of Books* on June 18, 1970).

the students who obtained generous scholarships for their commitment. As the war drew to a close and the draft disappeared from their lives, most students came to tolerate, if not respect, their few uniformed classmates.[93]

The university was also responsive to student concerns on more local but no less pressing issues. In 1967 all undergraduates were allowed, for the first time in forty years, to bring cars to school. Parietal rules were greatly loosened and then abolished in 1968–1969 to allow distaff visitors at any hour and off-campus living. In the fall of 1969, women moved into Princeton to stay. To further mark its modernity, the university also switched from an antiquated five-group grading system to the more familiar A–F.[94] But the biggest changes came in response to student demands for a voice in university decisions that affected them, if not total "student management of student affairs."[95]

At Reunions in 1969 the Alumni Council announced the newest alumni trustees: Brent Henry '69, who had participated in the respectful ABC occupation of New South, and Richard Cass '68, both Woodrow Wilson School graduates and students at Yale Law School. Their election initiated a new plan by which a graduating senior each year would be elected to the board by the two upperclasses and the two most recently graduated classes.[96]

Of even greater symbolic and practical moment was the creation in May 1969 of the Council of the Princeton University Community (CPUC or U-Council). The product of a Committee on the Structure of the University, eight faculty and seven students chaired by Professor of Politics Stanley Kelley, CPUC was a large "deliberative body with unrestricted opportunity to recommend action to any de-

[93] Jones, "Taps for ROTC," *PAW*, Sept. 29, 1970, 8–9; "ROTC Inquiry," *PAW*, Jan. 26, 1971, 5–6; Jones, "ROTC Marches Back," *PAW*, Feb. 1, 1972, 10–11; "ROTC Report," *PAW*, Sept. 26, 1972, 8.

[94] Weidlein, "On the Campus," *PAW*, Sept. 26, 1967, 6 ("Cars Permitted"); *PAW*, May 7, 1968, 6; "Letters" (Dean of Students Neil Rudenstine), *PAW*, Nov. 30, 1971, 3; "We Have Gone Coed," *PAW*, Apr. 29, 1969, 7.

[95] Dippel, "Student Power," *PAW*, Feb. 6, 1968, 10–12, 15; Weidlein, "On the Campus," *PAW*, May 7, 1968, 6.

[96] "New Trustees," *PAW*, July 1, 1969, 9–10.

cision-making element of the University." Its fifty-seven members included representatives from every constituency of the university; nearly 40 percent of the seats were held by undergraduates and graduate students. Working through several standing committees, such as Judicial, Priorities, and Governance, the council devoted—and still devotes—long monthly meetings (widely reported in the *Prince*) to sorting through the university's most vexing problems and offering timely advice that carried much weight with policymakers. During what may have been Princeton's "most perilous spring [1970] in a century," CPUC's lengthy meetings gave students "confidence that they were being listened to" and played a major role in helping the university to weather the political firestorm. Since then it has also served to inform administrators of potential sources of discontent before fuses and lids blew.[97]

In addition to the major restructuring effected by the Patterson (coeducation) and Kelley committees, a large, multigenerational Commission on the Future of the College, chaired by sociologist Marvin Bressler, was appointed in November 1970. After two-and-a-half years of study, it issued a 436-page report on the whole academic side of undergraduate life, from admissions, diversity, and college size to curriculum, teaching, and evaluation. Much of what Princeton already did well was confirmed and several reasonable changes were instituted. But many impractical suggestions, in tune with the prevailing pedagogical zeitgeist but inappropriate for Princeton, were largely ignored by the administration or roundly rejected by the faculty. Equal admissions access for men and women, the addition of a D to the pass-fail grading option, and the creation of a separate program in theater and dance met with approval, but

[97] During the tensest times in the late 1960s, the Kelley Committee issued two preliminary reports to inform the students in particular that meaningful reform was underway. The first, thirty-six pages long, came in mid-November 1968, six months after the appointment of the committee; the second appeared in May 1969 with an initial set of recommendations. The final 166-page report was published in May 1970, well after the effective work of the Council had begun. Durkee, "On the Campus," *PAW*, Dec. 10, 1968, 4, 24; "A Peaceful Revolution," *PAW*, June 3, 1969, 7; "Kelley Report," *PAW*, May 12, 1970, 6–9, 13; Jones, "Two Cheers for the University Council," *PAW*, June 1, 1971, 12–16; E-mail from Patricia Marks, former member of CPUC, Aug. 12, 2005.

an early start to the academic year and the report's major recommendation—a three-year curriculum—were quickly defeated.[98]

By the time the Bressler Report was published in April 1973, however, the war had ended and the draft had been eliminated. On campus the mood was exhausted relief and apathy as the students turned inward and back to their quotidian studies and pleasures. The five-year-old prediction of SDS leader Richard Fried—that "almost all student movements would fold ten weeks after the war ended"—had indeed been realized at Princeton.[99] But they had not folded on many other campuses, primarily because their administrators and faculty had not listened carefully to the full range of student voices, not just a vocal minority, or succeeded in educating and actively engaging the students in the responsibilities of running a complex institution with carefully defined purposes and mandates, as Princeton's had. "Princeton was the envy of most campuses," former president William Bowen remembered in 1995. "While we had stresses and strains, the fabric of the university was never torn. It remained one university, and even people who disagreed vehemently by and large respected each other."[100]

Other universities had played to student sympathies by giving honorary degrees to crusaders and countercultural celebrities such as Coretta Scott King and Bob Dylan, as Princeton did at its cicada-filled June commencement in 1970.[101] But few had taken so seriously and responded so positively and carefully to the real concerns and sensible demands of their students. Unlike most research universities, Princeton's unusual focus on undergraduate education, its close faculty-student involvement and rapport made possible by its luxurious student-faculty ratio, and its smart, tough, caring, and collegial administrators, combined with an equally smart and independent-

[98] PU, *The Report of the Commission on the Future of the College* (Princeton, Apr. 1973); "Highlights from The Report . . . ," *PAW*, May 15, 1973, between 14 and 15; "Bressler Commission," *PAW*, Oct. 8, 1974, 8. An extensive survey of the classes of 1954, 1964, and 1969 for the report was also published in *PAW*, Mar. 4, 1975, 9–12.

[99] Williams, "On the Campus," *PAW*, May 15, 1973, 7; Dippel, "Student Power," *PAW*, Feb. 6, 1968, 12.

[100] Tom Krattenmaker '70, "Season of Discontent," *PAW*, May 10, 1995, 17–22, at 20.

[101] "Honorary Degrees," *PAW*, June 30, 1970, 10.

minded student population, enabled it not only to survive the Sixties but to mature impressively, setting the stage for its steady academic ascendance on Bowen's fifteen-year watch.

One key issue did not get resolved, at least to some students' satisfaction, during the long and active Sixties. Black students in particular remained unhappy that the university would not disinvest in South Africa, even after President Bowen explained at length and with great precision, on numerous occasions, the complex issues involved, the principle of institutional neutrality, and the economic consequences of doing so.[102] Beginning in the spring of 1978 and continuing into the early 1990s, this and a variety of other, more local, issues sporadically propelled groups of protesters into Nassau Hall for sit-ins, as if the students were in search of historical valorization from their more pugnacious predecessors. Mostly the demonstrations fizzled.[103]

But the latest revival of student activism at Princeton took an imaginative turn in the spring of 2005 and earned it "The Protest of the Year" award from, appropriately, *Mother Jones* magazine, a left-leaning product of the Sixties.[104] When majority leader of the Senate William Frist '74 threatened to abolish the filibuster to prevent Democrats from blocking the appointment of ideologically extreme candidates for the federal bench, Princeton students launched a filibuster of their own in front of the Frist Campus Center, built with $25 million from Senator Frist and his family. Bucking "rain, cold weather, and harassment by inebriated Republicans," its sophomore creator said, the "Fristbusters" read, sang, and rapped for 384 continuous hours, attracting national media attention and "copycat protests on 50 campuses in 35 states." After the gabfest moved to Washington

[102] William G. Bowen, "The Case Against Divestiture," *PAW*, May 22, 1985, 24–26 (also in *Ever the Teacher: William G. Bowen's Writings as President of Princeton* [Princeton, 1987], 29–36).

[103] Danny Hoffman '94, "Turning Back the Tide: The Revival of Activism in the '80s," *The Orange & Black in Black & White*, 97–98; "The Nassau Hall Sit-In" issue, *PAW*, Apr. 24, 1978; "Nassau Hall Blockade" (letters), *PAW*, May 22, 1985, 6, 8, 11; "Nassau Hall Sit-In," *PAW*, Mar. 8, 1989, 12–13; Matthew T. Henshon '91, "On the Campus," *PAW*, June 13, 1990, 7.

[104] *Mother Jones* (online), Sept./Oct. 2005.

and held a final press conference in front of the Capitol, the Senate majority agreed to drop its "nuclear option" and the Democrats to be sparing in their resort to the filibuster.[105] Once again, the student mouse that roared proved to be, however briefly, a Tiger.

Pranks' Progress

Much of Princeton's student culture resembled that found on college campuses across America. It certainly had its own flavor and accent, but young Tigers were members of a national peer group and consumers of a national youth culture before and during their four-year stay in Princeton. Although their dress, dialect, religious behavior, and political activism all took on local coloring from the campus environment, the basic elements of their culture were widely shared. The most distinctive and original aspects of Princeton's student culture were its customs, traditions, and rituals. In form and function they, too, resembled counterparts on other campuses. But their content and performance were decidedly indigenous, which bound the students ever more tightly to their tribal identity as Princetonians.

The initiation of new students, interclass rivalry, rebellion against authority, the building of class spirit, and the sheer letting off of age-specific or academic steam are standard reasons for the formation of college traditions, long familiar to social anthropologists who study rites of passage and other aspects of group formation and maintenance in other "tribal" settings.[106] But each tribe goes about them in

[105] Ashley Johnson '05, "On the Campus," *PAW*, June 8, 2005, 17; Asheesh Kapur Siddique '07, "For Students, a Sense of Empowerment," *PAWPlus* (online), June 8, 2005; Dylan S. Hogarty '06, "Let's Have a Real Debate, Not Obstruction," *PAWPlus* (online), June 8, 2005.

[106] Helen Lefkowitz Horowitz, *Campus Life: Undergraduate Cultures from the End of the Eighteenth Century to the Present* (New York, 1987); Simon J. Bonner, *Piled Higher and Deeper: The Folklore of Campus Life* (Little Rock, 1990); Michael Moffatt, "Inventing the 'Time-Honored Traditions' of 'Old Rutgers': Rutgers Student Culture, 1858–1900," *Journal of the Rutgers University Libraries* 47:1 (1985): 1–11; Moffatt, *Coming of Age in New Jersey*; Arnold van Gennep, *The Rites of Passage*, trans. Monika B. Vizedom and Gabrielle L. Caffee (Chicago, 1960); Vizedom, *Rites and Relationships: Rites of Passage and Contemporary Anthropology* (Beverly Hills, 1976); Joseph Kett, *Rites of Passage: Adolescence in America, 1790 to the Present* (New York, 1977); Ray Raphael, *The*

ways that express its distinctive values, tensions, and goals. Princeton was no different. Many traditions began in the nineteenth century, and some still persist, though often in modified form. Several died natural deaths for lack of student interest or because they no longer performed a useful function in the ever-changing campus culture. And sometimes new traditions were born, because student imagination and daring continued to transform one-time pranks into durable customs.

To put the new freshmen in their place in the campus hierarchy, early-twentieth-century sophomores resorted to *horsing* in addition to enforcing the all-black dress regulations. Horsing was a milder form of hazing, which had made freshman lives miserable throughout the nineteenth century and much of the eighteenth. Hazing, as the sophomore class admitted in 1898, was "any molestation, intimidation or dictation to the members of the Freshmen class." After the near-drowning of a freshman during hazing in 1894, the students themselves gradually reduced hazing to horsing and placed its management in the hands of the Senior Council.[107] Easily identified by their dinks and dark duds, freshmen were made to perform acts of silly humiliation, often in small groups. When Ernest Poole arrived in 1898, he was told to "make love to a horse's hind leg" (which carried its own dangers) and, while perching on a gatepost, to "read the tenderest passages of 'Romeo and Juliet,' replacing Romeo's name by [his own], and Juliet's by that of stout Mrs. Doogan, who scrubbed floors in a dormitory close by." Seven years later, greenhorn Harold Medina was made to "scramble like an egg" in the middle of unpaved Nassau Street. His classmates had to do tricks like "performing Salomé's dance" in a tissue-paper skirt, "swimming on the sidewalk," and "milking a bicycle as though it were a cow." Others

---

Men from the Boys: Rites of Passage in Male America (Lincoln, 1988); David Berreby, "It Takes a Tribe," *New York Times Education Life*, Aug. 1, 2004, 22–23, 36; Rebekah Nathan [Cathy A. Small], *My Freshman Year: What a Professor Learned by Becoming a Student* (Ithaca, 2005); Nathan, "An Anthropologist Goes under Cover," *CHE*, July 29, 2005, B11–13.

[107] Elizabeth Greenberg, "Barely Remembered: A History of Princeton University Prank Traditions" (Senior thesis, Dept. of History, PU, 2002). (Thanks to Ms. Greenberg for a copy of her thesis and of her junior paper on a similar topic.)

ten years later hung their coats on air hooks and then wore them home inside out.[108]

In retrospect, most freshmen probably agreed that, as nonsensical and occasionally mean as it could be, horsing did "bring the boys together. They get excited," confessed one critic, "talk over their experiences, and it breaks the ice." For many homesick high schoolers and shy small-towners, it was the first thing they had in common with their classmates, at a time when "fitting in" was all-important. If a few "obnoxious" fellows were treated roughly, even "driven out," and others from big, well-known prep schools or promising athletes with husky friends got off lightly, those, too, were lessons in social education.[109]

Horsing died of natural causes over the summer of 1914, as Europe's guns of August made themselves heard even in pastoral New Jersey. But "to curb [the freshmen's] spirits and to make them realize that they are Freshmen in Princeton and not Seniors in a preparatory school," the Senior Council renewed the regulations embodying many of the "traditional customs" aimed at the newcomers. Freshmen were not allowed to smoke on the campus or on Nassau Street. They had to remain in their rooms after the 9:00 p.m. curfew bell. Tossing a baseball or football on campus (except on the athletic field) was prohibited. Walking on the grass or on Prospect Avenue, McCosh Walk, or in front of Nassau Hall, much less riding a bicycle, was an affront to upperclass dignity. Sitting around the Mather Sundial, the senior's preserve since its erection in 1907, was even worse. These and many of the dress restrictions were still going strong in the 1920s, when the freshman handbook published them annually as "unwritten laws" that a sophomore "Vigilance Committee" would enforce under the aegis of the Senior Council.[110]

[108] Benn, *Columbus—Undergraduate*, 21; Ernest Poole, *The Harbor* (New York, 1915), 50; J. Woodford Howard, Jr. *59, "Judge Medina's School Days," *PAW*, June 5, 1988, 22–25, at 23; also in *Best of PAW*, 90–94, at 92; Gauss, *Through College on Nothing a Year*, 36–37. For pictures of horsing and hazing, see Wheaton J. Lane, ed., *Pictorial History of Princeton* (Princeton, 1947), 130–31.

[109] "1909 Alumni Recall Campus in Wilson's Day," 10; Gauss, *Through College on Nothing a Year*, 37–38, 89–90.

[110] Stewart, "The Undergraduate Week," *PAW*, Sept. 30, 1914, 13–14; also in *Best of PAW*, 108–9; "College Customs for Freshmen in 1923," *PAW*, May 7, 1997, 39.

A year after horsing was pastured, another venerable species of interclass rivalry met its demise. For some forty years, *rushes* pitting the whole freshman class against the sophomore phalanx were an annual fall event. As the initial horsing period subsided, the freshmen secretly scheduled a meeting in old Dickinson Hall or the gymnasium to elect class officers. But the sophomores, catching wind of the date, sought to keep them out. The black-sweatered frosh, coached by the juniors, charged the white-shirted sophs blocking the way. "It was always a battered, clothesless group which elected equally bedraggled officers."[111]

The *Cannon Rush* was similar, except that the day was widely advertised. When night fell, the sophomores congregated at the large Revolutionary cannon buried muzzle down in the quadrangle behind Nassau Hall. In the flare of torches and fireworks, they attached a heavy leather belt around the cannon with ropes radiating from it like the spokes of a wheel. "They packed themselves in between the ropes," said a bipartisan veteran of two campaigns, "and the whole mass revolved slowly around the cannon, singing 'Oh we'll whoop'er up for Oughty Nine, etc., or whatever their class was, to give them courage and strike terror into the hearts of the Freshmen." The sophomore class president stood on the cannon with a length of rope in his hand to ward off any invaders who tried to usurp his position. Coached again by junior tacticians and often spearheaded by football linemen, the freshmen launched attacks from three directions. When the battalions met, "it was like colliding trains of cars"; the front ranks were actually "lifted into the air by the shock." Broken bones, torn clothing, and bloody noses were the usual casualties of war, but in 1915 one frosh with a weak heart died in the mêlée, which brought the brutal tradition to an abrupt end.[112]

[111] Lane, *Pictorial History of Princeton*, 133–34; William Zinsser, "Why Freshmen Have High Voices," *Nassau Sovereign* 4:1 (Oct. 1941): 12–13, 42, at 13; "Letters from a Self-Made Son," no. 3, p. 10.

[112] Leitch, *Princeton Companion*, 79–80; "The Diary of a Freshman," *PAW*, Oct. 7, 1914, 48; also in *Best of PAW*, 129–30, at 130; Poole, *The Bridge*, 55–56; James W. Alexander, *Princeton—Old and New: Recollections of Undergraduate Life* (New York, 1898), 27–28; Jesse Lynch Williams, *The Adventures of a Freshman* (New York, 1899), 32, 38, 40; "Letters from a Self-Made Son," no. 3, p. 10. After the cannon rush in 1906, "some enterprising, if slightly dishonest, Sophomores and upperclassmen made the rounds of the Freshman boarding houses and took up collections to straighten the cannon which

The goal of all these interclass clashes was to develop class spirit, to "cement the class into a solid unit."[113] This they did. But when they vanished or were erased from the scene, other traditions had to be reinforced or substitutes found, until the whole notion of class spirit became less important. For fifteen years the freshman class picture was such an occasion for continued, if less strenuous, class rivalry. Beginning around 1911, the freshmen assembled in their Sunday best on the steps of Whig Hall to be photographed. One earnest naïf put on his best blue suit, a fine new collar, and a dapper little bow tie and headed for the appointment. Having heard that the post-horsing, post-rush sophomores would pelt them with "flowers" by way of reconciliation, he had visions of pink carnations floating down as the photographer clicked away. Instead, he and subsequent generations (who heard better and came dressed down for the event) found themselves bombarded from the roof by paper sacks of *flour*, sand, eggs, treacle, and rotten fruit, all washed down with hosewater. The pictures taken in "Decorating 101" (as it was dubbed) were unlikely to have been sent home with any great frequency or pride.[114] Yet when the Senior Council tried to abolish the *Flour Picture* and other freshman customs in 1923, the undergraduate protest, especially from the Class of 1927, was so loud that they were immediately restored. Three years later an annual tug-of-war between the first- and second-year classes was substituted for the picture taking.[115]

The one steady sport that epitomized the underclass rivalry was the *Cane Spree*. In modified form it is still contested today, by men and women from each class, making it the oldest extant undergraduate tradition and perhaps the oldest intramural event in the country.

---

had been bent in the rush! They made quite a good thing of it too" (Brown Rolston '10, " 'The Good Old Days': Student Life and Customs in the Wilson Era," *PAW*, Jan. 15, 1960, 6–9, at 7; also in *Best of PAW*, 99–102, at 100).

[113] Rolston, "The Good Old Days," 7; Williams, "The Great Freshman-Sophomore Rush," *Adventures of a Freshman*, 41; Williams, *Princeton Stories*, 5–6.

[114] Gauss, *Through College on Nothing a Year*, 67–68; Benn, *Columbus—Undergraduate*, 23–24; Zinsser, "Why Freshmen Have High Voices," 13; Lane, *Pictorial History of Princeton*, 131, 134; Oberdorfer, *Princeton University*, 114–16; Greenberg, "Barely Remembered," 10; Burr, "Princeton in the Twenties," 11.

[115] Burr, "Princeton in the Twenties," 12.

FIGURE 21. Sophomores "decorate" the freshmen assembled on the steps of Whig Hall in the annual Flour Picture (c. 1920s).

It began in the 1860s, when freshmen sought to emulate their academic seniors by carrying fancy carved canes.[116] The jealous sophomores naturally sought to prohibit their use by such unworthies, which quickly led to individual wrestling matches for their possession. The class that seized the most canes got its way with the swagger sticks. By the 1870s, three pairs of spreers (light-, middle-, and heavyweight) would wrestle on behalf of their classes. But delegation did not prevent mass battles from erupting between and after the scheduled matches. These violent free-for-alls, staged at night on the lawn near Witherspoon Hall and in later years on the athletic field, led to numerous injuries to person and property.[117]

After 1892 the spree became part of an organized fall athletic program, for which elimination matches between seriously trained athletes determined the final contestants. Yet "full-fledged riots" continued to accompany the events. In the 1930s these were particularly brutal. The pre-war *Prince* published the official instructions, including "Dangerous missiles are not to be used by participants" and "After the conclusion of the Cane Spree, there will be no parading in the streets in an undressed condition." The latter warning was necessary because a mighty effort was made to disrobe the enemy, usually by ripping his clothes to shreds. As with a famous later event, this led to a certain amount of sportif spectating by both jeering upperclassmen and cheering townspeople.[118]

After World War II, the intramural athletic department took charge of the annual fall field day still called Cane Spree. Since canes went out of fashion in Wilson's day, the interclass tussle is now for a straight hickory stick and is conducted according to strict rules to prevent injury. No longer can it be said, as it could in the 1890s, that "to win a cane for one's class [is] an honor of a lifetime." Class spirit

[116] For a photograph of three elaborate nineteenth-century canes, see Oberdorfer, *Princeton University*, 88.

[117] Greenberg, "Barely Remembered," 14–21, at 21; "The History of the Cane Spree," *PAW*, Mar. 8, 1911, 349–50; T. E. Schulte, "Princetoniana: The Cane Spree," *Nassau Sovereign* 4:2 (Nov. 1941): 22; Alexander, *Princeton—Old and New*, 28–31; Lane, *Pictorial History of Princeton*, 132; Oberdorfer, *Princeton University*, 88.

[118] Greenberg, "Barely Remembered," 16–18; George H. Vaught, "Cane Sprees," *Nassau Sovereign* 8:1 (Sept. 1948): 16. See also Jesse Lynch Williams, "The Winning of the Cane," *Princeton Stories* (New York, 1895), 3–35.

has taken different, more subdued forms, and the spree itself now consists of seventeen events, such as tennis, swimming, field hockey, badminton, soccer, softball, volleyball, ultimate Frisbee, and tug-of-war, the final event of the day. Although the other events gradually became coeducational or offered both men's and women's competitions, cane wrestling remained all-male until 1993, when several doughty women talked their way into the fray. Thus the level of participation has again risen to pre-war levels, but the class rivalries are directed into "more modest and less sanguinary channels."[119]

Occasionally a custom emerges that involves only a few students but gains a surprising hold on a class's imagination and spirit. *Stealing the clapper* from the cupola bell atop Nassau Hall was one such prank that became a long, strong tradition for Princeton freshmen. Soon after the bell was hung in 1756, it became the target of undergraduates of all classes who resented its minute regulation of their daily lives, from the pre-dawn call to chapel to the equally early signal for curfew. When the clapper was stolen by a junior in 1864, the janitor had to strike the bell with a hammer until a replacement could be obtained.[120]

Even when the bell ceased to micromanage the students' lives, it was rung hourly, to announce classes, and to mark special university occasions. Silencing it by derring-do and stealth remained a challenge reserved by custom for freshmen. In 1898 a nostalgic alumnus remembered that in his day the class that failed to achieve this feat was "considered beneath contempt." Although the freshmen still were so regarded and would continue to be for some time, their class's failure to make off with the fifty-pound iron trophy entailed major loss of face through most of the twentieth century. In 1993 campus opinion-makers remembered (albeit incorrectly) that until the administration had ended the tradition two years earlier, "only the class of 1961 failed to obtain the clapper from its resting spot." Sixty-one had plenty of company, but the charge stung nevertheless.[121]

[119] Greenberg, "Barely Remembered," 20–21; Vaught, "Cane Sprees," 16.

[120] Greenberg, "Barely Remembered," 21–22.

[121] Greenberg, "Barely Remembered," 23–30; Leitch, *Princeton Companion*, 331–32; Alexander, *Princeton—Old and New*, 34; "First-Years Seek Out New Tradition to Replace Quest for Bell Clapper," *DP*, Sept. 17, 1993, 1, 5.

FIGURE 22. Triumphant clapper thieves J. D. Sparkman, J. P. Crutcher, J. Rockefeller, and J. C. Wright (all '52) display their booty and equipment before the silent bell tower of Nassau Hall in 1948.

Despite the high cost of clapper replacement and the danger of personal injury to the young cat burglars, the administration was ambivalent about and often inconsistent in dealing with the crime. In its paternalistic mode, it sought to support the class-inspiriting tradition. It restricted the game to freshmen and to one theft a year, but came down harder on offenders from other classes, especially those who exceeded the booty limit. From time to time, proctors and administrators were actually complicit, by leaving key doors unlocked, looking the other way while the caper was in progress, or securing the clapper with a simple nut and bolt instead of a permanent weld as publicized. It was also a well-known secret that the university kept a ready supply of replacement clappers.[122]

Until the 1970s, entry to the bell tower was largely an inside job, through Nassau Hall. When the administration finally managed to secure the bell tower against internal assault, freshmen newly talented in rock-climbing (often through the new Outdoor Action pre-orientation program) began to ascend three stories up the exterior walls and over a tricky overhanging slate roof to reach the prize. This understandably worried the university more because of the potential danger to life and limb and the liability that might result from a bad fall or accidental death. Firm believers in their own immortality, the freshmen showed no similar fears and continued their "self-indulgence," as President Harold Shapiro was to call it. Even after the bell ringing had been electrified in 1962 and the university sponsored a diversionary (and short-lived) freshman clapper hunt on the ground, the first-year classes sought to maintain their honor, prodded by upperclassmen who told them that "our class would be the laughingstock of the campus if we didn't steal the clapper."[123]

Finally, after numerous (mostly minor) injuries, near-misses, and increasingly foolish gang assaults on Nassau, the university reluctantly removed the clapper from the bell, after carefully recording its peals for playing henceforth from speakers on neighboring East Pyne

[122] Clinton Meneely '30, president of the family business that made the 1857 replacement bell, said that "his firm received more orders for clappers for the Princeton bell than for any other bell in the firm's history" (Leitch, *Princeton Companion*, 332).

[123] Greenberg, "Barely Remembered," 23–29.

Hall. Today the real Nassau bell, reclappered briefly for each occasion, rings for only a few university events annually, such as Baccalaureate, Commencement, Class Day, and the Reunions P-rade, when all the classes are reminded by its tintinnabulations of the heady pride or mild shame they once earned as freshmen.[124]

If the freshmen had their clapper caper to build class spirit, sophomores had the *Nude Olympics*. This act of midwinter madness certainly upped the ante in sheer chutzpah for nearly thirty years before succumbing to the kind of student excess and university liability jitters that killed the freshmen's sport not long before. It, too, began with a few brazen participants, but gradually built a "modest" class clientele and a much larger following of spectators and even state and national media. It was terminated in 1999 by an administration for which the event had created a public relations nightmare, a strain in town-gown relations, and a serious danger to many of its participants, especially women.

"The Nude Olympics was born at the intersection of many 1960s social movements," notes historical authority Elizabeth Greenberg '02, "from the counterculture and student rebellion to the 'playboy' philosophy, women's liberation, and the sexual revolution."[125] But all-male Princeton had a long tradition of naked exhibitionism before the Olympics got its semi-official start in 1970 and its name from the *Prince* two years later. The rugby team was famous for its annual springtime "jock runs" through campus, wearing either athletic supporters or nothing at all. Beginning in the mid-1960s, a "Red Baron," dressed only in World War I flier's helmet, ski mask, gog-

[124] Greenberg, "Barely Remembered," 29–30; "Bell in Nassau Hall Falls Silent as Proctors Seek to End Clapper Thefts," *PAW*, Oct. 23, 1991, 5–6. The student urge to scale campus buildings persists, despite stern administrative warnings. In 2004 a renewed phase of "buildering" struck Princeton. Encouraged by online climbing communities at Yale and other universities, Tigers mounted Pyne Hall and dreamed of conquering taller structures. Their ultimate goal was Nassau Hall because, one said, "The University has taken away so many traditions, and bringing back the clapper tradition would be great" (Elyse Graham, "Students Secretly 'Builder' Campus," *DP* [online], Sept. 30, 2004). For an earlier phase, semi-sanctioned by the administration if ropes were not used, see Susan Williams '74, "On the Campus," *PAW*, Nov. 14, 1972, 7.

[125] Greenberg, "Barely Remembered," 44–98, at 44.

gles, cape, and footwear, irregularly flew through large final-exam venues to alleviate the takers' stress (and maybe his own). After a hard day of Housepartying in 1966, Cannon Club members and their dates staged a post-midnight nude volleyball game. And random, late-night "streaking" across campus was not uncommon before and after the advent of coeducation.[126]

The Olympics, however, originated in and were long confined to Holder Courtyard, until 1982 an underclass precinct. Typically, at midnight on the first snow of the year, a few hardy men, fortified by warming spirits, dropped their clothes between neck and ankles and proceeded to cavort in the raw (weather) with calisthenics, wheelbarrow and relay races, Frisbee tossing, and an especially daring bonfire jump. When Holder went coed in 1971–1972, women cheered the athletes as loudspeakers, lacking the yet-unwritten "Chariots of Fire" theme, boomed out Wagner's "Ride of the Valkyries" and other "bombastic classics." By 1974, the short-lived national "streaking" craze had inspired not only more interest in the Olympics but a new "tradition" of skinny-dipping in the Woodrow Wilson School fountain.[127]

Until the mid-1980s, the event featured only thirty or so participants and attracted only local news coverage and minimal administrative attention. It was confined to Holder courtyard, except for a few breakaways into Firestone Library to give weary "grinds" an eye break. But since the mid-1970s a few women had joined in the frolic, which changed its dynamic as much as the 1983 raising of New Jersey's drinking age. The temptation to thumb one's sophomore nose at two serious taboos proved less and less resistible. By 1985 the Dionysian Olympians had multiplied to over a hundred, the spectators to four times that number, and T-shirts celebrating the event were hot items. In 1990 nearly 30 percent of the 200 buff athletes were women; the following year 100 women joined 300 male classmates for the follies. The combination of insobriety and nudity inevitably led to incidents of "hurtful and rude sexual behavior." This prompted public warnings from the Women's Center, student government, and

[126] Greenberg, "Barely Remembered," 49–50, 55.

[127] Greenberg, "Barely Remembered," 51–60.

SHARE, the university's sexual harassment education office, that "*women who participate in the Nude Olympics have not abdicated their right to be respected.*"[128]

Another change for the worse was escape from the Holder quadrangle. By 1990 the crowd had spilled onto Nassau Street, where they ran through bars, stores, and late-night eateries, even the staid Nassau Inn. This drew the unwanted attention of the local constabulary and the predictable glare of wire service and television coverage, none of which the university needed as it pursued its ambitious 250th Campaign among the alumni. When property damage and arrests for lewdness were added to the usual cases of frostbite, broken bones, and alcohol poisoning, the end of the Olympics was near, despite its status as a "necessary, defining moment of class identity."[129]

Despite earnest attempts by the university to control the event and to confine it to Holder, the crowds grew larger and less predictable. In January 1999, after a snowless and Olympics-free previous year, the mass assembly of nude revelers in Holder was so large and inexperienced in Olympic protocol that they just "ran amongst themselves." The result was innumerable acts of egregious sexual harassment, gross behavior, and even fornication, and large amounts of property damage to Rockefeller and Mathey Colleges, which bordered the courtyard. Having recently settled a $300,000 lawsuit with a former student who, in a drunken stupor, had climbed on top of the Dinky shuttle train, been electrocuted, and lost three limbs, the university was in no mood to risk further liability from a tradition that had clearly become counterproductive and dangerous to its participants. After the usual careful study, the administration regretfully closed the books on the Nude Olympics.[130]

[128] Greenberg, "Barely Remembered," 61–73 at 73.

[129] Greenberg, "Barely Remembered," 73–83; Greg Phillips '93, "On the Campus: Tracking a Once and Future Tradition: The Nude Olympics in Fact and Fiction," *PAW*, Mar. 18, 1992, 10–11, at 11.

[130] Greenberg, "Barely Remembered," 83–98. In an open forum during Reunions in May 2004, an alumnus from the Class of 2000 tried to make a case to President Shirley Tilghman for reinstituting the Nude Olympics. He argued that the current ban implied that Harvard students, who streak annually on their campus in January, are more mature than Princeton students, to which Tilghman replied, "Nice try" (*PAW*, July 7, 2004, 12). In December 2004 a new coed "Princeton University Varsity Streaking Team" barely

❁ ❁ ❁

One of the verities of college life is that undergraduate traditions come and go with some frequency. Yet to hear alumni and some current students tell it, all losses are regrettable and sure signs of the decline of campus culture and class spirit. The birth of "new" traditions is seldom recognized and hardly celebrated until they gain some weight and age. During the past century, Princeton traditions have come, stayed, and gone, in unequal proportions. More have disappeared from the scene, for three reasons: the administration outlawed them as too dangerous or beneath the dignity of a great university; the students themselves lost interest in maintaining them and found other ways to meet their social and emotional needs; and even short-term interruptions of academic life, such as world wars, broke the chain of student memory upon which tradition depends.

Despite the loss of several traditions, new ones emerged and old ones were modified to accommodate new generations and conditions. As American society and the university became less hierarchical and social relations less formal, Princeton freshmen could walk on Prospect Street and all campus sidewalks and sit around the Mather Sundial. They could dress, if they wished, in college colors, yellow slickers, or the latest college "uniform." They could palaver in the latest patois to prove they were not *dorks*, *dweebs*, or *meatballs*. They did not have to wait until senior year to sing on the steps of Nassau Hall, no more than they did to win a starting position on a varsity team, to sit in a front pew of the Chapel, or to take 400-level courses. They alone could participate in Outdoor Action programs before school began. And as they left the Chapel after Opening Exercises, beginning in September 2004, they participated in a new version of an old tradition: their own P-rade. Dubbed the "Pre-rade" by its sponsors, the Undergraduate Student Government and the three up-

---

made its debut. It was outlawed by the administration by late spring after being disgraced by a preemptive performance by the coed Hamilton College team in broad daylight. Grace Labatt, "Dare to Bare All," *DP* (online), Feb. 3, 2005; Sara Lipka, "Winning Streaks," *CHE*, Mar. 18, 2005, A6; May 6, 2005, A6; Viola Huang, "Streaking Team Disbanded," *DP* (online), Apr. 20, 2005.

perclass presidents, the freshmen exited the campus near the library, turned left up Nassau Street, and entered the newly refurbished FitzRandolph Gate, to the applause of the upper classes.[131]

At the same time, they could not bicker an eating club, major in the Woodrow Wilson School, write a JP (junior paper) or senior thesis, win the Pyne Prize for academic distinction, or wear a beer jacket. Like all other students, they had to wait until Commencement to exit the FitzRandolph Gate onto Nassau Street without jeopardizing their degrees and to march with their class in the P-rade. If by then they did not identify with a two-digit class or honor the university's tribal traditions, sacred and profane, they still had a chance to assimilate—convert—by reading the *Alumni Weekly* sixteen times a year and attending Reunions in a garish orange-and-black costume at least once every five years.

[131] Alexander Maugeri, "CPUC: Malkiel Details Implementation of Grade Plan," *DP* (online), Sept. 28, 2004; e-mail from Dean of Undergraduate Students Kathleen Deignan, Feb. 7, 2005. Early in the previous century, the freshmen used to march in their own P-rade. Adlai Stevenson '22 reported to his mother in October 1918 that on Saturday "at 3:00 all the regular freshmen [many were still in Army and Navy units] assembled in front of Witherspoon hall for the annual freshman P-rade. We P-raded around the campus singing Princeton songs and cheers. . . . We then went to the steps of Whig Hall for the freshman picture" (*The Papers of Adlai E. Stevenson*, ed. Walter Johnson, 8 vols. [Boston, 1972–1979], 1:69 [Oct. 27, 1918]).

Another relatively new tradition surrounds Dean's Date, the 5:00 p.m. deadline for delivering papers to faculty offices. In 2000 sophomore Rakesh Satyal began the tradition of handing out paper clips, staplers, and other supplies in McCosh Courtyard to students racing toward faculty offices. When he graduated in 2002, he requested administration help in continuing the event. By 2005 the Dean of Undergraduate Students office provided drinks and popcorn and the University Band offered appropriate tunes to run by. Hundreds of students attended to enjoy the end of a long week of paper-writing. E-mail from Kathleen Deignan, Feb. 7, 2005. See also Alexie Rothman, "University Community Develops New Traditions as Old Fade," *DP* (online), Jan. 10, 2005.

CHAPTER SEVEN

Higher Learning

[A graduate school] will do more than any other one thing to increase Princeton's reputation in the world of learning.

—Woodrow Wilson

For Andrew Fleming West it was a day of triumph long postponed. Ever since his appointment as Dean of the Graduate School in 1900, he had planned (and later plotted) for a magnificent medieval residence for his advanced students, well removed from the high-jinks of the undergraduate campus, and he had finally realized his ambition. As brilliant fall sunshine bathed the courts and towers of Ralph Adams Cram's design, "the best example of Collegiate Gothic ever done in this country" most agreed, three thousand guests witnessed one of "the most distinguished events in American academic history" to that time. The dedication of the Graduate College had been carefully planned to the last detail by the dean himself, just as he had orchestrated Princeton's university-launching sesquicentennial in 1896. As one European guest whispered to another, "these people" did indeed "have a genius for ceremonial."[1]

The festivities had begun on Monday, October 20, 1913, with four lectures by gray eminences from Oxford, Cambridge, Berlin, and Paris, each in his native tongue. The following evening three hundred academic guests dined under the soaring hammer beams of Procter Hall, with its stained-glass windows, oak wainscoting, and English-style high table. After-dinner speakers recounted the pre-

[1] "The Dedication of the Graduate College," *PAW*, Oct. 29, 1913, 87; Cram quoted in Thorp, *PGS*, 163; Arthur E. Shipley, "The Graduate College at Princeton," *PAW*, Nov. 19, 1913, 175–77, at 177.

West years when Princeton's few graduate students were, in "a certain sad and servile" sense, "beggars," forced to room and board as they could in the small country town. Former president Francis Landey Patton, on whose watch West had been appointed, warned against overspecialization and trivial research at the expense of "large general culture," and denied that "the highest intellectual development" was necessarily incompatible with "luxurious surroundings." "There will be a mental uplift in the very architectural environment in which [the student] lives," he predicted. Thanks to the donors' generosity, the luxury of the college (including semi-private bathrooms—"*more Americano*") was available to every graduate student for as little as $300 a year, as President John Grier Hibben was quick to assure the well-fed assembly.[2]

The dedication ceremonies on Wednesday morning eclipsed all the others in academic pomp. Over a hundred delegates from European and American colleges, universities, and learned societies, mostly male peacocks in polychromatic caps and gowns, processed into the main quadrangle behind President Hibben, ex-president Patton, outgoing U.S. President William Howard Taft, donors Moses Taylor Pyne '77, and William Cooper Procter '83, legal representatives of deceased donors Josephine Thomson Swann and Isaac C. Wyman '48, and, of course, a happy Dean West. Under the baton of Leopold Stokowski, the Philadelphia Orchestra played Tchaikovsky and the university choir sang a Latin hymn. After architect Cram passed the keys of the college to President Hibben, the audience stood while preacher Patton launched an interminable dedicatory prayer; when it was printed in the alumni magazine, it consumed forty-two column inches over four pages. This ordeal was immediately followed by Dean West's briefer address on "The Household of Knowledge," which he would deliver annually to the College inmates until he retired in 1928. As a cure for the "mediocrity of mind," premature professionalism, "persistent illiteracy," ungeneralized spe-

[2] *PAW*, Oct. 29, 1913, 113, 114, 116; Shipley, "The Graduate College," 176. The best rooms went for $450. Unfortunately, despite an endowment for operations, annual costs rose 32 percent by 1919. *Annual Report of the President . . . 1919, Official Register of Princeton University*, 11:2 (Dec. 1919): 52 (hereafter *President's Report* [year]).

cialization, and lack of "proper" provision for the "physical and social welfare" of American graduate students in the liberal (as opposed to professional) studies, he hoped that the new college would promote the "daily fellowship of kindred minds of rare promise, generous rivalry and high aspiration" and the interdisciplinary "communion which reveals the unity of knowledge."[3]

After a handful of congratulatory speeches by academic guests from far and near, the majestic 173-foot Cleveland Memorial Tower, built in part with pennies collected by America's schoolchildren, was dedicated by Republican President Taft, who handsomely eulogized his Democratic predecessor. With lunch and other needs on everyone's mind, the final introduction of a minister who had graduated from Princeton at the outbreak of the Civil War must have caused some concern. But he surprised them with a forty-three-word benediction upon the College and the deed was done. Dean West had his Gothic dream-house on a knoll overlooking the Springdale golf course, which its residents would soon dub "St. Andrew's-on-the-Links."[4]

One figure was conspicuous by his absence from the triumphal proceedings. When West drew up the guest list, he had the good sense not to ignore former president Woodrow Wilson, now in his first year in the White House. But West, we can be sure, also wanted to make his former friend squirm at his decanal victory, knowing full well that Wilson in his pride would not appear at the scene of his last and worst academic defeat. Although they had begun with virtually the same ideas in 1896, Wilson and West gradually formed sharply different visions of Princeton's graduate school, especially its

[3] *PAW*, Oct. 29, 1913, 87–94, at 94; Thorp, *PGS*, 174–76, 183. On dedication day, Princeton University Press published in book form a revised, expanded, and illustrated version of West's article in *Century Magazine* as *The Graduate College at Princeton, With Some Reflections on the Humanizing of Knowledge*. It adumbrated his philosophy of liberal education and aspirations for the Graduate College. It was probably given to the academic delegates as a keepsake.

[4] *PAW*, Oct. 29, 1913, 89–90, 95–103; David R. Coffin, *Princeton University's Graduate College* (Princeton: PU, Office of Communications, [2000]); Raymond P. Rhinehart, *The Campus Guide: Princeton University: An Architectural Tour* (New York, 1999), 130–43.

FIGURE 23. Aerial view of Ralph Adams Cram's striking Graduate College, overlooking the Springdale golf course: Cleveland Memorial Tower (near entrance), Procter (dining) Hall (far left), main Thomson Court (all completed in 1913), and North Quad (upper right), added by soap magnate William Procter in 1927.

character and location. West consistently sought to build and oversee a sumptuous Graduate *College*, like those he had seen and romanticized in Oxford and Cambridge. Wilson, on the other hand, although initially he had no major objection to such a facility if funds were available, was soon persuaded that gathering a distinguished faculty was the best and perhaps only way to thrust the Graduate *School* into national prominence.

They also came to differ strenuously over the ideal location for such a college. Initially, both had favored a central location on campus so that graduate seriousness and scholarship could stimulate the undergraduates. But West soon came to favor an off-campus site, both to protect the graduate students from undergraduate distractions and to nurture their "high thinking," not in "plain living" or "unsocial isolation," but in a "beautiful, even . . . stately home" of learning and culture.[5] In large measure, the history of Princeton's graduate school until the 1960s was framed by these competing visions.

❁ ❁ ❁

After Wilson returned to Princeton as professor of jurisprudence and politics in 1890, it was no surprise that he and "Andy" West became "cordial, personal friends." Besides their Princeton degrees, they had a great deal in common. Both were loyal family men, witty raconteurs given to puns and limericks, and generous to friends and extended family. They both believed in "liberal culture" and the primacy of the liberal arts college; both admired Oxford, especially its tutorials and its college system. Both were more English men of letters than Germanic scholars, stylists rather than deep researchers. They both preferred to lecture to undergraduates than to mix it up with graduate students in seminars. But underlying their eventual split was another strong resemblance: both were deeply religious sons of Presbyterian ministers, with somewhat Manichean views of right and wrong, friends and foes. Once they clarified their goals and made up their minds, they were tenacious and stubborn combatants.[6]

At that point, however, their styles diverged. Wilson's evangelical righteousness led him to direct, sometimes precipitous, action. He sought to win support for his policies largely through "eloquent speeches and compelling ideals." West, on the other hand, worked behind the scenes among friends and personal contacts, earning a reputation among admirers and critics alike as a "political intriguer," a veritable "Tammany politician" who loved to meddle in university affairs.[7] After watching West undermine Francis Patton's presidency,

[5] West, *The Graduate College*, 28.

[6] John D. Davies, "The 'Lost World' of Andrew Fleming West '74," *PAW*, Jan. 15, 1960, 10–14; John M. Mulder, *Woodrow Wilson: The Years of Preparation* (Princeton, 1978), 203–4.

[7] Mulder, *WW: Years of Preparation*, 204; Stockton Axson, "*Brother Woodrow*": *A Memoir of Woodrow Wilson*, ed. Arthur S. Link (Princeton, 1993), 71, 136; Henry W. Bragdon interviews with Oscar Veblen, June 9, 1939 (box 63, folder 54); Williamson U. Vreeland, Mar. 24, 1940 (box 63, folder 57); Charles Grosvenor Osgood, Apr. 14, 1939 (box 63, folder 24); Winthrop Daniels, Mar. 30, 1940 (box 62, folder 28), WWC.

Wilson became convinced that West was "not entirely to be trusted," with good reason. After Wilson himself assumed the presidency in 1902, West proved "by far the more skillful intriguer. No college president ever had to face a more resourceful and dangerous personal antagonist," one who was, according to their mutual friend Bliss Perry, "both unscrupulous and relentless."[8] As Wilson admitted more than once after leaving Princeton to tangle with state and national party pros, "those politicians are just children beside Andy West."[9]

The trouble began effectively when "Andy" West—"63 inches around the vest" as the seniors saw him—was appointed dean of the Graduate School by the trustees in December 1900 and took office the following September. His powers were radically different from those of most graduate deans, then or now. He was appointed solely by the trustees, he had jurisdiction over every aspect of graduate life and teaching, he appointed his own faculty committee (one of whose initial members was Wilson) merely to advise him, and he reported not to the president but to the trustees' Standing Committee on the Graduate School, of which he was an ex officio member. He asked for and was given this extraordinary authority to prevent the administratively lazy and somewhat "reactionary" incumbent, President Patton, from impeding the progress of graduate education. Predictably, under a more forceful and reform-minded president, the graduate dean's constitutional independence would prove a serious source of conflict.[10]

The new dean certainly had his work cut out for him. Earned doctoral degrees had been awarded at the College of New Jersey since 1879, but they were a small portion of the forty-eight doctorates handed out in the next twenty-two years; the rest were honorary.

[8] Bliss Perry to Ray Stannard Baker [RSB], Nov. 12, 1925, Baker Papers, container 113, reel 81, pp. 8–9; Bliss Perry, *And Gladly Teach: Reminiscences* (Boston and New York, 1935), 144, 158.

[9] Bragdon interview with Charles W. McIlwain, Jan. 2, 1940 (box 63, folder 11, p. 4), WWC; William Starr Myers, "Wilson in My Diary," in *Woodrow Wilson: Some Princeton Memories*, ed. Myers (Princeton, 1946), 47. Most of the following text to 394 is taken from my article, "The Dilettante Dean and the Origins of the Princeton Graduate School," *PULC* 62:2 (Winter 2001): 239–61.

[10] Thorp, *PGS*, 65–68.

FIGURE 24. Dean Andrew Fleming West, in a 1906 portrait.

The great majority of graduate students under presidents James McCosh and Patton were Princeton Theological "Seminoles," supplementing their theology with one or two courses in classical languages or philosophy next door, or master's degree students seeking an extra year or two of study before entering a profession.[11]

[11] Thorp, *PGS*, 37, 374n26. McCosh gave graduate study a major push in the late 1870s in an effort to propel Princeton toward university status. But his trustees blocked both efforts at the end of his tenure, thus promoting a counterrevolution under Patten.

The push toward a formalized graduate school had been gathering momentum since McCosh's later years, and particularly since the college's sesquicentennial celebration in October 1896, for which West raised $1.3 million and edited a large commemorative volume.[12] By declaring and renaming itself a university, Princeton was obliged to act like one. A faculty memorial to the trustees less than two months later, written by a small committee that included "Tommy" Wilson (as his classmates called him), argued that "the Graduate College"—then used synonymously with Graduate *School*—"is not only the proper completion of our Academic System, but is necessary if Princeton is to maintain its place as one of the leading American Universities."[13]

But when Wilson became president in 1902, both he and West made it clear to the trustees that Princeton had made very little progress in earning university status and, indeed, had fallen behind its old, and several new, rivals. Wilson was blunt: while Harvard and Yale had been transformed into true universities, Princeton had not kept pace and had "fallen out of the list"; and "while she lingered" newer institutions—Cornell, Johns Hopkins, and Chicago—had "pressed in ahead of her." West supplied the harsh facts: among nine comparable graduate programs in liberal studies, Princeton ranked sixth in the number of male graduate students (the women at other schools obviously did not count), sixth in library holdings, seventh in the number of graduate instructors, eighth in the number of graduate fellowships, and dead last in graduate scholarships (because it had none). As everyone in the administration realized, Princeton's "first and most obvious need" as a university was a greatly improved graduate school.[14]

J. David Hoeveler, Jr., *James McCosh and the Scottish Intellectual Tradition: From Glasgow to Princeton* (Princeton, 1981), 285–86, 295–97, 326–27, 338–41; Thomas Jefferson Wertenbaker, *Princeton, 1746–1896* (Princeton, 1946), chaps. 9–10.

[12] Thorp, *PGS*, 56; *Memorial Book of the Sesquicentennial Celebration of the Founding of the College of New Jersey and of the Ceremonies Inaugurating Princeton University* (New York, 1898).

[13] Faculty Memorial to the Trustees, c. Dec. 2, 1896, in *PWW*, 10:68–71. See also Thorp, *PGS*, 58, 59–60.

[14] Wilson, Report to the Trustees, Oct. 21, 1902, in *PWW*, 14:157; Thorp, *PGS*, 70.

Such a major enterprise would not come cheap. In a handsome book, *The Proposed Graduate College of Princeton University*, published early in 1903, Dean West put the price tag at a walloping $3.1 million, at a time when the Princeton endowment was under $2.9 million. His breakdown of costs made it clear that his title again referred broadly to the Graduate School. As he had more than once since writing his *Brief Account of Princeton University* in 1893, West acknowledged that a body of "eminent professors" was the "one true foundation" on which the Graduate School must be built. For fifteen new professorships at competitive salaries, the university would need an endowment of nearly $1.9 million. To endow at least forty graduate fellowships to attract the brightest and best from Princeton and other colleges would require another half-million dollars. But the feature that was and would remain closest to the dean's heart—at a cost of "at least" $600,000—was a residential quadrangle or Graduate *College*.[15]

Ever since West toured Europe for the first time in 1881 and again at the trustees' expense in 1902, he had been unduly impressed by the romantic "charm" of the Gothic architecture and bucolic settings of European universities, especially Oxford and Cambridge. There he found, in his own flushed words, "quadrangles enclosing sunny lawns, towers and gateways opening into quiet retreats, ivy-grown walls looking on sheltered gardens, vistas through avenues of arching elms, walks that wind through the groves of Academe . . . places where the affections linger and where memories cling like the ivies themselves." All of this he wanted to transplant to Princeton, largely to answer what he was certain were "the immemorial longings of academic generations back to the time when universities first began to build their homes."[16]

[15] [Andrew Fleming West], *The Proposed Graduate College of Princeton University* (Princeton, 1903), 20; *PWW*, 14:156 (general and special endowments as of Oct. 21, 1902).

[16] *The Proposed Graduate College*, 15; for West's sponsored tour in 1902, see 7, 10–11, 13, 15; "Professor West's Journey," *PAW*, Jan. 24, 1903, 263–64; *PWW*, 14:139–40, 245–46. On June 9, 1902, the full board of trustees, at the recommendation of the Standing Committee on the Graduate School, authorized $2,500 in private funds for West "to be used in promoting the establishment of the Graduate College" and requested him "to visit the European Universities in order to collect such material for a report on recent developments in higher instruction abroad as will be of service in commending

West was certainly not alone in his romanticization of Oxbridge. On two English bicycling trips in the late-1890s, Wilson had been equally smitten, as had many other faculty members on their own pilgrimages. So it is no surprise that when the university issued *Plans and Sketches of the New Buildings Erected or Proposed for Princeton* in 1897, the dominant architectural mode was Collegiate Gothic. The proposed plans included a quadrangle for the graduate school, "set at the heart" of the campus (where the Chapel and McCosh and Dickinson Halls now stand).[17] In a plan that hardly varied before it was realized sixteen years later, West envisioned an Oriel, Balliol, or Magdalen in southern New Jersey, replete with entrance tower, great dining hall, kitchen, servants' quarters (one Oxford-style "scout" for every five students), commons and breakfast rooms, master's house and garden, and individual suites for a hundred students, each with bedroom, large study, fireplace, built-in bookcases, window seat, and attached bathroom.[18] As President Wilson wrote in his first report to the trustees in October 1902 and repeated verbatim in his preface to West's *Proposed Graduate College* four months later, the dean's plan was "not merely a pleasing fancy of an English college placed in the midst of our campus;" but it was assuredly a fancy, one that fed West's imagination and drove his ambitions more than any other aspect of graduate education.[19]

Given West's own recognition of Princeton's urgent need for graduate fellowships and professorial endowments, we are left to wonder why he pressed so strongly for a somewhat luxurious—or, as he put it, "well-appointed"—residential college. The faculty memorial in 1896 made no mention of a building and compared Princeton only to other "graduate *schools* . . . in our greater Universities"; and

the plan for the Graduate College" (Minutes of the Trustees, vol. 10 [1901–1908], 163, [PUA]). West sailed on August 16 and returned on December 21.

[17] Thorp, *PGS*, 59–60.

[18] *The Proposed Graduate College*, 10–11, 18–19.

[19] *PWW*, 14:157–58; *The Proposed Graduate College*, preface (my emphasis). For the American infatuation with English Gothic colleges, see Alex Duke, *Importing Oxbridge: English Residential Colleges and American Universities* (New Haven, 1996); Lester F. Goodchild, "Oxbridge's Tudor Gothic Influences on American Academic Architecture," *Paedagogica Historica* [Ghent] 36:1 (2000), 267–98.

it pleaded for funds only for "two graduate professorships and several University fellowships." Within months, however, the faculty committee—after a signal substitution of West for Wilson—began to refer to the Graduate College as a physical structure as well. By 1903, in his *Proposed Graduate College*, West still talked about endowing professorships and fellowships, but he now argued that a "stately" quadrangle was "an *equal* necessity."[20]

West's public arguments for a tangible college differed somewhat from the private one he used with the trustees. In his published sales pitch, he tickled Princeton's pride with a challenge to build something truly new and "unique" in America: "a residential college devoted solely to the higher liberal studies." Such a place would centralize "all influences," concentrating the life of every student in his work, presumably away from undergraduate frivolity. But West fudged his description to imply that the college would also be a place of *instruction*, for "constant contact of an intimate personal character with professors of marked ability, sympathy, and efficiency." And the deciding factor—after good salaries—in persuading those professorial paragons to move to Princeton would be the new "environment," particularly the building in which, West said, they and the graduate students were to "*live* and *work*."[21]

Yet the Graduate College was never intended to house more than the occasional bachelor professor or to serve any curricular purpose. The 1897 plan mentioned that "*perhaps*" it might include "some small lecture halls *adjoining*," presumably in a separate building. But lecture halls were not what "intimate" graduate seminars required, and neither they nor any other classrooms were mentioned again in any of West's plans. A decent scholarly library might have served a pedagogical purpose as well, but it, too, went unmentioned, perhaps because the new Pyne Library, built in 1897 at the center of the undergraduate campus, was quickly outfitted with separate "seminaries," or reading rooms, for each graduate department.[22]

[20] Faculty Memorial to the Trustees, c. Dec. 2, 1896, in *PWW*, 10:69, 70, 70n1; *The Proposed Graduate College*, 7, 8, 9.

[21] *The Proposed Graduate College*, 8–9.

[22] Thorp, *PGS*, 60, 61–62 (my emphasis). As late as 1939–1940, William K. Prentice and Williamson U. Vreeland regarded the Graduate College as nothing but a glorified

It requires very little reading between the lines to realize that West's primary argument for a residential college was *social*, not intellectual. He was convinced that in the past twenty or thirty years American graduate schools had lost their ability to compete with the professions and business for the cream of the college crop, those young men with the "best brains," "strongest characters," and "finer spirits." Moreover, too many of the students entering graduate school were what he characterized as "erratic men of mediocre general abilities" whose specializations became "narrowly intense," lacking the "breadth of vision and richly diversified cultivation" of Europe's scholarly scions. The dean wanted to counter both trends by attracting "the *right kind* of men" to the scholarly life, which he would do, he told his committee frankly, by attending to their "physical and social comfort." But the way he couched his plan publicly was to insist that "the building in which they live and its surroundings should be the visible symbol of that dignity and charm which ought to accompany and enrich their life."[23] Whether graduate students should lead a *charmed* life would soon become a hotly contested issue on the Princeton campus and in the town's drawing rooms.

West's public reasons for a graduate college were also a gloss on a much more chauvinistic reality. The real reason West believed he needed a residential college was twofold: first, Princeton was "the only large old college [located] in a very small town," which lacked suitable or sufficient lodging and board even for its thirty-five bona fide graduate students; and second, twenty-two of these students had been recruited from Princeton's own senior class. West did not have to—but did anyway—remind the trustees that Princeton undergraduates had become accustomed to elegant eating clubs and new Gothic dormitories. Because he wanted only graduate students of "*fine* personal and intellectual quality," the products of "liberal *culture*"—*fine* and *cultured* were his two favorite adjectives—he was

dorm and boarding house without a "real library" or labs. Bragdon interviews with Prentice, June 6, 1939 (box 63, folder 31) and Vreeland, Mar. 24, 1940 (box 63, folder 57), WWC.

[23] *The Proposed Graduate College*, 9–10, 13–14; Dean's Report to the Trustees' Standing Committee on the Graduate School, June 2, 1903, Records of the Committee, series 5, box 49, PUA.

confident that "such students must be drawn from our own graduates." "It would be hard," he asserted with pardonable if myopic pride, "to name twenty [of the five-hundred-some American colleges] whose diplomas we could receive as acceptable in place of the Princeton diploma." Although fifty-five colleges were currently represented in the total graduate student population of 124 men, "the majority of them," West complained, "do not furnish an education which may be as approximately equivalent to that provided in our undergraduate course," particularly the institutions that produced the eighty-nine men who came over from the seminary.[24]

At this point Wilson and West were still friends and reading from the same text. Wilson, too, believed in "liberal culture" and in the strength, if not superiority, of the Princeton degree. He, too, had the Graduate School and even a residential graduate college as priorities in his grand plan to make Princeton the best university in the country. But graduate education, which involved fewer than forty degree candidates (compared with nearly thirteen hundred undergraduates), was not—could not be—at the top of his list. He needed to reform and revivify the undergraduate curriculum and the faculty first. In these tasks he had the willing and apparently wholehearted cooperation of his graduate dean, whose formative experience and essential loyalty lay in the undergraduate college nearly as much as Wilson's did. When the trustees sent West to Europe in 1902 to examine graduate colleges, he was also glad to oblige Wilson by looking at the Oxbridge tutorial system as a possible model for what in 1905 became Wilson's famous preceptorial innovations. When he returned, he addressed education and alumni groups and wrote glowing articles on the precept plan, knowing full well that its implementation would delay the realization of his graduate college dream.[25]

[24] *The Proposed Graduate College*, 15; Dean's Report to the Trustees' Standing Committee on the Graduate School, June 2, 1903, Records of the Committee, series 5, box 49, pp. 1–3, PUA; Dean's Report, Oct. 14, 1903, Records of the Committee, series 5, box 49, pp. 3–4, PUA.

[25] West to Wilson, Nov. 29, 1902, in *PWW*, 14:246; "Professor West's Journey," *PAW*, Jan. 24, 1903, 263. One of the many talks West gave on the preceptorial system was "The Tutorial System in College," published in his *Short Papers on American Liberal Education* (New York, 1907), 1–24. See also Mulder, *WW: Years of Preparation*, 168–69.

But West was not willing to postpone his plans indefinitely. As early as 1903 he began to lobby wealthy Princeton friends and trustees for a scaled-down "working model" of the proposed Graduate College.[26] In 1905 Moses Taylor Pyne, one of the most loyal and effective trustees in Princeton's history, secretly purchased a large, three-storey Victorian house and eleven landscaped acres on Bayard Lane to inaugurate West's experiment in gracious scholarly living. "Merwick," as it was called, was to West's mind the perfect location for a graduate residence. A brisk eight-minute walk to the northwestern edge of the campus and a few more minutes to the library and labs, the house was suitably distant from the alleged distractions of undergraduate life.

Obviously, West had changed his mind since 1903 about the desirability of locating the Graduate College at the heart of the campus to exercise a civilizing influence on the undergraduates—a change that did not endear him to the president, who sought to promote the "organic" social and intellectual "coordination" of the whole university. Now West seemed to be worried that the influences would flow in the opposite direction. A residence in the center of campus, he warned, without evidence, "puts serious and permanent obstacles in the way of developing a distinct graduate attitude in graduate students and therefore makes it harder to maintain graduate standards both in studies and conduct." There was no little irony in the situation, as Stockton Axson, West's friend and Wilson's brother-in-law, pointed out, where "the man who was contending for the aloof idea of the graduate college was much more of a mixer than was the man who was contending for the 'social' position of the graduate college."[27]

Merwick was not only separated from the university; it quickly earned a reputation for elitism and "effetism." The charges did not

[26] "History of Merwick" [1914–1915], p. 18, Graduate School Records, box 31, folder 9, PUA. Most of the section on "Life at Merwick" is reprinted in Thorp, *PGS*, 86–98, and Thorp, "When Merwick was the University's 'Graduate House,' 1905–1913," *Princeton History*, no. 1 (1971): 51–71.

[27] West and Butler critique of plan for Thomson Graduate College, Prospect Site, 1909, Exhibit F, Graduate School Records (box 27, folder 5), PUA; Axson, "*Brother Woodrow*," 135.

bother West; he was frank about his wish to develop at Merwick "the true spirit of scholarly life in fairly attractive surroundings and [to] prepare our graduates for what we hope will be the *finer*"—that word again—"scholarly life of those who are to reside in the proposed Graduate College." And most of the men he handpicked to live there each year were, to judge by their earned degrees and subsequent careers, first-rate self-starters.[28]

Nonetheless, critics soon recognized that Merwick was more than "fairly attractive" and that its emerging social forms—many the inspiration of the dean who lived across the street and sought to direct "all influences" upon the graduates in the name of "culture"—cast doubt on its, and his, intellectual seriousness. The building, refurbished and refitted to house only a dozen students and to feed as many more, was tastefully appointed with furniture from Wanamaker's department store in Philadelphia, to which the residents added a piano. The grounds, dotted with tall, spreading trees, featured a wide lawn, a large garden, a tennis court, and plenty of room for baseball games and medicine-ball exercises. According to one happy denizen, learning there occurred in a suitably and unapologetically "fine and rare setting," on the theory that "scholars are gentlemen."[29]

Yet even Dean West realized that an excess of graciousness might harm Merwick's reputation and future usefulness as a model of the Graduate College. Early on he told the trustees' graduate committee, somewhat disingenuously, that he was "very anxious that Merwick shall not take on anything of the character of a boarding house, a club, or a hotel, but shall preserve at all times the aspect of a quiet studious home."[30] He had some cause to worry when its routines

[28] Dean's Report to the Trustees' Standing Committee on the Graduate School, Oct. 14, 1903, p. 3, Records of the Committee, series 5, box 49, PUA; Howard Crosby Butler, "Graduate Students," *PAW*, Jan. 26, 1910, 247–50.

[29] *The Proposed Graduate College*, 10, 11; Thorp, *PGS*, 91; M. S. Burt, "Life at Merwick," *PAW*, May 8, 1907, 512–14, at 514.

[30] Thorp, *PGS*, 85. Even former students who admired West said that Merwick was "more like a beautiful planned club than a dormitory" and that his ideal of a graduate college was that it "accustom men to the refinement of a gracious social life, and give them an atmosphere of quiet association with other young scholars, rather than put upon them the pressure of the urgency of work" (James Southall Wilson, Graduate Dean of the University of Virginia, quoted in Donald L. Stone, "Andrew Fleming

and customs became known. Because the students took "very few classes"—there were not yet many to be had in most departments—they enjoyed daily and weekly schedules that would be the envy of today's graduate grinds. Plenty of sleep and leisurely meals were the order of the day. Lunch and dinner were always followed by conversation, cards, chess, music, or light reading. Work halted at four o'clock for two-and-a-half hours of recreation—long walks, cross-country runs, tennis matches, or field games. Then sumptuous dinners in academic gowns lasted until eight, followed by some study. On Wednesday evenings the residents wore formal clothes under their "democratic" gowns and dined in style with guests and the dean himself before listening to a learned talk by a faculty member or trustee. Sundays were not for study but for leisure, correspondence, church, and visits. In sum, the Merwickians savored "full days of work and play well tempered" and sought to keep what their chronicler called the "dessicating influence of books" and "pedanticism" at arm's length.[31]

After observing the Westian lifestyle of a third of the graduate students, four of Wilson's most eminent professors, including his dean of the faculty, Henry Fine, sent him a memorial in 1910 protesting the way (and, by implication, by whom) graduate education

---

West—The Man," in The Association of Princeton Graduate Alumni [APGA], *Report of the Second Conference held at the Graduate College of Princeton University on June 12–13, 1951*, 8, 11). In 1922 West admitted that "the cultural side of a man's character"—which he regarded *as important* as the intellectual side—"can best be brought out by a *club-like* atmosphere similar to that which [undergraduate] Princeton is trying to exert" (*DP*, "Andrew Fleming West Edition," Feb. 22, 1928, p. 29, cols. 1–2). West himself was a true clubman: he belonged to several, his house was a social center for faculty bachelors, and his own lonely life—made so by the early insanity and institutionalization of his wife—brought out his social and conversational side. After 1892 he would drop into his former bachelor quarters, dubbed "The Monastery," at the foot of University Place and play ferocious games of hearts until after midnight. Charles Freeman Williams McClure, "Recollections of Andrew Fleming West," in APGA, *Report of the Second Conference . . . 1951*, 109. When West was feeling lonely, he made a habit of dropping into Dean Fine's office to chat at length, which irritated the busier and less gregarious dean of the faculty. Bragdon interview with William F. Magie, Aug. 6, 1940 (box 63, folder 9, p. 10), WWC.

[31] Thorp, *PGS*, 87–91; Burt, "Life at Merwick," 513, 514.

at Princeton was directed. They reiterated their conviction that "all residential considerations should be duly subordinated to the one end of a graduate school, [namely] the work of study and research." Moreover, they questioned West's emphasis upon "the supervision and direction of the life of graduate students." Having come from mature urban universities such as Chicago, Penn, and Leipzig, they thought that "the conditions of life and residence of the normal graduate student should be as free and untrammeled as those of other professional students." But most important, they emphasized, "we cannot have a great graduate school without a great graduate faculty . . . and we cannot attract strong men [to the faculty] by adherence to *dilettante ideals*."[32]

From that day to this, Dean West has stood under that stinging, if partisan, indictment. Were his ideals for the Graduate School "*dilettante*"? Did he subordinate the academic to the social? Were his notions of graduate education out of step with or simply behind those held by the best scholar-teachers of the day? The best way to answer these questions is to look at his own graduate education (since autobiography often informs educational philosophy), his general notion of a college professor (to see what he wanted his graduates to become), his primary requirements for entering students, and his personal life of scholarship (which, we might assume, informed his standards for others).

Significantly, the founding dean of the Graduate School never attended graduate school himself. Moreover, he had only two-and-a-half years of study at Princeton before graduating with the class of 1874. A January matriculation, a broken hip, and two years at Centre College in Kentucky account for the truncation.[33] In lieu of graduate

[32] Edward Capps, E. G. Conklin, W. M. Daniels, and H. B. Fine to Wilson, Jan. 10, 1910, in *PWW*, 19:754–55. Conklin later revealed that he had coined *le mot juste* at the pro-Wilson caucus that met frequently at Dean Fine's house. Bragdon interview with Conklin, Mar. 24, 1923 (box 62, folder 21, p. 2), WWC; Axson, "*Brother Woodrow*," 138.

[33] Laurence R. Veysey, "Andrew Fleming West," *Dictionary of American Biography [DAB]*, Supplement 3, 1941–1945 (New York, 1973), 809–11; Davies, "Andrew Fleming West," in Alexander Leitch, ed., *A Princeton Companion* (Princeton, 1978), 501–4. The "West Edition" of the *Daily Princetonian* (Feb. 22, 1928, p. 1, col. 2) noted that West had to leave Princeton after commencement in his first year (1870) because of "a serious

school, he taught Latin in Cincinnati high schools for six-and-a-half years. Only in the spring of 1881 did he manage to take seven months' leave to travel in Europe—but not to study, as some biographers have tried to suggest. He may have tutored a young boy during a kind of grand tour and may have looked at medieval manuscripts with a view toward a future book.[34] Upon his return from Europe he became headmaster of the Morris Academy in Morristown, New Jersey, from which he was plucked two years later by then President McCosh to assume the Giger Chair of Latin. Rather than having a formative graduate education of any regular or even irregular kind, West was basically a schoolteacher and headmaster by experience and by instinct. Even his Princeton doctorate was unearned: McCosh gave him an honorary degree along with his chair, a fitting reward for one of "me boys," as the savvy Scot called his favorites.[35]

Of course West grew into his new role as a college professor. But at Princeton as elsewhere, there were many genera of the professorial species, and the one West evolved into and felt most comfortable with was closer to a Princeton preceptor than to a publishing research professor. As both he and Wilson characterized the type, the preceptor was a competent scholar who cared more about nurturing

---

injury to his hip, suffered in an accident on the campus." He returned two years later as a junior.

[34] West's own contribution to the Class of 1874's *Tenth Reunion Book* (Princeton, 1884), 83–84, says, "In January 1881, obtained leave of absence [from Hughes' High School, Cincinnati] and *traveled* for seven months in Europe." The editor of the *Fiftieth Reunion Book* (Princeton, 1924), however, transformed West's half-year of travel into "a year of *study* in Europe" (91, my emphases). The "West Edition" of the *Daily Princetonian* (Feb. 22, 1928, p. 1, col. 3) also confused travel with study by saying that "he went to Europe for a year to study and as a tutor to a young boy, his travels including the Balkan states, a journey down the Danube, London, and visits to other countries and cities." Because his edition of Richard de Bury's *Philobiblon* (1889) was based on a miscatalogued manuscript he rediscovered in the Bodleian Library at Oxford and was collated with twenty-five other European manuscripts, he may have done some of this work on his first trip to Europe in 1881. Charles Christopher Mierow "The Most Unforgettable Character I Have Ever Known," *Classical Outlook* 41:9 (May 1964): 1.

[35] Hoeveler, *James McCosh*, 285, 290. Only Laurence Veysey (*DAB*, suppl. 3, p. 809) and Willard Thorp (*PGS*, 58) seem to have noticed that West's Ph.D. was honorary, not earned.

the *spirit* of learning in his students than about stuffing their heads with "facts and figures" or learning itself. In order to inspire their students to independent reading and thought, preceptors had to be widely read, broadly cultured, and possessed of "personal qualities of association"; they had to be "gentlemen," affable, interesting, "companionable," and—a very telling word—"clubable."[36] The (over)-specialized, (over)intellectualized scholar was not the ideal, nor were Wilson's new expectations for faculty research and publication the right attitude. "As a rule," wrote West in an article, "True and False Standards of Graduate Work," "the best 'collected works' a scholar can leave is a group of great students." And maybe not even great ones, for West professed a fondness for the top and bottom groups of students; among the latter are "some of the most interesting and lovable fellows that ever come to college." To those boy-men he could act as "guide, philosopher, friend, critic, doctor, and physician all in one," much like the schoolmaster he once was.[37]

When West sought his "small company of picked men" for graduate work, he understandably looked for preceptor-like qualities. He wanted practical rather than theoretical men, sociable men. The ideal candidates were like—or *were*—choice Princeton seniors, known for their "strong personal attractiveness," "good minds and good manners"—"gentlemen who are scholars," rather than vice versa.[38] As the Graduate College was finally being constructed, he assured his critics that "the sole test of admission is mental and moral worth. To make social eligibility a test would be unjust and silly." But many observers must have remained skeptical, and rightly so. In 1927, the year before his retirement from the deanship, he told the assembled residents of the Graduate College that a graduate student had only two duties: "(1) to be a gentleman (2) to do a little work."[39]

[36] West, "The Tutorial System," 10; *The Proposed Graduate College*, 12; *PWW*, 14:299, 317, 16:50, 62.

[37] West, "True and False Standards of Graduate Work," in *Short Papers*, 47–64, at 56; West, "The Tutorial System," 15, 17.

[38] West, "True and False Standards," 57, 62, 63–64.

[39] West, *The Graduate College*, 29; Graduate College House Committee Minutes (1916–1932), Nov. 2, 1927, Graduate School Collection (box 28, folder 3), PUA.

Those were the expectations and priorities West had held consistently throughout his whole career.

"A little work" was a fair description of his own scholarship as the Giger Professor of Latin. His faculty colleagues best qualified to know regarded West as "no scholar" or only "a scholar of sorts," although he could appreciate the scholarship of others.[40] With one exception, his scholarship was thin and undistinguished and came early in his career at Princeton, yet well after his appointment to an endowed chair. Before he was appointed graduate dean in 1900, he had published only three books; a fourth was published two years later. His first book was an unmemorable and undistinguished Latin edition of Terence for school and college classrooms (1888), which was largely derivative and quickly superseded by better work.[41] The second and best, *Philobiblon* (1889), was a three-volume edition/translation of a short treatise on book collecting by the fourteenth-century English bishop Richard de Bury (1889); only three hundred copies were issued by the Grolier Club, so its numerous qualities were not widely appreciated except by reviewers. Nor was *Philobiblon* a major work in its own right, a standard that West later applied to the subjects of graduate dissertations and faculty scholarship.[42]

In 1892 West published a short title in a Scribners series on The Great Educators, *Alcuin and the Rise of the Christian Schools*, which was largely panned or damned with faint praise by the scholarly press

[40] Bragdon interviews with Thomas Marc Parrott, Sept. 15, 1942 (box 63, folder 25); David Magie, June 6, 1939 (box 63, folder 8); Charles Grosvenor Osgood, Apr. 14, 1938 (box 63, folder 24); Williamson Vreeland, Mar. 24, 1940 (box 63, folder 57); Edward Capps, Mar. 23, 1943 (box 62, folder 16); Charles H. McIlwain, Jan. 2, 1940 (box 63, folder 11), WWC; William Warner Bishop, "Reminiscences of Princeton, 1902–7," *PULC* 8:4 (June 1947): 147–63, at 161.

[41] *P. Terenti Afri Andria et Heavton timorvmenos*, ed. Andrew Fleming West (New York and London, 1888), reprinted in 1892 and 1898. According to the preface, the text was "substantially that of Umpfenbach (Berlin, 1870)."

[42] *The Philobiblon of Richard de Bury*, ed. and trans. Andrew F. West, 3 vols. (New York, 1889), was reviewed very favorably by a scholarly expert in the *Critic* (18, [n. s. 15], no. 375 [Mar. 7, 1891]: 120–21). In "True and False Standards," West objected not to specialization per se but to "the study of the unimportant," "trifles," or "the obvious" (54). *Philobiblon* has gained more importance recently with the development of the history of the book; it has long been of only minor interest to medieval historians.

and soon ignored by specialists.[43] His last work of scholarship, before giving himself over to educational advocacy, light verse, honorary degree citations, Latin inscriptions for public monuments and academic buildings, and a rearguard defense of the classics, was *A Latin Grammar for Schools*, published in 1902 and reissued two years later, despite some hard reviews.[44] In other words, West's scholarship fit perfectly well with the major concerns and qualifications of a schoolmaster of the classics, not a university scholar. It was no coincidence that he was also Princeton's only professor of pedagogy from 1885 to 1892, who taught a two-semester course to graduate students intending to teach, primarily at the secondary level.[45]

It is no wonder, then, that West increasingly disappointed and irritated the president of the newly proclaimed university, who believed, after attending two real ones (Virginia and Johns Hopkins), that a university's "only legitimate object" was "*intellectual* attainment."[46] Even West's friends and colleagues thought the dean had little idea of what a real university was because he had never attended one.[47] And when he persisted in regarding first Merwick and then

[43] Andrew Fleming West, *Alcuin and the Rise of the Christian Schools*, The Great Educators (New York, 1892). Although the book was reprinted seven times by 1969, it added nothing to J. Bass Mullinger's *The Schools of Charles the Great and the Restoration of Education in the 9th Century* (London, 1877) and was quickly superseded by C.J.B. Gaskoin's *Alcuin: His Life and His Work* (London, 1904). Contemporary experts and encyclopedias barely mentioned West's little book, which was aimed largely at a student audience. In an interview with Henry Bragdon, Edward S. Corwin, a former colleague of West, revealed that "some of [West's] opponents claimed he had received help" on the Alcuin book, but sought to disassociate himself from such a rumor (June 9, 1939 [box 62, folder 22], WWC).

[44] Andrew Fleming West, *A Latin Grammar for Schools* (New York, 1902). Some of his subsequent publications were *Short Papers on American Liberal Education* (1907), (ed.) *Value of the Classics* (Princeton, 1917), *Presentations for Honorary Degrees in Princeton University, 1905–1925* (Princeton, 1929), and *Stray Verses* (Princeton, 1931).

[45] Thorp, *PGS*, 36, 59. On West's retrograde chairmanship of the Classics Department, in which he stonewalled Wilson's call for curricular rationalization and reform, see W. Robert Connor, "Said Woodrow Wilson, 'My Dear West . . .': Reflections on a Century of Departmental Organization of Knowledge," The William Kelly Prentice Lecture, PU, Dec. 2, 2003 (thanks to Bob Connor for a copy).

[46] Wilson, Address to the Princeton Club of Chicago, Mar. 12, 1908, in *PWW*, 18:20.

[47] Bragdon interviews with William K. Prentice, June 6, 1939 (box 63, folder 31), and Edward Capps, Mar. 23, 1943 (box 62, folder 16), WWC.

the Graduate College as (in the words of a trustee) "a great big upper class Club," he found himself on the wrong side of the president, who was seeking to reduce, if not eliminate, the social snobbery and nonacademic "sideshows" on Prospect Avenue.[48]

❁ ❁ ❁

Wilson's arguments for a graduate school built more of brains than bricks and central to university life and work were heavily reinforced by several events between late 1907 and the fall of 1909. After warning Wilson in 1907 that he was about to give Princeton a "friendly whack" in his influential annual report, Henry S. Pritchett, president of the Carnegie Foundation for the Advancement of Teaching, upon whose board Wilson sat, questioned whether Princeton deserved university status. He implied that Princeton's underdeveloped graduate school was an unnecessary addition to the defining undergraduate college and did not make Princeton a true university in spirit, methods, or atmosphere like Johns Hopkins. Wilson replied defensively that "Princeton has been doing very serious graduate work for a long time, not in all departments, but in many departments, and since '96 has steadily increased her claim on the title even on German grounds." But such a public slap at one of Wilson's key plans for Princeton's primacy clearly stung, as did Pritchett's personal opinion that Wilson's forte was shaping "the greatest of our American colleges" and not graduate school copycatting.[49] Indirectly, both remarks undermined Princeton's right to belong to the elite Associa-

[48] Melancthon W. Jacobus to Wilson, Mar. 20, 1909, in *PWW*, 19:114. For Wilson's losing struggle with the eating clubs, see Mulder, *WW: Years of Preparation*, 187–203, and Henry Wilkinson Bragdon, *Woodrow Wilson: The Academic Years* (Cambridge, Mass., 1967), 316–36.

[49] *PWW*, 17:511–12, 527, 545–46; Carnegie Foundation for the Advancement of Teaching [CFAT], *Second Annual Report of the President and Treasurer* (New York, 1907), 83, 91. The CFAT, endowed by Andrew Carnegie, was newly in the business of giving pensions to retired academics, at first only those at private institutions, soon to those at public institutions; those at denominational institutions were excluded. See Ellen Condliffe Lagemann, *Private Power for the Public Good: A History of the Carnegie Foundation for the Advancement of Teaching* (New York, 1983), esp. chap. 3.

tion of American Universities, founded in 1900 by fourteen of the nation's leading research universities, including Princeton.[50]

If the quality and seriousness of Princeton's graduate work did not register in some circles in 1907, they were impossible to miss by 1909. With Dean West constitutionally outside the hiring loop, Wilson and Dean Fine put the Graduate School on the map by signing some of the biggest names in international research and scholarship and by promoting to professorships several preceptors whose academic talents and ambitions had outgrown their tutorial positions. The search for senior "stars" had begun in 1905–1906 when philosopher Norman Kemp Smith was persuaded to leave Glasgow and mathematical physicist James Jeans and physicist Owen Richardson to forsake the foggy fens of Cambridge. When Pritchett poked at Princeton's pretensions, the university had just lured Greek scholar Edward Capps from the University of Chicago and was about to land his Latin colleague Frank Abbott. Penn yielded up biologist Edwin G. Conklin in 1908 after fending off a preemptive strike from Yale. By 1908 Wilson could matter-of-factly tell the alumni that Princeton now had the top classics, physics, and mathematics departments in the country.[51] To add to its luster as an emerging center of science, Palmer and Guyot Halls were opened for business in 1908 and 1909, respectively. Carefully designed by the faculty who would use them, after visiting the competition Wilson bragged they were "equal to any in the university world."[52]

Landing the best scholars was not the same as keeping them. Princeton soon found that its prizes were eagerly sought by its com-

[50] See Hugh Hawkins, *Banding Together: The Rise of National Associations in American Higher Education, 1887–1950* (Baltimore, 1992), 10–15; William K. Selden, "The Association of American Universities: An Enigma in Higher Education," *Graduate Journal* [U. of Texas], 8:1 (1968): 199–209.

[51] Bragdon, *WW: Academic Years*, 295, 360–61; Hugh S. Taylor, "Princeton's Scientific Departments—Their Growth and Reputation, Their Aid to Princeton and America," *PAW*, Mar. 17, 1941, 7–10. Richardson's eight years of work on electron emissions at Princeton earned him the Nobel Prize in 1928.

[52] *PWW*, 18:572–74, 19:679–83, 20:232. Biologist Edwin Conklin, hired in 1907 while Guyot was being planned, asked for and got an extra storey, "much to the dismay of the architect" (Bragdon interview with Conklin, Mar. 24, 1943 [box 62, folder 21, p. 1], WWC).

petitors, just as they are today. Worse yet, some of them were impelled to leave—or did leave—because of the condition of the Graduate School and its leadership. In the winter of 1908–1909, Harvard put the rush on the classical company of Capps and Abbott. Capps actually received an offer, which he seriously considered, despite his real attachment to Princeton and Wilson, because he felt "very much discouraged about the prospects of graduate work" under West. In March, physicist Jeans did resign, largely because of "the failure of the Graduate Department" and lack of progress in his own research and "graduate teaching."[53]

The loss of one and the near-loss of another of his stellar graduate faculty prompted Wilson to seek a major change in the government of the Graduate School. At the April 1909 meeting of the trustees, Wilson's friends handily won a vote to transfer the extraordinary powers in Dean West's hands to a new Faculty Graduate School Committee.[54] This committee, which was instantly filled with Wilson's senior hires and allies, now oversaw graduate admissions, instruction, examinations, and fellowships, as well as the affairs of "the Residential Graduate Hall" (Merwick), whose master voted with them on relevant matters. This officially relegated West to his ex officio seat on the now-weakened trustees' committee on the Graduate School and to the chairmanship of the new faculty committee.[55] Yet within a short time, Wilson came to believe that West should not retain even that much authority and "must be absolutely eliminated, administratively." "He can break any man's heart," Wilson lamented, "who tries to administer the [Graduate School] in the true university spirit."[56]

If Wilson did not fully understand that spirit before, or realize how much his graduate dean did not, he certainly did by the spring

[53] *PWW*, 19:10–11, 115–16.

[54] The change was engineered by Dean Fine in Wilson's absence in February 1909. RSB interview with Fine, June 18, 1925, Baker Papers, container 105, reel 74, p. 4.

[55] Minutes of the Board of Trustees, Apr. 8, 1909, in *PWW*, 19:153–54. The by-law as passed was not an unmitigated victory for Wilson. A previous draft more to his liking said that the administration of the Graduate School "and of the residential Graduate College shall, under the President of the University" lie in the hands of the new faculty committee. *PWW*, 19:28–29.

[56] *PWW*, 19:631 (Dec. 27, 1909), 21:25–26 (July 26, 1910).

of 1909. Wilson's learning curve shot up in late March when he asked the members of the new faculty committee—Capps, Conklin, Winthrop Daniels, Hibben, and Dean Fine—for their views on the current operations of and plans for the Graduate School. Their replies formed the basis of their joint memorandum on "dilettante ideals" the following January and informed Wilson's strong appeal to the New York alumni in April 1910. The committee reminded him, if he had forgotten his own experience at Johns Hopkins, that graduate students were men of thoroughly professional goals and modest means, who sought the best possible "instruction, books, and equipment" but only "plain and simple living." As mature men who had "abandoned the outside interests of [their] undergraduate days," graduate students were "unreservedly" serious about study, which the committee thought could and should be pursued at the heart of the university.[57]

As for West's plans and Cram's designs for the Graduate College, the committee was unanimous that they were too elaborate, too expensive, and inappropriate. Dean Fine noted that the plans would cost nearly twice the rate per person of Princeton's poshest undergraduate dormitories. Edward Capps compared the proposed college to "the most expensive of the private dormitories at Harvard, erected as investments and patronized by wealthy undergraduates," on the so-called Gold Coast. This kind of subsidized luxury would do the graduate students no good and only prepare them for "lives of discontent in the future." Far better to give them comfortable but simple accommodations, the kind they could expect as professors "on a modest salary after eight or ten years of apprenticeship." Moreover, the graduate residence must accommodate all of the graduate students, not a privileged few as it did currently. Thus the committee wanted the Graduate College to hold at least a hundred students, not the sixty then planned for. Dean Fine in particular wanted to end the two-class system in the Graduate School that mirrored the undergraduate gulf between "Club and non-Club men."[58]

[57] *PWW*, 19:132–35, at 132, 133 (Mar. 30, 1909), 135–36, at 135 (Mar. 31, 1909), 141–44 (Apr. 1, 1909); Edwin Grant Conklin, "As a Scientist Saw Him," in Myers, *WW: Princeton Memories*, 59–60; Bragdon interview with Edward Capps, Mar. 23, 1943 (box 62, folder 16, p. 1), WWC.

[58] *PWW*, 19:133, 141–42.

The final concern of the faculty committee, who spoke for a large majority of the whole faculty, was the emphasis West laid upon the "supervision and direction" of graduate student life.[59] As they argued in their January 1910 memo to Wilson, graduate student life should be as "free and untrammeled" as that of other professional students (of which Princeton at that time had none and therefore no experience). Winthrop Daniels, a senior member of Wilson's department, was convinced that mature graduate students were keen on neither "family-living" nor "restrictions upon their freedom" that would seem irksome to undergraduates.[60]

By the time Wilson digested the committee's letters and memo and addressed the New York alumni in April 1910, he could not resist caricaturing West's program of general "cultivation" for Merwick and the proposed graduate college. First, he said, Princeton wanted the kind of graduate students—nine out of ten—who "do not wish to be looked after . . . cared for and mothered." Unlike undergraduates, these older scholars wanted "absolutely normal conditions, such as you find everywhere else in the academic world of America." Even more important, potential students were flocking to Yale and other rivals because they understood "(what is understood throughout the academic world) that we"—by which he meant Dean West—"want to do something peculiar with them." And mature men, he did not have to tell those in his audience, "do not choose to have anything peculiar done with them." "We must slowly build up a great graduate school, as we built up a great undergraduate body," he concluded, "before we can do peculiar Princetonian things with them." Yet even as he said it, his tone and choice of words declared that he entertained no thought of ever amending his vision of a graduate school of *intellectual* distinction in a "peculiar" direction.[61] The battle lines between Wilson and West that had been drawn in sand for at least four years were now unmistakably carved in stone.

[59] On faculty sentiment, see *PWW*, 19:628–29 (Dec. 25, 1909), 653–54 (Dec. 28, 1909); Bragdon, *WW: Academic Years*, 486n61; Axson, "*Brother Woodrow*," 138–39.

[60] *PWW*, 19:136, 754.

[61] Address in St. Louis to the Western Association of Princeton Clubs, Mar. 26, 1910, *PWW*, 20:293–96, at 295; Address to the Princeton Club of New York, Apr. 7, 1910, *PWW*, 20:341–45, at 342, 343.

But they had been for a year, since May 1909 when William Procter, the Cincinnati soap king, offered Princeton a half-million dollars for the Graduate College if the university would match that amount and he approved the site. Dean West and his friends on the Board of Trustees were, of course, thrilled by this development because it gave them a way to proceed with the long-delayed construction of a graduate residence. They sought to combine Procter's gift with that of Josephine Swann, who in 1906 had left Princeton at least $250,000 for a similar though more modest college "upon the grounds of the said University."[62] The snag with her donation was that no satisfactory site on the existing campus could be found; Merwick was deemed well off-campus, as it had been intended. But when Procter, after several visits and talks with West, decided that the site overlooking the golf course was best, legal experts were found to declare the newly purchased site to be on university property, thus unencumbering the Swann bequest.

On both principle and pique, Wilson dug in his heels and sought to prevent West from prevailing. The trustees divided even more sharply, and war broke out over "the location of a boarding-house" (as one trustee put it) in alumni meetings, pamphlets, the alumni magazine, and the national press.[63] The town itself split into Wilson and West camps; faculty wives and even children took sides and crossed the street to avoid "enemies."[64] Procter turned the heat up in February 1910 by withdrawing his offer after Wilson proposed to build two colleges, one on campus with Mrs. Swann's

[62] *PWW*, 16:457–58n1 (Oct. 15, 1906). For the long, bitter struggle over the Graduate School and College, see Thorp, *PGS*, chap. 5; Bragdon, *WW: Academic Years*, chap. 18; Mulder, *WW: Years of Preparation*, chap. 8.

[63] Axson, "*Brother Woodrow*," 135.

[64] Bragdon, *WW: Academic Years*, 372–73; Bragdon interviews with William Berryman Scott, June 9, 1939, (box 63, folder 44); Mrs. F. Scott Agar (Scott's daughter), July 20, 1940 (box 62, folder 4); Bliss Perry, Jan. 27, 1940 (box 63, folder 26, p. 4); David Magie, June 6, 1939 (box 63, folder 8), WWC. In 1999 Emily Stuart Perry, daughter of Professor Duane Stuart (who sided with Wilson rather than his classical colleague West) and playmate of Eleanor Wilson, remembered the children's divisions in town and crossing the street to avoid the burly dean's unwanted hugs. Personal interview, Aug. 2, 1999, Greenboro, Vt. (Thanks to Tim Breen for introducing me to Mrs. Perry).

money (which had grown to $320,000 by 1909) and another on the golf course.[65]

In an effort to break the stalemate, some trustees approached West in early May about resigning his deanship in favor of serving as master of the new Graduate College. But on May 18, a week after West refused, the fighting suddenly stopped: Isaac Wyman '48 died in Salem, Massachusetts, leaving his alma mater, it was reported, anywhere from $2 million to $30 million for the Graduate College. When Wilson learned that West had been named as one of two executor-trustees of the estate and would now be able to build his dream house, he laughed, perhaps with a touch of relief, and told his family, "We've beaten the living, but we can't fight the dead—the game is up." "I could lick a half-million, but I'm licked by ten millions."[66] Though the Wyman bequest eventually brought in only $794,000, it prompted Procter to renew his offer and to designate $200,000 for a dining hall, the rest to endow graduate fellowships and the preceptorial system; both were of great interest to the feuding president and dean.[67]

Although Dean West had clearly won the last skirmish in a drawn-out academic war, he had been stripped of much of his administrative power before Wilson quit the field in October 1910 to run for governor.[68] Indeed, just as West's beautiful pre-aged college

[65] Wilson's proposal, while it may have been a poor tactic at the time, was not as foolish as his enemies regarded it. If the Graduate School was expected to grow in a major way in the near future, a single graduate residence would have been "either inadequate or else inadvisedly large" (August Heckscher, *Woodrow Wilson* [New York, 1991], 190).

[66] Eleanor Wilson McAdoo, *The Woodrow Wilsons* (New York, 1937), 101; Axson, "*Brother Woodrow*," 142; Margaret Axson Elliott, *My Aunt Louisa and Woodrow Wilson* (Chapel Hill, 1944), 242. For Wilson the game was not quite up. On June 10 he recommended West for the presidency of Clark College, a counterpart of Clark University in Worcester, Massachusetts. Wilson was undoubtedly trying to correct his mistake in May 1906 of going along with the trustees' graduate committee in asking West to turn down MIT's offer of its presidency. *PWW*, 19:240; Axtell, "The Dilettante Dean," 255–59.

[67] Mulder, *WW: Years of Preparation*, 224; *PWW*, 20:464n3 (May 22, 1910), 506 (June 6, 1910).

[68] His authority remained circumscribed, despite his attempt to redraw the by-laws in his favor shortly after Hibben became president. Approved by Hibben, West's former junior partner in the minority camp of the Faculty Graduate Committee, the proposed

was being completed in record time in the summer of 1913, now U.S. President Wilson may have had the last laugh. When he and Mrs. Wilson read the news in the Princeton paper, they both found it "a joke too good to be invented" that "the tax assessors at Princeton are to tax the new Graduate School buildings on the ground that they are not to be devoted to educational uses."[69] To Wilson, the last part was old news.

❁ ❁ ❁

Having obtained his Oxford quad and a more malleable president, Dean West set out to transfer the young traditions of Merwick to the Graduate College and to create some new ones. His motives were subject to different interpretations. Critics thought he was "intrinsically snobbish" and paid more attention to gentlemanly "appearances" than to scholarly "essentials." The only way he could have been happier, one critic said, was to be the master of a *real* Oxford college, "passing around the port at the High Table and making Latin puns after dinner."[70]

His defenders, on the other hand, saw other goals and motives at work. Edward Corwin, a Wilson proponent, allowed that "West's emphasis was aesthetic partly, partly on the civilizing influence of the surroundings." The dean believed, not unreasonably, that "if men were crude and unsociable, they would not be effective" and "their brains would be useless." Despite the heavy leaven of "finer" Princetonians, West, like Dean of the Faculty William Magie, regarded the graduate students as "a heterogeneous mass of uncultivation," "hayseeds" in need of manners and polish. "He was familiar with

---

changes "practically made the Graduate School independent of the university" and would have restored to West "the powers which he had failed to get during . . . Wilson's regime." Trustee Melancthon Jacobus crushed the attempt by substituting a resolution that "carried out President Wilson's principles" (RSB interview with Jacobus, May 8, 1925, Baker Papers, container 108, reel 77, p. 2).

[69] *PWW*, 28:203 (Aug. 21, 1913), 220–21 (Aug. 25, 1913).

[70] Bragdon interviews with Robert McNutt McElroy, Nov. 20, 1940 (box 63, folder 13, p. 4), Edward S. Corwin, June 9, 1939 (box 62, folder 22), and Winthrop M. Daniels, Mar. 30, 1940 (box 62, folder 28, p. 8), WWC; Axtell, "The Dilettante Dean," 246–47, 249–50, 252–53.

the colleges and universities from which they came," an old friend recalled, and "knew that most of these put little emphasis on culture as he understood it." In short, West sought to do something "peculiar" with the students once they were under his influence. He created an environment and set of traditions designed to foster "refinement of thought and manner, with ease, balance, adaptability, skill, and aspiration—traits of the utmost value in every walk of life," he thought, "and in none more valuable than in the life of the scholar."[71] The last thing he wanted was to have his graduates regarded as "scholastic geniuses and social morons," as an undergraduate satire on "Goon Hill" dubbed them a few years after his death.[72]

The Westian process of "cultivation" began even before matriculation, by careful culling of degree candidates. Like his faculty committee and the admitting departments, West always paid serious attention to applicants' "general and special scholarly essentials." But he also emphasized, to a degree they did not, the young men's "personality, character and promise," code words for their social and academic pedigrees; with relatively small applicant pools, such personal assessment by the dean was still possible.[73] The academic elitism he displayed early in his deanship continued throughout his tenure. In part he was guided by the initially short list of institutions whose qualified graduates were approved for graduate work by the Association of American Universities, in which West played an active, even combative, role.[74] Thus, when future president Harold Dodds ap-

[71] Bragdon interviews with Corwin, June 9, 1939 (box 62, folder 22), Dean W. F. Magie, June 13, 1939 (box 63, folder 9, pp. 4, 6), Dean Luther Eisenhart, June 9, 1939 (box 62, folder 35, p. 2), President Karl Compton (MIT), May 22, 1939 (box 62, folder 20), WWC; Charles Freeman Williams McClure, "Recollections of Andrew Fleming West," in APGA, *Report of the Second Conference . . . 1951*, 112; *President's Report (1925)*, 23.

[72] "Goon Hill," *Nassau Sovereign* (Apr. 1948), copy in Grounds and Buildings (box 5A), PUA.

[73] *President's Report (1928)*, 25 (West's final report).

[74] Association of American Universities [AAU], *Journal of Proceedings and Addresses* [*J. of Procs.*] (1947), 79: "There was West, a pillar in the structure of graduate organization, fatherly, a fighter for his idealogy [*sic*]." The AAU stopped making the list in 1949 because it was increasingly meaningless as it became longer and the process consumed too much time and expense. It was also found that admittees from approved schools did no better than those with similar qualifications from other institutions. An extensive

plied to the program in History, Politics, and Economics in 1911, West scrawled across his application, with his favorite blue pencil, "Ineligible, college degree insufficient." Obviously, Pennsylvania's little Grove City College, where Dodds's father, a Presbyterian minister, taught Bible, was not up to snuff, despite the applicant's otherwise strong credentials and two years of high school teaching. West admitted him only after Dodds took a year of courses at the seminary and with Edward Corwin and Henry Jones Ford at the university. Perhaps significantly, Dodds chose to live at the seminary after he was admitted with a fellowship in 1913 and to transfer to the University of Pennsylvania for his doctorate.[75]

With even less reason, West rejected the applications of two MIT graduates who came to Princeton for an interview. They had the misfortune not to have had Latin, or enough of it to satisfy the dean, who regarded his second language as "the unprinted entrance requirement to the Graduate College." As he led them to the door, he put his arms around their shoulders, as he was wont to do, and dismissed them with, "You're nice boys, but you have never been to college." It was an odd, though perhaps not surprising, thing to say for a man who had been offered MIT's presidency.[76]

Despite a successor's defensive denial, there is good reason to think that West also applied unspoken social criteria to applicants.[77]

---

study of graduate students at the University of Chicago in the 1930s found that "the relatively small group of graduates from unaccredited institutions made, on the whole, distinctly the best showing [in the classroom], having the largest percentage of superior records and next to the smallest percentage of unsatisfactory records" (Floyd W. Reeves and John Dale Russell, *Admission and Retention of University Students*, University of Chicago Survey, 12 vols. [Chicago, 1933], 5:152).

[75] Dodds's application is in the Harold W. Dodds Papers, PUA (thanks to Dan Linke for alerting me to it); Leitch, *Princeton Companion*, 137; Hugh Taylor, *Graduate Education at Princeton, 1945 to 1958* [Princeton, 1958], 3, copy in Graduate School Records (box 41, folder 6), PUA.

[76] Bragdon interview with Kenneth T. Bainbridge (Ph.D. 1929; professor of physics, Harvard), Jan. 19, 1940 (box 62, folder 7), WWC; James Southall Wilson, in APGA, *Report of the Second Conference . . . 1951*, 9; Axtell, "The Dilettante Dean," 255–59.

[77] "Social characteristics played no part in [his] choice of graduate students" (Bragdon interview with Dean Luther Eisenhart, June 9, 1939 [box 62, folder 35, p. 2], WWC).

Several former students remembered acutely and perhaps painfully that West played favorites. Jacob Beam, a future colleague, testified that West "selected at the beginning of the year the men he regarded as outstanding, partly by the cut of their clothes and their relationship to prominent men. The ordinary young man, of obscure origins, seldom got a chance. . . . [West] never recognized ability except when it was properly introduced." Francis O'Neil, a double Princetonian ('21, *25) and one of West's "few favorites," confessed that "certainly, [West] would not have picked as one of his protégés an unattractive Jew; on the other hand he would not insist that the man be a blue-blood; he might be a raw-boned uncouth Middle Westerner, in which case West would undertake to civilize him." While the dean took good care of his favorites and saw that they got fellowships for work in Athens and Rome, he earned a reputation at home for unfairness. Harlow Shapley, who made the transition from Merwick to the Graduate College before going on to a brilliant career in astronomy at Harvard, came to dislike and distrust West not only because "he played favorites in awarding fellowships," but because he "tampered with amounts of scholarship and fellowship funds already granted."[78]

Once the students, however chosen, entered the Graduate School and its collegiate embodiment, they were subjected to the dean's carefully wrought process of enculturation. As West thought gentlemen-scholars deserved, the Graduate College offered all the comforts of a well-to-do home or club: "hot water" showers twenty-four hours a day; "glorious beds" with double mattresses; "ready heat" controlled from individual room thermostats; "nutritious food"; and "broad chance to exercise" on the local bowling alleys, tennis and handball courts, and golf course. But more to the point, West sought to "humanize" learning by "bringing it back from the libraries, seminars, and laboratories, and exposing it to salutary contact with individual human beings who are primarily interested in another subject." Although he may have thought the ten-hour workdays of most

[78] Bragdon interviews with Jacob Beam, Mar. 29, 1941 (box 62, folder 9, p. 2), Francis O'Neil, July 18, 1940 (box 63, folder 22); Harlow Shapley, Mar. 6, 1967 (box 63, folder 45), WWC.

students admirable, he sought to provide enough formality, ritual, and tradition to prevent his charges from becoming "queer" or "unclubable" from overwork, overspecialization, and overintellection.[79]

The first communal ritual was dinner in Procter Hall. Every evening at six a tower bell rang to call the College members to the commodious Common Room, where it was hoped they would practice the civil art of conversation, preferably on topics unrelated to their disciplines. At six-thirty the huge doors swung open and the hungry horde, attired in black bachelor's gowns, swept into the hall and stood behind their chairs at four long tables. There they poised for the dean or resident master to say grace. If Dean West was dining, the state of his hunger determined the length of his blessings, which were sometimes but not always in Latin. When he was absent, the master often used Latin in deference, but he had a choice of English versions; some were printed on a frame with a handle, others in a small booklet opposite the dean's impeccable Latin. All the blessings mentioned daily food, meat, or drink and concluded with "Christ our Lord." Not until the 1960s were prayers added to recognize the faiths of Jewish, Hindu, and other non-Christian diners.[80]

Dinner was then served on good china and white tablecloths by uniformed waitresses and a number of Greek or Middle Eastern servants, most hired by resident master Howard Crosby Butler during his frequent archaeological expeditions to Sardis. Following dessert, demitasse was served to add another layer of social polish. Initially, wine and other spirits were not served, out of respect for

[79] Richard F. Cleveland, "The Princeton Graduate School," *PAW*, Feb. 9, 1921, 385–87, at 385; Bragdon interview with Dean Luther Eisenhart, June 9, 1939 (box 62, folder 35, p. 2), WWC. In his final report to the president, West estimated that "the time definitely given to study averages between eight and nine hours daily." On "many" occasions, "intervention has been needed to save men from over-study at high pressure" (*President's Report* [*1928*], 26).

[80] Thorp, *PGS*, 183, 305; Bragdon interview with Francis O'Neil, July 18, 1940 (box 63, folder 22), WWC; Stone, "Andrew Fleming West," 13. A copy of the Latin-English booklet (1923) is in the Graduate School Records (box 41, folder 5), PUA. Bill Berry, who arrived at the Graduate College in 1967, remembered grace being said occasionally in Greek and Hebrew as well as Latin. "Class Southerner," *Virginia Quarterly Review* 65:2 (Spring 1989): 308–31, at 310.

students from already dry states. But as the heavy hand of Prohibition lifted, alcohol made its way into College cups on holidays and other festive occasions.[81]

Another tradition brought from Merwick was the Wednesday night forum, held in the Common Room. In the Graduate College, a subcommittee of the House Committee chose the weekly speakers, not only from the university (and later the Institute for Advanced Study) but from the worlds of art, politics, and literature beyond. World-class physicists Niels Bohr and J. Robert Oppenheimer (director of the Institute) and philosopher Jacques Maritain (who, like all speakers, came without honoraria and at their own expense) drew large and appreciative audiences. When experts or celebrities could not be found, foreign graduate students often filled the bill. Facetious debates posed by British students in the style of the Oxford Union were great favorites. One resolved "That the United States of America be invited to rejoin the British Commonwealth." At year's end, the chairman of the speakers committee sometimes prepared a report and report card for his successor, giving a letter grade to each speaker. In 1951–1952, Rudolph Bing, general manager of the Metropolitan Opera, received an A++ for his talk on the economics and management of a production. A plain A went to William F. Buckley, brash author of *God and Man at Yale*, for baiting Princetonians with equal disdain. Black "left-winger" W.E.B. DuBois's paper, "The Revolt in Africa," caused "a lot of talk and fireworks" and earned a B+. The C given to Professor William Baumol for "Some Remarks on Welfare Economics and the Theory of the State" may have contained an element of revenge for his own tough grading, although Professor Hubert Wilson reaped an A for his take on "The British Elections."[82]

None of these "refinements" in themselves were objectionable, but there was some legitimate grumbling about three features of West's

[81] Stone, "Andrew Fleming West," 13; Taylor, *Graduate Education at Princeton*, 3.

[82] Thorp, *PGS*, 259–60; Hugh Taylor, *The Forum Through the Arches of the Years: An Address . . . to the Graduate College Forum of Princeton University, Oct. 12, 1960* (Princeton, 1963), 5, 14–15, 18–19; "Report on Wednesday Evening Forum Speakers, 1951–1952," Graduate School Records (box 29, folder 4), PUA; *PAW*, Mar. 11, 1955, 8. Maritain's talk, *Truth and Human Fellowship*, was published by Princeton University Press in 1957.

civilizing plan. One was the prescribed hour of dinner, which pulled students from lab and library when they might have wished to continue their work. This could be particularly frustrating when the one-mile hike back to the Graduate College took fifteen or twenty minutes. If a student took all of his meals in college and worked on campus after dinner, he might make the trek six times a day, using up to two hours and considerable shoe leather. Scientists especially resented having to take bag lunches to their labs on the opposite side of campus. New cross streets, automobiles, and the westward expansion of the campus after 1913 seemed to some disinterested faculty members to lessen the distance of the Graduate College. But the "feeble limbs" of many graduates, one student wrote, continued to "deplore the one-mile commuter trip" from dorm to "books and apparatus," even as they acknowledged in "judicial calm" that exercise was "a good thing for the bodies of men."[83]

Another infringement on graduate student freedom may not have occurred often, particularly as the Graduate College population grew to fill and overflow Procter Hall, but it must have irritated those who felt its obtrusive touch. "Like a hotel room clerk" or "a genial headwaiter," thought Hugh Stott Taylor, the fourth graduate dean, or, more accurately, like a prep school headmaster, West used to "watch out for departmental groupings in entries and, in Procter Hall, . . . try to break up unconscious disciplinary segregation at meals." In his evangelical effort to foster "enough interdepartmental communication to prevent scholar's astigmatism," West tended to forget that even graduate students in the liberal arts and sciences were, by necessity and inclination, intensely professional and vocational in their

[83] Cleveland, "The Princeton Graduate College," 386; Bragdon interviews with Edwin G. Conklin, Mar. 24, 1943 (box 62, folder 21, p. 3), William F. Magie, June 12–13, 1939 (box 63, folder 9, p. 4), Robert McNutt McElroy, Nov. 20, 1940 (box 63, folder 13, p. 4), Kenneth T. Bainbridge, Jan. 19, 1940 (box 62, folder 7), WWC; Dean Henry Fine to RSB, Aug. 23, 1927, Baker Papers, container 105, reel 74, p. 5; Jason Brownlee, "New Leaders Can Link Graduate Community to Main Campus," *DP* (online), May 14, 2001. The majority of respondants to a centennial questionnaire distributed online to Graduate School alumni thought that the *physical* distance of the Graduate College from the main campus was not a problem. Centennial Questionnaires, Graduate School Records, PUA.

disciplinary focus. After heterogeneous studies in college, they were eager and determined to master a chosen discipline and a specialty within it. To be told like schoolboys to put their passions aside for the sake of a dilettantish dean's increasingly dated project could only have surprised and rankled.[84]

The third and most distinctive tradition in West's "peculiar" plan was the wearing of black gowns at dinner in Procter Hall. The students seem to have been divided in their attitude toward the custom from 1906, when West introduced it at Merwick; some of the elite lodgers there penned a poem and a declaration against gowns on classy Merwick stationery.[85] As any American who has attended Oxford or Cambridge can testify, the novelty and medieval romance of mandatory gowns soon wears off. The gowns the Princeton students were obliged to buy were, pragmatic critics complained, "cold in the winter, hot in the summer, clumsy at the dinner table, and profusely if endearingly grease-stained by the time they are retired from active duty." Even Princeton's tradition-prone seniors had doubts about the value of West's import, which they raised in their 1923 Faculty Song:

> Here's to Andrew Fleming West,
> Who says his students must be dressed
> In gowns at meals to please the Dean
> And keep their shirts and trousers clean.

But many graduate students welcomed the nightly ritual as a benign piece of Anglophilia, a visible mark of distinction from the undergraduates, and a simple, dignified way to submerge the diversi-

[84] Interview with Hugh Stott Taylor, in "The Graduate School: Prospect and Retrospect," *PAW*, May 23, 1958, 6–9, at 6; Alfred Schlesinger, "Life in the Graduate College," *PAW*, Apr. 8, 1925, 630–31, at 630; Harry C. Avery, "Life at the Graduate College," *PAW*, Feb. 20, 1959, 3–7, at 6; Robert H. Rehder, "The Two Princetons," *PAW*, Jan. 13, 1961, 7–10, 17. As early as 1909 West recommended that the Graduate College have "comparatively small residential units if the men are to be influenced intimately ["and individually" deleted], if the formation of [disciplinary] cliques is to be prevented, and if non-Princetonians are to taken into the general life of the College" (West and Butler critique of plans for the Thomson Graduate College, 1909, Graduate School Records [box 27, folder 5], PUA).

[85] Graduate School Records (boxes 27, 31), PUA.

ties of race, class, dress, and nationality in an ancient "fraternity of scholars," a "brotherhood of the gown." Even those who considered it whimsical to wear a dirty, tattered, or torn gown honored the letter, if not the spirit, of the sartorial law. This seemed to satisfy Dean West, who had seen enough English student gowns not to complain about the condition of his own men's, as long as they wore one.[86]

The gowns disappeared from the Graduate College with many of the students at the outbreak of World War II and did not reappear until 1953. After the war, Dean Taylor found the cost of gowns "extortionate," so he did not reinstate the tradition right away, as much as he admired West and his essential philosophy of humanized learning. Even more relevant was the resistance of the mature veterans who flooded the Graduate School and College on the G.I. Bill. Serious men who had postponed their education, traveled widely, experienced women, and been shot at had no tolerance for any form of scholastic dandyism or curtailment of their hard-earned freedom. Yet even in 1953, well after the last veterans had graduated, the students voted two-to-one against the reinstatement of gowns. Dean Taylor, an English-born High Catholic who retained his British passport and was knighted by Queen Elizabeth in that year, was forced to ignore the plebiscite, he said, because of "sadly deteriorating sartorial standards," even "T-shirts revealing hairy chests," in the dining hall. Those who were adamantly opposed to gowns—and to the Graduate College being ruled like a "Crown Colony" ("no robes without representation")—could dine on the same food in the contiguous breakfast rooms or take their chances downtown. But Sir Hugh had his way and most of the "would-be revolutionaries decided that eating in Procter Hall, gowned, was cheaper than equivalent meals on Nassau or Witherspoon Streets."[87]

[86] Marvin Harold Cheiten "The Graduate School," *PAW*, May 30, 1972, 27; Stone, "Andrew Fleming West," 13. Bill Berry, a history student in the late-1960s from Arkansas, recognized the value of ritual and regarded the gown as "a sort of fancy bib overalls" that "saved on laundry" ("Class Southerner," 310).

[87] Taylor, *The Forum*, 6–7; "The Graduate School," *PAW*, May 23, 1958, 6; Thorp, *PGS*, 256–58 (p. 257 contains a misprint: "1958" should read "1953"). See also Margaret Keenan, "Hugh Stott Taylor," *Princeton History* 8 (1989): 22–33.

Gowns were worn until the early 1970s, when they largely went the way of formal sit-down dinners, Latin grace, waitresses, and a communal sense of tradition and elitist distinction. But not without some lingering nostalgia for the "aesthetically pleasing sight" of the great flock of "black crows" bent over their bowls beneath Procter's sixty-foot gothic ceiling and then "lined up chatting on the wall outside . . . after dinner on pleasant October or May evenings."[88]

❁ ❁ ❁

Even before Dean West retired in 1928, the graduate school he sought to equate with his ritualized Graduate College would not fit that procrustean quad and continued to grow in intellectual stature under Wilson's successors, Hibben and Dodds. Despite the challenges of two world wars and a major economic depression, the Graduate School managed to compile an enviable academic record while remaining purposely small and focused on the liberal arts and sciences.

The school's accomplishments were perhaps the more remarkable for having been fashioned from a mixed set of resources. First, the library was "inadequate to the present and rapidly growing needs of the University" and "inferior to the libraries of [its] chief academic rivals." The "narrow facilities" Princeton offered, warned Professor of Art Frank Mather in 1914, "makes the place relatively unattractive" to both faculty and the "more mature and able" graduate students "habitually engaged in original research." And the situation only worsened until Firestone Library opened in 1948.[89] The book-deprived graduate faculty also put in comparatively long hours in the classroom, whether they taught freshmen or advanced doctoral students. In 1906 most Princeton professors taught ten hours or more; in 1922 they still did. Their colleagues at rival research universities

[88] Thorp, *PGS*, 356; Avery, "Life at the Graduate College," *PAW*, Feb. 20, 1959, 4; questionnaire response from Donald D. Kasarda (Ph.D. 1961), Centennial Questionnaires, Graduate School Records, PUA.

[89] Frank Jewett Mather, Jr., "The University Library," *PAW*, May 20, 1914, 662–64, at 662.

taught fewer hours, particularly when they offered graduate courses and supervised theses and dissertations. Moreover, by the early 1920s, the Princeton faculty still had no revolving funds to support their research, though there was some money to subsidize their publications once they managed to produce them.[90]

The students who were accepted by the departments and the dean and accepted Princeton's offer of admission were, it would appear, reasonably well qualified for graduate work. According to West, "only men of superior academic record in distinctively liberal studies" were admitted, except briefly at the end of World War I when he was "forced occasionally to admit insufficiently qualified students solely in order to avoid a deficit."[91] But the undergraduate origins of these students suggests that their academic records were, again, not the sole basis of his judgments. Until West retired and was replaced by stricter meritocrats, physicist Augustus Trowbridge (1928–1933) and mathematician Luther Eisenhart (1933–1945), most graduate students came from small eastern or midwestern liberal arts colleges, such as Williams, Hamilton, and Oberlin, schools closer to the Princeton model than to the larger research universities in producing "finer" minds and social adepts.[92]

By far the largest segment—at least a third—of each class came from Princeton itself. Indeed, at a time when a quarter of the Princeton faculty had degrees from the Graduate School, President Hibben could boast that the university could now recruit an "increasing number" of graduate students from its own graduating classes because the new upperclass plan of study had begun to turn out men of greater intellectual independence and advanced research skills.[93] Before the

[90] "Class-Room and Laboratory Instruction by Teachers," in CFAT, *Third Annual Report* (New York, 1908), 134–43, at 136; Committee B, "Encouragement of University Research," in American Association of University Professors, *Bulletin* 8 (Apr. 1922): 27–39, at 34. Princeton established a scientific research fund in 1928 with proceeds from the General Education Board's grant (see p. 413, below). But a general University Research Fund was not created until 1936. Thorp, *PGS*, 254.

[91] *President's Report (1919)*, 52, *(1921)*, 9.

[92] Thorp, *PGS*, 204, 210. For the undergraduate origins of the graduate students, see the *President's Reports* for 1921, 1923, and 1926, app. C, table III.

[93] *President's Report (1925)*, 10.

advent of the Graduate Record Examination (GRE) and other nationwide assessments, Princeton was not alone in relying on established college reputations, "old-boy" networks, and its own seniors to recruit graduate school classes; in the 1920s nearly 30 percent of the University of Chicago's Ph.D.s had passed their undergraduate years on the same campus.[94] Yet the ingrown quality of the Princeton graduate cohorts certainly reduced the amount and quality of interpersonal and interdisciplinary exchange desired by Dean West.

Another measure of graduate school quality today is the selectivity of the admission process. In the 1920s the American graduate population was not very large, only fifteen thousand in 1920 and under fifty thousand ten years later, before a major surge occurred during the Great Depression. The majority of doctoral degrees were awarded by a small number of large research universities.[95] Thus admission selectivity may not have been as important an indicator of institutional quality as it was in the seller's markets of the 1950s and late 1980s. Yet a low acceptance rate could still indicate something about the quality of a graduate school in the eyes of its applicants, particularly a small, focused school. In the late 1920s, Princeton accepted over half of its applicants, but awarded its generous and numerous fellowships to only one in six; these fellows were expected to give (in Dean West's words) "tone to the whole body."[96] In this instance, the dean meant only *intellectual* tone.

To judge by the nationally recognized achievements of Princeton's graduate students and faculty before World War II, academic expectations for the Graduate School were well met, though best, ironi-

[94] Reeves and Russell, *Admission and Retention of University Students*, 141 (table 50).

[95] Bernard Berelson, *Graduate Education in the United States* (New York, 1960), 26; Roger L. Geiger, *To Advance Knowledge: The Growth of American Research Universities, 1900–1940* (New York, 1986), 113; David Allan Robertson, "Graduate Study in the United States," in AAU, *J. of Procs.* (1927): 47–75, at 48–49 (tables I–III). As late as the mid-1930s only eleven universities conferred half of the doctorates. National Resources Committee [NRC], *Research—A National Resource. I.-Relation of the Federal Government to Research* (Washington, DC, Nov. 1938), 170. In 1938 the thirty members of the AAU accounted for 84 percent of the c. 3,000 doctorates. "Report of the Committee on Graduate Work," AAU, *J. of Procs.* (1938): 35–47, at 40.

[96] Thorp, *PGS*, 199 (table 4); *President's Report (1923)*, 32, *(1928)*, 26.

cally, in disciplines that neither West nor Wilson understood or particularly championed. In 1938 a federally appointed committee of scientists and scholars singled out Princeton for praise in limiting its graduate enrollment to 250 and encouraging "the less competent to drop out with a master's degree." "It seems probable that from this policy," committee spokesman Raymond M. Hughes concluded, "Princeton has 250 of the most promising graduate students in the country constantly enrolled."[97] It was no coincidence that Hughes, president of the State University of Iowa, had also been the author in 1925 of the first national rating of graduate programs, in which Princeton acquitted itself quite well, despite its small size and relatively recent development. According to twenty-five leading scholars in each discipline, Princeton's sixteen departments were ranked as high as second (classics) and no lower than twelfth (German); seven departments (including mathematics, astronomy, and physics) were among the top five, and fourteen in the top ten, in their fields.[98]

That Princeton's humanities departments—classics, French, Spanish, English, and philosophy—scored in the top six was probably no surprise to academic contemporaries. But the equally strong showing of its science and math departments, including zoology, may have been news to most outsiders. Princeton used these results to ask the Rockefeller-supported General Education Board in the same year for $3.5 million to endow research in the sciences, as part of its just-launched $20 million campaign. The university's application also pointed to another impressive record in these fields.

> In the number of its Ph.D.s who have been granted National Research Fellowships, Princeton stands first in the list of universities in physics, ties for first in mathematics, and stands third in chemistry, and has the distinction, we believe, of never having had an applicant who failed of appointment. Also in the number of National Research Fellows who have come to Princeton, as compared with other univer-

[97] NRC, *Research*, 184. In 1932 Dean Trowbridge increased West's original ceiling on enrollment from 200 to 250, where it remained until 1945. Thorp, *PGS*, 200.

[98] R. M. Hughes, *A Study of the Graduate Schools of America* (Oxford, Ohio, 1925); Thorp, *PGS*, 192 (table 3).

> sities, Princeton ranks first in mathematics and third in mathematics, physics and chemistry combined.[99]

The board looked favorably on Princeton's request, giving $1 million if the university raised another $2 million. By 1928 Princeton had the funds to establish five research professorships, four of which were filled with local faculty, two of them—physicist Karl Compton and astronomer Henry Norris Russell—products of the Graduate School.[100]

Within three years, Princeton also got a first-rate chemistry building from industrialist Henry Clay Frick and a handsome mathematics building, named for Dean of the Departments of Science Henry Fine; he had been killed by a car while riding his bicycle in 1928. After the Institute for Advanced Study was founded in 1930, its earliest members, including Albert Einstein, were given offices in Fine Hall; several lived in the Graduate College. The addition to the Princeton community of these brilliant thinkers, some of them refugees from Nazi Europe, lent considerable luster to Princeton's growing reputation as a world-class center of science and mathematics, even though they were not officially part of the university.[101]

Princeton's role in pursuing quantum mechanics (the mathematical foundation of atomic and subatomic physics) in the late 1920s also put the university at the forefront of both theoretical and experimental science and scientific education, particularly at the graduate

[99] Thorp, *PGS*, 193. See also Frank R. Lillie, "Post-Doctoral Training for Productive Scholarship," AAU, *J. of Procs.* (1935): 147–53, at 152 (table I).

[100] Thorp, *PGS*, 191–95.

[101] Thorp, *PGS*, 196, 218–19; Leitch, *Princeton Companion*, 179–80, 271–72, 278–79; Loren Butler Feffer, "Oswald Veblen and the Capitalization of American Mathematics: Raising Money for Research, 1923–1928," *Isis* 89:3 (Sept. 1998): 474–97; Laura Smith Porter, "From Intellectual Sanctuary to Social Responsibility: The Founding of the Institute for Advanced Study, 1930–1933" (Ph.D. diss., Dept. of History, PU, 1988); Murray H. Reich, "Emigrés and Students," *Princeton History*, no. 6 (1987): 6–18; Donald Fleming and Bernard Bailyn, eds., *The Intellectual Migration: Europe and America, 1930–1960* (Cambridge, Mass., 1969); Jarrell C. Jackman and Carla M. Borden, eds., *The Muses Flee Hitler: Cultural Transfer and Adaptation, 1930–1945* (Washington, D.C., 1983); Laura Fermi, *Illustrious Immigrants: The Intellectual Migration from Europe, 1930–41*, rev. ed. (Chicago, 1971 [1968]).

and postdoctoral level. By 1930 Princeton was one of only five or six American universities with theoretical physics faculties of the first order. When James McKeen Cattell published the sixth edition of his influential directory of *American Men of Science* in 1938, Princeton's share of "starred" members—the top 5–6 percent in twelve major fields—ranked eighth, up from thirteenth in 1906.[102]

Since Princeton has always required even distinguished research professors to teach at least graduate students, the Graduate School benefited in a major way from the university's rise to scientific eminence. Dean West, who played little or no part in these developments, was understandably ambivalent about them. Although he celebrated them briefly in his final report to the president, he was more concerned to stress the need for "additions to strengthen departments having less [*sic*] facilities, especially in certain humanistic studies where the death or retirement of professors has left us insufficiently equipped and in departments which have not had their proportionate development."[103] It was an appropriate time for the old-time classicist to step down and for a physicist, then a mathematician, to lead the Graduate School to the threshold of a different, more complex, and brighter era.

❁ ❁ ❁

Before the outbreak of World War II, the Graduate School under deans Trowbridge and Eisenhart not only grew beyond 250 students, but tightened its standards and rationalized its curriculum and procedures. The presence of seminarians and other "incidental" students who took courses only part-time was all but eliminated. The M.A. was no longer awarded for accumulating course credits, but only for

[102] Stanley Coben, "The Scientific Establishment and the Transmission of Quantum Mechanics to the United States, 1919–32," *American Historical Review* 76:2 (Apr. 1971): 442–66; Geiger, *To Advance Knowledge*, 233–45; Katherine Russell Sopka, *Quantum Physics in America, 1920–35* ([Ph.D. diss., School of Education, Harvard University, 1976], New York, 1980); Charles Weiner, "New Site for the Seminar: The Refugees and American Physics in the Thirties," in Fleming and Bailyn, eds., *The Intellectual Migration*, 190–234; NRC, *Research*, 170–71, 174 (table II), 175.

[103] *President's Report (1928)*, 27.

passing the newly reformed general examination for the Ph.D. Although a reading knowledge of two foreign languages was still required, a defensible substitute for either French or German was now permitted. The doctoral "thesis" became a heftier "dissertation," which was expected to "enlarge or modify what was previously known, or present a significant interpretation of its subject." Dissertations were still required to be published before acceptance, but microfilming slowly became an acceptable substitute. Pre- and postdoctoral fellowships multiplied with the support of private donors, foundations, corporations, and foreign governments. Likewise, scholarships for first-year students were inaugurated with university funds to enable Princeton to compete with increasingly generous rivals. Finally, Research Assistants, who had been hired by the newly endowed science departments to assist the faculty in their labs, were all placed under the aegis of the Graduate School and subjected to its requirements; similarly, students who taught or supervised undergraduate labs part-time were classified as Assistants in Instruction.[104]

On the eve of war in Europe, the Graduate School, like the university in general, was in relatively robust shape, despite the economic uncertainties of the lingering depression. Unlike the endowments of most universities, Princeton's conservatively managed portfolio actually rose in value throughout the 1930s, in spite of generally falling rates of return on stocks and even bonds. Between 1937 and 1939 the university raised $3.6 million to augment the proceeds of its major campaign of the late 1920s. Instead of firing faculty, Princeton was able to hire more, particularly in the sciences and mathematics. Graduate enrollments also increased, to a high of 277 in the trough of the Great Depression. Although the national cost of living fell, money was still in short supply and applications for fellowships jumped sharply; but the number awarded declined only slightly and the stipends not at all. With 360 faculty members, an increase of 17 percent since the Great Crash, Princeton in 1939 had a teacher for every seven-and-a-half students. Since the faculty greatly outnumbered the graduate students, classes remained small and su-

[104] Thorp, *PGS*, 198–217.

pervision close. In 1939, fifty-five new doctors were hooded at commencement, an increase of 78 percent in a troubled decade.[105]

In the middle of the Great Depression, Princeton's strength in research, scholarship, and graduate education received strong recognition in two public reports. In 1934 a committee of the American Council on Education (ACE), chaired by the ubiquitous Raymond Hughes, conducted a "reputational" survey of the nation's graduate schools by asking a hundred learned experts in thirty-five disciplines to rate the "distinguished" and the "adequate" departments in their fields. In the eyes of its peers, Princeton had seventeen noteworthy departments, fourteen of which were regarded as distinguished, that is, among the top 20 percent; only two departments (botany and sociology) failed to make the grade. Although several, much larger universities had many more departments of various qualities, Princeton had the highest ratio of best to good departments, electing, in the Wilsonian spirit, to do fewer things well.[106]

The following year, Edwin R. Embree published an article entitled "In Order of Their Eminence: An Appraisal of American Universities" in the *Atlantic Monthly*, which generated as much talk and teeth-gnashing as the appearance of *U.S. News & World Report*'s annual college issue does today. Making it clear that he was considering "university scholarship" and not "college life," Embree used the ACE ratings, the starred entries in *American Men of Science*, publications in scholarly journals, and consultation with "individual scholars and national committees . . . in a position to judge" to put Princeton in a "second bracket," in eighth place, behind and among much larger rivals. His assessment, however, was that "Princeton has the most brilliant recent history of all the universities" in the second group (which included Michigan, Cornell, and Wisconsin) and has

[105] Geiger, *To Advance Knowledge*, 246–52, 272 (app. B), 275 (app. C), 277 (app. D), 278 (app. E).

[106] American Council on Education, *Report of Committee on Graduate Instruction* (Washington, D.C., Apr. 1934); R. M. Hughes, "Report of Committee on Graduate Instruction," *Educational Record* 15 (Apr. 1934): 192–234; "Survey of Graduate Schools," *PAW*, Apr. 27, 1934, 646. The Hughes study found that 208 of the 226 distinguished departments in the country were located in research universities. Geiger, *To Advance Knowledge*, 262.

"in a single generation" become "one of the nation's centres of highest scholarship."[107] Although the article was not directly an evaluation of graduate schools, Embree's words could not fail to honor Princeton's and to draw applicants to it.

America's entry in the war signaled a temporary and uneven reversal of fortune for the Graduate School. Student and faculty populations declined as war work drew many men away. In 1943 only 119 graduate students remained. To fill empty rooms, the Graduate College took in a number of faculty families and housed military units training at the university. But some departments, especially mathematics, physics, and chemistry, actually gained in numbers by undertaking classified research for the federal government and armed services. Work done in Princeton labs and by Princeton faculty contributed to the successful Manhattan Project that brought the war to a terrible and decisive close.[108]

❁ ❁ ❁

The conclusion of the war and the tsunamic return of military personnel to academic life set in motion a quarter-century of long-term trends in the Graduate School, as they did in higher education generally. By 1970 they had ushered the Graduate School into a new stage of evolution that rendered virtually obsolete the Westian forms and style of graduate education and elevated to primacy the Wilsonian focus on intellectual attainment. Losses as well as gains resulted from this shift, but the shift itself was inexorable, with large consequences for the Graduate School's national and international reputation and its status within the Princeton family.

The immediate effect of the war's end and the passage of the G.I. Bill in 1944 was a huge increase in Graduate School enrollments.

[107] *Atlantic Monthly*, June 1935, 652–64, at 660–61.

[108] Thorp, *PGS*, 219–21; "Princeton and the Bomb," *PAW*, Sept. 28, 1945, 7, 12; Richard Rhodes, *The Making of the Atom Bomb* (New York, 1987). For the general impact of the war on the university, see Richard D. Challener, "Princeton and Pearl Harbor: Town and Gown," *Princeton History*, no. 11 (1992): 28–47, and "The Response to War," *Princeton History*, no. 11 (1992): 48–65; Robert K. Root, "The Princeton Campus in World War II" (1950), revised by Jeremiah Finch (1978), PUA; J. Douglas Brown, "Princeton and the War," *PAW*, Nov. 16, 1945, 5–6.

From only 132 in 1944–1945, the graduate population nearly quadrupled in two years and reached 548 by 1949–1950, when eighty-nine Ph.D.s were awarded. While the undergraduate veteran bulge receded by 1950, graduate numbers continued to climb in response to the country's call for more faculty members to serve the proliferation and expansion of colleges and universities produced by Cold War, post-Sputnik competition, and the thoroughly American drive for credentials and the "collegiate" experience. By 1967 the Graduate School was bursting with 1,543 members, who constituted for the first time nearly a third of all Princeton students. Save for a small setback during the recession of the early 1970s, graduate enrollments continued to grow steadily to a high of 1,866 in 1992, before being trimmed to 1,734 at century's end and then surging over 2,000 in 2003–2004. Since these totals included the members of three professional schools, Princeton's core arts and sciences enrollment continued to compare unfavorably with Yale's and Harvard's in sheer size, which in "reputational" ratings still conferred an undue advantage.[109]

An alumnus of Merwick or the early Graduate College, however, would have found the new graduate population quite different from his own. Rather than a small coterie of smooth young men from the best liberal arts colleges, he would have found at any time after 1970 a veritable United Nations of ethnicities, nationalities, and genders, hailing mainly from undergraduate universities more like Princeton and its larger research rivals. Particularly after the implementation of the GRE in 1951, "clubability" was thoroughly replaced by intellectual aptitude and academic performance as the sole criteria for admission.[110] This brought an influx of women, American blacks and other minorities, and international students, few or (in the female case) none of whom had been admitted before the Axis cracked open

[109] William G. Bowen, *The Federal Government and Princeton University* (Princeton, 1962), 223 (table 17); Roger L. Geiger, *Research and Relevant Knowledge: American Research Universities Since World War II* (New York, 1993), 214 (table 17); Thorp, *PGS*, 324–25; PU, *Profile, 2003–2004* (Princeton: Office of Communications, 2003), 18.

[110] Princeton helped to develop the GRE in 1937, but administered it only to first-year students already accepted. In 1941 the graduate faculty voted not to require it for admission, but joined with its co-producers Harvard, Yale, and Columbia in asking those who had already taken it to submit the results with their applications. The GRE was not required of all applicants until 1951. Thorp, *PGS*, 214–16.

America's complacent isolationism and the resulting war began to correct its social astigmatism.

Although a graduate faculty committee had recommended the admission of women as early as 1958, the first one, Sabra Meservey, a Douglass College instructor, Princeton faculty wife, and mother of three, did not receive her acceptance letter—which began "Dear Sir"—until 1961. Three years later, China-born T'sai-ying Cheng became the first woman to receive a doctoral diploma, whose phraseology had not yet been neutered by the university's Latin scribe. From these small beginnings there was no turning back. When undergraduate Princeton went coed in 1969, there were over two hundred graduate sisters to welcome the newcomers. By 1975 a quarter of the graduate population was female, by 1998 more than a third. Their lot in a formerly all-male university was not always easy, but they performed as well as their male classmates and made a salutary and enduring mark on the quality and tenor of graduate life.[111]

The active recruitment—as opposed to mere acceptance—of African-Americans for graduate work enjoyed much less success. Blacks who had been admitted since Simeon Moss earned an M.A. in 1949 could be counted each semester on one hand. Only in the 1960s did the Graduate School, especially black Assistant Dean Conrad Snowden, begin to solicit applications from black students, largely from historically black colleges and urban universities. But black students' relative lack of preparation and the scarcity of programs that appealed to disadvantaged blacks with more immediate vocational payoffs in mind, not to mention Princeton's reputation as a white suburban fortress with a southern student heritage, stalled the early momentum gained from the civil rights and "black power" movements. From a peak of seventy-nine in 1973, black enrollments declined precipitously for the rest of the century. When they hit bottom in 1983 with only twenty-five, however, they had been aug-

[111] Thorp, *PGS*, 285–89, 327–29. Yale had admitted women to its graduate school since 1892 and Harvard since 1933. Brooks Mather Kelley, *Yale: A History* (New Haven, 1974), 283–84; Morton and Phyllis Keller, *Making Harvard Modern: The Rise of America's University* (New York, 2001), 51–52. In the fall of 2004, women constituted 37 percent of the Princeton graduate population.

mented by thirty Hispanics and forty-five Asian-Americans. By 2004 the American minority enrollment of the Graduate School stood at 12 percent, only 2.1 percent of whom were African-Americans, far below their share of the national population.[112]

Diversity of another kind was achieved by the steady enrollment of international students. The Graduate School had admitted foreign students in small numbers after World War I, when Dean West sought a special endowment for graduate exchanges with America's French and British allies. In 1920, fourteen students (9 percent) matriculated from Canada, Belgium, China, Japan, Norway, and France. When West stepped down in 1928, the leaven of strangers had nearly doubled. Most of these visitors were English-speakers from Europe and the British Commonwealth, well within West's comfort zone, a trend that continued until the late 1960s. From a low point in 1976 of only 178 students (18 percent), foreign enrollments rose steadily to the new millennium, causing Princeton to add to its informal motto "and in the Service of All Nations." In the fall of 2004, students from abroad numbered 812, some 40 percent of degree candidates.[113]

As foreign students flocked to Princeton, their countries of origin shifted noticeably. By the mid-1980s, Asian conversations—Chinese, Indian, Korean—began to inflect Graduate College table talk. After 1987 the single largest contingent came from the People's Republic of China, despite its political and social oscillations. The presence of large numbers of foreign-speakers raised concerns about their ability to teach effectively, but these were addressed only in 1997 by requiring all students with English deficiencies to take one or more summer courses in English as a Second Language (ESL). The less serious problem of national cliquishness, thought to hamper

[112] Thorp, *PGS*, 317–19, 329–32; John M. Fenton, "Black Graduate Students," *PAW*, May 4, 1971, 5; Dean Theodore Ziolkowski, letter to the editor, *PAW*, June 14, 1989, 4; Fall Enrollment Statistics (2004).

[113] *President's Report (1919)*, 51, *(1921)*, 90–91 (app. C, table III), *(1928)*, 103 (app. C, table I); Thorp, *PGS*, 332–33; PU, *Profile, 2004–05*, 18; Larry Dubois, "The Foreign Graduate Student," *PAW*, Feb. 14, 1967, 6–11 (interviews with fifteen). During World War II, a number of Chinese students pursued degrees in the sciences, but gradually withdrew after the cessation of hostilities. Thorp, *PGS*, 221.

departmental collegiality and Graduate College sociability, has yet to find a solution.[114]

The flood of students obviously inundated the Graduate College and in the process destroyed the easy equation that Dean West made between the College and the Graduate School. The administration remained committed to providing as much graduate housing as possible, for between 70 and 80 percent of the students, because of the town's lack of affordable rental space, the racism of some landlords, and a chivalrous regard for the safety of female students.[115] So the university expanded or built new quarters to keep up with rising enrollments. Expansion had been necessary even before the war. In 1927 William Procter was persuaded to add a handsome North Court to the Graduate College to raise the Gothic facility's capacity to 160. That trend continued, in a more modern but compatible and less expensive style, with the addition in 1963 of a dormitory complex for 275 students; its twin quads were named for Procter and the stellar Compton brothers, Karl, Wilson, and Arthur, all of whom earned Princeton Ph.D.s.[116]

Even before the war, not all graduate students met West's preference for single men in their twenties or wanted—or could afford—to

[114] Thorp, *PGS*, 332–36.

[115] In 1998 Stanford housed about 46 percent of its 7,000 graduate students on campus; Yale managed only 12 percent and Harvard 26 percent. *Stanford*, May/June 1998, 37. In 2001 Princeton housed 80 percent. A surge in enrollment in 2002–2003 dropped the housing figure to 70 percent. But the addition of seven new buildings (346 beds) to the Lawrence Apartments raised the number again to 80 percent. Brian Henn, "University to Build Additional Housing for Grads Amid Concern Over Shortage," *DP* (online), Sept. 13, 2002; Deborah Arostsky, "University Expands Lawrence Apartments," *DP* (online), Feb. 12, 2004.

[116] Thorp, *PGS*, 182, 278–83; "New Graduate Dormitories," *PAW*, Oct. 1, 1963, 6–9; Coffin, *Princeton's Graduate College*, 28, 30–32. Karl T. Compton (Ph.D. 1912) was chairman of the Princeton physics department and later president of MIT. Wilson M. Compton (Ph.D. 1915) taught economics, served the lumber industry and the federal government, and later became president of the State College of Washington (later Washington State University). Arthur Compton (Ph.D. 1916) taught physics at the University of Chicago, won a Nobel Prize in 1927, and later took a leading part in the development of the atomic bomb. Leitch, *Princeton Companion*, 112. For a fascinating look at their upbringing in Wooster, Ohio, where their father taught philosophy and was dean of the College of Wooster, see James R. Blackwood, *The House on College Avenue: The Comptons at Wooster, 1891–1913* (Cambridge, Mass., 1968).

submit themselves to his social experiment in the Graduate College. Thrifty or impecunious students, like future president Harold Dodds, often roomed and boarded in town or at the seminary. Married students, of course, posed the greatest challenge to the Westian "residential principle" by dividing their loyalties and by introducing Eves into the monastic landscape. Before the war, fellowship- and scholarship-holders were forbidden to marry, and the rest were strongly encouraged not to.[117] After the war, many of the returning veterans brought wives, who could not, of course, be sheltered in the Graduate College. The university found a partial solution through a federal housing program, which erected rebuilt military barracks for nearly 250 families on the old polo field on the east side of town. Not only were they not torn down after five years, as the contract stipulated they should be, but fifty-eight new units were added in 1988. The "Butler Tract" now houses about a fifth of the graduate population, who enjoy a full and distinctive social life of their own far, and far different, from that of the Graduate College.[118]

Women students and spouses gained additional housing in the 1960s. In 1966 the university built the 150-unit Lawrence Apartments just below the golf course. Families with children occupied a cluster of two-storey buildings, while couples took the one-bedroom units in a twelve-storey high-rise. Two years later, "Goon Castle" lowered its drawbridge to allow coed occupation of its new quads and the following year its venerable Gothic quads. But many American

[117] Walter J. Kauzmann, who studied chemistry from 1937 to 1939, remembered that "all graduate students were required to sign a pledge that they would not marry while they were graduate students." A number of his contemporaries violated the pledge and were "penalized and severely criticized" (Marks, *Luminaries*, 313–14). Even the scientific genius Richard Feynman was told that he would lose his prestigious and badly needed Procter Fellowship if he married his fatally ill fiancée, Arline, before graduation. Contrary to Kauzmann's memory, he did neither. James Gleick, *Genius: The Life and Science of Richard Feynman* (New York, 1992), 135; John and Mary Gribbin, *Richard Feynman: A Life in Science* (New York, 1997), 66–67.

[118] Thorp, *PGS*, 190–91, 226–28, 277, 304, 355, 358–59; Donald R. Hamilton, "Some Graduate School Issues," *PAW*, Apr. 22, 1960, 3–5; Randolph Clarke, "A Graduate Student Government?" *PAW*, Oct. 12, 1988, 25. In 1991 all graduate housing beyond the Graduate College was opened to gay and unmarried couples, partly because the graduate ranks of legal marrieds fell from 41 percent in 1970–1971 to only 14 percent at the end of the century. Thorp, *PGS*, 358.

women regarded the privilege warily, increasingly as the College's demographics remained "heavily male" and grew "disproportionately foreign." The remainder of the graduate population was forced to find quarters in town and as far away as Hightstown, Hopewell, and Trenton, much to the chagrin of deans who still believed in the Westian ideal of communal learning.[119]

Princeton continued to attract high-quality students for several reasons, the most decisive of which was the quality of its graduate faculty and programs. But competitive, if not generous, financial support was also effective. In the 1950s and early 1960s, Princeton benefited from the increased largesse of the federal government, corporations, and foundations, which turned to America's universities for basic and sponsored research, graduate training, and faculty development. A large percentage of the university's graduate fellowships (over half in 1968) was dependent on outside sources, all of which were subject to economic cycles, social trends, and politics. In the early 1960s the National Science Foundation supported 35 percent of the graduate students in physics and 55 percent in mathematics; the National Institutes of Health funded over 70 percent of the graduate biologists. The National Defense Education Act of 1958 subsidized new programs in Near Eastern and Slavic studies. In 1965 sponsored research, mostly in the sciences and engineering, brought Princeton $28.5 million, which represented about one half of the total university research budget for the year; all but $1 million came from Washington, much of it from the Atomic Energy Commission. All of this "hire learning," as Professor of Physics Henry DeWolf Smyth called it affectionately, made it possible to "enlarge the graduate school, to improve graduate instruction, and to improve the quality of the faculty."[120]

[119] Thorp, *PGS*, 283, 304, 329 (quotation), 359.

[120] Thorp, *PGS*, 260–63, 272–77 (quotation 276), 295–96, 337–42. Between 1946 and 1958 Princeton also received $3.7 million in support of the social sciences from the four major foundations (Carnegie, Ford, Rockefeller, and the Social Science Research Council). This amount constituted only 4.3 percent of the foundations' disbursements; Harvard, Chicago, and Columbia together received 48 percent of the total. Geiger, *Research and Relevant Knowledge*, 105.

Although outside support was welcome, allowing the university to use more of its own funds for improvements in the humanities and social sciences, many academics worried about the propensity of piper-payers to call the tunes. Fortunately, a study conducted by then-Professor of Economics William Bowen found that 86 percent of the graduate students in the heavily sponsored sciences felt free to choose their own advisors and dissertation topics. But the influx of new wealth did result in some inequalities among the three academic divisions. Graduate students in the natural sciences received higher stipends and science faculty enjoyed higher salaries, more summer research grants, and lower teaching loads than their colleagues in the humanities and social sciences.[121]

The biggest danger in relying on outside support for graduate education became all too clear when the federal government slashed its funding for both research and graduate education between the late 1960s and mid-1970s. The share of federal funding for higher education that went to support graduate education dropped from 60 to 17 percent; support for graduate students was cut in half, to only 13 percent. Princeton alone lost over 30 percent of its federal research funds, as did Chicago, Columbia, and Michigan, though Princeton suffered fewer serious results.[122]

When the decanal members of the Association of Graduate Schools met annually during those years of recession, double-digit inflation, and cutbacks, depressing statistics and alarms filled the air. A Northwestern University dean suggested that "perhaps we had flown too close to the fickle flame of society's acclaim and got our wings singed." Princeton's dean Alvin Kernan (1970–1974) emphasized institutional integrity. "We all bent ourselves in pretzels," he chided, "so as to participate in government support money and yet not abandon the fundamental research that most of us still want to maintain." Perhaps the most sensible warning was sounded by

[121] Bowen, *The Federal Government and Princeton*, 208–9, 226 (table 18), 268 (table 28).

[122] William F. Gaul, "The Congressional Outlook for Graduate Education," AAU, *J. of Procs.* (1977): 30–36, at 32–33; Geiger, *Research and Relevant Knowledge*, 209 (table 16).

President Steven Muller of Johns Hopkins, who told his listeners that "there was not, is not, and will not be any consistent national policy with respect to graduate training. . . . Our representative democracy is too reactive to changeable public opinion and to short-term pressures to sustain that kind of . . . policy."[123]

Apparently heeding that warning, Princeton for the remainder of the century sought to shift the ratio of its graduate funding sources. Although government funds for graduate education and research soon reappeared in lesser amounts, sometimes in new guises, they fell again, along with the Soviet bloc, before stabilizing thereafter. Corporate funds fluctuated with the state of the economy and the need for applied research. Foundation grants were perhaps the most attractive external sources, but they tended to be relatively modest in size, earmarked for specific purposes, and of short duration. Therefore the university wisely took it upon itself to fund ever-larger numbers of students to compensate for the uncertainties in other sources.[124]

Thanks in large measure to a robust economy and to the success of the university's 250th anniversary campaign, the Graduate School at its centennial in 2000 was able to offer nearly 600 university fellowships (of which 247 were endowed and named) and 262 assis-

[123] Dean Robert H. Baker, "The President's Remarks," AAU, *J. of Procs.* (1972): 4–6, at 5; Dean Alvin B. Kernan, "Changing Criteria in Graduate Programs," AAU, *J. of Procs.* (1974): 28–31, at 31; President Steven Muller, "AGS Graduate Schools in 2001 A.D.," AAU, *J. of Procs.* (1976): 9–12, at 10.

[124] Thorp, *PGS*, 337. The Ford Foundation gave Princeton $4 million for graduate fellowships in the humanities and social sciences between 1967 and 1974. Similarly, on the eve of the university's campaign of 1981–1986, Dean Theodore Ziolkowski obtained from the Andrew F. Mellon Foundation a $1.2 million grant for graduate education. Before he stepped down, he received another grant to fund summer stipends for students in five humanities departments in an effort to speed up their completion rates. Thorp, *PGS*, 296–97, 340; Ziolkowski, Report to the President (1990–1991), 3–4, Office of the Dean of the Graduate School, Nassau Hall. For Princeton's benefits from the Woodrow Wilson Fellowship Program, begun at Princeton in 1945–1946, see Thorp, *PGS*, 227–31, 272–73; Whitney J. Oates, "Recruiting for an Academic Career," *PAW*, Mar. 14, 1947, 5–7; "Wilson Fellows," *PAW*, Jan. 20, 1961, 7; "25 (Full) Years of Woodrow Wilson Fellowships," *PAW*, Mar. 18, 1969, 21–22, 39–42; also in *University: A Princeton Quarterly* (Spring 1969).

tantships in instruction, compared to only 330 government-sponsored research assistantships. Quite unlike the situation at most of its academic rivals, only 16 percent of Princeton's graduate population earned their keep by teaching; fully 56 percent were on university fellowships that freed them to concentrate on their scholarship—almost exactly the proportion who were supported by *external* fellowships thirty years earlier. Even science students were being increasingly supported in their first year by university fellowships, instead of being funded out of their advisors' uncertain research contracts.[125]

The steady rise in graduate enrollments after World War II coincided with an equally steady increase in the size of the Princeton faculty. From an ample 360 on the eve of the war, the faculty grew to 449 by 1959–1960 and 789 by 1979–80. Over the last two decades of the century, while the student population remained stable, the tenure-track faculty in the arts and sciences grew by 20 percent; at Harvard they grew by only 6 percent and at Yale they actually fell by 14 percent. In 2004 there were over eight hundred faculty full-time-equivalents (FTEs) at Princeton, giving it the largest arts and sciences faculty among its peers.[126]

Much of the growth of the faculty was attributable to the exponential growth of knowledge in the twentieth century and the resulting "fission and fusion" of the curriculum. As the traditional bounds of knowledge were exploded by wars, social and political pressure, economic need, invention, and sheer genius, universities responded, usually quickly, by adding new courses of study, some taught by new faculty members who had learned or at least heard about the advances when they were in graduate school. Because most professors take a proprietary interest in the courses they teach, curricula seldom sloughed off old courses to make room for new ones; both course catalogues and the faculty just grew like Topsy. Typical was the growth between 1956 and 1962, when graduate courses mushroomed from 333 to 434, an increase of 30 percent.[127]

[125] Thorp, *PGS*, 341.

[126] Geiger, *To Advance Knowledge*, 272 (app. B); Bowen, *The Federal Government and Princeton*, 270 (table 29); The Trustees of PU, *Report of the Wythes Committee* (Jan. 29, 2000), 18, fig. 3.

[127] Thorp, *PGS*, 284.

Graduate curricula have grown not only in size but in complexity to reflect the increased specialization, theoretical tendencies, and interdisciplinary nature of modern learning. Departments fused and subdivided: Modern Languages split into Romance and Germanic Language and Literature, Statistics broke free from Mathematics, and Astronomy and the Plasma Physics Laboratory became Astrophysical Sciences. In 1983 the university created a world-class Department of Molecular Biology from a small Biochemical Sciences Department and an aging Biology Department. Not long after, Computer Science hived off from Electrical Engineering. Some departments even experienced a second life: ironically, the graduate program in Slavic Languages and Literatures, cut in 1970 for lack of student demand, was reborn in 1990 after the dissolution of the Soviet bloc.[128]

Since knowledge making would not confine itself to existing disciplinary boundaries, programs sprang up between and around disciplines to accommodate the new growth, at least temporarily. By 1965 Princeton had twenty-six programs, including Demography, Comparative Literature, and Slavic Studies. Eight years later, however, only eight programs had survived recession, departmentalization, or senescence; none combined more than two disciplinary names or areas of study, such as Afro-American Studies and Political Philosophy. Yet by 1998–1999 graduate students could choose from two dozen programs, only six of which had survived from the earlier period. Some were recognizable, such as East Asian Studies, the Philosophy of Science, and the Ancient World. The rest included such luxuriant growths as "Plasma Science and Technology" and "Statistics and Operations Research." These resembled and matched in complexity new programs such as "Atmospheric and Oceanic Sciences" and "Public Affairs and Demography."[129]

Beginning in the 1980s, this congeries of departments and programs was joined by a host of even more focused and acronymic research institutes and centers, which embodied new ideas about how to conduct research and scholarship outside the bounds of existing disciplines. POEM was not a literary bloom but the Center

[128] Thorp, *PGS*, 284, 343.

[129] Thorp, *PGS*, 284–85, 342–44.

for Photonics and Optoelectronic Materials that sprouted in 1989 in the School of Engineering. PMI, the Princeton Materials Institute, followed a year later and involves more than fifty faculty from a dozen departments and their graduate students. In the humanities, the University Center for Human Values was founded in 1990 to provide a colloquium for selected graduate students to receive multidisciplinary critiques of their dissertations. In 1999 a Center for the Study of Religion grew from an earlier center devoted to American religion. One of the latest additions to the Princeton intercurriculum is the Institute for Integrative Genomics, directed by Shirley Tilghman until she became president of the university in 2001.[130]

❁ ❁ ❁

After World War II, Princeton clearly gathered the demographic, economic, and curricular resources to achieve a special kind of academic distinction. But did its students and faculty rise to the occasion? Did they take the Graduate School to a level of "*intellectual* attainment" that not only President Wilson but his successors and their peers would have acknowledged?

Complete and comparable measures of graduate student performance are scarce, but two sets forty years apart allow some perspective. In 1957–1958, Dean Taylor's final year in office, he commissioned Assistant Dean James Thorpe to make a thorough study of the graduate program. Thorpe concluded, first, that graduate admissions were more selective (31.5 percent) than in the undergraduate college (40 percent), at a time when nationally even the top graduate departments took half of their applicants and the rest had virtually open enrollments; neighboring Penn accepted 90 percent in most departments.[131] Second, more than 90 percent of the Princeton students passed their general or comprehensive examinations on the first try, two-thirds of the stymied on the second. He also found that those who continued tended to complete their dissertations and graduate

[130] Thorp, *PGS*, 344–45.

[131] Geiger, *Research and Relevant Knowledge*, 221; Taylor, *Graduate Education at Princeton*, 12.

in reasonable order and good number: two-thirds obtained the Ph.D. (only half of Columbia's candidates did) and did so in an average time after their bachelor's degrees of five years, well above the Graduate School's published "norm" of three years established by Dean West.[132]

By the late 1990s the Graduate School was much harder to get into; it accepted about 17 percent of its applicants and persuaded over half of those to enroll, against keen competition from moneyed and storied rivals such as Harvard, Yale, UC-Berkeley, Stanford, and MIT.[133] The GRE scores of those accepted were in the high 630s verbal, around 730 quantitative, and over 700 analytical; those in the humanities scored about forty points higher on the verbal portion, as did scientists and engineers on the quantitative. Over 60 percent continued to earn their degrees within seven years, and 94 percent (since 1972) found immediate employment, two-thirds of them in academic settings.[134]

The only note of decline since the late 1950s was a creeping rise in time-to-degree, almost six years in 1988–1989, as Dean Theodore Ziolkowski (1979–1992) confessed in the pages of the *American Scholar*. By the end of the century, however, several factors, including more generous student support in the summer, had dropped the average time to five years and eight months, with half the degrees attained in just over five years. Still, it was one more sign that Dean West's graduate school was a faded memory. Not even in the sciences was his ideal of a one-year dissertation feasible. Students in the cumulative humanities and social sciences, in particular, now had a

[132] Taylor, *Graduate Education at Princeton*, 6–7, 10–11, 13.

[133] In 1956 Princeton's "yield" (the number of those accepted for admission who enrolled) was 75 percent; but between then and 1970, when it stabilized at around 50 percent, many more first-rate graduate schools had been established to compete for the nation's best students. In 2004 the yield was 62 percent in the humanities and 42 percent in the more competitive natural sciences. Donald Ross Hamilton, Summary Report to the President: The Graduate School, 1958–1965, Graduate School Collection, box 33, folder 12, p. 9, PUA; William G. Bowen and Neil L. Rudenstine, *In Pursuit of the PhD* (Princeton, 1992), 56–62; "By the Numbers: Graduate School Admissions," *PWB* (online), May 31, 2004.

[134] Thorp, *PGS*, 326, 347.

century of new facts, theories, and scholarship to contend with before making original contributions of their own. Moreover, graduates in all fields felt increasingly compelled by competition in tight job markets not only to perfect or bulk up their dissertations for quicker publication, but to build up their résumés with conference papers and articles before applying to even less-than-top-tier colleges and universities.[135]

The consistently high performance of Princeton's graduate students in good times and bad owes a great deal to the quality of their professors and departments, which have scored exceedingly well on national assessments of graduate education since the 1960s. Princeton's rankings are the more impressive because the university has no medical school to drive scientific research, it is the smallest of the top ten research universities, with federal research and development funds well below the rest, and its undergraduate population is nearly two-and-a-half times larger than the graduate population, whereas at most of its closest competitors graduate students nearly equal or outnumber the undergraduates.[136]

Since 1966, four major national assessments have measured Princeton's graduate programs and faculty against the competition. All of these studies relied heavily on the reputations of the various departments in the thinking of several thousand faculty members in those fields, which obviously has serious methodological flaws. But the last two studies, published in 1982 and 1995, went beyond mere reputation and factored in a variety of more objective measures of academic quality, such as library holdings and faculty publications, awards, and fellowships. In all of these studies, Princeton was rated the sixth or seventh best in the country, behind much larger rivals.

In Allan Cartter's 1966 assessment for the American Council on Education, a solely reputational study, eleven of Princeton's twenty-one doctoral programs studied were rated in the top five, sixteen

[135] Thorp, *PGS*, 346–48; Theodore J. Ziolkowski, "The Ph.D. Squid," *American Scholar* 59 (Spring 1990): 177–95, at 188.

[136] William G. Bowen, *Report of the President. Graduate Education in the Arts and Sciences: Prospects for the Future* (Princeton, Apr. 1981), 5 (table 1); Hugh Davis Graham and Nancy Diamond, *The Rise of American Research Universities: Elites and Challengers in the Postwar Era* (Baltimore, 1997), 223–24 (table apps. 1–2)

in the top ten. Three—Philosophy, Mathematics, and Physics—were regarded as the country's best. The faculties in those departments ranked just slightly lower: only nine were ranked in the top five, though fifteen made it into the top ten.[137] Nearly thirty years later, the multidimensional study by the National Research Council (NRC) awarded the Graduate School seventh place overall. Sixteen of Princeton's twenty-nine departments studied were rated in the top five for program effectiveness; twenty-four made it into the top ten. German, Philosophy, and Mathematics were regarded as the nation's best.[138] The first NRC survey in 1982 gave the Graduate School similarly high marks.[139] All of these rankings were consistent with the Graduate School's standing in seven assessments conducted between 1925 and 1982, in which Princeton enjoyed an average rank of eighth.[140]

The quality of the Princeton faculty was all the more impressive if their numbers were used to calculate a per capita index of research productivity based on awards, grants, and publications. Hugh Davis Graham and Nancy Diamond's 1997 study of the period after World War II, *The Rise of American Research Universities*, did just that, and ranked the Princeton faculty second in the country behind Stanford's. and UC-Berkeley's.[141]

[137] Allan M. Cartter, *An Assessment of Quality in Graduate Education* (Washington, D.C., 1966); "How Good Are We? A National Ranking of Graduate Schools," *PAW*, Oct. 4, 1966, 8–10; Thorp, *PGS*, 300. The study was conducted in 1964. Five years later, the ACE conducted a follow-up study. Princeton improved its ranking in ten departments, slipped in three, and in the other eight held on to already high positions. Kenneth D. Roose and Charles J. Anderson, *A Rating of Graduate Programs* (Washington, D.C., 1970); John M. Fenton, "A Rating of Graduate Schools," *PAW*, Jan. 26, 1971, 12–14; William G. Bowen, *Report of the President (1972)*, 14–15.

[138] Marvin L. Goldberger, Brendan A. Maher, and Pamela Ebert Flattau, eds., *Research-Doctorate Programs in the United States* (Washington, D.C., 1995); "Graduate Departments Rank High," *PAW*, Oct. 25, 1995, 6, 8; Nov. 8, 1995, 57; Mar. 20, 1996, 57; Thorp, *PGS*, 351.

[139] Lyle V. Jones, Garner Lindzey, and Porter E. Coggeshall, eds., *An Assessment of Research-Doctorate Programs in the United States*, 5 vols. (Washington, D.C., 1982); "Graduate Programs Rated," *PAW*, Dec. 1, 1982, 19; Thorp, *PGS*, 350–51.

[140] David S. Webster, "America's Highest Ranked Graduate Schools, 1925–1982," *Change: The Magazine of Higher Education* 15:4 (May–June 1983): 14–24, at 24.

[141] Graham and Diamond, *American Research Universities*, 167 (table 6.7), 188 (table 7.9).

❁ ❁ ❁

After more than a century, especially the last half, there can be little doubt that the Graduate School has done "more than any one thing to increase Princeton's reputation in the world of learning," as Woodrow Wilson and the other members of a faculty committee predicted it would in 1896. In 1960 Dean Donald R. Hamilton (1958–1965) reminded readers of the *Princeton Alumni Weekly* that "Princeton without the Graduate School could not be the vibrant national institution which it has become." Ten years later, in the same pages, Assistant Director of Admission John Friedman '68 sought to disabuse those who suggested that "graduate students may not be bona fide *Princetonians* at all" with a simple fact: "The graduate school is the single most important reason for the type of school Princeton is today. Without the scholarly community created by the graduate school and the funds which the school attracts from government, foundations and corporations, the university could never maintain the quality of faculty and facilities which give Princeton, because of its extremely small enrollment, such a unique position among American universities."[142]

Moreover, as Dean Ziolkowski argued during and after his long and fruitful term in office, the Graduate School was indispensable to "Princeton's image and reputation" not only in North America but in "the great world outside." "While Nassau Hall marks the center of the campus as seen from within and constitutes the landmark of the university in the eyes of many alumni, Cleveland Tower dominates the landscape for viewers regarding Princeton from afar." "In lands where football means soccer and the tiger is a beast of prey. . . ," he told a 250th anniversary audience, "Princeton is known primarily for achievements associated with advanced research in the arts and

[142] *PWW*, 10:68–70, at 69 (c. Dec. 2, 1896); Hamilton, "Some Graduate School Issues," 3; John M. Friedman, "A Report from the Graduate School," *PAW*, Oct. 6, 1970, 12–15, at 12. The trustees' Report of the Wythes Committee in 2000 reiterated Friedman's point: "Princeton's ability to attract the most distinguished faculty and to build departments of preeminent quality depends importantly on the vitality of the Graduate School" (15).

sciences." It is Princeton's active participation in the "international discourse" of learning that "attracts hundreds of graduate students each year from over sixty different countries."[143]

And yet, despite its longevity, accomplishments, and sporadic good press, the Graduate School seems to have a durable identity problem and difficulty finding recognition in the Princeton family as a full adult member. Dean Ziolkowski spoke for his nine predecessors in 1992 when he complained that "it is *always* a continuing battle for the dean of the Graduate School at Princeton to claim attention for his or her bailiwick—much more so," he emphasized, "because of our history and our size than at other major universities." Three years later, as his successor John F. Wilson (1994–2002) noted with characteristic understatement, the Graduate School still "tend[ed] to be underappreciated for the role it has played in Princeton's rise to eminence over the last generation."[144]

Deans are not alone in lamenting the Graduate School's lack of recognition on campus. Over the past several decades, students past and present and reporters have chimed in with complaints about the marginalization of the school and its students. Article titles such as "The Fate of the Graduate School," "The Alienated Graduate Student," "The Two Princetons," "Second Class Citizens?" and "The Other Side of the Golf Course" reflect the persistent "sense of alienation from the life of the University" that many graduate students have felt and still feel.[145] There is a broad consensus that the primary causes of this anomalous situation are, as Dean Ziolkowski noted, two: the Graduate School's history and its size. Unlike their

[143] Ziolkowski, Report to the President (1991–1992), 50; Ziolkowski, "The Graduate School," 250th Anniversary Lecture Series, Princeton University, 1996, 1 (thanks to Ted Ziolkowski for a copy).

[144] Ziolkowski, Report to the President (1991–1992), 50; Wilson, Report to the President (1994–1995), 1; Thorp, *PGS*, 359–62, at 360.

[145] Marvin H. Cheiten (Ph.D. 1971), "The Fate of the Graduate School: Reflections of a Graduate Alumnus," *PAW*, Dec. 4, 1991, 47–48; John M. Clum, ('63, Ph.D. 1967), "The Alienated Graduate Student," *PAW*, May 10, 1966, 13, 18–19; Robert H. Rehder ('57, Ph.D. 1970), "The Two Princetons," *PAW*, Jan. 13, 1961, 7–10, 17; Sam J. Cooper, "Second Class Citizens?" *DP* (online), Dec. 3, 2001; Maria LoBiondo, "The Other Side of the Golf Course," *PAW*, Jan. 24, 2001, 24–27.

peers at rival universities, particularly Harvard and Yale, Princeton's graduate students are a "distinct minority" on campus, comprising about 40 percent of the student population. Moreover, "the university's decision to create neither a law school nor a medical school—nor any other graduate division—has left the graduate students in the arts and sciences without any natural allies."[146] Since Princeton's modest size and steady focus on the higher liberal studies constitute a major part of its uniqueness in the academic universe, however, the university can hardly be faulted for choosing those paths.

The historical decision that has done more than any other to marginalize Princeton's graduate program was, in the words of one denizen of both, Dean West's "blunder of having the Graduate College campus built a mile from the main campus." "Historically," complained a loyal graduate alumnus, "graduate students' isolation began at the very inception of the Graduate School" when they "wound up on the other side of Springdale meadow—marginalized from the start."[147] Although only a quarter of the graduate students live in the Graduate College today, the symbolic, psychic, and physical distance of that beautiful, aloof, castellated compound has relegated the larger Graduate School to a peculiar kind of academic purgatory: intellectually, as Wilson wanted, very much *of* the university but, thanks to West, socially not quite *in* it. It is a paradoxical and unfortunate legacy, which Dean West could live with best.

[146] Cheiten, "Fate of the Graduate School," 48; Clum, "The Alienated Graduate Student," 13.

[147] Cheiten, "Fate of the Graduate School," 48; Clum, "The Alienated Graduate Student," 13.

CHAPTER EIGHT

The Bookish Heart

A great library is the most important element
in the formation of a great university.

—David Starr Jordan

At no time before 1948 was Princeton's library considered by anyone—faculty, students, or staff—"great." Although in the late nineteenth century local pride had not been altogether absent, by the mid-1920s and 1930s Pyne Library had earned sadly low marks from all who encountered its "weird layout" in the "dismal slum days of overcrowding and undersanitation."[1] The trouble was not so much the lack of books—though the collection trailed ever farther behind its major university rivals—than their inaccessibility and the acute lack of hospitable space in which to use them. The steady growth of the student population and faculty, coupled with the new demands generated by the curricular reforms of 1923, severely compromised the ability of the library to serve the needs of a modern research university.

The major culprit was the pre-Wilsonian structure itself. It consisted of two very different libraries, designed for different eras and uses by the same architect, and joined incongruously at the hip. Each in its own day was considered, if not great, at least impressive and capable of serving the college for generations to come. But even together they quickly proved unequal to their evolving tasks and served instead as a serious brake on Princeton's rise to academic prominence.

[1] Remarks by Robert F. Goheen in "The Firestone Addition of 1971: Symbol of Continuity and Change," *PULC* 33:2 (Winter 1972): 90; Willard Thorp, "The Confraternity of Books," *PULC* 10:4 (June 1949): 185.

The initial building was the Chancellor Green Library, built in 1873 on the front campus facing Nassau Street. It was designed by architect William A. Potter, a twenty-nine-year-old devotee of the High Victorian Gothic style inspired by the English critic and theorist John Ruskin. (A student wag later dubbed it an example of the "purest late General Grant gothic.")[2] Potter's confection was a polychromatic stone octagon, crowned by an octagonal lantern and stunning star skylight. Two smaller, elongated octagons flanked the larger on the east and west, with ornate Romanesque entrances in the ligatures. Each wall of the main structure was pierced by four slender lancet windows and capped by a pediment containing a cinquefoil window. With pardonable pride, President James McCosh declared it "the most beautiful [library] building in the country." William Cullen Bryant, the venerable poet-editor who spoke at its dedication, settled for "this beautiful building."[3]

Inside, readers were treated to what later Librarian Julian Boyd called "an open, intimate, accessible undergraduate library."[4] The walls and ceiling were richly decorated with floral and geometric

[2] John B. Oakes, "Try and Study! An Undergraduate's Candid View of the Present Library Building," *PAW*, May 11, 1934, 693. On Potter's Princeton designs, see Sarah Bradford Landau, *Edward T. and William A. Potter: American Victorian Architects* (New York, 1979) (Thanks to Wanda Gunning for this reference.) For the history of Princeton's book collections and their locations before 1873, see William S. Dix, "The University Library," in Alexander Leitch, *A Princeton Companion* (Princeton, 1978), 285–89; Steve Ferguson, ed., "History of the Princeton University Library: Documents and Pictures" (http://libweb2.princeton.edu/rbsc2/libraryhistory/main.html); "The University Library," *Princeton University Bulletin* 9:4 (May 1898): 73–80.

[3] William Milligan Sloane, ed., *The Life of James McCosh: A Record Chiefly Autobiographical* (New York, 1896), 193; William Cullen Bryant, "The Princeton Library," *PULC* 24:3 (Spring 1963): 179. In October 1877 the editors of *Library Journal* declared Chancellor Green "the finest *circular* library building in the country," a plan regarded by at least one optimistic expert as "the model for a reference library of continuing growth" (p. 63, my emphasis).

[4] Remarks by Julian Boyd in "Firestone Addition of 1971," 93. For photographs, see Susan Marcus, "Homage to Chancellor Green," *PAW*, Nov. 6, 1973, 10–13; Wheaton J. Lane, ed., *Pictorial History of Princeton* (Princeton, 1947), 42; *The Princeton Book: A Series of Sketches Pertaining to the History, Organization and Present Condition of the College of New Jersey. By Officers and Graduates of the College* (Boston, 1879), plates opposite 250, 256.

FIGURE 25. Crowded Reading Room of the octagonal Chancellor Green Library, built in 1873.

patterns. Carved butternut bookcases radiated from the walls into the space in and under a balustraded gallery that circled the room. Librarian Frederic Vinton, newly lured from the Library of Congress, oversaw the whole operation from an elevated circular desk at the great wheel's hub.

Readers and librarian were quick to notice the new building's drawbacks. The main floor was only sixty-four feet across, and the shelves and central platform left an alley only nine feet wide for too few periodical racks, chairs, and tables to serve the college's four hundred students. In the gallery, the bookcases allowed no reading room whatever. Throughout, the uppermost bookshelves were unreachable except by the tallest reader. The cast-iron spiral stairs leading up to the gallery were narrow and "perilous." In the absence of electricity, and in fear of fire, the limited reading done on site had to be illuminated by natural light. But all the windows and skylight were filled with stained glass, "too dark" even by the librarian's conservation-conscious standards. On sunny days, students' eyes had to cope with multicolored rays dancing across their pages. Even these annoyances were short-lived: initially (though fortunately not for long), the library was open only two hours five days a week, one hour in the morning (for checking out books) and one in the afternoon.[5]

Yet limited access may have been a small hardship, considering how relatively few books there were to borrow. In 1879, six years after Chancellor Green opened, Librarian Vinton remarked that the library "would give thorough satisfaction to the friends of the College if it were full of good books." He had begun with a paltry 20,000 volumes and currently counted 44,000, but the library was shelved for more than 80,000.[6] By 1888, however, the year before he retired, Vinton was complaining that his shelves were *over*crowded. Ernest C. Richardson, his successor, was chagrined to discover that "the cellar was nearly full of books, the reading-room accommodations had been reduced to nothing, and administration was located wherever it could find a clearing."[7] By 1897, with twice as many students and faculty to serve, Chancellor Green had clearly outlived its usefulness as the newly renamed university's house of knowledge.

[5] Oakes, "Try and Study!" 693; Vinton, "The College Library," in *The Princeton Book*, 250–57, esp. 256–57; "The University Library," 84. In 1877 Vinton referred to "*the* hour for registration." The following year the hours were increased to six daily, three for check-outs and returns. Frederic Vinton, "Hints for Improved Library Economy, Drawn from Usages at Princeton," *Library Journal* 2:2 (Oct. 1877): 56 (my emphasis).

[6] Vinton, "The College Library," 256. According to a Bureau of Education report in 1876, Princeton's holdings were 29,500 volumes in the college library and another 12,000 in society libraries. Harvard had 212,050 items (154,000 books, the rest pamphlets) in the library and 15,000 in societies. Yale claimed upward of 95,200; Brown, 45,000; Columbia, 31,390; Dartmouth, 25,550; and the University of Pennsylvania, 23,250. See U.S. Department of the Interior, Bureau of Education, *Public Libraries in the United States of America: Their History, Condition, and Management*, Special Report, pt. 1 (Washington, D.C., 1876), 103, 125–26.

[7] Ernest Cushing Richardson, "The Princeton University Library and Its Reorganizations," *Library Journal* 25 (May 1900): 220; "The University Library," 85. For Vinton's career, see *Dictionary of American Library Biography* (*DALB*), ed. Bohdan S. Wymer (Littleton, Colo., 1978), 537–38. For Richardson, see *DALB*, 430–35; Lewis C. Branscomb, "Ernest Cushing Richardson," in *Pioneering Leaders in Librarianship*, ed. Emily Miller Danton, 1st ser. (Chicago, 1953), 141–52; Branscomb, *Ernest Cushing Richardson: Research Librarian, Scholar, Theologian, 1860–1839* (Metuchen, N.J., 1993).

The best solution to Princeton's problem was to build a new library, near enough to the old one to incorporate its space, but on a new scale and plan to avoid its major deficiencies. William Potter had just finished Alexander Hall, an imposing Romanesque-Byzantine auditorium, and was asked to plan the new library. It would be his last commission for Princeton. As Alexander showed, Potter was still fond of rounded buildings, which are all but incapable of extension. He needed six full drafts to satisfy the cogent wishes of Librarian Richardson and trustee Moses Taylor Pyne for a large, hollow quadrangle in Tudor Gothic.

When the "New Library" (later Pyne Library) was completed in 1897, thanks to an anonymous gift of $600,000 from Pyne's mother, it was considered, at least locally, "one of the largest and most splendidly equipped college libraries in the country." Professor and Anglophile Andrew Fleming West rhapsodized that one "cannot help but think of Magdalen College in Oxford and the battlemented walls overlooking the gardens of St. John's in Cambridge." It was, to West's—and Wilson's—delight, the beginning of Collegiate Gothic on campus.[8]

Externally, the new library made a handsome appearance, with its clean lines, fraternally twinned towers over arches, high leaded windows, and rusticated stone. Its quadrangular shape was regarded by contemporary experts as "the only practical form for a library, allowing as it does indefinite extension in the same form and allowing light from both sides." As befitting a "country campus," the main building rose only two and one-half stories. A dry moat allowed daylight even into the lower level.[9]

Readers entered a long room that linked the two libraries, dubbed the "Carfax" after Oxford's busy intersection. There they could consult a card catalog and submit call slips at a grilled check-out/delivery

[8] John Rogers Williams, *The Handbook of Princeton* (New York, 1905), 56; Ernest Cushing Richardson, "The Pyne Library," *PAW*, May 29, 1936, 742–43; Raymond P. Rhinehart, *The Campus Guide: Princeton University* (New York, 1999), 33–34.

[9] "The University Library," 88; Richardson, "Pyne Library," 742. The only feature to give pause was the library's color. To blend the new building with its predecessor, the architect chose a dark brownstone, which unhappily has neither weathered well nor harmonized with the lighter gray façades of Princeton's other Gothic buildings.

desk. If they chose to wait for a page to fetch their books, they could park themselves on a long oak bench. An alternative was to browse in Chancellor Green, now converted to a somewhat ventilated and electrified reading room that allegedly could seat nearly two hundred and offered a working library of 35,000 volumes. A reference librarian held office to assist readers, who now enjoyed access to the library from eight in the morning until ten at night.

Readers who sought their own books and the serendipity of discovery might venture—with special tickets of admission—into Pyne's five levels of stacks. Richardson's innovative design called for stacks uniformly seven and one-half feet high, ingeniously adjustable, well-ventilated, fireproof, and separated by translucent glass floors to maximize natural light. But to study or conduct research near the ranges of one's subject was discouraged by the paucity of tables; "scattered here and there," they were reserved for "special readers." Likewise, only senior honors and graduate students were allowed to use the wood-paneled corner seminar rooms that held the major reference works and primary sources of the main "reading" departments. In a fit of optimism, planners "expected that the ample provisions for study outside the stack[s] will do away with much of the need of study within."[10]

Nor were undergraduates expected to need or want access to the university's small assemblage of rare books, manuscripts, and other "treasures," primarily the gifts of loyal alumni. Most of these objects—world-class collections of death masks, Japanese *netsuke* (small carvings), and Vergil editions alongside assortments of coins, papyri, stone and cylinder seals, clay tablets, and illuminated manuscripts—were locked away in a basement vault, behind fenced-in shelves, or within glass-enclosed table cases in an Exhibition Room behind the delivery desk.[11] They were to be admired but not touched or integrated into undergraduate studies. Understandably, most stu-

[10] "The University Library," 90, 92.

[11] Williams, *Handbook of Princeton*, 57–59, 61–62. Not every rarity made it into secure quarters. Several items that modern librarians would classify as rare were scattered through the open stacks for lack of more suitable housing. Chancellor Green was worse. In 1876 a student could find Ludolf of Saxony's fifteenth-century *Life of Christ*, in original boards, upon the shelves. (Thanks to Don C. Skemer, Curator of Manuscripts.)

dents paid them no attention, except at Commencement, when visiting parents were brought around to be impressed.

For all its architectural and technical features, which *were* impressive for the day, Princeton's newest library was basically a book warehouse. In response to a steady and often startling growth in numbers—of students, scholar-teachers, library staff, course offerings, and especially publications—the designers of Pyne had moved away from the intimate, accessible, and somewhat static circle of knowledge that was Chancellor Green to a more elastic and efficient concept. No longer could it be said, as Librarian Vinton did in 1877, that "at Princeton, the students are allowed free access to the shelves, and no privilege is so highly valued."[12] The new concept seemed to be the wave of the bibliothecal future, which many other colleges and universities were encouraging as they constructed monumental libraries with cavernous reading rooms segregated from the tools of scholarship and sources of knowledge.[13]

Most of all, the new library was designed to cope with the proliferation of books and periodicals that an emerging university required and desired. Originally it was intended to hold 1,250,000 volumes, but last-minute changes reduced that figure to fewer than 700,000 by not outfitting the south stacks. Still, it was widely believed that Princeton now had enough shelf space, at the current rate of increase, to last one, if not two, centuries.[14] With just over 100,000 books,

[12] Vinton, "Hints for Improved Library Economy," 55.

[13] David Kaser, *The Evolution of the American Academic Library Building* (Lanham, Md., 1997), chap. 4; Rhinehart, *Campus Guide: Princeton*, 34; Walter C. Allen, "Library Buildings," *Library Trends* 25:1 (July 1976): 89–112; Jerrold Orne, "Academic Library Buildings: A Century in Review," *College & Research Libraries* 37 (July 1976): 316–31; Helen A. Reynolds, "University Library Buildings in the United States, 1890–1939," *College & Research Libraries* 14 (Apr. 1953): 149–66; John Y. Cole, "Storehouses and Workshops: American Libraries and the Uses of Knowledge," in *The Organization of Knowledge in Modern America, 1860–1920*, ed. Alexandra Oleson and John Voss (Baltimore, 1979), 364–85.

[14] Richardson, "Pyne Library," 743; Charles Grosvenor Osgood, "The House of Sapience," *PULC* 10:4 (June 1949): 161 ("hundred years"); Robert S. Fraser, "Building from a Bookcase: A History of the Princeton University Library," *PULC* 36:3 (Spring 1975): 218 ("two centuries"); "The Harvey S. Firestone Memorial Library" issue, *PAW*, Apr. 22, 1949, 6 ("200 years"), 8 ("two centuries"); Thomas Jefferson Wertenbaker,

housed loosely in the much smaller of two stack areas, and with annual additions of fewer than 4,000 volumes, Pyne Library seemed destined to a long and happy service.[15]

Unfortunately, academics are notoriously poor prophets. In just twenty-eight years, Princeton outgrew its library. Librarian James Thayer Gerould, who had succeeded Richardson in 1920, made the public announcement in the *Alumni Weekly* in Apr. 1925: "Both the Chancellor Green and the Pyne buildings are filled from cellar to garret . . . a literal fact." The university was in serious need of book storage for its approximately 545,000 volumes, and that space "has had to be taken from the inadequate reading-room facilities." Instead of the estimated five hundred seats needed to serve twenty-five hundred students, the reading room provided only a hundred. There was a constant unmet demand from the students for individual study space, where they could assemble their materials and leave them unattended without fear of loss or disturbance. The library had fourteen departmental "seminary rooms," but thirty were needed; the mathematicians had to move out altogether. Special-purpose rooms—to house important new and old collections of manuscripts, rare books, newspapers, and maps—were in extremely short supply. And the staff had only half the space it needed to process the books that flowed in a never-ending stream into Pyne.[16]

In arguing for a library "commensurate with the needs of the greater post-war Princeton," Gerould made several telling points to potential benefactors. He began with the academic librarian's truism, but one that many of his older readers, graduates of a more relaxed collegiate era, may not have fully appreciated: "Nothing is more essential to a university than a library." He reinforced the point by

---

Princeton, 1746–1896 (Princeton, 1946), 352, quoting the *Alumni Princetonian*, Nov. 11, 1897 ("two centuries").

[15] "The University Library," 76; Richardson, "Pyne Library," 742; Osgood, "House of Sapience," 161; [James Thayer Gerould], "How the University Library Has Outgrown Its Plant," *PAW*, Apr. 8, 1925, 625. The south stacks were finally equipped c. 1916.

[16] [Gerould], "Library Has Outgrown Its Plant," 625–26. For Gerould's career, see *DALB*, 192–94; Lawrence Heyl, "James Thayer Gerould: Some Recollections of an Associate," *PULC* 14:2 (Winter 1953): 91–93; William Warner Bishop, "Reminiscences of Princeton: 1902–7," *PULC* 8:4 (June 1947): 147–63, esp. 153–56.

noting that "if Princeton University were in a city where other great collections of books were at hand, its own deficiency in this direction might easily be counteracted." However, "situated as the University is"—advantages of which he did not have to elaborate—"a continued and rapid growth of its library is indispensable and inevitable." To clinch his argument, Gerould played his Big Three competition card. "It is significant," he noted without further explanation, "that Yale, even now, has a library which contains 1,500,000 volumes and is today planning a new library building; while Harvard has a library of 2,250,000 volumes and has recently erected a new building at a cost of about $3,000,000."[17]

Under John Grier Hibben, however, Princeton had other priorities for its limited funds. Nothing was done about the library, except some interior juggling to accommodate as many students as possible. When the Great Depression hit, further postponing progress, a broad coalition of friends and users began to describe the library's condition in public to embarrass the alumni and persuade them to endow a worthy replacement. In contrast to the Librarian's measured and matter-of-fact assessment, these advocates were not above using satire, pathos, and incriminating photographs to drive home their point.

Leading the charge for change were the Friends of the Princeton University Library, formed in 1930 by an affluent group of alumni book collectors. In their handsome publications, *Biblia* (1930–1939) and the *Princeton University Library Chronicle* (1939–), and in various fund- and interest-raising meetings and annual dinners, they supported emerging university plans for a new library. But mostly they sought to enlarge and improve Princeton's collections, even in the existing cramped quarters.[18] One of their early committees, chaired by Andrew Imbrie '95, enlisted the help of six students to inform the Friends and alumni of "the difficulties confronting the undergradu-

[17] [Gerould], "Library Has Outgrown Its Plant," 625–26.

[18] "Friends of the Princeton University Library Fiftieth Anniversary, 1930–1980" issue, *PULC* 41:2 (Winter 1980); Patricia H. Marks, "Bringing Gifts to the Library: The 75th Anniversary of the Friends of the Princeton University Library," *PULC* 67:1 (Autumn 2005), 9–35.

ates in their use of the library." The report they published in the *Alumni Weekly* in February 1931 was echoed and extended by several other exposés throughout the Great Depression.[19] All of them painted an unflattering picture of Princeton's response to Woodrow Wilson's academic innovation and to student demand for educational excellence.

The key element in Princeton's library problem was the change in curriculum inaugurated by Wilson's preceptorial system and completed by the four-course plan of 1923. As junior Allen Whipple accurately diagnosed the problem, "The Princeton library was designed to meet the needs of an entirely different system of education in a smaller and entirely different Princeton."[20] Andrew Imbrie, recalling student life before the building of Pyne, remembered "any number of students of the 'nineties who were quite able to, and did, graduate almost without knowing what the inside of the library looked like." He went on to explain that "we bought or borrowed our text-books, we took our own lecture notes or used our roommate's, and by the mere exercise of memory passed our examinations." The more studious might indulge in "[s]ome collateral reading," he admitted, but "most of these who used the library at all merely dropped in to get books to take to their rooms. The library, for the mass of the undergraduates, was not in any sense a workshop. It was just a big bookshop where the service was free."[21]

That attitude began to change with the arrival of Wilson's fifty preceptors in 1905. V. Lansing Collins '92, one of the original preceptors and a reference librarian simultaneously, testified that Wilson's desire to "make a reading man of [the student] instead of a mere pupil" had an immediate effect on the library. Once the faculty submitted lists of required and recommended reading for the semester, the library staff assembled several hundred titles for an overnight

[19] Andrew C. Imbrie, "The Undergraduate and the Library," *PAW*, Feb. 20, 1931, 471–72. These criticisms are discussed in more detail below.

[20] Allen O. Whipple, Jr., "Undergraduates and the Library," *PAW*, Apr. 1, 1938, 576. In 1941 Librarian Julian Boyd regretted that "a twentieth-century educational institution is obliged to carry on its teaching and research with a nineteenth-century library building" (PU, *Annual Report of the Librarian for the Year Ending June 30, 1941*, 3).

[21] Imbrie, "The Undergraduate and the Library," 471.

reserve desk. For larger classes, an average of two and as many as eight duplicate copies had to be purchased. Of the 179 duplicates bought for the first term of 1905, "scarcely any could be classed as mere textbooks." They were, Collins noted, "rather solid mental pabulum": Smith's *Wealth of Nations*; Carlyle's *Frederick the Great*; Mommsen on Roman law and James on psychology; Hakluyt Society editions of Drake, Raleigh, and Frobisher; Shaler's *Aspects of the Earth*; Morley's *Voltaire*; Balzac, Marlowe, and Shakespeare; and President Wilson's own tomes on American history. On average, each of the 1,053 "preceptees" read (or at least borrowed) one and a half books every month to supplement his texts. This "enforced serious reading" in the precepts had the effect of raising intellectual "shop talk" at some of the eating clubs to an alarming new level and making the library "one of the most frequented resorts on the campus."[22]

Even greater demands on the library were generated by the reforms of 1923. Comprehensive departmental exams required seniors to prepare for broad questions, not just from the specific courses they had taken, but on whole areas of their major discipline. Likewise, senior theses in the humanities and social sciences (and reference work for those in the sciences)—and soon serious papers and essays in all underclass courses—could be prepared only with the resources of a large and accommodating library. In the new pedagogy of independent study, advanced undergraduates were largely indistinguishable from graduate students and faculty scholars in their library needs. As Librarian William Dix later affirmed, "Each undergraduate in his own area of specialization requires a research collection." In truth, the library had become "the heart of the Princeton education," as important as—or, many students thought, more so than—"all the classrooms, lecture halls, and laboratories."[23]

Anyone who doubted that the new curriculum placed major new demands on the library had only to look at the circulation statistics

[22] V. Lansing Collins, "The Preceptorial System and the University Library," *PAW*, Mar. 24, 1906, 453–56.

[23] William S. Dix, "10 Years of Firestone Library," *PAW*, Apr. 25, 1958, 11; Whipple, "Undergraduates and the Library," 576.

the reformers happily provided. In Pyne's first year of operation, each student borrowed an average of twenty-two books a year. By 1923–1924, the year the four-course plan was launched, the number leaped to fifty-four. By 1937 each graduate student and undergraduate was checking out nearly ninety books a year.[24] That figure has stayed remarkably steady ever since and sets the standard for North American universities. Many Princetonians were convinced, as Librarian Gerould was, that "the circulation of the Library reflects, as no other figures can, an enlargement and intensification of the intellectual interests of our students" and serves as "an index of the success of the faculty in stimulating them."[25]

Undergraduates were not only pulled into the library, they were pushed. Unlike members of the previous generation, who took the occasional book back to their rooms to read, students in the "roaring" twenties and beyond inhabited dorms that were too noisy for studious seclusion. The culprits were "the radios, the phonographs, and the inconsiderate callers with which the dormitories abound." An apt symbol of the serious student's dilemma is a gargoyle that overlooks the great court added to the Graduate College in 1927: an attentive undergraduate has his ear eternally glued to a radio speaker.[26]

Similar distractions were portrayed in a short play performed by a group of undergraduates at the annual black-tie dinner of the Friends at New York's Plaza Hotel in April 1934. In a set-up for President Harold Dodds's major speech on the need for a new library, the curtain opens on a Princeton dorm room where a group of "sophomores" (including the recently graduated José Ferrer) are playing bridge, discussing the club system, and listening to a loud

[24] [Gerould], "Library Has Outgrown Its Plant," 625; Whipple, "Undergraduates and the Library," 577. For total circulation figures, see [Gerould], "Library Has Outgrown Its Plant," 625; Imbrie, "The Undergraduate and the Library," 472; G. Vinton Duffield, "Library Circulation," *PAW*, Mar. 13, 1936, 507–8.

[25] PUL, *Report of the Librarian for the Year Ending July 31, 1932* (to the Trustees' Committee on the Library), quoted in *PAW*, May 11, 1934, 693.

[26] Imbrie, "The Undergraduate and the Library," 472; Harold Willis Dodds, "Princeton's Future Library," *PAW*, May 11, 1934, 685–87, 694. See also Charles Rufus Morey, "Planning the New Library," *PAW*, Apr. 15, 1932, 625: "The Princeton campus, what with radios and gramophones, is not the quiet place it used to be."

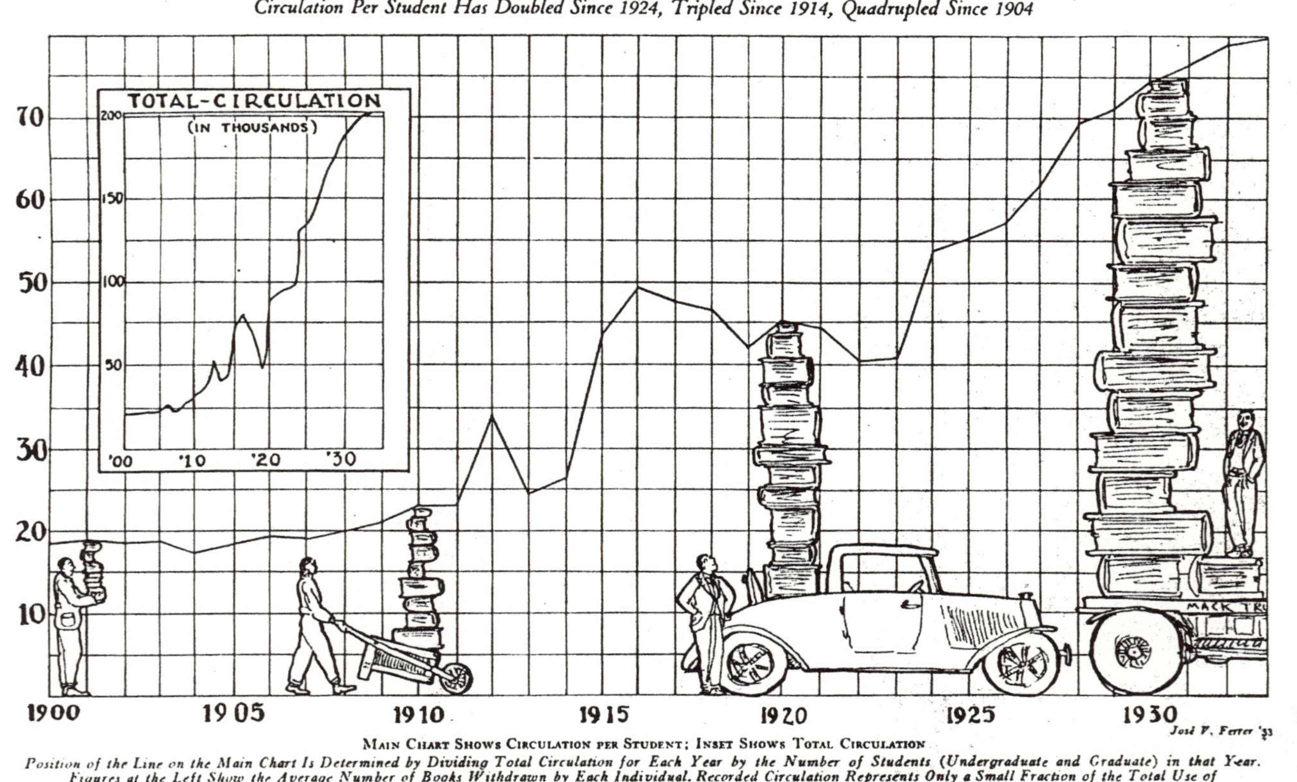

FIGURE 26. Future actor José Ferrer '33's cartoon in the *Princeton Alumni Magazine* illustrated the increase in student use of the library, particularly after the implementation of the four-course plan in 1923–24.

trumpet riff on a late-model phonograph. One studious fellow, with a precept book report due the next day, had been driven by the din to the library. He returns to regale his friends with a harrowing tale of trying and failing to find a volume in the great Pyne forest.[27]

Whether driven or drawn into the library, students found conditions there that gave them little reason to want to stay. The library staff did their best to make the students welcome. They created an additional reading room in Pyne, opened the stacks to all comers, and kept the library open until midnight. They also gave instruction on the use of the library, mounted small exhibitions of rare materials for specific classes, and sponsored an annual undergraduate book-collecting contest.[28] But these efforts could only palliate the essential problem of inadequate space for both books and readers, caused in large part by Pyne's once-heralded design.

Because of the great overflow of books, many were stored "all over town—in garrets, basements, storerooms, and dormitories." By the mid-1930s, 50,000 volumes were kept in the basements of Holder, Brown, and Dickinson Halls and in the attic of Palmer Physical Laboratory. Others found refuge at 20 Nassau Street and in the crypt of the new University Chapel. Messengers retrieved books from all of these fugitive locations twice a day. But if a student was in a hurry, he often had to undergo daunting rites of passage among steam pipes, packing crates, and roof timbers. "This library tires you out" was a common student refrain. A disgruntled junior explained that "many an undergraduate has spent a good part of his study time

[27] *PAW*, May 11, 1934, 694.

[28] Since 1922 the library had showcased outstanding student collections in the Exhibition Room, although a contest did not become an annual event until 1939. In 1964 the contest was named for Elmer Adler (1884–1962), the great bookman who had created the Graphics Arts Department and taught the history and art of books and prints from 1940 to 1952. Donald Farren, "What Is Book Collecting? The Case of Student Book-Collecting Contests: Their Origins," *RBM: A Journal of Rare Books, Manuscripts, and Cultural Heritage* 2:1 (2001): 55–58; *Biblia* [occasional publication of the Friends of the Princeton University Library] 6:2 (June 1935): n.p.; Lawrance Thompson, *Elmer Adler at Princeton* (Princeton: Friends of the PUL, 1952), reprinted in *Elmer Adler in the World of Books*, ed. Paul A. Bennett (Princeton: PUL, 1964), 23–46; Desiree Fowler, "Elmer Adler Book Collecting Prize Draws Campus Bibliophiles," *DP* (online), Nov. 18, 2004.

wandering around the town looking for a missing link in his thesis or term paper." Indeed, "enlightened" seniors were known to flee Princeton to do their thesis work in the libraries of Columbia, Penn, and Rutgers.[29]

Even in the library itself, book stalking was a strenuous sport. To reach room A in the south stacks of Pyne, for example, the hunter had to descend to the basement, pass through a dark, head-banging tunnel, climb four flights of iron stairs and then another to reach the makeshift room tucked under the eaves. The newspaper room containing unbound editions was "a hot, dusty hole in the very cellar of the building," yet the bound copies were kept in an entirely different section of the library. All of the glass and iron stack floors in Pyne had narrow catwalks between ranges, which also lent an air of derring-do to the quest.[30]

If the student found the books he needed, he struggled to find a place to use them. In the early 1930s the Pyne stacks held only fifty-two tables for study, forty of which were reserved for seniors writing theses. A faculty member remembered most of them as "little desks about the size of a placemat at the end of each row. You could rest a book on them and take a brief note, but you couldn't sit down and read anything." Other spots were seldom better. Undergraduates who found unoccupied space in "makeshift aeries under the eaves" would sometimes strip to the waist to cope with the spring sun beating upon the slate roof. Wherever they sat, readers had to squint in bad lighting. One freshman swore that the library stocked only twenty-five-watt bulbs.[31]

Retreat to the jerry-rigged reading room in Pyne brought little relief. Not only was it too small, but its floor, like the stacks from which it was reclaimed, was almost all glass. A man in leather shoes

[29] *Biblia* 6:2 (June 1935): n.p.; Whipple, "Undergraduates and the Library," 576; Duffield, "Library Circulation," 508.

[30] Oakes, "Try and Study!" 693, 694; *PAW*, May 11, 1934, 689; Peggy Meyer Sherry, "Firestone at Fifty: History with a Human Face," *PULC* 60:1 (Autumn 1998): 16 (interview with Professor Charles Gillispie, who arrived as a faculty member in 1947, when Pyne was still in use).

[31] Imbrie, "The Undergraduate and the Library," 471, 472; Duffield, "Library Circulation," 508; Sherry, "Firestone at Fifty," 16; Oakes, "Try and Study!" 693.

or a "Lorelei" (female page) in high heels walking across the room "produces a sound not unlike the well-known troop of cavalry charging across the tin bridge," complained a seasoned senior. "Any undergraduate who has attempted to study there, amidst the stamping of passersby upon the glass floor (this room serves as a passageway to remote parts of the building, too), amidst the clacking of ubiquitous typewriters, amidst the murmur of voices rising a few yards away at the call and information desks, can testify to the hopeless cacophony that makes the library hardly a refuge from the madding crowd of the campus." Should a reader hear the call of nature, the men's room was stashed in "the most distant corner" of the basement. In short, concluded the chairman of the Undergraduate Library Committee in 1934, "the inadequacy and the inconvenience of our library, which ought to be the heart of Princeton's intellectual life, . . . repels the undergraduate and acts as a damper upon whatever intellectual curiosity he may have."[32]

Other constituents as well were adversely affected by the university's "ridiculously inadequate" library facilities.[33] The most important were the faculty, whose scholarship and upperclass teaching required a first-class library. Thanks in large part to the forceful Henry Fine, Wilson's dean of the faculty and longtime dean of the departments of science, Princeton was amply supplied with excellent facilities for advanced scientific work. The recent addition of the John C. Green Engineering Building (1928), the Henry Clay Frick Chemical Laboratory (1929), Fine Hall for mathematics (1930), and the new astronomical observatory (1934) helped to maintain Princeton's strong reputation in math and science, which had been laid during Wilson's presidency with the building of the Palmer Physics Laboratory (1908) and Guyot Hall for geology, biology, and the natural history museum (1909).[34] Such facilities had lured and retained "the eminent scientists whom we wished to have," said art historian Charles Rufus

[32] Whipple, "Undergraduates and the Library," 575, 576; Oakes, "Try and Study!" 693; Thorp, "The Confraternity of Books," 185.

[33] Whipple, "Undergraduates and the Library," 575.

[34] For photographs of these buildings, see Lane, *Pictorial History of Princeton*, 83, 84, 97, 98.

Morey. But future recruiting in the bookish disciplines would depend on the speed with which Princeton could provide a real university library.[35]

More than salaries or housing, a superior library acts as a lodestone for academic talent, Morey and others argued. "[T]he best of humanistic scholars will gravitate to the great library," Morey affirmed, "just as surely as the best scientists find their way inevitably to the laboratories of maximum equipment." All of the planning for a new library in the 1930s and early 1940s was predicated on this symmetrical proposition, that "the library is to the teacher of the Humanities and the Social Sciences what the laboratory is to the teacher of science." Even a decade after a new library was finally built, its head spoke of the constant improvements in space, collections, and service that had to be made if Princeton was to maintain for the future "the great teaching and research instrument that its library must be if it is to attract and hold the faculty members it must have."[36]

Another key group that would be drawn to a new and improved library encompassed private collectors of rare books and manuscripts, who were "naturally concerned about the preservation and use of the libraries which they have built up so carefully." As early as 1896, Moses Pyne and Librarian Richardson had recognized that a new library would result in "a large increase in gifts" of and for books. By 1925 Librarian Gerould was lamenting the lack of "properly protected rooms for the collections of rare books which the University is already fortunate enough to possess, and for others which proper facilities for installation would bring to Princeton." Ten years later, faculty planners were confident that when the new Princeton library was built, collectors would "welcome the opportunity of installing their books" there.[37]

[35] C. Rufus Morey, "University in the Country," *PAW*, May 11, 1934, 691.

[36] C. Rufus Morey, *The New Princeton Library* (Princeton, 1935), 11; PU, Committee on New Library, *A Laboratory-Workshop Library for Princeton, 1746–1946* (Princeton, 1944), 11–12; Dix, "10 Years of Firestone Library," 13.

[37] *New Princeton Library*, 23; Richardson, "Pyne Library," 742; [Gerould], "Library Has Outgrown Its Plant," 626; *Laboratory-Workshop Library*, 5. On the eve of Firestone's completion, Librarian Julian Boyd firmly believed that "a new library building properly equipped to safeguard rare collections and to make the scholarly resources accessible to

In fact, many of them, alumni and nonalumni alike, did lend credence to William Dix's later proposition that "one of the functions of a great library building is . . . to attract notable gifts." Still, it was felt that older generations of collegiate alumni might need some educating in the importance of special collections. Speaking for the library committee of the faculty, art historian E. Baldwin Smith urged the uninitiated to appreciate that "special collections are, *of course*, the very life-blood of scholarship and will attract to Princeton scholars in various fields. As a means of enlarging the sphere of Princeton as a center of learning, nothing," he assured them, "can surpass the gift of collections of rare books."[38]

Before the Friends organized in 1930, as Willard Thorp recalled, Princeton "had very little we could boast of," especially "when your faculty friends at Harvard or Yale asked you what valuable collections there were in the Princeton Library." Although the budget was wisely spent on badly needed current publications and learned journals, Pyne Library's small Treasure Room did house the outstanding editions of Vergil collected by Junius Spencer Morgan '88, the equally fine editions of Horace donated by Robert Patterson '76, and one of the finest collections of George Cruikshank books and drawings in America, given by Richard W. Meirs '88. But "there you stuck" in the rare-book roll call, said Thorp with only slight exaggeration, "unable to go further," unless you remembered Laurence Hutton's collection of death masks of English and American literary and political figures, which "shed their pallor on our meager rarities." The gathering of the Friends was intended to remedy this humiliating state of affairs.[39]

It was wounding to Princeton's pride to be unable to hold its own with its principal rivals, even though Princeton was smaller, not located in a major city, and innocent of the usual professional schools

---

use will result in still further growth at an accelerated rate" (PU, *Annual Report of the Librarian*, 1947, 18).

[38] William S. Dix, "A Note on the Exhibition," in Robert S. Fraser, *One Hundred Notable Acquisitions, 1948–1973: An Exhibition to Commemorate the Twenty-fifth Anniversary of Firestone Library* (Princeton: PUL, 1973); *New Princeton Library*, 23 (my emphasis).

[39] Willard Thorp, "The First Twenty-five Years," *PULC* 16:4 (Summer 1955): 157–65; reprinted in *PULC* 41:2 (Winter 1980): 98–99.

that produced wealthy alumni. Dix cautioned that "library development is not, or should not be, recognized as one of the official Ivy League competitive sports," but he did not have to operate out of Pyne and Chancellor Green. Those who did took it exceedingly hard that, "with possibly a single exception, there is no other university library in the country so inadequately housed as ours."[40] They were not unwilling to make painful comparisons with the likes of Harvard and Yale in their efforts to sell the alumni on the urgent need for a new library. Nearly every publication written toward that end used statistics or sets of photographs to rub alumni noses in the shameful contrasts.

What alumni learned from the promotional literature was that Princeton lagged well behind its Big Three and other rivals in library holdings and was quickly losing ground. In his address to the Friends at the Plaza Hotel in 1934, President Dodds warned that "the position of the Princeton library among the twelve leading universities has fallen from seventh to eleventh in the past twenty years."[41] In the same issue of the *Alumni Weekly* that printed Dodds's talk, a bar graph plotted Princeton's numerical distance not only from Harvard and Yale but also from Columbia, Penn, Chicago, and several state universities in the West and Midwest. Even more stinging was a two-page layout of photos. The lefthand page featured spacious and well-appointed reading rooms at Minnesota, Michigan, Dartmouth, Harvard, and Yale. On the right were various scenes from "Princeton's chamber of horrors": Pyne's "murky" tunnel, the newspaper "dungeon," cramped and tiny study desks, boiler room storage shelves, and Chancellor Green's "dingy, ill-aired, fantastically constructed reference room."[42] The following year the faculty's library

[40] Dix, "10 Years of Firestone Library," 13; James Thayer Gerould and E. Baldwin Smith, "The Faculty Library Plan," *PAW*, Jan. 19, 1934, 355.

[41] Dodds, "Princeton's Future Library," 686. Two years later, a large graph informed alumni that, compared with eighteen rivals, Princeton held "undisputed last place" in the rate of increase of its library holds—a lowly 94 percent between 1915 and 1935. Even latecomer Stanford was making a run at Princeton with a 137 percent jump. *PAW*, Feb. 21, 1936, 443.

[42] *PAW*, May 11, 1934, 688–89, 691. *A Laboratory-Workshop Library for Princeton*, a fundraising document from 1944, included enviable photos of some of Princeton's world rivals: Harvard's Widener Library, Yale's Sterling, Michigan's Clements, Oxford's Bodleian, and the Folger Shakespeare Library in Washington, D.C.

committee could not propose a gentlemanly "browsing room" for the new library without pointing to similar fixtures at Dartmouth, Minnesota, and, of course, Harvard and Yale.[43]

Not every library advocate reveled in Princeton's competitive disadvantages. Two even tried to put a positive spin on the situation. E. Baldwin Smith, professor of the history of architecture, suggested that although "Princeton is the last of the great American universities to build a modern library," it "may profit by the experience of others."[44] An even more ingenious attempt to minimize Princeton's egregious delay was Charles Morey's argument that a carefully planned modern library would restore the institution to "a certain amount of leadership in the university education of America." The placement of abundant and commodious study spaces for students and offices for faculty within the stacks devoted to their disciplines would create an "intellectual 'house plan' " superior to Harvard's and Yale's largely *social* quads and better suited to the unique character of Princeton. Whereas the Harvard "houses" and Yale "colleges" fostered "fortuitous and artificial" associations of students and faculty, a "departmental set-up" in the new Princeton library would supply "a naturally selective and intellectual common basis for grouping the students and stimulating their relations with books and faculty."[45] Although such reasoning did nothing to solve the problem of the eating clubs, it did partially assuage local guilt over failing to secure some of Edward Harkness's millions for Wilson's residential reforms before they went to Cambridge and New Haven.[46]

Although lamentations over the defects of Princeton's library mounted steadily during the Great Depression, they abated once it

[43] *New Princeton Library*, 19.

[44] E. Baldwin Smith, "The Idea of the New Princeton Library and Its Plan," in *New Princeton Library*, 11.

[45] C. R. Morey, *A Laboratory-Library* (Princeton, [1932]), 2, 7; Gerould and Smith, "Faculty Library Plan," 356–57; Morey, "University in the Country," 690.

[46] On the Harkness benefactions, see Alex Duke, *Importing Oxbridge: English Residential Colleges and American Universities* (New Haven, 1996), chap. 4. In a letter to Wilson biographer Henry Bragdon on Apr. 26, 1939, Harkness wanted it understood that "my idea of the House Plan at Harvard, and the College Plan at Yale" was *not* "inspired by Woodrow Wilson and what he had done at Princeton" (box 62, folder 53, WWC).

became clear that Adolf Hitler constituted a greater threat to higher education than one imperfect book house. But the situation had become so untenable that the trustees decided to proceed with a new building even before the outcome of the war was certain and all of the funds for construction were in hand. They were able to begin because they had been planning a new library since 1920 and collecting funds since the mid-1930s. For the rest, they would trust in providence and in the power of the American armed forces that Princeton was helping to train on its campus and in its classrooms.[47]

When James Gerould arrived from the University of Minnesota in 1920, his negative assessment of the Princeton library prompted the trustees to appoint a committee to study building needs. This group in turn engaged architect Charles Z. Klauder, who had designed several of Princeton's most handsome Gothic dorms, to try to extend the existing libraries or to incorporate them into a new one. After six sets of unworkable plans, it became obvious that a whole new structure was the only option. Fierce infighting among the trustees, Klauder, and supervising architect Ralph Adams Cram over the best site was resolved in 1928 by the conflagration that consumed the John C. Green School of Science, "that architectural delirium," as Professor Charles Osgood called it. Its removal, coupled with the similar destruction of the equally unloved Dickinson Hall eight years earlier, effectively cleared the whole northeastern corner of the front campus near the soaring new Gothic Chapel, completed in 1928.[48]

In tune with the interwar trend toward monumental libraries, Klauder's initial plans envisioned a four-storey Gothic building topped by a massive 153-foot tower that would have dwarfed Nassau Hall and competed with the Chapel for symbolic attention.[49] Like

[47] Richard D. Challener, "Princeton and Pearl Harbor: Town and Gown," *Princeton History* 11 (1992): 28–65; Robert K. Root, "The Princeton Campus in World War II" (1950), bound typescript with added notes by Jeremiah Finch (Princeton, 1978), PUA.

[48] Osgood, "House of Sapience," 168. For photographs of the earlier buildings, see Lane, *Pictorial History of Princeton*, 41, 44, 95.

[49] Klauder's tower resembled the skyscraping "Cathedral of Learning" he had designed for the University of Pittsburgh; see *PAW*, Apr. 29, 1932, 665. On library building trends, see Kaser, *Evolution of the American Academic Library Building*, chap. 6; Arthur T. Hamlin, *The University Library in the United States: Its Origin and Develop-*

similar libraries at Columbia, Harvard, and elsewhere, it featured a "noble" entrance hall (thirty feet tall), one main reading room (three-quarters the length of a football field), a browsing room for clublike pleasure reading, and a reserve reading room for class assignments. Sixty-six small offices on the third and fourth floors were designated for faculty, who might teach or precept in some three dozen seminar rooms dotting the premises. Each floor of the twenty-one-storey tower, which housed the open book stacks, was surrounded by numerous carrels for upperclassmen and graduate students.[50] Klauder's library, in short, was an inflexible, generic building scarcely adapted to Princeton's particularities.

In 1932, as Librarian Gerould was leaning toward Klauder's design, Charles Morey publicly challenged it with the concept of a humanistic "laboratory-library." This idea was not a Princeton innovation, local chauvinism notwithstanding. Notions of the university library as the scholar's "workshop" or the humanist's equivalent of the scientist's lab had been current for nearly half a century, particularly at rival Harvard, Columbia, and Chicago.[51] Yet each library, even if regarded generically as "the heart of the university," had to be tailored to the institution's particular educational philosophy and constituents. After a decade of witnessing the creative synergy of books, students, and faculty in art and archaeology that centered on the Marquand Art Library in McCormick Hall, Morey was convinced that the Princeton curriculum demanded a more distinctive building than Klauder's "conventional type of circulating library."[52]

Princeton's emerging academic psychology, said Morey, was a "departmental sense of solidarity, a corporate feeling of mutual support and interdependence, transcending distinction of age or rank." His sensible premise was that "people interested in the same subject wish

---

ment (Philadelphia, 1981), chaps. 3–5; Reynolds, "University Library Buildings"; Orne, "Academic Library Buildings"; Allen, "Library Buildings."

[50] Gerould, "Planning the New Library," 665.

[51] Kenneth J. Brough, *Scholar's Workshop: Evolving Conceptions of Library Service* (Urbana, 1953), chap. 2; Cole, "Storehouses and Workshops." Even Frederic Vinton, Princeton's first professional librarian, wrote in 1877 of the library as the institution's "workshop" ("Hints for Improved Library Economy," 57).

[52] Morey, *A Laboratory-Library*, 5, 7; Morey, "Planning the New Library," 623.

to work near their books and near each other." Accordingly, a new Princeton library should foster departmental esprit de corps by placing student carrels, graduate reading rooms, faculty offices, and seminar rooms in the midst of the book stacks of mutual interest. This philosophy was the core of Morey's plan, which won approval of the faculty in October 1933 and of the trustees the following January.[53]

Morey's proposal also contained preliminary sketches of a building to realize his ideal. Although the structure featured more flexibility and less grandeur than Klauder's, it was still an inelegant attempt to relate departments to books. Four large open courts plunging through the bulk of the building wasted precious space and drove study areas and offices to the periphery. Worst of all, nine floors of books in an eighty-foot tower were separated from collections on eight lower levels. Its chief benefits were its capacity (nearly two million volumes, with the possibility of an extension for another three million) and its relative economy ($2.5 million for an efficient building calculated to serve Princeton's needs for "at least a half-century).[54]

Refinements were clearly needed in both philosophy and execution, and they were forthcoming. By 1935 the Faculty Plan, as it was being called, was being articulated with increasing confidence and finesse, particularly in a fundraising prospectus for *The New Princeton Library*, published by the faculty and trustee library committees. Charles Klauder's frontispiece drawing, however, like his latest blueprints, showed that he had neither reduced his obtrusive stack tower nor incorporated the latest and best thinking of the faculty. He was eventually relieved of the assignment.[55]

It is probably fortunate, given the university's architectural unreadiness to build a great and enduring library, that a sudden offer of funds did not materialize in the mid-1930s. In the summer of 1935 Professor of Classics Edward Capps, one of Wilson's star hires,

[53] Gerould and Smith, "Faculty Library Plan," 355–57; "Planning the Library," *PAW*, Apr. 22, 1949, 220; Jennifer S. Kron, "To Further the Advancement of Learning: A History of the Harvey S. Firestone Memorial Library" (http://meca.princeton.edu/CampusWWW/Studentdocs/Firestone.html).

[54] Morey, "Planning the New Library," 623, 624; Morey, *A Laboratory-Library*, 2, 4–5, 6, plates 1–8.

[55] *New Princeton Library*, frontispiece.

sailed to Europe on a ship carrying President Dodds. According to Capps, Dodds told him excitedly that Cyrus McCormick '79 and Cleveland Dodge '09 had pledged most of the $2 million cost of a new library—if it were named as a memorial to Woodrow Wilson, under whom McCormick and Dodge's father had served as devoted trustees. When Capps saw Dodds again in the fall, the offer had been rejected because Wilson's lingering enemies on the board—a full quarter-century after they had forced him from office—would not permit any memorial to their nemesis.[56]

Although it was obvious that a new library would not be built any time soon, the plans continued to be modified as if it might. Klauder was replaced by the new partnership of Walter Kilham, Jr., a Harvard M.A. in architecture, and Ides van der Gracht, Princeton '23, who had worked with Klauder for many years. Over the course of three years, before the war intervened, Kilham visited several important libraries at home and abroad to give the Princeton project additional perspective.[57]

By the fall of 1944, nearly ten years after approval of the faculty plan, Princeton was inclined to re-examine its assumptions in some detail. The trustees hired the new partnership of Kilham and Robert O'Connor, a Princeton M.F.A. and parent of an All-American stroke on the heavyweight crew, to design a library with greater flexibility and capacity for expansion than earlier plans allowed.[58] Science labs developed during the war to adapt easily to new conditions were the trustees' inspiration. Working closely with the librarians and the faculty, the new architects believed they needed to "discard preconceived ideas and work in terms of what is wanted." They made cardboard and then four actual-sized mock-ups of the modular sections or bays, each eighteen by twenty-four feet, into which the stack

[56] The official minutes of the board of trustees are silent on this unhappy episode in Princeton's most bitter feud. Henry Bragdon interview with Edward Capps, Mar. 23, 1943, pp. 4–5; Bragdon to Capps, Apr. 2, 1943; Capps to Bragdon, June 28, 1943, box 62, folder 16, WWC.

[57] *PAW*, Nov. 17, 1944, 3; Apr. 22, 1949, 25–26.

[58] O'Connor would be named supervising architect of the university in 1949. *PAW*, Apr. 22, 1949, 23, 25–26.

floors were to be conceptually divided to maximize flexibility.[59] The principal users of the library could then choose the optimal height (8′4″), lighting (incandescent), floor coverings, furniture, and configurations of the various bays. Only after the whole functional interior had been planned was the exterior considered, a major departure from previous exercises.[60]

Another group of library experts contributed their recommendations as Kilham and O'Connor vigorously returned to the drawing board. At the suggestion of Librarian Julian Boyd, President Dodds in 1944 invited representatives from fifteen colleges and universities to form a "Cooperative Committee" to assess common problems involved in designing new libraries on their campuses. Before the members from institutions as varied as Harvard, Rice, and the University of Maine disbanded four years later, they had met six times in various locations, twice in Princeton (December 1944 and June 1946). Princeton's plans were well advanced and accorded well with the principles of "simplicity, efficiency, economy, flexibility, functional usefulness, and the avoidance of monumentality" that emerged from the group's seminars. Accordingly, the Princeton library, before and after completion, served as a model not of the ideal library, but of a library extremely well adapted to its particular educational environment and mission, and it influenced future libraries at MIT, Duke, Rutgers, Penn, Cornell, and elsewhere.[61]

As the war ground to a close and the blueprints were completed, the major problem of finding enough funds to begin construction had to be faced. Over time, the estimated cost of the new library

[59] There is some disagreement in the sources over the exact size of Princeton's modular bays. The Firestone issue of *PAW* (Apr. 22, 1949) consistently says 18′ x 24′ (pp. 2, 20, 22), as does architect Kilham in "Planning the Princeton Library," *Journal of Higher Education* 19:9 (Dec. 1948): 451. The figure 18′ x 25′ appears both in the keepsake *The Harvey S. Firestone Memorial Library, Issued on the Occasion of a Tour of Inspection by Members of the American Library Association, June 19, 1948*, [1], and in John E. Burchard, Charles W. David, and Julian Boyd, eds., *Planning the University Library Building: A Survey of Discussions by Librarians, Architects, and Engineers* (Princeton, 1949), 47.

[60] Kilham, "Planning the Princeton Library," 451.

[61] Burchard, David, and Boyd, eds., *Planning the University Library Building*; remarks by Goheen in "Firestone Addition of 1971," 98–99.

had grown alarmingly. In the early 1930s, $2 million had seemed sufficient. The Presidential Campaign of 1935 put the figure for construction and endowment for operations and books at $4 million, an estimate that jumped to nearly $5 million by groundbreaking in January 1946. By the time the structure was completed in late 1948, the tab came to more than $6 million, driven by postwar inflation, material shortages, and strikes.[62]

The financial solution lay in the legendary generosity of Princeton's alumni and friends. In the midst of economic depression and war, they had put $600,000 into the library account by December 1943. A year later, the family of the late Harvey S. Firestone, whose five sons had all graduated from Princeton, donated $1 million of their tire earnings to the library, which now took the father's name in gratitude. Shortly thereafter, the trustees of the Institute for Advanced Study wrote a check for $500,000—"not a gift but a payment" for the full library privileges their members and fellows had always been accorded.[63]

These contributions galvanized the alumni into generous action. Seven classes from the 1920s cashed in the "memorial insurance" policies they had purchased at graduation. With more than 150 Princetonians killed in the latest war alone, there were "almost limitless opportunities" for memorial gifts of all sizes. A whole floor could be dedicated for $850,000, the manuscript room for $100,000, and 494 senior carrels for only $1,000 apiece. In all, twenty-one classes from 1890 to 1943 chipped in $1.5 million. Before the books closed, some 1,250 groups and individuals, including a large number

[62] Morey, *A Laboratory-Library*, 6; "Financing the New Library," *PAW*, Apr. 22, 1949, 11; "Princeton's New Program," *PAW*, Oct. 11, 1935, 62; Kron, "To Further the Advancement of Learning," 10; *Laboratory-Workshop Library*, 13; Sherry, "Firestone at Fifty," 21.

[63] For the Institute's generosity, a conference room on floor A of the new library was reserved for the use of its members. In 1949 the Institute transferred custody of the Garrett collection of Meso-American manuscripts. As soon as Firestone was built, it also transferred the world-class Gest Oriental Library, which it had acquired from McGill University in 1937. Earle E. Coleman, "The Department of Rare Books and Special Collections at Princeton," *PULC* 32:1 (Autumn 1970): 53; Hu Shih, "The Gest Oriental Library at Princeton University," *PULC* 15:3 (Spring 1954): 114–15; D. E. Perushek, "The Gest Chinese Research Library," *PULC* 48:3 (Spring 1987): 248–49.

of *non*-Princetonians, had raised more than $5.5 million. Significantly, the Firestones contributed an additional $228,000, and Cyrus McCormick '12, whose father had made the earlier offer of $1 million for a Wilson Memorial Library and been rebuffed, joined with his brother Gordon '17 to give $366,000 to an endowment fund. Amazingly, contributions to the vital Annual Fund had been not only sustained but even raised to record levels throughout the library campaign.[64]

With sufficient funds in hand, the Turner Construction Company broke ground on January 2, 1946. The job was an enormous undertaking because Firestone is deceptively large, a "stealth building," as architectural historian Raymond Rhinehart calls it—nearly four million cubic feet, with three floors for the main book stacks largely underground.[65] The roofline of its various sections is terraced in such a way that only an aerial view can convey an accurate picture of its huge volume. (The terracing led art historian Erwin Panofsky to describe the architecture as "pueblo Gothic.")[66]

The excavation of 100,000 cubic yards of soil and rock from as deep as thirty-one feet produced daily dramas for spectators. The dynamiting that shook the campus for six months skewed the Frick chemistry scales; it also had to be closely calibrated to avoid fracturing the stained-glass windows in the chapel. The demolition of the superannuated Class of 1877 Biological Laboratory and the Brackett Dynamo Building on site was worth watching, as was the moving of the Joseph Henry House, the dean of the college's residence, for the third time in its history. The latter prompted a faculty wit to suggest that if Henry, one of America's greatest scientists in the nineteenth century, "had been the really great inventor that history says he was, he would have built his damned house on wheels."[67]

The biggest excitement was the discovery of a whole school of 175-million-year-old fossil fish in the hard shale and soft clay under

[64] "Financing the New Library," 11, 12, 14; *Laboratory-Workshop Library*, 3, 13; Harold W. Dodds, "The New Princeton Library," *PULC* 10:4 (June 1949): 150–51.

[65] Rhinehart, *Campus Guide: Princeton*, 57.

[66] Peggy Meyer Sherry, interview with Professor Charles Gillispie, Feb. 27, 1998, [3]. (I am grateful to Dr. Sherry for a copy of the transcript in her possession.)

[67] "Building the Firestone Library," *PAW*, Apr. 22, 1949, 32.

the former School of Science. These one- to eight-inch specimens of the coelacanth, or lung fish—the best fossil examples in the Western Hemisphere—brought the sharp-eyed geologist Glenn Jepsen to the spotlight when the media, including the *New York Times*, got wind of his find. Members of the course in vertebrate paleontology got invaluable hands-on experience in helping to retrieve the fossils. Other students put up signs to indicate good fishing spots. When Librarian Boyd told one faculty colleague about the *Times* story, the latter riposted, "What on earth ever gave you the idea that it was *news* to find fossils on the Princeton campus?"[68]

When the big dig was completed, Turner's men poured 18,500 cubic yards of concrete for the walls and floors of the three lower levels. Support columns, spaced to accommodate the standard-sized bays, allowed the interior spaces to be arranged in any combination of shelves, carrels, and studies. By virtue of being built on a downward slope toward Nassau Street, all of the lower levels enjoyed natural light on at least one side.[69]

Once the superstructure was in place, the exterior was (block and) tackled. In an understated—some critics have said timid—way, Firestone was the penultimate expression of Collegiate Gothic on the Princeton campus (1915 Hall, dedicated in 1949, was the last before Whitman College is completed in 2007). The front, or southern, façade facing the Chapel was designated the permanent side and accordingly received the most suggestively medieval treatment. Thirty-nine Italian masons applied 5,200 tons of gray Foxcroft stone and 1,440 tons of Indiana limestone trim to the steel frame of the upper stories and a handsome 127-foot tower near the entrance. The Pennsylvania stone complemented the colors and textures of the neighboring Chapel, McCosh Hall, and engineering building

[68] The fossils were shared with several museums and universities in North America and England. *PAW*, May 17, 1946, 7; Apr. 22, 1949, 2, 31, 37; remarks by Boyd in "Firestone Addition of 1971," 97. The coelacanth, older than the dinosaurs and long thought to be extinct, has been caught in small numbers in the Indian Ocean at least since 1938. Some specimens have been as long as five feet. Samantha Weinberg, *A Fish Caught in Time: The Search for the Coelacanth* (New York, 2000); Keith Stewart Thomson, *Living Fossil: The Story of the Coelacanth* (New York, 1991).

[69] *PAW*, Apr. 22, 1949, 4, 30–31.

(across Washington Road). As well, it could be obtained in relatively large sizes, which served to reduce the scale of the building and to naturalize 30-inch windows instead of the usual Gothic 16- to 18-inch frames. The well-proportioned tower, the architects' only bow to monumentality, echoed the height of the Chapel opposite without challenging it.[70]

Finally, in early July 1948, the library was finished enough to receive its raison d'être: Princeton's one million-plus books. The reception was prepared by the erection of forty-one miles of metal shelves and the installation on the main floor of 3,288 catalog card trays. The physical transfer of books and other treasures was contracted to the university's Bureau of Student Employment, which hired thirty-seven undergraduates, most of them war veterans with a tolerance for hard work and strict order. In ten weeks, the crew moved the contents of Pyne and Chancellor Green in carts on a hundred-yard covered ramp. (Gathering the rest of the books from around campus and town took until December.) The work was hot and hard—one worker remembered feeling "like one of the Jewish slaves who helped to build the pyramids"—but the pay was good. Although they found the job immensely satisfying, there must have been times when the crew wished for some campuswide contribution to the effort. One suggestion was that over the summer "everybody on the faculty and all the students should be asked to charge out 200 books apiece and then return them in the fall to the new building."[71]

When the doors swung open for business on September 7, 1948, Princeton at long last had a library whose singular excellence could not be denied. It was not as big as some state university libraries, nor could it count as many volumes as several of its Ivy rivals. But it was the largest open-stack library in the world, and it realized to near perfection Princeton's distinctive educational philosophy and aims. Indeed, it was considered "a liberal arts university in itself" in the way it brought "teachers, students and books into a harmonious

[70] *PAW*, Apr. 22, 1949, 22, 24–25, 30; Rhinehart, *Campus Guide: Princeton*, 55–56; Kron, "To Further the Advancement of Learning," 7–8.

[71] "Operation Firestone—Moving the Books," *PAW*, Apr. 22, 1949, 34, 36–38; Sherry, "Firestone at Fifty," 18, 20.

FIGURE 27. The newly opened Harvey S. Firestone Memorial Library in 1948, as seen from the roof of the former Pyne Library.

relationship, as free of artificial obstructions as possible."[72] Every graduate student in the reading departments had a room in which to read; every senior in the humanities and social sciences, a locked carrel in which to write his thesis; any student who wanted one, a comfortable seat and light among the books he favored. According to Willard Thorp, who spoke for them at the dedication, "the members of the Princeton Faculty got the library they wanted." After being consulted so fully, "They will never be able to blame an architect or trustee for a misplaced bay or an irrational staircase." Moreover, unlike its predecessors, Firestone was built to last. It was capable of being extended up and out without diminishing its central focus and character. In 1971 Librarian Dix, normally a cautious man, saw no reason why Firestone could not be the "heart of Princeton's libraries in the year 2325."[73]

[72] *PAW*, Apr. 22, 1949, 1; *The Harvey S. Firestone Memorial Library . . . 1948*, [1].

[73] Thorp, "Confraternity of Books," 190; remarks by William Dix in "Firestone Addition of 1971," 103.

❋ ❋ ❋

The completion of Firestone had an immediate and magnetic effect on the university. Although, as Julian Boyd cautioned, "The true value of the Library . . . in promoting intellectual growth and in fostering research cannot be reduced to figures," the dramatic increase in its use was a clue to the intangibles. In 1939–1940, for example, the old library had drawn 3,906 borrowers, who checked out some 360,000 books from the stacks and the reserve desk. Ten years later, in Firestone's first full year, 5,630 users (minus 1,214 non-borrowing visitors, many from other universities) checked out some 476,000 titles. Of greatest significance, perhaps, were the 25,000 volumes charged to the senior carrels—about 50 books each. Clearly, Princeton was not a textbook college.[74] By 1957 the Librarian could boast in a national journal that at Princeton the new building had "more than doubled the circulation of books." "The Library is swarming with students," he said, because it is open, efficient, and welcoming.[75]

As Princeton embraced Firestone like a long-lost relative, no one did more to promote and ease the relationship than William Dix, the University Librarian from 1953 to 1975. Dix was the perfect librarian for post-Pyne Princeton. His academic credentials were exemplary. Virginia-born, he took his B.A. (Phi Beta Kappa) and M.A. from Mr. Jefferson's university. After heading a distinguished Georgia prep school for seven years, he earned a Ph.D. in American literature from the University of Chicago, writing two dissertations because someone preempted his first topic by publication. Then he taught briefly at Western Reserve, Williams, and Harvard before landing at Rice Institute (as it was known) in 1947. A year later he also became Rice's librarian and gradually traded one kind of teaching for another. When Princeton called in 1953, he was presi-

[74] PU, *Annual Report of the Librarian . . . June 30, 1940*, 1; *Annual Report of the Librarian . . . June 30, 1950*, 10–12.

[75] William S. Dix, "Catching Fire with a Book," *Wilson Library Bulletin* 31 (Feb. 1957): 451; Dix, "10 Years of Firestone Library," 12.

FIGURE 28. Librarian William Dix congratulates Murray Smith '54, the four-millionth person to use Firestone Library (1954). Dix holds a copy of the *Princeton University Library Chronicle.*

dent-elect of the Texas Library Association and chairman of the Intellectual Freedom Committee of the American Library Association (ALA), appointments that gave some indication of the kind of service and national prestige he would bring to the university. Before he retired in 1975, he had served as chairman of the elite Association of Research Libraries, president of the ALA, and member of the U.S. National Commission to UNESCO, a service that took him all over the world. In approaching Congress for support for a national program of cataloging and other assistance, Dix was, said his Harvard counterpart Douglas Bryant, "the most effective witness librarians could send to the Hill." Respected for his acumen and diplomacy on a worldwide stage, he was also "unquestionably one of the most loved of America's academic librarians" during his years at Princeton.[76]

Even more important was Dix's tailored fit with Princeton, including the tweed jacket and ubiquitous pipe. "Of all the academic librarians I have known," Bryant testified, "Bill Dix is the one who became the strongest force in his university, whose spirit and influence pervaded the affairs of the institution." The faculty accepted him as one of their own because of his academic pedigree and teaching experience—and, no doubt, his lack of formal library schooling.[77] They clearly approved of the way he ran the library and built the collections. In 1968, when testiness had become a national virus, 78 percent of the faculty rated their satisfaction with the library as "high"—the highest mark given to any part of the university. "The most demanding library users," recalled President William Bowen, "were [Dix's] strong supporters; even [economist and intellectual historian] Jack Viner thought he was the most estimable Librarian."[78] In the real crunch (over money), Dix slyly confided to a fellow university librarian that "with most [Princeton] faculty members the library comes next after the faculty themselves." The faculty also trusted him in hot seats of university governance. When Secretary

[76] *Current Biography Yearbook 1969* (New York, 1969), 126–28; Janet Harbison, "More Books for More People," *Presbyterian Life* 21:2 (Jan. 15, 1968): 6–9, 40; Douglas W. Bryant, "A Tribute to Bill Dix, 1910–1978," *Wilson Library Bulletin* 52 (Apr. 1978): 614; Michael H. Harris and Mary Ann Tourjee, "William S. Dix," in *Leaders in American Academic Librarianship: 1925–1975*, ed. Wayne A. Wiegand (Pittsburgh, 1983), 63.

[77] For his own part, Dix wished he *had* attended a professional library school, "not exclusively, but additionally." When he chose key staff members, he preferred those with a graduate library degree. Bryant, "Tribute to Bill Dix," 614; Harbison, "More Books for More People," 8.

[78] A colleague described Jacob Viner as "a living encyclopedia." "Few if any amateur 'reference librarians' of our time, and probably no professionals, could have matched his wide-ranging erudition." When he died, he left behind 24 drawers and 20 Florsheim shoe boxes of 4 x 6 note and bibliography cards. Fritz Machlup, "What Was Left on Viner's Desk," *Journal of Political Economy* 80 (Mar. 1972): 353–64. See also William G. Bowen, "Dedication of the Dix Alcove," *PULC* 46:1 (Autumn 1984): 99; PU, *Report of the President (Mar. 1986): The Princeton Library*, 18; tribute by Bowen in "William S. Dix (1910–1978)," *PULC* 39:3 (Spring 1978): 131.

of the Interior Walter Hickel was heckled and not allowed to speak by a rowdy group of student radicals in the mad Cambodian spring of 1970, Dix chaired the judicial committee of the newly created Council of the Princeton University Community that adjudicated the fates of thirteen of the worst offenders. His composure under tremendous provocation, firm defense of intellectual freedom, and transparent fairness only increased the regard in which the faculty and the rest of the community held him.[79]

Yet they reserved their greatest respect for what he did to lead Princeton to "a clearer understanding of the central position of the Library in the educational and scholarly purposes of a university." "Under his guidance," Bowen explained, "Firestone Library grew not only in size, not only in quality and scholarly importance, but in our consciousness as an essential educational resource."[80] Dix was in total accord with the Princeton philosophy as it was practiced in Firestone, and he tried only to realize its full potential for the kind of university Princeton was. In numerous speeches and articles, he articulated his and Princeton's vision of independent study as the heart of the curriculum and a superior library as the indispensable source and site for independent study.

While Dix was still at Rice, he argued that separate undergraduate libraries were unnecessary and undesirable, except in the very largest universities, such as Harvard. If the collection was housed in one building, with open stacks and strict Library of Congress subject classification, the student would profit from being "constantly confronted by books a little beyond his grasp" and from the example of graduate students and faculty working the same shelves. Whether

[79] *The Librarian Speaking: Interviews with University Librarians*, ed. Guy R. Lyle (Athens, Ga., 1970), 28; Landon Y. Jones, "A Matter of Discipline," *PAW*, Apr. 28, 1970, 6–15; Bowen, "William S. Dix," 132–33; Bowen, "Dedication of the Dix Alcove," 100; Bryant, "Tribute to Bill Dix," 614.

[80] Bowen, "Dedication of the Dix Alcove," 99. In his first year as Librarian (1940), Julian Boyd also argued that the university library was "an instrument of teaching" that must "integrate its policy with the whole educational program." As "the one center to which all students and all members of the faculty must inevitably resort," the library is "the chief hope for the unification of the educational process" ("Books Make the College," *PAW*, May 24, 1940, 746).

the student found a specific book did not concern Dix so much as "instructing him to learn to think, to use the library, and to grow intellectually"—objectives "identical with those of the teaching faculty." From such a perspective, the library and librarians were leading educators on campus, and "the closer the librarian approaches the ideal of the teacher-scholar the better."[81]

Whenever he had the chance, Dix underlined the point for the Princeton community. In 1969 he published a short article in the *Alumni Weekly*, "Firestone Library as a Teaching Instrument," which made many of the same points he had covered in a retrospective piece on Firestone eleven years earlier. In his annual report for 1970, he reminded President Robert Goheen that "in an educational institution the library can become an active, and sometimes an equal partner with the classroom teacher in the actual learning process." "When it works," as he thought it did at Princeton, "this partnership can produce teaching at its best."[82] Significantly, it was *learning*, not teaching, that was important to Dix, "that magic contact between book and reader which is at the indispensable center of education" at Princeton. "The essential function of a library building [is] to facilitate that contact," he believed, and Firestone accomplished that goal "magnificently." It did so by imaginatively obeying the "First Law of Bibliodynamics," which is "to get into the hands of the reader the book he wants when he wants it." And all things considered, "the odds of success," Dix wagered, "are obviously better if we have more books . . . all the books we can."[83]

When Dix was hired, a major part of his charge was to develop Princeton's collections. A merely large, workaday selection of books for student use did not confer the prestige that a distinguished library

[81] William S. Dix, "Undergraduate Libraries," *College & Research Libraries* 14 (July 1954): 271; Dix, "Leadership in Academic Libraries," *College & Research Libraries* 21:4 (Sept. 1960): 373, 377.

[82] *PAW*, Apr. 25, 1958, 10–13; Apr. 29, 1969, 11; PU, *Annual Report of the Librarian . . . June 30, 1970*, 10.

[83] Remarks by Dix in "Firestone Addition of 1971," 102; William S. Dix, "Of the Arrangement of Books," *College & Research Libraries* 25 (Mar. 1964): 87. See also Dix, "New Challenges to University Libraries," *University: A Princeton Quarterly* 26 (Fall 1965): 6–7.

like Firestone and an ambitious university like Princeton sought in the postwar years. Because acquisition budgets are always too small, the best solution was to solicit major gifts of rare books and manuscripts. There was no substitute for money, Dix acknowledged, but "[a] steady flow of gifts of important books and manuscripts solves a few of the problems which money eases." Although rare and special collections are used primarily by scholars and graduate students, Princeton juniors and seniors could and did consult them on a regular basis for their papers and theses. In 1973, after two decades of Dix's open-door policy, undergraduate visitors to Firestone's rare book room outnumbered graduate students two-to-one and faculty members four-to-one.[84]

Major gifts also conferred two additional benefits. They enabled Princeton to compete for the attention of the international book-writing and book-collecting worlds, and thereby to attract more resources in the future. By concentrating on selected subject areas where faculty were active (or soon would be) and building collections in some depth, Princeton could also compensate sensibly for its slippage in the national rankings of total volumes held. Although Firestone ranked twelfth in numbers in 1958, Dix could boast: "In few university libraries can one find better book collections in geology, in certain narrow fields of literature [English and American] and history [American and European], in classics, in mathematics and theoretical physics, in Arabic and Persian studies, [and] in mediaeval art."[85] Thanks in large part to Dix, the list of Princeton's special

[84] Dix, "Leadership in Academic Libraries," 375; Gerald Eades Bentley, "Libraries and Librarians," *PULC* 37:1 (Autumn 1975): 9.

[85] Dix, "10 Years of Firestone Library," 10. In 1906, Princeton's library ranked sixth in number of volumes. By 1930 it had dropped to eleventh. In the 1970s it hovered between seventeenth (at Dix's departure) and nineteenth. In 2002–2003, with over 6.2 million volumes, it had the fifteenth-largest collection in North America (the University of Toronto included). All fourteen of its leading rivals had law schools, ten had medical schools, and two had business schools, all of which required substantial libraries of their own. *CHE Almanac 2004–2005*, Aug. 27, 2004, 34. In 2001, for example, 17 percent of Yale's monographs alone (excluding bound periodicals)—nearly 1.8 million volumes—were held by its five professional school libraries. Firestone and Yale's Sterling Memorial Library hold virtually the same number of volumes. (Thanks to Danuta Nitecki, Yale's associate university librarian, for these figures.)

strengths grew dramatically. When the Librarian retired in 1975, Professor of English Gerald Bentley acknowledged at a dinner of the Friends of the Library "the scores of collections of books and manuscripts whose acquisition by Princeton must be largely (or in some cases wholly) attributed to Bill Dix."[86]

Bentley did not have time to enumerate even the major collections acquired during the Dix era. They were numerous and newsworthy, and they put Princeton near the top of the roster of great university libraries. The two headline collections were those of Robert H. Taylor '30 and William H. Scheide '36, alumni who read their books as carefully as they collected them.

The Scheide Library is the living creation of three generations. It was begun by William T. Scheide, a Pennsylvania oilman who retired at forty-two, and continued by his tubercular son, John H. '96, and very active grandson, William H. Remarkably, all three Scheides pursued in their own very disciplined ways books and manuscripts relating to three themes: the history of printing and the progress of the Word (especially biblical), the discovery of America, and great moments in human thought and action. Altogether, the Scheide Library encompasses some five thousand items, whose significance and rarity have led many to regard it as "the finest private library in North America and one of the finest in the world." To give just a glimpse of its treasures, it has a two-volume Gutenberg Bible;[87] the ca. A.D.

[86] Bentley, "Libraries and Librarians," 9. By 1986 President Bowen noted that Princeton also ranked among the best five or six libraries in the country in art and archaeology, medieval and Renaissance studies, population research, East Asian studies, and plasma physics. [Bowen], *Report of the President [1986]*, 12. Dix was ably and quietly assisted by Assistant University Librarian for Acquisitions Alexander D. Wainwright, and several area bibliographers. Dix also built on the outstanding legacy of Julian Boyd in collecting "the records that serve to illuminate and document the contemporary American scene" (Julian Boyd, "The Princeton Archives of American Letters: A Program to Meet an Obligation to Future Historians," *PULC* 2:4 [June 1941]: 133–36).

[87] In January 2001, studying the Gutenberg Bible (ca. 1455) and another Gutenberg item, Paul Needham, the Scheide Librarian, and Blaise Agüera y Arcas, a 1998 Princeton physics graduate, used computer enhancement of the printer's letters to demonstrate that Gutenberg had not employed metal mold casting but a cruder, more variable form of sand-casting. The exact replicability of metal molds did not appear in Europe for several years. Dinitia Smith, "Has History Been Too Generous to Gutenberg?" *New York Times*, Jan. 27, 2001, A15–16. On May 31, 2002, the Scheide Library mounted a

1000 "Blickling Homilies," the only complete Anglo-Saxon manuscript in the Western Hemisphere; a late fourth- or early fifth-century Coptic codex of the complete Gospel of Matthew, one of the four oldest known copies of the whole text; the Columbus letter (Rome, 1493) describing his first voyage; the first surviving books printed in Mexico and South America; the extremely rare *Indian Grammar* by missionary John Eliot (Cambridge, 1666); and a pristine copy of the first broadside of the Declaration of Independence. In 1965, grandson Scheide underwrote a handsome addition to Firestone adjacent to the Department of Rare Books and Special Collections to house his private collection. It has its own librarian, its holdings are listed in the general library catalog, and its treasures can be used by any serious student or scholar.[88]

A collection of a somewhat different sort came to Princeton shortly after the Scheide library was installed. When they were deposited in Firestone in 1971, Robert Taylor's 4,000 volumes and 3,300 manuscripts were regarded by the *Times* of London as "the most distinguished collection . . . of English literature made in this century." In 1934, four years after graduating from Princeton in architecture, Taylor inherited a fortune that allowed him to devote his life to books, which he did generously. As if his own collection were not gift enough, he continued to donate valuable items to other Princeton collections, to upgrade the condition of Princeton copies, and to underwrite, alone or in company, the purchase of major collections

---

special exhibition of "The First Four Printed Bibles." Only six libraries in the world (five of them in Europe) own copies of all four, and William H. Scheide is just the third private collector in history to possess them. Dinitia Smith, "Collector Assembles a Rare Quartet of Bibles," *New York Times*, June 10, 2002, A1, A17; *The First Four Printed Bibles in the Scheide Library* (keepsake brochure).

[88] Nicholas A. Basbanes, *A Gentle Madness: Bibliophiles, Bibliomanes, and the Eternal Passion for Books* (New York, 1995), 264; William H. Scheide, "John Hinsdale Scheide, 1875–1942," in *Grolier 75: A Biographical Retrospective to Celebrate the Seventy-fifth Anniversary of the Grolier Club* (New York, 1959), 191–93; Julian P. Boyd, *The Scheide Library* (privately printed, 1947); "The Scheide Library" issue of *PULC* 37:2 (Winter 1976); "The Scheide Collection," *PAW*, May 4, 1965, 11–13; *The Same Purposeful Instinct*, ed. William P. Stoneman (Princeton: PUL, 1994), issued originally as *PULC* 55:2 (Winter 1994); *For William H. Scheide: Fifty Years of Collecting, 6 January 2004* (Princeton: PUL, 2004).

for Princeton as—or before—they appeared on the market. His loyalty to Princeton—and to its librarian—led him to help secure the Hannay collection of the eighteenth-century English poet William Cowper (the best in the world): the Helmingham Hall or Tollemache Chaucer, a fifteenth-century manuscript of the *Canterbury Tales* (one of only five complete versions in the United States); the Hall collection of Handel (the fourth largest in the world); the nearly complete Aiken collection of books and pamphlets on the Glorious Revolution of 1688; and the Troxell collection of more than 3,000 letters and 800 printed items relating to the Rossetti family (one of the seven best in North America).[89]

Dix went about securing these and other gifts for the library the way he went about everything—with "persuasive charm." After adumbrating the Princeton philosophy of library education with "firm conviction," he did not hesitate to ask key collectors and potential donors to contribute their special resources to the Firestone cause. Often working through the Council of the Friends of the Library, he cultivated likely prospects with all the "amiable geniality that characterize[d] him." Robert Taylor, longtime chairman of the council, testified that Dix always "made himself so pleasant to donors that they were rarely willing to see anyone else."[90]

If donors did not come to him, he would seek them out in their own habitats. As rare books grew rarer, Dix and many of his university competitors increasingly congregated where dealers and collectors appeared, "assuming more every year the position of alert robins on a lawn." He attended so many well-watered Friends meetings that he worried that "cirrhosis of the liver may yet become an occupational disease." He even visited Sylvia Beach in her famous Paris

[89] *The Tradition of Princeton Collecting* (a keepsake to accompany the 1994 Firestone exhibition "The Treasure Room Revisited"), 14; the "Robert H. Taylor Collection" issues of *PULC* 38:2–3 (Winter–Spring 1977), and 47:2 (Winter 1986); Alexander D. Wainwright, "Robert H. Taylor," in *Grolier 2000: A Further Grolier Club Biographical Retrospective in Celebration of the Millennium* (New York, 2000), 376–78; Robert H. Taylor, *Certain Small Works*, intro. Jeremiah S. Finch (Princeton: PUL, 1980).

[90] Edward Naumburg Jr., "The Second Twenty-five Years," *PULC* 41:2 (Winter 1980): 112; Robert H. Taylor, "William S. Dix—A Tribute," *PULC* 36:3 (Spring 1975): 225.

bookshop, Shakespeare and Company, to suggest that she leave her extensive archive of Lost Generation and modernist writers to a library in "her home town." It did no harm that Dix was an elder in the First Presbyterian Church, in whose parsonage she had spent her teenage years.[91]

When in 1954 Dix persuaded Kenneth Rockey '16 to donate a large collection of books on fish and fishing, a subject dear to the Librarian's outdoor heart, the gift included "a generous endowment to perpetuate it." Most librarians would have been content with that much, but Dix boldly pushed for more. He urged Rockey to designate a part of the endowment income "to provide staff time for acquisition and maintenance," a provision that reflected, as Dix graciously put it, "the understanding of library problems which Mr. Rockey has gained through active participation on the Council of the Friends as well as his desire that the Angling Collection place no additional burden upon the Library."[92]

Catches like Rockey reflected the energy and care that Dix gave to Firestone's acquisitions. In 1920 Pyne Library's small Exhibition Room held only eighteen named collections of any importance, and the acquisitions budget for the whole library was a modest $37,643, little of it endowed. By 1980, five years after Dix stepped down, Princeton enjoyed the fruits of more than 260 endowed book funds, which yielded nearly $1 million and contributed 40 percent of the library's total acquisitions budget.[93] Yet the library under Dix (and

[91] Dix, "New Challenges to University Libraries," 15; Dix, "Four Notable Acquisitions," *PULC* 26:1 (Autumn 1964): 3. See also Sylvia Beach, *Shakespeare and Company* (New York, 1959); Howard C. Rice, Jr., "The Sylvia Beach Collection," *PULC* 26:1 (Autumn 1964): 7–13, repr. in Rice, "The Papers of Sylvia Beach," *PAW*, Feb.16, 1965, 12–14, 17–18; Mimi Chubb, "Bringing the Epic Home: Beach's Literary Legacy and Her Traces in Princeton," *DP* (online), Apr. 1, 2004.

[92] William S. Dix, "The Rockey Angling Collection," *PULC* 15:3 (Spring 1954): 161. Twenty years later Dix noted that "the staff costs of acquisitions and cataloguing consume as much as one third of the annual budgets of university libraries" (William S. Dix, "The Financing of the Research Library," *College & Research Libraries* 35 [July 1974]: 257).

[93] Robert E. Molyneux, *The Gerould Statistics, 1907/8–1961/62*, 2d ed. (Charlottesville, 1998) (http://fisher.lib.virginia.edu/gerould/data/prince.html); Alexander D. Wainwright, "Endowed Library Funds," *PULC* 41:2 (Winter 1980): 147. In 2004 more than 350 endowed funds provided the lion's share of the acquisitions budget. (Thanks to

his successors) sought to cultivate donors of all sizes, even before they were able to contribute in any significant way. Besides supporting the undergraduate book-collecting club and the annual collecting contest, the librarian sought to make lifelong readers, collectors, and potential donors of students and alumni by exhibition and, to a lesser extent, publication of many of its most interesting and valuable holdings.

Firestone was planned and built with a long exhibition gallery leading to the Department of Rare Books and Special Collections. Eventually, a few glass cases outside the gallery entrance and many more one floor up in the Graphic Arts Department allowed the librarians to mount a series of large and small exhibitions, usually around historical or literary themes. Dix was a champion of exhibitions, which he regarded as "another kind of teaching by the Library." They "offer sample displays of the library's resources, instruct the many casual visitors, and suggest to students and scholars new possibilities for study and research."[94] His principal ally in this mission was Howard C. Rice, Jr., Assistant Librarian for Rare Books and Special Collections until 1970.[95] Rice and his colleagues usually mounted a half-dozen shows a year, often accompanied by well-printed brochures or catalogs. The richness of their themes could not fail to convey some of Firestone's wealth of resources still to be seen and used.

Since Firestone opened in 1948, there have been major displays on such topics as Byzantium; "The Illustrated Book"; Audubon; "The Horsemen of the Americas"; early New Jersey; "Americans in Paris" (Sylvia Beach and others); literary "Fathers and Sons" and "Women

---

Assistant University Librarian for Rare Books and Special Collections Stephen Ferguson for the latest figures and so much else.) Harvard's 1,300 endowed funds provided 38 percent of the library's total budget. "Leaner Libraries," *Harvard Magazine*, Mar.–Apr. 2005, 70–72, at 72.

[94] Dix, "Firestone Library as a Teaching Instrument," 11; Dix, "10 Years of Firestone Library," 12.

[95] Alfred L. Bush, retired curator of Western Americana and Historic Maps, called Rice "the master behind a most distinguished series of exhibitions in the library's exhibition gallery" (Bush, "Howard Crosby Rice, Jr., 1904–1980," *PULC* 42:3 [Spring 1981]: 187).

and Writing: A Thousand Years" (both after coeducation); Judaica; Mormons; "The Book in Imperial China" (featuring the Gest Oriental Library); the centennial history of the Graduate School; and, of course, Woodrow Wilson '79 and F. Scott Fitzgerald '17. Many of these reached the notice of alumni who could not attend through illustrated articles in the *Alumni Weekly*.

One exhibition in the spring of 1959—"100 Notable American Books"—was the boldest effort yet to stimulate gifts. The original idea for a "best list" was concocted in 1936, when the English Department managed to compromise on "The Hundred Great English Books." When this list was published in *Biblia*, the Friends' newsletter, the Librarian made certain that potential donors knew that Harvard had seventy-nine and Yale seventy-four first editions of these titles, whereas Princeton had a piddling eighteen.[96] The American list was hammered out in 1957 from a number of different criteria: obvious masterpieces (*Walden*, *Moby Dick*), first publications (Hemingway's *Three Stories & Ten Poems*) or mature works (Parkman's *Oregon Trail*) of masters, vivid reports of episodes in American history (Lewis and Clark's *History of the Expedition*), and books with significant consequences (Bowditch's *Practical Navigator*, Webster's *American Dictionary*). As soon as Willard Thorp published the list in the *Princeton University Library Chronicle* in the winter of 1958, the librarians decided to make an exhibition around it the following spring. Apparently, it had the desired effect. By the following winter, Firestone had added seven titles to the sixty-six in its possession. Three were bought with endowed funds, but four were gifts from friends or alumni who had seen the show.[97]

Although "great" books do not by themselves make a great collection, the targeting of specific books, manuscripts, and authors by the library staff does have the advantage of appealing to individual donor tastes and bank accounts. The Friends—from the beginning

[96] "A Sad Story," *Biblia* 7:1 (Feb. 1936), n.p. At the end of 2004, Firestone's tally stood at ninety-two.

[97] Willard Thorp, introduction to "One Hundred Notable American Books," *PULC* 19:2 (Winter 1958): 87–91; "One Hundred Notable American Books," *PULC* 20:2 (Winter 1959): 115–16. At the end of 2004, the library lacked only five American "Notables."

a broadly based organization, one of the largest in academe—have done the most to answer the librarians' calls for specific help. Many issues of *Biblia* in the 1930s featured "want lists" in a variety of fields.[98] When Dix arrived, he saw the need to revive the target approach to bibliographical begging. *Needs: An Occasional Discursive List of Books and Manuscripts* Earnestly *Desired by the Library* was the result. Eighteen numbers were published between 1954 and 1965 by the so-called Needs Committee of the Friends of the Library, of which—no surprise—Dix was the chairman and addressee of all checks. The list was sent not to all Friends but to a smaller number "who presumably are more interested in the satisfaction that comes from helping the Library than in getting their money's worth in material things." The titles listed fell under the aegis of a "Revolving Fund," established by Friends in 1954 "to enable the Library to acquire desirable items . . . which must ordinarily be acquired quickly or not at all." Once an item was purchased, it was announced in *Needs*, and the first person to replenish the fund for its cost had a bookplate featuring his or her name pasted in the volume. Surprisingly, only the occasional manuscript, reference tool, or set of microfilm cost more than $100. Princetoniana was always popular. For a mere $35 a loyal Tiger could underwrite the purchase of a 1910 letter from President Wilson thanking an author—with a wry smile, no doubt—for a copy of his *How to Develop Power and Personality in Speaking*.[99]

Dix also believed that the library could pursue its double goal of teaching and solicitation by publishing unique or scarce items from its collections from time to time. Many of the choicest selections were beautifully designed by P. J. Conkwright, the Princeton University Press's prize-winning typographer-designer.[100] The library's third publication, for example—Howard Rice's history of *The Rittenhouse Orrery*, Princeton's 1771 astronomical instrument recently restored to working order—was selected by the American Institute of Graphic Arts as one of the fifty best-designed books in 1954.

[98] See, for example, the History Department's list in *Biblia* 10:1 (Dec. 1938), n.p.

[99] *Needs* 18 (May 1965): 5.

[100] For more, see the P. J. Conkwright issue of *PULC* 56:2 (Winter 1995), also issued in book form, and chapter 10, pp. 574–78, below.

Among the other publications during Dix's tenure were two works by F. Scott Fitzgerald; two selections of Booth Tarkington's correspondence; the unique William Faithorne pastel portrait of sightless John Milton (1670); a Cowper poem; an Otomi (Indian) catechism; essays on English illustrator George Cruikshank, Thomas Mann, the Rossettis; and the first American novel, penned in Nassau Hall by two Princeton juniors, Philip Freneau and Hugh Henry Brackenridge (both Class of 1771).[101] The possibility that Princeton might publish something from an outstanding collection was a small but real incentive to collectors to contribute to Firestone's richness.

Dix's success in collection building had a downside: Firestone soon needed to let out its seams. With a wealth of new gifts and endowments and a healthy percentage of the university's educational and general budget, the library grew at a steady pace, though much more slowly than many of the large state university libraries, which were responding to the higher education boom of the late 1950s and early 1960s. While following Princeton's philosophy of focusing on a limited number of goals but doing each of them well, the library still managed to push the limits of its original capacity. Fortunately, it was designed for expansion, which it underwent on five occasions during Dix's tenure. The major one, in 1971, extended the bottom two stack floors underground—but around a central garden court—northward toward Nassau Street, adding 13 percent more floor space and ten miles of open stack shelves. Perhaps predictably, the Firestone family again responded generously when Dix "explained our needs," saying "the original building was so good that what we wanted was more of the same."[102] Few librarians in Princeton's history were likely to say such a thing.

[101] Jay K. Lucker, "Princeton University Library as Publisher, 1953 to 1974," *PULC* 36:3 (Spring 1975): 201–16; "Occasional Publications Sponsored by the Friends," *PULC* 41:2 (Winter 1980): 160–62.

[102] William S. Dix, "Princeton University Library," in *Encyclopedia of Library and Information Science*, vol. 23 (New York and Basel, 1978), 268; remarks by Goheen and by Dix, "Firestone Addition of 1971," 92, 102. Two other additions were the John Foster Dulles '08 Library of Diplomatic History (1962) and the Scheide Library (1965), both added to the Department of Rare Books and Special Collections. *PAW*, May 29, 1959, 9; May 25, 1962, 10–15 (Dulles). A beautiful two-storey, day-lit atrium for study was the principal feature of another large underground addition north to Nassau Street and east to Washington Road in 1988. It added 15 percent more floor space and nineteen miles

Even with new additions, shelf space was taken up by books that were little used or needed only by a distinct group of borrowers. This situation prompted Dix in 1968 to build an annex library on university land (the Forrestal Campus) a few miles from the main campus. The initial 200,000 volumes were shelved by size (though strictly by classification to allow browsing) in taller, cooler, and narrower stacks; they could be recalled to Firestone within twenty-four hours and were available to visitors, who could work in the attached reading room.[103] More space was freed up in Firestone by the completion of the Seeley G. Mudd Manuscript Library in 1976. This modern-style building received the extensive manuscript collection of the Center for Twentieth-Century American Statecraft and Public Policy, which features the papers of such public figures as Adlai Stevenson, George McGovern, Bernard Baruch, and David Lilienthal. Also moved to Mudd were the University Archives, the incredible and indispensable trove of objects, printed materials, and manuscripts relating to Princeton's long history.[104]

Other centrifugal forces—obeying the Princeton ethos of uniting books with readers where the latter worked—spun library holdings away from Firestone, the home primarily of tools for the humanities and social sciences. By 1975 the library had built seven new subject

---

of shelving, much of which on the lowest level (C floor) consisted of movable compact shelves. Harold Shapiro, "An Expanding Firestone," *PAW*, May 18, 1988, inside front cover; "Firestone's Enlightened Addition," *PAW*, Oct. 26, 1988, cover, 8–10; John V. Fleming, "Laboratory, Quarry, Pleasure-Dome, and Plaisance: Remarks on the Dedication of the Addition to Firestone Library," *PULC* 50:3 (Spring 1989): 195–205.

[103] "Library Expansion," *PAW*, Nov. 14, 1967, 5; "New Library," *PAW*, Nov. 28, 1967, 7; *The Librarian Speaking*, 18–20; "The Annex Library," *PULC* 30:3 (Spring 1969): 189–90; Lucinda Conger, "The Annex Library at Princeton University: The Development of a Compact Storage Library," *College & Research Libraries* 31 (May 1970): 160–68. In 2001 a new eight-million-volume storage facility was built by Columbia, the New York Public Library, and Princeton on the Forrestal Campus. *CHE*, Apr. 30, 1999, A26; *PAW*, June 9, 1999, 14; http://recap1.princeton.edu/about/general.html; Marilyn Marks, "University Libraries Have Designs on the Future," *PWB* (online), June 17, 2002.

[104] Nancy Bressler, "The Seeley G. Mudd Manuscript Library: A Home Fit for Statesmen," *PULC* 39:1 (Autumn 1977): 1–10; Tom Krattenmaker, "Princeton's Attic," *PAW*, Feb. 24, 1993, 9–12; Ben Primer, "Princeton University Archives: Notes for a History," *PULC* 58:1 (Autumn 1996): 9–31; *PAW*, Sept. 27, 1976, 6.

libraries and moved, remodeled, or enlarged five others around campus to be nearer their users, mostly scientists, mathematicians, and applied social scientists. These were not mere working collections but essentially the total collection of the university in those fields. They ranged in size from the world-class Marquand Library for art and archaeology (some 280,000 volumes and 150 seats) to the equally world-class Plasma Physics Library, with 5,000 volumes and 20 seats. In response to the first two residential colleges, formed in 1968 and 1970, the library also created a campus precedent by establishing libraries of 10,000 nonspecialist volumes in Wilson College and Princeton Inn (now Forbes) College in an effort to stimulate student extracurricular reading and to provide oases of quiet for study.[105]

When Dix stepped down as Librarian in 1975, he left behind a formidable instrument of teaching and research, acknowledged by even its larger rivals as one of the very best in the country. But academic excellence, whether in pedagogy, scholarship, or libraries, is a rolling concept. It has to be earned continually, day after day, semester after semester. Good enough never is, and complacency, while natural, is a plague. Even before Dix left, America's research libraries and Princeton's in particular were feeling the effects of economic and cultural trends that made the librarian's job much more stressful. Those trends were not strong enough to erode seriously the established excellence of the Princeton library, but they were capable of retarding its ascent and freezing its relative standing among its peers.

Much of the bad news was economic. Worst of all was inflation, which spiked in double digits four times between 1974 and 1981. Book and serial prices rose even faster than prices in general, between 10 and 15 percent a year. By 1976, serials were consuming 46 percent of Princeton's acquisitions budget, and book orders dropped from nearly 70,000 to just over 50,000 a year. Overseas publications also cost more as the dollar faded against stronger currencies. The expensive advent of microform publications and computer systems for cataloging and circulation (the first of which performed poorly

[105] Dix, "Princeton University Library," 268–69; *The Librarian Speaking*, 14–17; Warren B. Kuhn, comp., *The Julian Street Library: A Preliminary List of Titles* (New York, 1966).

and had to be replaced) only compounded the economic damage. In the meantime, Princeton entered the 1970s in an austerity mode, which entailed reductions in the rate of budget increases and some deficit financing. The library, accustomed to receiving between 7 and 8 percent of the university's educational funds, quickly slipped to 5 percent (the ALA norm) in 1978. To make matters worse, the library assistants unionized for higher wages, and the library reached only half its target in the otherwise successful endowment campaign that ended in 1977.[106]

A change in library culture also took its toll. In depressing numbers, students with disdain for authority and for each other stole books or mutilated journals, often by razoring assigned articles rather than photocopying them. Princeton's open stacks and generous admission policy were prey to abuse by both students and visitors, some of them professional book thieves. "Although a sign near the entrance of Firestone ask[ed] guests to identify themselves, no well-balanced person [was] ever approached to show identification or to justify his [or her] existence in any way." An inventory in 1977 revealed that nearly 4 percent of Firestone's volumes and almost 10 percent of the branch library holdings—a total of 150,000 volumes—were missing. "Stealing a book is not considered a serious offense any more by students," fumed the math librarian. "They don't care."[107]

All of this bad news was enough to make a librarian decide to bolt for greener pastures. Dix's successor, Dutch-born Richard W. Boss, did just that in December 1977, after only two years in Firestone. He cited as his reasons for leaving a general "feeling of frustration," low job satisfaction, "a pressured environment," and widespread resistance to the innovations, particularly computerized automation, he sought to introduce into the library system.[108]

106 Dix, "New Challenges to University Libraries"; Virginia Kays Creesy, "A Library in Trauma Searches for Remedies," *PAW*, Jan. 30, 1978, 11–17; "Unionization and the University," *PAW*, Feb. 21, 1977, 6.

107 "Crime in the Stacks," *PAW*, Jan. 30, 1978, 14, 17. Before coeducation, women were frequently asked for identification. On weekends in particular, groups of female visitors and dates were escorted to the Librarian's office to wait while their IDs were verified. (Thanks to Wanda Gunning for this intelligence.)

108 *PAW*, Dec. 19, 1977, 9. In fact, it was Boss who selected the first computer system, which failed miserably and had to be replaced at great expense.

Fortunately, his successors, Donald Koepp (1978–1995) and Karin Trainer (1996–), were made of sterner (and more resourceful) stuff, and both the academic economy and student ethos repaired themselves in time with the astute help of President Bowen.[109] Having fallen behind during the economic downturn, the library was restored to its nation-leading share of the university budget (7–8 percent). In turn, the library after 1978 allocated a greater portion of its budget to acquisitions in an attempt to peg its purchases at a fixed percentage of the books published worldwide and to make retrospective purchases of publications not bought earlier. Making much of this progress possible was A Campaign for Princeton (1981–1986), which overshot its target of $8 million for library endowment by nearly $4 million. Theft and mutilation of books and periodicals were reduced dramatically, not only by a new generation of students but also by electronic security systems in the branch libraries and a tightening of access to Firestone.[110] To help defray mounting costs, non-Princeton users (some 20 percent) were required to pay a fee after 1982 or to demonstrate legitimate library needs that a free, short-term pass from a new access office could satisfy.[111]

When Princeton celebrated its 250th year in 1996, the library gave the university one of its best reasons to rejoice. Even as the library was increasingly wired for the brave new world of automation, digi-

[109] On Koepp, a University of California, Berkeley, doctor of library science, see *PAW*, May 8, 1978, 22–23; Donald W. Koepp, "From the Library: Challenges of the Eighties," *PAW*, Nov. 3, 1980, 8–9. On Trainer, who worked under Dix during part of her first tenure at Princeton from 1972 to 1978 and served as Yale's associate librarian from 1983 to 1996, see *PAW*, Apr. 17, 1996, 9; Ann Waldron, "The University's New Librarian Sets Priorities," *PAW*, Oct. 23, 1996, 7; Waldron, "Lighting Up Firestone," *PAW*, Sept. 8, 1999, 18–25.

[110] [Bowen], *Report of the President (1986)*, 18–20; William McCleery, *The Story of A Campaign for Princeton, 1981–1986* (Princeton: PU, 1987), [113]; Koepp, "From the Library," 9.

[111] [Bowen], *Report of the President (1986)*, 21–22; "Reconsidering Library Access," *PAW*, Apr. 19, 1982, 11; Letters to the Editor, *PAW*, May 3, 1982, 3–4; June 14, 1982, 3–4 (comparing Princeton's proposed fees with Harvard's and Yale's, which were already in place and considerably higher), 8 (the faculty approves the new restrictions); Dec. 1, 1982, 13–14 (a new entrance barrier and employees to check materials leaving the building).

talization, and the Web, the circulation of books and attendance continued to climb (as it has ever since). In a year, Princeton's 5,000 students checked out as many books as Michigan's 33,000 students did.[112] Fully half the student body could find seats in Firestone or its eighteen branch libraries, most of them near the books they needed, whereas the ALA thought that space for a quarter of an institution's students was ample. And the university community could openly browse or consult nearly 5 million books, 4 million microforms, 250,000 rare books, 300,000 maps, 18,000 prints and drawings, 236 newspapers, 18,000 periodicals, and 36,000 linear feet of manuscripts and archives, not to mention the world's largest collection of plaster masks of famous dead people.[113]

Since 1996 the library's book count has passed 6 million, and several striking additions to its collections and facilities have been made. In 1997, in a space initially occupied by the reserve book room, one of the world's largest collections of children's literature came to Firestone, the gift of charter trustee Lloyd Cotsen '50. Besides providing a habitat designed to accommodate and delight young readers and listeners, the Cotsen Children's Library offers scholars more than 50,000 printed books, drawings, manuscripts, and educational toys dating from the fifteenth century to the present in more than forty languages. An endowment supports scholarship and conferences.[114] In 2002 the children's space was totally redesigned as an interactive

[112] In 1999 Princeton students and faculty borrowed, on average, 132 books each to lead the Ivy League; Harvard was second with only 84 books. Michael Stein, "Turning a New Page, Firestone Rethinks Its Role on Campus," *DP*, Jan. 9, 2002, 3.

[113] Office of the University Librarian, "A Statistical Abstract of the Princeton University Libraries: Detailed Statistics for the Year Ending June 30, 1997" (which contains a full set of corrected figures for 1996), 1–3 (thanks to Librarian Karin Trainer for a copy and many other courtesies); [Bowen], *Report of the President (1986)*, 31 (ALA); Waldron, "The University's New Librarian," 7 (circulation); Waldron, "Lighting Up Firestone," 18–25; "The Princeton Death-Masks," *PAW*, Feb. 13, 1953, cover, 7, 11–13; Wes Tooke, "Immortality in Plaster," *PAW*, Dec. 16, 1998, 8–11. For an evocation and appreciation of Princeton's rare-book collections, see Natasha D'Schommer (photographs) and Anthony Grafton (text), *Ex Libris: A Glimpse into Some Rare Books at Princeton University* (Princeton: PU, Office of Communications, 1997).

[114] Some of the conference papers have been published in *PULC* 60:2 (Winter 1999), and 62:1 (Autumn 2000).

and contemplative "Bookscape" to entice young users to its treasures. A bookshelf that doubles as a staircase to a reading loft in a miniature house contains carved wooden books with titles such as *If I Ran the University*, by Shirley Tilghman.[115]

Even more high-tech but equally designed for (slightly older) readers in the twenty-first century is the Friend Center for Engineering Education, the gift of trustee Dennis Keller '63. The gleaming metal and glass building attached to the postmodern Computer Science Building was designed after extensive consultation with students and faculty. It features power outlets for laptop computers at every seat, more than two thousand electronic books, myriad online journals, and classrooms and study spaces designed for the highly collaborative projects of engineers and applied scientists.[116]

The same versatile concept is being followed in a new science library on the lower campus. Designed by adventurous Frank Gehry and funded by trustee Peter Lewis '55, the library will connect underground with Fine Hall's math and physics collections and will consolidate the departmental libraries of Chemistry, Molecular Biology, Ecology and Evolutionary Biology, and Geosciences. It will also house the popular Digital Map and Geospatial Information Center and the Education Technology Center, which help faculty develop computer tools for teaching and distance-learning courses. Gehry's gravity-defying sculptural design of metal and glass features a central tower half as tall as Fine, surrounded by two sweeping, birdlike wings, a major departure from Collegiate Gothic.[117]

[115] Harold T. Shapiro, "The Cotsen Children's Library," *PAW*, Mar. 19, 1997, 57; Mary Caffrey, "Cotsen Children's Library Unveiled," *PAW*, Dec. 3, 1997, 4, 6–7; Jennifer Greenstein Altmann, " 'Bookscape' Brightens Literary Landscape in Children's Library," *PWB* (online), Sept. 16, 2002.

[116] Shirley Tilghman, "Evolving Libraries," *PAW*, Dec. 5, 2001, 4; Marks, "University Libraries Have Designs." Although 90 percent of its acquisitions budget still goes for printed works (books and journals) and microfilm, the university library has, "not the largest, but the most comprehensive" electronic data library in the country. Waldron, "Lighting Up Firestone," 20, 24.

[117] Tilghman, "Evolving Libraries"; Marks, "University Libraries Have Designs"; Ruth Stevens, "A Study in Contrasts: Initial Plans Revealed for Whitman College, Science Library," *PWB* (online), Oct. 21, 2002; Raj Hathiramani, "Gehry-Designed Library To Be Built Soon," *DP* (online), Dec. 10, 2003; Steve Armenti, "Gehry's Sci-

Despite—or because of—the new contents, uses, and looks of Princeton's library system, students and faculty still regard it as the intellectual heart of the university, in no small part because the librarians continue to take seriously their role as teachers. Professor of English John Fleming has argued, with only slight exaggeration, that "the three most important factors in undergraduate education in the humanities at Princeton are the reference librarian, the circulation librarian, and the reserve librarian." It is their "educational *vocation*" to "help people *read* books." This is not to minimize the library's importance to the faculty, who must study in order to teach. For many faculty, as for Fleming, the library is their "Laboratory, Quarry, Pleasure-Dome, and Plaisance," the indispensable tool for their teaching and their scholarship. Sooner or later students, too, fall under its spell. Despite or because of the many papers they research and write there, undergraduates confess their affection for Firestone as "the most wonderful place on campus." Although they admit that they find it "supremely overwhelming at times," it is a "fabulous resource," a "veritable superstore" of the material—printed, manuscript, digital, and rare—they need to educate themselves.[118]

A vivid demonstration of the students' unabashed regard for the library could be found not long ago on the night of the first snow of winter. After the university's famous Nude Olympians finished their calisthenics and cavorting amid the falling flakes, they would make a traditional dash through the campus and into Firestone. There, as one reveler confessed, "We just jogged around and kissed the books." It is difficult, if not impossible, to imagine a scene of such naked and worthy affection for a library at any other university.[119]

---

ence Project," *DP* (online), Feb. 2, 2005; Sophia Ahern Dwosh, "As Volumes Go Digital, Firestone Here to Stay," *DP* (online), Feb. 8, 2005. In 2002–2003 the Marquand Library of Art and Archaeology was renovated and expanded to provide a larger reading room, ubiquitous Internet access, and sophisticated projection equipment in its seminar and classrooms. Callen Blair, "Renovated Marquand Art Library Attracts Students and Scholars," *DP* (online), Oct. 13, 2003.

[118] Fleming, "Laboratory, Quarry, Pleasure-Dome, and Plaisance," 197, 198; John Lurz, "Exploring the World Hoard," *DP* (online), Dec. 10, 2001.

[119] "Cheek to Cheek," *PAW*, Jan. 28, 1987, 5.

CHAPTER NINE

The Tiger's Eye

In the world of visual images, the museum
is *the* primary source for education.

—SHERMAN E. LEE

HIGHER EDUCATION in Woodrow Wilson's day, as in the medieval university and Tudor Oxbridge, was predominantly an apprenticeship in letters, in the meanings conveyed by the arbitrary visual symbols of oral sounds manipulated by capricious codes of grammar, syntax, and punctuation. From early home and school immersion in broad pools of visual and aural experience, students who moved on to college found their academic experience narrowed to the printed word of books and the spoken word of lectures (immediately transcribed), both of which were then analyzed in the written word of examinations and essays. Symptomatic of this scholastic squinting was the large number of students who acquired their first pair of eyeglasses in college.[1]

Although Wilson was not obviously among them, some educators in late nineteenth- and early twentieth-century America thought that students who never raised their eyes from the printed page were deprived not only of manifold experiences and pleasures of man-made beauty, but of the unique ability of the visual arts to contribute to the goals of liberal education. Fortunately for Princeton students, newly arrived president James McCosh was in the vanguard of such thinking. From the moment he took office in 1868, he acknowledged the need for an "art gallery" because, he said, "man has other endow-

[1] In 1915, 40 percent of Princeton's seniors wore glasses; 22 percent had acquired them in college. Weir Stewart, "The Undergraduate Week," *PAW*, Apr. 28, 1915, 706–7, at 707.

ments than [rational] understanding." In addition to imagination, humans have "taste and sensibility which can appreciate beauty and sublimity" in representational art as well as literary prose and poetry, all of which should be "cultivated in our academic groves." Fourteen years later, on the eve of launching an art department and securing a collection to begin an art museum, he told alumni and other potential donors, "I believe that the Fine Arts should have a place, along with Literature, Philosophy and Science, in every advanced College. If the students are required to know the literature of Greece, England, Germany, and France," he asked rhetorically, "why should they not have the means of becoming acquainted with their paintings, sculpture and architecture, which have an equally refining and elevating character."[2]

Once it was decided that Princeton students should have an opportunity to be educated in the visual arts, future and current faculty continued to make the case for the serious study of art history, though in terms somewhat different from those employed by the enlightened Scot. In 1882 General George B. McClellan, former governor of New Jersey, and William C. Prime '43, lawyer, editor, author, world traveler, founding trustee and acting president of the Metropolitan Museum of Art, and major collector of pottery and porcelain, published—at McCosh's urging—a pamphlet, *Suggestions on the Establishment of a Department of Art Instruction in the College of New Jersey*, to present to the college trustees.[3] Eschewing an aesthete's definition, they regarded art as "whatever man has made, of whatever material." As, in effect, "another form of . . literature," works of art record people's "thoughts, purposes, wants, necessities, habits, customs, [and] tastes," not in "phonetic or hieroglyphic characters" but in objects plain and fancy. These could be understood,

[2] Quoted in Betsy Rosasco, "The Teaching of Art and the Museum Tradition: Joseph Henry to Allan Marquand," *An Art Museum for Princeton: The Early Years, Record of The Art Museum, Princeton University* 55:1–2 (1996): 44, nn. 35, 41.

[3] (Trenton, 1882). For Prime's role in the founding and development of the Metropolitan Museum of Art, see Calvin Tomkins, *Merchants and Masterpieces: The Story of the Metropolitan Museum of Art*, rev. and updated ed. (New York, 1989).

the authors were confident, by "every ordinary intellect" with proper instruction, whether the objects were handicrafts of common utility or statues, architecture, and paintings that documented the "cultivated and educated tastes" of historical peoples and their variable standards of beauty.[4]

Indispensable to Princeton's foray into art education was a museum, the foundation of which Prime had promised to make his own large collection of decorative arts. "The foundations of any system of education in Historic Art," he and McClellan believed, "must obviously be in object study. A museum of art objects is so necessary to the system that without it we are of [the] opinion it would be of small utility to introduce the proposed department. Courses of lectures, while conveying some instruction, would be of little practical benefit," they warned, "without objects to be seen and studied in connection with the instruction." Although such a museum might begin on a small scale, they fully expected it to grow "by small accretions from gifts, bequests and purchases. Certainly Princeton may look with confidence to her sons, . . . at home and abroad, for contributions to her educational power in this department."[5]

Their arguments apparently won over the trustees and McCosh got his way. Almost immediately the board accepted Prime's generous gift, promising to build a fireproof museum to hold it, and in 1883 McCosh appointed him the college's first (albeit nonresident and largely titular) professor of art and archaeology. As the effective instructor of art history he appointed Allan Marquand '74, the Seminary graduate and Johns Hopkins Ph.D. in philosophy, who had taught Greek and logic at Princeton before realizing that his heart was in art. Marquand came by his passion honestly. His wealthy father, Henry G. Marquand, was a founder and major supporter of the Metropolitan Museum of Art, and the family homes in New York and Newport were filled with master works of the world's fine

[4] McClellan and Prime, *Suggestions*, 3–5, quoted in Rosasco, "The Teaching of Art," 24.

[5] McClellan and Prime, *Suggestions*, 7–8, quoted in Rosasco, "The Teaching of Art," 24–25.

FIGURE 29. John Flanagan's bronze sculpture of Allan Marquand '74, first director of the Art Museum and founder of the world-class Marquand Art Library.

art. After a year in Europe and the Near East retooling his knowledge of ancient art and architecture and another convalescing from a serious bout of "Roman [malignant] fever," he launched the third art history department in the United States in the fall of 1884.[6]

Both the trip and the department were financed largely by a bequest from Marquand's equally rich uncle Frederick, who had died the previous summer. This allowed his nephew to hire archaeologist Arthur L. Frothingham, Jr., a Leipzig Ph.D. and expert in Semitic languages, as a colleague at "no charge on the [straitened] general funds of the College." It also enabled him to accumulate a large personal library in art and archaeology, which he transferred to the college museum in 1900, deeded to the university in 1908, and continued to fund until he retired in 1922. This became the Marquand Library, one of the best art libraries in the world and the crucial third leg of Princeton's "system" of visual education.[7] Without a specialized library of books, periodicals, and reproductions of art not owned by the university's art museum, students and scholars simply could not pursue or contribute to the history of art, however narrowly or generously it was defined.

As the department grew and its offerings in art, architecture, and archaeology proliferated, faculty members sought to articulate its mission and the educational benefits of art history. In 1909 preceptor Charles Rufus Morey told the alumni that the department had three

[6] Craig Hugh Smyth and Peter M. Lukehart, eds., *The Early Years of Art History in the United States* (Princeton: Department of Art and Archaeology, 1993). The accepted order seems to be Vassar, Harvard, Princeton, Yale, and Smith (xi).

[7] Rosasco, "The Teaching of Art," 26–33; Marilyn Aronberg Lavin, *The Eye of the Tiger: The Founding and Development of the Department of Art and Archaeology, 1883–1923, Princeton University* (Princeton: Dept. of Art and Arch. and The Art Museum, 1983); Charles Rufus Morey, "Allan Marquand, Founder of the Department of Art and Archaeology," *Art and Archaeology* [Princeton Number] 20:3 (Sept. 1925): 105–12. The Marquand Library's noncirculating collection of some 300,000 books, now housed in sumptuous new quarters in McCormick Hall, is made possible by an acquisition endowment equal to that of the Getty Museum and larger than those of Harvard and Yale's art libraries. (Thanks to Librarian Janice Powell for informative interviews in August 2001 and Mar. 2004 and for generous archival access.) See Alexander Leitch, *A Princeton Companion* (Princeton, 1978), 314–16; Callen Bair, "Renovated Marquand Art Library Attracts Students and Scholars," *DP* (online), Oct. 13, 2003.

goals for its undergraduate curriculum. The first was to acquaint the student with "the acme of human achievement in the domain of art" throughout the course predominantly of European history. The second aim was to form the student's taste, to make him an "intelligent layman in matters artistic." The faculty thought this could be done most effectively by beginning with the study of antiquity and the Middle Ages before proceeding to the "contradictions of the highly personal Renaissance," where the powerful appeal of the "artist's personality" allegedly complicated the task of applying the more "abstract" and "universal" standards of antique art. The ability to judge art by classical norms was thought to be "the prime requisite for intelligent rating" of works of modern art, which process Morey in particular regarded as "subjective in the extreme." And third, the department sought to make each course "a means to the clearer understanding of the peoples and periods with whose art it deals, a short-cut, so to speak, of the *Zeitgeist*" of each epoch. "A student can learn more of what is meant by the 'Greek Spirit' in a half hour's study of the Parthenon marbles," Morey argued, "than many months of Greek [language study] may teach him."[8]

As Morey matured and moved into a twenty-one-year chairmanship of the department (1924–1945) and professional leadership nationally, he continued to tout the intellectual virtues of art history. In a 1937 address at the University of Michigan, his alma mater, he testified from his long Princeton experience that "the history of art appeals to the student as the single humanistic subject in the modern curriculum which gives him an adequate survey of the history of the human race." Historians specialized too narrowly, philosophers were too abstract, and literary study was confined to "outstanding" but often unrepresentative "mentalities." The history of art, by contrast, illustrated human history by "concrete example" as no other discipline could. Because the artist is "the very child of his time," moreover, his is "the only effective universal language that was ever invented." For many students, as Morey (and other experts) noted in

[8] Charles Rufus Morey, "The Department of Art and Archaeology," *PAW*, June 9, 1909, 553–55. See also Morey's colleague, Frank Jewett Mather, Jr., "Old Art or New," *College Art Journal* 1:2 (Jan. 1942): 31–33.

1944, "the verbal symbols of language cannot communicate feelings and ideas with the compelling power of the concrete imagery of the visual arts." "I have never known a student to really understand the Renaissance," he said, "through its literature alone, or from reading its historians." Thus the synoptic scope and accessibility of art history made it indispensable as "the correlating discipline among the humanities" and "no less fundamental to liberal education than any other field."[9]

The subject also enjoyed several pedagogical advantages over other branches of the humanities. In 1944 an august committee of the College Art Association, including Morey and Erwin Panofsky, his colleague at the Institute for Advanced Study, elaborated on some of them. "Whereas pieces of music or of literature unfold in *time*," the committee noted, the objects of art "exist in *space*" and may therefore be seen "instantaneously" in their entirety. "Thus it is possible to apprehend the structure and coherence of a painting or a statue more quickly than that of a novel or symphony." Classroom or museum study of an art object can shift rapidly between object and discussion. "With few exceptions, all parts or qualities of a work are actually present throughout the study—as they cannot be in literature or music." Two or more works, in one or more media, can also be seen together, enabling valuable comparisons to be made about the early and late works of Renoir, for example, or the decorative styles of the Escorial and Chartres Cathedral.[10]

From their own experience, the Princeton faculty knew that the best teachers of art history were the objects themselves, not photographs, slides, or plaster casts. To house a collection of such objects, the college (as it was still called) built a stolid, three-storey Romanesque Revival museum in 1889. Measuring a mere seventy-five by twenty-five feet, it was designed to be only "a beginning of a Museum of Art, with proper regard for future extension." Faculty wit Andrew Fleming West thought it looked "wingless [and] tail-

[9] Charles R. Morey, "The Fine Arts in Higher Education," *College Art Journal* 3:1 (Nov. 1943): 2–10, at 3–5; "A Statement on the Place of the History of Art in the Liberal Arts Curriculum," *College Art Journal* 3:3 (Mar. 1944): 82–87, at 86–87.

[10] "A Statement" (my emphasis).

less," which it remained for more than thirty years. With only four thousand square feet of display space, no running water (except through the leaky skylighted roof), no control over its heating, no storage, no conservation facilities, and no proper classrooms, it was quickly outgrown. The growing department, the Marquand library, and a large collection of sculptural casts (a gift of the Class of 1881 at its decennial reunion) were all squeezed into the building made smaller by the arrival also in 1891 of the sprawling Trumbull-Prime collection of ceramics.[11]

By 1895 the collection, with small additions by gift and purchase, and the classes were already competing for space. During Wilson's presidency, some professors were forced to carry their lantern slides to the lecture room in Nassau Hall or to McCosh Hall. As enrollments climbed in the 1910s and 1920s, along with the size of the library and the study photograph collection, "the art collections were literally driven to the wall." Blackboards were set up in front of display cases and movable cases were shoved into corners to make room for tablet chairs. When Frank Jewett Mather, Jr., became director of the museum in 1922, he inherited what he called "the oddest kingdom of shreds and patches imaginable." And this was *after* the Art Department, the undergraduates, the new School of Architecture, the Index of Christian Art (Morey's 1917 brainchild),[12] materials

[11] *The Art Museum, Princeton University: An Illustrated History* (Princeton, c. 1978), [5]; Francis F. Jones, "The Making of a Museum," *PAW*, June 11, 1979, 21–26, at 21–22 (repr. in *Selections from The Art Museum, Princeton University* [Princeton, 1986], 11–17); Sara E. Bush, "Architectural History of The Art Museum," *Record of The Art Museum PU*, 55:1–2 (1996): 77–106, at 83–86, 97. The collection's formal name is Trumbull-Prime, in honor of his wife Mary's contributions to ceramic collecting and research. Her father, Gurdon Trumbull, assembled a collection of ceramics now in the Wadsworth Atheneum in Hartford. Rosasco, "The Teaching of Art," 21.

[12] The Index, the largest archive of medieval art in the world, is a photographic file and subject index of the iconography of Christian art without geographical limit from early apostolic times to A.D. 1400. Begun by Morey in a shoebox, it has grown to more than 200,000 images and more than 26,000 index terms, from Christ and Isaiah to bread, fools, and crocodiles. Since 1991 the collection has been gradually digitized and placed online, but copies of the full index are also available in Dumbarton Oaks, Utrecht, at UCLA, and at the Vatican. C. R. Morey, "An Important Instrument of Research," *PAW*, Dec. 4, 1931, 236–37; Rosalie B. Green, "The Index of Christian Art," *PAW*, Mar. 1, 1963, 8–11, 16–17; Ann Waldron, "Medieval Art Goes Online," *PAW*, Jan.

and mosaics from the department's archaeological expeditions in Syria, the photographs, and the library had all moved the following year into a large new attached Venetian Gothic building named McCormick Hall, in honor of the family of Mrs. Cyrus H. McCormick, the wife of Wilson's close friend and classmate, who funded most of it.[13]

With a newly liberated building and characteristic vigor, Mather sought to renew the museum's teaching mission. He framed a policy of "build[ing] the collections around the art courses, to provide fine objects of a characteristic sort so that the student may get the actual look of the thing and free himself from the partial and often false impression gained by working too much with reproductions. The hope," he said in 1925, "is to give the Museum a definite teaching value, and to avoid objects, however fine intrinsically, from which the beginner can learn little." Five years later, he was humming the same tune. "Our aim at Princeton," he wrote in the department *Bulletin*, among whose readers were members of the department's numerous and august Visiting Committee, "is a visible history of art in brief epitome, in original and fine examples. . . . We buy only such objects as we think have teaching value for the undergraduates, and such objects," he added, "being usually published"—often in the department's distinguished series *Princeton Monographs in Art and Archaeology*—"have also a value of research to our graduate students."[14]

26, 2000, 11; Isa Ragusa, "Observations on the History of the Index: In Two Parts," *Visual Resources* 13:3–4 (1998): 215–51; Colum Hourihane, " 'They stand on his shoulders': Morey, Iconography, and the Index of Christian Art," in Hourihane, ed., *Insights and Interpretations: Studies in Celebration of the Eighty-Fifth Anniversary of the Index of Christian Art*, Index of Christian Art Occasional Papers 5 (Princeton: Index of Christian Art, 2002), 3–16.

[13] Bush, "Architectural History," 86, 87; Allan Marquand, "The Needs of the Art Department," *PAW*, Feb. 4, 1920, 393–95, at 394; Frank Jewett Mather, Jr., "An Art Museum at Princeton," *PAW*, Feb. 11, 1925, 417–20, at 417; Mather, "The Museum of Historic Art," *Art and Archaeology* 20:3 (Sept. 1925): 113; Lavin, *Eye of the Tiger*, 18, 20, 23, 24, 25.

[14] Mather, "The Museum of Historic Art," 114; Mather, "A New Museum," *Bulletin of the Department of Art & Archaeology*, Sept. 1930: 9–11, at 11. See also William B. McCormick, "The Princeton Museum, A Workshop," *PAW*, Nov. 11, 1925, 163 (repr. from *International Studio*, Sept. 1925).

FIGURE 30. The Museum of Historic Art (1889), designed by Arthur Page Brown, conjoined with Ralph Adams Cram's Venetian Gothic McCormick Hall (1923). The squat Romanesque Revival museum was demolished to make way for the new one dedicated in 1966.

From Mather's day to this, the director and the department have regarded the museum largely, if not exclusively, as a teaching museum. From the perspective of the department chair, Charles Morey told potential donors in 1925, the museum was intended only to be "an instrument collateral to the undergraduate courses in art history, and to contain a sufficiently wide selection of originals of paintings, sculptures, and the minor arts, to give reality to the impressions evoked in the lecture room." In an address to the College Art Association nine years later, Mather boasted that he knew of only two American college museums that were being built up "specifically for teaching purposes—Smith and Princeton" (and he might have added Oberlin, another "isolated college").[15] When considering any

[15] As Mather reiterated frequently, "All universities and colleges, except such as are located near great museums, must have their own museums if their teaching of art is to

object for his museum, he said, "I always ask myself the question, 'Would this have meant a lot to me when I was twenty?' If the answer is *no*, I do not buy, however tempting the opportunity or however much the object may mean to me now." And the purpose of such a collection? Mather and his departmental colleagues agreed that it was "merely to give the student assurance that we tell the truth in the class room, merely to give him something of the first hand experience upon which our own tastes and convictions rest, merely to bring visually alive the necessarily verbal exercises of the class room."[16]

But the small, "old and unfinished" museum was never able to realize its full potential as a teaching museum. "Under grave disadvantages," Mather managed to acquire "nearly half" of "a visible history of art in brief epitome, in original and fine examples" by 1930. By 1944 he thought he was "perhaps three-quarters" of the way there. The problem was less the collections, which continued to grow despite their unappealing quarters, than the space to display them properly and in which students and scholars could view them, even in storage.[17] By 1953 the museum situation was truly "desperate," according to new director Ernest T. DeWald, a marked decline from mere "distress" in 1930. What had been small in 1889 was "ridiculous" in 1953. Exhibition space was so limited that DeWald could display relatively few objects of outstanding quality at once, having to rotate them periodically with other material needed for departmental courses. One small gallery was reserved for special exhibitions, bor-

---

have any vitality." Certainly at Princeton, he argued in 1934, "though for years we have arranged trips to the museums and great private galleries of New York, we could not teach effectively without our own museum." Frank Jewett Mather, Jr., "The Museum of Historic Art at Princeton University," *Art in America* 32:4 (Oct. 1944): 189–98, at 189; Mather, "The College Art Museum," *Parnassus* 6:4 (Apr. 1934): 18–20, at 18; also Mather, "A New Museum," 11.

[16] Barbara T. Ross, "The Mather Years, 1922–1946," *Record of The Art Museum* 55:1–2 (1996): 53–76, at 55; Mather, "The College Art Museum," 18, 19, 20.

[17] In 1944 Mather noted that Princeton owned "possibly the largest and most important collection" of Early Christian and "Dark Ages" pagan art "on this side of the Atlantic," but that it languished in storage for "lack of space and facilities for exhibition" ("The Museum of Historic Art at Princeton University," 196).

rowed to offer diversity or drawn from the museum's own collections in storage, which overflowed "in flagrant violation of codes, written and unwritten." Some of the overflow wound up in a barn, a warehouse, and the basements of a dormitory and Nassau Hall, none of which was conducive to its proper preservation.[18]

The museum's situation would have been worse had its collection been larger. Patrick J. Kelleher, DeWald's successor, lamented in 1962 that "Princeton has lost major works of art in the past for fear on the part of potential donors that 'the building was insecure, unprepossessing, unfireproof,' and for a number of other reasons." One was that with so many objects and collections in storage, donors arriving to see their gifts on display were frequently embarrassed—perhaps no more so than the staff—by their absence. Like the university library before Firestone, the old museum was simply not a good bet for philanthropically minded collectors.[19]

The only solution was to build a new museum, which the university finally did in 1966 and greatly enlarged and renovated between 1984 and 1989.[20] These improvements gained the museum some thirty thousand additional square feet of display space, storage and teaching spaces for the departments of photography and of prints and drawings, conservation labs for paintings and paper, and five study-storage rooms where precepts and seminars may be held

[18] Memorandum on "Museum Priority" from E. T. DeWald to President Harold W. Dodds, Jan. 19, 1953, 1, in Historical Subject Files: "Art Museum," box 7 (PUA); Mather, "A New Museum," 11; Bush, "Architectural History of The Art Museum," 97; *The Art Museum, PU* [12], [15]; Jones, "The Making of a Museum," 25; Patrick J. Kelleher, "Interim Notes for a New Art Museum," *PAW*, Nov. 9, 1962, 9–10, at 9.

[19] Kelleher, "Interim Notes," 10; DeWald memorandum to Dodds, 1–2; *The Art Museum, PU*, [14]; *A Statement Prepared to Describe the Part of the Department of Art & Archaeology in the Campaign for $53 Million for Princeton University* [1959], 2, in "Department of Art & Archaeology," box 12 ("Dept. History—Published Sources") (PUA). For the pre-Firestone library situation, see chapter 8, pp. 443, 449–51, 454.

[20] The extension of the new museum was strongly supported by Provost Neil Rudenstine, who was "not only enormously sophisticated about art but also ambitious for the Museum" ("Letter from Allen Rosenbaum on His Retirement," The Art Museum, PU, *Newsletter* [Fall 1998], 1). He got the project added to the university's "Campaign for Princeton" in the late 1970s. William McCleery, *The Story of A Campaign for Princeton, 1981–1986* (Princeton: PU, 1987).

among the original objects.[21] More than ever, the Princeton art community regarded the museum not only as a "teaching tool" but as a "humanistic laboratory," a concept that had already been applied in the Firestone and Marquand libraries. By the time the museum had largely realized its potential as a teaching museum, it was no longer literally "unique among college and university museums," as department chairman Rensselaer Lee '20 had predicted it would be in 1957, but it was a notable rarity. It enabled faculty and students to take full advantage of its collections, not only in the galleries but in nearby precept rooms located in "live" or "study" storage areas.[22]

❁ ❁ ❁

Although space is never a minor consideration, the significance of any art museum is measured primarily by the quality of its collections. And among competitive universities, comparisons are inevitable. Although Princeton was handicapped from the start by a building too small, it could not resist measuring its museum against those at Harvard and Yale. Only department chairman Charles Morey

[21] Bush, "Architectural History," 97–104; Hedy Backlin-Landman, "The New Art Museum at Princeton," *Art Journal* 26:1 (Fall 1966): 30–31; Backlin-Landman, "The Art Museum at Princeton University: A Selection from the Collections," *Art Journal* 26:2 (Winter 1966–1967): 172–78; "The New Art Museum," *PAW*, Nov. 8, 1966, 6–11; "Art Museum Reopens," *PAW*, May 3 and 17, 1989, 26–28. For the museum's conservation facilities and staff, see Norman Muller, "Slowing the Clock: Art Conservation at The Art Museum," *Record of the Princeton University Art Museum* 59:1–2 (2000): 2–15.

[22] Patrick J. Kelleher, "The Art Museum as a Teaching Tool," *PAW*, Sept. 20, 1966, 18–21; Bush, "Architectural History," 97; "Princeton Portraits: Rensselaer W. Lee '20: The Need for a New Art Museum," *PAW*, Nov. 15, 1957, 8–9; Harold T. Shapiro, "The President's Page: A Teaching Museum," *PAW*, Mar. 7, 2001. The concept of a "humanistic laboratory" was Charles Morey's. See "A Humanistic Laboratory," *Bull. of the Dept. of Art & Arch.*, Oct. 1929: 5–15; Morey, "Desiderata for a Humanistic Laboratory," *Bull. of the Dept. of Art & Arch.*, Sept. 1930, 5–9. In the former article, Morey admitted that "the exploitation of the [old] Museum as an undergraduate laboratory has only begun, and its further development must await better installation of our collections"(13). The fullest realization of the concept was in Firestone Library, whose planning was guided by Morey's early booklet *A Laboratory-Library* (Princeton, [1932]). See chapter 8, pp. 451–52, 455, 457–58.

seemed to shrink from comparisons. His emphasis on the museum's teaching mission led him in 1925 to deny that Princeton had any intention of trying to "rival the collection of so fine a university museum as the Fogg Art Museum . . . at Harvard."[23]

Director Allan Marquand and his successors suffered from no such inhibitions. In 1920 Marquand told the alumni that "what Princeton ought to have in the Museum is what Yale and Harvard already have: a real art-gallery filled not only with [plaster] casts, but also with a reasonable number of representative originals, which would afford the illustration and stimulus which Yale and Harvard students of art derive from the Jarves Collection [of Italian paintings] and the Fogg Art Museum." Frank Mather, Marquand's successor, was even more ambitious. In 1925, in the national journal *Art and Archaeology*, Mather spoke frankly about Princeton's aim to build its collection around its art courses, but to fill it with "fine objects." "It already begins to be representative," he said, but "we hope also to make it rich . . . at least on an equality with those of Harvard and Yale."[24]

Just how it could become competitively rich he revealed to the alumni the same year. He first baited them with notice that "it will be years before the Princeton Art Museum can rival such galleries as those of Harvard, Yale, University of Pennsylvania, and University of Toronto," the last two names thrown in to embarrass sons of one of the Big Three. Then he informed them (perhaps disingenuously) that although Princeton did not want a big museum, it did want "the finest things of their kind," the things that great museums want and trained collectors hate to lose. "And we shall get them," he appealed, "when our collecting friends and alumni realize that to give Princeton a fine work of art is to assure it worthy and permanent exhibition in best company."[25]

Although Princeton's collection grew nicely despite the Great Depression, it was clear that the inadequate museum building ham-

[23] *Record of The Art Museum* 55:1–2 (1996): 6.

[24] Allan Marquand, "The Needs of the Art Department," *PAW*, Feb. 4, 1920, 393–95, at 394; Mather, "The Museum of Historic Art," 114.

[25] Mather, "Art Museum at Princeton," 420; Mather, "Art Museum Progress," *PAW*, Dec. 6, 1935, 246.

pered growth and that rival targets would not stand still. After the donation in 1932 of a group of red-figure Greek vases and a large collection of early prints from Junius S. Morgan '88 and fifty Italian paintings from Henry W. Cannon, Jr. '10 three years later, Mather acknowledged the museum's substantial progress in "its long, stern chase with the art museums of Harvard and Yale." Both had gotten off to quicker starts with appreciably larger donor bases. In 1944 a *Nassau Sovereign* article on the increasingly visited "Campus Treasure Cache" again reminded the administration that "a new building or an addition to the present one is necessary if the Museum is to reach its full efficiency and rank with Yale and Harvard in this field."[26] When undergraduates preoccupied with war began to feel heat from their Big Three sports rivals over the art museum, it was past time to do something about it.

Unfortunately, nothing was done until the $53 Million Campaign provided for a new museum, which would not be completed until 1966. In the meantime, new director Joseph Kelleher (1960–1973) continued to make the case for Princeton's strong potential. After a frank assessment of its collection strengths and weaknesses in the pages of the alumni magazine, he played *his* Big Three trump card. In the 1940s, he admitted, Harvard's younger Fogg Museum (1895) grew to become "the leading University Museum in America and perhaps anywhere." And "recently the Yale Museum has made enormous strides as a rival." But Kelleher was convinced that Princeton's art museum "belongs in the league with the best," even though the *New York Times* art critic in 1960 had failed to mention it in a list of Fogg's closest rivals—the museums at Yale, Smith, and Oberlin. Borrowing an idea from a recent, "startlingly spectacular" Yale exhibition, he invited Princeton alumni to lend their best works of art to the new museum when it opened. As for the suggestion that "Yale men are richer than Princeton men" and such an exhibition would therefore suffer in comparison, he very much doubted it. He ended by hoping that the Princeton motto *Dei sub numine viget*

[26] Harold Saunders, "Campus Treasure Cache," *Nassau Sovereign* 8:8 (May 1949): 20, 29–30, at 30.

("Under God she flourishes") would have future application to the Art Museum.[27]

From then on the battle was joined, as Presidents Goheen and Bowen and their successors made art education a more conspicuous Princeton priority and dared to engage Harvard and Yale head-on. Today there is widespread agreement that Princeton's "art-gallery" is not only the third-oldest university museum in America, but the third-best, with an endowed acquisition budget that actually exceeds those of its two Ivy rivals. Although it is still smaller than the other two, it gives away little if anything in the "fineness" and representative breadth of its collection and nothing in its teaching capacity.[28]

❁ ❁ ❁

Museum collections grow in three ways: by gifts, by purchases on endowed or special funds, and, temporarily, by loans and traveling exhibitions from other museums or collectors. Directors Marquand and Mather not only solicited gifts and acquisition funds but collected and donated large numbers of art objects to the museum themselves. Mather was especially energetic in both regards. Having taught in the Art Department since 1910, he knew firsthand the museum's gaps and weaknesses. With a keen eye developed as a popular New York art critic, writer, and collector, the Johns Hopkins Ph.D. in English acquired choice bargains—and some speculative mistakes—around the world. For years he claimed that he never spent more than $25 for a drawing, thus making a virtue of necessity. In

[27] Patrick J. Kelleher, "The Art Museum," *PAW*, Sept. 23, 1960, 10–11, 18–19. On Harvard's inexorable lead, see James Cuno et al., *Harvard's Art Museums: 100 Years of Collecting* (Cambridge, Mass. and New York, 1996).

[28] Harvard and Yale's lead was noticeable but not overwhelming in 1955 by just one measure of collection quality. When John D. Morse inventoried forty "Old Masters" in American museums, Harvard had 16 (by 15 painters), Yale had 13 (by 9 painters), and Princeton had 11 (by 9 painters). *Old Masters in America* (Chicago, 1955), 182, 185, 187. By 2004, according to their respective Web sites, Princeton's museum held some 60,000 registered objects; Harvard's collections, housed in three museums, had grown to more than 200,000 objects, Yale's to 90,000. Smith alone had 25,000 items (80,000 with the Five College Consortium and Historic Deerfield) and Oberlin perhaps 13,000.

1925 his budget for purchases was less than $1,000 (about $10,000 in 2003 buying power), up from only $300 five years earlier, but Mather was able to boast that he made 150 acquisitions in the previous two years.[29] Although he garnered some of the museum's foundational collections, he was, like Marquand, extremely generous with his own possessions and funds. In addition to donating hundreds of rare books to the university and Marquand libraries, before his second retirement in 1946 (the first was from teaching in 1933) he gave "over 400 drawings and water-colors, nearly 400 fine prints, 39 paintings, 24 sheets of Medieval illumination, 8 pieces of sculpture, 23 pieces of Ancient, Medieval, and Renaissance pottery, 12 bone and ivory objects," and more. Many of his gifts launched Princeton's venture into both contemporary and American art, subjects in which he taught in addition to his Renaissance specialty.[30] And to increase Princeton's chances in the Big Three art competition, he and three siblings established in 1923 the museum's second endowment, the Caroline G. Mather Fund, in memory of their mother.[31]

As Mather and his successors pursued donors, both the museum's endowment and its collections grew apace, though always behind Harvard and Yale. By the mid-1930s Mather had about $7,000 a year (less than $100,000 in 2003 purchasing power) to spend on new objects. One of his greatest allies was Carl Otto von Kienbusch '06, the beneficiary of a New York tobacco business. Von Kienbusch not only made donations from his personal collection, he regularly asked

[29] Jones, "The Making of a Museum," 23; Ross, "The Mather Years," 56; Mather, "An Art Museum at Princeton," 420.

[30] In the winter of 1942–1943 Mather gave his collection of sixty drawings by American artists to the museum in conjunction with the inauguration of the university's Program of Study in American Civilization. Princeton University Art Museum [PUAM], "Exhibitions (Museum, Department, Architecture)" [1892/3–1946], 34 (typescript) (thanks to Jill Guthrie for a copy of this detailed list, culled primarily from *PAW* and the *Bull. of the Dept. of Art & Arch.*).

[31] E. Baldwin Smith, "Frank Jewett Mather: An Expression of Appreciation to 'An Enthusiastic Princetonian,' " *PAW*, May 23, 1947, 7; Ross, "The Mather Years," 53, 54, 63, 67, 68–69, 76n74; Mather, "The Museum of Historic Art," 195–96; John Wilmerding, *American Art in the Princeton University Art Museum. Volume 1: Drawings and Watercolors* (Princeton: PUAM, 2004), 5–7 (thanks to John Wilmerding for an advance copy of his introduction and to Jill Guthrie for a copy of the published catalogue).

the director, "Is there anything you feel you cannot live without?" and promptly wrote a check for it. He also established a memorial collection for an infant son that brought to Princeton three dozen sculptures and numerous pieces of three-dimensional art. To make the collections better known, in 1942 he initiated and financed the *Record of the Museum of Historic Art*, a distinguished biannual journal devoted to studies of museum objects and collections. And last but far from least, he contributed $250,000 to the construction of the new museum and guaranteed the future publication of the *Record* under its simpler new names.[32]

Enterprising directors and generous benefactors slowly but steadily added cubits to Princeton's stature in the art world. In 1939 department chairman E. Baldwin Smith noted once again the disparity between the museum's collections and its ability to properly show and preserve them. "If exception is made of the support of a very small group of generous and discerning alumni," he wrote in the department *Bulletin*, the museum "has shared the incredible neglect experienced by the University Library during the past twenty-five years, and deserves it no more than that other step-child of Princeton." Although many Princetonians were vague even about the museum's existence, he assured readers that "it is well-known to art-lovers and scholars of this country and abroad as one of the best small collections in America." Many of its highlights—a thirteenth-century stained-glass window depicting the *Martyrdom of St. George* from Chartres Cathedral, the grotesque *Christ before Pilate* by (now thought to be the atelier of) Hieronymus Bosch, mosaics from Princeton's joint excavations of Antioch, the Veronese Cannon paintings—"make it a place that foreign connoisseurs feel that they must not omit from their itineraries in the United States."[33]

[32] Mather, "The College Art Museum," 20; *The Art Museum, PU*, 4–5; Jones, "The Making of a Museum," 22, 23. In 1948 the Museum of Historic Art became the Art Museum at the suggestion of Director Ernest DeWald (1947–1960). *The Art Museum, PU*, 12. In 2000 new Director Susan M. Taylor changed it to the Princeton University Art Museum, for which bibliographers are grateful.

[33] [E. Baldwin Smith], "Space," *Bull. of the Dept. of Art & Arch.* (June 1939): 15–16. For illustrations, see *Selections from The Art Museum*, 47, 57, 78, 93.

FIGURE 31. *Christ before Pilate*, one of the Art Museum's major works, was a gift of Allan Marquand in the early 1920s. The wonderfully grotesque oil painting is attributed to the atelier Hieronymous Bosch (c. 1450–1516). Photo by Bruce M. White.

By the time Princeton decided to embrace its artistic stepchild by building a new museum, the collection was literally bursting the seams of the old one. To make way for the demolition of the old building, the museum staff moved into Green Hall Annex in 1963 and sent many objects into temporary asylum in other museums, such as Colonial Williamsburg, Oberlin, the Baltimore Museum of Art, and the Metropolitan. As part of the process, the collection was thoroughly inventoried, yielding a minimum count of 22,000 items. Among the art that was shipped off or stored were 1,200 paintings, 450 sculptures, 1,500 pieces of pottery and porcelain (about 40 percent ancient), 700 pieces of glass, and more than 3,000 coins, mostly Greek and Roman.[34]

[34] "The Green Years," *Record of The Art Museum*, 22:2 (1963): 57–59.

The new museum led not only to a tremendous increase in visitors (double in the first year) but a freshet of gifts and loans. Many had long been promised, but the lack of a safe and attractive space to exhibit them had delayed their release. As early as 1939 Baldwin Smith had hoped that an addition to McCormick Hall would help secure for the university several "fine collections that are ready to come to it when assured of proper housing. (An excellent collection of modern art"—the museum's most glaring weakness—"was offered under such conditions this spring.) The proffer of such contingent gifts is becoming more and more frequent; the impossibility of accepting them . . . all the more distressing."[35]

The new museum of 1966 attracted new endowments as well as gifts in kind. The Friends of the Art Museum, formed in 1950, took on renewed energy, using a newsletter to publicize museum needs and philanthropic opportunities.[36] In 1973 two gifts enabled Princeton to hold its own in the increasingly heated world art market. The Surdna Foundation, interested mainly in supporting the library's collection of rare books and manuscripts, also gave $100,000 (worth more than $400,000 in 2003 dollars) to endow the purchase of British art. This came just in time for the museum to obtain a stained glass panel depicting Saint Cecilia, designed by Sir Edward Burne-Jones and executed by the William Morris atelier.[37]

The museum's single largest endowment, however, came from the estate of Fowler McCormick '21, the grandson of Cyrus, Sr., and John D. Rockefeller, Sr., freshman rower, and former chairman of

[35] [Smith], "Space," 15–16.

[36] Jones, "The Making of a Museum," 26; Renata Stepanov, "Guiding Visitors Through the World of Art," *DP*, Nov. 7, 2003, 3; Indre Vengris, "Uncharted Territory: Taking a Tour of the Art Museum, Princeton's Hidden Treasure," *DP* (online), Sept. 18, 2003. In 1966 the University League, a social and service group of faculty and staff wives, was asked by the Art Department to establish a Docent Association to lead tours of the museum. Eighteen women inaugurated the tours after suitable training; today nearly 80 docents serve, including a number of student guides. In 1975 students formed their own friends organization, which for $5.00 sent subscribers a newsletter and invited them to exhibition openings.

[37] Jones, "The Making of a Museum," 26; *Selections from The Art Museum*, 103; *The Art Museum, PU*, 17–18.

International Harvester. In addition to a separate fund to support research in the history of photography (Peter C. Bunnell had just been lured from the Museum of Modern Art in New York by the new David H. McAlpin '20 chair in the subject), McCormick's will left the museum a $2.7 million endowment for collection development.[38] It has enabled Princeton to acquire such "fine" and teachable objects as a bronze bust of a woman coiffed in a hair net from second-century Rome, a doleful painting, *Christ as Redeemer*, by Hendrik Goltzius (Dutch, 1558–1617), a spiral-decorated red-clay Chinese jar (2500–2000 B.C.), an elaborate late-nineteenth-century gold badge of honor from Ghana, and an Art Deco–like window from a 1904 Frank Lloyd Wright house.[39]

By 2004 Princeton's collection had reached some sixty thousand items, not counting thousands of archaeological shards from the Art Department's early Turkish and Syrian excavations. Although it is populated by individual masterworks by many of the world's best artists, its pedagogical and research value lies as much in the range and depth of its various subcollections. More than seven thousand drawings, for example, allow students access to the equivalent of the artist's "private notes, revealing intimately his true aims and ideas, as yet unveiled by the conventions of a finished technique or the public demands that become imposed on the final painting." Many drawings were not meant to be seen but only used and discarded. If they are not particularly "good," they are still invaluable to students seeking to understand the artistic process, with its often false starts and wrong turns. They are particularly revealing when a series of sketches by the same artist can be studied as the artist makes his or her uncertain way toward a finished painting or print.[40]

[38] Peter T. Joseph '72, "Photography as Art," *PAW*, Nov. 28, 1972, 8–11; "The Bunnell Years, 1973–1978," *The Art Museum, PU*, 17–18; Bunnell, *Photography at Princeton: Celebrating Twenty-Five Years of Collecting and Teaching the History of Photography* (Princeton: The Art Museum, 1998).

[39] "Art Museum Receives $2.5 Million Bequest," *Princeton Packet*, Jan. 7, 1976, 37; *Selections from The Art Museum*, 43, 84, 191, 241, 285; for other McCormick Fund purchases, see 39, 77, 80, 96, 99, 210, 227.

[40] Felton Gibbons, "To the Student, Drawings Are an Artist's Private Notes," *University: A Princeton Quarterly* 44 (Spring 1970), inserted in *PAW*, Mar. 17, 1970, 31–41. Susan Taylor, the museum's current director, notes that in drawings, as in watercolors,

Many drawings are turned into prints, by the artist or a professional printmaker. Since any college or university museum is necessarily limited in the number of great paintings it can own, less expensive original prints can be used to reveal "another facet of a master's talent, one in which the imagery is expressed more intimately," usually in black and white. Princeton's more than eight thousand prints—the majority collected in the 1920s and 1930s by Frank Mather and Dan Fellows Platt '25—put students in direct touch with painter-printmakers such as Dürer, Tiepolo, Rembrandt, Van Dyck, Goya, Manet, and Picasso. Junius Morgan's donations during Mather's tenure included 2,500 prints from the fifteenth to the nineteenth century, among which was a nearly complete set of Jacques Callot (c. 1592–1635), some in several states, and a large selection of the Haarlem Mannerist Goltzius, two of the most famous printmakers of all time. Twenty-two posters by Toulouse-Lautrec evoking the Montmartre theater district of Paris also document the advent of color lithography in the late nineteenth century.[41]

Although painting has long been regarded as the queen of the visual arts, sculpture has an equally long pedigree. As one of man's earliest attempts to express himself aesthetically in visual terms, it presents to the viewer the tactile immediacy of three-dimensional objects, small and large. Works on paper and canvas cannot be seen from the side or behind as sculptures can, which gives the student direct access to the objects' rounded intentionality. Princeton's

---

"the hand of the maker is often more evident and more telling than in a large-scale finished work. The connection between the artist's intent and its expression on paper is never closer than in a drawing" (Wilmerding, *American Art in the Princeton University Art Museum*, vii). See also *Selections from The Art Museum*, 110–27, 136, 138–40.

[41] Robert A. Koch, "The Importance of Prints in a Teaching Museum," *University* 42 (Fall 1969), inserted in *PAW*, Sept. 23, 1969, 23–33, at 23; Barbara T. Ross, "The Prints and Drawings Collection: The Early Years," *Record of The Art Museum* 55:1–2 (1996): 135–55. In 2004, according to their museum Web sites, Harvard's Fogg Museum had 10,000 drawings, 60,000 prints, and 70,000 photographs; Yale owned a total of 30,000 prints, drawings, and photographs. In addition to its more than 15,000 drawings and prints, Princeton had more than 20,000 photographs by some 900 artists. Before 1971, when David McAlpin donated more than 500 images, the museum's permanent collection had only 19 photographs. Bunnell, *Photography at Princeton*, 1–2.

sculptures range from an elegant wooden arm from an Eighteenth Dynasty (c. 1580 B.C.) Egyptian tomb, a caravan of Chinese tomb figures (Third–Sixth century A.D.), and Mayan effigy pots to a busy Red Grooms scene of New York's painter-friendly Cedar Bar and a collection of twenty-one modern sculptures placed outdoors around campus.[42]

The latter, the John B. Putnam, Jr., Memorial Collection, owned by the university but administered by the museum, consists of impressive works by such modern masters as Jacques Lipchitz, Alexander Calder, Henry Moore, and Isamu Noguchi. Since its installation in the early 1970s, it has left daily reminders to the campus population that sculpture is for quotidian pleasure, although studies or maquettes of ten of the outsized objects may be studied in the museum. When it was erected near the museum's entrance in 1971, Picasso's cast-concrete *Head of a Woman* drew the most attention. But since its removal to a site near the "Dinky" station to make way for the underground extension of Marquand Library, Henry Moore's 2 ½-ton bronze *Oval with Points* near the Admission Office in West College has become the overwhelming favorite of students and visitors, most of whom cannot resist rubbing or perching in it (with the university's tacit approval).[43]

The university's collection of outdoor art continues to grow. In 1998 Scott Burton's "Public Table" and two years later Richard Serra's outsized rippling steel ribbons, "The Hedgehog and the Fox," were added to the campus art show. Since 2004 the new ellipse dor-

[42] Patrick J. Kelleher, "The Uses of Sculpture in a Teaching Museum," *University* 48 (Spring 1971), inserted in *PAW*, Mar. 23, 1971, 17–26. For numerous examples, see *Selections from The Art Museum*, and Brunilde S. Ridgway, *Greek Sculpture in The Art Museum, Princeton University: Greek Originals, Roman Copies and Variants* (Princeton: The Art Museum, 1994). Red Grooms' *Maquette for the Cedar Bar* (1986) is pictured in *In Celebration: Works of Art from the Collections of Princeton Alumni and Friends of The Art Museum, Princeton University* (Princeton: The Art Museum, 1997), 328–29.

[43] Patrick J. Kelleher, *Living with Modern Sculpture: The John B. Putnam, Jr., Memorial Collection, Princeton University* (Princeton: The Art Museum, 1982); John M. Fenton, "The Putnam Sculptures," *PAW*, Dec. 14, 1971, 6–13. For a profile of the enigmatic physicist-philosopher Peter Putnam '46, *60, who funded the outdoor sculptures in his brother's name, see Ann Waldron, "Brilliant Enigma," *PAW*, May 15, 1991, 22–26.

FIGURE 32. Henry Moore's bronze *Oval with Points*, cast in England, was installed near West College in 1971. A 5½-inch version is in the John B. Putnam, Jr., Memorial Collection of artists' maquettes in the Art Museum.

mitory on the south campus has sported an eye-catching painting by Connecticut artist Sol LeWitt on the ceiling of the large archway leading from Elm Drive to Poe Field. Entitled "Wall Drawing No. 1134 Whirls and Twirls," its "undulating skeins of juicy, electric color" greet students daily as well as reuning P-raders who now pass under it annually.[44]

The museum's strongest collections today are in the arts of Western Europe, the ancient Mediterranean region, China, the United States, and the pre-Columbian Americas. But to fulfill its teaching mandate, it has also purchased and been given collections from other parts of the world—Japan, India, Africa, the Middle East, and Byzantium. Two examples suggest the breadth and quality of Princeton's collections.

Under Charles Morey, Kurt Weitzmann, and music historian Oliver Strunk, Princeton became one of the leading centers of Byzantine studies in the country, second only to Harvard's Dumbarton Oaks in Washington, D.C. The Art Museum kept pace with that reputation in its collections and its encouragement of Weitzmann's expeditions to Orthodox monasteries on Mount Athos and Mount Sinai to photograph their rich and rare holdings of illuminated manuscripts and icons. In 1986 architectural historian Slobodan Ćurčić, Weitzmann's belated successor in the Art Department, organized an exhibition in Firestone Library, *Byzantium at Princeton*, to coincide with an international meeting of Byzantinists in Washington. Firestone contributed illuminated manuscripts from the Robert Garrett collection and coins, the Art Department lent numerous photographs and drawings, and the Art Museum provided an extensive array of artistic, archaeological, and architectural objects. Although the exhibition spoke for itself, Weitzmann contributed an historical essay to the published catalogue describing "The Contribution of the Princeton University Department of Art and Archaeology to the Study of Byzantine Art," much of it his own.[45]

[44] Ruth Stevens, "Bright Surprise Awaits Students in Ellipse Dorm," *PWB* (online), Sept. 5, 2004. For a view of Serra's "Hedgehog," see Wilmerding, "American Arts at Princeton," 9 (fig. 5).

[45] Slobodan Ćurčić and Archer St. Clair, eds., *Byzantium at Princeton: Byzantine Art and Archaeology at Princeton University* (Princeton, 1986). Weitzmann's essay is on pp.

Princeton's Chinese holdings began with trade pottery in the founding Trumbull-Prime collection, to which were later added three hundred pieces from Clement K. Corbin '02. These export tea service items were made and decorated to accord with conventional Western assumptions about the Far East as "exotic" or "droll" (George Washington's term). The five hundred snuff bottles received in 1934 from Col. James A. Blair '03 were a step up in both artistic quality and authentic design. The following year in London an international exhibition of Chinese art, much of it from former imperial palace collections, brought to the West for the first time art of high quality that reflected indigenous aesthetic values. Princeton benefited from this enlightenment when it received five hundred paintings from Dubois S. Morris '93, longtime Presbyterian missionary in China, at the 1947 bicentennial conference on Far Eastern Culture and Society. Previously on loan for twenty years, the Morris collection also formed the basis of Professor and first Curator of Far Eastern Art George Rowley's influential *Principles of Chinese Painting* (Princeton, 1947). Rowley's own collection of Chinese rubbings of engraved stones with figure representations came to the museum ten years later.[46]

Rowley's successor, Wen C. Fong '51, *57 was instrumental in securing several major additions to the museum's Chinese collection. He encouraged Mr. and Mrs. Earl Morse (who had no Princeton connection) to collect the works of seventeenth-century painter Wang Hui and his contemporaries, who worked in the styles of the old Chinese masters. When the new museum staged a special exhibition of the Morse collection in 1969, it published a scholarly catalogue entitled *In Pursuit of Antiquity*, in which Mr. Morse promised

---

11–30. A much fuller account is in his *Sailing with Byzantium from Europe to America: The Memoirs of an Art Historian* (Munich, 1994). In 1973 the Art Museum published *Illuminated Greek Manuscripts from American Collections: An Exhibition in Honor of Kurt Weitzmann*, edited by Gary Vikan; many of the entries were written by Weitzmann's former students.

[46] Cary Y. Liu, "Asian Art Collection: From Exotica to Art and History," *Record of The Art Museum* 55:1–2 (1996): 125–36; "Morris Collection Presented to Princeton," *PAW*, May 23, 1947, 8–9; George Rowley, "The Morris Collection of Chinese Paintings," *Record of the Museum of Historic Art* 6:1–2 (1947): 2–3; *The Art Museum, PU*, 7, 8, 11.

his group of paintings by Wang Hui. In the 1970s an extended family of Elliotts, particularly that of Fong's classmate John B. Elliott '51, gave a rich array of calligraphic art, from the fourteenth to the nineteenth century. This, too, eventually resulted in a major exhibition and catalogue, *Images of the Mind* (1984), in which Fong explained the philosophical connection between calligraphy and painting in the world of Tao.[47]

Another of Fong's successes came in 1965 when oil executive Chester Dale Carter was persuaded by his lawyer John Howley '29 to sell his extremely rare collection of eighty-four ancient Chinese ritual bronzes to Princeton. Assembled while Carter was posted to Japan after World War II, the bronzes, spanning the whole Chinese Bronze Age (fourteenth century B.C. to the first century A.D.), feature a menagerie of snakes, monsters, birds, and animals and the earliest known form of Chinese writing on them. Harvard's Oriental art expert Max Loehr could hardly contain his Ivy envy after appraising the collection from photographs. He told Fong that it was an "astonishingly large" collection of "rare and magnificent specimens" and of consuming "historical and artistic importance." Princeton had a rare chance to secure a private collection of such high quality, which he and Fong agreed could "probably never be assembled again." Fortunately for Princeton, a number of the museum's faithful supporters stepped forward to make the purchase.[48]

[47] *The Art Museum, PU*, 13, 21; Margaret M. Keenan, "Images of the Mind," *PAW*, May 16, 1984, 22–25; Wen C. Fong, *Images of the Mind: Selections from the Edward L. Elliott Family and John B. Elliott Collection of Chinese Calligraphy and Painting at The Art Museum, Princeton University* (Princeton: The Art Museum, 1984). See also *Selections from The Art Museum*, 212–19. In 1999 the museum staged another exhibition, *The Embodied Image*, featuring calligraphy from John B. Elliott's recent bequest. A year later the show doubled in size and went to the Metropolitan Museum of Art, where Wen Fong had become Curator of Chinese Art. Holland Cotter, "Not Penmanship, Cultural Treasure," *New York Times*, June 4, 1999, E31.

[48] *The Art Museum, PU*, 16; PU, press release, Feb. 17, 1965; Max Loehr, Abby Aldrich Rockefeller Professor of Oriental Art, Fogg Art Museum, Harvard University, to Wen Fong, June 3, 1964, Hist. Subj. Files: "Art Museum," box 1 (PUA); Roderick Whitfield, "The Carter Collection," *PAW*, Feb. 23, 1965, 10–13 (illus.). For more examples, see *Selections from The Art Museum*, 192, 194.

One of those supporters was Arthur M. Sackler, a New York physician and generous Harvard donor, whose family and foundation not only footed a third of the Carter collection cost but gave another collection and funded a gallery in the Far Eastern section of the new museum. The best works were sixteen paintings by Tao-chi (b. 1641), a well-born monk who developed a nontraditional style of self-expression. The Sackler collection, according to Fong, was "the largest, and the last possible, comprehensive collection" of this Chinese Rembrandt.[49]

❁ ❁ ❁

As extensive as the Princeton collection was, the scope of the world's art far exceeded it. The only way to extend the museum's array of originals for teaching purposes was to bring to Princeton temporary exhibits of art from other collections—private, public, and academic. The first major loan show was mounted in 1928 to introduce "Masterpieces of Nineteenth-Century Art" from the Metropolitan Museum, the Phillips Collection in Washington, and various dealers. A key object, Director Mather said, was to show "the friends of the Museum the sort of pictures"—Renoir, Cézanne, Constable, Delacroix, Manet—"which should eventually comprise its permanent collections. Alumni art collectors please take notice."[50] Before World War II, lack of space limited most exhibitions to small loans of a week or two. The primary lenders were major art dealers in New York such as Knoedler & Co., local, faculty, and alumni collectors (including student members of the Princeton Camera Club), and faculty and students of the School of Architecture and, after 1941, the Creative Arts Program.[51] Between 1947 and 1992 (less two three-year periods when the new museum was under construction and then renovation), the museum mounted some fifty exhibitions from collections other than its own, about 8 percent of its exhibitions during

[49] *The Art Museum, PU*, 16; "The Sackler Collection," PU, press release, June 24, 1968; "Princeton Gains Rare Chinese Art," *New York Times*, June 25, 1968, 38.

[50] *PAW*, May 25, 1928, 1002, quoted in *In Celebration*, xvi.

[51] PUAM, "Exhibitions" [1892/3–1946].

that period. The added gallery space in the new museum made room for thirty-four loan shows in the twenty years after its opening. Many lenders were alumni, but other works came from Paris, the Smithsonian, the Wadsworth Atheneum in Hartford, the Museum of African Art in Washington, and a variety of colleges and universities, from Pomona in the West to Syracuse, Williams, and Harvard in the East.[52]

One of the museum's most popular loans came in late 1972 at the initiative of President William Bowen, who had broached the idea with Norton Simon at a trustees' meeting of the Institute for Advanced Study. Simon, the wealthy and civic-minded head of a major food and industrial conglomerate, had assembled (according to department chairman Fong) "the greatest single group of works of European art still without a permanent home." Rather than build his own museum, Simon and the president of his foundation, Robert S. Macfarlane, Jr., a 1954 graduate of the Art Department, decided to lend holdings from the collection for yearlong exhibitions around the country. Thanks to Bowen's persuasions, Princeton was the first university to receive this corporate benefaction, and the first to publish a catalogue of the collection. Simon, a Berkeley dropout (after only six weeks), was also clearly impressed that at Princeton "one of four undergraduates attends at least one course in the Department of Art and Archaeology during his college years."[53]

The hundred-plus works that were on display for a full year brought to Princeton some of the most beautiful and original works in existence and galvanized visitor attendance and student attention. The show's highlight was the newly purchased *Madonna and Child with Book*—one of only six Raphaels in the United States—which made its first public appearance after decades in an English country house. But superb paintings, watercolors, and sculptures from the

[52] The Art Museum, "Past Exhibits" [1947–1992] (typescript). This is a rough list that is being revised and updated, but for illustrative purposes it is reasonably accurate, if not complete. (Thanks to Jill Guthrie for a copy.)

[53] "A Major Resource for a Teaching Museum," *PAW*, Feb. 6, 1973, 8–13; David W. Steadman, ed., *Selections from the Norton Simon, Inc. Museum of Art* (Princeton: The Art Museum, 1972), 9–10, 12; William McCleery, "A Businessman & Art Collector Talks of Art (& Business)," *University* 60 (Spring 1974): 8–13, 27–28.

late fifteenth to the twentieth century drew suburban crowds (attendance jumped 70 percent over the previous year), spawned special class visits, paper topics, and senior theses, and inspired a ten-week course in the Princeton Adult School, a community enterprise. Jan Steen's rendering of an inebriated woman being loaded into a wheelbarrow by mocking villagers may even have served as a cautionary tale for Princeton's new coeds, male and female. More likely, they and other visitors were captivated by the large number of sculptures and paintings of the human figure—portraits by Cézanne, Rubens, Bellini, Renoir, and Van Gogh, nude sculptures by Maillol, Degas, Rodin, Picasso, Matisse, and Henry Moore.[54]

More typical were large loan exhibitions that originated in other museums before coming to Princeton or were organized in Princeton, with numerous contributions from the museum's collections and curators, before traveling to other venues. In the winter of 1992–1993 a rich show called *Gates of Mystery: The Art of Holy Russia*, organized by the State Russian Museum in St. Petersburg and the Walters Art Gallery in Baltimore, came to Princeton for two months, the second stop on a six-museum tour. The exhibition reintroduced Princeton to nearly a hundred new manifestations of iconic Byzantine art that the museum had displayed from time to time in the days of Morey and Weitzmann. As was often the case with major exhibitions, *Gates of Mystery* extended its intellectual reach with an international scholarly conference and the publication of a sumptuous color catalogue, including ten essays by Russian and British scholars.[55]

A similarly evocative exhibition of ancient Greek art was organized by Princeton's Curator of Ancient Art J. Michael Padgett for a three-month showing in 2003–2004. Before traveling to the Museum of Fine Arts in Houston, the exhibition dazzled viewers with its imaginative and learned display of artistic renderings of composite human-animals from ancient Greek mythology: centaurs, satyrs,

[54] "A Major Resource," 8; Peter C. Bunnell, "On the Showing of Simon Works at Princeton Art Museum," *University* 60 (Spring 1974): 4–7; David W. Steadman, "The Norton Simon Exhibition at Princeton," *Art Journal* 32:1 (Fall 1972): 34–40; Steadman, *Selections*; Marian Burleigh-Motley, "The Human Image in Art," *University* 54 (Fall 1972): 19–24.

[55] Roderick Grierson, *Gates of Mystery: The Art of Holy Russia* (Fort Worth 1992).

sphinxes, sirens, Gorgons, and various gods and demons. The inspiration for this complex and beautifully installed show arose in a Princeton seminar on *Mischwesen*, or mixed creatures, taught by Padgett and Professor of Art William Childs in the spring of 1999. This was followed by the gathering of 101 objects from 37 lenders around the world, 21 of them from Princeton's own collection of Greek art, and the production by the museum staff of a stunning 5 ½-pound, 426-page catalogue, largely in color. Although most of the catalogue entries were written by an international cast of curators, Princeton graduate student Kyriaki Karoglou wrote three gallery handouts for the exhibition and Nathan Arrington '02, Padgett's curatorial research assistant, wrote the entry on Princeton's red-figure vase depicting Oedipus and the Sphinx.[56]

Another source of loans was Princeton-associated collectors. Particularly before the new museum opened in 1966, many loans were small collections belonging to individual alumni or local denizens, such as St. Louis lawyer J. Lionberger Davis '00, who retired to Princeton, Institute director J. Robert Oppenheimer, who was inordinately proud of his inherited Van Gogh, *Enclosed Field with Rising Sun*, and Paul Oppenheim, resident aficionado of nineteenth-century French painting.[57] On three occasions, however, after the university resolved to pick up its pace in art education, the museum organized major exhibitions of alumni-owned art, partly in hopes of beating Yale at its own game (as Director Kelleher planned) and of securing later gifts and bequests.

Around commencement in 1972 the museum honored retiring President and Mrs. Goheen (she a docent and member of the Friends' board) with a 137-piece show of European and American art, the most ambitious exhibition it had thus far attempted. Out-

[56] J. Michael Padgett et al., *The Centaur's Smile: The Human Animal in Early Greek Art* (Princeton: PUAM, 2003). For appreciative reviews, see Benjamin Genocchio, "Creatures of Mystery, Some Friendly, Some Not," *New York Times*, Nov. 2, 2003, sec. 14 (New Jersey), 9; Ken Johnson, "Finding the Beast Within, And Portraying It Without," *New York Times*, Nov. 7, 2003, sec. E, pt. 2, 32.

[57] Jeremy Bernstein, *Oppenheimer: Portrait of an Enigma* (Chicago, 2004), 6, 193, 197. After Oppenheimer's death, the picture was sold at Sotheby's in 1985 to a private collector for $9 million.

standing works from nine centuries were lent by discerning alumni such as Malcolm Forbes '41, John D. Rockefeller III '29, Charles Scribner, Jr. '43, and George L. Shultz '40. Kelleher, who also contributed, was gratified that over seventy of the artists in the show were not represented in the museum's collection, and particularly that several exhibitors had agreed to extended loans and three outstanding paintings had already been promised as gifts.[58]

Nine years later, the museum gathered more than two hundred *Works on Paper*—drawings, watercolors, pastels, and collages—from a hundred alumni collectors for a big if less dramatic show. The exhibition, which also resulted in a published catalogue, was dedicated to A. Hyatt Mayor '22, the late curator of prints at the Metropolitan and an involved as well as distinguished member of the advisory councils of both the Art Department and the museum. Text from his classic *Prints & People: A Social History of Printed Pictures* (New York, 1971) furnished several labels to describe prints from the museum collection that were also on view.[59]

For the university's 250th anniversary, however, Director Allen Rosenbaum (1980–1998) and the Art Museum pulled out all the stops for an alumni exhibition unprecedented in breadth and quality. Taking the art of the world (except prints) as its subject, *In Celebration* was built upon more than 370 works lent by some two hundred members of the wider Princeton community, including parents, private collectors, honorary class members, neighbors, and even a freshman. Conspicuous for their generosity to the university on other occasions were lenders such as Lloyd Cotsen '50, Roger S. Berlind

[58] Hedy B. Landsman, ed., *European and American Art from Princeton Alumni Collections* (Princeton: The Art Museum, 1972), xiii, xvi–xvii; "Alumni Art Show," *PAW*, May 9, 1972, 10–14. Among the show's highlights were Rembrandt's *Portrait of a Man* (1635), theretofore never shown publicly and inaccessible even to scholars; Rubens's *Cupid Supplicating Jupiter*, two Winslow Homers; a Murillo self-portrait; Houdon's terracotta *Head of Voltaire* (1782); Manet's earthy *Gitane à la cigarette* (1862); and Monet's *Waterlilies and Japanese Bridge*.

[59] *Princeton Alumni Collections: Works on Paper* (Princeton: Princeton Art Museum, 1981); "Exhibiting Alumni Art Collections," *PAW*, Dec. 3, 1979, 24–25; "Works on Paper," *PAW*, May 18, 1981, 10–11. On the museum's collection of works on paper, see Ross, "The Prints and Drawings Collection," 135–55; Wilmerding, "American Art at Princeton," 3–22.

'52, Leonard L. Milberg '53, Carl C. Icahn '57, Mitchell Wolfson, Jr. '63, the major donor of the new 27,000-square-foot wing of the museum in 1989, and Peter B. Lewis '55, who funded a gallery in the new wing devoted to contemporary art. Welcoming visitors appropriately to the first gallery was George Stubbs's large *Portrait of a Royal Tiger* (c. 1770–1780). Beyond lay such visual pleasures as an encaustic portrait on wood of a curly-headed young man before mummification from mid-second century A.D. Egypt; a colorful Bolivian textile (370 B.C.–A.D. 450) covered with toothy llamas; an elaborate fourteenth-century French ivory *Six Scenes from the Life of Christ*; a luminous portrait of *Saint Jerome* contemplating mortality by Dutch painter Jacques de Rousseau (c. 1600–1638); Rubens's sensual rendering of *Leda and the Swan* (c. 1600); Degas's bronze *Dancer Looking at the Sole of Her Right Foot*; a tender self-portrait of Gaugin nuzzling his son; a hypnotic Frank Stella '58 green-and-white triangle, *Valparaiso Green* (1963); and, in a popular bow, E. H. Shepard's pen-ink-and-watercolor drawings for illustrations for *Winnie the Pooh* and *The House at Pooh Corner* (1928), featuring, of course, Tigger.[60]

❁ ❁ ❁

If collections are the heart of a museum, exhibitions are the lifeblood that sustains and renews it. In the thirty-nine years between 1947 and 1992 when the museum was fully open, for example, the staff mounted at least 634 exhibitions. Nearly 19 percent of them were regarded as major, and nearly 12 percent gave rise to published catalogues, which continued to educate students and art lovers long after the shows were dismantled. Some fifty shows (8 percent) were lent by other collectors or institutions. But by far the greatest number of exhibitions—fully one-third—were prepared specifically for undergraduate courses in the history of art and, less often, the creative arts.[61] This was entirely appropriate for a teaching museum, and

[60] *In Celebration*, xvii, 8, 99, 135, 155, 166, 213, 214, 220–21, 311; Harold T. Shapiro, "The President's Page: A Sumptuous Feast for the Eye and Mind," *PAW*, Feb. 19, 1997, 57; "Art Museum Reopens," *PAW*, May 3 and 17, 1989, 26–28. As in the previous alumni shows, several works—twenty-three—were promised to Princeton as gifts or bequests.

[61] The Art Museum, "Past Exhibits" [1947–1992].

nonacademic visitors could profit from the installations and labels as well as the students, whether accompanied by a knowledgeable docent or not.

The first exhibitions for classes were mounted in the old museum, where space was at a premium. After McCormick Hall was completed in 1923, however, the Art Department itself often prepared exhibitions for classes in its own spacious precincts. The creation in 1935 of a modest gallery in the enclosed Antioch Court within the museum-McCormick quadrangle and exhibition space in a new two-storey addition allowed the faculty to expose their classes to small and large groups of artworks, as often as fifteen to twenty-five times a year. Three hundred Chinese paintings from the Morris collection, for example, were "shown in smaller groups, in chronological order to parallel the graduate course in Chinese painting" taught by George Rowley. The Museum of Modern Art regularly sent one–three paintings from New York. And ninety-five Dürer etchings, engravings, and dry-points from the Lessing Rosenwald collection managed to be displayed all at the same time. Although these exhibitions were arranged "for the benefit of students . . . to supplement courses in the curriculum," they were also "open to, and much visited by, the public of Princeton."[62]

When the new museum opened in 1966, it provided several permanent study collections and spaces for changing exhibitions for classes, particularly in an L-shaped gallery on the lower level. After the major expansion and remodeling of 1984–1989, small flexible spaces on the upper level and a handful of precept rooms encouraged even greater use of the collections for teaching purposes.[63] Between late 1966 and the beginning of 1986, when the museum closed for renovations, 119 exhibitions were mounted specifically for Princeton

[62] Ross, "The Mather Years," 56, 58; Bush, "Architectural History," 90; "Exhibitions," *Bull. of the Dept. of Art and Arch.*, June 1939: 10. In 1950 museum holdings were exhibited for classes in American art (twice), Italian drawings, Chinese paintings, medieval art, and European painters of the nineteenth and twentieth century. [E. Baldwin Smith], Chairman's Report to the Advisory Committee of the Department of Art and Archaeology, Nov. 3, 1950, "Dept. of Art & Arch.," box 11: "History of Department" (PUA).

[63] Backlin-Landman, "The New Art Museum at Princeton," 32; "Art Museum Reopens," 26–28.

classes, an average of six a year. But classes and individual students also visited the galleries and storage collections, the thirty-four loan shows, and the ninety-two major exhibitions available during that period. Others hopped the "Dinky" for pedagogical pilgrimages to New York or Philadelphia museums.[64]

Teaching exhibitions are arranged with the museum staff several months in advance. The director and the appropriate curators, often with Marquand's librarian and the head of the recently renamed Visual Resources Collection, meet with the Art Department to determine what faculty members will need for their courses. Some classes need small exhibits for only ten days or three weeks; others need to reserve the photographic suite or one of the five storage-precept rooms at a regular time for the whole semester. For a large course like John Wilmerding's on modern American art, twenty to thirty works on paper will be hung in a small gallery off the main floor, where he can explain their subtleties and students can revisit them for closer examination. When the museum is closed, students can now study all of the images seen in class, on slides or exhibition, in digital form from any computer port on or off campus. In today's art world, Wilmerding and his colleagues see the value of having images "available at all times for students to use, to zoom in on, and to print out."[65]

Before the advent of digital images and the Internet, art history students had to either remember the slides shown in class or resort to study rooms in McCormick Hall to examine cardboard-mounted photographs of the images, not all of which were reproduced. Around exam times, the study rooms were crowded and photographs (if no one walked off with them) were hard to approach or look at for long. Throughout the better part of the last century, the Princeton faculty, like most art faculties, relied heavily on photographs for

[64] The Art Museum, "Past Exhibits" [1947–1992].

[65] Ann Waldron, "The Magic Classroom," *PAW*, Apr. 7, 1999, 18–22, at 22. (Thanks to John Wilmerding for an extended telephone interview about department-museum synergy, Aug. 4, 2004). See also Waldron, "Enlightened Scholar of Luminous Artistry," *PAW*, Dec. 5, 1990, 12–16; Franklin Kelly, "Scholar, Teacher, Collector: John Wilmerding and American Art," in Kelly et al., *American Masters from Bingham to Eakins: The John Wilmerding Collection* (Washington, D.C., 2004), 3–30.

teaching purposes, especially in their larger survey courses. Photographs of the major monuments in the history of art were two-dimensional extensions of the museum's own collections. Yet the faculty's reliance on them was also a necessity, for two reasons. First, the museum was still very much a work-in-progress. Its collections, while broadly representative by midcentury, still had obvious gaps and lacked depth in several areas. It did not and could not provide students with even a fraction of the world's great art, to which the faculty wanted to expose them. Second, until 1966, the physical museum was grossly unequal to the collections. It was unable to exhibit to maximum advantage the objects it did own, to conserve them properly, or to give access to them in storage. The use of photographs for class study was thus a reasonable and economical alternative. But at least one purist thought Princeton's reliance on them excessive, even given its special circumstances.

Upon his arrival in 1935 to join the Institute and the Art Department, émigré scholar Kurt Weitzmann, the product of the famous University of Berlin art history faculty and Europe's rich museums, found his colleagues' "exclusive use of photographs" regrettable and claimed to be "the first to bring about [a] change." When he inherited the medieval art course from Charles Morey at the end of World War II, for example, Weitzmann changed the final exam. For the traditional "shotgun questions" and identifications, he substituted a take-home essay on any one of several objects in a small exhibition he arranged in the museum. Likewise, in his precepts, he ended each class by pulling from his pocket and putting on the table an object he had borrowed from the museum. This encouraged the students to "see and handle" original artworks from which they acquired lessons in iconography and connoisseurship, if not in conservation.[66]

In one auspicious precept, Weitzmann remembered, sophomore "Tom" Hoving '53 fingered a small Romanesque ivory of a Virgin enthroned "with great fascination. It was this kind of experience which induced him to major in art history, to go on to graduate study [in the department], and to write a Ph.D. thesis on ivories under my

[66] Weitzmann, *Sailing with Byzantium*, 154–55. Today, students would either not be allowed to handle most objects or could do so only with cotton archival gloves.

supervision."[67] Hoving, who became the attention-getting director of the Metropolitan Museum, credited Weitzmann with teaching him "how to look at a work of art, not just *see* it. How to probe, examine, and peel a work of art like an onion, stripping its multiple layers right down to the very core of its meaning . . . how to distinguish between real and fake, truth and forgery. Watching Weitzmann, whose eyes and fingers seemed capable of stroking inner secrets from a mute medieval work of art," he said, "I soaked up connoisseurship, gradually learning how to recognize artistic quality in all its subtle gradations."[68]

Weitzmann obviously exaggerated his own priority at Princeton in using museum objects to teach his courses. The Art Department had since its beginnings emphasized such use, and the museum collections were built accordingly. Between 1947 and 1963 (Weitzmann's heyday), seventy-four exhibitions (43 percent of the total) were prepared specially for university classes.[69] And the trend has continued, especially with the growth of faculty specialties, course offerings, student enrollments, museum staff, and the collections themselves, in number and richness.[70]

[67] Weitzmann, *Sailing with Byzantium*, 155.

[68] Thomas Hoving, *King of the Confessors* (New York, 1981), 24–25. As a sophomore, Hoving had another decisive engagement with original art objects in Frederick Stohlman's course on sculpture from the Renaissance to the present. In a precept of five upperclassmen and two graduate students, Hoving was the only person to deny that a graceful piece of metalwork (an obstetrical speculum) mounted on a base of polished hardwood was sculpture. Later in the semester Stohlman placed in Hoving's eager hands a piece of Roman glass, which also did much to persuade the hitherto aimless and lackluster student to major and excel in art history. Hoving's grade-point average went from 4.46 (on a 7-point scale, 1 being the highest) at the end of his sophomore year to a straight 1 in the department and summa cum laude at graduation. John McPhee, *A Roomful of Hovings and Other Profiles* (New York, 1968), 46–50.

[69] The Art Museum, "Past Exhibits" [1947–1992].

[70] Enrollments in art courses rose from between four and eight hundred throughout the 1920s and 1930s to highs of between eleven and fifteen hundred throughout the rest of the century before declining substantially in the new millennium. Since the early 1980s, women have increasingly outnumbered men in art history courses and in choosing art majors. Marquand, "Needs of the Art Department," 394; *Art and Archaeology* 20:3 (Sept. 1925): 107–8; "Dept. of Art & Arch.," box 11: "History of Dept." folder (PUA) [course elections between 1928–1929 and 1938–1939]; *Bull. of the Dept. of Art & Arch.*,

In addition to regular art courses and precepts, students have availed themselves of numerous other ways to further their visual education in the museum. Undergraduates volunteer and are trained as docents and serve as summer interns in various museum departments. Like graduate students, majors in the Art Department pursue research for junior papers and senior theses in the museum collections and the rich recesses of Marquand Library. Doctoral candidates not only develop expertise in analysis, connoisseurship, and conservation in the museum, but are given opportunities to put it to work in the museum's published catalogues, exhibition guides, and newsletter, in exhibitions, and in public gallery talks and lectures.

Three examples of student scholarship suggest the rare but not uncommon opportunities afforded by the museum's teaching mission. In June 1974, four seniors in the Art Department, guided and encouraged by Professors David Steadman and Rona Goffen, mounted a clever exhibition and wrote a catalogue on *Copies as Originals: Translations in Media and Techniques*. Beginning with twenty-six original works of art—paintings, engravings, etchings, photographs, frescoes, drawings, and sculpture—the exhibition showed the interpretive "translation" of those images into other media with other techniques. Unlike mere replicas and blatant forgeries, these copies, the students suggested, became in the hands of new artists "originals" in their own right.[71] In the early spring of 1990, a month-long exhibition of eleven Winslow Homer drawings, paintings, and watercolors from the 1870s drew appreciative viewers to the museum, mainly by the charm of his depictions of young farm children in bucolic settings. Although it was organized by Professor John Wilmerding rather than by students, the show was accompanied by a handsome catalogue, which sold briskly. Two Princeton graduate

---

Sept. 1930: 5; John R. Martin, "Art and Archaeology at Princeton," *PAW*, Apr. 30, 1948, 5–7, at 7; [Smith], Chairman's Report to the Advisory Council (Nov. 3, 1950), 1; Lee, "The Need for a New Art Museum," 9; *Department Statement for the Campaign for $53 Million* (1959), 5; Office of the Registrar, *Report to the President*: Statistical Appendix (1972–1973), 16; (1982–1983), 18–19; (1992–1993), 13; (2002–2003), 13.

[71] Princeton: The Art Museum, 1974.

students and a senior art major contributed the descriptive entries for all of the pictures.[72]

The most ambitious involvement of students in a museum exhibition began in Institute fellow and sometime Professor of Art Irving Lavin's 1978–1979 seminar on the drawings of Gianlorenzo Bernini. During that year, Lavin twice visited the incomparable Bernini collection in the Museum der Bildenden Künste in Leipzig, still then in Communist East Germany, with the idea of producing an exhibition that would begin in Princeton before moving to five other major American museums. For three years his seminarians—four Princetonians and two students from New York University, where Lavin had taught previously—continued to meet to organize the exhibition and to write what proved to be a 384-page catalogue to accompany it. When the six-week show opened in Princeton in early October 1981, the catalogue drew special attention to the two major essays on function and style in Bernini's work and to the catalogue entries for the 30 main drawings and 120 comparative illustrations written by the six students.[73]

❁ ❁ ❁

The productive synergy between the Art Department and the museum has attracted members of other departments. Civil engineers Robert Mark and David Billington worked with museum curators to organize exhibitions initially for teaching purposes, both of which extended their pedagogical influence with published catalogues. For two months in the winter of 1984–1985, Mark's show focused on the technology of *High Gothic Structure*, particularly of European cathedrals with their vaulted ceilings and flying buttresses. It then traveled to nine other college museums. Billington's three-month

[72] John Wilmerding and Linda Ayres, *Winslow Homer in the 1870s: Selections from the Valentine-Pulsifer Collection* (Princeton: The Art Museum, 1990). The exhibition also traveled to the Wadsworth Atheneum, its co-sponsor, in Hartford.

[73] Irving Lavin et al., *Drawings by Gianlorenzo Bernini from the Museum der Bildenden Künste, Leipzig, German Democratic Republic* (Princeton: The Art Museum, 1981). The book was designed by Bruce Campbell, who designed many of the museum's prize-winning catalogues and publications.

exhibition of photographs, drawings, and models in the spring of 2003 illustrated *The Art of Structural Design: A Swiss Legacy.* Revolving around the work of four Swiss bridge-builders and two of their teachers, it and a handsome catalogue moved to four college museums before finishing in Zurich. One of the artist-engineers, Robert Maillart, was the subject of an earlier book by Billington, who was struck by the sheer beauty of Maillart's Alpine suspension bridges.[74]

In the fall of 2003 Assistant Professor of History Peter Silver first took the students in his junior seminar on "The Atlantic World's Long Revolution, 1690–1800" to the museum for a single visit to see period pieces of art. He had heard glowing reports about John Wilmerding's expert use of the museum in his course on art and American nationalism and wanted to promote the use of interdisciplinary sources and methods in his own. After advance consultation with Silver, Research Curator of Later Western Art Betsy Rosasco began the tour in the permanent collection of paintings and busts, including the large Edward D. Balken, Class of 1897, collection of post-Revolutionary folk paintings of New England families, furnishings, and children.[75] The class then moved to a precept room where she had laid out several items from the founding Trumbull-Prime collection of ceramics. Particularly evocative were a large Staffordshire pitcher commemorating George Washington, an exquisite Sèvres model of Franklin and Louis XVI signing the Franco-American treaty, and an original Wedgwood antislavery medallion. A short trip to the print study room found Curator of Prints and Drawings Laura Giles, who showed the class stacks of Hogarth and other late eighteenth-century English engravings and cartoons. William Blake's bold engravings of John Stedman's experiences in Suriname, especially the cruelties of black slavery, made a palpable im-

[74] Robert Mark, *High Gothic Structure: A Technological Reinterpretation* (Princeton: The Art Museum, 1983); David P. Billington, *The Art of Structural Design: A Swiss Legacy* (New Haven, 2003); Billington, *Robert Maillart's Bridges: The Art of Engineering* (Princeton, 1979).

[75] George R. Clay, "Children of Young America as Illustrated in The Edward Duff Balken '97 Collection," *PAW,* Dec. 2, 1960, 8–11, 15; "A Window into Collecting American Folk Art: The Edward Duff Balken Collection," *Record of The Art Museum* 57:1–2 (1998).

pression on the students.[76] Although few of the students' papers integrated material artifacts into their analyses, Silver became a convert to the museum as a key source for teaching history and began plans to take his class on Early America to 1740 for a similar visit.[77]

Michael Cook, professor of Near Eastern studies, made more extensive use of museum collections in his course on "What Happened in History?," a survey of the past ten thousand years that resulted in his book *A Brief History of the Human Race* (New York, 2003). In an earlier freshman seminar, Cook, who has a pair of archaeologists in his family tree, had occasionally brought in objects he happened to own to liven up discussion. But when the course became an upperclass offering, Director Susan Taylor invited him to use the museum for his weekly classes. His initial host was Curator of Ancient Art Michael Padgett, whose precept room served as the classroom for most of the semester. But Curator of Asian Art Cary Liu and Faculty Curator of Pre-Columbian Art Gillett Griffin also lent their storage rooms and objects. Several of Griffin's loans were his own possessions, including a four-thousand-year-old Mediterranean relief of a coupling couple.[78]

Each week Cook would introduce the class to several objects, usually ten to fifteen, from the cultures under discussion. The objects ranged from a bizarre Jomon clay object (possibly a lantern) to a wooden crosspiece from an Eighteenth Dynasty Egyptian stool (and a modern Danish lookalike for comparison) and a quattrocento medal (c. 1489) of sex- and revenge-driven Caterina Sforza-Riario

[76] John Gabriel Stedman, *Narrative of a Five Years Expedition Against the Revolted Negroes of Surinam* [London, 1790], ed. Richard Price and Sally Price (Baltimore, 1988).

[77] Thanks to Peter Silver for a long e-mail (July 1, 2004) describing his museum experience.

[78] Griffin, former book designer, Firestone librarian, traveler, collector, popular lecturer on pre-Columbian Mexican art, and friend of Einstein, retired in 2004 and gave more of his extraordinary collection of ancient and pre-Columbian artifacts to the museum. For many years he had been donating objects, so many that he said, "In a way, it was like being curator of my own collection" (Jean Stratton, "Princeton Personality: Gillett Griffin, Curator of Pre-Columbian Collection, Has Had a Long Love Affair with Art," *Town Topics* [Princeton], Mar. 10, 2004, 18–20, at 19; Raj Hathiramani, "Faculty: Curator to Leave Rich Legacy," *DP* [online], Apr. 16, 2004).

with Victory in a chariot, dressed in a widow's veil—her husband had just been assassinated—but by then already deep into another affair. From his own modest collection Cook added Greek loom-weights, pottery shards from Jericho, and a late Ottoman Turkish bowl to accompany one of his Turkish manuscripts and a Moroccan Koranic recitation. Even his wife contributed her mid-twentieth-century East Asian mortar and pestle, which he placed among a dozen objects for a cautionary class exercise in dating during the first week. (The students tended to date it somewhere between the Lower Paleolithic and the Neolithic.) Although textual scholar Cook pretended to be "a card-carrying philistine" in matters artistic, he, too, is a convert to museum teaching.[79]

Faculty in other departments, from German to Classics, have gravitated to the museum because they, like their colleagues in the Art Department, believe that "learning to look" is as important a goal for liberally educated Princetonians as learning to read, write, and compute. As George Rowley described the aims of Art I in 1948, a course built around artistic objects was "training in pictorial language," so that the student experienced them "directly through his eyes and not through words." Ideally, through visits to the museum, the student would "enter into the creative imagination of a culture, period, or artist in artistic terms" before hearing about it in class.[80] Thus one aim of art history has always been to promote some level of appreciation or connoisseurship, to train students' eyes "to judge quality and evaluate the significance of works of art in the larger context of history."[81]

But object and context are mutually dependent. Just as objects are defined by their contexts, contexts are formed by objects. Each is capable of informing us about the other. Since the late nineteenth century, art historians at Princeton have used the historical background of artworks primarily to illuminate their aesthetic significance and value. But as Charles Morey and others have argued since

[79] Thanks to Michael Cook for a long e-mail (July 7, 2004) about his museum forays.

[80] George Rowley, "Art I at Princeton," *College Art Journal* 7:3 (Spring 1948): 195–98, at 195–96.

[81] Kelleher, "The Art Museum as a Teaching Tool," 9.

Wilson's day, artistic objects could also be used as visual shortcuts to the spirit and character of historical societies and cultures.

As the increasingly active partner of Firestone Library in collecting, conserving, and making available to students and scholars Princeton's rich troves of artistic objects, the Art Museum operates on the working assumption that animated Fritz Saxl, the longtime director of the Warburg Institute in London (one of the Marquand Library's very few rivals worldwide). Like the latest generation of Princeton historians who have found their way to the museum, Saxl believed that "visual images should and could be used as historical documents and that the insights they may give are in no way inferior to those derived from the study of written sources."[82] As long as history and appreciation remain the twin core of visual education at Princeton, the Art Museum will have no dearth of users, visitors, or supporters.

[82] E. H. Gombrich, in Fritz Saxl et al., *A Heritage of Images: A Selection of Lectures* (Harmondsworth, Eng., 1970), quoted in John Pope-Hennessy, *Learning to Look* (New York, 1991), 71.

CHAPTER TEN

Coin of the Realm

Publication is not unrelated to the purposes for which a university exists.

—Ralph Barton Perry

Most students and many alumni, even some faculty, are unaware that one of the important agents of Princeton's educational mission and a key contributor to the university's reputation in the learned world is its press. They do know that the faculty teaches what is already known and pursues research and scholarship to discover what is not. Most, especially habitués of the humanities and social sciences, also realize that the library is the active repository of knowledge old and new. But relatively few appreciate the university's need to complete the circle by helping to publish the results of those researches for the future use and enlightenment of students, faculty, and the world at large.

Even a man as broadly educated as J. Robert Oppenheimer, nuclear physicist and later director of the Institute for Advanced Study, had trouble grasping the need for the university itself to be involved in the dissemination of research results. As a scientist, Oppenheimer resorted to specialized journals and face-to-face colloquia to publish his research and to learn about that of his lab-and-blackboard colleagues. It took a canny humanist to make him acknowledge the utility of and need for university presses. Wilmarth S. Lewis, bibliophile, leading authority on Horace Walpole, and Yale trustee, secured the skeptic's conversion by simply chalking on the board, "Faculty + Library = Publication."[1]

[1] William H. Honan, "Obituaries: Chester Brooks Kerr, 86, Scholars' Editor," *New York Times*, Aug. 26, 1999, A15.

The case for university presses was made less succinctly but no less persuasively as soon as American universities in the last quarter of the nineteenth century began to emphasize their research function and to demand that their faculties "publish or perish" (or at least not flourish). Johns Hopkins, Wilson's graduate alma mater, led the ambitious new universities in that period, inspired at least in part by German research institutions and ideals. In 1878, two years after its founding, Hopkins president Daniel Coit Gilman reminded his faculty and trustees that "it is one of the noblest duties of a university to advance knowledge, and to diffuse it not merely among those who can attend daily lectures—but far and wide." Whereupon he established a Publication Agency to produce scholarly journals to publish the results of faculty research; three years later it became the Johns Hopkins Press and moved into book publication in a serious way.[2] Counterparts at the University of Chicago (1891), the University of California (1893), and Columbia University (1893) soon followed. In 1918 Nicholas Murray Butler, the president of both Columbia and its press, emphasized in his annual report that "a university has three functions to perform: It is to conserve knowledge; to advance knowledge; and to disseminate knowledge. It falls short of the full realization of its aim unless, having provided for the conservation and advancement of knowledge, it makes provision for its dissemination as well."[3]

The rapid spread of university presses before 1895 was not duplicated until after 1905, when Princeton established its own, followed by Yale (1908), Harvard (1913), and six other universities before 1920.[4] By then it was clear that commercial, or "trade," publishing houses, pinched by rising manufacturing costs, were increasingly unable or unwilling to handle the outpouring of new scholarship from the na-

[2] Dale Keiger, "Pressing On," *Johns Hopkins Magazine*, Apr. 2003, 46–55, at 48. "University" was not added to the press's name until 1972.

[3] Gene R. Hawes, *To Advance Knowledge: A Handbook on American University Press Publishing* (New York, 1967), 30–32, 34, at 32. Cornell had established a university press, largely for printing and journalistic purposes, in 1869, but it closed for financial reasons in 1884 and did not reopen until 1930. The University of Pennsylvania opened a press in 1890, but it, too, failed within ten years and was not fully resurrected until 1927.

[4] Hawes, *To Advance Knowledge*, 35–39.

tion's research universities. Scholarly print runs were too small and profits too low, if not written in red ink. If universities had not established, and often subsidized, their own presses, much worthy scholarship, some of it written to appeal to intelligent but nonspecialist audiences, would simply have remained unpublished, unread, and therefore unapplied to society's vital questions and problems. Unlike trade books, scholarly books seldom make a big splash or initial profit; they tend instead to accumulate sales slowly over time as "backlist" titles, on the strength of persistent classroom sales.[5] Only a university press has the relative luxury of being able to put quality before profits because it's in business "to break even." As a former Harvard director put it, "A university press should publish as many good books as possible, short of bankruptcy."[6]

The prime mover behind Princeton's university press, appropriately, was New York publisher Charles W. Scribner, Class of 1875, whose firm published the popular works of a few Princeton faculty but who realized that more recondite scholarship had far less sales potential. In March 1905 he summoned Whitney Darrow '03, the enterprising young business manager of the *Princeton Alumni Weekly*, to his office to discuss the possibility of establishing a university press. Such an idea had been bandied about by the magazine staff for a year or two, but no practical plans had emerged. Darrow had the notion that a university press could be started by buying out the equipment of the press at 2 Nassau Street where the *PAW* was printed. This appealed to Scribner, who told Darrow that "for many years I have had the idea of a Princeton University Press. . . . I didn't want to start with publishing, which should be a gradual development. I think it should start with manufacturing," he continued,

[5] In 1948, 59 percent of the sales of the top thirty-three university presses came from backlist titles. Chester Kerr, "The American University as Publisher," *Saturday Review of Literature*, May 14, 1949, 10–16, 38–40, at 11. Princeton's backlist sales comprised 70 percent of its total sales in 1949–1950; 43 percent had been published two or more years earlier. PUP, "Report to the President" (1949–1950), 172–73 (PUA). In the mid-1980s its backlist sales were slightly over 60 percent. Loren Hoekzema, "Repackaging Scholarly Books," *Scholarly Publishing* 15 (Apr. 1984): 237.

[6] Kerr, "The American University as Publisher," 16; Herbert S. Bailey, Jr., "Implications of the Cartter Report for University Presses," *Scholarly Publishing* 6:3 (Apr. 1975): 207–9, at 207.

"and ultimately produce the best of printing. I think also that the Press should pay its own way and that we shouldn't start another 'one of those things' which would mean continually calling on alumni for money to keep it going."[7]

With a $1,000 stake from Scribner, Darrow raised another $4,000 from a handful of other *PAW* trustees to purchase the press by November 1905, from which date Princeton University Press (PUP) calculates its anniversaries. It was renamed the Alumni Press to prevent confusion with the Princeton Press, the other printing establishment in town. Within two months, Darrow had effected the buy-out of that press as well. Scribner had contributed $5,000, and "much the same people" ponied up the other $4,500. This gave the new entity—officially incorporated in October 1906 as the Princeton University Press—the business of printing the town newspaper, the alumni magazine, the *Nassau Lit*, the *University Catalogue*, the *Daily Princetonian*, examination papers, and much of the job printing of the university. After sloughing off the printing of the weekly *Princeton Packet* (as it was renamed), the new press gradually took up president Scribner's strong suggestion that it improve the quality of its printing so that "the Press may become noted for the excellence of its work."[8]

As early as 1907 Scribner also sought to "more definitely make the Press a University concern." In the fall of 1909 he encouraged Darrow to look around Princeton for a "suitable property where a University Press building might some day be put up." Darrow quickly found one at the corner of William and Charlton Streets, "on the eastern outskirts of the fast-growing campus." Scribner paid $25,000 for it sight unseen, convinced by a Darrow sketch that it held great promise and, after some minor land swapping with the university, room for growth.[9]

[7] Whitney Darrow, *Princeton University Press: An Informal Account of Its Growing Pains, Casually Put Together at the Point of a Gun for the Intimate Friends of the Press* (Princeton, 1951), 18–20.

[8] Darrow, *Princeton University Press*, 20, 22–25; *Letters from Charles Scribner, '75 to Whitney Darrow, '03 in the Early Days of Princeton University Press* (Princeton, 1968), n.p., Jan. 11, 1907.

[9] *Letters from Scribner to Darrow*, May 7, 1907; Oct. 22, 1909; Darrow, *Princeton University Press*, 35–36, 45–46.

Nothing was done with the property until the following summer, when Scribner left for his regular European vacation to hunt books and authors. As he left the Press office in Princeton, he casually suggested to Darrow that he get together with Ernest Flagg, "a pretty well known architect—in fact, a very good architect," to work out plans for a building. Darrow soon learned that Flagg was Scribner's brother-in-law and had designed not only the Beaux-Arts Scribner Building in New York but the Singer Building, New York's first great skyscraper, and the Corcoran Gallery of Art in Washington. But the publisher was not without his own ideas for the Princeton building: "it might possibly be built around a court like the Plantin Museum," he offered. Later that summer he sent Darrow a postcard of the famous printing museum in Antwerp to register the strength of his suggestion.[10]

Since the university had shown its commitment to the Press by giving it all of its printing business, Scribner sought to bind the Press to the university as he had originally proposed. On October 4, 1910, the Press was reincorporated as "an association not for pecuniary profit . . . [but] in the interest of Princeton University, to establish, maintain, and operate a printing and publishing plant for the promotion of education and scholarship, and to serve the University by manufacturing and distributing its publications." The by-laws required Press trustees to be trustees, faculty, or alumni of the university; the university president was an ex officio member. To link the Press and the university even more closely, papers were drawn and filed with the university trustees, stipulating (in Darrow's words) that "if at any time the University wants to take over the Press for any reason whatsoever they can do so by giving sixty days' notice to the Press and at the expiration of that time the University owns the Press, lock, stock, and barrel."[11]

Scribner liked his brother-in-law's plans and by December 1910 ground had been broken for a Gothic press building, featuring a high

[10] Darrow, *Princeton University Press*, 36–37; Charles Scribner, Jr., *In the Company of Writers: A Life in Publishing* (New York, 1990), 4–5.

[11] *Letters from Scribner to Darrow*, Oct. 4, 1910; Darrow, *Princeton University Press*, 48–49.

cantilevered-ceiling press room flanked by two office wings; a walled archway at the entrance formed a Plantinesque courtyard. Scribner again picked up the tab: $53,000 for the building proper, "not counting excavations or architect's fees," and a grand total "rather more" than his original $75,000 deposit. In November 1911 the Press moved into its new quarters at 41 William Street and has not left since.[12] Only in 1965, after a new printing plant was built in nearby Lawrenceville, did the actual bookmaking and bookkeeping operations move out of the tardily renamed Scribner Building. This then underwent a major renovation to accommodate the expanding editorial, sales, and administrative staff, and in 2001 a twelve-thousand-square-foot, two-storey expansion at the back and another thoroughgoing renovation for the same reason.[13]

Spurred by their new building and equipment, the Press staff was eager to produce printing and books of fine quality. Manager Darrow was not much help on that score. He admitted that he knew nothing about "good bookmaking" and still didn't when he left Princeton in 1917 to join the Scribner company as business manager. According to Charles Scribner, Jr., Scribner's grandson, books were to Darrow "the necessary price to pay for the pleasure of running the press as a business concern." That attitude distressed the elder Scribner, "whose primary interest was the books" and who "saw the whole purpose of the press as service to scholarship."[14]

Under Darrow, accordingly, the primary emphasis of the Press was printing, not publishing. From the first, the printing business almost always made money, "in some years," the manager boasted, "a very considerable amount." This enabled the Press, unlike the vast majority of university presses then or today, never to need or accept a contribution from the university. Moreover, in the first

[12] Darrow, *Princeton University Press*, 37–38; *Letters from Scribner to Darrow*, Dec. 22, 1910; Jan. 30, 1911.

[13] Herbert S. Bailey, Jr. '42, "Princeton University Press: For Sixty Years Publishers for the World of Learning," *PAW*, Nov. 30, 1965, 8–11, 17–18; "The 'New' University Press," *PAW*, Feb. 27, 1968, 10–11; Ann Waldron, "Of Books and the Bottom Line," *PAW*, Oct. 24, 2001, 18–20.

[14] Darrow, *Princeton University Press*, 40; Scribner, *In the Company of Writers*, 46–47, 117–18.

three decades, the losses the Press "deliberately incurred" in publishing scholarly books were in most years met by its profits from printing. This situation pleased Scribner just fine: "He never at any time had in mind that the Press would 'make money.' On the other hand," Darrow insisted, "he wanted to make sure the Press would not lose money."[15]

But with many of the relatively few books the Press did publish, Scribner was less pleased. "With his feeling for fine book work," Darrow lamented, "he must often have been greatly upset over our making of books up to the time I left." Without a book designer or even a manager who cared about books, the Press was in sore need of quality control and publishing experience. Scribner felt obliged to provide some of both. When Art Museum director Allan Marquand went to see Scribner about a proposed series of monographs on art and archaeology, the publisher assured him that the Press could have the "full assistance" of Scribner's art department in making the illustrations. He also sent Darrow a batch of Scribner books as possible models for design of the art volumes, asking that he be sent page proofs of the first one so he could examine "the front matter and the first page and some of the binding details, upon which I place importance." Well aware that "the University of Chicago is far ahead of us on the Press question and that Yale and Columbia are actually issuing valuable books in behalf of their respective Universities," Scribner was eager to get PUP in the race, without sacrificing form to speed.[16]

It was obvious to Scribner and other trustees that the scholarly quality of the Press's books could only be guaranteed by active faculty involvement. A year before the new building was completed, Scribner saw no "competent publishing committee in sight." But as soon as the Press was up and running early in 1912, a five-man committee was found and formed under the chairmanship of biologist Edwin G. Conklin, one of Wilson's star hires and a leading proponent of faculty research. Early members of the committee were clas-

[15] Darrow, *Princeton University Press*, 39–41.

[16] Darrow, *Princeton University Press*, 39; *Letters from Scribner to Darrow*, Nov. 5, 1910; Feb. 9, 1912; June 2, 1912.

sicist Edward Capps, economist F. A. Fetter, mathematician W. F. Magie, art historian Frank Mather, Jr., and popular Scribner author and *littérateur* Henry van Dyke. Primarily they served as a conduit for promising manuscripts and a source of suggestions for new book projects. The Press manager then presented their report, along with his own proposals, to the trustees, who made the final decision to publish or not.[17]

In the first few years of the Press, Darrow confessed, the selection process was somewhat haphazard and the books were published in "a very amateurish way." A "real editorial program," he suggested, did not get under way until 1937, when the Committee on Publications became an editorial board of three members, appointed in rotation by the president of the university, one man retiring each year.[18] The by-laws were rewritten to make its members voting members of the board of trustees, who retained the final say on what was published. But no book could be published and bear the PUP imprint without the recommendation of the Committee on Publications, later called the Editorial Board. The trustees spent long hours discussing these recommendations, but as of 1951, Darrow had "yet to know of any book being strongly and unanimously recommended as a work most necessary and important" that had not been accepted by the trustees "without regard to cost."[19] Manuscripts with less support, however, were not so fortunate.

Darrow's memory of the "amateurish" publication process in his own day was reasonably accurate. The publications committee en-

[17] *Letters from Scribner to Darrow*, Nov. 5, 1910; May 20, 1913; *Princeton University Press, 1905–1935* (Princeton, [1935]), 11, in PUP Records, DRBSC (#CO728), box 44, folder 1 (PUL). After a meeting with the new Committee on Publications in May 1913, Scribner wrote Darrow to assure the members that "the future of the Press in its publishing dept. rests with them—that they will be supported as far as possible. It occurs to me," he continued, "that the provision about the approval of the trustees must seem to them a great limitation upon their work. I have told them that the provision is for the safety of the Press only and that we shall support them when we have the money" (*Letters from Scribner to Darrow*, May 20, 1913).

[18] Darrow's memory was faulty: the Committee on Publications still functioned under that name until 1954.

[19] Darrow, *Princeton University Press*, 42–43.

joyed the services of some of the university's most learned and discerning faculty, but the Press had no publishing profile or goals other than to publish the best manuscripts that came over the transom. In its early years, it did not have the luxury of being able to specialize in selected disciplines, as it would by midcentury when its reputation had grown along with its distinctive backlist of titles. Its first book—in 1912—was a 173-page reprint of colonial President John Witherspoon's *Lectures on Moral Philosophy*, first published in Philadelphia in 1800 in his posthumous *Works*. The book was issued under the auspices of the American Philosophical Association as the first volume in a series of works by "Early American Philosophers," each published by the institution with which the thinker was most closely associated. It was expertly introduced and annotated by Varnum L. Collins '92, professor of French and later Secretary of the University and author of a two-volume biography of Witherspoon (1925). But it was no best-seller, despite the clear, neat printing of the text. Of the 500 copies printed, 399 remained unsold after three years.[20] The dull maroon cloth binding and minuscule lettering on the spine may have done as much as the contents to discourage sales.

Much more inviting was Allan Marquand's inventory of *Della Robbias in America* (1912), the inaugural volume of "Princeton Monographs in Art and Archaeology." Printed on lightly coated paper to capture the quality of seventy-two black-and-white illustrations, the quarto's generous margins, legible typeface, and handsome blue quarter-cloth binding bore the marks of Charles Scribner's personal oversight and standards. That it also carried the imprint of Oxford University Press as its English co-publisher, as many PUP books would throughout the next half-century, was another good omen for the Press's future.

Actions taken by the publications committee at its first two meetings in 1913 also augured well for Press standards and belied Darrow's assessment of Press operations after his departure. With Dean William Magie in the chair, members Capps, Mather, and Collins sent two manuscripts out to faculty readers, rejected a set of "Renaissance

[20] Datus C. Smith, Jr. '29, "Promoting Education and Scholarship: A Premier University Press at Princeton," *PAW*, Dec. 15, 1980, 12–17, at 13.

Lectures" (with an explanation to President Hibben, who may have encouraged the submission), and recommended the publication of "The Graduate College of Princeton," which was to mark the opening of Dean West's Gothic castle above the golf course. A month later the gatekeepers rejected "Twenty Years of Princeton Debating," but accepted Professor of History Thomas Jefferson Wertenbaker's "Virginia Under the Stuarts," though they doubted the wisdom of publishing it "from the free funds of the Press at this time"; they favored "an arrangement relieving the Press of a considerable portion of the cost." Such cost-consciousness would seem inconsistent with another committee recommendation, that "any Doctor's [Ph.D.] thesis regularly passed by the University" be accepted for publication "without further reference in any case to the Committee." Although every Princeton dissertation, no matter how esoteric, unreadable, or unsaleable, had to be "published" (printed) before formal acceptance, their impecunious authors had to foot the bill.[21]

The publications committee's zeal for maintaining standards and the Press's eclecticism in the books it published continued well into the managership of Paul Tomlinson '09, Ivy Club member, attorney, financial writer, and (like his father) author of boys' books, who replaced Darrow in 1917 and presided until 1938. Under Tomlinson the Press was still more printer than publisher, making consistent profits from the *PAW*, several other magazines and journals, binding books and periodicals for the university library, and job printing for the university and a host of other organizations, institutions, and individuals. But Tomlinson also modernized the printing plant and operated without endowment income or university subsidy, plowing all profits back into book publishing.[22] He also sought to raise the production standards for the 261 books published on his watch, an average of just twelve titles a year. For two-and-a-half years he employed

[21] PUP, "Minutes of the Meeting of the Committee on Publications, 1913–1926" (typescript), Sept. 30, Oct. 30, 1913, DRBSC (#CO728), box 24 (PUL).

[22] "Princeton's Press Typifies Growth of American University Publishing," *Publisher's Weekly*, May 21, 1949, 2053–57, at 2053; *Princeton University Press, 1905–1935*, 9–10, 13–14; Smith, "Promoting Education and Scholarship," 13; Darrow, *Princeton University Press*, 41, 50; Bailey, "Princeton University Press," 10; *Princeton University Press Almanac for . . . 1922* (Princeton, 1922), n.p.

high-end typographer and self-described perfectionist Frederic Warde to add some panache to PUP volumes. But Warde's arty, underinked pages and classy designs proved too expensive, even as they won five awards for book design from the American Institute of Graphic Arts (AIGA).[23]

Tomlinson also sought to raise the Press's profile in the university and in the learned world in general. Between 1922 and 1938 the Press published the *Princeton University Press Almanac*, containing a calendar of university events, historical tidbits, occasional humor, ads for Press books, pictures and short biographies of faculty authors, and numerous essays, mostly by Tomlinson himself, on publishing, books, and reading. In the initial volumes, the manager argued that Press books were "the best kind of publicity Princeton can have. It is not spectacular advertising," he admitted, "but it brings to the attention of thoughtful people everywhere the fact that Princeton is a seat of scholarship and learning. . . . Many people consider that the Princeton University Press can do more to secure Princeton's fame as an institution of learning and to make that fame enduring than is possible in any other way."[24] In the 1930s he also led the Press into substantial foreign sales, which would remain a PUP hallmark thereafter. The Dutch firm Nijhoff distributed PUP titles in Europe and firms in Tokyo and Shanghai pushed them in the Far East. To reach the Middle East, the Press began to publish in Arabic. The first volume in the "Princeton Oriental Texts" series, and the first Arabic book to be published by an American university press, appeared in 1930, when Professor of Oriental Languages and Literature Philip K. Hitti edited the unique Escorial manuscript of a memoir by a twelfth-century Arab gentleman of letters and warrior who fought Christian crusaders in Syria.[25]

[23] Smith, "Promoting Education and Scholarship," 13; Darrow, *Princeton University Press*, 39–40; *A Century in Books: Princeton University Press, 1905–2005* (Princeton, 2005), 61. Press employees still retail the story of how Warde, furious with the head pressman over the quality of the "makeready," threw his hat into the press and ruined everything. E-mail interview with Michael Burton, Dec. 8, 2002, 7.

[24] *PUP Almanac for . . . 1922*, opposite February.

[25] *Princeton University Press, 1905–1935*, 14; *PAW*, Oct. 17, 1930, 83. See also Oleg Grabar, "Philip Khûdri Hitti," in Marks, *Luminaries*, 119–24.

On the home front, Tomlinson furthered relations with the university by primarily publishing books by Princeton faculty. In 1930, a typical year, fourteen of the twenty-one new titles (67 percent) were written by Princeton professors. The local monopoly persisted even as the Press increased its co-publication work with universities that lacked a press, such as the University of Cincinnati. In 1935 Tomlinson (re-titled director two years earlier) offered "book credit"—a gratis selection of Press books—to the five members of the Committee on Publications, a perquisite that remains. He also approved the committee's recommendation that the dean of the Graduate School be made an ex officio member of the trustees and the larger Council.[26] Relations were further tightened in 1939 when Tomlinson's successor, Joseph A. Brandt, former Rhodes Scholar, historian of nineteenth-century Spain, and founding director of the University of Oklahoma Press, was given faculty status by the university, recognition that was also extended to his successor when Brandt returned to Oklahoma three years later to assume the university presidency.[27]

Although the Press under Tomlinson published a relatively small number of books and most of them by local faculty, the publications committee—reduced to three members in 1937—continued to guard the PUP imprint as best it could and to give its imprimatur to a goodly number of outstanding books, such as Henri Pirenne's *Medieval Cities* (1925), Albert Einstein's Stafford Little Lectures at Princeton, *The Meaning of Relativity* (1922), and many others still regarded as classics in their fields. The committee was not afraid to send books back to colleagues for revisions or to reject submissions that did not meet their scholarly standards. In 1928, Professor Hitti's English translation of Usamah Ibn-Munqidh's Arabic memoir was returned "with the suggestion that it had best be rewritten."[28] A fe-

[26] Smith, "Promoting Education and Scholarship," 13; PU, *Report of the President (1930)*, 66–67; *(1935)*, 225; PUP, "Minutes of the Committee on Publications. Dec. 1926–June 1940" (bound typescript), Dec. 16, 1935, DRBSC (#CO728), box 25 (PUL).

[27] PU, *Report of the President (1939)*, 193; Darrow, *Princeton University Press*, 50; "Princeton's Press Typifies Growth," 2054.

[28] Hitti took his manuscript to Columbia University Press instead, where it was published in 1929 as a volume in the "Records of Western Civilization" series. It was reissued

male author's manuscript entitled "Arms and the Men in Geneva" was rejected as "a competent but not profound work, inclining to be emotional and journalistic." A negative reader's report from religious philosopher Paul Elmer More led to the return of a manuscript on "The Fine Arts in the Education of Hellenic Boys." The committee saw no need to resort to outside readers to reject "The Writings of Geraldine" by Mrs. Geraldine Camp Tibbetts and "Milk: A Dangerous Drink." They were equally relieved to learn that "Direct Mail Advertising" had been withdrawn from consideration because it had found a slot with another publisher.[29]

Yet in its eagerness to forge strong links with the faculty, the committee and the Press sometimes accepted local manuscripts of marginal scholarship and even less vendibility. Dean Andrew West's *Presentations for Honorary Degrees* (1930) was clearly a vanity publication that the committee could hardly turn down. Tomlinson's own *History of the Trenton Banking Company, 1804–1929*, though subsidized by the subject, fell into the same category. Although it may have done a service for the young man's bid for tenure, an economics instructor's *Building and Loan Associations in New Jersey* (1930) was equally suspect. When he came on board in 1938, Director Brandt inherited a troubling project involving a beloved faculty member. To honor the long service and recent retirement of Woodrow Wilson Professor of English Literature George McLean Harper, his colleagues had organized a "memorial volume" of essays (although he was far from deceased), which the committee had accepted. Even if all 500 copies had been sold—only 137 had been reserved by subscribers—the "irrecoverable loss" would have amounted to $874.66. Fortunately for the Press, President Harold Dodds offered to cover the loss. But Brandt let it be known that "he did not approve of memorial volumes; that the best monument to any teacher was the students

in paperback in 2000. Philip K. Hitti, trans., *An Arab-Syrian Gentleman and Warrior in the Period of the Crusades: Memoirs of Usamah Ibn-Munqidh* (New York, 1929; 2000).

[29] "Minutes of the Committee on Publications," Feb. 13, 1928; Feb. 24, 1930; Nov. 24, 1930; Oct. 5, 1938. *Wordsworth and Coleridge—Studies in Honor of George McLean Harper*, ed. Earl Leslie Griggs, was published in 1939.

he trained." The committee "agreed in principle" but gave the go-ahead anyway.[30]

The outgoing director had also recognized that, among his scholarly successes and occasional best-sellers, the Press list harbored some clinkers. In 1935, as the Press turned thirty and found itself in its best financial shape ever, despite the Great Depression, Tomlinson had vowed to publish books "of more importance and wider appeal." He might have been thinking negatively of loss-leaders such as a translation from the Swedish of *Selected Short Stories* by Hjalmar Söderberg, *Kentucky Superstitions*, or a drama-themed festschrift for Professor of English Thomas Marc Parrott.[31] What he must have had in mind were more books like Edward S. Corwin's *The Constitution and What It Means Today* (1920), which in its updated versions has seen fourteen editions; Edward W. Kemmerer's *The ABC of the Federal Reserve System* (1918), an unlikely best-seller that went through ten editions and sold 65,000 copies by 1940; J. Franklin Jameson's *The American Revolution Considered as a Social Movement* (1926), based on four Princeton lectures; and Frank Lloyd Wright's *Modern Architecture* (1931), an Art-Deco rendition of his six Kahn Lectures at Princeton.[32]

Tomlinson must also have yearned for another book like Professor Harper's brief but headline-grabbing *Wordsworth's French Daughter* (1921), the story of the poet's natural child Caroline by his young French lover Annette Vallon. Few PUP books enjoyed the double fortune of selling well around the world and being immortalized in Princeton seniors' song:

[30] PU, *Report of the President (1930)*, 66–67; "Minutes of the Committee on Publications," Nov. 2, 1938; Dec. 2, 1938.

[31] PU, *Report of the President (1920)*, 66; (1935), 225–26; Hjalmar Söderberg, *Selected Short Stories*, trans. Charles Wharton Stork (Princeton: PUP and New York: American-Scandinavian Foundation, 1935); Daniel Lindsey Thomas and Lucy Blayney Thomas, *Kentucky Superstitions* (Princeton, 1920); Hardin Craig, ed., *Essays in Dramatic Literature: The Parrott Presentation Volume* . . . (Princeton, 1935), underwritten by several classmates in the Class of 1888.

[32] *A Century in Books*, 9–12, 14–16; Thomas Dugan and John Meiners, "The PUP," *Nassau Sovereign* 2:8 (May 1940): 15.

Harper went to France to get
The red-hot dope on dear Annette;
And there performed a deed of note,
Revealing Wordsworth's one wild oat.

He found no such book in his last years, but he must have taken considerable pleasure in knowing that he had signed several authors—philosopher Paul Weiss, political scientist Alpheus T. Mason, sociologist Robert S. Lynd, mathematician Hermann Weyl—whose names would reverberate through academe and beyond for many decades.[33]

❁ ❁ ❁

As books were being banned and burned in contemporary Europe, Brandt modernized the Press and moved book publishing to the forefront, forging in the process the closest ties yet with the Princeton faculty. In only three years, he swept the cobwebs out of the operation and invigorated the staff and the publishing program; the Press began to assume something like its present form.

He began with the plant and the administration. After installing a new high-speed book press, he added a five-thousand-square-foot extension at the back of the building and remodeled the office wing, adding a comfortable lounge area where authors might consult with editors. To streamline decision making, he engineered the abolition of the Council (the equivalent of the Press stockholders) and the creation of a more inclusive group of Associates. These actions placed corporate responsibility in the hands of the smaller board of trustees, now limited to between nine and fifteen members, including the university president ex officio.[34] The director himself

[33] Leitch, *Princeton Companion*, 241–42; PU, *Report of the President (1939)*, 194–95. *Wordsworth's French Daughter* was only forty-one pages long, but it contained transcriptions and translations of Caroline's birth and marriage certificates, which proved conclusively that the poet was her father.

[34] PU, *Report of the President (1939)*, 193–94; PUP, "Report to the President" (1940–1941), 239. The original Council of fifteen met annually. Later a smaller board of trustees was elected by and from the Council members to enact business between the annual meetings. The new Associates consisted of "all those who have been at any time officers

began to play a larger role in the proceedings of the publications committee. In order to increase the Press's scholarly output, especially of serious books with wider appeal, he altered policy: no dissertations that were not equal in quality and breadth to real books, no festschrifts unless their costs were covered up front, no foreign-language translations of English books, publishing losses no longer the printing department's sole responsibility—"profitable" books to make up the difference. Fortunately, he did not listen to the management consultants who had recommended, shortly before he came, the closure of the publishing department because "that's the only place you are losing money."[35]

Brandt's desire to increase book production depended on fuller cooperation from the faculty, who continued to contribute half of the manuscripts published. In his first report to the president of the university, he emphasized that the faculty "must realize that the Press is their own." In the winter of 1938–1939 the still-intact Council invited younger faculty members to dine at the Princeton Inn to solicit suggestions for "increasing the scope of scholarly writing at Princeton." Brandt proposed to make semi-annual reports on Press activities and policies to the whole faculty.[36] Hugh Stott Taylor, the chairman of the publications committee, agreed that "a great deal of missionary work yet remained to be done with the faculty," many of whom "still believed that the Press made money when the manufacturing cost of a book was obtained by the Press in sales," completely ignoring the substantial cost of editorial work to acquire, vet, contract, edit, prepare, and proofread the manuscript.[37]

An augmented sales force under energetic Norvell Samuels '24 pushed book sales up 50 percent in Brandt's first two years and another 25 percent in his last. With sales representatives visiting nearly

---

or members of the council, the trustees, or the various editorial committees of the Press." They met once a year to elect the trustees. Darrow, *Princeton University Press*, 46–47.

[35] "Minutes of the Committee on Publications," Nov. 2, 1938, 4–5; Smith, "Promoting Education and Scholarship," 13.

[36] Whether he ever did so is uncertain, but his two successors did make occasional written reports until the mid-1960s.

[37] PU, *Report of the President (1938)*, 191, *(1939)*, 193; "Minutes of the Committee on Publications," Jan. 18, 1939, 1.

eight hundred stores, the average sale of a Press book shot up from 1,000 to 1,450 copies. Each year the list of new titles increased, from twenty-five in 1938–1939 to fifty-six two years later.[38] To stimulate alumni interest in buying PUP books, Brandt launched the Princeton Book Club. Graduates were obliged to buy, for as little as $12 a year, a minimum of four Press books, many of which had also been recommended by the Book-of-the-Month Club (twenty-five by October 1941), the Scientific Book Club, and the Literary Guild.[39] Brandt also inaugurated the first Press series to be sold by subscription—a twenty-volume collection of "America's Lost Plays"—as well as a similarly voluminous "Princeton History of New Jersey" and an occasional "American Peoples Series." Two other new series—the Princeton Mathematical Series and Annals of Mathematics Studies, both printed in offset from typescript to reduce costs—sold surprisingly well to another class of readers. Initially the authors were offered no royalties, but the books sold so well worldwide that payments were soon made retroactively.[40] Both math series are alive and well, numbering well over two hundred volumes between them at the end of 2004.

Despite the doubling of book production, Brandt, his editors, and the publications committee managed not only to avoid any dilution of the list's quality but to enhance it. Some of America's Lost Plays might have remained so, and *Paul Elmer More: A Bibliography* added more to More's stature than to PUP's; but in general the 161 books published during Brandt's tenure were solid, serious works of scholarship and increasingly accessible and appealing to a literate, nonspecialist audience. The Press obviously worked hard to make them so. In February 1939, for instance, the publications troika returned

[38] PU, *Report of the President (1939)*, 193, *(1940)*, 190; PUP, "Report to the President" (1940–1941), 237 (PUA); Dugan and Meiners, "The PUP," 29.

[39] PU, *Report of the President (1940)*, 192; PUP, "Princeton Book Club," Historical Subject Files (#AC109), box 271 (PUA); Lawrance Thompson, "Princeton Books: A Challenge to Alumni," *PAW*, Oct. 20, 1939, 93–95.

[40] Smith, "Promoting Education and Scholarship," 13; Bailey, "Princeton University Press," 11; PU, *Report of the President (1940)*, 190–91; PUP, "Report to the President" (1940–1941), 238–39 (PUA). Between 1939 and 1949, 8 percent of PUP's books were published in offset from typewritten copy. "Princeton's Press Typifies Growth," 2056.

the manuscript of "Catholics and Unbelievers in Eighteenth-Century France" to its thirty-year-old author in Dickinson Hall for "substantial enrichment and revision," with a recommendation that he "consult with Dean [Christian] Gauss on the style . . . and with Mr. [Gilbert] Chinard on the intellectual background." Apparently, R. R. Palmer was a quick study because the revised manuscript was accepted within five weeks.

Whether the committee's next piece of advice struck Palmer as wise career counseling or as an expression of academic timidity is not recorded; but the committee thought that his new proposal for an ambitious book covering a more extended period was inappropriate and urged him to "undertake to do some other work with greater appeal as his second book for the Press."[41] They must have been pleased two years later when PUP published *Twelve Who Ruled: The Committee of Safety during the Terror*, a groundbreaking study of Robespierre and his fellow autocrats who caused the death of thirty thousand Frenchmen during the Revolution, which became a classroom classic and helped earn its author tenure at Princeton. Postponing the larger project probably had its benefits. When PUP brought out Palmer's two-volume, Bancroft Prize-winning *The Age of the Democratic Revolution* in 1959 and 1964, the book was the finished product of a mature master of his field and a veteran of the PUP editorial board.

Both Brandt and the publications committee underestimated the sales potential of *Twelve Who Ruled*—only five hundred copies were printed—but they were generally more accurate about books they had chosen for their broad appeal.[42] Good titles made some of the difference. A publisher could hardly miss with titles such as *The Invasion from Mars* (1940), Associate Professor of Psychology Hadley Cantrill's study of the national hysteria created by Orson Welles's famous 1938 radio drama that was mistaken for a news report from the landing site near Princeton, or *Why Men Behave Like Apes, and*

[41] "Minutes of the Committee on Publications," Feb. 13, 1939, 2; Mar. 22, 1939, 1.

[42] *A Century in Books*, 23–24; "Minutes of the Committee on Publications," Mar. 22, 1939, 2; *Prizes Awarded to Princeton University Press under the Directorship of Herbert S. Bailey, Jr., 1954–1986*, 21.

Vice Versa (1941), E. A. Hooten's inviting primer on animal behavior. *Chip Off My Shoulder* (1940), Pultizer Prize-winning journalist Thomas L. Stokes's feisty memoir of the Washington scene, garnered gratifying sales from both the Book-of-the-Month and the Princeton Book Clubs.[43]

A trio of Brandt-era books attracted attention and customers for other reasons. Hermann Weyl's *The Classical Groups: Their Invariants and Representations* (1939), the initial volume in the "Annals of Mathematics Studies," provided an unexpectedly creative introduction to the new and thereafter seminal subject of group theory by using history and biography as well as theorems and proofs. Angie Debo's *And Still the Waters Run: The Betrayal of the Five Civilized Tribes* (1940) was an unlikely book for an elite Eastern university press at the time; but Brandt had brought it with him from Oklahoma where it had been rejected as too hot a treatment of Sooner politicians, still guilt-ridden if not still embroiled in chicanery over Indian lands. To its credit, Princeton's publications committee accepted the manuscript in 1939, though with the prudent proviso "subject to elimination of possible libel and the approval of the revised manuscript by some competent attorney." The book quickly became a catalyst for the scholarly history of American Indians. *The Gang's All Here* (1941) by Harvey Smith, the Class of 1917's longtime secretary, caused more excitement in the smaller universe of Princeton alumni with its fictional version of a twenty-fifth-reunion classbook written by a let-it-all-hang-out secretary. End papers featuring "Dear Old Nostalgia" (the ersatz university's bibulous anthem), a title-page coat of arms (six bottles, a beer stein, a rep tie, and a football) above the motto *Per facilia ad mediocria* ("With ease to mediocrity"), and a purple spine festooned with a stack of gold mortarboards were apt expressions of the book's wicked wit. The Princeton Book Club did a predictably brisk business with the title.[44]

[43] Dugan and Meiners, "The PUP," 15; PU, *Report of the President (1940)*, 193; PUP, "Report to the President" (1940–1941), 237 (PUA).

[44] *A Century in Books*, 17–20; "Minutes of the Committee on Publications," Nov. 24, 1939, 1; Bailey, "Princeton University Press," 11; Nathaniel Burt, "The Princeton Novel: 1920–1978," *PULC* 40:3 (Spring 1979): 215–33, at 222–23; Ann Waldron, "The Fictive Princeton," *PAW*, Nov. 4, 1998, 16–24, at 21–22.

Having come to PUP in its uncertain adolescence, Brandt made two personnel decisions that ushered it into vigorous maturity and enhanced its standing in the learned world for years to come. The first decision was to persuade master typographer and book designer Pleasant Jefferson Conkwright in 1939 to follow him from Oklahoma to Princeton, where P. J. (as he was known universally) remained until he retired at the end of 1970. Conkwright's classically handsome, often witty, and always reader-friendly book designs made PUP books immediately recognizable and attracted authors to the Press as well as customers to its products. Brandt's second decision was to lure Datus C. Smith, Jr. '29 from the tiny *PAW* editor's office down the hall to an editor's desk in the publications department. When Brandt returned to Oklahoma in 1941, Smith was chosen as his successor—after a brief period of looking at outside candidates—and led the Press through the next dozen years, in war and peace, to major accomplishments and wide recognition at home and abroad.

❁ ❁ ❁

To the Princeton faculty and Press authors, Datus Smith was "the scholar's ideal of a university publisher"—imaginative, courageous, energetic, yet patient and informally efficient. Perhaps his greatest quality was good judgment, of books and people. "I am no scholar," he once told a nonacademic author. "But I have acquired a kind of feel for scholarship and think I know a good piece of goods when I see it."[45] The staff he inherited and assembled regarded him with respect and affection because he consulted and cooperated with them at every turn and encouraged them to see the whole publishing picture by allowing them to perform more than one specialized job. Although the war thinned their ranks substantially, they willingly produced more volumes than ever before and with virtually no loss

[45] *Putting Knowledge to Work, 1942–1952: A Tribute to Datus C. Smith, Jr., on the Occasion of His Tenth Anniversary as Director of Princeton University Press* (Princeton, 1952), 11; *Journey with Joy: Letters from Datus C. Smith, Jr.*, ed. Dorothy Smith (Princeton: privately printed, 1972), 72.

of quality, despite frequent paper and metal type shortages. To Smith, the Press, and the university, the publishing of books in wartime was no luxury that could or ought to be sacrificed.[46]

Wartime publishing at PUP differed surprisingly little from peacetime operations. Printing profits continued to outdo those from book publishing. More than a third of the authors published were Princeton faculty, though each manuscript continued to receive at least one outside reading. As Smith told the faculty in a war-end report, "It has been the thought of the Press for a long time that the best thing we can do for Princeton is to maintain the highest possible standards of scholarship in our list without shading decisions in favor of Princeton authors." This kind of vigilance persisted after the war as well. When English professor and former member of the publications committee Donald Stauffer looked back on Smith's directorial decade, he found the list of 450 titles published "singularly free from revamped doctoral theses published simply because they were written here, and—more difficult to avoid—free from the books that creep on press lists because the author is a good sort who has taught loyally and long at his alma mater and whose sensitive nature would be deeply hurt by a rejection."[47]

During the war, the Press undertook as part of its duty to publish a number of books of "special wartime usefulness." In many months, 75 percent of the printing work was government-related, some of it reports on classified research that had been conducted in campus labs and the rest reports and manuals for the federal government, the army, and the navy. As the war proceeded, the Press's output increased while the staff decreased. The staff fell from eighty-five to sixty, including several men declared 4-F, a half-dozen military wives, and a deaf-mute linotype operator. Since Press work was considered "essential activity" by the War Manpower Commission, the plant often operated seven days a week.[48]

One of the first war titles off the presses was Dartmouth professor Bernard Brodie's *A (Layman's) Guide to Naval Strategy* (1942). Brodie

[46] "Princeton's Press Typifies Growth," 2054; PUP, *Report to the University Faculty* (Dec. 7, 1941–Dec. 7, 1945), 1, 3, DRBSC (#CO728), box 44, folder 1 (PUL).

[47] PUP, *Report to the Faculty (1941–1945)*, 10; *Putting Knowledge to Work*, 37.

[48] PUP, *Report to the Faculty (1941–1945)*, 1–3.

had published *Sea Power in the Machine Age* with PUP the year before, but Smith had some additional advice to offer after seeing the prospectus for the *Guide*: "Your job is to be as 'relaxed' and unpedantic as possible in your prose style, and at the same time to have sufficient precision of statement to meet with the approval of the scholar." When the Press returned the copyedited manuscript to Brodie nine months later after a critical reading by an outside expert, Smith, in the guise of "the Layman Himself," counseled the budding author to "go through the whole damn manuscript and excise the yah-yah swearwords about your fellow critics of naval strategy. . . . Particularly, I'd try to get across my point about [Admiral Alfred T.] Mahan without seeming to call anybody an s.o.b. or a nincompoop. Don't change one idea, don't retract an inch in your convictions, but don't deny yourself a hearing by making anybody mad *needlessly*." Smith's advice was apparently well taken because the book (minus the "Layman's" parenthesis) was immediately adopted by the navy and placed on every ship and in the curriculum of the Naval War College. By the end of the war, 60,000 copies had been sold, a surprise best-seller even by trade press standards.[49]

Thanks to military purchases, other PUP books did nearly as well or better. Philip Hitti's *The Arabs: A Short History* (1943) found 7,500 civilian customers and space in the backpacks of 50,000 American soldiers headed for North Africa and other theaters in the Near East. PUP titles in meteorology, helicopter design, ore deposits, and military strategy proved popular in the Pentagon and its research facilities and academic affiliates. *Makers of Modern Strategy: Military Thought from Machiavelli to Hitler* (1943), twenty essays edited by Institute fellow Edward Mead Earle, began in 1934 as an annual seminar at the Institute and helped move military history from amateur "battle history" status to scholarly acceptance as a bona fide branch of Clio's craft.[50]

Two books published at the tail end of the war also became unlikely best-sellers. *Foundations of National Power: Readings on World Politics and American Security* (1945) was edited by Professor of Poli-

[49] *Journey with Joy*, 47, 49–50; PUP, *Report to the Faculty (1941–1945)*, 5.

[50] *A Century in Books*, 36–37; *Putting Knowledge to Work*, 51.

tics Harold Sprout and his wife, Margaret, at the request of Secretary of the Navy James V. Forrestal '15. Before it was republished by a trade house the following year, the 800-page tome had become a staple in fifty-two Navy ROTC courses and sold 45,000 copies.[51] *Atomic Energy for Military Purposes* (1945), written by Professor of Physics Henry DeWolf Smyth '18, had a more extraordinary genesis and delivery.[52]

In the eyes of many, Smyth had been given "the most difficult job of authorship and editorship ever assigned to an American scientist," namely, to tell the complex story of the Manhattan Project with meticulous accuracy and fairness but without giving away any state secrets. Appointed by Major General Leslie Groves in the spring of 1944, Smyth, a double Ph.D. in physics and chairman of the Princeton Physics Department, had a complete version ready by July 30, 1945. On August 11, two days after the second atomic bomb was dropped on Nagasaki, President Truman ordered the "Smyth Report" (as it came to be called universally) published for all the world to see, without copyright restrictions. Since Smyth had written the semi-technical report with a "nonexpert audience in mind," the President wanted it published as widely as possible beyond the Government Printing Office's own cheap printing. Indeed, back in June, Smyth had broached the possibility of having the government use PUP's summer-vacated facilities for two weeks for a "Top Secret" job that might become headlines overnight. Because of previous commitments and other concerns, Smith declined. But when he read—on the only vacation he had had in four years—a *New York Times* article on Truman's publication order, he guessed the nature of the job Smyth had referred to and rushed back to Princeton with an offer to publish.[53]

[51] PUP, *Report to the Faculty (1941–45)*, 7; Vincent Davis, Maurice A. East, and James N. Rosenau, "Harold and Margaret Sprout," in Marks, *Luminaries*, 285–96.

[52] Henry DeWolf Smyth, *Atomic Energy for Military Purposes: The Official Report on the Development of the Atomic Bomb under the Auspices of the United States Government, 1940–1945* (Princeton, 1945); H. D. Smyth '18, "The 'Smyth Report,'" *PULC* 37:3 (Spring 1976): 173–89; Datus C. Smith, Jr. '29, "The Publishing History of the 'Smyth Report,'" *PULC* 37:3 (Spring 1976): 191–203.

[53] *Journey with Joy*, 57–58, 61; George T. Reynolds, "Henry DeWolf Smyth," in Marks, *Luminaries*, 273–84, at 274n1, 280; Smith, "Publishing History," 191–92.

After gaining "informal assent to a bypassing of our normal procedure for authorizing publication," a Press investment of $15,000, and countless phone calls to procure enough paper to print the first 60,000 copies at a Pennsylvania printing plant (PUP's was tied up with priority orders), Smith and company produced the 250-page book from manuscript in exactly *three weeks*. The cloth edition sold for $2, the paperback for 75 cents less. Although the text was in the public domain, publishers all over the world asked PUP's permission to translate it and were "thrown for a loop" when told that it was "anyone's for the taking." Translations in some forty languages soon appeared. Nevertheless, PUP sold not only the whole first printing on the day of publication—September 15—but nine printings and 126,741 copies before it went out of print in 1973, nearly thirty years later. Some of the briskest sales were to closeted scientists and technicians at the hard-to-reach Oak Ridge, Richland, and Los Alamos labs where the bomb had its fateful birth.[54]

PUP's interest in books relating to the war—and how to avoid another—continued well after the hot global conflict turned colder. The first two of four multi-authored volumes of *The American Soldier*, a groundbreaking social-psychological study of America's fighting men, appeared in 1949. Institute fellow Herbert Feis's *The Road to Pearl Harbor* was released the following year, the first of five books of diplomatic history that Feis would publish with PUP before going to a commercial press.[55] Two books received unusual fast-track approval because of their timeliness. In 1947 Frank Monaghan's *Heritage of Freedom* was hustled into print as a companion volume to 122 "basic documents of American liberty" circulating the country on the Freedom Train, sponsored by the American Heritage Foundation; Princeton's Librarian Julian Boyd had served on the

[54] *Journey with Joy*, 58–61; Smith, "Publishing History," 193–200; *A Century in Books*, 48–49. A copy autographed by eighteen eminent scientists associated with the Manhattan Project, including five Nobel laureates, Institute director J. Robert Oppenheimer, and four Princeton faculty members, is in the Department of Rare Books and Special Collections in Firestone Library. The signed copy—minus Smyth's own signature—was in PUP's library until 1982, when Smyth was invited to a Press ceremony to sign it before it was deposited in Firestone. "Autographed Edition," *PAW*, Sept. 8, 1982, 7.

[55] *Putting Knowledge to Work*, 15, 54, 72–73, 83; "Princeton's Press Typifies Growth," 2056; *Journey with Joy*, 71–72; *A Century in Books*, 57–58.

committee that chose the documents. By 1949 the large quarto had sold 59,000 copies.[56]

In the summer of 1948 Datus Smith informed Sherman Kent, Yale historian and the most effective operative in the Office of Strategic Service's Research and Analysis branch during the war, that the Press had accepted his "Strategic Intelligence for American World Policy" for publication the following year. "This action," he explained, "was authorized by our executive committee which used extraordinary measures to short-circuit our normal procedure for handling manuscripts," a procedure reserved for only three manuscripts in the previous ten years. But the director also took care to caution Kent that "we do not expect your book to sell anything like those." Yet because of its intrinsic importance, the Press had "placed it in the procedural category of those best-sellers."[57]

A single title that few noticed or purchased was a precursor to a later series with worldwide, even galactic, applications. One of the first manuscripts accepted by newly hired Herbert S. Bailey, Jr. '42, PUP's first science editor, was "Jet Propulsion in Commercial Air Transportation" by Robert E. Hage. After it was published in 1948, the Pentagon asked the university and the Press to organize and publish a multivolume series on "High Speed Aerodynamics and Jet Propulsion." The proposed nine volumes were to be written by a hundred experts at "an advanced level," primarily for "research scientists entering these new areas of transportation." The first volume, *General Theory of High Speed Aerodynamics*, was published in the fall of 1954. That it happened to be the Press's one-thousandth book gave its appearance only slightly more publicity than its title would have garnered. But the series (which grew to twelve volumes) had staying power and reach. After Sputnik was launched in 1957, an enterprising twelve-year-old American boy who wanted to build a rocket wrote to the head of the Russian space program in Moscow

[56] *Putting Knowledge to Work*, 82; "Princeton's Press Typifies Growth," 2055. On the Freedom Train, see David Hackett Fischer, *Liberty and Freedom: A Visual History of America's Founding Ideas* (New York, 2005), 567–73.

[57] *Journey with Joy*, 69–71, at 70. On Kent's career in the OSS and later the CIA, see Robin W. Winks, *Cloak & Gown: Scholars in the Secret War, 1939–1961* (New York, 1987), chap. 2, esp. 82–96.

for information. When some weeks later the boy excitedly opened his mail, the Russian rocketeer politely informed him that the best book on the subject was published in a place called "Prinston."[58]

Not every category of book published by the Press was of national or international import. Some volumes were unabashedly local and chauvinistic. Prompted largely by Princeton's bicentennial in 1947, PUP published eleven university-related titles—historical, bibliographical, and pictorial. The most important were Wertenbaker's truncated history of *Princeton, 1746–1896* (1946) and Donald Drew Egbert's *Princeton Portraits* (1947), a scholarly study of the subjects and artists of the university's large and historically important collection. *Planning the University Library Building* (1949), edited by Librarian Boyd, was no page-turner or best-seller, but it effectively analyzed the conferences and the conclusions of the many American librarians who worked cooperatively for many years to design the most efficient and effective libraries for postwar universities. At Princeton, its ideas led to the durable adaptability of Firestone.[59] A slim volume of informal memories of Woodrow Wilson's presidency by seven faculty members, most of whom he had recruited, has proven invaluable to later historians and biographers.[60]

Despite the urgencies of war and local celebration, PUP felt obliged mainly to publish "books of long-term significance" and managed to do so with impressive rigor and regularity.[61] Ironically, the war brought extraordinary talent to the Press list. When Hitler shook the tree, Princeton collected much of the best fruit. Many Jewish émigrés and refugees, most notably mathematicians and historians of art, found succor in the university and the Institute, and their works were welcomed by the university press.[62] Charles de

[58] *Putting Knowledge to Work*, 68, 88; "P.U.P.'s 1000th," *PAW*, Dec. 3, 1954, 14; [John D. Davies,] "Princeton University Press: The University as Publisher," *PAW*, Apr. 20, 1962, 10–13, at 13.

[59] See chapter 8, p. 460.

[60] *Putting Knowledge to Work*, 32–33, 72–74, 81–83; William Starr Myers, ed., *Woodrow Wilson: Some Princeton Memories* (Princeton, 1946).

[61] PUP, *Report to the Faculty (1941–45)*, 1.

[62] Erwin Panofsky, "Three Decades of Art History in the United States: Impressions of a Transplanted European," in *Meaning in the Visual Arts: Papers in and on Art History* (Garden City, N.Y., 1955), 321–46, at 332 ("Hitler is my best friend," New York Universi-

Tolnay from Hungary published the first two of five monumental volumes on Michelangelo during the war (riling not a few editors and designers in the process with his demands).[63] Erwin Panofsky, the German-born master of artistic iconology and English prose, was grateful for the appearance of his two-volume *The Life and Art of Albrecht Dürer* in 1943, but had to wait three years for his edition and translation of *Abbot Suger* on Saint-Denis to be published.[64] Likewise, Kurt Weitzmann began to publish a series of monographs on Byzantine art that made his reputation as the leading authority.[65]

Several other works contributed to PUP's growing distinction and, by virtue of the Press's name, to the university's as well. Professor of Economics Oskar Morgenstern, Viennese aristocrat and professional boat-rocker, joined forces with the Institute's brilliant mathematician John von Neumann to produce *Theory of Games and Economic Behavior* (1944) from a short collaborative paper. Their revolutionary application of strategic decision making to economics sold only two hundred copies in the first year; but thanks largely to an effusive front-page article in the *New York Times*, its implications and Cold War uses gained notoriety and the edition sold out within the second year.[66] In music circles, Alfred (not Albert) Einstein's definitive three-volume *The Italian Madrigal* (1949) made a similar

ty's Institute of Fine Arts chairman Walter Cook used to say, "he shakes the tree and I collect the apples."); Colin Eisler, "*Kunstgeschichte* American Style: A Study in Migration," in Donald Fleming and Bernard Bailyn, eds., *The Intellectual Migration: Europe and America, 1930–1960* (Cambridge, Mass., 1969), 544–629; Laura Fermi, *Illustrious Immigrants: The Intellectual Migration from Europe, 1930–41* (Chicago, 1968), 247–54.

[63] Datus C. Smith, Jr., and Herbert S. Bailey, Jr., "Some Personal Recollections of 'P.J.'," *PULC* 56:2 (Winter 1995): 175–82, at 177.

[64] On the delays caused by the war and related impediments, including the extraordinary print runs needed for the "Smyth Report," see *Dr Panofsky & Mr Tarkington: An Exchange of Letters, 1938–1946*, ed. Richard M. Ludwig (Princeton: PUL, 1974), 17, 23–25, 33, 41, 77, 83, 116, 128.

[65] *Putting Knowledge to Work*, 28–30, 74–75.

[66] *A Century in Books*, 40–41, 110–11; *Putting Knowledge to Work*, 61, 87; Martin Shubik, "Oskar Morgenstern," in Marks, *Luminaries*, 198–203. The Press originally thought to publish the manuscript in a multilithed edition of three hundred copies because of its esoteric nature and 1,200-page bulk. "Princeton University Press," 13.

impression. And Julian Boyd's close study of the textual evolution of the document in *The Declaration of Independence* (1945) served to elevate Thomas Jefferson's stature as thinker and writer. Even more so did the monumental *Papers of Thomas Jefferson*, a projected 52-volume series conceived and edited by Boyd. Slated for completion in 1963, the series was the first of PUP's ambitious "papers" and "works" projects, which now treat Thoreau, Auden, Kierkegaard, Einstein, Jung, Coleridge, and Woodrow Wilson among others. The initial volume appeared in 1950 to great fanfare, including a reception at the Library of Congress with President Truman. By the end of 2004, however, only thirty-two volumes had been published, the projected series had grown to seventy-five volumes, and the completion date had jumped to an optimistic 2026, the bicentennial of Jefferson's death.[67]

University presses are meant to publish books of esoteric scholarship, but even PUP must have had doubts about *The Pylos Tablets* (1951), one of the volumes it published for the University of Cincinnati. The book consisted of painstaking hand-drawn transcriptions of the unknown script (called Linear B) of an unknown language incised on eleven hundred clay tablets found at the turn of the century on Late Bronze Age sites in Pylos on the Greek mainland. A translation volume was supposed to follow, but, awkwardly, no one in the world could read the script or knew the language. So PUP had published a literally unreadable book, all in the hope that someone, someday, would be able to decipher it and establish its lineage. Surprisingly, the volume quickly sold out its first edition of two thousand copies. One of those copies enabled full-time architect and part-time cryptographer Michael Ventris and classical archaeologist John Chadwick to partially crack the code within a year. Linear A, a related script found at Knossos in Crete, remains unbroken.[68]

[67] *Putting Knowledge to Work*, 83–84; *A Century in Books*, 59–60; "The Papers of Thomas Jefferson," *PAW*, Apr. 7, 1950, 8–9; *PAW*, May 26, 1950, 7–10; Mark F. Bernstein '83, "History, Letter by Letter," *PAW*, May 14, 2003, 20–23; Eric Meng, "University Press Publishes Thomas Jefferson's Papers," *DP* (online), Nov. 17, 2004.

[68] *The Pylos Tablets: A Preliminary Transcription*, ed. Emmett L. Bennett, Jr. (Princeton, 1951); *The Pylos Tablets: Texts of the Transcriptions Found 1939–1954*, ed. Bennett (Princeton, 1955). Unhappily, the tablets turned out to be mundane bookkeeping records. *Putting Knowledge to Work*, 26, 75; Trevor Lipscombe, "The Unreadable Book:

As the Press moved into the 1950s and celebrated Datus Smith's decade in the director's chair (he went on leave in 1952, resigned in late 1953, and was replaced in 1954), it could point to a marked increase in overall quality, public awareness of its books, and stature in the learned world. Although PUP still published fewer than forty-five titles a year, and 35–40 percent of those were by Princeton authors, its publications committee could afford to be increasingly choosy. Because postwar and Cold War faculties at Princeton and elsewhere were expanding, university presses had many more authors from whom to choose. At Princeton the temporary impairment of scholarship had been reversed with a vigorous reassertion of "publish or perish" expectations for promotion and tenure by such leaders as Hugh Taylor, dean of the Graduate School and ex officio Press trustee from 1945 to 1958.[69] While the Press's war-related best-sellers helped to subsidize what Smith called the "saleless wonders" among the specialized monographs, better marketing and distribution led to a fifteen-fold increase in sales between 1937 and 1957; nearly a quarter of that income came from overseas, where most university presses gleaned no more than eleven percent and trade publishers only five. As Smith's successor told the faculty, "In some countries Princeton is known to scholars mainly through the Press's publications—and is judged by those publications, whether or not the books were written by Princeton faculty members."[70] An equally good sign for the long-term health of the Press was that about 70 percent of its sales came from titles on the backlist.[71] Smith may have startled a few readers of the *Atlantic Monthly* in 1949 when he argued that "the scholarly vigor of the whole backlist is of far greater importance

Minoans, Math Phobia, and Modern Publishing," *Journal of Scholarly Publishing* 30:1 (Oct. 1998): 3–10; John Chadwick, *The Decipherment of Linear B* (Cambridge, 1958).

[69] In 1951 President Harold Dodds could boast that "departmental reports record the highest level of . . . scholarly productivity since the war" ("President's Report," *PAW*, Nov. 30, 1951, 5). On Taylor, see above, chapter 2, pp. 89–91; Walter J. Kauzmann, "Hugh Stott Taylor," in Marks, *Luminaries*, 311–18.

[70] PUP, *A Report to the University Faculty, Nov. 1, 1955*, [4], Hist. Subj. Files (#AC109), box 271 (PUA).

[71] PU, *Report of the President (1952)*, 13; PUP, "Report to the President" (1949–1950), 172–73 (PUA).

to the financial well-being of a press than the pyrotechnics, however beautiful, of a few current titles."[72]

When Smith submitted his resignation in 1953, he admitted that he was leaving "the best publishing job in America." It could also be said—and was—that he had *done* one of the best publishing jobs in the country. As his colleague and successor Herbert Bailey appraised the work of the Press in 1965, after more than a decade of his own successes, he still regarded Smith's decade as "the Press's greatest period of growth and achievement."[73]

❁ ❁ ❁

Even Bailey would have been forced to admit upon retiring in 1986 that the Press during his own tenure of thirty-two years had surpassed any previous performance. It had done so with fiscal responsibility, increased productivity, a scrupulous concern for quality, and a distinctive style of management and book design, all of which enhanced PUP's considerable reputation at home and abroad. But the achievements did not come easily. Halfway through Bailey's term, the publishing world, particularly that of university presses, was buffeted by runaway inflation, severe cuts in federal aid to university research and libraries, and technological challenges to the book and its traditional modes of production. PUP responded with imagination and resolve but cautiously, taking care to protect its scholarly mission and economic viability.

After graduating from Princeton in 1942 and three years of service as a naval radar instructor in the war, crew-cut "Herb" Bailey joined the PUP crew as its first science editor (1946–1952) and then as its editor-in-chief for two years while Datus Smith was on leave. When he was chosen to succeed Smith in 1954, he was—at thirty-two—the youngest director of a major press in the nation. Having taken

[72] Or, as publisher Jason Epstein put it, "the function of the frontlist is to enhance the backlist" (*Book Business: Publishing Past Present and Future* [New York, 2002], 60). Datus C. Smith, Jr., "Putting Knowledge to Work," *Atlantic Monthly* (Mar. 1949), 76–78, at 77.

[73] *Journey with Joy*, 75; Bailey, "Princeton University Press," 11.

FIGURE 33. Herbert S. Bailey, Jr., Director of the Princeton University Press from 1954 to 1986 and a recognized force in the publishing world.

several electrical engineering electives as an English major, a sign of his broad and keen curiosity, he proved a natural leader of a wide-ranging scholarly press. Understandably, he built up PUP's math and science offerings, creating twelve new series and maintaining the vigor of three that predated his arrival. But he also launched two poetry series and the Princeton Library of Asian Translations and moved the Press energetically into anthropology, economics, and political philosophy, in addition to building on its strengths in literary criticism, classical studies, history, art and archaeology, and regional and area studies.[74]

[74] Herbert S. Bailey, Jr., "A Brief History," in *Princeton University Press, 1905–1980* (Princeton, 1980), 38–39.

At the same time, he ran a "tight ship" by exercising discipline over costs and growth. His nonpatented "Bailey Formula," invented in 1954, allocated to each book a fixed dollar portion of nonmanufacturing costs (such as editing, design, and proofreading), not, as was customary in the trade, a percentage of the selling price, which could change. The formula quickly spread throughout the university-press world, particularly after he explained its utility in *The Art and Science of Book Publishing* in 1970. Other lessons learned were passed on in witty poems published in *Publisher's Weekly* and widely reprinted in accounting textbooks.[75] Yet Bailey always made it clear that cash flow and the bottom line were not the point of a university press. "A publisher is known not by the skill with which he runs his business," his book concluded, "but by the books he publishes." "What makes a great publishing house are great books, written by great authors, edited by great editors, designed with taste, produced with skill and efficiency, and energetically and widely sold." "Although a university press looks like a business and must have businesslike efficiency," he reminded his university press colleagues in 1975, "it is *not* a business." "Quality," not potential profit, "must be *the* criterion for acceptance." His best advice to fiscally challenged directors was to "manage conservatively and shoot for the moon in quality" because "only high quality can justify the financial support we need. . . . Our publications must be of such high quality that they constitute an essential part of our culture, so that society cannot afford to let them go unpublished."[76]

Bailey could well afford his own idealistic advice. Although the Press continued its unusual financial independence from the university, it enjoyed a comfortable and growing endowment and a profitable printing business with which to subsidize "saleless wonders" and to make improvements. Only half of its printing operations were devoted to its own books; the other half was split evenly between

[75] (New York: Harper & Row, 1970). The book was reprinted in 1980 by Ohio University Press and in 1990 by the University of Texas Press, directed by former PUP managing editor Joanna Hitchcock. The formula is explicated in chapter 4. The poems are reprinted in the Ohio University Press edition (Athens, 1980), xv–xvii.

[76] Bailey, *Art and Science of Book Publishing* (Athens, Ohio, 1980), 5, 195; Bailey, "Implications of the Cartter Report for University Presses," *Scholarly Publishing* 6:3 (Apr. 1975): 207–9.

university work and even more profitable outside jobs.[77] Founder Charles Scribner's testamentary bequest of $50,000 in 1930 and the establishment of a Whitney Darrow Fund in 1956 to underwrite specialized books of low profitability eventually grew to enviable proportions because they were invested wisely and not drawn upon for many years. These funds were supplemented as book profits accrued on steadily increased sales.[78] Timely grants from the Ford Foundation (1956–1965) and the Andrew W. Mellon Foundation (1982–1985) allowed the Press to publish titles in the humanities and social sciences of high quality and low sales potential without drawing subsidies from the reserve fund. Under Bailey's careful management and that of his controller, William C. Becker, widely regarded as "the wisest business analyst in university press work," PUP became one of the best-financed presses in the country.[79]

The thirty-year-long "Golden Age" of American higher education after World War II swept most university presses, including Princeton's, along in its growth and prosperity. It was hard for a press not to acquire and sell good scholarly books when the number of institutions grew 55 percent to 2,747, students multiplied six times to over eleven million, tenure-hungry faculty tripled to 628,000, federal aid to higher education—largely for research, graduate education, and libraries—more than sextupled to over $3 billion, and, not least, library expenditures as a percentage of university education and general budgets rose from 2 to 3 percent.[80] On this general tide PUP's

[77] PUP, *A Report to the University Faculty, Nov. 1, 1955*, [7]; [Bailey], "A Report to the Association of Princeton University Press, Dec. 9, 1960," fig. 2, in Hist. Subj. Files (#AC109), box 271 (PUA).

[78] In 1983, for example, after a number of outstanding years, the trustees moved $500,000 in publishing profits into the Scribner and Darrow funds. Three years later, the Press had $388,050 in endowment interest available for book subsidies; in the fall of 1986 it allocated $74,900 to underwrite twenty-two books. "Minutes of the PUP Trustees," Mar. 17, 1983, 1; "Report on Subsidy Allocation, Aug. 1–Dec. 1, 1986" (PUP). (Thanks to Director Walter Lippincott for generous access to the Press records at 41 William Street.)

[79] Smith, "Promoting Education and Scholarship," 15; interview with Walter Lippincott, June 14, 2004, Princeton.

[80] Arthur M. Cohen, *The Shaping of American Higher Education: Emergence and Growth of the Contemporary System* (San Francisco, 1998), 176 (table 4.1), 226 (table 4.3), 253, 264 (table 4.5).

average first printing grew from 2,000 copies in 1962 to 2,500 in three years. Bailey also recognized that the Press would have to increase its output to serve its major constituents. In 1962 he told the alumni that "as Princeton's faculty and graduate school expand, and as other American universities expand, we will have to expand too if we are to do our job. But we intend to expand reluctantly and slowly, keeping our emphasis on quality."[81]

Circumstances changed so fast that in 1965 Bailey reported to President Robert Goheen that, although PUP was "not yet meeting the challenges or realizing the opportunities that lie before us as a leading American university press," the past year had marked "a transition into a new era" for the Press.[82] The most visible change was the completion in that year of a sixty-thousand-square-foot printing plant and warehouse on ten acres near Lawrenceville. The move not only secured the latest offset equipment for PUP's printers, it freed up badly needed space in the Scribner Building for expanded publishing staff and activities. Within three years, full renovations gave PUP a fresh new face and amenities to go with its growing reputation for superior publishing. The *Saturday Review* called it "the aristocrat of university presses." The *Yale Review* described PUP as "notoriously alert" for scholarly research of distinction.[83]

The new facilities allowed the Press to produce more titles each year and to launch—somewhat tardily—a paperback line of its own in 1965, having hitherto leased about a hundred titles to other publishers, notably Atheneum.[84] When Bailey became director in 1954,

[81] [Davies], "Princeton University Press," 12, 13. He delivered a similar message to the faculty the following year. PUP, *A Report to the Faculty* (Oct. 1, 1963), 2, Hist. Subj. Files (#AC109), box 271 (PUA).

[82] PUP, "Report to the President" (1964–1965), 519–20.

[83] Bailey, "Princeton University Press," 9; *A Miscellany of Princeton Printing Compiled to Celebrate the Dedication of the Henry A. Laughlin Building of the Princeton University Press and the Sixtieth Anniversary of the Founding of the Press* (Dec. 3, 1965), 3–6; "The 'New' University Press," *PAW*, Feb. 27, 1968, 10–11.

[84] In 1972 Bailey also launched Limited Paperback Editions for very specialized titles, chiefly in math and science. The same size as clothbound books, they cost 40 percent less. The idea of limited editions subsequently caught on at many other presses. "PUP: From a Humble Start, An Illustrious Institution," *PWB*, Feb. 16, 1976, 2; telephone interview with Bailey, Jan. 24, 2005.

PUP had issued only 37 new titles; a decade later the year's output was a healthy 69. By 1979 the director could report 125 new scholarly titles and 50 new paperbacks. When he retired in 1986, the fall and spring catalogues together boasted 142 new hardbacks.[85] While significant and steady, Princeton's gains were not as pronounced as those registered by its rivals at Yale, Chicago, California, Cornell, and the trade-like behemoths at Oxford and Cambridge, in keeping with Bailey's desire to maintain quality throughout his list.[86]

But the Press was able to maintain quality control over the increased output on the strength of greatly enhanced sales, even throughout the difficult early 1970s and early 1980s. By 1980 Bailey had orchestrated a twenty-fold dollar growth in sales, the proceeds of moving 750,000 copies a year, more than half of them paperbacks. Foreign sales, one of PUP's traditional strengths, constituted some 30 percent of hardback sales. Goheen liked to tell the story of when he was introduced to a scholar in New Delhi as the president of Princeton, the Indian said, "Oh very interesting. And does that university have any connection with Princeton University Press?"[87]

PUP's reluctance to expand except under pressure, its conservative fiscal management, and its steady focus on its traditional scholarly mission enabled it to survive the economic downturns of the 1970s and 1980s. When federal funding for college libraries dropped 56 percent in three years and inflation eroded their buying power still further, the average first printing at the Press dropped from 2,400 copies in 1970 to 2,000 in 1975 (17 percent) and the list price rose from $11 to $16 (45 percent), further pinching the libraries. Hardbacks that on average sold 1,660 copies after five years in 1969 sold only 1,003 in 1984, a decline of 40 percent.[88] Since libraries then constituted 65

[85] "Publisher Par Excellence," *PAW*, July 16, 1986, 18–19, at 18; PUP, *Memorandum to Princeton Faculty*, Jan. 10, 1965, 1, insert in the Spring 1965 PUP catalogue, Hist. Subj. Files (# AC109), box 271 (PUA); Bailey, "A Brief History," 33.

[86] "University Press Growth, 1979–1999" (chart), *Change*, May–June 2001, 7.

[87] Smith, "Promoting Education and Scholarship," 15; Bailey, "A Brief History," 33.

[88] William B. Harvey, Herbert S. Bailey, Jr., William C. Becker, and John B. Putnam, "The Impending Crisis in University Publishing," *Scholarly Publishing* 3:3 (Apr. 1972): 195–200, at 196; Bailey, "Economics of Publishing in the Humanities," *Scholarly Publishing* 8:3 (Apr. 1977): 223–31, at 225; Bailey, "The Future of University Press Publishing," *Scholarly Publishing* 19:2 (Jan. 1988): 63–69, at 63–64.

percent of most university press sales, the search for solutions took some presses into awkward and expensive competition for fiction and other "best-seller" trade books, and several into extinction.

Princeton chose another route, in part because of its general economic health, in larger part because of Bailey's firm belief in the power of a strong backlist, rigorous standards, and the true calling of a university press. In an interview upon his election as president of the Association of American University Presses (AAUP) in 1972, he warned that "to seek out books for their apparent money-making potential would be to subvert our primary purpose. . . . But," he added, "like falling in love with a girl who happens to be rich, this doesn't mean that commercially attractive books have to be turned down." Yet he was also convinced, like his predecessor, that "the most successful frontlist for a university publisher is one that will become a strong backlist in years ahead."[89]

When Datus Smith surveyed the Press's progress for the alumni magazine in 1980, he acknowledged that he knew of no publishing list in the country "holding so rigorously to the standards of scholarly purity." Indeed, he argued, it was "*because* of that adherence to scholarly standards" that PUP was "probably in sounder financial condition than most other university presses." The watchdogs of quality were the senior faculty members of the renamed Editorial Board, increased to four members when Bailey took office. Since Press books carried the name of the university, Bailey, like his predecessors, insisted that the board was ultimately responsible for the imprint, which all agreed was "the Press's most valuable possession."[90]

Bailey received an early and unforgettable lesson in scholarly standards at his first meeting with the Editorial Board after he became editor-in-chief in 1952. On the three-man board that year was the formidably learned and fearless economist Jacob Viner, then one of

[89] Smith, "Promoting Education and Scholarship," 15 (library sales); Michael Mok, "PW Interviews: Herbert S. Bailey, Jr.," *Publisher's Weekly*, July 17, 1972, 62–63, at 62.

[90] Smith, "Promoting Education and Scholarship," 15; Bailey, "A Brief History," 34; *Putting Knowledge to Work*, 5 (Julian Boyd). See also John Dreyfus, "On Printing and Design," in *A Miscellany of Princeton Printing*, 19: "The books produced by a university press differ from those of commercial publishers in that they derive additional authority from the imprint of the sponsoring body."

the few faculty members known to frequent Firestone Library on Sundays.[91] When Bailey, all of thirty years old, presented seven book proposals for approval, Viner and his colleagues promptly shot down four as unworthy. This left the embarrassed editor with a shortage of manuscripts for the production queue—and a newfound determination to toughen up his own standards before sending any more proposals to the board. When he became director two years later, it also convinced him to give the board more proposals than could feasibly be published in order to keep them on their mettle. As Professor of English Gerald Bentley remembered at the end of his stint on the board, during which he had read 20–25 manuscripts each year and debated the merits of all the rest, the board's primary responsibility was negative—"to say NO" to less than the best proposals each month. In so doing, the board heeded Bailey's constant reminder that "it is more important to fail to recognize—and thus miss publishing—good books than to fail by publishing weak or mediocre ones."[92] From the start of his directorship, Bailey kept an eye on the board's rejection rate and compared it with those of Princeton's rivals.[93]

He also required a minimum of two expert readers' reports on every promising manuscript, at least one from outside the university for Princeton authors. This allowed the acquisition editors (later called "listbuilders"), particularly after 1963, to weed out weaker manuscripts before sending proposals to the editorial board. The procedure was necessitated in part by the daunting if flattering in-

[91] Fritz Machlup, "What the World Thought of Jacob Viner," *Journal of Political Economy* 80 (Jan. 1972): 1–4; Machlup, "What Was Left on Viner's Desk," *Journal of Political Economy* 80 (Mar. 1972): 353–64; Donald Winch, "Teaching: Jacob Viner," *American Scholar* 50 (Autumn 1981): 519–25; Lionel Robbins, *Jacob Viner: A Tribute* (Princeton, 1970).

[92] [Davies], "Princeton University Press," 12; "Publisher Par Excellence," 19. By the 1980s, according to member and trustee Alvin Kernan, "the board members did not read the manuscripts, unless there was a particular interest or problem, but made decisions on the basis of the reports of two or three outside specialists and the recommendations of the editors" (*In Plato's Cave* [New Haven, 1999], 235).

[93] "Publisher Par Excellence," 18; e-mail interviews with former PUP science editor Edward Tenner, June 22, 2004, and former controller William C. Becker, July 16, 2002, 13; telephone interview with Herbert S. Bailey, Jr., June 10, 2002.

crease in manuscript submissions as "the Ph.D. octopus and tenure torpedo" (as Bailey called them) intensified academe's "publish-or-perish" imperative.[94] But Press procedures, regarded by many as "the most rigorous scholarly review process anywhere in academic publishing," did have a downside: they were slow and therefore discouraged some "important thinkers" who expected their work to receive fast-track treatment.[95]

That PUP did not suffer unduly from author impatience is suggested by the 224 prizes won by the 2,948 clothbound books published on Bailey's watch, when prizes were less profuse than they are today. Institute fellow and diplomat George F. Kennan garnered a Pulitzer Prize, a Bancroft Prize, and a National Book Award for *Russia Leaves the War: Soviet-American Relations, 1917–1920* (1956). PUP books won back-to-back National Book Awards for Translation in 1974 and 1975. The second volume of Joseph Frank's monumental five-volume biography of Dostoevsky, *The Years of Ordeal, 1850–1859* (1983), carried away the National Book Critics Circle Award in 1985, which more than justified the editorial board's "enthusiastic" approval of the manuscript three years earlier and the Press's somewhat generous 12½ percent royalty.[96] Among Princeton's four other Pulitzer winners were Press loyalist Herbert Feis for *Between War and Peace: The Potsdam Conference* (1960) and Constance McLaughlin Green for the first volume of her two-part history of Washington, *Village and Capital, 1800–1878* (1962). Columbia University's Bancroft Prize for History also went to Institute fellow Felix Gilbert's succinct *To the Farewell Address: Ideas of Early American Foreign Policy* (1961) and to R. R. Palmer's ambitious first volume of *The Age of the Democratic Revolution* (1959), which the publications committee twenty years before had wisely urged him to postpone.

[94] In 1962, c. 300 manuscripts crossed the editors' desks; a decade later, 740; in 1981, 1,129 poured in, of which only 81 (7 percent) were accepted. Tenner interview; [Davies], "Princeton University Press," 12; Kernan, *In Plato's Cave*, 235. See also Robert Darnton, "Publishing: A Survival Strategy for Academic Authors," *American Scholar* (Autumn 1983): 533–37.

[95] Sanford G. Thatcher, "Remarks on the Occasion of Herb Bailey's Retirement Dinner, May 16, 1986" (typescript; thanks to Sandy Thatcher for a copy); Tenner interview.

[96] PUP, "Minutes of the Editorial Board," July–Aug. 1982, 14 (PUP).

It was not only in history that the Press won top honors. In 1981 the Association of American Publishers gave its prestigious Professional & Scholarly Publishing Award to two PUP science books, Wayne Johnson's *Helicopter Theory* (1980) and Princeton biologist John T. Bonner's *The Evolution of Culture in Animals* (1980); three years later, two Princeton books shared the award in the physical sciences and Warren F. Kimball's splendid edition of *Churchill & Roosevelt: The Complete Correspondence* (1984) claimed the social sciences prize. The indefatigable Fritz Machlup, Princeton professor of economics and author of *The Production and Distribution of Knowledge in the United States* (1962), was given a lifetime achievement award by the American Society for Information Science for opening that new field.[97] In his late sixties, he began, with Bailey's encouragement, a projected ten-volume updating of his groundbreaking study entitled *Knowledge: Its Creation, Distribution, and Economic Significance*. He lived to see only three volumes published, but they stand as apt symbols of his brilliant energy and Bailey's courageous foresight in fostering large, seminal projects.[98]

The *Papers of Thomas Jefferson*, begun under Datus Smith but sustained by Bailey's help in obtaining important funding from the National Historic Publications and Records Commission, is PUP's largest multivolume papers project, but the *Papers of Woodrow Wilson* (1966–1994) is the most successful. Not only did its editorial standards equal those of Julian Boyd and his successors at the Jefferson papers, its incredibly disciplined editor Arthur S. Link managed, despite a debilitating back ailment, to complete all sixty-nine volumes in just thirty-five years, as if, colleagues said and Link believed, he "had God on his side." That he also wrote five substantial volumes toward a biography of Wilson, two of which won Bancroft Prizes, only added to PUP's reflected renown.[99]

[97] *Prizes Awarded to Princeton University Press under Bailey*; Sanford G. Thatcher, "Some of the Outstanding Scholarly Books Published During Herbert S. Bailey, Jr.'s Tenure" [Jan. 1986] (typescript), 1–2; *A Century in Books*, 87–88, 91–92, 101–4, 156–57.

[98] Burton G. Malkiel, "Fritz Machlup," in Marks, *Luminaries*, 182–89.

[99] Richard W. Leopold, "Arthur S. Link at Northwestern: The Maturing of a Scholar," in John Milton Cooper, Jr., and Charles E. Neu, eds., *The Wilson Era: Essays in Honor of Arthur S. Link* (Arlington Heights, Ill., 1991), 30–51; Terry Teachout, "35 Years with Woodrow Wilson: The Journey of a Long-Distance Editor," *New York Times*

Bailey also threw his support behind—and often his personal energy into—several other long-term commitments, all of which spoke eloquently for PUP's mature confidence and unusual focus. It was owing to Bailey's financial sagacity that these projects also proved to be "cash cows," because they were well funded by foundations from the outset and, with one brief exception, their editorial offices were not located in or paid for by the Press.[100] Having published the first English translations of Søren Kierkegaard in the 1930s, it seemed only natural for PUP to undertake a completely reworked scholarly edition by Howard Hong and others beginning in the 1970s. As a devotee of naturalist Henry David Thoreau, Bailey fought hard to win the contract for the twenty-five-volume *Writings*, which for many years was edited in an office in Firestone Library. He also helped to obtain funding from the National Endowment for the Humanities and sponsorship of the project from the Modern Language Association's Center for Editions of American Authors.[101]

To land *The Collected Papers of Albert Einstein*, a projected twenty-five volumes, required a "superhuman effort" on Bailey's part. Beginning in 1971, PUP's agreement with the Einstein estate was contested for years and finally resolved by arbitration in the Press's favor in 1980. Then the editorial structure, initially housed in the Press building and underwritten by a million-dollar gift from Press trustee Harold McGraw, underwent five upheavals before the first volume was published to critical acclaim in 1987. Its offices have migrated from Princeton to Boston University and most recently to the California Institute of Technology, where the editors are now trying to bring

---

Book Review, Oct. 1, 1993, 33, 49–50; John Milton Cooper, Jr., "Arthur S. Link," in *Clio's Favorites: Leading Historians of the United States, 1945–2000*, ed. Robert Allen Rutland (Columbia, Mo., 2000), 111–25, at 113; James Robert Carroll, *The Real Woodrow Wilson: An Interview with Arthur S. Link, Editor of the Wilson Papers* (Bennington, Vt., 2001). In Carroll's interview, Link confessed that he knew of "only two typographical errors in those sixty-nine volumes" (28).

[100] E-mail interview with Charles Creesy, PUP's director of computing and publishing technologies, June 21, 2004; Lippincott interview.

[101] Bailey interview; Saralinda Hooker '73, "The Thoreau Papers," *PAW*, Dec. 4, 1973, 8–9, 14; Ann Waldron, "Compiling the Definitive Thoreau Edition," *PAW*, Sept. 8, 1980, 8; Bailey, "Thoreau and Us," *Scholarly Publishing* 2:4 (July 1971): 327–28.

the volumes out in a timely fashion.[102] In the meantime, PUP has published four popular anthologies of Einstein quotations for readers ill-equipped to navigate the German originals or indisposed to tackle the translated esoterica of the *Papers*.[103]

The biggest coup in Press history, and the most surprising boon to its economic well-being, was the cost-free acquisition of the Bollingen Series from Pantheon Books and the Bollingen Foundation in 1969. The series and the foundation were the inspiration of Mary and Paul Mellon, who had been attracted in the late 1930s to the Swiss psychologist C. G. Jung and an international circle of his friends and admirers. Financed by Paul Mellon, who had recently inherited a fortune from his father, financier Andrew W. Mellon, the foundation set out to underwrite research and publish books in psychology, mythology, religion, philosophy, symbolism, art, archaeology, cultural history, aesthetics, and literature that bore on "the evolution of human consciousness." By 1969 the "extraordinarily prestigious" series numbered more than 250 volumes, including the collected works of Jung, Nobel Prize–winner in literature Paul Valéry, Samuel Taylor Coleridge, and Miguel de Unamuno.[104]

Although Bailey was no fan of the Jungian goals or flavor of half the series, he had pursued it for seven years before bringing it lock, stock, and future volumes to Princeton, beating out Harvard and Yale, Paul's alma mater, in the process. Well-designed but poorly marketed and underpriced by Pantheon, which had handled it since

[102] Becker interview; Herbert Smith Bailey, Jr., "On the Collected Papers of Albert Einstein: The Development of the Project," *Proceedings of the American Philosophical Society* 133:3 (1989): 347–59; Daniel J. Kevles, "Albert Einstein: Relativity, War, and Fame," in *A Century in Books*, 186–200; see also 184–85.

[103] Helen Dukas and Banesh Hoffmann, eds., *Albert Einstein, The Human Side: New Glimpses from His Archives* (1979); Alice Calaprice, ed., *The Quotable Einstein* (1996); Calaprice, ed., *The Expanded Quotable Einstein* (2000); Calaprice, ed., *The New Quotable Einstein* (2005).

[104] The legal transfer to PUP was finalized in 1967, but the book inventory did not arrive until 1969. William McGuire, *Bollingen: An Adventure in Collecting the Past* (Princeton, 1982; rev. ed. 1989); McGuire, "The Bollingen Adventure," *PAW*, Sept. 21, 1983, 15–19; Bailey, "A Brief History," 36; "Bollingen Series, 1943–2002," *A Century in Books*, 142–49. The volumes as of 1982 are listed in McGuire's book, pp. 295–310.

the 1940s, the series had lost a million dollars a year before the move. To ensure that it would not become a financial drain on the Press, Bailey secured from the foundation $1.5 million to continue the unfinished work, to which Paul Mellon added another million to complete the series. By 1982, however, the series was not completed, but the invested funds had grown far larger than needed. Because the Bollingen Fund had been successfully invested with the university's endowments, the university trustees decided to allocate $2 million to the university library (for purchases in British and American art, history, and literature, all interests of Paul Mellon) and $2 million to the Press (to support scholarly publications outside the Bollingen series). A residue of $1.8 million was reserved to complete the series, which was finally accomplished in 2002 with the publication of the 275th volume. This unexpected windfall (in the understated words of its long-time controller) "measurably improved the Press's financial soundness."[105]

So did several Bollingen titles, which happened to click with many "New Age" readers during the heyday of "consciousness raising" and experiments in "alternative living." In handsomely redesigned formats and paper covers and, ironically, with increased (cost-covering) prices, youthful readers and other seekers flocked to Joseph Campbell's *The Hero with a Thousand Faces* (1968), particularly after Campbell was interviewed in 1989 by Bill Moyers on national television, and to the oracular *I Ching, or Book of Changes* (1967), a perhaps three-thousand-year-old Chinese guide involving sixty-four hexagrams and three coins or a bundle of yarrow stalks. The *I Ching* had begun a modest ascent in sales in the early 1960s. But after songwriter (and future Princeton honorary-degree recipient) Bob Dylan and Harvard guru Timothy Leary endorsed its use, sales skyrocketed. Annual sales of thirty thousand copies or more continued throughout the 1970s, well after the "counterculture" phenomenon had waned. By 1982 total sales of the ancient divination device had passed the half-million mark; by 2004 it had sold more than a million copies, confounding the *Boston Globe* book reviewer who had once predicted that "the whole *I Ching* fad will probably last no longer

[105] McGuire, *Bollingen*, 287; Bailey interview; Becker interview, 5–6.

than Mah Jong" (which Princeton students had played in the 1920s) and persuading many in publishing of Bailey's occidental clairvoyance.[106] By the late 1970s Bollingen books had so tapped into the zeitgeist that they constituted more than 20 percent of PUP's total sales, and they continue to earn far more than their keep as stalwarts on the Press's backlist. Small wonder that Bailey only half-jokingly regarded the series as Princeton's "Louisiana Purchase."[107]

The Press's successes during Bailey's long tenure owed a great deal to his collegial management style and to P. J. Conkwright's peerless book designs. By all accounts, Bailey was "a leader par-excellence," "a terrific boss" who created a working environment in which "people thrived, enjoyed themselves, and took great pride in what they were doing." The Press staff "always operated as a team." Bailey chose talented people and then encouraged them to exercise their talents, without undue interference. He also involved everyone, junior and senior, in the planning and decision making of the Press. When newcomers joined the staff, they were amazed to be sent regularly a pink folder containing copies of all the business correspondence that the director had exchanged and, moreover, invited to write him memos or comments in the margins. This immersion in the processes and prospects of the Press, and the humane treatment the staff received from Bailey and his key associates, fostered an unusual degree of staff loyalty and long records of service. Many of the staff worked at PUP with other family members and many more received twenty-five-year medals at festive retirement dinners.[108]

Another characteristic Bailey touch was a special Press medal for exceptional exercise of initiative or imagination, awarded ceremoniously before the whole administrative staff and worn by the recipient around the neck for a day.[109] The same sense of esprit-

[106] McGuire, *Bollingen*, 18–19, 142, 180–81; "Minutes of the PUP Trustees," June 2, 1988, 4 (PUP); McGuire, "The 'I Ching' Story," *PAW*, May 7, 1974, 10–13, at 12–13.

[107] Smith, "Promoting Education and Scholarship," 17; *A Century in Books*, 143.

[108] Becker interview; Becker, "Remarks for Herb Bailey's Retirement Dinner," May 16, 1986; ("Remarks" hereafter) Joanna Hitchcock, former PUP managing editor, "Remarks."

[109] Becker, "Remarks;" Hitchcock, director of the University of Texas Press, telephone interview, Nov. 12, 2002.

building fun went into various staff productions, with Bailey's blessings and often connivance. For many years the editorial staff published an occasional in-house newsletter called *Jellied Constellations*, the title taken from a political science manuscript that contained the sentence, "What was needed to jell this incipient constellation was an ideological catalyst and umbrella." The newsletter, which exposed mostly auctorial malaprops, bloopers, and blather, also received wider notice in the trade journal *Scholarly Publishing*, with which *JC*'s editor sporadically shared excerpts.[110] In 1980 the staff compiled and published a forty-page *Princeton University Press Seventy-Fifth Anniversary Cookbook*. In the preface Bailey confessed that the book had not been approved by the editorial board because "we like to put something over on them once in a while." He also contributed the initial recipe, "The Bollingen Martini," in which he instructed the reader how to properly pronounce the series' namesake (*ng* as in *sing*, hence *Bälingen*).

But Bailey's almost paterfamilial concern for and involvement with his staff had a better measure in his development of their careers, especially those of women. Every year he led a staff contingent to the professional meetings of the AAUP, of which he was president in 1972–1973, and encouraged them to give papers and publish articles, as he did frequently. He treated men and women equally, promoting women to top positions in Press management.[111] He was an early member of "Women in Scholarly Publishing" and helped two of his associates (R. Miriam Brokaw and Joanna Hitchcock) become the first female presidents of the AAUP.[112] To foster the creativity of top performers, he inaugurated a leave policy in 1964–1965. Those with at least ten years of service who had special projects requiring study or travel could apply for six months' paid leave, which required the trustees' approval. As the staff felt more pressure to produce more books each year without a drop in quality, these

[110] Carol Orr, "Jellied Constellations," *Scholarly Publishing* 6:1 (Oct. 1974): 66–68; 7:4 (July 1976), 333–35; 8:4 (July 1977), 354–56; 12:3 (Apr. 1986), 245–47.

[111] R. Miriam Brokaw, longtime editor, shared associate director duties with controller William Becker; Joanna Hitchcock was managing editor for many years, lending gender balance to Sanford Thatcher in the editor-in-chief's seat.

[112] Hitchcock, "Remarks."

generous changes of scene and tempo paid noticeable dividends in morale and productivity.[113]

One department head was too valuable to the Press's ongoing operations and success to lose for half a year; fortunately, P. J. Conkwright had earned his own eight-month leave in 1956–1957 by winning a Guggenheim fellowship, for travel to Europe to study letter forms and the history of printing. It is emblematic of his stature in the scholarly, not just the publishing, world that he is the only typographer to have done so. To the three directors with whom P. J. worked, he was "our real superstar," an "original" artist-craftsman. As early as 1941, Joseph Brandt assured him that he was "a typographic eminence" in his own right. By the 1970s P. J. was a veritable institution in the university press world, so much so that a major press advertised for a book designer with a preference for a "P. J. Conkwright type." By then his books had won places in the AIGA's Fifty Best Books of the Year competition an unprecedented and still unrivaled fifty-two times, and had been featured in exhibitions at the Princeton University Library three times, the Metropolitan Museum of Art, the University of Kentucky Library, and the Grolier Club. For accomplishments such as these he received the AIGA Gold Medal, honorary degrees from Kentucky and Princeton, and election to the American Academy of Arts and Sciences and Phi Beta Kappa.[114]

For all the personal kudos, P. J. was the quintessential "reader's designer." He believed that printing was a "servant art, like architecture," and that "self-effacement" was "the etiquette of the good printer." He saw his primary job as one of conveying the author's thought as clearly as possible. The design of the book must therefore be transparent, unobtrusive, drawing no attention to itself but only to the content. This is no easy task because "a book's function . . . lies precisely in how it looks." P. J.'s books are easily identified by their distinctive style, freshness, and "unflagging attentiveness to the

[113] PUP, "Reports to the President" (1964–1965), 520; Hitchcock interview.

[114] Mark Argetsinger, "Harmony Discovered: P. J. Conkwright in the Tradition of Classical Typography," *PULC* 56:2 (Winter 1995): 183–252, at 202, 206, 239, 246.

FIGURE 34. A shelf of books designed by the Press's prize-winning designer, P. J. Conkwright. His distinctive spine labels and artistic treatments are as noticeable as the clarity of his type fonts and reader-friendly layouts.

reader's essential needs."[115] Black or contrasting color labels on the spine highlight the horizontal title and author in genuine gold leaf or, less frequently, silver. Durable polished cloth and acid-free paper (introduced by Bailey in 1960) guarantee long life in library circulation. Sewn signatures ensure that the book lies open in the reader's lap and when put down. Margins, particularly at the foot, allow comfortable holding without obscuring any text.

The heart of a book is the text and its arrangement, and P. J. was a masterful servant of the former and a serviceable master of the second. Before designing a book, he believed, the designer must acquire "a sympathetic and complete understanding of the author's message" by reading the manuscript. Although P. J. looked at books "with the eye of an artist," noted British designer John Dreyfus, he maintained "a scholar's reverence for their content." Once he had a feel for the author's message and intent, he could select type and lay out the pages. P. J. preferred classically roman typefaces with quiet "personality" and

[115] Datus C. Smith, Jr., and Herbert S. Bailey, Jr., "Some Personal Recollections of 'P. J.,' " *PULC* 56:2 (Winter 1995) 175–82, at 178–79; John Dreyfus, "P. J. Conkwright and University Press Book Design," pamphlet to accompany an exhibition of P. J.'s books at the Princeton University Library in 1963, reprinted in *PULC* 32:2 (Winter 1971): 74–78.

a touch of age, such as Caslon, Baskerville, Granjon, Caledonia, and Monticello, the font he helped create for the Jefferson Papers. He avoided boldface and contemporary design clichés at all costs and any "mannered" fonts that drew attention to themselves and were unlikely to appeal to the traditional tastes of later generations of scholarly readers. But he was no fetishist and loved all kinds of lettering. He did not hesitate to have some books set in sans serif "modern" fonts, particularly books in math and science that required offset printing rather than his preferred letterpress.[116]

The most obvious characteristics of P. J.'s work, argued John F. Peckham, who trained under him before joining the Meriden Gravure Company, are "an appearance of cleanness or freshness in his pages, a feeling of balance and an almost calligraphic rhythm in the use of type, and—most easily recognized of all—the liveliness of appropriate decorative ornaments." An eighteenth-century fleuron, a stylish border, a subtle touch of color in either or in the title, or just a small stylized acorn or leaf could set his classically proportioned, centered, and incredibly crisp title pages apart from the crowd.[117] Most noticeable, perhaps, is his visual wit, which momentarily illuminates the subject. His delicate touch can be seen on the spine of Alfred Einstein's *The Italian Madrigal*, where medieval notes on musical staves denote volumes one, two, and three; in the chapter headings of Øystein Ore's *Cardano the Gambling Scholar*, where the faces of typographically produced dice announce the chapter numbers; on the title page and spine of Stanley L. Payne's *The Art of*

[116] P. J. Conkwright, *Some Notes from the Journal of a Book Designer* (Rochester, N.Y.: Press of the Good Mountain, [1974]), 6; Dreyfus, "P. J. Conkwright and University Press Book Design," 74, 75; Humphrey Stone and Jan Lilly, illustrated talks on P. J. at the annual meeting of the AAUP, Seattle, 1999 (thanks to Gretchen Oberfranc and Chuck Creesy for a videotape of the session); Argetsinger, "Harmony Discovered," 244–46; P. J. Conkwright, "Types and Time," *Scholarly Publishing* 5:2 (Jan. 1974): 121–28, at 128. P. J.'s favorite typefaces are most easily identified on his work specifications, catalogued on manila file folders in the Conkwright Papers, DRBSP (#CO665), box 15, folder 6 (PUL)

[117] Always flexible and imaginative, P. J. created some handsome flush-left title pages, such as those for Jay Martin's *Conrad Aiken: A Life of His Art* (1962) and *The Writings of Henry D. Thoreau* (1971–).

Asking Questions, framed by a 3–4-line border composed of question marks; and on the title page of Howard Robinson's history, *The British Post Office*, which extends over two pages as a cancelled envelope with the title as addressee and the publisher's imprint as the return address. Most were regarded, even by abstemious fellow designers, as delightful and appropriate "grace notes."[118]

Some have argued that the high quality of P. J.'s books was uneconomical, a luxury more suitable to a private press. It is true that his audience for designs at Princeton was "institutional, captive, and conservative" and that his ideals were underwritten by "the patronage of a great university." But he knew, as he taught his friend Julian Boyd, that "cheap printing is a false economy" and "indifference to form" can easily slip into "indifference to substance." Moreover, unlike his predecessor Frederic Warde, he possessed "a practical business understanding one does not often find in an artist," admired the supremely practical Whitney Darrow.[119] When the Press ordered new fonts, P. J. chose them with an eye to readability and stylistic longevity; he developed a house style based on Caslon that still resonates, with computerized variation, today. He also worked with standard paper sizes to reduce costs.[120]

P. J.'s modus operandi did entail some extra expense: he always paid "close personal attention to every detail of a project." Constantly before the transfer of the printing shop to Lawrenceville in 1965 and at least once a week thereafter, he would pop into the shop to hand-set a title-page the way he wanted it or to pull extra proofs until he was satisfied. Bailey sought to curb this practice on economic grounds, but in the end he knew he had to give in to P. J.'s unrivaled judgment and skill. According to the Press's controller, P. J.'s design extras—high-quality gold leaf, two-color title pages, double

[118] John F. Peckham, "P. J.," *Scholarly Publishing* 5:2 (Jan. 1974): 137–43, at 140; Argetsinger, "Harmony Discovered," 241–42; O. J. Rothrock, "P. J. Conkwright. Style & Tradition: Book Designs, 1940–1970," *PULC* 32:2 (Winter 1971): 79–80, at 79; "Take a Bow: P. J. Conkwright," *Publisher's Weekly*, May 21, 1949, 2062–63, at 2063.

[119] Argetsinger, "Harmony Discovered," 245, 247 (quoting Julian Boyd); Darrow, *Princeton University Press*, 40.

[120] Lilly talk; Tenner interview; Peckham, "P. J.," 141; Smith and Bailey, "Some Personal Recollections," 179.

stamping, colored endpapers—were not major cost considerations. In the budget for *each* book, Bailey included two or three "frills" for the designer to use as he or she saw fit. Similarly, *all* PUP books were budgeted for long-lasting, high-quality materials. If P. J.'s designs entailed some added expense, they were felt to be "well worth the cost."[121]

P. J.'s worth was measured in several ways. One was that his distinctive designs and awards gave the Press "an edge in competing with other university presses for the most sought after manuscripts, particularly in the humanities," whose scholarly practitioners put a premium on the physical appearance of their books. P. J.'s personal coordination of the design, composition, and printing arms of the Press also attracted complicated projects in art and archaeology and the presidential papers.[122] His extraordinary skills drew invitations from other presses, university and commercial. He freelanced individual volumes for Rutgers, the University of Kentucky, the State University of New York, Holt, Rinehart and Winston, MIT, Vassar, and Colonial Williamsburg, and designed the collected papers or works of Abraham Lincoln, Louis Brandeis, John Milton, and Charles Francis Adams, in addition to Princeton's own Jefferson and Wilson projects.

P. J. and PUP were a great match. His designs were a signal part of the Press's success, noted Jan Lilly, his closest protégé, and he in turn "was allowed to use his skills to the fullest because of the scholarly success of [the Press's] list." Even if his designs cannot be proven to have sold more books, they enhanced PUP's prestige by demonstrating that the Press cared deeply about its products, physical and intellectual. More than three decades after his retirement, a longtime staff member observes, "PUP still benefits from the lingering reputation for good design and quality of production that he won for us," although the market no longer seems to place as much value on them as it once did.[123]

[121] Argetsinger, "Harmony Discovered," 197, 205–6; Lilly interview; Becker interview, 9.

[122] Becker interview, 9; Lilly interview.

[123] Lilly interview; Creesy interview. Along with Elmer Adler, who came to Princeton at nearly the same time to direct the Graphic Arts division of the university library,

As inflation and the declining market for scholarly monographs put pressures on the finances of the Press in the early 1980s, Bailey was forced to adjust in ways that were not always to his or his staff's liking. To keep nonmanufacturing costs in check while increasing the number of titles published, he asked designer Frank Mahood to develop a "model book" program to cut down on design time.[124] Before computers became standard in the industry, Mahood created four standard templates for the design and layout of books with uncomplicated texts. Special books still received handcrafted artistic treatment, but the rest were allocated fewer "frills" and less costly attention. Simple typographic clarity and high-quality paper and cloth remained standard on all PUP books.[125]

To recruit the best scholarly books, especially those with sales potential and backlist longevity, PUP had to give its "listbuilders" (acquisition editors) greater initiative and autonomy in seeking out, securing, vetting, and preparing the best manuscripts in an increasingly competitive environment. To beat its traditional rivals, especially Harvard, Yale, Chicago, and California, the Press had to offer more advance contracts, bigger advances, and more generous royalties. After the listbuilders had done their jobs in screening and preparing the manuscripts, the editorial board was given fewer proposals and expected to approve at least 90 percent.[126] And to avoid the appear-

---

P. J. raised Princeton's consciousness about good design. He redesigned the university stationery to create uniform letterheads for its departments. He designed the new *Princeton University Library Chronicle* and the masthead for the local newspaper *Town Topics*. He designed countless cards, announcements, stationery, bookplates, pamphlets, and brochures for local citizens and university faculty and staff. Some of his most beautiful work was for books published by the Friends of the Princeton University Library, which often featured colorful decorative paper bindings. Argetsinger, "Harmony Discovered," 191–95; "P. J. Conkwright and the Princeton University Library," *PULC* 32:2 (Winter 1971): 73, illustrations between 78 and 79; Rothrock, "P. J. Conkwright," 79–80; Peckham, "P. J.," 142–43; "Take a Bow," 2063.

[124] "Frank Mahood," *PUProfiles* [a staff-produced newsletter], Dec. 1996, 1–2.

[125] Bailey phone interviews, June 10, 2002, Dec. 23, 2004; Lilly interview. Mahood described the program in *Scholarly Publishing* 5:3 (Apr. 1974): 265–69.

[126] "Minutes of the Editorial Board," Aug. 3, 1982; Memo from Bailey and Sandy Thatcher to Ed. Bd., July 2, 1985: "We must take more risks than in the past, especially with proven authors, and particularly with past PUP authors" (2).

ance of serving as a vanity publisher, the Press reduced the percentage of Princeton-related authors to 10–15 percent, where it remains today.[127] Overall, Bailey expected the Press to maintain a balanced list by filling rough quotas in various fields: about one-third humanities and a quarter history, followed by social sciences and natural sciences (18 percent each) and a handful of poetry (4–6 titles).[128]

When Bailey retired in the summer of 1986, the Press's financial position remained "very strong," although the printing plant was showing signs of inefficiency and underutilization and occasional red ink. And yet the publishing world had changed faster than PUP could or was willing to accommodate. The global economy, production techniques, marketing, scholarly research, and writing itself were all very different from what they were when Bailey began to build PUP's list in math and science forty years earlier. Accordingly, the Press trustees chose a new director for new times.

❁ ❁ ❁

Walter Lippincott, Philadelphia-born, Princeton-educated ('60) opera and soccer aficionado, came to university press publishing after a three-year stint in banking and eleven years at Harper & Row, largely in the College Department. In 1974 he became editorial director of the American branch of Cambridge University Press, where he oversaw the increase of American acquisitions from fewer than twenty to well over a hundred titles a year. Nine years later, he moved to Ithaca as director of Cornell University Press after two years as executive editor in New York City. In 1986 he moved back to Princeton (where his uncle, William Lippincott, had served as the first dean of students) to begin PUP's remodeling.[129] Although he inher-

[127] Between 1975 and 1980, only 79 of 621 PUP books (13 percent) were written by Princeton-associated authors. Smith, "Promoting Education and Scholarship," 16; "Minutes of the PUP Trustees," Mar. 17, 1983, 3; Waldron, "Of Books and the Bottom Line," *PAW*, Oct. 24, 2001, 20.

[128] "Minutes of the Ed. Bd.," Aug. 3, 1982.

[129] *PUProfiles: Walter Lippincott* (Oct. 1997); Waldron, "Of Books and the Bottom Line."

ited a hefty Press endowment, his assignment was difficult and became only more so with time.

Academic presses faced increasingly serious challenges throughout Lippincott's nineteen-year tenure (1986–2005), and PUP's performance was predicated in no small measure on how well he rose to them. The biggest single problem was that the sale of scholarly monographs continued to drop, precipitously, as library orders declined. Library book budgets contracted largely because scholarly journals proliferated and were increasingly produced by large, consolidated, commercial publishers (such as Reed Elsevier in Holland) and sold at prices that rose well above inflation; these costs commandeered a greater proportion of total library budgets.[130] Funds for book purchases also declined as libraries moved heavily into expensive new information technology and digital collections of all sorts. Sporadic national recessions, which adversely affected university budgets, and unfavorable exchange rates abroad, which drove up the libraries' cost of international books, only increased the libraries', and therefore the presses', woes.

Although PUP enjoyed financial independence from its host institution, it had to change to maintain its identity and fundamental mission, as did all of its rivals and counterparts. To the same predicament, university presses offered different solutions. Basic to all was the need to cut costs and to find ways to compensate for the loss of monograph sales, particularly in certain fields, such as literary criticism, British and European history, and the softer social sciences (sociology and anthropology). One opportunity to address the latter problem was provided indirectly by the consolidation of numerous trade houses within a few, often foreign-owned, media conglomer-

[130] In 1997, journals were thirty times more expensive than they were in 1970, an average annual price increase of 13 percent; in the eleven years between 1986 and 1997, the average increase was 15.5 percent a year. In 122 major research libraries, the number of monographs purchased dropped 17 percent between 1986 and 2000; expenditure on serials increased 192 percent. John B. Thompson, *Books in the Digital Age: The Transformation of Academic and Higher Education Publishing in Britain and the United States* (Cambridge, 2005), 99–100, 103–4 (thanks to Brigitta van Rheinberg for an advance copy of the typescript). For a lengthy synopsis of the book, see Thompson, "Survival Strategies for Academic Publishing," *CHE*, June 17, 2005, B6–B9.

ates, such as Bertelsmann and Holtzbrinck. As the smaller houses increasingly sought huge sales from "blockbuster" titles to meet their new owners' expectations and debt obligations, "midlist" titles with better-than-academic sales potential became more available to—and the object of keen competition among—university presses. Another door was opened by the large new bookstore chains—Borders and Barnes and Noble—and later online dealers such as Amazon. Giant stores with space for 100,000 titles needed university press books to help fill their shelves.[131]

To address their common conundrum, academic presses resorted to various combinations of price raising and cost cutting. Between 1986 and 1992 the average price of scholarly monographs—the presses' mainstay—rose 50 percent before leveling off at 16 percent between 1992 and 2000; both figures exceeded the growth of the Consumer Price Index. The prices of backlist titles were also raised regularly to equal the current costs of producing them.[132] Yet university presses were reluctant to go too far in that direction because of their traditional mission of making scholarship available at affordable prices. They preferred to seek ways to trim costs and to increase sales.

From the 1980s, cost cutting took an inventive array of forms. Editing and typesetting went desktop and digital. Production was streamlined and better coordinated, often under one manager. Many functions, particularly copy editing, printing, and binding, were outsourced to reduce overhead. Book-design templates, camera-ready-copy produced on authors' computers, and notch-and-glue rather than Smyth-sewn bindings were resorted to for the same purpose. Authors' royalties were reduced by calculating them on net proceeds rather than list price.

In an effort to boost sales, the presses devised several publishing strategies. They published paperback originals as well as simultane-

[131] Yet when academic titles, despite their colorful new jackets, did not sell as anticipated, the presses were obliged to give full refunds for returned books, which had sold at risky 40–50 percent trade discounts rather than traditional academic discounts of 20–30 percent. As a proportion of sales, returns to university presses constituted 10 percent in 1969 and 22 percent in 2001. Thompson, *Books in the Digital Age*, 170–71.

[132] Thompson, *Books in the Digital Age*, 116–17.

ous cloth and paperback editions, instead of waiting for cloth sales to peak and decline before bringing the title out in paper. Although reluctant to purchase paperbacks, cash-strapped libraries were often forced to buy the cheaper versions, which library wholesalers (such as Yankee Book Peddler) would re-bind for a total cost less than that of the cloth original.[133] Some presses tried to "raise the quality threshold" for the books they accepted by cutting back on unrevised (and even revised) dissertations, canceling some monograph series, and placing informal quotas on the subject areas they published.[134]

In search of greater selectivity, most presses chose two related tactics. One was to broaden the generic mix of books they published. Without reducing in a major way the number of scholarly monographs they produced, they added new kinds of books to their lists: reference, anthologies, regional, professional, midlist trade or "academic-trade," and texts, not for underclass survey courses (which were the monopoly of specialized textbook publishers) but for upperclass and graduate courses. All of these required editing and marketing skills different from those demanded by traditional monographs, and all involved economic and reputational risks. But "mixed portfolios" became vital to the continued support of the presses' scholarly mission.[135]

So, too, did a refocusing of press specialties, away from the "disciplinary catholicism" prompted by the host university's faculty and curriculum. In general, the presses shifted their main attention from the humanities and softer social sciences to math and the natural sciences, the harder social sciences, particularly economics, linguistics, and some areas of philosophy and classics, all of which managed

[133] By 1995 half of the new university press books were in paper. Paperback originals constituted 27 percent of their new books by 2000, when 32 percent were published in cloth and paper simultaneously. Since the resort to paperbacks had the ironic effect of driving down hardback sales still further, many presses began to rethink this particular strategy. Thompson, *Books in the Digital Age*, 118–22.

[134] Thompson, *Books in the Digital Age*, 125–28.

[135] John Thompson pointed to the new publishing paradox: "It is possible to survive as an academic publisher only in so far as you are able and willing to move beyond the field of academic publishing per se and to publish different kinds of books for different kinds of markets" (Thompson, *Books in the Digital Age*, 139; also 169).

to sustain library sales, retain the loyalty of scholars willing to invest in personal libraries, and enjoy robust international sales. The larger presses, such as those of Harvard, Chicago, and Princeton, continued to publish across the disciplinary (and interdisciplinary) spectrum, but even they altered their portfolios to take advantage of new scholarship and new markets.[136]

The heated competition for the best books in the "hottest" fields led to a more active acquisitions process. Acquisition editors now traveled widely to locate and sign books with the greatest intellectual and sales potential. To look out for the latter, sales, marketing, and production personnel were increasingly involved in "preselection screening." Thus, "questions of quality"—which remained central—were "supplemented in myriad ways by considerations of sales potential and financial viability of new book projects." Books with this combination of strengths were sometimes sought abroad. But more often they were nurtured at home by editors who urged academic authors to paint on a broader canvas, to choose better (usually shorter) titles, and to write, without jargon, for intelligent but nonspecialized readers.[137]

The challenges of the last two decades were not met successfully by every university press and a few were forced to close their doors. But PUP under Lippincott responded with ingenuity and energy to retain its position among the six largest and best university presses in the country, a place it had held for more than four decades. Although Lippincott sometimes gave the impression that he had taken PUP in a brave new direction, toward New York's serious trade houses such as W. W. Norton, John Wiley, and Penguin, he kept the Press very much on its scholarly course while making a number of occasionally unsettling changes in its organization and culture. He could not duplicate the policies or styles of his predecessors in the rough new environment, but he was successful in responding to the formidable challenges posed by the publishing world as he assumed the direction of the Press in 1986.

[136] Thompson, *Books in the Digital Age*, 129–30.

[137] Thompson, *Books in the Digital Age*, 133–38, at 136, 137.

Having watched print runs and sales of scholarly monographs decline to fewer than eight hundred copies and megastores decline to carry them as they initially had, Lippincott sought to make PUP more competitive.[138] His personal pleasure, he said, came not from bookmaking per se but from the competitive "game of publishing," of acquiring manuscripts from "very smart and interesting people"—"the best and the brightest" in their fields—and of forecasting who would be the best in the future."[139] The prizes sought were less awards for book design and traditional scholarship, though these continued to be important, but for capturing the biggest names in academe whose books had the potential to become "mid list" or even best-sellers and to produce relatively sudden paradigm shifts in their disciplines.

This shift in emphasis also put a premium on individual titles rather than long-term, multivolume works. Largely because he inherited them and they more than paid their way, Lippincott continued the Bollingen series and the Jefferson and Einstein papers projects. The sole complex project undertaken by the Press during his tenure was the *Barrington Atlas of the Greek and Roman World* (2000), a magnificent companion to and correction of the *Princeton Encyclopedia of Classical Sites* (1976). Costing $4.5 million (of which the Press itself contributed $350,000), the atlas was produced in twelve years by editor Richard J. A. Talbert, more than seventy scholars, and as many consultants around the world. The first printing of six thousand copies quickly sold out even with a $325 price tag.[140]

[138] "Minutes of the PUP Trustees," Oct. 18, 1988, 2; Sept. 11, 2003, 5.

[139] Lippincott interview; Lippincott e-mail, June 23, 2004; *PUProfiles: Lippincott*; e-mail interview with Michael P. Burton, Dec. 8, 2002, 11; Creesy interview.

[140] "Minutes of the PUP Trustees," Mar. 23, 2000, 3; Lippincott interview; *A Century in Books*, 245–46. The eight-volume *Complete Works of W. H. Auden*, conceived and edited by Auden's literary executor Edward Mendelson (1988—) was not particularly complicated to produce; by the end of 2004, only four volumes had been published. By the same token, Bruce Redford's five-volume *The Letters of Samuel Johnson* (1992) was initiated and generously underwritten by Mary Hyde Eccles, the owner of many of the letters. Beautifully designed by Mark Argetsinger, it was printed at the Stinehour Press in Lunenburg, Vermont. Characteristically, it was begun during Bailey's tenure.

The thrust of Lippincott's Press was expansion through contraction. Ironically, one of his first acts was to purchase a new printing press for the Lawrenceville plant. Another was to consolidate the copyediting, design, and production departments under one manager, the better to regulate the workflow in the publishing division. In order to obtain services at more competitive prices, some were outsourced to freelancers or to specialized suppliers. The in-house copyediting staff was disbanded, the small reference library was sold off, and the model book program was expanded to include virtually all books, which desktop computers and sophisticated graphics software made possible and financially desirable. The biggest cost-saving came in 1993 from the sale of the printing plant and three years later of the Lawrenceville administration building and its land. This was preceded in 1990 by the severing of eighty-five-year-old ties with the *Princeton Alumni Weekly*, which became independent and moved to a Nassau Street office building. All of these decisions were calculated to focus PUP's energy on the publishing of books, not on printing which had once subsidized many of its books. The lucrative sale of PUP's only remaining journal, *Philosophy & Public Affairs*, to Blackwell's in 2003 further concentrated the book-production mission of the Press.[141]

The expansion made possible by these contractions took several forms, beyond the extension and renovation of the Scribner Building in 2001. The first was a steady increase in new titles to more than two hundred by the mid-1990s. Another was a subsequent 50-percent rise in sales revenue, from $12 million to $18.7 million at the end of fiscal year 2004, even with a slight decrease in titles. This resulted from backlist price increases, greater attention to marketing and publicity around the world, and a noticeable shift in the Press's publishing profile. Specialized monographs in some areas of the humanities, history, and area and regional studies (Latin America, Asia,

[141] Waldron, "Of Books and the Bottom Line;" Lippincott, "Princeton University Press: Recent History" (draft, May 2004), 1–2; Becker interview, 12; "Minutes of the PUP Trustees," Mar. 27, 2003, 5. A few presses, particularly those of the University of Chicago and Johns Hopkins, took on more journals to achieve economies of scale and specialization.

and the Middle East), which now sold in minuscule numbers, were scaled back to make room for titles written mostly by senior scholars in fields with large international markets, such as math, economics, finance, and science, and vendible at high prices. Religion and Jewish studies, two of the university's strengths, were given new attention. In part because of former university president William Bowen, the Press became the publisher of a distinguished series of books on higher education sponsored by the Andrew F. Mellon Foundation, of which Bowen was the presiding officer and the co-author of four of its best-selling, attention-getting studies.[142]

Art was another promising field for prestige and profit, and PUP entered it heavily in the 1990s, publishing glossy museum catalogues as well as monographs. But Yale's lead in the field could not be overtaken and Princeton cut back in 2003, happy to save the high costs and trouble of obtaining permissions for illustrations.[143] With more success PUP went after popular science, for which television often generated large audiences. Sir David Attenborough's *The Private Life of Plants* (1995) and *The Life of Birds* (1998), both acquired from England where they were best-sellers, sold over thirty thousand copies each in the United States after national book tours and atypical publicity campaigns.[144] Rather than radical departures, these books were simply the latest additions to a long line of bird books and field guides begun by bird-watcher Bailey. Books in popular—and midlevel—science also complemented PUP's long lists of professional and scholarly titles in math and the natural sciences.

To attract more international authors in the new fields of emphasis, the Press opened a small English branch in Woodstock near

[142] William G. Bowen and Neil L. Rudenstine, *In Pursuit of the PhD* (1992); Bowen and Derek Bok, *The Shape of the River: Long-Term Consequences of Considering Race in College and University Admissions* (1998); James L. Shulman and Bowen, *The Game of Life: College Sports and Educational Values* (2001); Bowen and Sarah A. Levin, *Reclaiming the Game: College Sports and Educational Values* (2003).

[143] Waldron, "Of Books and the Bottom Line," 19; Lippincott interview; Lippincott, "PUP: Recent History," 2. Lippincott has now published fuller "Reflections on the Occasion of the Centenary" in *Princeton University Press, 1905–2005* (Princeton, 2005), 43–70.

[144] "Minutes of the PUP Trustees," Sept. 14, 1995; Dec. 15, 1995, 5; Mar. 30, 1999.

Oxford in 1999. This was meant to recruit, publicize, and market PUP books in Europe and the United Kingdom, as well as to compete with Yale, the only other American university press with an English branch. One of the most successful books signed in England, Elroy Dimson's *The Triumph of the Optimists: 101 Years of Global Investment Returns* (2002), sold six thousand copies in its first six weeks at $99.50 apiece.[145] Back home, cooperation rather than competition fueled the creation in 1992 of a fulfillment service with the University of California Press in Ewing, New Jersey. After three years of losses, the facility became profitable and further reduced the Press's costs for its essential publishing services.[146]

Desktop publishing, which PUP was among the first to introduce after taking lessons in the early 1980s from the trend-setting *Alumni Weekly* down the hall, was also calculated to save money and to accelerate production schedules. It did both, but only after a number of false starts and widely shared failures to anticipate developments in the rapidly changing world of computers, digital typesetting, and the Internet. Relative compatibility in operating systems and global connectivity has now tamed the wildcat frontier of piecemeal innovations, but waves of the technological future too often subsided into mere puddles of misplaced investment and optimism.[147]

Much more promising was an extensive online catalogue of PUP books, with tables of contents, cover images, sample chapters, and reviewers' quotes. At the end of 2004 over three hundred titles were available as E-books for purchase and downloading through Amazon.com; 650 in- and out-of-print titles were available through an on-demand printing service, whose ability to produce a small number of bound copies obviated the Press's need to reprint larger numbers or to maintain expensive (and taxable) inventory. Having so many books available digitally also allowed PUP to sell its titles easily to large databases or "content aggregators," who largely serviced college and university libraries. The hope was that exposure to numer-

[145] "Minutes of the PUP Trustees," Mar. 30, 1999; Dec. 15, 1999; Lippincott interview.

[146] Lippincott interview; Lippincott, telephone interview, Jan. 14, 2005.

[147] Just as the industry's enthusiasm for CD-ROMs crested and broke, PUP invested $200,000 in one for the ever-popular *I Ching*; today the technology to run it is nearly obsolete. "Minutes of the PUP Trustees," Dec. 15, 1995, 2; Mar. 28, 1996, 4.

ous Press titles online would lead to increased sales of its other titles, in digital and printed form.[148]

For all its organizational and operational changes, Princeton remained one of the university presses most committed to scholarly quality and to the scholarly monograph. It maintained its traditional commitment to monographs by subsidizing the least saleable of them with endowment proceeds and with the robust sales of other kinds of scholarly books in its newly mixed portfolio. By choosing manuscripts with potential to change the conversation or direction of their fields, PUP's editors frequently discovered books that sold extremely well. Robert Putnam's *Making Democracy Work* (1993), a study of twentieth-century Italian politics, became an unlikely paradigm-shifter and paperback best-seller. *Neighbors* (2001), Jan Gross's sobering analysis of why one half of a Polish village exterminated the other during World War II, sold 22,000 copies by early 2005 and drew much media attention at home and abroad. For economist Robert Shiller's *Irrational Exuberance* (2000), timing was (almost) everything. The book appeared just before the technology bubble burst and the overheated stock market slid awkwardly into recession. By the time PUP sold the paperback rights to a New York firm for a very large sum, it had sold 50,000 cloth copies. Former Harvard president Derek Bok and Princeton's ex, William Bowen, wrote *The Shape of the River* (1998) to reshape the American debate on affirmative action and they did just that, selling nearly 30,000 copies in the process by early 2005. And when Princeton philosopher-emeritus Harry G. Frankfurt's 67-page treatise *On Bullshit* (2005) landed at the top of the *New York Times* best-seller list, the Press was as surprised as the author.[149]

The quality of PUP's list can also be judged by the awards its titles have won for best scholarly or professional books at the annual conferences of the Association of American Publishers. In the judgment of expert eight-person committees consisting of scholars, li-

[148] *PUProfiles: Chuck Creesy . . . In His Own Words* (Jan. 1999), 1–3; Creesy and Adam Fortgang, "The History of Electronic Publishing at PUP" (draft essay, 2004); Creesy, "The Use of Technology at PUP" (draft essay, 2004).

[149] Jim Holt, "A Critic at Large: Say Anything," *New Yorker*, Aug. 22, 2005, 69–70, 73–75.

brarians, and working publishers who were once academics, Princeton walked away with 28 first prizes and 16 honorable mentions in the first five years of the new millennium; the closest runner-up was much larger and more diverse Oxford University Press, with only 23 firsts and 21 honorable mentions. In the 2004 competition, perhaps the most apropos PUP winner was Gérard Liger-Belair's *Uncorked: The Science of Champagne* in the Physics and Astronomy category. More typical of Princeton and Press scholarship was the 2003 winner in the Philosophy division, *Philosophical Analysis in the Twentieth Century*, a two-volume opus by Princeton philosopher Scott Soames.[150]

The guardians and guarantors of the Press's quality were the acquisition editors and the editorial board, which was expanded from four to five rotating members in 1987. Many of the new editors were armed with Ph.D.s and a broad knowledge of the disciplines for which they were responsible, from promising graduate students to gray eminences. When Bailey stepped down, there were four listbuilders in the humanities, two in the sciences, and two in the social sciences; on the eve of Lippincott's departure, the lineup was twelve (including two in England): three in the humanities, one in history, one in reference, three in math and science, and four in the social sciences (two-plus in economics alone).[151] Not content to wait for manuscripts to come over the transom, they traveled regularly, visiting universities and attending scholarly conferences from coast to coast.

The acquisition editors also worked more closely than ever before with the editorial board, particularly during the pre-selection process. Before rendering a final judgment, board members were frequently called upon to help the editors mold and secure revisions of promising submissions, especially from junior scholars. They still rejected proposals, but they were now more likely to demand additional readers' reports to clarify some of their misgivings. For their services, each member received a modest honorarium for each of the

[150] The awards are posted on the AAP's Web site (http://www.aap.org) and were published in the *Chronicle of Higher Education*, Mar. 25, 2005, A7. In the 2004 competition, Harry Frankfurt's *The Reasons of Love* won in the Philosophy division, just as his 1986 article "On Bullshit" was becoming an improbable best-seller in book form.

[151] Lippincott, "PUP: Recent History," 2; PUP Website (http://www.pupress.princeton.edu): Staff (July 1, 2004).

monthly board meetings he or she attended and, perhaps more fitting and welcome, a liberal selection of Press books, the true coin of the scholarly realm.[152]

It may be some time before Lippincott's Press can be fairly and fully evaluated. But its strengths are discernible even at close range. PUP remains one of the best university presses in the country. It still enjoys the largest endowment of any American university press, which enables it to take publishing risks that leaner presses cannot afford. Its books continue to win scholarly awards in abundance and to draw substantially more reviews in the national and scholarly press than in the past.[153] And the Press carries the university's name into more of the world's bookstores, libraries, and studies than ever before, bringing the university recognition comparable to that garnered by Einstein's posthumous fame and by the international alumni of the Graduate School.

Of course, PUP's response to the uncertainties of the new publishing climate will likely entail some costs it cannot foresee. Under Lippincott, one cost was staff turnover, which was high and may have signaled a loss of loyalty and longevity of experience. Some was due to the hard-driving atmosphere that supplanted Bailey's more familial ambience, some to the developed excellence of staff who were lured away by rival presses.[154] Book designers were among the first to leave. Long before the design department lost its autonomy, some of the most creative designers left when their skills were underused in the model book program and they were forced largely to

[152] In the early 1980s, editorial board members were handed "two new twenty dollar bills at the beginning of each meeting" (Kernan, *In Plato's Cave*, 234). In 1995, perhaps chafing under the new acquisition procedures, board member and former dean of the Graduate School Theodore Ziolkowski waxed nostalgic for the board's former mandate, which he said (with some exaggeration) was to cut one-third to one-half of the books proposed. "Minutes of the Ed. Bd.," Sept. 14, 1995, 7–8.

[153] In 2002 PUP books won 49 prizes and awards, up from just 16 and 15 in the previous two years; trackable reviews were up 54 percent. The April 10, 2003, edition of the *New York Review of Books* contained a full-page ad listing the year's award-winning books and authors. "Minutes of the PUP Trustees," Mar. 27, 2003, 6; June 5, 2003, 4.

[154] In a report to the trustees, Lippincott explained the turnover as the benign result of the Press's operation as "an incubator system, taking bright young people, training them, and creating a group of desirable editors who are attractive to other presses" ("Minutes of the PUP Trustees," Sept. 14, 2000, 4).

produce multicolored jackets to catch the eye of megastore browsers and paperback buyers. PUP's desktop-designed books are as serviceable, durable, and clear as any in the business, but the short time in which they must be designed often results in little to distinguish them from its rivals' books or to capture the eye and heart.[155]

❁ ❁ ❁

For most of the past century, PUP has sought to contribute to the reputation of its parent university in the learned world. It has done so almost exclusively by sending into that world "roving ambassadors of the University, with the single word 'Princeton' branded on their spines." How well they represented the university abroad is important to know but nearly impossible to determine, particularly over the course of a century. It may be enough to realize that it is "the *cumulative* effect of a publishing program" that contributes to "how well the parent university is thought of in general." By that measure, Princeton in the twenty-first century has undoubtedly had its "membership in the guild of great universities" confirmed by PUP's powerful products and productivity. In that select company, Princeton without a press was and is virtually "unthinkable," thanks to Charles Scribner, Whitney Darrow, and their successors.[156]

[155] E-mail interviews with Mark Argetsinger, May 15, 2002, June 3, 2002; Lilly interview; Oberfranc interview; Burton interview, 10.

[156] [Davies], "Princeton University Press," 12; Morris Philipson (then director of the University of Chicago Press), "American Chronicle: What Is a University Press Worth?" *Encounter* 40:5 (May 1973): 41–49, at 44 (my emphasis); John V. Lombardi (then president of the University of Florida), "Elegant Artefact or Auxiliary Enterprise: Universities' Presses," *Scholarly Publishing* 27:2 (Jan. 1992): 67–76, at 70, 72. Lippincott's successor, Peter J. Dougherty, was social sciences editor at the Press for thirteen years. Before that he had learned the trade for twenty years at six other (mostly trade) presses. Like Bailey, he has published numerous articles on economics and publishing and a well-received book, *Who's Afraid of Adam Smith* (New York, 2002). Richard Byrne, "Princeton U. Press Names New Director, Who Says Remaining Scholarly Is His Top Goal," *CHE* (online), Mar. 28, 2005; Ruth Stevens, "Dougherty Selected as Director of Princeton University Press," PU, press release, Mar. 24, 2005.

CONCLUSION

She Flourishes

This university simply wouldn't be what it is,
or work as it does, if its history were different.

—William G. Bowen

Princeton's assumption of university name and status in 1896 seemed to some an arrogation of honors rather than just desserts. Despite Wilson's restless ambition to make Princeton one of the nation's best, the recently crystallized features of a university were lacking as late as 1910, as Edwin Slosson acknowledged even as he included the college in his anthology, *Great American Universities.*[1] Princeton did not belong among the foremost American universities, the Chicago Ph.D. admitted, if the criteria were "age, size, wealth, cosmopolitanism, publications, graduate students, professional courses, or public services." Yet Slosson could not omit Princeton, any more than the founding presidents of the elite Association of American Universities could in 1900, because of its colonial heritage, collegiate mystique, and socially prominent clientele. The best he could say for it was that "if it is not a university now, it is going to become one in the fullest sense of the word."[2] For other skeptics, the question was when.

Their doubts were not unfounded. In 1907 Henry S. Pritchett, the head of the influential Carnegie Foundation for the Advancement of Teaching, got under Wilson's skin by telling him frankly that although Princeton was "the greatest American college," it did not deserve the university name because its graduate program was simply not comparable to the more German-inspired graduate schools of

[1] Laurence R. Veysey, *The Emergence of the American University* (Chicago, 1965).

[2] Edwin E. Slosson, *Great American Universities* (New York, 1910), 104–5.

authentic universities such as Johns Hopkins.[3] Wilson may have been particularly sensitive on the point because more public skepticism had appeared in the widely read *Saturday Evening Post* three months before. In a series entitled "Which College for the Boy?" Princeton-admirer John Corbin (or his editor) described Princeton as a "Collegiate University." Lamenting that Princeton had "wrought confusion . . . when it changed its ancient title of college for that of university," Corbin was chagrinned that "once Princeton stood as the foremost of our collegiate institutions. . . . Now, in name if not in fact, it is one of the least considerable of our universities. In any real sense of the word it is not a university, and it is not likely to become one."[4]

Similar doubts emerged even locally, not only from old-time faculty threatened by Wilson's academic upgrading. In 1947 William Warner Bishop, a key Princeton librarian during Wilson's presidency and later president of the American Library Association, remembered that "Princeton in 1902 was essentially an American liberal arts college." It had "no law school, no medical school, [and] few professional faculties or students." The Graduate School, established only in 1900, was "rather slow in developing." In fact, he concluded after World War II, Princeton was "a university chiefly in name, the principal emphasis still being placed on undergraduate teaching"—"a man's college only."[5] A sympathetic graduate of Wilson's era was equally disappointed. Just before America entered the war, Norman S. Mackie '09 regretted that "Wilson promised Princeton a great future which has not been realized."[6]

Although skeptics had some cause to doubt Princeton's bona fides as a university, they were all, with the partial exception of librarian Bishop, outsiders, nonacademics whose concept of a university was patterned after larger, more complex institutions, such as Harvard, Columbia, and the state universities of the Midwest and West. They

[3] WW to Pritchett, Nov. 27, 1907, *PWW*, 17:527; see also 17:545.

[4] John Corbin, "Which College for the Boy? Princeton: The Collegiate University," *Saturday Evening Post*, Aug. 17, 1907, 6–7, 23, at 6.

[5] William Warner Bishop, "Reminiscences of Princeton: 1902–7," *PULC* 8:4 (June 1947): 147–63, at 149.

[6] Bragdon interview with Mackie, Feb. 21, 1940, box 63, folder 7, p. 2, WWC.

expected to see big graduate and professional schools attracting large numbers of postgraduate students, perhaps equaling or outnumbering the undergraduates, in pursuit of specialized degrees for specific jobs and careers. When they didn't see in Wilson's Princeton what they and most Americans imagined a university to be, they found it—and him—wanting.

But those close to Wilson, particularly his faculty, understood better what he intended to do and how different the university he sought to build was even from his own graduate alma mater, Johns Hopkins. They knew not only that "Wilson *made* Princeton" into "one of the strongest universities in the country," as his dean of the faculty Henry Fine insisted in 1925, but that "all the developments since, except the Graduate College, have been based upon foundations Wilson laid," as English professor Thomas Marc Parrott argued in 1942. Historian Arthur Link, Wilson's biographer and the indefatigable editor of his papers, went even further in a flush of understandable hyperbole. In 1986 he told an interviewer that modern Princeton "reflects Wilson almost perfectly. . . . Everything he stood for is being vindicated and realized. . . . He seemingly lost some big battles. . . . But he has won 'in the fullness of time' . . . because those ideas, though buried, stayed alive in the institutional memory."[7]

What these faculty members understood was that the Princeton Wilson made and sought to make was a university of a special kind, which had not appeared on the American scene, as Slosson noted, and has yet to be fully duplicated, despite numerous admirers and would-be imitators. Wilson wanted Princeton to be modestly sized, devoted primarily to face-to-face undergraduate teaching, grounded in the liberal arts and sciences, and intellectually powerful; but above all else, he wanted it to be *distinctive*. "Princeton is not like Harvard," he told a Harvard audience, "and she does not wish to be." To alumni audiences he preached that "Princeton is noticeable because of her

[7] Baker interview with Henry B. Fine, June 18, 1925, Baker Papers, container 105, reel 74; Bragdon interview with Thomas Marc Parrott, Sept. 15, 1942, box 63, folder 25, WWC; interview with Arthur S. Link, in William McCleery, *Conversations on the Character of Princeton* (Princeton, 1986, 1990), 77.

individuality, because she stands for something different."[8] He reassured them that "we can afford to be one of the lesser universities in number if we are one of the foremost in power and quality." And by power he meant *intellectual* power as manifested in "scholarship—broad, luminous, thorough, catholic, masterful scholarship."[9]

Although he regarded his message as an "utter commonplace of the history of education," he worked hard to convince Princeton's alumni from an earlier, collegiate era that a modern university "has as its only legitimate object intellectual attainment." He coveted "all the glory there is for Princeton," he said, but the glory he sought was "intellectual distinction and intellectual primacy in the country."[10] To those who still believed that colleges should breed character, he stressed that study was the direct "object" and character only the indirect "result." This was a difficult message to swallow for Princetonians who had attended or taught in President Patton's Protestant "country club." But Wilson hammered away at the theme throughout his presidency and put his major efforts into building a faculty and a student body for whom scholarship was their "chief duty" and their "chief glory."[11]

Princeton today, as Wilson would be quick to recognize, is quite different from the university he left in 1910. It is considerably larger, better financed, more heterogeneous in its social makeup, more athletic, more variegated in its architecture, stronger in the sciences and engineering, more research-oriented, more interdisciplinary, more *serious*. In these aspects it resembles most American research univer-

[8] WW, Address at Harvard University, June 26, 1907, *PWW*, 17:226–28, at 227; WW, Address to Princeton Alumni in Washington, D.C., Mar. 27, 1903, *PWW*, 14:400–403, at 402.

[9] WW, Address to Princeton Alumni of Western Pennsylvania, Pittsburgh, Mar. 7, 1903, *PWW*, 14:383, 385–86, at 385; WW, Address at Opening Exercises, PU, Sept. 17, 1902, *PWW*, 14:132.

[10] WW, Address to the Western Association of Princeton Clubs, Pittsburgh, May 2, 1908, *PWW*, 18:280–85, at 284; WW, Address to the Princeton Club of Chicago, Mar. 12, 1908, *PWW*, 18:17–34, at 20; WW, Address to the Western Assoc. of Princeton Clubs, Cleveland, May 19, 1906, *PWW*, 16:406–11, at 408; *PWW*, 18:20 (Mar. 12, 1908).

[11] WW, "The Training of Intellect," Address to Yale Phi Beta Kappa, Mar. 18, 1908, *PWW*, 18:55–59, at 55; *PWW*, 14:132 (Sept. 18, 1902).

sities. But Wilson would also want to know if Princeton, after all its many changes, was still *distinctive*. What, if anything, distinguishes Princeton from the other top one hundred research universities in the country, from Stanford, Michigan, and MIT, but particularly from its Big Three rivals, Harvard and Yale? Some of our best testimony comes from forty faculty and administrators and one coach who were interviewed about Princeton's "character" by William McCleery in 1986. Most had attended or taught at other elite universities, which tempered their local chauvinism. What they had to say about Princeton's distinguishing features supports the evidence presented in the previous chapters.[12]

Compared to most of its peers, Princeton is still by choice quite small, a face-to-face community located on a beautiful, tree-filled campus in an exurban colonial town. Its fewer than seven thousand students are taught and mentored by a faculty of over eleven hundred, giving it a 5:1 student-faculty ratio (in full-time equivalents), one of the lowest in the nation.[13] This low ratio stems directly from Princeton's philosophy of maintaining close personal contact between teachers and learners, and not only in innumerable Wilson-inspired precepts and seminars. The four-course plan, with its demanding (of both students and faculty) junior papers and senior theses, and comprehensive exams were, as Professor of English Charles G. Osgood emphasized on the eve of World War II, "natural results" of the preceptorial system, Wilson's reorganization of the curriculum, and "the personal efforts of men whom Wilson brought to Princeton or advanced."[14]

Such a system of close faculty-student contact requires not only a faculty unusually devoted to teaching but extraordinary resources. "Let's face it," Professor of Politics Alpheus Mason half-boasted, "The Princeton method is damned expensive!" As a private university with limited ability to raise tuition and other fees (and no univer-

[12] McCleery, *Conversations*.

[13] PU, *Profile 2004–05* (Princeton, 2004), 2, 4.

[14] McCleery, *Conversations*, 22, 83; Bragdon interview with Osgood, Apr. 14, 1939, box 63, folder 24, WWC; also Bragdon interview with professor of Greek William Kelly Prentice, June 6, 1939, box 63, folder 31, WWC.

sity charges its students anything like the full cost of their education), Princeton has to rely largely on its endowment and other forms of alumni generosity to fuel its educational fires. At the end of 2005, Princeton's endowment of more than $11 billion was the nation's fourth largest, behind Harvard, Yale, and the whole Texas system. But each Princeton student had over $1.6 million of endowment behind him or her, by far the biggest bankroll in the country. The major cause of Princeton's good fortune was the loyalty and open (and often deep) pockets of its now coeducated alumni. Annual giving provided about 10 percent of the university's education and general budget, and traditionally over 60 percent of Princeton's former undergraduates contribute, the highest rate in the country.[15] The rest of the university's economic cushion was provided by Princeton's prudently aggressive money managers, who had earned over 14 percent on investments since 1976, better than their Harvard and Yale competitors.[16] It did not hurt that two of the last three Princeton presidents were astute economists with extensive experience in university finance, William Bowen as Princeton's provost and Harold Shapiro as president of the University of Michigan.

Princeton's ample resources allowed the university to go first-class virtually across the board, a luxury Wilson was never able to afford. Admissions continued to be need-blind, enabling the university to select the nation's best students without regard to their ability to pay. A new financial-aid policy in 1998, resulting from the extraordinarily successful campaign for the 250th anniversary, replaced loans for

[15] McCleery, *Conversations*, 86; PU, *Profile 2003–04*, 29–30; *CHE Almanac Issue 2004–05*, Aug. 26, 2004, 26–27. During the 1981–1986 campaign, which raised over $410 million, "the largest campaign per capita in the history of American higher education," 74 percent of the undergraduate alumni contributed either to the capital fund or annually; in the 250th campaign, which raised $1.14 billion, 78 percent did. William McCleery, *The Story of A Campaign for Princeton, 1981–1986* (Princeton, 1987), vii; *PAW*, Sept. 11, 1996, 12; Sept. 13, 2000, 2; *U.S. News & World Report*, Sept. 16, 1996, 111.

[16] PU, *Profile 2003–04*, 29; Brian Henn, "Endowment Increases by $400 Million," *DP* (online), Sept. 25, 2003. Princeton's rate of return over the ten years before 2004 was 14.3 percent, third behind Yale's 16 percent and Harvard's 14.7 percent. Stephanie Strom, "Some Alumni Balk Over Harvard's Pay To Money Managers," *New York Times*, June 4, 2004, A1, A20.

lower-income students with outright grants and reduced the amount they, middle-income students, and their families were expected to contribute. Three years later, Princeton increased the pressure on its elite competitors by offering grants instead of loans to all students, thus providing greater economic as well as racial and ethnic diversity in the student experience.[17] Faculty salaries stayed highly competitive with those of its chief rivals in more expensive settings, and newly endowed chairs in abundance upped the ante. Princeton was also able to build first-class laboratories, such as the postmodern Thomas Laboratory for molecular biology, and to expand its rich library and art museum, largely on the proceeds of the special campaign of 1981–1986.[18] Likewise, for the 250th anniversary, the family of aerospace pioneer James S. McDonnell '21 gave $8 million toward a state-of-the-art building for the teaching of physics, and Chinese developer Gordon Wu '58 committed $100 million to revitalize the School of Engineering and Applied Science and to improve the Graduate College. Philanthropic emulators soon provided funds for a long-delayed campus center, a social sciences building, a gleaming glass teaching center and library for engineering, a bold new science library designed by Frank Gehry, a new interdisciplinary lab for molecular genetics, a new football stadium and track, a music library in a renovated music center, a new center for Jewish life, a humanities center incorporating a renovated Chancellor Green Library, and a new modified-Gothic residential college to house undergraduates from all four classes—the belated downpayment on Wilson's original quad plan.[19]

[17] Ben Gose, "Princeton Plans Major Increase in Aid for Middle- and Low-Income Students, " *CHE*, Jan. 30, 1998, A35–36; Andrew Brownstein, "Upping the Ante for Student Aid," *CHE*, Feb. 16, 2001, A47–49; Pamela Burdman '84, "Dollars and Sense," *PAW*, Apr. 23, 2003, 16–17.

[18] In 2004–2005, full professors at Princeton were the third-highest paid in the country, behind those at Harvard and tiny Rockefeller University, both top-heavy with better paid professional-school faculty. Salaries for Princeton's associate and assistant professors were somewhat less competitive. Charlie Stone, "Professors' Salaries Third Highest in Nation," *DP* (online), Apr. 27, 2005. The 1981–1986 campaign endowed thirty-eight new professorships and twelve preceptorships. McCleery, *Story of A Campaign*, 118–20.

[19] *Princeton: With One Accord*, Summer 1996, 1, 6; Winter 1996, 1, 6, 7; Summer 1997, 1, 7; Fall 1997, 1, 6, 7; Summer 1998, 1, 7; Winter 1998, 1; Fall 1999, 1, 3; Winter 2002, 1,

After midcentury, Princeton's unusual wealth, actual and potential, could have allowed it to add one or more traditional professional schools (a law school was frequently mentioned). Instead, the university remained true to Wilson's philosophy of selective excellence by maintaining only three somewhat unconventional offshoots in engineering and applied science, architecture, and public and international affairs. The last two together enroll only 250, or less than 13 percent of all Princeton graduate students; graduate engineers number well under 500. Together with those of the Graduate School in arts and sciences, their numbers constitute only 43 percent of the undergraduate enrollment, minuscule by rivals' standards. In keeping with Princeton's long-standing focus on undergraduate education, the architecture and engineering schools have as many or more undergraduate majors, as did the Woodrow Wilson School until recently.[20]

Princeton is also unusual in being what former dean and provost J. Douglas Brown called a "liberal university," which has graduate programs only in the liberal arts and sciences and in professional fields that lean heavily on the arts and sciences. And by choice, its professional schools all emphasize the practical value of theory over the theoretical value of practice. According to former dean Robert Jahn, Princeton offers "surely the most *liberal* engineering education one can find." About half of its BSEs "don't go into professional engineering careers, but into medicine, law, business, and other sectors."[21] Scientist Robert May, former chairman of the powerful University Research Board, acknowledged that "Princeton has been especially drawn to theoretical research through the years, partly

---

7; Spring 2002, 1, 3; Fred Bernstein '77, "One Campus, Different Faces," *PAW*, Dec. 18, 2002, 10–14; Brian Henn, "Genomics Institute Opens to Bridge Scientific Community," *DP* (online), May 9, 2003.

[20] PU, *Profile 2003–04*, 7, 18, 21, 23. In 2003–2004, graduate and professional students greatly outnumbered undergraduates at Yale, Harvard, Chicago, Pennsylvania, Stanford, and MIT in percentages ranging from 115 percent at Yale to 209 percent at Chicago. *Barron's Profiles of American Colleges 2005*, 26th ed. (Hauppauge, N.Y., 2004), 363, 418, 562, 762, 768, 1328.

[21] McCleery, *Conversations*, 50–54.

because of its size: You don't need large groups of people or large pieces of machinery or a large and costly administrative infrastructure to support theoretical research."[22]

One large token of the university's belief in the long-range efficacy of theory and basic science is the federally funded Princeton Plasma Physics Laboratory, the largest center for the development of fusion energy in the hemisphere. In operation on the university's James Forrestal Campus since 1951, its giant Tokamak reactor had produced world-record levels of fusion power, though few immediate applications, before it was replaced in 1999 by a smaller, more efficient model. Its 400-plus employees collaborate with university faculty and graduate students to make both theoretical and empirical advances.[23]

The university's penchant for theoretical research also draws support from the Institute for Advanced Study, founded in 1930 on land near the campus. The Institute was and is the home of some of the most brilliant mathematicians and theoretical physicists in the world, Einstein being only the most recognizable. Although it accommodates advanced scholars, permanent and visiting, in the natural sciences, historical studies, and social sciences, its lack of laboratories reinforces its preference for intellectual work that requires only computers and blackboards. Some Princeton faculty enjoy multiyear, half-time appointments at the Institute, and Institute faculty often teach graduate or undergraduate courses at the university, albeit "surreptitiously" (as art historian Erwin Panofsky quipped).[24] The Insti-

[22] McCleery, *Conversations*, 95.

[23] PU, *Profile 2003–04*, 27; Don Oberdorfer, *Princeton University: The First 250 Years* (Princeton, 1995), 167–71; Ken Howard, "PPPL Dedicates NSTX," *PWB*, Mar. 8, 1999, 1; J. I. Merritt '66, *Princeton's James Forrestal Campus: Fifty Years of Sponsored Research* (Princeton: PU, 2002), 60–61; Steven Schultz, "Abraham: U.S. Participation in International Fusion Effort Builds on Success at PPPL," *PWB* (online), Feb. 19, 2003. In 2004 the PPPL was chosen as the U.S. project office for a $5 billion international fusion experiment to be built in France or Japan. The ITER test reactor will draw on PPPL's reputation for the "highest-quality science and top-flight management" ("PPPL to Host Office for New Reactor," *Princeton Packet*, Aug. 6, 2004 7A).

[24] Panofsky said that the Institute's unusual reputation stemmed from the fact that "its members do their research work openly and their teaching surreptitiously" (Erwin

tute's 150 visiting scholars annually add a rich layer to the local community of intellect, as do the students and faculty of the Princeton Theological Seminary (1812) and the research staffs of several high-tech and biotech companies that surround Princeton.[25]

Much of Princeton's distinctiveness is owed to several other academic features. Since its opening in 1948, Firestone Library has been one of the most user-friendly and adaptable university libraries in the country. With fully open stacks, locked carrels for nearly every senior thesis-writer in the humanities and social sciences, and vast holdings with departmental seminar rooms, offices, and study spaces interspersed in the appropriate collections, it was perfectly designed to reflect Princeton's educational philosophy of self-discovery and to promote scholarship at every academic level, from freshman paper to *magnum* faculty *opus*. Likewise, the Art Museum has been one of the most teaching-oriented university museums since the nineteenth century. Its extensive collections, frequent exhibitions, numerous storage-area precept rooms, and now digital study collections—to-

---

Panofsky, "Three Decades of Art History in the United States: Impressions of a Transplanted European," in *Meaning in the Visual Arts: Papers in and on Art History* [Garden City, N.Y., 1955], 322). See also Laura Smith Porter *88, "From Intellectual Sanctuary to Social Responsibility: The Founding of the Institute for Advanced Study" (Ph.D. diss., Dept. of History, PU, 1988); Alexia Maizel, "Journey Out of Eden: The Institute for Advanced Study (1939–1945)" (Senior thesis, Dept. of History, Rutgers University, May 1998); Landon Y. Jones, Jr., "Bad Days on Mount Olympus," *Atlantic Monhtly* Feb. 1974, 37–46, 51–53; Ed Regis, *Who Got Einstein's Office? Eccentricity and Genius at the Institute for Advanced Study* (Reading, Mass., 1987); Harry Woolf, "A Community of Scholars: The Institute for Advanced Study, 1930–1980" (paper delivered to Phi Beta Kappa at Brown University, Mar. 25, 1981); Liz McMillen, "The Science Wars Flare at the Institute for Advanced Study," *CHE*, May 16, 1997, A13. The 1994 Hollywood film "I.Q.," starring Walter Matthau as Einstein, traded on the Institute's reputation for sheer braininess.

[25] The Gallup polling organization (1935), RCA Laboratories (1942), and the Educational Testing Service (1947) add to Princeton's reputation as "brains town," in geographer Jean Gottman's idiom, "a prestige location for high-brow intellectual and advanced scientific activities" (Michael H. Ebner, "Experiencing Megalopolis in Princeton," *Princeton History* 12 [1994]: 19–43, at 19). See also Carlos Baker, "The Princeton Constellation: The Town of Princeton as a Research Center, Academic & Industrial," *PAW*, Feb. 12, 1960, 8–10, 14, 16; Deborah Arotsky, "Increasingly, Biotech Firms Are Calling Princeton Home," *DP*, Nov. 28, 2001, 3.

gether with Marquand Library's world-class holdings and the Index of Christian Art—are all designed to promote the visual education of Princeton's students and faculty with maximum efficiency and effectiveness.

Princeton's Graduate School bears a strong resemblance to most of its peers, except in three regards: its faculty all teach undergraduates as well, which grounds their specializations in fundamentals; many of its students live in America's first residential graduate college, a stately Gothic "castle" overlooking a manicured golf course; and all of its students, humanists and scientists alike, are extremely well funded by fellowships, teaching and research assistantships, and summer research grants.

The Princeton University Press, which publishes some of the best work of the university's faculty and doctoral graduates, has been legally and financially independent of the university since its founding in 1905; the great majority of university presses are not. Yet the books and series that spread the university name around the world are chosen by a small editorial board of Princeton faculty, nominated by the Press director but appointed by the university president.

Most of these distinctive features appeared after Wilson left his presidency for the governorship of New Jersey. But several of Princeton's defining attributes were put in place while he was a faculty member or during his tenure as president. An honor system, instigated in 1893 by students who were disturbed by the flagrant cheating of their classmates, still governs the conduct of exams, but the reluctance of students to turn in offending classmates remains a problem. Although honor codes are now widespread in American colleges, they are less so in major universities, and Princeton's was one of the first to be enforced solely by students. At Princeton, as former Provost Neil Rudenstine noted, the honor code is part of the "ritualistic context" of hard academic work, along with "preceptorials, the library, and the relationship between faculty and students," that every class shares en route to senior theses and graduation.[26]

[26] McCleery, *Conversations*, 99; PU, *Undergraduate Announcement, 2004–05*, 19–25; Leitch, *Princeton Companion*, 260–61; "Commitment to Honor Code Tenets Shaky," *PAW*, Dec. 11, 1996, 8, 10; Jeremy Caplan, "The Honor Code," *PAW*, Dec. 25, 1996, 7; Joshua Tauberer, "Two Systems Hold Students to Their Honor," *DP*, Mar. 3, 2003, 3.

Ten eating clubs still hold social sway over Prospect Avenue, but all are now coed, half are nonselective, and only three-fourths of the upperclasses join, mostly for lack of culinary and social alternatives. For similar reasons, small, informal eating clubs sprang up on many American campuses in the nineteenth and twentieth centuries; most were evanescent. Only Princeton's developed so fully into social monopolies and arbiters of campus prestige, privately owned and sumptuously housed. With enduring reputations for hurtful and superficial selection procedures and alcoholic malfeasance, the clubs define—for better or worse—social life at Princeton for prospective applicants. Underclass counterweights to the club ethos are five colleges (one aptly named for Wilson), in which freshmen and sophomores live and dine; a sixth will be completed in 2007. Three will house all four classes and all six will host a smattering of graduate students. Unlike Harvard's "houses" and Yale's colleges, all of which are truly quadrangular as Wilson wanted his to be, Princeton's latter-day colleges are nonetheless distinctive in being confined to the first two years. Their denizens move on to conventional heterogeneous dormitories, from which they hike to more expensive club meals three times a day or to the more affordable cuisine of the Frist Campus Center.

Princeton's informal motto "In the Nation's Service"—the title of Wilson's sesquicentennial address—has been extended to read "and in the Service of All Nations," as befitting the university's increasingly cosmopolitan student body, curriculum, and mission. It also testifies to the university's self-confidence and ambition, to the global enlargement of Wilson's goal of training leaders of all kinds for the nation's business. As Princeton has consciously become an international university since its bicentennial observances in 1946–1947, its alumni have been roused to recognize the importance and implications of the transformation by the most frequently published

---

Stockton Axson, Wilson's brother-in-law, attributed the honor code to his sister Ellen, who was shocked by what the students told her of cheating; he was wrong. Stockton Axson, "*Brother Woodrow*": *A Memoir of Woodrow Wilson*, ed. Arthur S. Link (Princeton, 1993), 67–68; Edward Tenner, "The Honor Code Through Wilson's Spectacles," *PULC* 64:3 (Spring 2003): 425–44.

FIGURE 35. Architect's drawing of four-year Whitman College (2007). Designed by Demetri Porphyrios *80, it is the first of Princeton's colleges to be built from the ground up rather than assembled from existing structures.

alumni magazine in the country. The feistily independent *Princeton Alumni Weekly* (since 1900) appears sixteen times a year. Keeping alumni well informed and giving them an outlet for frequent comment, criticism, and horn-tooting does much to sustain their extraordinary personal and financial investment in the university. An intellectually fortified Alumni Weekend in February, admission work on an extensive Schools Committee, the annual pre-commencement Reunions, and the one-of-a-kind orange-and-black "P-rade" of classes, not just those in five-year cycles, all bolster the graduates' "transcendent feeling of kinship" with one another and their alma mater.[27] None of which is diminished by the domination of Ivy League sports and numerous national titles won by Tiger athletes, male and female, over the past quarter-century.

Last but not least, Princeton may be best known to the general public as the only American university whose president moved to the White House, with hardly a breather for career counseling. The public would be half-wrong, forgetting that Dwight Eisenhower

[27] Robert K. Durkee '69, "Reunion Reflections," *Princeton: With One Accord* (Summer 2004), 8.

presided over Columbia University briefly and ineffectually before being elected President on the strength of his reputation as the Supreme Allied Commander and redeemer of Europe in World War II.[28] Nor was he a widely published college professor, master orator, and the leading spokesman for higher education in his time, as Wilson was. In the public mind, Princeton will always be "Wilson's University," the meaning of which we have tried to explicate but also complicate.

Although Wilson would be pleased by most if not all of Princeton's continuing and acquired distinctions, the one he cared most about—intellectual distinction—is the most difficult to assess. Wilson aimed high. He wanted every department to be "at the very front, not only in scholarship, but in influence and leadership." And to (literally) man those departments, he sought faculty "whom advanced students cannot afford not to study under"—published and polished stars in the academic firmament.[29] But judging scholarly quality—depth and breadth of research, focused energy, originality, logical power, imagination, verbal virtuosity—can never be quantified because it is always a matter of human judgment, as variable as its individual makers.

The most reliable judges, it has long been assumed, are academic peers, qualified and tested. Yet in judging collectivities of scholars, in academic departments or whole universities, even peers resort to breezy generalizations, quasi-quantified measures of quality, or quantifiable substitutes for it. Any attempts to *rank* academic institutions by outsiders and even by peers must therefore be taken with a large grain of salt. But no less than the gambling public, academics are prone to playing the numbers. Lacking sounder, more careful assessments, we, too, are forced to fall back on half-measures.[30]

[28] Travis B. Jacobs, *Eisenhower at Columbia* (New Brunswick, N.J., 2001); Robert A. McCaughey, *Stand Columbia: A History of Columbia University in the City of New York, 1754–2004* (New York, 2004), 338–41.

[29] *PWW*, 17:117 (Apr. 24, 1907); 18:20 (Mar. 12, 1908).

[30] Nicholas Thompson, "Playing with Numbers," *Washington Monthly* 32:9 (Sept. 2000): 16–23; Paul Boyer, *College Rankings Exposed: Getting Beyond the Rankings* (New York, 2003); Nancy Diamond and Hugh Davis Graham, "How Should We Rate Research Universities?" *Change* 32:4 (July–Aug. 2000): 21–33.

By the most relevant and meaningful measures we do have for assessing the quality of universities and their faculties, Princeton earns very high marks, especially when calculations are made on a per capita basis. In absolute numbers, Princeton often runs behind Harvard, Yale, Stanford, or the larger state universities of California and the Midwest. But relative to its modest size, it frequently outscores the academic giants with whom it competes for students, faculty, and honors.

Although it uses several criteria of questionable worth, *U.S. News & World Report* for the first five years of the twenty-first century (2001–2005) rated Princeton the best doctoral university in the country, slightly ahead of Harvard (with whom it tied twice), Yale, and MIT.[31] To interpret "best," we should remember that as a popular consumer guide for undergraduates, the *U.S. News* "America's Best Colleges" issue focuses on the learning rather than the teaching and research end of university business by looking primarily at class sizes, freshman retention and graduation rates, incoming freshman statistics, and student-faculty ratios. On-campus student opinion of Princeton's quality was no less favorable. In a poll of 65,000 undergraduates at 331 universities in 2002, the *Princeton Review* (the exam prep company unrelated to the university) found that Princeton, according to the registered enthusiasm of its current students, provided the "best academic experience" in the country.[32] In 2001 and 2003, surveys of Princeton sophomores and seniors found equally positive results. In both years, 80–82 percent of the students who responded described their overall experience as "very satisfactory" or "outstanding." In 2003, 87 percent rated "Academics" the feature they most liked about Princeton; the second most popular answer was "People."[33]

[31] Because the magazine altered its criteria and weights slightly every year (partly to create interest and increase sales), the Big Three (Harvard, Yale, and Princeton) alternated in the top spot through most of the 1990s. Anne Machung, "Playing the Rankings Game," *Change* 30:4 (July–August 1998): 12–16; Thompson, "Playing with Numbers."

[32] The Princeton Review, *The Best 331 Colleges* (online, 2002).

[33] *The Summary Report of The Princeton Experience Survey, Spring 2003, Class of 2003 and Class of 2005* (PU, Office of the Provost, Nov. 8, 2004), 3, 5–6, 48–49.

On its graduate education and research side, Princeton fares nearly as well. In 1993 the National Research Council, using a combination of reputational and objective criteria, measured Princeton's twenty-nine graduate departments against their national peers, the great majority of which were much larger. The average rank of Princeton's programs for "faculty quality" was seventh, a remarkable score for a relatively small university with more than twice as many undergraduates as graduate students and with no medical school to boost research productivity. The math and philosophy programs were rated the nation's best, and seven of ten departments in the arts and humanities ranked among the top five.[34]

Of more recent vintage and employing slightly different criteria, the University of Florida's Lombardi Program on Measuring University Performance in 2004 ranked Princeton in a tie for ninth among all American research universities but tied for fourth among private institutions. The difference stems from the criteria used: many count the sheer *size* or *numbers* of things, such as total and federal research budgets, doctorates awarded, and postdoctoral appointees. Large state universities score well in these areas, smaller private ones such as Princeton less well. Even in absolute numbers, Princeton ranks high in endowment assets, faculty members of the National Academies of Sciences and Engineering, and prestigious awards, fellowships, and grants.[35]

On an international scale, Princeton also carries weight, despite its relatively modest size. In 2004 the *Times* of London's *Higher Education Supplement*, using four objective indicators and the opinion of thirteen hundred academics in eighty-eight countries, ranked

[34] Marvin L. Goldberger, Brendan A. Maher, and Pamela Ebert Flattau, eds., *Research-Doctorate Programs in the United States: Continuity and Change* (Washington, D.C., 1995), app. (tables H, I, P). In seven different assessments of leading doctoral universities between 1925 and 1982, Princeton was ranked sixth on average for "faculty quality," behind much larger Chicago, Harvard, Columbia, Yale, and Wisconsin; Princeton's overall reputational average was eighth. David S. Webster, *Academic Quality Rankings of American Colleges and Universities* (Springfield, Ill., 1986), 127 (table IV), 137 (table XII).

[35] John V. Lombardi et al., *TheCenter: The Top American Research Universities* (Gainesville, 2003), 86–87, 90–91, 244–45.

Princeton ninth among the world's universities; it trailed six of its traditional American rivals and Oxford and Cambridge. In the same year, the solely objective rankings of Shanghai Jiao Tong University's Institute of Higher Education moved Princeton up to seventh place. When President Shirley Tilghman and three top university officials visited alumni groups in China, Korea, and Japan in the fall of that year, they discovered the reason for Princeton's difficulty in recruiting students (graduate and undergraduate) and other resources in East Asia: Princeton lacked large and visible professional schools and therefore groups of alumni, to whom university delegations made fewer visits. In that part of the world, orange and black was simply less visible than Harvard crimson, Stanford cardinal, and Yale blue.[36]

Although the quality of any university faculty as a whole is nearly immeasurable, some notion of the Princeton professoriate can be gained from its collective productivity and the magnitude of some of its stars. Between 1986 and 1990, two researchers found, Princeton ranked third behind Stanford and UC-Berkeley in per capita research productivity as measured empirically by research grants and fellowships, scholarly publications, and peer citation of those publications in professional journals. Princeton's humanities faculty had by far the best record in winning fellowships from the National Endowment for the Humanities, the American Council of Learned Societies, and the John Simon Guggenheim Foundation. Other studies of citation indices discovered that between 1997 and 2001, for example, Princeton's philosophers and geoscientists, despite their small numbers, were the third-most prolific departments in the country; geoscience and psychology papers written by Princeton faculty were the most frequently cited in other scholars' papers. Princetonians were second only to Berkeley's more numerous space scientists in articular prolificacy. And between 1911 and 1990, Princeton practitioners of the "dismal science" were the second-most

[36] Hannah Charlick, "University Places Ninth in International Rankings," *DP* (online), Nov. 9, 2004; Institute of Higher Education, Shanghai Jiao Tong University, "Academic Rankings of World Universities 2004"; Mike Hsu, "Administrators Visit Asia, Seek to Improve University Profile," *DP* (online), Nov. 23, 2004.

published in the flagship *American Economic Review*; from 1951 Professor William Baumol stacked the deck by publishing a record seventeen articles.[37]

Even more impressive are Princeton's winners of various international prizes, honorary memberships, and special fellowships. As of 2004, Princeton faculty had taken home nineteen Nobel Prizes. Five—in four different fields—were won in the four years leading up to the 250th anniversary in 1996. Others were earned for work done previously at Princeton. The Fields Medal, awarded every four years at the International Congress of Mathematicians, is the equivalent of the Nobel in the numbers game for those under forty. Of the forty-five medalists since 1936, seven came from the Princeton faculty and four more from the university's symbiotic neighbor, the Institute for Advanced Study; Harvard, the runner-up, took home four medals. Fifteen Princeton scientists had received the National Medal of Science at the White House; geologist Jason Morgan, the authority on plate tectonics, was the most recent.[38]

Between 1981 and 2005, twenty-five Princetonians and one Institute fellow had received telephone calls from the MacArthur Foundation informing them that they had been selected anonymously for five-year, no-strings "genius" fellowships; five additional winners subsequently joined the Princeton faculty. Nearly as fortuitous, four of the first fifteen winners of the Andrew W. Mellon Foundation Distinguished Achievement Award in the humanities, worth $1.5 million of institutional and research support over three years, went to Princeton professors; one of the latest recipients was historian Anthony Grafton, who also won the 2002 international Balzan Prize for the humanities. Perhaps more emblematic of the faculty's eminence was membership in the prestigious American Academy of

[37] Hugh Davis Graham and Nancy Diamond, *The Rise of American Research Universities: Elites and Challengers in the Postwar Era* (Baltimore, 1997), 167 (table 6.7), 186 (table 7.8), 188 (table 7.9); Lynn C. Hattendorf Westrey, ed., *Educational Rankings Annual 2004* (Detroit, 2004), 247–49, 336, 348, 482.

[38] Oberdorfer, *Princeton University*, 230–31; PU, *Profile 2003–04*, 4; "Fields Medal Winners" (http://www.icm2004.org.cn/general/prize/pre_winners.htm); *PAW*, Dec. 20, 2000, 9; Steven Schultz, "Morgan to Receive National Medal of Science. . ." *PWB* (online), Nov. 3, 2003.

Arts and Sciences: 130 honorees were on the Princeton faculty, which meant that about one-quarter of its full professors were members. Over sixty scientists and mathematicians were fellows of the National Academy of Sciences, as were eleven from the Institute. Seven faculty artists and writers, such as Toni Morrison, Joyce Carol Oates, and John McPhee, were also members of the smaller but equally selective American Academy of Arts and Letters.[39]

The cumulative weight of independent evidence such as this suggests that Princeton has indeed become "one of the foremost" American universities "in power and quality." The caliber and quantity of scholarship its faculty and students generate in "the spirit of learning" have long since met—and likely exceeded—Wilson's expectations. In 1976, for instance, the university prepared a six-page brief entitled "Some Reasons for Princeton's Standing as One of the World's Great Universities." It, too, drew attention to Princeton's distinctive size, the rankings of its graduate departments, its meritorious and devoted teaching faculty, and the premium it placed on undergraduate education in preceptorials and independent study before adding a page on its successful alumni, many "in the Nation's Service." The document's centerpiece was an evaluation by Clark Kerr, former chancellor of UC-Berkeley (1952–1958) and president of California's university system (1958–1967), one of America's most knowledgeable educators. He asserted that "Princeton, while a rather small university, is in the absolute top rank in terms of the scholarly quality of its faculty. . . . Among the great universities of the nation," Princeton was also "the best balanced overall if you look at both teaching and research and the attention given to both graduates and undergraduates. . . . Perhaps the ultimate compliment which could be made to an academic community is its ability to hold the

[39] MacArthur Fellowship Winners, 1981–2005 (http://www.macfound.org/programs/fel/winners_overview.htm); "Grafton Chosen for Mellon Distinguished Achievement Award," PU, press release, Dec. 16, 2003; Lindsey White, "History Professor Grafton Awarded Prestigious Balzan Prize for Study," *DP* (online), Sept. 12, 2002; American Academy of Arts and Sciences, *Bulletin* 58:1 (Fall 2004): 58–93; National Academy of Sciences database for Oct. 2004; Louis Auchincloss et al., *A Century of Arts & Letters* (New York, 1998), 293–96.

greatest scholars. At that," he concluded, "I would rank Princeton first in the nation."[40]

Head-turning assessments like Kerr's have been Princeton's lot since it began its push to become a truly national university of meritocratic excellence after World War II. Even earlier, in the 1920s, it began to earn bragging rights for the star-power of its scientific and mathematical faculties and their ability to draw many of the nation's best graduate students and postdoctoral award-winners. But the risk in success is always hubris, particularly in the highly competitive groves of academe. In 1933 Einstein famously referred to his new academic neighbors in Princeton as "puny demigods on stilts."[41] A half-century later, several faculty with academic pedigrees and experience elsewhere drew attention to the downside of Princeton's achievements. Sociologist Marvin Bressler admitted that it was easy to lampoon Princeton's "exaggerated sense of self." "Our intense self-consciousness, our invincible conviction that we are a chosen instrument of a higher purpose, and our insularity are an invitation to satire." (He went on to argue that "if Princeton had had a more accurate sense of its location in the cosmos, its very real achievements would have been far less substantial.") Poet Theodore Weiss, a fan of big-city cultural life, confessed that to live and work in Princeton "is so rare an experience that smugness can be a problem." Weiss was seconded by former dean and provost J. Douglas Brown. But Princeton's hubris, he offered, was usually tempered by its formidable competition. "Luckily for us there are Harvard and Yale, MIT, Stanford, Cal Tech, and other great universities out there. . . . We're kept modest by knowing that because of their sheer size they can do things we can't, and by having to compete with them for faculty and students—and not always winning!"[42]

While much of Princeton's modern growth and stature has been and is easily attributed to Wilson, we should not exaggerate his in-

[40] "Some Reasons for Princeton's Standing as One of the World's Great Universities" (June 1976), typescript in Historical Subject Files, #A–109, "History: Princeton in the 1970s" (PUA).

[41] Alice Calaprice, ed., *The Expanded Quotable Einstein* (Princeton, 2000), 56.

[42] McCleery, *Conversations*, 14, 24, 137.

fluence or its persistence. Well into the 1930s, trustees who had opposed him in the rancorous fights over his quad plan and the Graduate School sustained their animus and blocked any attempts to publicly honor his name on campus. The School of Public and International Affairs, though founded in 1930, was not renamed for Wilson until 1948, after some of his political ideas had found renewed favor in another postwar world and most of his enemies were gone from the scene. Until that time, no public statue or building was erected to carry his name. Even with a desperate need for a new library, his old enemies on the board rejected a generous donation that would have built a fitting memorial to his intellectual leadership.[43]

But Wilson's academic hopes and dreams had staying power because they were realistic and right for Princeton and were expressed with uncommon eloquence and cogency. Yet they could have been jettisoned or simply ignored by subsequent presidents and faculties who might have wished to pursue new institutional goals or educational fashions. That they were not speaks as well for his successors' skill in translating his dream into a contemporary idiom as it does for the power of his original vision. In 1986 former president Robert Goheen assessed the question of legacy with characteristic insight. "Wilson really had an enormous impact on Princeton," he acknowledged. "He may not have 'made Princeton what it is today'—other people had key roles in that—" he said, "but it wouldn't be what it is without him."[44]

The key player in Princeton's modern making, Goheen's provost (1967–1972) and successor (1972–1988) William Bowen, also acknowledged Princeton's debt to Wilson. "We are his descendants, the beneficiaries of his ideas. . . . The influence of a man like that is powerful, but subtle," he noted. "We each have to do things in our own way in our own time, with a clear sense of current objectives." His conclusion was that "the influence of Wilson is so evident that we don't have to overdo the explicit announcement of it, and that is, in a way, the greatest compliment we could pay him."[45]

[43] See chapter 7, pp. 458–59.

[44] McCleery, *Conversations*, 47.

[45] McCleery, *Conversations*, 10.

As Princeton makes its way through the uncertainties and challenges of the new millennium, it will have not only Wilson's ambitious vision to guide it, but a recent century of transformative change and accomplishment to give it courage. If the university's new leaders provide the will and its alumni and friends the means, Princeton will have an enviable combination of strengths with which to enact the next chapter of its history.

Selected Bibliography

Woodrow Wilson

Axson, Stockton. *"Brother Woodrow": A Memoir of Woodrow Wilson*, ed. Arthur S. Link. Princeton: Princeton University Press, 1993.

Baker, Ray Stannard. *Woodrow Wilson: Life and Letters*. 8 vols. Garden City, N.Y.: Doubleday, Page, & Co., 1927.

Bragdon, Henry Wilkinson. *Woodrow Wilson: The Academic Years*. Cambridge, Mass.: Harvard University Press, Belknap, 1967.

Bundy, McGeorge. *An Atmosphere to Breathe: Woodrow Wilson and the Life of the American University College*. New York: The Woodrow Wilson Foundation, 1959.

Carroll, James Robert. *The Real Woodrow Wilson: An Interview with Arthur S. Link, Editor of the Wilson Papers*. Bennington, Vt.: Images from the Past, 2001.

Cooper, John Milton, Jr. *The Warrior and the Priest: Woodrow Wilson and Theodore Roosevelt*. Cambridge, Mass.: Harvard University Press, Belknap, 1983.

Craig, Hardin. *Woodrow Wilson at Princeton*. Norman: University of Oklahoma Press, 1960.

Daniels, Winthrop M. *Recollections of Woodrow Wilson*. New Haven: Privately printed, 1944.

Elliott, Margaret Axson. *My Aunt Louisa and Woodrow Wilson*. Chapel Hill: University of North Carolina Press, 1944.

Hale, William Bayard. *Woodrow Wilson: The Story of His Life*. Garden City, N.Y.: Doubleday, Page, and Co., 1912.

Heckscher, August. *Woodrow Wilson*. New York: Charles Scribner's Sons, 1991.

Kraig, Robert Alexander. *Woodrow Wilson and the Lost World of the Oratorical Statesman*. College Station: Texas A&M University Press, 2004.

Link, Arthur S. *Wilson: The Road to the White House*. Princeton: Princeton University Press, 1947.

———, et al., eds. *The Papers of Woodrow Wilson*. 69 vols. Princeton: Princeton University Press, 1966–1994.

McAdoo, Eleanor Wilson. *The Woodrow Wilsons*. New York: Macmillan Co., 1937.

McAdoo, Eleanor Wilson, ed. *The Priceless Gift: The Love Letters of Woodrow Wilson and Ellen Axson Wilson.* New York: McGraw-Hill Book Co., 1962.

McMillan, Lewis. *Woodrow Wilson of Princeton.* Narbeth, Pa.: Privately printed, 1952.

Mulder, John M. *Woodrow Wilson: The Years of Preparation.* Princeton: Princeton University Press, 1978.

———. Ernest M. White, and Ethel S. White. *Woodrow Wilson: A Bibliography.* Westport, Conn.: Greenwood Press, 1997.

Myers, William Starr, ed. *Woodrow Wilson: Some Princeton Memories.* Princeton: Princeton University Press, 1946.

Osborn, George C. *Woodrow Wilson: The Early Years.* Baton Rouge: Louisiana State University Press, 1968.

Reid, Edith Gittings. *Woodrow Wilson: The Caricature, the Myth, and the Man.* New York: Oxford University Press, 1934.

Saunders, Frances Wright. *Ellen Axson Wilson: First Lady Between Two Worlds.* Chapel Hill: University of North Carolina Press, 1985.

Thorsen, Niels Aage. *The Political Thought of Woodrow Wilson, 1875–1910.* Princeton: Princeton University Press, 1988.

Weinstein, Edwin A. *Woodrow Wilson: A Medical and Psychological Biography.* Princeton: Princeton University Press, 1981.

Princeton

An Art Museum for Princeton: The Early Years. Record of The Art Museum, Princeton University, vol. 55, nos. 1–2 (1996).

Baker, Carlos. *A Friend in Power.* New York: Charles Scribner's Sons, 1958. (Fiction)

Bowen, William G. *Ever the Teacher: William G. Bowen's Writings as President of Princeton.* Princeton: Princeton University Press, 1987.

———, and Derek Bok. *The Shape of the River: Long-Term Consequences of Considering Race in College and University Admissions.* Princeton: Princeton University Press, 1998.

———, and Sarah A. Levin. *Reclaiming the Game: College Sports and Educational Values.* Princeton: Princeton University Press, 2003.

Benn, John A. *Columbus—Undergraduate.* Philadelphia: J. B. Lippincott Co., 1928.

Breese, Gerald. *Princeton University Land, 1752–1984.* Princeton: Trustees of Princeton University, 1986.

Brown, J. Douglas. *The Liberal University: An Institutional Analysis.* New York: McGraw-Hill Book Co., 1969.

———. *The Commonplace Book of an Academic Dean.* Princeton: Industrial Relations Section, Princeton University, 1978.

Butz, Otto, ed. *The Unsilent Generation: An Anonymous Symposium in Which Eleven College Seniors Look at Themselves and Their World.* New York: Rinehart and Co., 1958.

Caldwell, Ian, and Dustin Thomason. *The Rule of Four.* New York: Dial Press, 2004. (Fiction)

[Campbell, Bruce, compiler.] *Princeton Reflections: Contemplations in Color.* Princeton: Princeton University Press, 1982. (Photographs)

Chamberlain, Samuel. *Princeton in Spring: Camera Impressions.* New York: Hastings House, 1950. (Photographs)

Collins, Varnum Lansing. *Princeton.* American College and University Series. New York: Oxford University Press, 1914.

———. *Princeton: Past and Present.* Princeton: Princeton University Press, 1931.

Condit, Kenneth W. *History of the Engineering School of Princeton University, 1875–1955.* Princeton: Princeton University Press, 1962.

Daily Princetonian. The Orange & Black in Black & White: A Century of Princeton Through the Eyes of The Daily Princetonian. Princeton: Daily Princetonian Publishing Co., 1992.

Darrow, Whitney. *Princeton University Press: An Informal Account of Its Growing Pains, Casually Put Together at the Point of a Gun for the Intimate Friends of the Press.* Princeton: Princeton University Press, 1951.

DeVorkin, David H. *Henry Norris Russell: Dean of American Astronomers.* Princeton: Princeton University Press, 2000.

Dodds, Harold W. *The Academic President—Educator or Caretaker?* Carnegie Series in American Education. New York: McGraw-Hill Book Co., 1962.

Edgar, Day. *In Princeton Town.* New York: Charles Scribner's Sons, 1929. (Fiction)

Eisenhart, Luther Pfahler. *The Educational Process.* Princeton: Princeton University Press, 1945.

Fitzgerald, F. Scott. *This Side of Paradise.* New York: Charles Scribner's Sons, 1920. (Fiction)

Gambee, Richard. *Princeton.* New York: W. W. Norton and Co., 1993. (Photographs)

Gauss, Christian. *Through College on Nothing a Year: Literally Recorded from a Student's Story.* New York: Charles Scribner's Sons, 1915.

———. *Life in College.* New York: Charles Scribner's Sons, 1930.

Gauss, Christian. *The Papers of Christian Gauss*, ed. Katherine Gauss Jackson and Hiram Haydn. New York: Random House, 1957.

Gellman, Barton, and Beth English. *In the Nation's Service: Seventy-Five Years at the Woodrow Wilson School*. Princeton: Woodrow Wilson School of Public and International Affairs, 2005.

Goheen, Robert F. *The Human Nature of a University*. Princeton: Princeton University Press, 1969.

Greiff, Constance M., Mary W. Gibbons, and Elizabeth G. C. Menzies. *Princeton Architecture: A Pictorial History of Town and Campus*. Princeton: Princeton University Press, 1967.

Heath, Roy. *Princeton Retrospectives: Twenty-Fifth-Year Reflections on a College Education*. Princeton: Princeton University, The Class of 1954, 1979.

Hoeveler, J. David, Jr. *James McCosh and the Scottish Intellectual Tradition: From Glasgow to Princeton*. Princeton: Princeton University Press, 1981.

Karabel, Jerome. *The Chosen: The Hidden History of Admission and Exclusion at Harvard, Yale, and Princeton*. Boston: Houghton Mifflin, 2005.

Kemeny, P. C. *Princeton in the Nation's Service: Religious Ideals and Educational Practice, 1868–1928*. New York: Oxford University Press, 1998.

Keyser, Catherine. *Transforming the Tiger: A Celebration of Undergraduate Women at Princeton University*. Princeton: Office of Printing and Mailing Services, Princeton University, 2001.

Lane, Wheaton J. *Pictorial History of Princeton*. Princeton: Princeton University Press, 1947.

Lavin, Marilyn Aronberg. *The Eye of the Tiger: The Founding and Development of the Department of Art and Archaeology, 1883–1923, Princeton University*. Princeton: Department of Art and Archaeology, 1983.

Leitch, Alexander. *A Princeton Companion*. Princeton: Princeton University Press, 1978.

Leslie, W. Bruce. *Gentlemen and Scholars: College and Community in the "Age of the University," 1865–1917*. University Park: Penn State University Press, 1992; New Brunswick: Transaction Books, 2005.

Looney, J. Jefferson. *Nurseries of Letters and Republicanism: A Brief History of the American Whig-Cliosophic Society and Its Predecessors, 1765–1941*. Princeton: American Whig-Cliosophic Society, 1996.

MacAyeal, H. S. *Tiger! Tiger!* London: Minerva Press, 1996. (Fiction)

Marks, Patricia H., ed. *Luminaries: Princeton Faculty Remembered*. Princeton: Association of Princeton Graduate Alumni, 1996.

Marsden, Donald. *The Long Kickline: A History of the Princeton Triangle Club*. Princeton: Princeton Triangle Club, 1968.

McCleery, William. *Conversations on the Character of Princeton*. Princeton: Office of Communications/Publications, Princeton University, 1987.

———. *The Story of A Campaign for Princeton, 1981–1986*. Princeton: Office of Communications/Publications, 1987.

Merritt, J. I., ed. *The Best of PAW: 100 Years of the Princeton Alumni Weekly*. Princeton: Princeton Alumni Weekly, 2000.

Nasar, Sylvia. *A Beautiful Mind: A Biography of John Forbes Nash, Jr., Winner of the Nobel Prize in Economics, 1994*. New York: Simon & Schuster, 1998.

Norris, Edwin M. *The Story of Princeton*. Boston: Little, Brown, and Co., 1917.

Oberdorfer, Don. *Princeton University: The First 250 Years*. Princeton: Trustees of Princeton University, 1995. (Pictorial history)

Osgood, Charles G., et al. *The Modern Princeton*. Princeton: Princeton University Press, 1947.

———. *Lights in Nassau Hall*. Princeton: Princeton University Press, 1951.

Paul, Bill. *Getting In: Inside the College Admissions Process*. Reading, Mass.: Addison-Wesley Publishing Co., 1995.

Perry, Bliss. *And Gladly Teach: Reminiscences*. Boston and New York: Houghton Mifflin Co., 1935.

Phillips, John Aristotle, and David Michaelis. *Mushroom: The Story of the A-Bomb Kid*. New York: William Morrow and Co., 1978.

Princeton Tiger. Roaring at One Hundred: The Princeton Tiger Magazine Centennial Album. Princeton: The Princeton Tiger, 1983.

Princeton University Press, 1905–2005: Whitney Darrow, *The Founding of Princeton University Press* (1951), Herbert S. Bailey, Jr., *A Brief History of Princeton University Press* (1981), Walter H. Lippincott, *Reflections on the Occasion of the Centenary* (2005). Princeton: Princeton University Press, 2005.

Rhinehart, Raymond P. *The Campus Guide: Princeton University*. New York: Princeton Architectural Press, 1999.

Rich, Frederic C. *The First Hundred Years of the Ivy Club, 1879–1979: A Centennial History*. Princeton: The Ivy Club, 1979.

[Rivinus, Willis M., comp. and ed.] *The Colonial Club of Princeton University, 1891–1991*. Princeton: Privately printed, 1991.

———. *The Princeton Tower Club*. Princeton: Privately printed, 1995.

Savage, Henry Lyttleton. *Nassau Hall, 1756–1956*. Princeton: Princeton University Press, 1956.

Schmitt, Judy Piper, ed. *The* Prince *Remembers: One Hundred Years of* The Daily Princetonian [*1876–1976*]. Princeton: The Daily Princetonian Publishing Co., 1976.

Schreiner, Samuel A., Jr. *A Place Called Princeton.* New York: Arbor House, 1984.

Scott, William Berryman. *Some Memories of a Palaeontologist.* Princeton: Princeton University Press, 1939.

Selden, William K. *Woodrow Wilson School of Public and International Affairs, Princeton University: Conception and Early Development, 1930–1943*. Princeton: Woodrow Wilson School of Public and International Affairs, 1984.

———. *Princeton—The Best Old Place of All: Vignettes of Princeton University, 1884, 1934, 1984*. Princeton: Privately printed, 1987.

———. *Princeton Theological Seminary: A Narrative History, 1812–1992*. Princeton: Privately printed, 1992.

———. *Club Life at Princeton: An Historical Account of the Eating Clubs at Princeton University.* Princeton: Princeton Prospect Foundation, 1996.

———. *Women at Princeton, 1746–1969*. Princeton: Privately printed, 2000.

Shulman, James, and William G. Bowen. *The Game of Life: College Sports and Educational Values*. Princeton: Princeton University Press, 2001.

Slosson, Edwin E. *Great American Universities.* New York: Macmillan Co., 1910.

Smith, Richard D. *Princeton*. Images of America. Dover, N. H.: Arcadia Publishing, 1997. (Historical photographs)

———. *Princeton University.* The Campus History Series. Charleston, S.C.: Arcadia Publishing, 2005. (Historical photographs)

Stillwell, Richard. *The Chapel of Princeton University.* Princeton: Princeton University Press, 1971.

Synnott, Marcia Graham. *The Half-Opened Door: Discrimination and Admissions at Harvard, Yale, and Princeton, 1900–1970*. Westport, Conn.: Greenwood Press, 1979.

Thorp, Willard, ed. *The Lives of Eighteen from Princeton*. Princeton: Princeton University Press, 1946.

———, Minor Myers, Jr., Jeremiah Stanton Finch, and James Axtell. *The Princeton Graduate School: A History*, ed. Patricia H. Marks. Princeton: Association of Princeton Graduate Alumni, 2000.

Van Zandt, Helen, with Jan Lilly. *The Princeton University Campus: A Guide.* Princeton: Princeton University Press, 1964, 1970. (Photographs)

Wertenbaker, Thomas Jefferson. *Princeton, 1746–1896*. Princeton: Princeton University Press, 1946.

West, Andrew Fleming. *Short Papers on American Liberal Education*. New York: Charles Scribner's Sons, 1907.

Williams, Jesse Lynch. *Princeton Stories.* New York: Charles Scribner's Sons, 1895. (Fiction)

———. *The Adventures of a Freshman*. New York: Charles Scribner's Sons, 1899. (Fiction)

Williams, John Rogers. *The Handbook of Princeton*. With an Introduction by Woodrow Wilson. New York: Grafton Press, 1905.

Wilson, Edmund. *A Prelude: Landscapes, Characters and Conversations from the Earlier Years of My Life*. New York: Farrar, Straus, and Giroux, 1967.

Wolff, Geoffrey. *The Final Club*. New York: Alfred A. Knopf, 1990. (Fiction)

Index